# OCR

# Advanced economics

Peter Smith

philip allan
UPDATES

Philip Allan Updates
Market Place
Deddington
Oxfordshire
OX15 0SE

**Orders**

Bookpoint Ltd, 130 Milton Park, Abingdon, Oxfordshire, OX14 4SB
tel: (44) 01235 827720
fax: (44) 01235 400454
e-mail: uk.orders@bookpoint.co.uk
Lines are open 9.00 a.m.–5.00 p.m., Monday to Saturday, with a 24-hour message answering service. You can also order through the Philip Allan Updates website: www.philipallan.co.uk

ISBN-13: 978-1-84489-421-5
ISBN-10: 1-84489-421-5

This textbook has been written specifically to support students studying OCR Advanced Economics. The content has been neither approved nor endorsed by OCR and remains the sole responsibility of the author.

All website addresses included in this book are correct at the time of going to press but may subsequently change.

All photographs are reproduced by permission of TopFoto, except where otherwise specified.

Design and artwork by Juha Sorsa and Dianne Shaw
Printed in Great Britain by CPI Bath

**Environmental information**
The paper on which this title is printed is sourced from managed, sustainable forests.

P00644

# Contents

# Introduction

This textbook provides an introduction to economics. It has been tailored explicitly to cover the content of the OCR specification for AS and A-level economics, module by module. The text provides the foundation for studying OCR economics, but you will no doubt wish to keep up to date by referring to additional topical sources of information about economic events. This can be done by reading the serious newspapers, visiting key sites on the internet, and by reading such magazines as *Economic Review.*

The core content of the text is as follows:

| OCR module | Text |
|---|---|
| **AS Unit 2881**<br>The market system | **Part 1:** The market system<br>Chapters 1–4 |
| **AS Unit 2882**<br>Market failure and government intervention | **Part 2:** Market failure and government intervention<br>Chapters 5–8 |
| **AS Unit 2883**<br>The national and international economy | **Part 3:** The national and international economy<br>Chapters 9–13 |
| **Common material for units 2884 and 2885**<br>Market structure | **Part 4:** Market structure<br>Chapters 14 and 15 |
| **Advanced Unit 2884 (option)**<br>Economics of work and leisure | **Part 5:** The economics of work and leisure<br>Chapters 16–19 |
| **Advanced Unit 2885 (option)**<br>Transport economics | **Part 6:** Transport economics<br>Chapters 20–23 |
| **Advanced Unit 2886 (option)**<br>Economics of development | **Part 7:** Economics of development<br>Chapters 24–28 |
| **Advanced Unit 2887 (option)**<br>The UK economy | **Part 8:** The UK economy<br>Chapters 29–33 |
| **Advanced Unit 2888**<br>Economics in a European context | **Part 9:** Economics in a European context<br>Chapters 34–37 |

The text features the following:
- ➤ a statement of the intended learning outcomes for each chapter
- ➤ clear and concise but comprehensive explanation and analysis of economic terms and concepts
- ➤ definitions of key terms
- ➤ examples to show these concepts applied to real world situations
- ➤ exercises to provide active engagement with economic analysis

The structure of the optional Modules means that some topics appear in more than one place in the book.

## Assessment objectives

In common with other economics specifications, OCR economics entails four assessment objectives. Candidates will thus be expected to:
- ➤ demonstrate knowledge and understanding of the specified content
- ➤ apply knowledge and critical understanding to problems and issues arising from both familiar and unfamiliar situations
- ➤ analyse economic problems and issues
- ➤ evaluate economic arguments and evidence, making informed judgements

In the overall assessment of the A-level, the four assessment objectives count equally. However, there is a greater weighting given to the first two objectives in AS, and a greater weighting to the final two objectives in A2.

In addition, the final Unit 2888 is designated as a *synoptic* unit, which tests understanding of the connections between different elements of the subject, and which relates to all of the assessment objectives. This will test the ability to:
- ➤ understand the interrelatedness of many economic issues, problems and institutions
- ➤ understand how certain economic concepts, theories and techniques may be relevant to a range of different contexts
- ➤ apply such concepts, theories and techniques in analysing economic issues and problems and in evaluating arguments and evidence

*(See the OCR AS/A GCE Economics Specification at **www.ocr.org.uk**.)*

## Economics

Economics is different from some other A-level subjects in that relatively few students will have studied it before embarking on the AS course. The text thus begins from the beginning, and provides a thorough foundation in the subject and its applications. By studying this book, you should develop an awareness of the economist's approach to issues and problems, and the economist's way of thinking about the world.

The study of economics also requires a familiarity with recent economic events in the UK and elsewhere, and candidates will be expected to show familiarity with 'recent historical data' — broadly defined as the last 7 to 10 years. The following websites will help you to keep up to date with recent trends and events.

Recent and historical data about the UK economy can be found at the website of the Office for National Statistics (ONS) at:
**www.statistics.gov.uk/**

Also helpful is the site of HM Treasury at:
**www.hm-treasury.gov.uk/**

The Bank of England site is well worth a visit, especially the *Inflation Report* and the Minutes of the Monetary Policy Committee:
**www.bankofengland.co.uk/**

The Institute for Fiscal Studies offers an independent view of a range of economic topics:
**www.ifs.org.uk**

For information about other countries, visit the following:
**www.oecd.org/home/**
**http://europa.eu.int/**
**www.worldbank.org/**
**www.undp.org/**

Another way of keeping up to date with economic topics and events is to read *Economic Review*, a magazine specifically written for A-level economics students, also published by Philip Allan Updates.

## How to study economics

There are two crucial aspects of studying economics. The first stage is to study the theory, which helps us to explain economic behaviour. However, in studying AS and A2 economics it is equally important to be able to *apply* the theories and concepts that you meet, and to see just how these relate to the real world.

If you are to become competent at this, it is vital that you get plenty of practice. In part, this means carrying out the exercises that you will find in this text. However, it also means thinking about how economics helps us to explain news items and data that appear in the newspapers and on the television. Make sure that you practise as much as you can.

In economics, it is also important to be able to produce examples of economic phenomena. In reading this text, you will find some examples that help to illustrate ideas and concepts. Do not rely solely on the examples provided here, but look around the world to find your own examples, and keep a note of these ready for use in essays and exams. This will help to convince the examiners that you have understood economics. It will also help you to understand the theories.

## Enjoy economics

Most important of all, I hope you will enjoy your study of economics. I have always been fascinated by the subject, and hope that you will capture something of the excitement and challenge of learning about how markets and the economy operate. I also wish you every success with your AS/A-level studies.

# Acknowledgements

I would like to express my deep gratitude to Mark Russell, whose thorough reading of the first draft of the book and insightful and helpful comments were invaluable in improving the scope and focus of the book. I would also like to thank everyone at Philip Allan Updates, especially Penny Fisher, David Cross, Ash Allan and Dianne Shaw, for their efficiency in production of this book, for their support and encouragement, and for putting up with my inability to meet deadlines. Chris Bessant's editing was also much appreciated.

Many of the data series shown in figures in this book were drawn from the data obtained from the National Statistics website: **www.statistics.gov.uk** Crown copyright material is reproduced with the permission of the Controller of HMSO.

Other data were from various sources, including OECD, World Bank, United Nations Development Programme and other sources as specified.

Whilst every effort has been made to trace the owners of copyright material, I would like to apologise to any copyright holders whose rights may have unwittingly been infringed.

*Peter Smith*

OCR Advanced Economics

# The market system

# Part 1

# *Chapter 1*
# Introducing economics

*Welcome to economics. Many of you opening this book will be meeting economics for the first time, and you will want to know what is in store for you as you set out to study the subject. This opening chapter sets the scene by introducing you to some key ideas and identifying the scope of economic analysis. As you learn more of the subject, you will find that economics is a way of thinking that will broaden your perspective on the world around you.*

## Learning outcomes

This chapter will introduce you to:
- the nature and scope of economic analysis
- the concept of opportunity cost
- market, centrally-planned and mixed economies
- the distinction between microeconomics and macroeconomics
- the notion of factors of production
- the role of models and assumptions in economics
- the production possibility curve
- the concept of the division of labour
- how specialisation can improve productivity
- the role of markets
- the importance of money and exchange in an economy
- positive and normative statements

## The economic problem

For any society in the world, the fundamental economic problem faced is that of **scarcity**. You might think that this is obvious for some societies in the less developed world, where poverty and hunger are rife. But it is also true for relatively prosperous economies such as those of Switzerland, the USA or the UK.

**Key term**

**scarcity:** a situation that arises because people have unlimited wants in the face of limited resources

It is true in the sense that all societies have *finite resources*, but people have *unlimited wants*. A big claim? Not really. There is no country in the world in which all wants can be met, and this is clearly true at the global level.

Talking about *scarcity* in this sense is not the same as talking about *poverty*. Poverty might be seen as an extreme form of scarcity, in which individuals lack the basic necessities of life — whereas even relatively prosperous people face scarcity because resources are limited.

### Scarcity and choice

The key issue that arises from the existence of scarcity is that it forces people to make choices. Each individual must choose which goods and services to consume. In other words, everyone needs to prioritise the consumption of whatever commodities they need or would like to have, as they cannot satisfy all their wants. Similarly, at the national level, governments have to make choices between alternative uses of resources.

It is this need to choose that underlies the subject matter of economics. Economic analysis is about analysing those choices made by individual people, firms or governments.

### Opportunity cost

This raises one of the most important concepts in all of economic analysis — the notion of **opportunity cost**. When an individual chooses to consume one good, she does so at the cost of the item that would have been next in her list of priorities. For example, suppose you are on a strict diet and at the end of the day you can 'afford' either one chocolate or a piece of cheese. If you choose the cheese, the opportunity cost of the cheese is the chocolate that you could have had instead. In other words, the opportunity cost is the value of the next best alternative forgone.

 **Key term**

**opportunity cost:** in decision making, the value of the next-best alternative forgone

This important notion can be applied in many different contexts because, whenever you make a decision, you reject an alternative in favour of your chosen option. You have chosen to read this book — when instead you could be watching television or meeting friends.

### Exercise 1.1

Andrew has just started his AS courses, and has chosen to take economics, mathematics, geography and French. Although he was certain about the first three, it was a close call between French and English. What is Andrew's opportunity cost of choosing French?

As you move further into studying economics, you will encounter this notion of opportunity cost again and again. For example, firms take decisions about the sort of economic activity in which to engage. A market gardener with limited land available has to decide whether to plant onions or potatoes; if he decides to grow

onions, he has to forgo the opportunity to grow potatoes. From the government's point of view, if it decides to devote more resources to the National Health Service, it will have fewer resources available for, say, defence.

## The coordination problem

With so many different individuals and organisations (consumers, firms, governments) all taking decisions, a major question is how it all comes together. How are all these separate decisions coordinated so that the overall allocation of resources in a society is coherent? In other words, how can it be ensured that firms produce the commodities that consumers wish to consume? And how can the distribution of these products be organised? These are some of the basic questions that economics sets out to answer.

A **market economy** is one in which market forces are allowed to guide the allocation of resources within a society. Prices play a key role in this sort of system.

In contrast, a **centrally planned economy** is one in which the government undertakes the coordination role, planning and directing the allocation of resources. The collapse of the Soviet bloc in the 1990s largely discredited this approach, although a small number of countries (such as North Korea and Cuba) continue to stick with central planning.

Most economies operate a **mixed economy** system, in which market forces are complemented by some state intervention. It has been argued that any such state intervention should be *market-friendly*: in other words, when governments do intervene in the economy, they should do so in a way that helps markets to work, rather than trying to have the government replace market forces.

## Factors of production

People in a society play two quite different roles. On the one hand, they are the consumers, the ultimate beneficiaries of the process of production. On the other, they are a key part of the production process in that they are instrumental in producing goods and services.

More generally, it is clear that both *human resources* and *physical resources* are required as part of the production process. These productive resources are known as the **factors of production**.

The most obvious human resource is *labour*. Labour is a key input into production. Of course, there are many different types of labour, encompassing different skill levels and working in different ways. *Entrepreneurship* is another human resource.

*Factors of production — labour (workers), capital (buildings) and land*

An entrepreneur is someone who organises production and identifies projects to be undertaken, bearing the risk of the activity. *Management* is also sometimes classified as a human resource, although it might be seen as a particular form of labour. *Natural resources* are also inputs into the production process. In particular, all economic activities require some use of *land*, and most use some raw materials. An important distinction here is between *renewable resources* such as forests, and *non-renewable resources* such as oil or coal.

There are also *produced resources* — inputs that are the product of a previous manufacturing process. If you like, these can be regarded as a stock of past production used to aid current production. For example, machines are used in the production process; they are resources manufactured for the purpose of producing other goods. These inputs are referred to as *capital*, which includes things like factory buildings and transport equipment as well as plant and machinery.

The way in which these inputs are combined in order to produce output is another important part of the allocation of resources. Firms need to take decisions about the mix of inputs used in order to produce their output. Such decisions are required in whatever form of economic activity a firm is engaged.

## Exercise 1.2

Classify each of the following as human, natural (renewable or non-renewable) or produced resources:

a  timber
b  services of a window cleaner
c  natural gas
d  solar energy
e  a combine harvester
f  a computer programmer who sets up a company to market his software
g  a computer

By now you should be getting some idea of the subject matter of economics. The US economist Paul Samuelson (who won the Nobel Prize for Economic Sciences in 1970) identified three key questions that economics sets out to investigate:

1 *What?* What goods and services should be produced in a society from its scarce resources? In other words, how should resources be allocated among producing DVD players, potatoes, banking services and so on?

2 *How?* How should the productive resources of the economy be used to produce these various goods and services?

3 *For whom?* Having produced a range of goods and services, how should these be allocated among the population for consumption?

## Summary

➤ The fundamental problem faced by any society is scarcity, because resources are finite but wants are unlimited. As a result, choices need to be made.

➤ Each choice has an opportunity cost — the value of the next-best alternative.

➤ Decisions need to be coordinated within a society, either by market forces or by state intervention, or a mixture of the two.

➤ The amount of output produced in a period depends upon the inputs of factors of production.

➤ Economics deals with the questions of what should be produced, how it should be produced, and for whom.

## Models and assumptions

**Key term**

**model:** a simplified representation of reality used to provide insight into economic decisions and events

Economics sets out to tackle some complex issues concerning what is a very complex real world. This complexity is such that it is essential to simplify reality in some way; otherwise the task would be overwhelming. Economists thus work with **models**. These are simplified versions of reality that are more tractable for analysis, allowing economists to focus on some key aspects of the world.

Often this works by allowing them to focus on one thing at a time. A model almost always begins with assumptions that help economists to simplify their questions. These assumptions can then be gradually relaxed so that the effect of each one of them can be observed. In this way, economists can gradually move towards a more complicated version of reality.

In evaluating a model, it is not a requirement that it be totally realistic. The model's desired objectives may be to predict future behaviour, or test empirical evidence collected from the real world. If a model provides insights into how individuals take decisions or helps to explain economic events, then it has some value, even if it seems remote from reality.

However, it is always important to examine the assumptions that are made, and to ask what happens if these assumptions do not hold.

## Opportunity cost and the production possibility curve

Economists rely heavily on diagrams to help in their analysis. In exploring the notion of opportunity cost, a helpful diagram is the **production possibility curve (PPC)**, also known as the production possibility frontier. This shows the maximum combinations of goods that can be produced with a given set of resources.

> **Key term**
>
> **production possibility curve:** a curve showing the maximum combinations of goods or services that can be produced in a set period of time given available resources

First consider a simple example. In Exercise 1.1, Andrew was studying for his AS. Suppose now that he has got behind with his homework. He has limited time available, and has five economics questions to answer and five maths exercises to do. An economics question takes the same time to answer as a maths exercise.

What are the options? Suppose he knows that in the time available he can either tackle all of the maths and none of the economics, or all of the economics and none of the maths. Alternatively, he can try to keep both teachers happy by doing some of each. Figure 1.1 shows his options. He can devote all of his efforts to maths, and leave the economics for another day. He will then be at point *A* in the figure. Alternatively, he can do all the economics exercises and no maths, and be at point *B*. The line joining these two extreme points shows the intermediate possibilities. For example, at *C* he does 2 economics exercises and 3 maths problems.

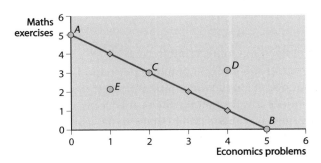

**Figure 1.1**
*The production possibility curve*

The line shows the maximum combinations that Andrew can tackle — which is why it is sometimes called a 'frontier'. There is no way he can manage to be beyond the frontier (for example, at point *D*), as he does not have the time (i.e. resources) to do so. However, he could end up *inside* the frontier, at a point such as *E*. This could happen if he gives up, and squanders his time by watching television; that would be an inefficient use of his resources — at least in terms of tackling his homework.

As Andrew moves down the line from left to right, he is spending more time on economics and less on maths. The opportunity cost of tackling an additional economics question is an additional maths exercise forgone.

Figure 1.2 shows how the *PPC* provides information about opportunity cost. Suppose we have a farmer with 10 hectares of land who is choosing between growing potatoes and onions. The *PPC* shows the combinations of the two crops that could be produced. For example, if the farmer produces 300 tonnes of onions on part of the land, then 180 tonnes of potatoes could be produced from the remaining land. In order to increase production of potatoes by 70 tonnes from 180 to 250, 50 tonnes of onions must be given up. Thus, the opportunity cost of 70 extra tonnes of potatoes is seen to be 50 tonnes of onions.

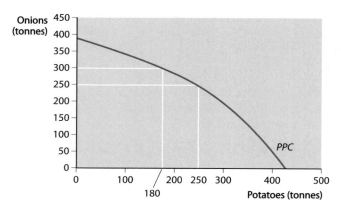

*Figure 1.2*
*Opportunity cost and the PPC*

## Consumption and investment

To move from thinking about an individual to thinking about an economy as a whole, it is first necessary to simplify reality. Assume an economy that produces just two types of good: capital goods and consumer goods. Consumer goods are for present use, whereas the capital goods are to be used to increase the future capacity of the economy — in other words, for investment.

Figure 1.3 illustrates society's options in a particular period. Given the resources available, society can produce any combination of capital and consumer goods along the *PPC*. Thus, point *A* represents one possible combination of outputs, in which the economy produces $C_1$ consumer goods and $K_1$ capital goods.

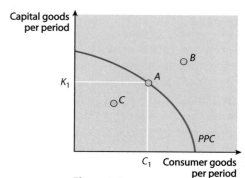

*Figure 1.3*
*Capital and consumer goods*

As with the simpler examples, if society were to move to the right along the *PPC*, it would produce more consumer goods — but at the expense of capital goods. Thus, it can be seen that the opportunity cost of producing consumer goods is in terms of forgone opportunities to produce capital goods. Notice that the *PPC* has been drawn as a curve instead of a straight line. This is because not all factors of production are equally suited to the production of both sorts of good. When the economy is well balanced, as at *A*, the factors can be allocated to the uses for which they are best equipped. However, as the economy moves towards complete specialisation in one of the types of good, factors are no longer being best used, and the opportunity cost changes. For example, if nearly all of the workers are engaged in producing consumer goods, it becomes more difficult to produce still more of these, whereas those workers producing machinery find they have too few resources with which to work. In other words, the more consumer goods are being produced, the higher is their opportunity cost.

It is now possible to interpret points *B* and *C*. Point *B* is unreachable given present resources, so the economy cannot produce that combination of goods. This applies to any point outside the *PPC*. On the other hand, at point *C* society is not using its resources efficiently. In this position there is *unemployment* of some resources in the economy. By making better use of the resources available, the economy can move towards the frontier, reducing unemployment in the process.

## Economic growth

Figure 1.3 focused on a single period. However, if the economy is producing capital goods, then in the following period its capacity to produce should increase, as it will have more resources available for production. How can this be shown on the diagram? An expansion in the available inputs suggests that in the next period the economy should be able to produce more of both goods. This is shown in Figure 1.4.

**Key** *term*

**economic growth:** an expansion in the productive capacity of the economy

Suppose that in the year 2006 the production possibility curve was at $PPC_{2006}$. However, in the following year the increased availability of resources enables greater production, and the frontier moves to $PPC_{2007}$. This is a process of **economic growth**, an expansion of the economy's productive capacity through the increased availability of inputs. Notice that the decision to produce more capital goods today means that fewer consumer goods will be produced today. People must choose between 'more jam today' or 'more jam tomorrow'.

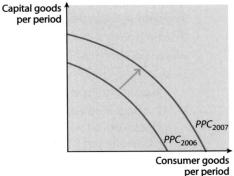

*Figure 1.4*
*Economic growth*

## Total output in an economy

Remember that the PPC is a model: a much simplified version of reality. In a real economy there are many different goods and services produced by a wide range of different factors of production — but it is not possible to draw diagrams to show all of them. The total output of an economy like the UK is measured by its **gross domestic product (GDP)**.

**Key** *term*

**gross domestic product (GDP):** a measure of the economic activity carried out in an economy during a period

## Exercise 1.3

Beverly has been cast away on a desert island, and has to survive by spending her time either fishing or climbing trees to get coconuts. The *PPC* in Figure 1.5 shows the maximum combinations of fish and coconuts that she can gather during a day. Which of the points A to E represent each of the following?

**a** a situation where Beverly spends all her time fishing

**b** an unreachable position

**c** a day when Beverly goes for a balanced diet — a mixture of coconuts and fish

**d** a day when Beverly does not fancy fish, and spends all day collecting coconuts

**e** a day when Beverly spends some of the time trying to attract the attention of a passing ship

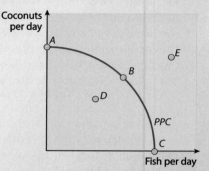

**Figure 1.5** *Fish and coconuts*

## Summary

➤ The production possibility curve shows the maximum combinations of goods or services that can be produced in a period by a given set of resources.

➤ At any point on the *PPC*, society is making full use of all resources.

➤ At any point inside the *PPC*, there is unemployment of some resources.

➤ Points beyond the *PPC* are unattainable.

➤ In a simple society producing two goods (consumer goods and capital goods), the choice is between consumption, and investment for the future.

➤ As society increases its stock of capital goods, the productive capacity of the economy increases, and the production possibility curve moves outwards: this may be termed 'economic growth'.

## Specialisation

How many workers does it take to make a pin? The eighteenth-century economist Adam Smith figured that 10 was about the right number. He argued that when a worker was producing pins on his own, carrying out all the various stages involved in the production process, the maximum number of pins that could be produced in one day was 20 — given the technology of his day, of course. This would imply that 10 workers could produce about 200 pins if they worked in the same way as the lone worker. However, if the pin production process were broken into 10 separate stages, with one worker specialising in each stage, the maximum production for a day's work would be a staggering 48,000. This is known as **division of labour**.

The division of labour is effective because individual workers become skilled at performing specialised tasks. By focusing on a particular stage, they can become highly adept, and thus more efficient, at carrying out that task. In any case, people are not all the same, so some are better at certain activities. Furthermore, this specialisation is more efficient because workers do not spend time moving from one activity to another. Specialisation may also enable firms to operate on a larger scale of production. You will see later that this may be advantageous.

> **Key term**
>
> **division of labour:** a process whereby the production procedure is broken down into a sequence of stages, and workers are assigned to particular stages

This can be seen in practice in many businesses today, where there is considerable specialisation of functions. Workers are hired for particular tasks and activities. You do not see Michael Owen pulling on the goalkeeper's jersey at half time because he fancies a change. Earlier in the chapter, it was argued that 'labour' is considered a factor of production. This idea will now be developed further by arguing that there are different types of labour, having different skills and functions. At another level, firms and even nations specialise in particular kinds of activity.

## The benefits from specialisation

Everyone is different. Individuals have different natural talents and abilities that make them good at different things. Indeed, there are some lucky people who seem to be good at everything.

Consider this example. Colin and Debbie try to supplement their incomes by working at weekends. They have both been to evening classes and have attended pottery and jewellery-making classes. At weekends they make pots and bracelets. Depending on how they divide their time, they can make differing combinations of these goods; some of the possibilities are shown in Table 1.1.

| | Colin | | | Debbie | |
|---|---|---|---|---|---|
| **Pots** | **Bracelets** | | **Pots** | **Bracelets** | |
| 12 | 0 | | 18 | 0 | |
| 9 | 3 | | 12 | 12 | |
| 6 | 6 | | 6 | 24 | |
| 3 | 9 | | 3 | 30 | |
| 0 | 12 | | 0 | 36 | |

*Table 1.1*
*Colin and Debbie's production*

The first point to notice is that Debbie is much better at both activities than Colin. If they each devote all their time to producing pots, Colin produces only 12 to Debbie's 18. If they each produce only bracelets, Colin produces 12 and Debbie, 36. There is another significant feature of this table. Although Debbie is better at producing both goods, the difference is much more marked in the case of bracelet production than pot production. So Debbie is relatively more proficient in bracelet production: in other words, she faces a lower opportunity cost in making bracelets. If Debbie switches from producing pots to producing bracelets, she

gives up 6 pots for every 12 additional bracelets that she makes. The opportunity cost of an additional bracelet is thus 6/12 = 0.5 pots. For Colin, there is a one-to-one trade-off between the two, so his opportunity cost of a bracelet is 1 pot.

More interesting is what happens if the same calculation is made for Colin and pot making. Although Debbie is absolutely better at making pots, if Colin increases his production of pots, his opportunity cost in terms of bracelets is still 1. But for Debbie the opportunity cost of making pots in terms of bracelets is 12/6 = 2, so Colin has the lower opportunity cost.

Why does this matter? It illustrates the potential benefits to be gained from special-isation. Suppose that both Colin and Debbie divide their time between the two activities in such a way that Colin produces 6 pots and 6 bracelets, and Debbie produces 6 pots and 24 bracelets. Between them, they will have produced 12 pots and 30 bracelets. However, if they each specialise in the product in which they face the lower opportunity cost, their joint production will increase. If Colin devotes all his time to pottery, he produces 12 pots, while Debbie, focusing only on bracelets, produces 36. So between them they will have produced the same number of pots as before — but 6 extra bracelets.

One final point before leaving Colin and Debbie. Figure 1.6 shows their respective production possibility curves. You can check this by graphing the points in Table 1.1 and joining them up. In this case the *PPC*s are straight lines. You can see that because Debbie is better at both activities, her *PPC* lies entirely above Colin's. The differences in opportunity cost are shown by the fact that the two *PPC*s have different slopes, as the opportunity cost element is related to the slope of the *PPC* — the rate at which one good is sacrificed for more of the other.

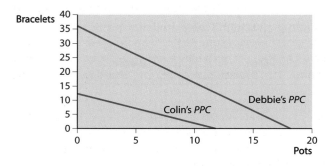

*Figure 1.6*
*Colin and Debbie's*
*production*
*possibilities*

## Summary

➤ Adam Smith introduced the notion of division of labour, which suggests that workers can become more productive by specialising in stages of the production process.

➤ Specialisation opens up the possibility of trade.

➤ The gains from specialisation and trade result from differences in opportunity cost.

# chapter 7

## Markets

You will find that in economics the term **market** is used frequently, so it is important to be absolutely clear about what is meant by it.

A market need not be a physical location (although it could be — you might regard the local farmers' market as an example of 'a set of arrangements that allows transactions to take place'). With the growth of the internet, everyone is becoming accustomed to ways of buying and selling that do not involve direct physical contact between buyer and seller, so the notion of an abstract market should not be too alien a concept.

In relation to a particular product, a market brings together potential buyers and sellers. This will be explored in the next chapter.

> **Key term**
>
> **market:** a set of arrangements that allows transactions to take place

## Money and exchange

Imagine a world without money. It is lunchtime, and you fancy a banana. In your bag you have an apple. Perhaps you can find someone with a banana who fancies an apple? But the only person with a banana available fancies an ice cream. The problem with such a *barter economy* is that you need to find someone who wants what you have and who has what you want — a *double coincidence of wants*. If this problem were to be faced by a whole economic system, undertaking transactions would be so inefficient as to be impossible. Hence the importance of *money* as a *medium of exchange*.

In order to fulfil this role, money must be something that is acceptable to both buyers and sellers. Nobody would accept money in payment for goods or services if they did not trust that they could proceed to use money for further transactions. Money must thus also act as a *store of value*: it must be possible to use it for future transactions. This quality of money means that it can be used as one way of storing wealth for future purchases. Money also allows the value of goods, services and other assets to be compared — it provides a *unit of account*. In this sense, prices of goods reflect the value that society places on them, and must be expressed in money terms.

A further role for money is that it acts as a *standard of deferred payment*. For example, a firm may wish to agree a contract for the future delivery of a good, or may wish to hire a worker to be paid at the end of the month. Such contracts are typically agreed in terms of a money value.

All of these *functions of money* are important to the smooth operation of markets, and are crucial if prices are to fulfil their role in allocating resources within society. This will become apparent as you learn more about economics.

## Microeconomics and macroeconomics

The discussion so far has focused sometimes on individual decisions, and sometimes on the decisions of governments, or of 'society' as a whole. Economic

thinking is applied in different ways, depending on whether the focus is on the decisions taken by individual agents in the economy or on the interaction between economic variables at the level of the whole economy.

**Microeconomics** deals with individual decisions taken by households or firms, or in particular markets.

**Macroeconomics** examines the interactions between economic variables at the level of the aggregate economy. For example, it might examine the effect of a change in income taxes on the level of unemployment, or of the interest rate on total demand and the rate of inflation.

**Key terms**

**microeconomics:** the study of economic decisions taken by individual economic agents, including households and firms

**macroeconomics:** the study of the interrelationships between economic variables at an aggregate (economy-wide) level

In some ways the division between the two types of analysis is artificial. The same sort of economic reasoning is applied in both types, but the focus is different.

## Positive and normative statements

Economics tries to be objective in analysis. However, some of its subject matter requires careful attention in order to retain an objective distance. In this connection, it is important to be clear about the difference between **positive** and **normative statements**.

**Key terms**

**positive statement:** a statement about what *is*, i.e. about *facts*

**normative statement:** a statement about what *ought to be*

In short, a positive statement is about *facts.* In contrast, a normative statement is about *what ought to be.* Another way of looking at this is that a statement becomes normative when it involves a *value judgement.*

Suppose the government is considering raising the tax on cigarettes. It may legitimately consult economists to discover what effect a higher tobacco tax will have on the consumption of cigarettes and on government revenues. This would be a *positive* investigation, in that the economists are being asked to use economic analysis to forecast what will happen when the tax is increased.

*Increasing taxes on tobacco affects consumption of cigarettes and government revenue*

A very different situation will arise if the government asks whether it *should* raise the tax on cigarettes. This moves the economists beyond positive analysis because it entails a value judgement — so it is now a *normative* analysis. There are some words that betray normative statements, such as 'should' or 'ought to' — watch for these.

Most of this book is about positive economics. However, you should be aware that positive

analysis is often called upon to inform normative judgements. If the aim of a policy is to stop people from smoking (which reflects a normative judgement about what *ought* to happen), then economic analysis may be used to highlight the strengths and weaknesses of alternative policy measures in a purely positive fashion.

Critics of economics often joke that economists always disagree with one another: for example, it has been said that if you put five economists in a room together, they will come up with at least six conflicting opinions. However, although economists may arrive at different value judgements, and thus have differences when it comes to normative issues, there is much greater agreement when it comes to positive analysis.

## Summary

➤ A market is a set of arrangements that allows transactions to take place.

➤ A barter economy is a highly inefficient way of conducting transactions, hence the importance of money in enabling exchange to take place.

➤ Money plays key roles as a medium of exchange, a store of value, a unit of account, and a standard of deferred payment.

➤ By fulfilling these various roles, money enables the smooth operation of markets, and allows prices to act as a guide in allocating resources.

➤ Microeconomics deals with individual decisions made by consumers and producers, whereas macroeconomics analyses the interactions between economic variables in the aggregate — but both use similar ways of thinking.

➤ Positive statements are about *what is*, whereas normative statements are about *what ought to be*.

# Chapter 2
# Demand, supply and equilibrium

*The demand and supply model is perhaps the most famous of all pieces of economic analysis; it is also one of the most useful. It has many applications that help explain the way markets work in the real world. It is thus central to understanding economics. This chapter introduces the model. Some applications will be investigated in Chapter 3.*

## Learning outcomes

After studying this chapter, you should:
➤ be familiar with the demand curve and the factors that influence its shape and position
➤ be aware of the supply curve and the factors that influence its shape and position
➤ be able to distinguish between movements *of* and *along* the demand and supply curves
➤ understand the notion of equilibrium and its relevance in the demand and supply model
➤ be aware of the distinction between normal and inferior goods

## Demand

Consider an individual consumer. Think of yourself, and a product that you consume regularly. What factors influence your **demand** for that product? Put another way, what factors influence how much of the product you choose to buy?

When thinking about the factors that influence your demand for your chosen product, common sense will probably mean that you focus on a range of different points. You may think about why you enjoy consuming the product. You may focus on how much it will cost to buy the product, and whether you can afford it. You may decide that you have consumed a product so much that you are ready for a change; or perhaps you will decide to try something advertised on TV, or being bought by a friend.

>  **term**
>
> **demand:** the quantity of a good or service that consumers choose to buy at any possible price in a given period

Whatever the influences you come up with, they can probably be categorised under four headings that ultimately determine your demand for a good. First, the *price* of the good is an important influence on your demand for it, and will affect the quantity of it that you choose to buy. Second, the *price of other goods* may be significant. Third, *your income* will determine how much of the good you can afford to purchase. Finally, almost any other factors that you may have thought of can be listed as part of your *preferences*.

### Individual and market demand

A similar line of argument may apply if we think in terms of the demand for a particular product — say, DVDs. The market for DVDs can thus be seen as bringing together all the potential buyers (and sellers) of the product, and market demand can be analysed in terms of the factors that influence all potential buyers of that good or service. In other words, market demand can be seen as the total quantity of a good or service that all potential buyers would choose to buy at any given price. The same four factors that influence your own individual decision to buy will also influence the total market demand for a product. In addition, the number of potential buyers in the market will clearly influence the size of total demand at any price.

R. Parkes/Ontanet

### Demand and the price of a good

Assume for the moment that the influences mentioned above, other than the price of the good, are held constant, so that the focus is only on the extent to which the price of a good influences the demand for it. This is a common assumption in economics, which is sometimes expressed by the Latin phrase **ceteris paribus**, meaning 'other things being equal'. Given the complexity of the real world, it is often helpful to focus on one thing at a time.

 **term**

**ceteris paribus:** a Latin phrase meaning 'other things being equal'; it is used in economics when we focus on changes in one variable while holding other influences constant

This ceteris paribus assumption is used a lot in economics, and is a powerful tool. Focusing on one influence at a time is a way of coping with the complexities of the real world and makes the analysis of economic issues much clearer than if we try to analyse everything at once. You will see many instances of it as the course proceeds.

So how is the demand for DVDs influenced by their price? Other things being equal (ceteris paribus), you would expect the demand for DVDs to be higher when the price is low and lower when the price is high. In other words, you would expect an inverse relationship between the price and the quantity demanded. This is such a strong phenomenon that it is referred to as the **law of demand**.

If you were to compile a list that showed how many DVDs would be bought at any possible price and plot these on a diagram, this would be called the **demand curve**. Figure 2.1 shows what this might look like. As it is an inverse relationship, the demand curve slopes downwards. Notice that this need not be a straight line: its shape depends upon how consumers react at different prices. According to this curve, if price were to be set at £40, the quantity demanded would be 20,000 per period. However, if the price were only £20, the demand would be higher, at 60,000.

**Key terms**

**law of demand:** a law that states that there is an inverse relationship between quantity demanded and the price of a good or service, ceteris paribus

**demand curve:** a graph showing how much of a good will be demanded by consumers at any given price

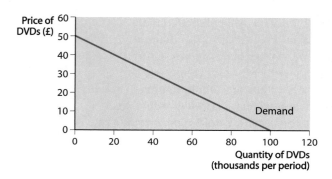

*Figure 2.1*
*A demand curve for DVDs*

## Extension point

An analysis of why the demand curve should be downward sloping would reveal that there are two important forces at work. At a higher price, a consumer buying a DVD has less income left over. This is referred to as the *real income effect* of a price increase. In addition, if the price of DVDs goes up, consumers may find other goods more attractive and choose to buy something else instead of DVDs. This is referred to as the *substitution effect* of a price increase.

As the price of a good changes, a movement along the demand curve can be observed as consumers adjust their buying pattern in response to the price change.

Notice that the demand curve has been drawn under the ceteris paribus assumption. In other words, it was assumed that all other influences on demand were held constant in order to focus on the relationship between demand and price. There are two important implications of this procedure.

First, the price drawn on the vertical axis of a diagram such as Figure 2.1 is the *relative* price — it is the price of DVDs under the assumption that all other prices are constant.

Second, if any of the other influences on demand change, you would expect to see a movement of the whole demand curve. It is very important to distinguish between factors that induce a movement *along* a curve, and factors that induce a movement *of* a curve. This applies not only in the case of the demand curve — there are many other instances where this is important.

### Snob effects

It is sometimes argued that for some goods a 'snob effect' may lead to the demand curve sloping upwards. The argument is that some people may value certain goods more highly simply because their price is high, especially if they know that other people will observe them consuming these goods; an example might be Rolex watches. In other words, people gain value from having other people notice that they are rich enough to afford to consume a particular good. There is thus a *conspicuous consumption* effect, which was first pointed out by Thorstein Veblen at the end of the nineteenth century.

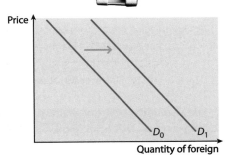

*Rolex watches may benefit from the conspicuous consumption effect*

However, although there may be some individual consumers who react to price in this way, there is no evidence to suggest that there are whole markets that display an upward-sloping demand curve for this reason. In other words, most consumers would react normally to the price of such goods.

### Demand and consumer incomes

The second influence on demand is consumer incomes. For a **normal good**, an increase in consumer incomes will, ceteris paribus, lead to an increase in the quantity demanded at any given price. Foreign holidays are an example of a normal good because, as people's incomes rise, they will tend to demand more foreign holidays at any given price.

Figure 2.2 illustrates this. $D_0$ here represents the initial demand curve for foreign holidays. An increase in consumers' incomes causes demand to be higher at any given price, and the demand curve shifts to the right — to $D_1$.

However, demand does not always respond in this way. For example, think about bus journeys. As incomes rise in a society, more people can afford to have a car, or to use taxis. This means that, as incomes rise, the demand for bus journeys may tend to fall. Such goods are known as **inferior goods**.

*Figure 2.2*
*A movement of the demand curve following an increase in consumer incomes (a normal good)*

**Key terms**

**normal good:** one where the quantity demanded increases in response to an increase in consumer incomes
**inferior good:** one where the quantity demanded decreases in response to an increase in consumer incomes

This time an increase in consumers' incomes in Figure 2.3 causes the demand curve to shift to the left, from its initial position at $D_0$, to $D_1$ where less is demanded at any given price.

The relationship between quantity demanded and income can be shown more directly on a diagram. Panel (a) of Figure 2.4 shows how this would look for a normal good. It is upward sloping, showing that the quantity demanded is higher when consumer incomes are higher. In contrast, the income demand curve for an inferior good, shown in panel (b) of the diagram, slopes downwards, indicating that the quantity demanded will be lower when consumer incomes are relatively high.

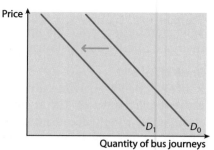

**Figure 2.3**
*A movement of the demand curve following an increase in consumer incomes: an inferior good*

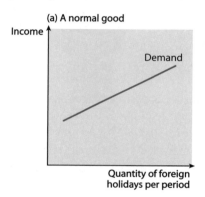

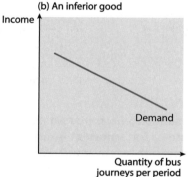

**Figure 2.4**
*Demand and income*

## Exercise 2.1

Identify each of the following products as being either a normal good or an inferior good:

a digital camera     c potatoes     e fine wine

b magazine     d bicycle     f cheap wine

## Extension point: a Giffen good

Remember that a consumer's response to a change in the price of a good is made up of a substitution effect and a real income effect (see the extension point on page 18). The substitution effect always acts in the opposite direction to the price change: in other words, an increase in the price of a good always induces a switch *away* from the good towards other goods. However, it can now be seen that the real income effect may operate in either direction, depending on whether it is a normal good or an inferior good that is being considered.

Suppose there is a good that is *very* inferior. A fall in the price of a good induces a substitution effect towards the good, but the real income effect works in the opposite direction. The fall in price is equivalent to a rise in real income, so consumers will consume less of the good. If this effect is really strong, it could overwhelm the substitution effect, and the fall in price could induce a *fall* in the quantity demanded: in other words, for such a good the demand curve could be upward sloping.

Such goods are known as *Giffen goods*, after Sir Robert Giffen, who pointed out that this could happen. However, in spite of stories about the reaction of demand to a rise in the price of potatoes during the great Irish potato famine, there have been no authenticated sightings of Giffen goods. The notion remains a theoretical curiosity.

### Demand and the price of other goods

The demand for a good may respond to changes in the price of other related goods, of which there are two main types. On the one hand, two goods may be **substitutes** for each other. For example, consider two different (but similar) breakfast cereals. If there is an increase in the price of one of the cereals, consumers may switch their consumption to the other, as the two are likely to be close substitutes for each other.

Not all consumers will switch, of course — some may be deeply committed to one particular brand — but some of them are certainly likely to change over.

On the other hand, there may also be goods that are **complements** — for example, products that are consumed jointly, such as breakfast cereals and milk, or cars and petrol. Here a fall in the price of one good may lead to an increase in demand for *both* products.

> **Key terms**
>
> **substitutes:** two goods are said to be substitutes if the demand for one good is likely to rise if the price of the other good rises
>
> **complements:** two goods are said to be complements if an increase in the price of one good causes the demand for the other good to fall

Whether goods are substitutes or complements determines how the demand for one good responds to a change in the price of another. Figure 2.5 shows the demand curves (per period) for two goods that are substitutes — tea and coffee.

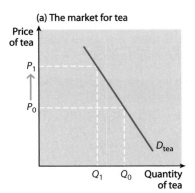

(a) The market for tea

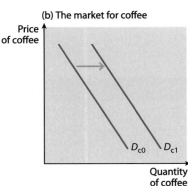

(b) The market for coffee

*Figure 2.5*
*A movement of the demand curve following an increase in the price of a substitute good*

If there is an increase in the price of tea from $P_0$ to $P_1$ in panel (a), more consumers will switch to coffee and the demand curve in panel (b) will move to the right — say, from $D_{c0}$ to $D_{c1}$.

For complements the situation is the reverse: in Figure 2.6 an increase in the price of tea from $P_0$ to $P_1$ in panel (a) causes the demand curve for milk to move leftwards, from $D_{m0}$ to $D_{m1}$.

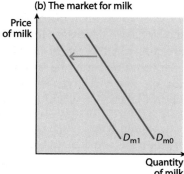

*Figure 2.6*
*A movement of the demand curve following an increase in the price of a complementary good*

### Demand, consumer preferences and other influences

The discussion has shown how the demand for a good is influenced by the price of the good, the price of other goods, and by consumer incomes. It was stated earlier that almost everything else that determines demand for a good can be represented as 'consumer preferences'. In particular, this refers to whether you like or dislike a good. There may be many things that influence whether you like or dislike a product. In part it simply depends upon your own personal inclinations — some people like dark chocolate, others prefer milk chocolate. However, firms may try to influence your preferences through advertising, and sometimes they succeed. Or you might be one of those people who get so irritated by television advertising that you compile a blacklist of products that you will never buy! Even this is an influence on your demand.

In some cases your preferences may be swayed by other people's demand — again, this may be positive or negative. Fashions may influence demand, but some people like to buck (or lead) the trend.

You may also see a movement of the demand curve if there is a sudden surge in the popularity of a good — or, indeed, a sudden collapse in demand.

### Exercise 2.2

Sketch some demand curves for the following situations, and think about how you would expect the demand curve to change (if at all):

a   the demand for chocolate following a campaign highlighting the dangers of obesity

b   the demand for oranges following an increase in the price of apples

    **c** the demand for oranges following a decrease in the price of oranges

    **d** the demand for DVDs following a decrease in the price of DVD players

    **e** the demand for VCRs following a decrease in the price of DVD recorders

    **f** the demand for private transport following an increase in consumer incomes

    **g** the demand for public transport following an increase in consumer incomes

The above discussion has covered most of the factors that influence the demand for a good. However, in some cases it is necessary to take a time element into account. Not all of the goods bought are consumed instantly. In some cases, consumption is spread over long periods of time. Indeed, there may be instances where goods are not bought for consumption at all, but are seen by the buyer as an investment, perhaps for resale at a later date. In these circumstances, expectations about future price changes may be relevant. For example, people may buy fine wine or works of art in the expectation that prices will rise in the future. There may also be goods whose prices are expected to fall in the future. This has been common with many hi-tech products; initially a newly launched product may sell at a high price, but as production levels rise, costs may fall, and prices also. People may therefore delay purchase in the expectation of future price reductions.

## Summary

➤ A market is a set of arrangements that enables transactions to take place.

➤ The market demand for a good depends upon the price of the good, the price of other goods, consumers' incomes and preferences and the number of potential consumers.

➤ The demand curve shows the relationship between demand for a product and its price, ceteris paribus.

➤ The demand curve is downward sloping, as the relationship between demand and price is an inverse one.

➤ A change in price induces a movement *along* the demand curve, whereas a change in the other determinants of demand induces a movement *of* the demand curve.

➤ When the demand for a good rises as consumer incomes rise, that good is referred to as a *normal good*; when demand falls as income rises, the good is referred to as an *inferior good*.

➤ A good or service may be related to other goods by being either a *substitute* or a *complement*.

➤ For some products, demand may be related to expected future prices.

## Supply

The demand curve shows a relationship between quantity demanded and the price of a good or service. A similar relationship between the quantity supplied by firms and the price of a good can be identified in relation to the behaviour of firms in a competitive market — that is, a market in which individual firms cannot influence

the price of the good or service that they are selling, because of competition from other firms.

In order to analyse how firms decide how much of a product to supply, it is necessary to make an assumption about what it is that firms are trying to achieve. Assume that they aim to maximise their profits, where 'profits' are defined as the difference between a firm's total revenue and its total costs.

In such a market it may well be supposed that firms will be prepared to supply more goods at a high price than at a lower one (ceteris paribus), as this will increase their profits. The **supply curve** illustrates how much the firms in a market will supply at any given price, as shown in Figure 2.7. As firms are expected to supply more goods at a high price than at a lower price, the supply curve will be upward sloping, reflecting this positive relationship between quantity and price.

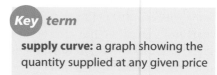

**supply curve:** a graph showing the quantity supplied at any given price

Notice that, again, the focus is on the relationship between quantity supplied and the price of a good in a given period, ceteris paribus — that is, holding other things constant. As with the demand curve, there are other factors affecting the quantity supplied. These other influences on supply will determine the position of the supply curve: if any of them changes, the supply curve can be expected to move.

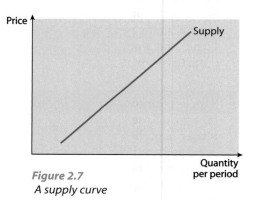

*Figure 2.7*
*A supply curve*

### What influences supply?

We can identify five important influences on the quantity that firms will be prepared to supply to the market at any given price:
➤ production costs
➤ the technology of production
➤ taxes and subsidies
➤ the price of related goods
➤ firms' expectations about future prices

### Costs and technology

If firms are aiming to maximise profits, an important influence on their supply decision will be the costs of production that they face. Chapter 1 explained that in order to produce output, firms need to use inputs of the factors of production — labour, capital, land etc. If the cost of those inputs increases, firms will in general be expected to supply less output at any given price. The effect of this is shown in Figure 2.8, where an increase in production costs induces firms to supply less output at each price. The curve shifts from its initial position at $S_0$ to a new position at $S_1$. For example, suppose the original price was £10 per unit; before the increase in costs, firms would have been prepared to supply 100 units of the product to the market. An increase in costs of £6 per unit that shifted the supply curve from $S_0$ to $S_1$ would mean that, at the same price, firms would now supply only 50 units of the good. Notice that the vertical distance between $S_0$ and $S_1$ is the amount of the change in cost per unit.

In contrast, if a new technology of production is introduced, which means that firms can produce more cost effectively, this could have the opposite effect, moving the supply curve to the right. This is shown in Figure 2.9, where improved technology induces firms to supply more output at any given price, and the supply curve moves from its initial position at $S_0$ to a new position at $S_1$. Thus, if firms in the initial situation were supplying 50 units with the price at £10 per unit, then a fall in costs of £6 per unit would induce firms to increase supply to 100 units (if the price remained at £10).

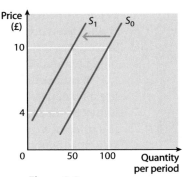

**Figure 2.8**
*The supply curve shifts to the left if production costs increase*

### Taxes and subsidies

Suppose the government imposes a sales tax such as VAT on a good or service. The price paid by consumers will be higher than the revenue received by firms, as the tax has to be paid to the government. This means that firms will (ceteris paribus) be prepared to supply less output at any given market price. Again, the supply curve shifts to the left. This is shown in panel (a) of Figure 2.10, which

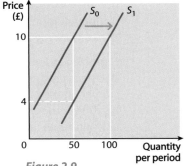

**Figure 2.9**
*The supply curve shifts to the right if production costs fall*

assumes a fixed per unit tax. The supply curve shifts, as firms supply less at any given market price. This will be analysed more carefully in the next chapter. On the other hand, if the government pays firms a subsidy to produce a particular good, this will reduce their costs, and induce them to supply more output at any given price. The supply curve will then shift to the right, as shown in panel (b).

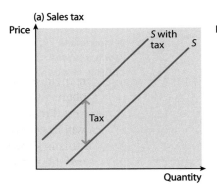

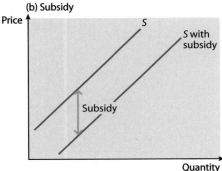

**Figure 2.10**
*The effects of taxes and subsidies on supply*

### Prices of other goods

It was shown earlier that from the consumers' perspective, two goods may be substitutes for each other, such that if the price of one good increases, consumers may be induced to switch their consumption to substitute goods. Similarly, there may be substitution on the supply side. A firm may face a situation in which there are alternative uses to which its factors of production may be put: in other words, it may be able to choose between producing a range of different products. A rise in the price of a good raises its profitability, and therefore may encourage a firm to switch production from other goods. This may happen even if there are high switching costs, provided the increase in price is sufficiently large. For example, a change in relative prices of potatoes and organic swedes might encourage a farmer to stop planting potatoes and grow organic swedes instead.

In other circumstances, a firm may produce a range of goods jointly. Perhaps one good is a by-product of the production process of another. An increase in the price of one of the goods may mean that the firm will produce more of both goods. This notion of joint supply is similar to the situation on the demand side where consumers regard two goods as complements.

### Expected prices

Because production takes time, firms often take decisions about how much to supply on the basis of expected future prices. Indeed, if their product is one that can be stored, there may be times when a firm will decide to allow stocks of a product to build up in anticipation of a higher price in the future, perhaps by holding back some of its production from current sales.

## Movements along and movements of the supply curve

As with the demand curve, it is very important to remember that there is a distinction between movements *along* the supply curve, and movements *of* the supply curve. If there is a change in the market price, this induces a movement along the supply curve. After all, the supply curve is designed to reveal how firms will react to a change in the price of the good. For example, in Figure 2.11, if the price is initially at $P_0$ firms will be prepared to supply the quantity $Q_0$, but if the price then increases to $P_1$ this will induce a movement along the supply curve as firms increase supply to $Q_1$.

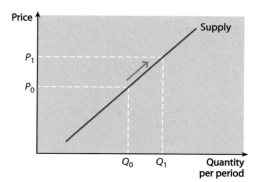

*Figure 2.11*
*A movement along a supply curve in response to a price change*

In contrast, as seen in the previous section, a change in any of the other influences on supply will induce a movement of the whole supply curve, as this affects the firms' willingness to supply at any given price.

## Exercise 2.3

For each of the following, decide whether the demand curve or the supply curve will move, and in which direction:

a Consumers are convinced by arguments about the benefits of organic vegetables.

b A new process is developed that reduces the amount of inputs that firms need in order to produce bicycles.

c There is a severe frost in Brazil that affects the coffee crop.

d The government increases the rate of value added tax.

e Real incomes rise.

f The price of tea falls: what happens in the market for coffee?

g The price of sugar falls: what happens in the market for coffee?

## Summary

➤ Other things being equal, firms in a competitive market can be expected to supply more output at a higher price.

➤ The supply curve traces out this positive relationship between price and quantity supplied.

➤ Changes in the costs of production, technology, taxes and subsidies or the prices of related goods may induce movements of the supply curve, with firms being prepared to sell more (or less) output at any given price.

➤ Expectations about future prices may affect current supply decisions.

## Market equilibrium

The previous sections in this chapter have described the components of the demand and supply model. It only remains to bring them together, for this is how the power of the model can be appreciated. Figure 2.12 shows the demand for and supply of butter.

Suppose that the price were to be set at a relatively high price (above $P^*$). At such a price, firms wish to supply lots of butter to the market. However, consumers are not very keen on butter at such a high price,

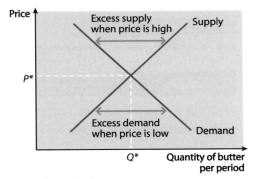

**Figure 2.12**
*Bringing demand and supply together*

so demand is not strong. Firms now have a problem: they find that their stocks of butter are building up. What has happened is that the price has been set at a level that exceeds the value that most consumers place on butter, so they will not buy it. There is *excess supply*. The only thing that the firms can do is to reduce the price in order to clear their stocks.

Suppose they now set their price relatively low (below *P\**). Now it is the consumers who have a problem, because they would like to buy more butter at the low price than firms are prepared to supply. There is *excess demand*. Some consumers may offer to pay more than the going price in order to obtain their butter supplies, and firms realise that they can raise the price.

How will it all end? When the price settles at *P\** in Figure 2.12, there is a balance in the market between the quantity that consumers wish to demand and the quantity that firms wish to supply, namely *Q\**. This is the **market equilibrium**. In a free market the price can be expected to converge on this equilibrium level, through movements along both demand and supply curves.

**Key term**

**market equilibrium:** a situation that occurs in a market when the price is such that the quantity that consumers wish to buy is exactly balanced by the quantity that firms wish to supply

## Exercise 2.4

Identify the equilibrium market price if demand and supply are as in Figure 2.13.

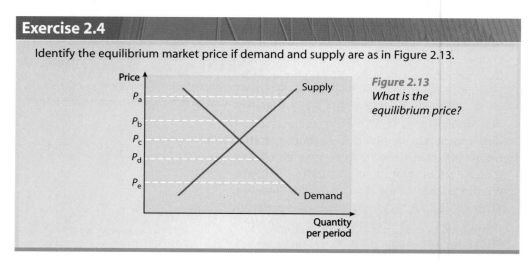

*Figure 2.13*
*What is the equilibrium price?*

## Summary

➤ Bringing demand and supply together, you can identify the market equilibrium.

➤ The equilibrium price is the unique point at which the quantity demanded by consumers is just balanced by the quantity that firms wish to supply.

➤ In a free market, natural forces can be expected to encourage prices to adjust to the equilibrium level.

OCR Advanced Economics

## The labour market

Within the economy, firms demand labour and employees supply labour — so why not use demand and supply to analyse the market? This can indeed be done.

From the firms' point of view, the demand for labour is a *derived demand*. In other words, firms want labour not for its own sake, but for the output that it produces. When the 'price' of labour is low, firms will tend to demand more of it than when the 'price' of labour is high. The wage rate can be regarded as this 'price' of labour. On the employee side, it is argued that more people tend to offer themselves for work when the wage is relatively high.

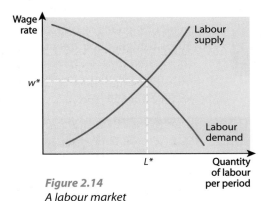

**Figure 2.14**
*A labour market*

On this basis, the demand for labour is expected to be downward sloping and the supply of labour upward sloping, as in Figure 2.14. As usual, the equilibrium in a free market will be at the intersection of demand and supply, so firms will hire $L^*$ labour at a wage rate of $w^*$.

The consequences of such a market being away from equilibrium are important. Consider Figure 2.15. Suppose the wage rate is set above the equilibrium level at $w_1$. The high wage rate encourages more people to offer themselves for work — up to the amount of labour $L_s$. However, at this wage rate employers are prepared to hire only up to $L_d$ labour. Think about what is happening here. There are people offering themselves for work who cannot find employment: in other words, there is **unemployment**. Thus, one possible cause of unemployment is a wage rate that is set above the equilibrium level.

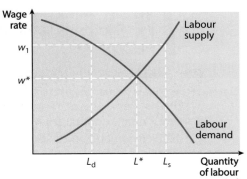

**Figure 2.15**
*A labour market out of equilibrium*

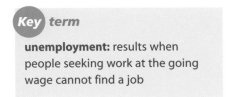

**Key term**

**unemployment:** results when people seeking work at the going wage cannot find a job

## The foreign exchange market

When you take your holidays in Spain, you need to buy euros. Equally, when German tourists come to visit London, they need to buy pounds. If there is buying going on, then there must be a market — remember from Chapter 1 that a market is a set of arrangements that enable transactions to be undertaken. So here is another sort of market to be considered. The exchange rate is the price at which two currencies exchange, and it can be analysed using demand and supply.

Consider the market for pounds, and focus on the exchange rate between pounds and euros, as shown in Figure 2.16. Think first about what gives rise to a demand for pounds. It is not just German tourists who need pounds to spend on holiday: anyone holding euros who wants to buy UK goods needs pounds in order to pay for them. So the demand for pounds comes from people in the euro area who want to buy UK goods or services — or assets. When the exchange rate for the pound in euros is high, potential buyers of UK goods get relatively few pounds per euro, so the demand will be relatively low, whereas if the euro per pound rate is relatively low, they get more for their money. Hence the demand curve is expected to be downward sloping.

Currencies are traded on the foreign exchange market

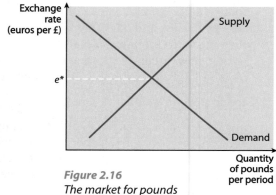

**Figure 2.16**
The market for pounds

One point to notice from this is that foreign exchange is another example of a derived demand, in the sense that people want pounds not for their own sake, but for the goods or services that they can buy. One way of viewing the exchange rate is as a means by which to learn about the international competitiveness of UK exports. When the exchange rate is high, UK goods are less competitive in Europe, ceteris paribus. Notice the ceteris paribus assumption here. This is important because the exchange rate is not the only determinant of the competitiveness of UK goods: they also depend on the relative price levels in the UK and Europe.

How about the supply of pounds? Pounds are supplied by UK residents wanting euros to buy goods or services from Europe. From this point of view, when the euro/pound rate is high, UK residents get more euros for their pounds and therefore will tend to supply more pounds.

If the exchange market is in equilibrium, the exchange rate will be at $e^*$, where the demand for pounds is matched by the supply.

## The money market

Chapter 1 highlighted the importance of money in enabling exchange to take place through the operation of markets. This implies that people have a **demand for money**. This demand for money is associated with the functions of money set out on page 13 — as a medium of exchange, store of value, unit of account and standard of deferred payment. If there is a demand for money, then perhaps there should also be a market for money?

We can think of the demand for money depending on a number of factors — in particular, upon the number of transactions that people wish to undertake — which probably depends upon income. But is there a price of money? The price of money can be viewed in terms of opportunity cost. When people choose to hold money, they incur an opportunity cost, which can be seen as the next best alternative to holding money. For example, instead of holding money, you could decide to purchase a financial asset that would provide a rate of return, represented by the rate of interest. This rate of interest can thus be interpreted as the price of holding money.

How about the supply of money? This will be discussed much later in the course, but for now, it can be assumed that the supply of money is determined by the Bank of England, and it can be assumed that this money supply will not depend upon the rate of interest. Figure 2.17 illustrates the market for money. The demand for money is shown to be downward sloping, as the higher the rate of interest, the greater the return that is sacrificed by holding money, so the smaller will be the demand for money. The supply of money does not depend upon the rate of interest (by assumption), so is shown as a vertical line. The market is in equilibrium when the rate of interest is at $r^*$, the level at which the demand and supply of money are equal.

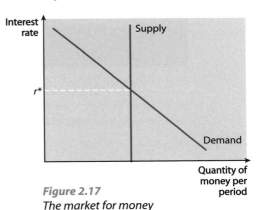

**Figure 2.17**
*The market for money*

## Summary

➤ In the labour market, equilibrium is achieved through the wage rate. If the wage rate is set too high, it leads to unemployment.

➤ Demand and supply enable you to examine how the foreign exchange rate is determined.

➤ The model can also be applied to analyse the money market.

## Exercise 2.5 Profits and superships

In August 2001 *The Financial Times* reported that ship-owners were facing serious problems. Shipping rates (the prices that ship-owners charge for carrying freight) had fallen drastically in the second quarter of 2001. For example, on the Europe–Asia route, rates fell by 8% eastbound and 6% westbound, causing the ship-owners' profits to be squeezed. Overleaf are some relevant facts and issues:

*In 2001 shipping rates fell drastically*

**a** New 'superships', having been ordered a few years earlier, were coming into service with enhanced capacity for transporting freight.

**b** A worldwide economic slowdown was taking place; Japan was in lengthy recession and the US economy was also slowing, affecting the growth of world trade.

**c** Fuel prices were falling.

**d** The structure of the industry is fragmented, with ship-owners watching each other's orders for new ships.

**e** New ships take a long time to build.

**f** Shipping lines face high fixed costs with slender margins.

Assume that the market is competitive. (This will allow you to draw supply and demand curves for the market.) There is some evidence for this, as shipping lines face 'slender margins' (see f). This suggests that the firms face competition from each other, and are unable to use market power to increase profit margins.

How would you expect the demand and supply curves to move in response to the first three factors mentioned (i.e. a, b and c)? Sketch a diagram for yourself.

Why should the shipping lines undertake a large-scale expansion at a time of falling or stagnant demand?

# Chapter 3
# Developing the supply and demand model

*The previous chapter introduced the notions of demand and supply, together with the key concept of market equilibrium. It is now time to begin to develop this model further to see how it provides insights into how markets operate. You will encounter demand and supply in a wide variety of contexts, and begin to glimpse some of the ways in which the model can help to explain how the economic world works.*

## Learning outcomes

After studying this chapter, you should:
- ➤ understand what is meant by comparative static analysis
- ➤ understand the concept of elasticity measures and appreciate their importance and applications
- ➤ have an overview of how the price mechanism works to allocate resources
- ➤ understand the meaning and significance of consumer surplus
- ➤ be able to see how prices provide incentives to producers
- ➤ understand the meaning and significance of producer surplus
- ➤ understand the effects of the entry and exit of firms into and out of a market

The previous chapter introduced the supply and demand model, and showed equilibrium in a range of different markets. In this chapter the model will be developed further, and you will start to see some important applications of the model.

## Comparative statics

First, however, it is necessary to introduce another of the economist's key tools — comparative static analysis. Chapter 2 described the way in which a market moves towards equilibrium between demand and supply through price adjustments and movements along the demand and supply curves. This is called static analysis, in the sense that a ceteris paribus assumption is imposed by holding constant the factors that influence demand and supply, and focusing on the way in which the market reaches equilibrium.

In the next stage, one of these background factors is changed, and the effect of this change on the market equilibrium is then analysed. In other words, beginning with a market in equilibrium, one of the factors affecting either demand or supply is altered, and the new market equilibrium is then studied. In this way, two static equilibrium positions — before and after — will be compared. This approach is known as **comparative static analysis**.

**Key term**

**comparative static analysis:** examines the effect on equilibrium of a change in the external conditions affecting a market

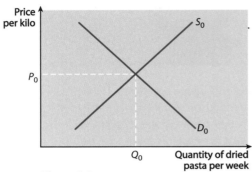

*Figure 3.1*
*A market for dried pasta*

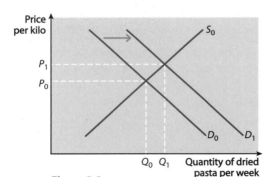

*Figure 3.2*
*A change in consumer preferences for dried pasta*

*Dried pasta in production*

## A market for dried pasta

Begin with a simple market for dried pasta, a basic staple foodstuff obtainable in any supermarket. Figure 3.1 shows the market in equilibrium. $D_0$ represents the demand curve in this initial situation, and $S_0$ is the supply curve. The market is in equilibrium with the price at $P_0$, and the quantity being traded is $Q_0$. It is equilibrium in the sense that pasta producers are supplying just the amount of pasta that consumers wish to buy at that price. This is the 'before' position. Some experiments will now be carried out with this market by disturbing the equilibrium.

### A change in consumer preferences

Suppose that a study is published highlighting the health benefits of eating pasta, backed up with an advertising campaign. The effect of this is likely to be an increase in the demand for pasta at any given price. In other words, this change in consumer preferences will shift the demand curve to the right, as shown in Figure 3.2.

The market now adjusts to a new equilibrium, with a new price $P_1$, and a new quantity traded at $Q_1$. In this case, both price and quantity have increased as a result of the change in preferences.

### A change in the price of a substitute

A second possibility is that there is a fall in the price of fresh pasta. This is likely to be a close substitute for dried pasta, so the probable result is that some former

OCR Advanced Economics

consumers of dried pasta will switch their allegiance to the fresh variety. This time the demand curve for dried pasta moves in the opposite direction, as can be seen in Figure 3.3. Here the starting point is the original position, with market equilibrium at price $P_0$ and a quantity traded $Q_0$. After the shift in the demand curve from $D_0$ to $D_2$, the market settles again with a price of $P_2$ and a quantity traded of $Q_2$. Both price and quantity traded are now lower than in the original position.

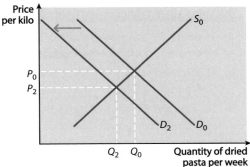

**Figure 3.3**
*A change in the price of a substitute for dried pasta*

### An improvement in pasta technology

Next, suppose that a new pasta-making machine is produced, enabling dried pasta makers to produce at a lower cost than before. This advancement reduces firms' costs, and consequently they are prepared to supply more dried pasta at any given price. The starting point is the same initial position, but now it is the supply curve that moves — to the right. This is shown in Figure 3.4.

Again, comparative static analysis can be undertaken. The new market equilibrium is at price $P_3$, which is lower than the original equilibrium, but the quantity traded is higher at $Q_3$.

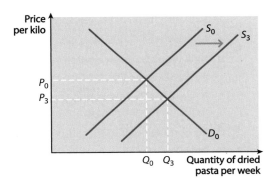

**Figure 3.4**
*New pasta-making technology*

### An increase in labour costs

Finally, suppose that pasta producers face an increase in their labour costs. Perhaps the Pasta Workers' Union has negotiated higher wages, or the pasta producers have become subject to stricter health and safety legislation, which raises their production costs. Figure 3.5 starts as usual with equilibrium at price $P_0$ and quantity $Q_0$.

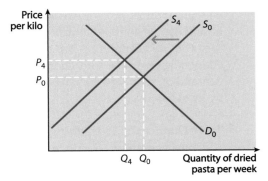

**Figure 3.5**
*An increase in labour costs*

The increase in production costs means that pasta producers are prepared to supply less dried pasta at any given price, so the supply curve shifts to the left — to $S_4$. This takes the market to a new equilibrium at a higher price than before ($P_4$), but with a lower quantity traded ($Q_4$).

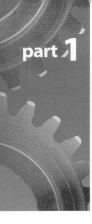

**part 1**

## Summary

➤ Comparative static analysis enables you to analyse the way in which markets respond to external shocks, by comparing market equilibrium before and after a shock.

➤ All you need to do is to figure out whether the shock affects demand or supply, and in which direction.

➤ The size and direction of the movements of the demand and supply curves determine the overall effect on equilibrium price and quantity traded.

## Exercise 3.1

For each of the following market situations, sketch a demand and supply diagram, and undertake a comparative static analysis to see what happens to the equilibrium price and quantity. Explain your answers.

**a** An increase in consumer incomes affects the demand for bus travel.

**b** New regulations on environmental pollution force a firm making paint to increase outlay on reducing its emission of toxic fumes.

**c** A firm of accountants brings in new, faster computers, which have the effect of reducing the firm's costs.

**d** An outbreak of bird flu causes consumers of chicken to buy burgers instead. (What is the effect on both markets?)

## Elasticity: the sensitivity of demand and supply

Both the demand for and the supply of a good or service can be expected to depend upon its price as well as other factors. It is often interesting to know just how sensitive demand and/or supply will be to a change in either price or one of the other determinants — for example, in predicting how market equilibrium will change in response to a change in the market environment. The sensitivity of demand or supply to a change in one of its determining factors can be measured by its **elasticity**.

### The price elasticity of demand

The most common elasticity measure is the **price elasticity of demand (*PED*)**. This measures the sensitivity of the quantity demanded of a good or service to a change in its price.

The elasticity is defined as the percentage change in quantity demanded divided by the percentage change in the price.

> **Key terms**
>
> **elasticity:** a measure of the sensitivity of one variable to changes in another variable
>
> **price elasticity of demand (*PED*):** a measure of the sensitivity of quantity demanded to a change in the price of a good or service. It is measured as:
>
>
>
> $$\frac{\% \text{ change in quantity demanded}}{\% \text{ change in price}}$$

OCR Advanced Economics

We define the percentage change in price as $100 \times \Delta P/P$ (where $\Delta$ means 'change in' and $P$ stands for 'price'). Similarly, the percentage change in quantity demanded is $100 \times \Delta Q/Q$.

When the demand is highly price sensitive, the percentage change in quantity demanded following a price change will be large relative to the percentage change in price. In this case, *PED* will take on a value that is numerically greater than 1. For example, suppose that a 2% change in price leads to a 5% change in quantity demanded; the elasticity is then −5 divided by 2 = −2.5. When the elasticity is numerically greater than 1, demand is referred to as being *price elastic*.

There are two important things to notice about this. First, because the demand curve is downward sloping, the elasticity will always be negative. This is because the changes in price and quantity are always in the opposite direction. Second, you should try to calculate the elasticity only for a relatively small change in price, as it becomes unreliable for very large changes.

When demand is not very sensitive to price, the percentage change in quantity demanded will be smaller than the original percentage change in price, and the elasticity will then be numerically less than 1. For example, if a 2% change in price leads to a 1% change in quantity demanded, then the value of the elasticity will be −1 divided by 2 = −0.5. In this case, demand is referred to as being *price inelastic*.

### An example

Figure 3.6 shows a demand curve for pencils. When the price of a pencil is 40p, the quantity demanded will be 20. If the price falls to 35p, the quantity demanded will rise to 30. The percentage change in quantity is $100 \times 10/20 = 50$ and the percentage change in price is $100 \times -5/40 = -12.5$. Thus, the elasticity can be calculated as $(50/-12.5) = -4$. At this price, demand is highly price elastic.

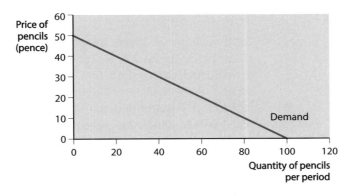

**Figure 3.6**
*A demand curve for pencils*

At a lower price, the result is quite different. Suppose that price is initially 10p, at which price the quantity demanded is 80. If the price falls to 9p, demand increases

to 82. The percentage change in quantity is now $100 \times 2/80 = 2.5$, and the percentage change in price is $100 \times -1/10 = -10$, so the elasticity is calculated as $2.5/-10 = -0.25$, and demand is now price inelastic.

This phenomenon is true for any straight-line demand curve: in other words, demand is price elastic at higher prices and inelastic at lower prices. At the halfway point the elasticity is exactly $-1$, which is referred to as *unit elasticity*.

Why should this happen? The key is to remember that elasticity is defined in terms of the percentage changes in price and quantity. Thus, when price is relatively high, a 1p change in price is a small percentage change, and the percentage change in quantity is relatively large — because when price is relatively high, the initial quantity is relatively low. The reverse is the case when price is relatively low. Figure 3.7 shows how the elasticity of demand varies along a straight-line demand curve.

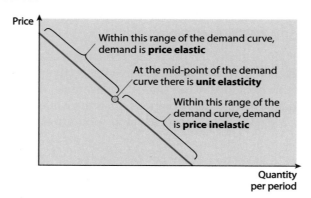

Within this range of the demand curve, demand is **price elastic**

At the mid-point of the demand curve there is **unit elasticity**

Within this range of the demand curve, demand is **price inelastic**

*Figure 3.7*
*The own-price elasticity of demand varies along a straight line*

### The price elasticity of demand and total revenue

One reason why firms may have an interest in the price elasticity of demand is that, if they are considering changing their prices, they will be eager to know the extent to which demand will be affected. For example, they may want to know how a change in price will affect their total revenue. As it happens there is a consistent relationship between the price elasticity of demand and total revenue.

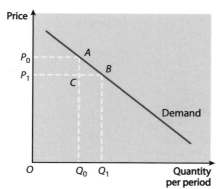

*Figure 3.8*
*Demand and total revenue*

Total revenue is given by price multiplied by quantity. In Figure 3.8, if price is at $P_0$, quantity demanded is at $Q_0$ and total revenue is given by the area of the rectangle $OP_0AQ_0$. If price falls to $P_1$ the quantity demanded rises to $Q_1$, and you can see that total revenue has increased, as it is now given by the area $OP_1BQ_1$. This is larger than at price $P_1$, because in moving from $P_0$ to $P_1$ the area $P_1P_0AC$ is lost, but the area $Q_0CBQ_1$ is gained, and the latter is the larger. As you move down the demand curve, total revenue at first increases like this, but then decreases — try sketching this for yourself to check that it is so.

For the case of a straight-line demand curve the relationship is illustrated in Figure 3.9. Remember that demand is price elastic when price is relatively high. This is the range of the demand curve in which total revenue rises as price falls. This makes sense, as in this range the quantity demanded is sensitive to a change in price and increases by more (in percentage terms) than the price falls. This implies that, as you move to the right in this segment, total revenue rises. The increase in quantity sold more than compensates for the fall in price. However, when the mid-point is reached and demand becomes unit elastic, total revenue stops rising — it is at its maximum at this point. The remaining part of the curve is inelastic: that is, the increase in quantity demanded is no longer sufficient to compensate for the decrease in price, and total revenue falls. Table 3.1 summarises the situation.

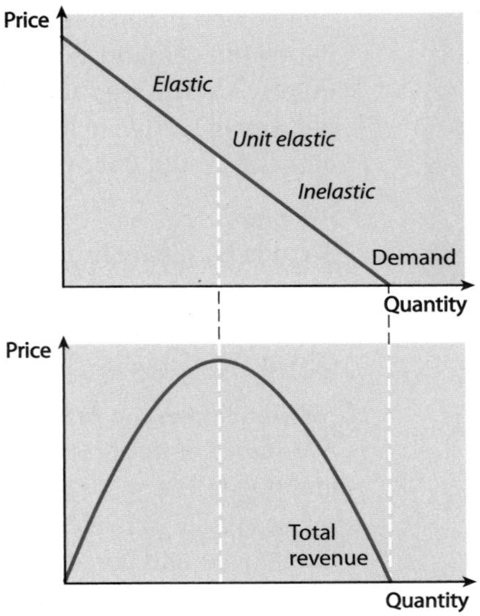

**Figure 3.9**
*Elasticity and total revenue*

| Price elasticity of demand | For a price increase, total revenue... | For a price decrease, total revenue ... |
| --- | --- | --- |
| Elastic | falls | rises |
| Unit elastic | does not change | does not change |
| Inelastic | rises | falls |

**Table 3.1**
*Total revenue, elasticity and a price change*

Thus, if a firm is aware of the price elasticity of demand for its product, it can anticipate consumer response to its price changes, which may be a powerful strategic tool.

One very important point must be made here. If the price elasticity of demand varies along a straight-line demand curve, such a curve cannot be referred to as either elastic or inelastic. To do so is to confuse the elasticity with the *slope* of the demand curve. It is not only the steepness of the demand curve that determines the elasticity, but also the point on the curve at which the elasticity is measured.

Two extreme cases of the price elasticity of demand should also be mentioned. Demand may sometimes be totally insensitive to price, so that the same quantity will be demanded whatever price is set for it. In such a situation, demand is said to be *perfectly inelastic*. The demand curve in this case is vertical — as in $D_i$ in Figure 3.10. In this situation, the numerical value of the price elasticity is zero, as quantity demanded does not change in response to a change in the price of the good.

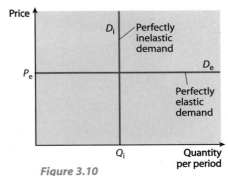

**Figure 3.10**
*Perfectly elastic and inelastic demand*

The other extreme is shown on the same figure, where $D_e$ is a horizontal demand curve and demand is *perfectly elastic*. The numerical value of the elasticity here is infinity. Consumers demand an unlimited quantity of the good at price $P_e$. No firm has any incentive to lower price below this level, but if price were to rise above $P_e$, demand would fall to zero.

### An example

A study by the Institute for Fiscal Studies for the UK found that the price elasticity of demand for wine was −1.69. This means that demand for wine is elastic. If the price of wine were to increase by 10%, there would be a fall of 16.9% in the quantity of wine demanded.

### Influences on the price elasticity of demand

A number of important influences on the price elasticity of demand can now be identified. The most important is the availability of substitutes for the good or service under consideration. For example, think about the demand for cauliflower. Cauliflower and broccoli are often seen as being very similar, so if the price of cauliflower is high one week, people might quite readily switch to broccoli. The demand for cauliflower can be said to be price sensitive (elastic), as consumers can readily substitute an alternative product. On the other hand, if the price of all vegetables rises, demand will not change very much, as there are no substitutes for vegetables in the diet. Thus, goods that have close substitutes available will tend to exhibit elastic demand, whereas the demand for goods for which there are no substitutes will tend to be more inelastic.

Hemera Technologies

Associated with this is the question of whether an individual regards a good or service as a necessity or as a luxury item. If a good is a necessity, then demand for it will tend to be inelastic, whereas if a good is regarded as a luxury, consumers will tend to be more price-sensitive. This is closely related to the question of substitutes, as by labelling a good as a necessity one is essentially saying that there are no substitutes for it.

A second influence on the price elasticity of demand is the relative share of the good or service in overall expenditure. You may tend not to notice small changes in the price of an inexpensive item that is a small part of overall expenditure, such as salt or sugar. This tends to mean that demand for that good is relatively inelastic. On the other hand, an item that figures large in the household budget will be seen very differently, and consumers will tend to be much more sensitive to price when a significant proportion of their income is involved.

Finally, the time period under consideration may be important. Consumers may respond

*Demand for wine is price elastic*

more strongly to a price change in the long run than to one in the short run. An increase in the price of petrol may have limited effects in the short run; however, in the long run, consumers may buy smaller cars or switch to diesel. Thus, the elasticity of demand tends to be more elastic in the long run than in the short run. Habit or commitment to a certain pattern of consumption may dictate the short-run pattern of consumption, but people do eventually adjust to price changes.

## Summary

➤ The price elasticity of demand measures the sensitivity of the quantity of a good demanded to a change in its price.

➤ As there is an inverse relationship between quantity demanded and price, the price elasticity of demand is always negative.

➤ Where consumers are sensitive to a change in price, the percentage change in quantity demanded will exceed the percentage change in price. The elasticity of demand then takes on a value that is numerically greater than 1, and demand is said to be elastic.

➤ Where consumers are not very sensitive to a change in price, the percentage change in quantity demanded will be smaller than the percentage change in price. Elasticity of demand then takes on a value that is numerically smaller than 1, and demand is said to be inelastic.

➤ When demand is elastic, a fall (rise) in price leads to a rise (fall) in total revenue.

➤ When demand is inelastic, a fall (rise) in price leads to a fall (rise) in total revenue.

➤ The size of the price elasticity of demand is influenced by the availability of substitutes for a good, the relative share of expenditure on the good in the consumer's budget and the time that consumers have to adjust.

## Exercise 3.2

Examine Table 3.2, which shows the demand for a particular red wine at different prices.

| Price (£) | Quantity demanded (bottles per week) |
|---|---|
| 10 | 20 |
| 8 | 40 |
| 6 | 60 |
| 4 | 80 |
| 2 | 100 |

*Table 3.2*
*Demand for Château Econ*

a  Draw the demand curve.

b  Calculate the price elasticity of demand when the initial price is £8.

c  Calculate the price elasticity of demand when the initial price is £6.

d  Calculate the price elasticity of demand when the initial price is £4.

part 1

## The income elasticity of demand

Elasticity is a measure of the sensitivity of a variable to changes in another variable. In the same way as the price elasticity of demand is determined, an elasticity measure can be calculated for any other influence on demand or supply. **Income elasticity of demand (YED)** is therefore defined as:

$$YED = \frac{\% \text{ change in quantity demanded}}{\% \text{ change in consumer income}}$$

**income elasticity of demand (YED):** a measure of the sensitivity of quantity demanded to a change in consumer incomes

Unlike the price elasticity of demand, the income elasticity of demand may be either positive or negative. Remember the distinction between normal and inferior goods? For normal goods the quantity demanded will increase as consumer income rises, whereas for inferior goods the quantity demanded will tend to fall as income rises. Thus, for normal goods the *YED* will be positive, whereas for inferior goods it will be negative.

Suppose you discover that the *YED* for wine is 0.7. How do you interpret this number? If consumer incomes were to increase by 10%, the demand for wine would increase by 10 × 0.7 = 7%. This example of a normal good may be helpful information for wine merchants, if they know that consumer incomes are rising over time.

On the other hand, if the *YED* for coach travel is −0.3, that means that a 10% increase in consumer incomes will lead to a 3% fall in the demand for coach travel — perhaps because more people are travelling by car. In this instance, coach travel would be regarded as an inferior good.

In some cases the *YED* may be very strongly positive. For example, suppose that the *YED* for digital cameras is +2. This implies that the quantity demanded of such cameras will increase by 20% for every 10% increase in incomes. An increase in income is encouraging people to devote more of their incomes to this product, which increases its share in total expenditure. Such goods are referred to as **luxury goods**.

**luxury good:** one for which the income elasticity of demand is positive, and greater than one, such that as income rises, consumers spend proportionally more on the good

**cross-price elasticity of demand (XED):** a measure of the sensitivity of quantity demanded of a good or service to a change in the price of some other good or service

## Cross-price elasticity of demand

Another useful measure is the **cross-price elasticity of demand (XED)**. This is helpful in revealing the interrelationships between goods. Again, this measure may be either positive or negative, depending on the relationship between the goods. It is defined as:

$$XED = \frac{\% \text{ change in quantity demanded of good X}}{\% \text{ change in price of good Y}}$$

If the *XED* is seen to be positive, it means that an increase in the price of good Y leads to an increase

OCR Advanced Economics

in the quantity demanded of good X. For example, an increase in the price of apples may lead to an increase in the demand for pears. Here apples and pears are regarded as substitutes for each other; if one becomes relatively more expensive, consumers will switch to the other. A high value for the *XED* indicates that two goods are very close substitutes. This information may be useful in helping a firm to identify its close competitors.

On the other hand, if an increase in the price of one good leads to a fall in the quantity demanded of another good, this suggests that they are likely to be complements. The XED in this case will be negative. An example of such a relationship would be that between coffee and sugar, which tend to be consumed together.

### Examples

A study by the Institute for Fiscal Studies using data for the UK found that the cross-price elasticity of demand for wine with respect to a change in the price of beer was −0.60, whereas the cross-price elasticity with respect to the price of spirits was +0.77. The negative cross-price elasticity with beer suggests that wine and beer are complements: a 10% increase in the price of beer would lead to a 6% fall in the quantity demanded of wine. In contrast, the cross-price elasticity of demand for wine with respect to the price of spirits is positive, suggesting that wine and spirits are substitutes. An increase in the price of spirits leads to an increase in the quantity demanded of wine.

## Price elasticity of supply

As elasticity is a measure of sensitivity, its use need not be confined to influences on demand, but can also be turned to evaluating the sensitivity of quantity *supplied* to a change in its determinants — price in particular.

It was argued in Chapter 2 that the supply curve is likely to be upward sloping, so the price elasticity of supply can be expected to be positive. In other words, an increase in the market price will induce firms to supply more output to the market. The **price elasticity of supply (PES)** is defined as:

$$PES = \frac{\% \text{ change in the quantity supplied}}{\% \text{ change in price}}$$

> **Key term**
>
> **price elasticity of supply (PES):** a measure of the sensitivity of quantity supplied of a good or service to a change in the price of that good or service

So, if the price elasticity of supply is 0.8, an increase in price of 10% will encourage firms to supply 8% more. As with the price elasticity of demand, if the elasticity is greater than 1, supply is referred to as being elastic, whereas if the value is between 0 and 1, supply is considered inelastic. *Unit elasticity* occurs when the price elasticity of supply is exactly 1, so that a 10% increase in price induces a 10% increase in quantity supplied.

The value of the elasticity will depend on how willing and able firms are to increase their supply. For example, if firms are operating close to the capacity of their

existing plant and machinery, they may be unable to respond to an increase in price, at least in the short run. So here again, supply can be expected to be more elastic in the long run than in the short run. Figure 3.11 illustrates this. In the short run, firms may be able to respond to an increase in price only in a limited way, and so supply may be relatively inelastic, as shown by $S_s$ in the figure. However, firms can become more flexible in the long run by installing new machinery or building new factories, so supply can then become more elastic, moving to $S_l$.

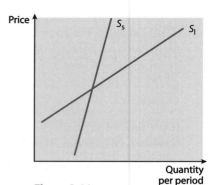

*Figure 3.11*
*Short- and long-run supply*

There are two limiting cases of supply elasticity. For some reason, supply may be fixed such that, no matter how much price increases, firms will not be able to supply any more. For example, it could be that a certain amount of fish is available in a market, and however high the price goes, no more can be obtained. Equally, if the fishermen know that the fish they do not sell today cannot be stored for another day, they have an incentive to sell however low the price goes. In these cases, supply is perfectly inelastic. At the other extreme is perfectly elastic supply, where firms would be prepared to supply any amount of the good at the going price.

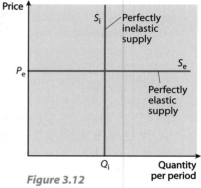

*Figure 3.12*
*Perfectly elastic and inelastic supply*

These two possibilities are shown in Figure 3.12. Here $S_i$ represents a perfectly inelastic supply curve: firms will supply $Q_i$ whatever the price, perhaps because that is the amount available for sale. Supply here is vertical. At the opposite extreme, if supply is perfectly elastic then firms are prepared to supply any amount at the price $P_e$, and the supply curve is given by the horizontal line $S_e$.

## Exercise 3.3

Imagine the following scenario. You are considering a pricing strategy for a bus company. The economy is heading into recession, and the company is running at a loss. Your local rail service provider has announced an increase in rail fares. How (if at all) do you use the following information concerning the elasticity of bus travel with respect to various variables to inform your decision on price? Do you raise or lower price?

➤ price elasticity of demand     −1.58
➤ income elasticity of demand     −2.43
➤ cross-price elasticity of demand with respect to rail fares     +2.21
➤ your price elasticity of supply     +1.15

OCR Advanced Economics

## Summary

➤ The income elasticity of demand (*YED*) measures the sensitivity of quantity demanded to a change in consumer incomes. It serves to distinguish between normal, luxury and inferior goods.

➤ The cross-price elasticity of demand (*XED*) measures the sensitivity of the quantity demanded of one good or service to a change in the price of some other good or service. It can serve to distinguish between substitutes and complements.

➤ The price elasticity of supply (*PES*) measures the sensitivity of the quantity supplied to a change in the price of a good or service. The price elasticity of supply can be expected to be greater in the long run than in the short run, as firms have more flexibility to adjust their production decisions in the long run.

## Prices and resource allocation

### The coordination problem

As Chapter 1 indicated, all societies face the fundamental economic problem of scarcity. Because there are unlimited wants but finite resources, it is necessary to take decisions on which goods and services should be produced, how they should be produced and for whom they should be produced. For an economy the size of the UK, there is thus an immense coordination problem. Another way of looking at this is to ask how consumers can express their preferences between alternative goods so that producers can produce the best mix of goods and services.

Some alternative possibilities for handling this problem will now be considered. In a **free market economy**, market forces are allowed to allocate resources. At the other extreme, in a centrally planned economy the state plans and directs resources into a range of uses. In between there is the mixed economy. In order to evaluate these alternatives, it is necessary to explore how each of them operates.

> **Key term**
>
> **free market economy:** one in which resource allocation is guided by market forces without intervention by the state

In a free market economy, prices play the key role; this is sometimes referred to as the *laissez-faire* approach to resource allocation.

## Prices and preferences

How can consumers signal their preferences to producers? Demand and supply analysis provides the clue. Figure 3.13 shows the demand and supply for laptop computers. These have become popular goods in recent years. That is to say, over time there has been a rightward shift in the demand curve — in the figure, from $D_0$ to $D_1$. This simply means that consumers are placing a

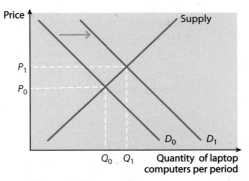

*Figure 3.13*
*The market for laptop computers*

higher value on these goods; they are prepared to demand more at any given price. The result, as you know from comparative static analysis, is that the market will move to a new equilibrium, with price rising from $P_0$ to $P_1$ and quantity traded from $Q_0$ to $Q_1$: there is a movement along the supply curve.

The movement of the demand curve is an expression of consumers' preferences; it embodies the fact that they value laptop computers more highly now than before. The price that consumers are willing to pay represents their valuation of laptop computers.

*Consumer demand for laptops has risen over the last few years*

### Consumer surplus

Think a little more carefully about what the demand curve represents. Figure 3.14 again shows the demand curve for laptop computers. Suppose that the price is set at $P^*$ and quantity demanded is thus $Q^*$. $P^*$ can be seen as the value that the last customer places on a laptop. In other words, if the price were even slightly above $P^*$, there would be one consumer who would choose not to buy: this individual will be referred to as the *marginal consumer.*

To that marginal consumer, $P^*$ represents the marginal benefit derived from consuming this good — it is the price that just reflects the consumer's benefit from a laptop, as it is the price that just induces her to buy. Thinking of the society as a whole (which is made up of all the consumers within it), $P^*$ can be regarded as the **marginal social benefit** (*MSB*) derived from consuming this good. The same argument could be made about any point along the demand curve, so the demand curve can be interpreted as the marginal benefit to be derived from consuming laptop computers.

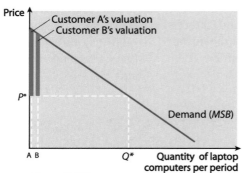

*Figure 3.14*
*Price as marginal benefit*

**Key term**

**marginal benefit:** the additional benefit that society gains from consuming an extra unit of a good

In most markets, all consumers face the same prices for goods and services. This leads to an important concept in economic analysis. $P^*$ may represent the value of laptops to the *marginal* consumer, but what about all the other consumers who are also buying laptops at $P^*$? They would all be willing to pay a higher price for a laptop. Indeed, consumer A in Figure 3.14 would pay a very high price indeed, and thus values a laptop much more highly than $P^*$. When consumer A pays $P^*$ for a laptop, he gets a great deal, as he values the good so much more highly — as represented by the vertical green line on Figure 3.14. Consumer B also gains a surplus above her willingness to pay (the blue line).

If all these surplus values are added up, they sum to the total surplus that society gains from consuming laptops. This is known as the **consumer surplus**, represented by the shaded triangle in Figure 3.15. It can be interpreted as the welfare that society gains from consuming the good, over and above the price that has to be paid for it.

**Key term**

**consumer surplus:** the value that consumers gain from consuming a good or service over and above the price paid

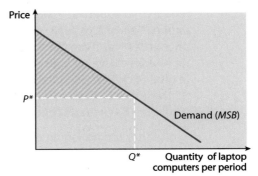

*Figure 3.15*
*Consumer surplus*

## Prices as signals and incentives

From the producers' perspective, the question is how they receive signals from consumers about their changing preferences. Price is the key. Figure 3.13 shows how an increase in demand for laptop computers leads to an increase in the equilibrium market price. That increase in price encourages producers to supply more computers — there is a movement *along* the supply curve. This is really saying that producers find it profitable to increase their output of laptop computers at that higher price. The price level is thus a signal to producers about consumer preferences.

Notice that the price signal works equally well when there is a *decrease* in the demand for a good or service. Figure 3.16, for example, shows the market for video recordings. With the advent of DVDs, there has been a large fall in the demand for video recordings, so the demand for them has shifted to the left — consumers are demanding fewer videos at any price. Thus, the demand curve shifts from $D_0$ to $D_1$. Producers of video recordings are beginning to find that they cannot sell as many videos at the original price as before, so they have to reduce their price to avoid an increase in their unsold stocks. They have less incentive to produce videos, and will supply less. There is a movement *along* the supply curve to a lower equilibrium price at $P_1$, and a lower quantity traded at $Q_1$. You may like to think of this as a movement along the firm's production possibility curve for DVDs and videos.

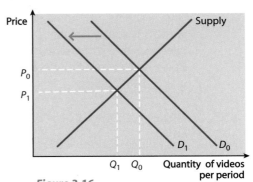

*Figure 3.16*
*The market for video recordings*

Thus, you can see how existing producers in a market receive signals from consumers in the form of changes in the equilibrium price, and respond to these signals by adjusting their output levels.

### Producer surplus

Parallel to the notion of consumer surplus is the concept of **producer surplus**. Think about the nature of the supply curve: it reveals how much output firms are prepared to supply at any given price in a competitive market. Figure 3.17 depicts a supply curve. Assume the price is at $P^*$, and that all units are sold at that price. $P^*$ represents the value to firms of the marginal unit sold. In other words, if the price had been set slightly below $P^*$, the last unit would not have been supplied, as firms would not have found this profitable.

> **Key term**
>
> **producer surplus:** the difference between the price received by firms for a good or service and the price at which they would have been prepared to supply that good or service

Notice that the threshold at which a firm will decide it is not profitable to supply is the point at which the price received by the firm reaches the cost to the firm of producing the last unit of the good. Thus, in a competitive market the supply curve reflects marginal cost. This will be discussed in more detail in Chapter 14.

The supply curve shows that, in the range of prices between point $A$ and $P^*$, firms would have been willing to supply positive amounts of this good or service. So at $P^*$, they would gain a surplus value on all units of the good supplied below $Q^*$. The total area is shown in Figure 3.18 – it is the area above the supply curve and below $P^*$, shown as the shaded triangle.

One way of defining this producer surplus is as the surplus earned by firms over and above the minimum that would have kept them in the market. It is the *raison d'être* of firms.

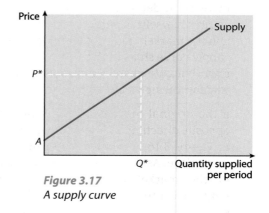

*Figure 3.17*
*A supply curve*

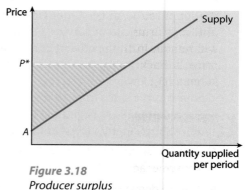

*Figure 3.18*
*Producer surplus*

## Entry and exit of firms

The discussion so far has focused on the reactions of existing firms in a market to changes in consumer preferences. However, this is only part of the picture. Think back to Figure 3.13, where there was an increase in demand for laptop computers following a change in consumer preferences. The equilibrium price rose, and existing firms expanded the quantity supplied in response. Those firms are now earning a higher producer surplus than before. Other firms not currently in the market will be attracted by these surpluses, perceiving this to be a profitable market in which to operate.

If there are no barriers to entry, more firms will join the market. This in turn will tend to move the supply curve to the right, as there will then be more firms prepared to supply. As a result, the equilibrium market price will tend to drift down again, until the market reaches a position in which there is no further incentive for new firms to enter the market. This will occur when the rate of return for firms in the laptop market is no better than in other markets.

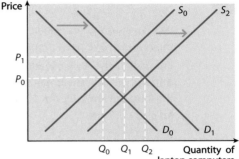

**Figure 3.19**
*The market for laptop computers revisited*

Figure 3.19 illustrates this situation. The original increase in demand leads, as before, to a new equilibrium with a higher price $P_1$. As new firms join the market in quest of producer surplus, the supply curve shifts to the right to $S_2$, pushing the price back down to $P_0$, but with the quantity traded now up at $Q_2$.

If the original movement in demand is in the opposite direction, as it was for video recordings in Figure 3.16, a similar long-run adjustment takes place. As the market price falls, some firms in the market may decide that they no longer wish to remain in production, and will exit from the market altogether. This will move the supply curve to the left in Figure 3.20 (to $S_2$) until only firms that continue to find it profitable will remain in the market. In the final position price is back to $P_0$, and quantity traded has fallen to $Q_2$.

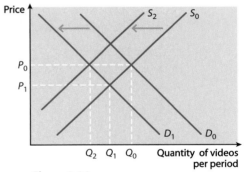

**Figure 3.20**
*The market for video recordings*

## Exercise 3.4

a  Sketch a demand and supply diagram and mark on it the areas that represent consumer and producer surplus.

b  Using a demand and supply diagram, explain the process that provides incentives for firms to adjust to a decrease in the demand for fountain pens in a competitive market.

c  Think about how you could use demand and supply analysis to explain recent movements in the world price of oil.

## Summary

➤ If market forces are to allocate resources effectively, consumers need to be able to express their preferences for goods and services in such a way that producers can respond.

➤ Consumers express their preferences through prices, as prices will adjust to equilibrium levels following a change in consumer demand.

➤ Consumer surplus represents the benefit that consumers gain from consuming a product over and above the price they pay for that product.

➤ Producer surplus represents the benefit gained by firms over and above the price at which they would have been prepared to supply a product.

➤ Producers have an incentive to respond to changes in prices. In the short run this occurs through output adjustments of existing firms (movements along the supply curve), but in the long run firms will enter the market (or exit from it) until there are no further incentives for entry or exit.

# Chapter 4
# Firms and how they operate

*The focus so far has been mainly on demand. However, the supply side of markets is equally important. The role of firms in this context is crucial, and this chapter investigates how firms operate, and how they take decisions designed to achieve their objectives. This requires some discussion of the costs and revenues faced by firms at different levels of output. In addition, the chapter shows how firms' decisions are influenced by the market environment in which they operate.*

## Learning outcomes

After studying this chapter, you should:
- ➤ be aware of the reason for the birth of firms, and the desire for their growth
- ➤ be aware of the need for firms to grow if they wish to compete in global markets
- ➤ be familiar with short- and long-run cost curves and their characteristics
- ➤ understand the significance of economies of scale in the context of the growth of firms
- ➤ understand the profit maximisation motive and its implications for firms' behaviour
- ➤ be aware of the principal–agent issue, and its influence on the motivations of firms
- ➤ be familiar with alternative motivations for firms and how these affect decision making
- ➤ understand what is meant by market structure, and why it is important for firms
- ➤ appreciate the significance of barriers to entry to a market in influencing the market structure

## What is a firm?

One way of answering this question is to say that **firms** exist in order to organise production: they bring together various factors of production, and organise the production process in order to produce output.

There are various forms that the organisation of a firm can take. The simplest is perhaps that of *sole proprietor*, in which the owner of the firm also runs the firm. Examples would be

>  **Key** *term*
>
> **firm:** an organisation that brings together factors of production in order to produce output

*Publishing Pictures*

*Independent newsagents are often run by sole proprietors*

an independent newsagent/corner shop, plumber or hairdresser, where the owner is liable for the debts of the enterprise, but also gets to keep any profits.

In some professions, firms are operated on a *partnership* basis. Examples here are doctors', dentists' and solicitors' practices. Profits are shared between the partners, as are debts, according to the contract drawn up between them. Some non-professional enterprises, such as some builders and hardware stores, also operate in this way.

Private *joint stock companies* are owned by shareholders, each of whom has contributed funds to the business by buying shares. However, each shareholder's responsibility for the debts of the company is limited to the amount he or she paid for the shares. Profits are distributed to shareholders as dividends. The shares in a private company of this kind are not traded on the stock exchange, and the firms tend to be controlled by the shareholders themselves. Many local businesses are operated on this basis: for example, double glazing installation firms and computer consultancies. If you look in your local *Yellow Pages*, you will see that some firms indicate that they are this sort of company by adding 'Ltd' after their name, referring to the fact that shareholders have *limited liability* for the firm's debts, as mentioned above. Many family firms operate in this way, with the families maintaining control through their ownership of shares.

Firms that are owned by shareholders, but are listed on the stock exchange are *public joint stock companies*. Again, the liability of the shareholders is limited to the amount they have paid for their shares. However, such companies are required to publish their annual accounts and also to publish an annual report to their shareholders. Day-to-day decision making is normally delegated to a board of directors (who are not major shareholders), appointed at the annual general meeting (AGM) of the shareholders. Examples of this sort of company abound — Tesco, HSBC, BP and so on. Again, your local *Yellow Pages* will reveal the names of some companies with 'plc' after the name, standing for *public limited company*.

## Firm size

An important decision facing any firm is to choose its scale of operation. If you look around the economy, you will see that the size of firms varies enormously, from small one-person operations up to mega-sized multinational corporations. Such firms may need to continue to grow in order to compete with other large-scale competitors in global markets. There may be many reasons why firms wish to expand their operations. This chapter will begin to explain why this is so, and show how the decision about how much output to produce depends upon what it is that a firm is trying to achieve, and on the market environment in which it is operating.

## Summary

➤ A firm is an organisation that exists to bring together factors of production in order to produce goods or services.

➤ Firms range, in the complexity of their organisation, from sole proprietors to public limited companies.

➤ Firms vary in size, from one-person concerns to large multinational corporations operating in global markets.

## Costs facing firms

To understand why firms wish to grow, it is first important to examine the costs of production that they face. This section focuses on the relationship between costs and the level of output produced by a firm. Diagrams will illustrate this relationship using a series of cost curves that apply in various circumstances.

For simplicity, it is assumed that the firm under consideration produces a single product — analysis of conglomerates is a little more complicated. It is also assumed that the firm uses just two factors of production — labour ($L$) and capital ($K$). This seems a stronger assumption, but again is made for simplicity. 'Labour' and 'capital' can be thought of as the representative factors of production, although in real life a firm organises a whole range of factors of production — including different types of labour and capital.

These two factors are representative in a particular way. In the short run, the firm faces limited flexibility. Varying the quantity of labour input the firm uses may be relatively straightforward — it can increase the use of overtime, or hire more workers, fairly quickly. However, varying the amount of capital the firm has at its disposal may take longer. For example, it takes time to commission a new piece of machinery, or to build a new factory — or a Channel Tunnel! Hence labour is regarded as a flexible factor and capital as a fixed factor. This may not always be correct: for example, it may sometimes be easier to bring in new computers than to train new staff to use them. However, in this chapter 'labour' will be regarded as flexible and 'capital' as inflexible, and the definitions of the **short run** and **long run** are based on this assumption.

 **Key** *terms*

**short run:** the period over which a firm is free to vary its input of one factor of production (labour), but faces fixed inputs of the other (capital)

**long run:** the period over which the firm is able to vary the inputs of all its factors of production

## The production function

As the firm changes its volume of production, it needs to vary the inputs of its factors of production. Thus, the total amount of output produced in a given period depends upon the inputs of labour and capital used in the production process. Of course, there are many different ways of combining labour and capital inputs, some combinations being more efficient than others. The **production function** summarises the technically most efficient combinations for any given output level. It specifies how the level of output produced by a firm depends upon the quantities of inputs of the factors of production that are utilised.

The nature of technology in an industry will determine the way in which output varies with the quantity of inputs. However, one thing is certain. If the firm increases the amount of inputs of the variable factor (labour) while holding constant the input of the other factor (capital), it will gradually derive less additional output per unit of labour for each further increase. This is known as the **law of diminishing returns**, and is one of the few 'laws' in economics. It is a *short-run* concept, as it relies on the assumption that capital is fixed.

### Key terms

**production function:** relationship that embodies information about technically efficient ways of combining labour and capital to produce output

**law of diminishing returns:** law stating that if a firm increases its inputs of one factor of production whilst holding inputs of the other factor fixed, eventually the firm will get diminishing marginal returns from the variable factor

It can readily be seen why this should be the case. Suppose a firm has 10 computer programmers working in an office, using 10 computers. The 11th worker may add some extra output, as the workers may be able to 'hot-desk' and take their coffee breaks at different times. The 12th worker may also add some extra output, perhaps by keeping the printers stocked with paper. However, if the firm keeps adding programmers without increasing the number of computers, each extra worker will be adding less additional output to the office. Indeed, the 20th worker may add nothing at all, being unable to get access to a computer.

*Computer programmers add to production provided they have machines to use*

Figure 4.1 illustrates the short-run relationship between labour input and total physical product ($TPP_L$), with capital held constant. The shape of the $TPP_L$ relationship reflects the law of diminishing returns: as labour input increases, the amount of additional output produced gets smaller. An increase in the amount of capital available will raise the amount of output produced for any given labour input, so the $TPP_L$ will shift upwards, as shown in Figure 4.2.

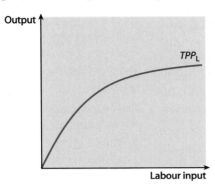

**Figure 4.1**
*A short-run production function*

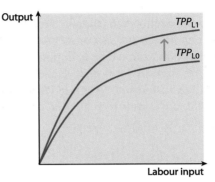

**Figure 4.2**
*The effect of an increase in capital*

The production function thus carries information about the physical relationship between the inputs of the factors of production and the physical quantity of output. With this information and a knowledge of the prices that the firm must pay for its inputs of the factors of production, it is possible to map out the way in which costs will change with the level of output.

We can view the firm's decision process as a three-stage procedure. First, the firm needs to decide how much output it wants to produce. Second, it chooses an appropriate combination of factors of production given that intended scale of production. Third, it attempts to produce as much output as possible given those inputs. Another way of expressing this is that, having chosen the intended scale of output, the firm tries to minimise its costs of production. These decisions are part of the response to the question of *how* output should be produced.

### Total, marginal and average costs

In talking about costs, economists distinguish between total, marginal and average costs. **Total cost** is the sum of all costs that are incurred in order to produce a given level of output. Total cost will always increase as the firm increases its level of production, as this will require more inputs of factors of production, materials and so on.

**Average cost** is simply the cost per unit of output — it is total cost divided by the level of output produced.

 **terms**

**total cost:** the sum of all costs that are incurred in producing a given level of output

**average cost:** total cost divided by the quantity produced; sometimes known as unit cost

Equally important as these measures is the concept of **marginal cost**. Indeed, as you learn more about economics, you will realise that economists rely heavily on the idea that firms, consumers and other economic actors can make good decisions by thinking in terms of the margin. This is known as the **marginal principle**. For example, a firm may examine whether a small change in its behaviour makes matters better or worse. In this context, marginal cost is important. It is defined as the change in total cost associated with a small change in output. In other words, it is the additional cost incurred by the firm if it increases output by 1 unit.

## Costs in the short run

Because the firm cannot vary some of its inputs in the short run, some costs may be regarded as fixed, and some as variable. In this short run, some **fixed costs** are **sunk costs**: that is, they are costs that the firm cannot avoid paying even if it chooses to produce no output. Total costs are the sum of fixed and **variable costs**:

total costs = total fixed costs + total variable costs

Total costs will increase as the firm increases the volume of production because more of the variable input is needed to increase output. The way in which the costs will vary depends on the nature of the production function, and on whether the prices of labour or capital alter as output increases.

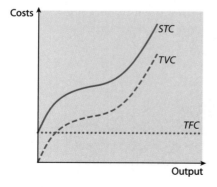

*Figure 4.3*
*Costs in the short run*

A common assumption made by economists is that in the short run, at very low levels of output, total costs will rise more slowly than output, but that as diminishing returns set in, total costs will accelerate, as shown in Figure 4.3.

Table 4.1 provides an arithmetic example to illustrate the relationship between these different aspects of costs. The firm represented here faces fixed costs of £225 per week. The table shows the costs of production for up to 6,000 units of the firm's product per week. Column 3 shows total variable costs of production: you can see that these rise quite steeply as the volume of production increases.

Adding fixed and variable costs gives the short-run total costs (*STC*) at each output level. This is shown in column 4, which is the sum of columns 2 and 3.

OCR Advanced Economics

| (1) Output ('000 units per week) | (2) Fixed costs | (3) Total variable costs | (4) Short-run total costs (2) + (3) | (5) Short-run average total cost (4)/(1) | (6) Short-run marginal cost Δ(4)/Δ(1) | (7) Short-run average variable cost (3)/(1) | (8) Short-run average fixed cost (2)/(1) |
|---|---|---|---|---|---|---|---|
| 1 | 225 | 85 | 310 | 310 | | 85 | 225 |
| | | | | | 65 | | |
| 2 | 225 | 150 | 375 | 187.5 | | 75 | 112.5 |
| | | | | | 60 | | |
| 3 | 225 | 210 | 435 | 145 | | 70 | 75 |
| | | | | | 90 | | |
| 4 | 225 | 300 | 525 | 131.25 | | 75 | 56.25 |
| | | | | | 175 | | |
| 5 | 225 | 475 | 700 | 140 | | 95 | 45 |
| | | | | | 395 | | |
| 6 | 225 | 870 | 1095 | 182.5 | | 145 | 37.5 |

*Table 4.1 The short-run relationship between output and costs (in £s)*

The short-run average total cost (*SATC* — column 5) is calculated as short-run total cost divided by output. To calculate short-run marginal cost, you need to work out the additional cost of producing an extra unit of output at each output level. This is calculated as the change in costs divided by the change in output (Δ column 4 divided by Δ column 1, where Δ means 'change in').

Finally, average variable costs (*SAVC*, i.e. column 3/column 1) and average fixed costs (*SAFC*, i.e. column 2/column 1) can be calculated.

These relationships are plotted in Figure 4.4, which shows how they relate to each other. First, notice that short-run average total costs (*SATC*) takes on a U-shape. This is the form often assumed in economic analysis. *SATC* is the sum of average fixed and variable costs (*SAFC* and *SAVC*, respectively). Average fixed costs slope downwards throughout — this is because fixed costs do not vary with the level of output, so as output increases, *SAFC* must always get smaller, as the fixed costs are spread over more and more units of output. However, *SAVC* also shows a U-shape, and it is this that gives the U-shape to *SATC*.

A very important aspect of Figure 4.4 is that the short-run marginal cost curve (*SMC*) cuts both *SAVC* and *SATC* at their minimum points. This is always the case. If you think about this for a moment, you will realise that it makes good sense. If you are adding on something that is greater than the average, the average must always increase. For a firm, when the marginal cost of producing an additional unit of a good is higher than the average cost of doing so, the average cost must rise. If the marginal cost is the same as the average cost, then average cost will not change. This is quite simply an arithmetic property of the average and the marginal, and always holds true. So when you draw the average and marginal cost curves for a firm, the

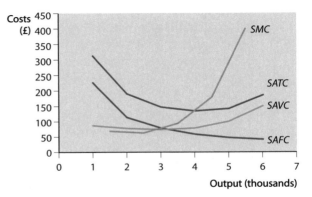

*Figure 4.4 Short-run cost curves*

marginal cost curve will always cut average cost at the minimum point of average cost. Another way of viewing marginal cost is as the *slope* or gradient of the total cost curve.

Remember that the short-run cost curves show the relationship between the volume of production and costs under the assumption that the quantity of capital is fixed, so that in order to change output the firm has to vary the amount of labour. The *position* of the cost curves thus depends on the quantity of capital. In other words, there is a short-run average total cost curve for each given level of capital.

### Costs in the long run

In the long run, a firm is able to vary both capital and labour. It is thus likely to choose the level of capital that is appropriate for the level of output that it expects to produce. Figure 4.5 shows a number of short-run average total cost curves corresponding to different expected output levels.

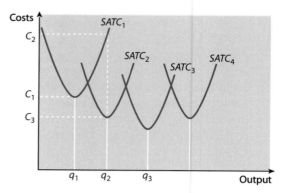

*Figure 4.5* Short-run cost curves with different levels of capital input

## Extension material

For the firm in Figure 4.5, the choice of capital is important. Suppose the firm wants to produce the quantity of output $q_1$. It would choose to install the amount of capital corresponding to the short-run total cost curve $SATC_1$, and could then produce $q_1$ at an average cost of $C_1$ in the short run. However, if the firm finds that demand is more buoyant than expected, and so wants to increase output to $q_2$, in the short run it has no option but to increase labour input and expand output along $SATC_1$, taking cost per unit to $C_2$.

In the longer term, the firm will be able to adjust its capital stock and move on to $SATC_2$, reducing average cost to $C_3$. Thus, as soon as the firm moves away from the output level for which its capital stock is designed, it incurs a higher average cost in the short run than it needs to in the long run.

In this way a long-run average cost curve can be derived to illustrate how the firm chooses to vary its capital stock for any given level of output. Figure 4.6 shows what such a curve would look like for the firm of the previous figure under the

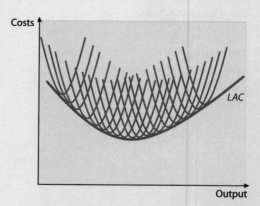

*Figure 4.6*
*The long-run average cost curve*

assumption that there is an infinite number of short-run costs curves, each corresponding to a particular desired output level, of which only some are shown. The long-run average cost curve just touches each of the short-run average cost curves, and is known as the 'envelope' of the *SATC* curves.

With the set of *SATC* curves in Figure 4.5, the long-run average cost curve also takes on a U-shape.

### Economies of scale

One of the reasons why firms find it beneficial to be large is the existence of **economies of scale**. These occur when a firm finds that it is more efficient in cost terms to produce on a larger scale.

**economies of scale:** occur for a firm when an increase in the scale of production leads to production at lower long-run average cost

It is not difficult to imagine industries in which economies of scale are likely to arise. Chapter 1 introduced the notion of division of labour. When a firm expands, it reaches a certain scale of production at which it becomes worthwhile to take advantage of division of labour. Workers begin to specialise in certain stages of the production process, and their productivity increases. Because this is only possible for relatively large-scale production, this is an example of economies of scale. It is the size of the firm (in terms of its output level) that enables it to produce more efficiently — that is, at lower average cost.

Although the division of labour is one source of economies of scale, it is by no means the only cause, and there are several explanations of cost benefits from producing on a large scale. Some of these are industry-specific, and thus some sectors of the economy exhibit more significant economies of scale than others — it is in these activities that the larger firms tend to be found. There are no hairdressing salons that come into the top ten largest firms, but there are plenty of oil companies.

#### Technology

One source of economies of scale is in the technology of production. There are many activities in which the technology is such that large-scale production is more efficient.

One source of technical economies of scale arises from the physical properties of the universe. There is a physical relationship between the volume and surface area of an object, whereby the storage capacity of an object increases proportionately more than its surface area. Consider the volume of a cube. If the cube is 2 metres each way, its surface area is $6 \times 2 \times 2 = 24$ square metres, while its volume is $2 \times 2 \times 2 = 8$ cubic metres. If the dimension of the cube is 3 metres, the surface area is 54 square metres (more than double the surface area of the smaller cube) but the volume is 27 cubic metres (more than three times the volume of the smaller cube).

Thus the larger the cube, the lower the average cost of storage. A similar relationship applies to other shapes of storage containers, whether they be barrels or ships.

What this means in practice is that a large ship can transport proportionally more than a small ship, or that large barrels hold more wine relative to the surface area of the barrel than small barrels. Hence there may be benefits in operating on a large scale.

Furthermore, some capital equipment is designed for large-scale production, and would only be viable for a firm operating at a high volume of production. Combine harvesters cannot be used in small fields; a production line for car production would not be viable for small levels of output. In other words, there may be *indivisibilities* in the production process.

In addition to indivisibilities, there are many economic activities in which there are high *overhead* expenditures. Such components of a firm's costs do not vary directly with the scale of production. For example, having built a factory, the cost of that factory is the same regardless of the amount of output that is produced in it. Expenditure on research and development could be seen as such an overhead, which may be viable only when a firm reaches a certain size.

Notice that there are some economic activities in which these overhead costs are highly significant. For example, think about the Channel Tunnel. The construction (overhead) costs were enormous compared to the costs of running trains through the tunnel. Thus the overhead cost element is substantial — and the economies of scale will also be significant for such an industry.

There are other examples of this sort of cost structure, such as railway networks and electricity supply. The largest firm in such a market will always be able to produce at a lower average cost than smaller firms. This could prove such a competitive advantage that no other firms will be able to become established in that market, which may therefore constitute a **natural monopoly**. Intuitively, this

 **Key** *term*

**natural monopoly:** monopoly that arises in an industry in which there are such substantial economies of scale that only one firm is viable

*The Channel Tunnel — the construction costs were enormous compared to the costs of running trains through the tunnel*

makes sense. Imagine having several underground railway systems operating in a single city, all competing against each other!

### Management and marketing

A second source of economies of scale pertains to the management of firms. One of the key factors of production is managerial input. A certain number of managers are required to oversee the production process. As the firm expands, there is a range of volumes of output over which the management team does not need to grow as rapidly as the overall volume of the firm, as a large firm can be managed more efficiently. Notice that there are likely to be limits to this process. At some point, the organisation begins to get so large and complex that management finds it more difficult to manage. At this point **diseconomies of scale** are likely to cut in — in other words, average costs may begin to rise with an increase in output at some volume of production.

**Key term**

**diseconomies of scale:** occur for a firm when an increase in the scale of production leads to higher long-run average costs

Similarly, the cost of marketing a product may not rise as rapidly as the volume of production, leading to further scale economies. One interpretation of this is that we might see marketing expenses as a component of fixed costs — or at least as having a substantial fixed cost element.

### Finance and procurement

Large firms may have advantages in a number of other areas. For example, a large firm with a strong reputation may be able to raise finance for further expansion on more favourable terms than a small firm. This, of course, reinforces the market position of the largest firms in a sector and makes it more difficult for relative newcomers to become established.

Once a firm has grown to the point where it is operating on a relatively large scale, it will also be purchasing its inputs in relatively large volumes. In particular, this relates to raw materials, energy and transport services. When buying in bulk in this way, firms may be able to negotiate good deals with their suppliers, and thus again reduce average cost as output increases.

It may even be the case that some of the firm's suppliers will find it beneficial to locate in proximity to the firm's factory, which would reduce costs even more.

### External economies of scale

The factors listed so far that may lead to economies of scale arise from the internal expansion of a firm. If the firm is in an industry that is itself expanding, there may also be external economies of scale.

Some of the most successful firms of recent years have been in activities that require high levels of technology and skills. The computer industry is one example of an economic activity that has expanded rapidly. As the sector expands, a pool of skilled labour is built up that all the firms can draw upon. The very success of the sector encourages people to acquire the skills needed to enter it, colleges may

provide courses and so on. Each individual firm benefits in this way from the overall expansion of the sector. The greater availability of skilled workers reduces the amount that individual firms need to spend on training.

Computer engineering is by no means the only example of this. Formula 1 development teams, pharmaceutical companies and others similarly enjoy external economies of scale. A similar argument has been used to help understand the rapid growth of the East Asian region, so these effects are not confined to particular sectors.

### Economies of scope

There are various ways in which firms expand their scale of operations. Some do so within a relatively focused market, but others are multi-product firms that produce a range of different products, sometimes in quite different markets.

> **Key term**
>
> **economies of scope:** economies arising when average cost falls as a firm increases output across a range of different products

For example, look at Nestlé. You may immediately think of instant coffee, and indeed Nestlé produces 200 different brands of instant coffee worldwide. However, Nestlé also produces baby milk powder, mineral water, ice cream and pet food, and has diversified into hotels and restaurants — not to mention locally popular items such as lemon cheesecake-flavoured Kit Kats (a strong seller in Japan).

Such conglomerate companies can benefit from **economies of scope**, whereby there may be benefits of size across a range of different products. These economies may arise because there are activities that can be shared across the product range. For example, a company may not need a finance or accounting section for each different product, nor human resource or marketing departments. There is thus scope for economies to be made as the firm expands.

## Exercise 4.1

Which of the following reflects a movement *along* a long-run average cost curve, and which would cause a movement *of* a long-run average cost curve?

a A firm becomes established in a market, learning the best ways of utilising its factors of production.

b A firm observes that average cost falls as it expands its scale of production.

c The larger a firm becomes, the more difficult it becomes to manage, causing average cost to rise.

d A firm operating in the financial sector installs new, faster computers, enabling its average cost to fall for any given level of service that it provides.

### Returns to scale

In Figure 4.7, if the firm expands its output up to $q^*$, long-run average cost falls. Up to $q^*$ of output is the range over which there are economies of scale. To the right of $q^*$, however, long-run average cost rises as output continues to be increased, and the firm experiences diseconomies of scale. The output $q^*$ itself is at the intermediate state of **constant returns to scale**.

It is important not to confuse the notion of returns to scale with the idea introduced earlier of diminishing marginal returns to a factor. The two concepts arise in different circumstances. The law of diminishing returns to a factor applies in the *short run*, when a firm increases its inputs of one factor of production while facing fixed amounts of other factors. It is thus solely a short-run phenomenon. Diseconomies of scale (sometimes known as *decreasing returns to scale*), can occur in the *long run*, and the term refers to how output changes as a firm varies the quantities of *all* factors.

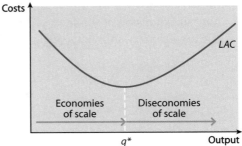

**Figure 4.7**
*Economies and diseconomies of scale*

**Key** *term*

**constant returns to scale:** found when long-run average cost remains constant with an increase in output — in other words, when output and costs rise at the same rate

If the firm is operating at the lowest possible level of long-run average costs, it is in a position of *productive efficiency*. For example, in Figure 4.7 the point $q^*$ may be regarded as the optimum level of output, in the sense that it minimises average cost per unit of output.

## Summary

➤ A firm may face inflexibility in the short run, with some factors being fixed in quantity and only some being variable.

➤ The short run is defined in this context as the period over which a firm is free to vary some factors, but not others.

➤ The long run is defined as the period over which the firm is able to vary the input of all of its factors of production.

➤ The production function shows how output can be efficiently produced through the input of factors of production.

➤ The law of diminishing returns states that, if a firm increases the input of a variable factor while holding input of the fixed factor constant, eventually the firm will get diminishing marginal returns from the variable factor.

➤ Short-run costs can be separated into fixed, sunk and variable costs.

➤ There is a clear and immutable relationship between total, average and marginal costs.

➤ For a U-shaped average cost curve, marginal cost always cuts the minimum point of average cost.

## Exercise 4.2

A firm faces long-run total cost conditions as in Table 4.2.

| Output ('000 units per week) | Total cost (£'000) |
|---|---|
| 0 | 0 |
| 1 | 32 |
| 2 | 48 |
| 3 | 82 |
| 4 | 140 |
| 5 | 228 |
| 6 | 352 |

*Table 4.2 Output and long-run costs*

**a** Calculate long-run average cost and long-run marginal cost for each level of output.

**b** Plot long-run average cost and long-run marginal cost curves on a graph. (*Hint:* don't forget to plot *LMC* at points that are halfway between the corresponding output levels.)

**c** Identify the output level at which long-run average cost is at a minimum.

**d** Identify the output level at which $LAC = LMC$.

**e** Within what range of output does this firm enjoy economies of scale?

**f** Within what range of output does the firm experience diseconomies of scale?

**g** If you could measure the nature of returns to scale, what would characterise the point where *LAC* is at a minimum?

## Revenue of firms

Chapter 3 showed how the total revenue received by a firm varies along the demand curve, according to the price elasticity of demand. In the same way that there is a relationship between total, average and marginal cost, there is also a relationship between **total revenue**, **average revenue** and **marginal revenue**.

Figure 4.8 reminds you of the relationship between total revenue and the *PED*. The marginal revenue (*MR*) curve has also been added to the figure, and has a fixed relationship with the average revenue (*AR*) curve. This is for similar mathematical reasons as the relationship between marginal and average costs explained earlier in the chapter. *MR* shares the intercept point on the vertical axis (at point *A* on

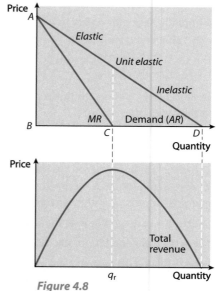

*Figure 4.8*
*Elasticity and total revenue*

OCR Advanced Economics

Figure 4.8), and has exactly twice the slope of *AR*. Whenever you have to draw this figure, remember that *MR* and *AR* have this relationship, meeting at *A*, and with the distance *BC* being the same as the distance *CD*. *MR* is zero (meets the horizontal axis) at the maximum point of the total revenue curve.

## Motivations of firms

The opening section of this chapter stated that firms exist to organise production by bringing together the factors of production in order to produce output. This begs the question of what motivates them to produce particular *levels* of output, and at what price. This section considers alternative objectives that firms may set out to achieve.

> **Key terms**
>
> **total revenue:** the revenue received by a firm from its sales of a good or service; it is the quantity sold, multiplied by the price
>
> **average revenue:** the average revenue received by the firm per unit of output; it is total revenue divided by the quantity sold
>
> **marginal revenue:** the additional revenue received by the firm if it sells an additional unit of output

### Profit maximisation

Traditional economic analysis has tended to start from the premise that firms set out with the objective of maximising profits. In analysing this, economists define profits as the difference between the total revenue received by a firm and the total costs that it incurs in production:

profits = total revenue − total cost

Total revenue here is seen in terms of the quantity of the product that is sold multiplied by the price. Total cost includes the fixed and variable costs that have already been discussed. However, one important item of costs should be highlighted before going any further.

Consider the case of a sole proprietor — a small local business. It seems reasonable to assume that such a firm will set out to maximise its profits. However, from the entrepreneur's perspective there is an *opportunity cost* of being in business, which may be seen in terms of the earnings that the proprietor could make in an alternative occupation. This required rate of return is regarded as a fixed cost, and is included in the total cost of production.

The same procedure applies to cost curves for other sorts of firm. In other words, when economists refer to costs, they include the rate of return that a firm needs to make it stay in a particular market in the long run. Accountants dislike this, as 'opportunity cost' cannot be identified as an explicit item in the accounts. This part of costs is known as **normal profit**.

> **Key terms**
>
> **normal profit:** the return needed for a firm to stay in a market in the long run
>
> **abnormal, supernormal or economic profits:** profits above normal profits

Profits made by a firm above that level are known as **supernormal profits**, **abnormal profits** or **economic profits**.

part 1

In the short run, a firm may choose to remain in a market even if it is not covering its opportunity costs, provided its revenues are covering its variable costs. Since the firm has already incurred fixed costs, if it can cover its variable costs in the short run, it will be better off remaining in business and paying off part of the fixed costs than exiting the market and losing all of its fixed costs. Thus, the level of average variable costs represents the shut-down price, below which the firm will exit from the market in the short run. In situations where firms in a market are making abnormal profits, it is likely that other firms will be attracted to enter the market. The absence or existence of abnormal profits will thus be important in influencing the way in which a market may evolve over time.

How does a firm choose its output level if it wishes to maximise profits? An application of the marginal principle shows how. Suppose a firm realises that its marginal revenue is higher than its marginal cost of production. What does this mean for profits? If it were to sell an additional unit of its output, it would gain more in revenue than it would incur additional cost, so its profits would increase. Similarly, if it found that its marginal revenue was less than marginal cost, it would be making a loss on the marginal unit of output, and profits would increase if the firm sold less. This leads to the conclusion that profits will be maximised at the level of output at which marginal revenue ($MR$) is equal to marginal cost ($MC$). Indeed, this $MR = MC$ rule is a general rule that tells a firm how to maximise profits in any market situation.

### The principal–agent problem

The discussion so far seems reasonable when considering a relatively small owner-managed firm. In this context, profit maximisation makes good sense as the firm's motivation.

However, for many larger firms — especially public limited companies — the owners may not be involved in running the business. This gives rise to the **principal–agent (or agency) problem**. In a public limited company, the shareholders delegate the day-to-day decisions concerning the operation of the firm to managers who act on their behalf. In this case the shareholders are the *principals*, and the managers are the *agents* who run things for them. In other words, there is a divorce of ownership from control.

 **term**

**principal–agent problem:** arises from conflict between the objectives of the principals and their agents, who take decisions on their behalf

If the agents are in full sympathy with the objectives of the owners, there is no problem and the managers will take exactly the decisions that the owners would like. Problems arise when there is conflict between the aims of the owners and those of the managers.

One simple explanation of why this problem arises is that the managers like a quiet life, and therefore do not push for the absolute profit-maximising position, but do just enough to keep the shareholders off their backs. Herbert Simon referred to this

OCR Advanced Economics

as '**satisficing**' behaviour, where managers aim to produce satisfactory profits rather than maximum profits.

Another possibility is that managers become negligent because they are not fully accountable. One manifestation of this may be *organisational slack*: costs will not be minimised, as the firm is not operating as efficiently as it could. This is an example of what is called **X-inefficiency**. For example, in Figure 4.9 *LAC* represents the long-run average cost curve showing the most efficient cost positions for the firm at any output level. With X-inefficiency, a firm could end up producing output $q_1$ at average cost $AC_1$. Thus, in the presence of X-inefficiency the firm will be operating *above* its long-run average cost curve.

Some writers have argued that the managers may be pursuing other objectives. For example, some managers may enjoy being involved in the running of a *large* business, and may prefer to see the firm gaining market share — perhaps beyond the profit-maximising level. Others may like to see their status rewarded and so will want to divert part of the profits into managerial perks — large offices, company cars and so on. Or they may feel that having a large staff working for them increases their prestige inside the company. These sorts of activity tend to reduce the profitability of firms.

**Key terms**

**satisficing:** behaviour under which the managers of firms aim to produce satisfactory results for the firm — for example, in terms of profits — rather than trying to maximise them

**X-inefficiency:** occurs when a firm is not operating at minimum cost, perhaps because of organisational slack

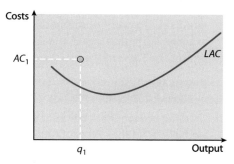

*Figure 4.9*
*X-inefficiency*

## Revenue maximisation

William Baumol argued that managers may set out with the objective of maximising revenue. One reason is that in some firms managerial salaries are related to turnover rather than profits. The effects of this can be seen by looking back at Figure 4.8. You can see that total revenue is maximised at the peak of the *TR* curve (where $MR = 0$) at $q_r$. A revenue-maximising firm will produce more output than a profit-maximising one, and will need to charge a lower price in order to sell the extra output. This should be apparent from the fact that profits are maximised where $MR = MC$, which must be at a positive level of $MR$ — and thus to the left of $q_r$ in Figure 4.8.

Baumol pointed out that the shareholders might not be too pleased about this. The way the firm behaves then depends upon the degree of accountability that the agents (managers) have to the principals (shareholders). For example, the

shareholders may have sufficient power over their agents to be able to insist on some minimum level of profits. The result may then be a compromise solution.

## Sales maximisation

In some cases, managers may focus more on the volume of sales than on the resulting revenues. This could lead to output being set even higher, to the point at which total revenue only just covers total cost. Remember that total cost includes normal profit — the opportunity cost of the resources tied up in the firm. The firm would have to close down if it did not cover this opportunity cost.

Again, the extent to which the managers will be able to pursue this objective without endangering their positions with the shareholders depends on how accountable the managers are to the shareholders. Remember that the managers are likely to have much better information about the market conditions and the internal functioning of the firm than the shareholders, who view the firm only remotely. This may be to the managers' advantage.

## Summary

➤ Traditional economic analysis assumes that firms set out to maximise profits, where profits are defined as the excess of total revenue over total cost.

➤ This analysis treats the opportunity cost of a firm's resources as a part of fixed costs. The opportunity cost is known as normal profit.

➤ Profits above this level are known as abnormal profits.

➤ A firm maximises profits by choosing a level of output such that marginal revenue is equal to marginal cost.

➤ For many larger firms, where day-to-day control is delegated to managers, a principal–agent problem may arise if there is conflict between the objectives of owners (principals) and those of the managers (agents).

➤ This may lead to satisficing behaviour and to X-inefficiency.

➤ William Baumol suggested that managers may set out to maximise revenue rather than profits; others have suggested that sales or the growth of the firm may be the managers' objectives.

## Market structure

Firms cannot take decisions without some awareness of the market in which they are operating. In some markets, firms find themselves to be such a small player that they cannot influence the price at which they sell. In others, a firm may find itself to be the only firm, which clearly gives it much more discretion in devising a price and output strategy. There may also be many intermediate situations where the firm has some control over price, but needs to be aware of rival firms in the market.

Economists have devised a range of models that allow such different **market structures** to be analysed. A detailed discussion of these market structures will follow in the A2 part of the course, but for now it is important to introduce the key characteristics of alternative market structures. The main models are summarised in Table 4.3. In many ways, we can regard these as a spectrum of markets with different characteristics.

> **Key term**
>
> **market structure:** the market environment within which firms operate

| | Perfect competition | Monopolistic competition | Oligopoly | Monopoly |
|---|---|---|---|---|
| **Number of firms** | Many | Many | Few | One |
| **Freedom of entry** | Not restricted | Not restricted | Some barriers to entry | High barriers to entry |
| **Firm's influence over price** | None | Some | Some | Price maker, subject to the demand curve |
| **Nature of product** | Homogeneous | Differentiated | Varied | No close substitutes |
| **Examples** | Cauliflowers | Fast-food outlets | Cars | PC operating systems |
| | Carrots | Travel agents | Mobile phones | Local water supply |

*Table 4.3  A spectrum of market structures*

## Perfect competition

At one extreme is **perfect competition**. This is a market in which each individual firm is a *price taker*. This means that there is no individual firm that is large enough to be able to influence the price, which is set by the market as a whole. This situation would arise where there are many firms operating in a market, producing a product that is much the same whichever firm produces it. You might think of a market for a particular sort of vegetable, for example. One cauliflower is very much like another, and it would not be possible for a particular cauliflower-grower to set a premium price for its product.

Such markets are also typified by freedom of entry and exit. In other words, it is relatively easy for new firms to enter the market, or for existing firms to leave it to produce something else. The market price in such a market will be driven down to that at which the typical firm in the market just makes enough profit to stay in business. If firms make more than this, other firms will be attracted in, and thus abnormal profits will be competed away. If some firms in the market do not make sufficient profit to want to remain in the market, they will exit, allowing price to drift up until again the typical firm just makes enough to stay in business. In Chapter 14 it will be shown that this characteristic of a market is highly desirable from society's point of view.

> **Key term**
>
> **perfect competition:** an extreme form of market structure in which no individual seller (or buyer) is able to influence the price of the product

## Monopoly

At the other extreme of the spectrum of market structures is **monopoly**. This is a market where there is only one firm in operation. Such a firm has some influence over price, and can choose a combination of price and output in order to maximise its profits. The monopolist is not entirely free to set any price that it wants, as it must remain aware of the demand curve for its product. Nonetheless, it has the freedom to choose a point along its demand curve.

The nature of a monopolist's product is that it has no close substitutes — either actual or potential — so faces no competition. An example might be Microsoft, which for a long time held a global monopoly for operating systems for PC computers. At the time of the famous trial in 1998, Microsoft was said to supply operating systems for about 95% of the world's PCs.

 **term**

**monopoly:** a form of market structure in which there is only one seller of a good

*Bill Gates held a global monopoly on PC operating systems through his company, Microsoft*

Another condition of a monopoly market is that there are barriers to the entry of new firms. This means that the firm is able to set its price such as to make profits that are above the minimum needed to keep the firm in business, without attracting new rivals into the market.

## Monopolistic competition

Between the two extreme forms of market structure are many intermediate situations in which firms may have some influence over their selling price, but still have to take account of the fact that there are other firms in the market. One such market is known as **monopolistic competition**. This is a market in which there are many firms operating, each producing similar but not identical products, so that there is some scope for influencing price, perhaps because of brand loyalty. However, firms in such a market are likely to be relatively small. Such firms may find it profitable to make sure that their own product is differentiated from other goods, and may advertise in order to convince potential customers that this is the case. For example, small-scale local restaurants may offer different styles of cooking.

 **terms**

**monopolistic competition:** a form of market structure with some features of perfect competition (many firms) and some characteristics of monopoly (firms have some influence over price)

**oligopoly:** a form of market structure in which there are a few firms operating

## Oligopoly

Another intermediate form of market structure is **oligopoly**, which literally means 'few sellers'.

OCR Advanced Economics

*Small-scale local restaurants differentiate what they have to offer by serving particular kinds of food*

This is a market in which there are just a few firms that supply the market. Each firm will take decisions in close awareness of how other firms in the market may react to their actions. In some cases, the firms may try to collude — to work together in order to behave as if they were a monopolist — thus making higher profits. In other cases, they may be intense rivals, which will tend to result in abnormal profits being competed away. The question of whether firms in an oligopoly collude or compete has a substantial impact on how the overall market performs in terms of resource allocation, and whether consumers will be disadvantaged as a result of the actions of the firms in the market.

## Barriers to entry

It has been argued that if firms in a market are able to make abnormal profits this will act as an inducement for new firms to try to gain entry into that market in order to share in those profits. A **barrier to entry** is a characteristic of a market that prevents new firms from joining the market. The existence of such barriers is thus of great importance in influencing the market structure that will evolve.

**Key** *term*

**barrier to entry:**
a characteristic of a market that prevents new firms from easily joining the market

For example, if a firm holds a patent on a particular good, this means that no other firm is permitted by law to produce the product, and the patent-holding firm thus has a monopoly. The firm may then be able to set price such as to make abnormal profits without fear of rival firms competing away those profits. On the other hand, if there are no barriers to entry in a market, then if the existing firms set price to make abnormal profits, new firms will join the market, and the increase in market supply will push price down until no abnormal profits are being made. Barriers to entry will be discussed in more detail in Chapter 7.

## Summary

➤ The decisions made by firms must be taken in the context of the market environment in which they operate.

➤ Under conditions of perfect competition, each firm must accept the market price as given, but can choose how much output to produce in order to maximise profits.

➤ In a monopoly market, where there is only one producer, the firm can choose output and price (subject to the demand curve).

➤ Monopolistic competition combines some features of perfect competition, and some characteristics of monopoly. Firms have some influence over price, and will produce a differentiated product in order to maintain this influence.

➤ Oligopoly exists where a market is occupied by just a few firms. In some cases, these few firms may work together to maximise their joint profits; in other cases, they may seek to outmanoeuvre each other.

## Exercise 4.3

For each of the market situations listed below, select the form of market structure that is most likely to apply. In each case, comment on the way in which the firm's actions may be influenced by the market structure.

Forms of market structure:    A  perfect competition

                                 B  monopoly

                                 C  monopolistic competition

                                 D  oligopoly

a  A fairly large number of fast-food outlets in a city centre, offering various different styles of cooking (Indian, Chinese, fish and chips, burgers, etc.) at broadly similar prices.

b  An island's only airport.

c  A large number of farmers selling parsnips at the same price.

d  A small number of large firms that between them supply most of the market for commercial vans.

# Market failure and government intervention

# Part 2

# Chapter 5
# Prices, resource allocation and market failure

Part 1 described how markets work to reconcile producers' decisions about what to produce with consumers' preferences about the goods and services that they want to consume. In this discussion it was hinted that there would be circumstances in which governments might need to intervene to make sure that markets work effectively. Part 2 begins to explore some of the reasons why markets may fail to produce the best possible outcome for resource allocation in a society. This chapter begins with an important discussion of what economists mean by efficiency.

## Learning outcomes

After studying this chapter, you should:
➤ understand the concepts of productive and allocative efficiency
➤ be familiar with the way in which resources are allocated in a free market economy
➤ appreciate the situations in which markets may fail to allocate resources effectively

## Aspects of efficiency

In tackling the fundamental economic problem of scarcity, a society needs to find a way of using its limited resources as effectively as possible. In normal parlance it might be natural to refer to this as a quest for *efficiency*. From an economist's point of view there are two key aspects of efficiency, both of which are important in evaluating whether markets in an economy are working effectively.

Chapter 1 introduced one of these aspects in relation to the production possibility curve (PPC). Figure 5.1 shows a country's production possibility curve. One of the choices to be made in allocating resources in this country is between producing agricultural or manufactured goods.

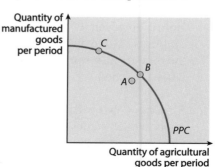

**Figure 5.1**
*Productive efficiency*

In Chapter 1 it was seen that at a production point such as *A* the economy would not be using its resources fully, since by moving to a point *on* the PPC it would be possible to produce more of both types of good. For example, if production took place at point *B*, then more of both agricultural and manufactured goods could be produced, so that society would be better off than at *A*.

A similar claim could be made for any point along the PPC: it is more efficient to be at a point *on* the frontier than at some points *within* it. However, if you compare point *B* with point *C*, you will notice that the economy produces more manufactured goods at *C* than at *B* — but only at the expense of producing fewer agricultural goods.

This draws attention to the trade-off between the production of the two sorts of goods. It is difficult to judge whether society is better off at *B* or at *C* without knowing more about the preferences of consumers.

This discussion highlights the two aspects of efficiency. On the one hand, there is the question of whether society is operating on the PPC, and thus using its resources effectively. On the other hand, there is the question of whether society is producing the balance of goods that consumers wish to consume. These two aspects of efficiency are known as **productive efficiency** and **allocative efficiency**, and are discussed in more detail below.

In terms of Figure 5.1, both *B* and *C* are on the PPC, so both are productively efficient points, but it is not possible to judge which of the two is better without knowing consumers' preferences.

An efficient point for a society would be one in which no redistribution of resources could make any individual better off without making some other individual worse off. This is known as the *Pareto criterion*, after the nineteenth-century economist Vilfredo Pareto, who first introduced the concept.

Notice, however, that *any* point along the PPC is a **Pareto optimum**: with a different distribution of income among individuals in a society, a different overall equilibrium will be reached.

> **Key terms**
>
> **productive efficiency:** attained when a firm operates at minimum average total cost, choosing an appropriate combination of inputs (cost efficiency) and producing the maximum output possible from those inputs (technical efficiency)
>
> **allocative efficiency:** achieved when society is producing an appropriate bundle of goods relative to consumer preferences
>
> **Pareto optimum:** an allocation of resources is said to be a Pareto optimum if no reallocation of resources can make an individual better off without making some other individual worse off

## Efficiency in a market
Aspects of efficiency can be explored further by considering an individual market. First, however, it is necessary to identify the conditions under which productive and allocative efficiency can be attained.

### Productive efficiency
The production process entails combining a range of inputs of factors of production

in order to produce output. One way of measuring productive efficiency is in terms of the **average total cost** of production, as introduced in Chapter 4. This is simply the total cost of production divided by the quantity of output produced. Productive efficiency can then be defined in terms of the minimum average cost at which output can be produced, noting that average cost is likely to vary at different scales of output.

There are two aspects to productive efficiency. One entails making the best possible use of the inputs of factors of production: in other words, it is about producing as much output as possible from a given set of inputs. This is sometimes known as **technical efficiency**. However, there is also the question of whether the *best* set of inputs has been chosen. For example, there may be techniques of production that use mainly capital and not much labour, and alternative techniques that are more labour intensive. The firm's choice between these techniques will depend crucially on the relative prices of capital and labour. This is sometimes known as **cost efficiency**.

 **terms**

**average total cost:** total cost divided by the quantity produced

**technical efficiency:** attaining the maximum possible output from a given set of inputs

**cost efficiency:** the appropriate combination of inputs of factors of production, given the relative prices of those factors

To attain productive efficiency, both technical efficiency and cost efficiency need to be achieved. In other words, productive efficiency is attained when a firm chooses the appropriate combination of inputs (cost efficiency) and produces the maximum output possible from those inputs (technical efficiency).

It is worth noting that the choice of technique of production may depend crucially upon the level of output that the firm wishes to produce. The balance of factors of production may well change according to the scale of activity. If the firm is producing very small amounts of output, it may well choose a different combination of capital and labour than if it were planning mass production on a large scale.

Thus, the firm's decision process is a three-stage procedure. First, the firm needs to decide how much output it wants to produce. Second, it has to choose an appropriate combination of factors of production, given that intended scale of production. Third, it needs to produce as much output as possible, given those inputs. Once the intended scale of output has been decided, the firm has to minimise its costs of production. These decisions are part of the response to the question of *how* output should be produced. Remember also the concept of *marginal cost* (page 56), which refers to the cost faced by a firm in changing the output level by a small amount. This becomes an important part of the discussion.

### Allocative efficiency

Allocative efficiency is about whether an economy allocates its resources in such a way as to produce a balance of goods and services that matches consumer preferences. In a complex modern economy, it is clearly difficult to identify such an ideal result. How can an appropriate balance of goods and services be identified?

Take the market for an individual product. Chapter 3 considered the market for laptop computers and argued that, in the long run, the market could be expected to arrive at an equilibrium price and quantity at which there was no incentive for firms either to enter the market or to exit from it. Figure 5.2 will remind you of the market situation.

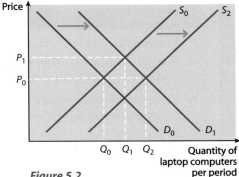

**Figure 5.2**
*The market for laptop computers revisited again*

The sequence of events in the diagram shows that, from an initial equilibrium with price at $P_0$ and quantity traded at $Q_0$, there was an increase in demand, with the demand curve moving to $D_1$. In response, existing firms expanded their supply, moving up the supply curve. However, the lure of the producer surplus (abnormal profits) that was being made by these firms then attracted more firms into the market, such that the supply curve moved to $S_2$, a process that brought the price back down to the original level of $P_0$.

Now think about that price from the point of view of a firm. $P_0$ is at a level where there is no further incentive to attract new firms, but no firm wishes to leave the market. In other words, no surplus is being made on that marginal unit, and the marginal firm is just breaking even on it. The price in this context would seem to be just covering the marginal cost of production.

However, it was also argued that from the consumers' point of view any point along the demand curve could be regarded as the marginal benefit received from consuming a good or service.

Where is all this leading? Putting together the arguments, it would seem that market forces can carry a market to a position in which, from the firms' point of view, the price is equal to marginal cost, and from the consumers' point of view, the price is equal to marginal benefit.

This is an important result. Suppose that the marginal benefit from consuming a good were higher than the marginal cost to society of producing it. It could then be argued that society would be better off producing more of the good because, by increasing production, more could be added to benefits than to costs. Equally, if the marginal cost were above the marginal benefit from consuming a good, society would be producing too much of the good and would benefit from producing less. The best possible position is thus where marginal benefit is equal to marginal cost — in other words, where *price is set equal to marginal cost.*

If all markets in an economy operated in this way, resources would be used so effectively that no reallocation of resources could generate an overall improvement. Allocative efficiency would be attained. The key question is whether the market mechanism will work sufficiently well to ensure that this happens — or whether it will fail. In other words, are there conditions that could arise in a market, in which price would not be set at marginal cost?

## Summary

➤ A society needs to find a way of using its limited resources as efficiently as possible.

➤ Productive efficiency occurs when firms have chosen appropriate combinations of factors of production and produce the maximum output possible from those inputs.

➤ Allocative efficiency occurs when firms produce an appropriate bundle of goods and services, given consumer preferences.

➤ An allocation of resources is said to be a Pareto optimum if no reallocation of resources can make an individual better off without making some other individual worse off.

➤ An individual market exhibits aspects of allocative efficiency when the marginal benefit received by society from consuming a good or service matches the marginal cost of producing it — that is, when price is equal to marginal cost.

## Exercise 5.1

Consider Figure 5.3, which shows a production possibility curve (*PPC*) for an economy that produces consumer goods and investment goods.

Identify each of the following (*Hint*: in some cases more than one answer is possible):

**a** a point of productive inefficiency

**b** a point that is Pareto-superior to *B*

**c** a point of productive efficiency

**d** a point of allocative efficiency

**e** an unattainable point (*Hint*: think about what would need to happen for society to reach such a point)

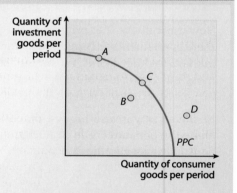

**Figure 5.3** *A production possibility curve*

## The working of a market economy

The previous section showed that the price mechanism allows a society to allocate its resources effectively if firms respond to changes in prices. Consumers express changes in their preferences by their decisions to buy (or not to buy) at the going price, which leads to a change in the equilibrium price. Firms thus respond to changes in consumer demand, given the incentive of profitability, which is related to price. In the short run, existing firms adjust their output levels along the supply curve. In the long run, firms enter into markets (or exit from them) in response to the relative profitability of the various economic activities that take place in the economy. But how does this work out in practice in a 'real-life' economy?

One way of viewing this system is through the notion of opportunity cost, introduced in Chapter 1. For example, in choosing to be active in the market for video

recordings, a firm faces an opportunity cost. If it uses its resources to produce video recordings, it is *not* using those resources to produce DVDs. There may come a point at which the cost of producing video recordings becomes too high, if the profitability of DVDs is so much higher than that for video recordings, because of changes in the pattern of consumer demand. When the firm finds that it is not covering its opportunity costs, it will transfer production from the video market to the DVD market.

This sort of system of resource allocation is often referred to as **capitalism**. The key characteristic of capitalism is that individuals own the means of production, and can pursue whatever activities they choose — subject, of course, to the legal framework within which they operate.

The government's role in a free capitalist economy is relatively limited, but nonetheless important. A basic framework of *property rights* is essential, together with a basic legal framework. However, the state does not intervene in the production process directly. Secure property rights are significant, as this assures the incentives for the owners of capital.

Within such a system, consumers try to maximise the satisfaction they gain from consuming a range of products, and firms seek to maximise their profits by responding to consumer demand through the medium of price signals.

As has been shown, this is a potentially effective way of allocating resources. In the eighteenth century Adam Smith discussed this mechanism, arguing that when consumers and firms respond to incentives in this way resources are allocated effectively through the operation of an **invisible hand**, which guides firms to produce the goods and services that consumers wish to consume. Although individuals pursue their self-interest, the market mechanism ensures that their actions will bring about a good result for society overall. A solution to the coordination problem is thus found through the free operation of markets. Such market adjustments provide a solution to Samuelson's three fundamental economic questions of what? how? and for whom?

However, Adam Smith also sounded a word of warning. He felt that there were too many factors that interfered with the free market system, such as over-protectionism and restrictions on trade. At the same time, he was not utterly convinced that a free market economy would be wholly effective, noting also that firms might at times collude to prevent the free operation of the market mechanism:

> People of the same trade seldom meet together, even for merriment and diversion, but the conversation ends in a conspiracy against the public, or in some contrivance to raise prices...

> Adam Smith, *The Wealth of Nations*, Vol. I

> **Key** *terms*
>
> **capitalism:** a system of production in which there is private ownership of productive resources, and individuals are free to pursue their objectives with minimal interference from government
>
> **invisible hand:** term used by Adam Smith to describe the way in which resources are allocated in a market economy

So there may be situations in which consumer interests need to be protected, if there is some sort of **market failure** that prevents the best outcome from being achieved.

## Causes of market failure

The following chapters explore a number of ways in which markets may fail to bring the best result for society as a whole. In each case, the failure will arise because a market settles in a position in which marginal social cost diverges from marginal social benefit. The remainder of this chapter introduces the most important reasons for market failure.

 **term**

**market failure:** a situation in which the free market mechanism does not lead to an optimal allocation of resources — for example, where there is a divergence between marginal social benefit and marginal social cost

### Imperfect competition

The discussion of market adjustment outlined above argued that the entry and exit of firms ensures that a market will evolve towards a situation in which price is equal to marginal cost. However, this rested on the assumption that markets are competitive. Firms were fairly passive actors in these markets, responding perhaps rather tamely to changes in consumer preferences. The real world is not necessarily like that, and in many markets, firms have more power over their actions than has so far been suggested.

In the extreme, there are markets in which production is dominated by a single firm. In 1998 Microsoft was taken to court in the USA, accused of abusing its dominant position. At the time, Microsoft was said to control 95% of the market for operating systems for PC computers — and not just in the USA: this was 95% of the *world* market. When a firm achieves such dominance, there is no guarantee that it will not try to exploit its position at the expense of consumers.

The very fact that there was a court case against Microsoft bears witness to the need to protect consumers against dominant firms. In the UK, the Office of Fair Trading (OFT) and the Competition Commission have a brief to monitor the way in which markets operate and to guard against anti-competitive acts by firms.

This is one example of how imperfect competition can lead to a distortion in the allocation of resources. Firms with a dominant position in a market may be able to drive prices to a level that is above marginal cost; consumers then lose out in terms of allocative efficiency. Chapter 7 explores these issues more carefully, and outlines the measures that a government can take to try to deal with the problem.

### Externalities

If market forces are to guide the allocation of resources, it is crucial that the costs that firms face and the prices to which they respond fully reflect the actual costs and benefits associated with the production and consumption of goods. However, there are a number of situations and markets in which this does not happen because of **externalities**. These cause a divergence between marginal social cost and

*Pollution is a cost to society that may not be reflected in a good's market price*

marginal social benefit in a market equilibrium situation. In the presence of such externalities, a price will emerge that is not equal to the 'true' marginal cost.

There are many examples of such externalities. An obvious one is pollution. A firm that causes pollution in the course of its production process imposes costs on others, but does not have to pay these costs. As a result, these costs are not reflected in market prices. This causes a distortion in the allocation of resources.

**externality:**
a cost or a benefit
that is external to
a market
transaction, and is
thus not reflected
in market prices

Not all externalities are negative. There may be situations in which a firm takes an action that benefits others. For example, if a firm chose to upgrade the road that ran past its factory, this would benefit other users of the road, even though they did not have to contribute to the cost of the upgraded road.

Not all externalities are on the supply side of the market. There may also be externalities in consumption, which may be positive or negative. If your neighbours mount an excellent firework display on 5 November, you can benefit without having to pay.

Externalities are discussed in Chapter 6.

### Information failure

If markets are to perform a role in allocating resources, it is extremely important that all relevant economic agents (buyers and sellers) have good information about market conditions; otherwise they may not be able to take rational decisions.

It is important that consumers can clearly perceive the benefits to be gained by their consuming particular goods or services, in order to determine their own

willingness to pay. Such benefits may not always be clear. For example, people may not fully perceive the benefits to be gained from education — or they may fail to appreciate the harmfulness of smoking tobacco.

In other market situations, economic agents on one side of the market may have different information from those on the other side: for example, sellers may have information about the goods that they are providing that buyers cannot discern. Chapter 7 explains that such information failure can also lead to a suboptimal allocation of resources.

### Public goods

There is a category of goods known as public goods, which because of their characteristics cannot be provided by a purely free market. Street lighting is one example: there is no obvious way in which a private firm could charge all the users of street lighting for the benefits that they receive from it. Such goods are also discussed in Chapter 7.

### Income distribution

Chapter 8 will discuss equity. It is commonly accepted that safeguards need to be in place in any economy to ensure that the distribution of income does not become so skewed that poverty escalates. If there is substantial poverty in a society, the allocation of resources is unlikely to be optimal. Chapter 8 examines the extent to which inequality in the distribution of income can be considered a form of market failure that requires some intervention by government. In addition, Chapter 8 also examines some ways in which government intervention may have unintended effects — in other words, situations in which there may be *government failure*.

## Summary

➤ Free markets do not always lead to the best possible allocation of resources: there may be market failure.

➤ Markets may fail when there is imperfect competition, so that firms are able to utilise market power to disadvantage consumers.

➤ When there are costs or benefits that are external to the price mechanism, the economy will not reach allocative efficiency.

➤ Markets can operate effectively only when participants in the market have full information about market conditions.

➤ Public goods have characteristics that prevent markets from supplying the appropriate quantity.

➤ Most societies are concerned to some extent with notions of equity.

# Chapter 6
# Externalities

*If markets are to be effective in guiding the allocation of resources in society, a precondition is that market prices are able to reflect the full costs and benefits associated with market trans-actions. However, there are many situations in which this is not so, and there are costs or benefits that are external to the workings of the market mechanism. This chapter examines the circumstances in which this may happen, and provides a justification for government inter-vention to improve the workings of the market.*

## Learning outcomes

After studying this chapter, you should:
- ➤ recognise situations in which the free market mechanism may fail to take account of costs or benefits that are associated with market transactions
- ➤ be familiar with situations in which there may be a divergence between private and social costs or benefits, such that price is not set equal to marginal cost
- ➤ be able to use diagrams to analyse positive and negative externalities in either production or consumption
- ➤ appreciate reasons why government may need to intervene in markets in which exter-nalities are present
- ➤ be familiar with a wide range of examples of externalities
- ➤ recognise ways in which external costs or benefits may be valued
- ➤ be familiar with possible solutions to the problem of externalities

## What is an externality?

**Externality** is one of those ugly words invented by econ-omists, which says exactly what it means. It simply describes a cost or a benefit that is external to the market mechanism.

An externality will lead to a form of market failure because, if the cost or benefit is not reflected in market

**Key** *term*

**externality:** a cost or a benefit that is external to a market transaction, and is thus not reflected in market prices

part **2**

prices, it cannot be taken into consideration by all parties to a transaction. In other words, there may be costs or benefits resulting from a transaction that are borne (or enjoyed) by some third party not directly involved in that transaction. This in turn implies that decisions will not be aligned with the best interests of society.

For example, if there is an element of costs that is not borne by producers, it is likely that 'too much' of the good will be produced. Where there are benefits that are not included, it is likely that too little will be produced. Later in the chapter, it will be shown that this is exactly what does happen. Externalities can affect either demand or supply in a market: that is to say, they may arise either in **consumption** or in **production**.

In approaching this topic, begin by tackling Exercise 6.1, which offers an example of each type of externality.

 **terms**

**consumption externality:** an externality that impacts on the consumption side of a market, which may be either positive or negative

**production externality:** an externality that impacts on the production side of a market, which may be either positive or negative

## Exercise 6.1

Each of the following situations describes a type of externality. Do they affect production or consumption?

**a** A factory situated in the centre of a town, and close to a residential district, emits toxic fumes through a chimney during its production process. As a result, residents living nearby have to wash their clothes more frequently, and incur higher medical bills as a result of breathing in the fumes.

**b** Residents living along a main road festoon their houses with lavish Christmas lights and decorations during the month of December, helping passers-by to capture the festive spirit.

### Toxic fumes

Example (a) is a negative production externality. The factory emits toxic fumes that impose costs on the residents (third parties) living nearby, who incur high washing and medical bills. The households face costs as a result of the production activities of the firm, so the firm does not face the full costs of its activity.

Thus, the **private costs** faced by the producer are lower than the social costs: that is, the costs faced by society as a whole. The producer will take decisions based only on its private costs, ignoring the **external costs** it imposes on society.

**terms**

**private cost:** a cost incurred by an individual (firm or consumer) as part of its production or other economic activities

**external cost:** a cost that is associated with an individual's (a firm or household's) production or other economic activities, which is borne by a third party

Figure 6.1 illustrates this situation under the assumption that firms operate in a competitive market (i.e. there is not a monopoly). Here, $D$ ($MSB$) represents the demand curve, which was characterised in Chapter 3 as representing the marginal social benefit derived from consuming a good. In other words, the demand curve represents consumers' willingness to pay for the good, and thus reflects their marginal valuation of the product.

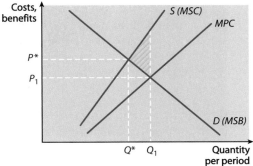

**Figure 6.1**
*A negative production externality*

Producers face marginal private costs given by the line $MPC$, but in fact impose higher costs than this on society. Thus $S$ represents the supply curve that includes these additional costs imposed on society. This may be regarded as being the marginal social cost ($MSC$) of the firms' production.

If the market is unregulated by the government, firms will choose how much to supply on the basis of the marginal (private) cost they face, shown by $MPC$ in Figure 6.1. The market equilibrium will thus be at quantity traded $Q_1$, where firms just break even on the marginal unit sold; price will be set at $P_1$.

This is not a good outcome for society, as it is clear that there is a divergence between the price in the market and the 'true' marginal cost — in other words, a divergence between marginal social benefit and marginal social cost. It is this divergence that is at the heart of the market failure. The last unit of this good sold imposes higher costs on society than the marginal benefit derived from consuming it. Too much is being produced.

In fact, the optimum position is at $Q^*$, where marginal social benefit is equal to marginal social cost. This will be reached if the price is set equal to (social) marginal cost at $P^*$. Less of the good will be consumed, but also less pollution will be created, and society will be better off than at $Q_1$.

The extent of the welfare loss that society suffers can be identified: it is shown by the shaded triangle in Figure 6.1. Each unit of output that is produced above $Q^*$ imposes a cost equal to the vertical distance between $MSC$ and $MPC$. The shaded area thus represents the difference between marginal social cost and marginal benefit over the range of output between the optimum output and the free market level of output.

### Christmas lights

Example (b) in Exercise 6.1 is an example of a positive consumption externality. Residents of this street decorate their homes in order to share the Christmas spirit with passers-by. The benefit they gain from the decorations spills over and adds to the enjoyment of others. In other words, the social benefits from the residents'

*Christmas lights have a positive consumption externality*

decision to provide Christmas decorations go beyond the private enjoyment that they receive.

Figure 6.2 illustrates this situation. *MPB* represents the marginal private benefits gained by residents from the Christmas lights; but *MSB* represents the full marginal social benefit that the community gains, which is higher than the *MPB*. Residents will provide decorations up to the point $Q_2$, where their marginal private benefit is just balanced by the marginal cost of the lights. However, if the full social benefits received are taken into account, $Q^*$ would be the optimum point: the residents do not provide enough décor for the community to reach the optimum. The shaded triangle in Figure 6.2 shows the welfare loss, that is, the amount of social benefit forgone if the outcome is at $Q_2$ instead of $Q^*$.

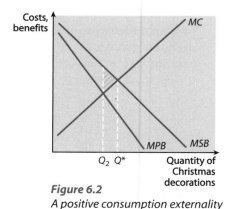

**Figure 6.2**
*A positive consumption externality*

### Positive and normative revisited

Example (b) is a reminder of the distinction between positive and normative analysis, which was introduced in Chapter 1. Economists would agree that Figure 6.2 shows the effects of a beneficial consumption externality. However, probably not everyone would agree that the lavish Christmas decorations are providing such benefits. This is where a *normative judgement* comes into play. It

could equally be argued that the lavish Christmas decorations are unsightly and inappropriate, or that they constitute a distraction for drivers and are therefore likely to cause accidents. After all, not everyone enjoys the garish.

---

### Exercise 6.1 (continued)

Discussion has centred around two examples of externalities: a production externality that had negative effects, and a consumption externality that was beneficial to society. In fact, there are two other possibilities.

c   A factory that produces chemicals, which is located on the banks of a river, installs a new water purification plant that improves the quality of water discharged into the river. A trout farm located downstream finds that its productivity increases, and that it has to spend less on filtering the water.

d   Liz, a 'metal' enthusiast, enjoys playing her music at high volume late at night, in spite of the fact that she lives in a flat with inadequate sound insulation. The neighbours prefer rock, but cannot escape the metal.

---

### Water purification

Example (c) is a production externality that has *positive* effects. The action taken by the chemical firm to purify its waste water has beneficial effects on the trout farm, which finds that its costs have been reduced without it having taken any action whatsoever. Indeed, it finds that it has to spend less on filtering the water.

Figure 6.3 shows the position facing the chemicals firm. It faces relatively high marginal private costs given by *MPC*. However, its actions have reduced the costs faced by the trout farm, so the 'social' cost of the firm's production activities is lower than its private cost. Thus, in this case marginal social cost, shown by *MSC* in the figure, is lower than marginal private cost. The firm will produce up to the point where *MPC* equals marginal social benefit: that is, at $Q_3$.

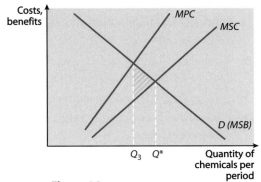

**Figure 6.3**
*A positive production externality*

In this market position, notice that the marginal benefit that society receives from consuming the product is higher than the marginal social cost of producing it, so too little of the product is being consumed for society's good. Society would be better off at $Q^*$, where marginal social benefit is equal to marginal social cost.

Again, the shaded triangle in Figure 6.3 represents the extent of the inefficiency: it is given by the excess of marginal social benefit over marginal social cost over the range of output between the market outcome and society's optimum position.

### Rock and metal

Example (d) is a *negative* consumption externality. Liz, the metal fan, gains benefit from listening to her music at high volume, but the neighbours also hear her music and suffer as a result. Indeed, it may be that when they try to listen to rock, the metal interferes with their enjoyment. Their benefit is reduced by having to hear the metal.

Figure 6.4 illustrates this. The situation can be interpreted in terms of the benefits that accrue as a result of Liz's consumption of loud metal music. Liz gains benefit as shown by the line *MPB*, which represents marginal private benefit. However, the social benefit is lower than this if the vexation suffered by the neighbours is taken into account, so *MSB* in Figure 6.4 represents the marginal social benefits from Liz's metal.

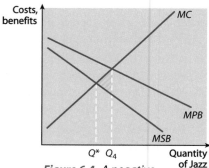

**Figure 6.4** *A negative consumption externality*

Liz will listen to metal up to the point where her marginal private benefit is just equal to the marginal cost of playing it, at $Q_4$. However, the optimal position that takes the neighbours into consideration is where marginal social benefit is equal to marginal cost — at $Q^*$. Thus, Liz plays too much metal for the good of society.

## Summary

➤ Markets can operate effectively only if all relevant costs and benefits are taken into account in decision making.

➤ Some costs and benefits are external to the market mechanism, and are thus neglected, causing a distortion in resource allocation.

➤ Such external costs and benefits are known as 'externalities'.

➤ Externalities may occur in either production or consumption, thereby affecting either demand or supply.

➤ Externalities may be either positive or negative, but either way resources will not be optimally allocated if they are present.

## Exercise 6.2

Discuss examples of some externalities that you meet in everyday situations, and classify them as affecting either production or consumption.

Externalities occur in a wide variety of market situations, and constitute an important source of market failure. This means that externalities may hinder the achievement of good resource allocation from society's perspective. The final section of this chapter explores some ways in which attempts have been made to

measure the social costs imposed by externalities. First, however, a number of other externalities that appear in various parts of the economy will be examined.

## Externalities and the environment

Concern for the environment has been growing in recent years, with 'green' lobbyist groups demanding attention, sometimes through demonstrations and protests. There are so many different facets to this question that it is sometimes difficult to isolate the core issues. Externalities lie at the heart of much of the debate.

Some of the issues are international in nature, such as the debate over global warming. At the heart of this concern is the way in which emissions of greenhouse gases are said to be warming up the planet. Sea levels are rising and major climate change seems imminent.

One reason why this question is especially difficult to tackle is that actions taken by one country can have effects on other countries. Scientists argue that the problem is caused mainly by pollution created by transport and industry, especially in the richer countries of the world. However, poorer countries suffer the consequences as well, especially countries such as Bangladesh, where much of the land is low lying and prone to severe flooding — indeed, two-thirds of the country was under water during the floods of 2004.

In principle, this is very similar to example (a) in Exercise 6.1: it is an example of a negative production externality, in which the nations causing most of the damage face only part of the costs caused by their lifestyles and production processes. The inevitable result in an unregulated market is that too much pollution is produced.

When externalities cross international borders in this way, the problem can be tackled only through international cooperation. For example, at the Kyoto World Climate Summit held in Japan in 1997, almost every developed nation agreed to cut greenhouse gas emissions by 6% by 2010. (The USA, the largest emitter of carbon dioxide, withdrew from the agreement in early 2001, fearing the consequences of such a restriction on the US economy.)

Global warming is not the only example of international externality effects. Scandinavian countries have suffered from acid rain caused by pollution in other European countries, including the UK. Forest fires left to burn in Indonesia have caused air pollution in neighbouring Singapore.

Another environmental issue concerns rivers. Some of the big rivers of the world, such as the Nile in Africa, pass through several countries on their way to the sea. For Egypt, through which the river runs at the end of its journey, the Nile is crucial for the livelihood of the economy. If countries further upstream were to increase their usage of the river, perhaps through new irrigation projects, this could have disastrous effects on Egypt. Again, the actions of one set of economic agents would be having damaging effects on others, and these effects would not be reflected in

market prices, in the sense that the upstream countries would not have to face the full cost of their actions.

Part of the problem here can be traced back to the difficulty of enforcing property rights. If the countries imposing the costs could be forced to make appropriate payment for their actions, this would help to bring the costs back within the market mechanism. Such a process is known in economics as 'internalising the externality', and will be examined later in this chapter.

Concern has also been expressed about the loss of *biodiversity*, a word that is shorthand for 'biological diversity'. The issue here is that when a section of rainforest is cleared to plant soya, or for timber, it is possible that species of plants, insects or even animals whose existence is not even known at present may be wiped out. Many modern medicines are based on chemicals that occur naturally in the wild. By eradicating species before they have been discovered, possible scientific advances will be forgone. Notice that when it comes to measuring the value of what is being destroyed, biodiversity offers particular challenges — namely, the problem of putting a value on something that might not even be there!

## Externalities and transport

With the introduction of the congestion charge in parts of central London, the London authorities have been attempting to tackle congestion. When traffic on the roads reaches a certain volume, congestion imposes heavy costs on road users. This is another example of an externality.

Figure 6.5 illustrates the situation. Suppose that $D$ ($MSB$) represents the demand curve for car journeys along a particular stretch of road. When deciding whether or not to undertake a journey, drivers will balance the marginal benefit gained from making the journey against the marginal cost that they face. This is given by $MPC$ — the marginal private cost of undertaking journeys. When the road is congested, a motorist who decides to undertake the journey adds to the congestion, and slows the traffic. The $MPC$ curve incorporates the cost to the motorist of joining a congested road, and the chosen number of journeys will be at $Q_1$.

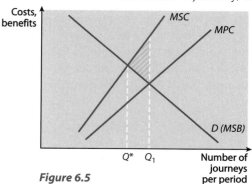

**Figure 6.5**
*Traffic congestion*

However, in adding to the congestion the motorist not only suffers the costs of congestion, but also imposes some marginal increase in costs on all other users of the road, as everyone suffers from the slower journeys resulting from the extra congestion. Thus, the marginal social costs ($MSC$) of undertaking journeys are higher than the cost faced by any individual motorist. $MSC$ is therefore higher than $MPC$. Society would be better off with lower congestion: that is, with the number of journeys undertaken being limited to $Q^*$, where marginal social benefit equals marginal social cost.

# Externalities and health

Healthcare is a sector in which there is often public provision, or at least some state intervention in support of the health services. In the UK, the National Health Service is the prime provider of healthcare, but private healthcare is also available, and the use of private health insurance schemes is on the increase. Again, externalities can help to explain why there should be a need for government to intervene.

Consider the case of vaccination against a disease such as measles. Suppose an individual is considering whether or not to be vaccinated. Being vaccinated reduces the probability of that individual contracting the disease, so there are palpable potential benefits. However, these benefits must be balanced against the costs. There may

*There are palpable potential benefits to being vaccinated*

be a direct charge for the vaccine; some individuals may have a phobia against needles; or they may be concerned about possible side-effects. Individuals will opt to be vaccinated only if the marginal expected benefit to them is at least as large as the marginal cost.

From society's point of view, however, there are potential benefits that individuals will not take into account. After all, if they do contract measles, there is a chance of their passing it on to others. Indeed, if lots of people decide not to be vaccinated, there is the possibility of a widespread epidemic, which would be costly and damaging to many.

Figure 6.6 illustrates this point. The previous paragraph argues that the social benefits to society of having people vaccinated against measles exceed the private benefits that will be perceived by individuals, so that marginal social benefits exceed marginal private benefits. Private individuals will choose to balance marginal private benefit against marginal private cost at $Q_1$, whereas society would prefer more people to be vaccinated at $Q^*$. This parallels the discussion of a positive consumption externality. Chapter 7 returns to consider another aspect of healthcare provision.

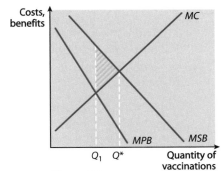

**Figure 6.6**
*Vaccination*

# Externalities and education

As you are reading this textbook, it is reasonably safe to assume that you are following a course in AS/A-level economics. You have decided to demand education. This is yet another area in which externalities may be important.

When you decided to take A-levels (including economics), there were probably a number of factors that influenced your decision. Perhaps you intend to demand even more education in the future, by proceeding to study at university. Part of your decision process probably takes into account the fact that education improves your future earnings potential. Your expected lifetime earnings depend in part upon the level of educational qualifications that you attain. Research has shown that, on average, graduates earn more during their lifetimes than non-graduates. This is partly because there is a productivity effect: by becoming educated, you cultivate a range of skills that in later life will make you more productive, and this helps to explain why you can expect higher lifetime earnings than someone who chooses not to demand education.

What does society get out of this? Evidence suggests that, not only does education improve productivity, but a *group* of educated workers cooperating with each other become even more productive. This is an externality effect, as it depends upon interaction between educated workers — but each individual perceives only the individual benefit, and not the benefits of cooperation.

In other words, when you decide to undertake education, you do so on the basis of the expected private benefits that you hope to gain from education. However, you do not take into account the additional benefits through cooperation that society will reap. So here is another example of a positive consumption externality. As with healthcare, some other aspects of education will be discussed in Chapter 7.

## Externalities and tourism

As international transport has become easier and cheaper, more people are wanting to travel to new and different destinations. For less developed countries, this offers an opportunity to earn much-needed foreign exchange.

There has been some criticism of this. The building of luxury hotels in the midst of the poverty that characterises many less developed countries is said to have damaging effects on the local population by emphasising differences in living standards.

However, constructing the infrastructure that tourists need may have beneficial effects on the domestic economy. Improved roads and communication systems can benefit local businesses. This effect can be interpreted as an externality, in the sense that the local firms will face lower costs as a result of the facilities provided for the tourist sector.

## Social cost–benefit analysis

The importance of externalities in regard to environmental issues means that it is especially important to be aware of externalities when taking decisions that are likely to affect the environment. One area in which this has been especially contentious in recent years is road-building programmes. If decisions to build new roads, or to expand existing ones such as the M25, are taken only by reference to commercial considerations, there could be serious implications for resource allocation.

In taking such decisions, it is desirable to weigh up the costs and benefits of a scheme. If it turns out that the benefits exceed the costs, it might be thought appropriate to go ahead. However, in valuing the costs and the benefits, it is clearly important to include some estimate for the externalities involved in order that the decision can be based on all relevant factors. In other words, it is important to take a 'long and wide view' and not to focus too narrowly on purely financial costs and benefits.

A further complication is that with many such schemes the costs and benefits will be spread out over a long period of time, and it is important to come to a reasonable balance between the interests of present and future generations.

**Social cost–benefit analysis** is a procedure for bringing together the information needed to make appropriate decisions on such large-scale schemes. This entails a sequence of key steps.

### 1   Identify relevant costs and benefits
The first step is to identify all relevant costs and benefits. This needs to cover all of the direct costs of the project. These can probably be identified relatively easily, and include the production costs, labour costs and so on. The indirect costs also need to be identified, and this is where externality effects need to be considered. For example, in a road-building scheme, it is important to think in terms not only of the costs of construction, but also of the opportunity cost — how else could the land being used for the road have been used? How will the increase in traffic affect the quality of life enjoyed by local residents? For example, they may suffer from noise from the traffic using the road, or from the traffic fumes. Similarly, direct and indirect benefits need to be identified.

 **terms**

**social cost–benefit analysis:** a process of evaluating the worth of a project by comparing its costs and benefits, including both direct and social costs and benefits — including externality effects

**shadow price:** an estimate of the monetary value of an item that does not carry a market price

### 2   Valuation
If the costs and benefits are to be compared, they all need to be given a monetary valuation. It is likely that some of them will be items that have a market price attached to them. For these, valuation is not a problem. However, for externalities, or for other indirect costs and benefits without a market valuation, it is necessary to establish a **shadow price** — an estimate of the monetary value of each item.

### 3   Discounting the future
It is also important to recognise that costs and benefits that will flow from the project at some point in the future need to be expressed in terms of their value in the present. From today's perspective, a benefit that is immediate is more

valuable than one that will only become relevant in 20 years' time. In order to incorporate this notion into the calculations, we need to **discount** the future at an appropriate rate, and calculate the **net present value** of the future stream of costs and benefits associated with the project under consideration.

**Key terms**

**discount:** a process whereby the future valuation of a cost or benefit is reduced (discounted) in order to provide an estimate of its present value

**net present value:** the estimated value in the current time period of the discounted future net benefit of a project

## Summary

➤ Externalities arise in many aspects of economic life.

➤ Environmental issues are especially prone to externality effects, as market prices do not always incorporate environmental issues, especially where property rights are not assigned.

➤ Congestion on the roads can also be seen as a form of externality.

➤ Externalities also arise in the areas of healthcare provision and education, where individuals do not always perceive the full social benefits that arise.

➤ A number of approaches have been proposed to measure externalities. Measurement may enable a social cost–benefit analysis to be made of projects involving a substantial externality element.

## Exercise 6.3

Suppose there is a proposal to construct a new industrial estate close to where you live. Identify the costs and benefits of the scheme, including direct costs and benefits and not forgetting externalities.

## Dealing with externalities

Externalities arise in situations where there are items of cost or benefit associated with transactions, and these are not reflected in market prices. In these circumstances a free market will not lead to an optimum allocation of resources. One approach to dealing with such market situations is to bring those externalities into the market mechanism — a process known as **internalising an externality**. For example, in the case of pollution this principle would entail forcing the polluting firms to face the full social cost of their production activities. This is sometimes known as the *polluter pays* principle.

**Key term**

**internalising an externality:** an attempt to deal with an externality by bringing an external cost or benefit into the price system

### Pollution

Figure 6.7 illustrates a negative production externality: pollution. Suppose that firms in the market for chemicals use a production process that emits toxic fumes, thereby imposing costs on society that the firms themselves do not face. In other words, the marginal private costs faced by these firms are less than the marginal social costs that are inflicted on society. As explained earlier in the chapter, firms in this market will choose to produce up to point $Q_1$ and charge a price of $P_1$ to consumers. At this point, marginal social benefit is below the marginal cost of producing the chemicals, so it can be claimed that 'too much' of the product is being produced — that society would be better off if production were at $Q^*$, with a price charged at $P^*$.

Note that this optimum position is not characterised by *zero* pollution. In other words, from society's point of view it pays to abate pollution only *up to* the level where the marginal benefit of reducing pollution is matched by the marginal cost of doing so. Reducing pollution to zero would be too costly.

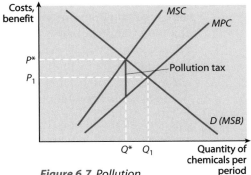

*Figure 6.7* Pollution

How can society reach the optimum output of chemicals at $Q^*$? In line with the principle that the polluter should pay, one approach would be to impose a tax on firms such that polluters face the full cost of their actions. In Figure 6.7, if firms were required to pay a tax equivalent to the vertical distance between marginal private cost (*MPC*) and marginal social cost (*MSC*), they would choose to produce at $Q^*$, paying a tax equal to the green line on the figure.

An alternative way of looking at this question is via a diagram showing the marginal benefit and marginal cost of emissions reduction. In Figure 6.8, *MB* represents the marginal social benefits from reducing emissions of some pollutant and *MC* is the marginal costs of reducing emissions. The optimum amount of reduction

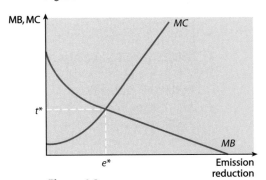

*Figure 6.8*
*Reducing the emission of toxic fumes*

is found where marginal benefit equals marginal cost, at $e^*$. Up to this point, the marginal benefit to society of reducing emissions exceeds the marginal cost of the reduction, so it is in the interest of society to reduce pollution. However, beyond that point the marginal cost of reducing the amount of pollution exceeds the benefits that accrue, so society will be worse off. Setting a tax equal to $t^*$ in Figure 6.8 will induce firms to undertake the appropriate amount of emission reduction.

This is not the only way of reaching the objective, however. Figure 6.8 suggests that there is another possibility — namely, to impose environmental standards, and to prohibit emissions beyond $e^*$. This amounts to controlling quantity rather than price; and, if the government has full information about marginal costs and marginal benefits, the two policies will produce the equivalent result.

Either of the approaches outlined above will be effective — *if* the authorities have full information about the marginal costs and benefits. But how likely is this? There are many problems with this proviso. The measurement of both marginal benefits and marginal costs is fraught with difficulties.

The marginal social benefits of reducing pollution cannot be measured with great precision, for many reasons. It may be argued that there are significant gains to be made in terms of improved health and lower death rates if pollution can be reduced, but quantifying this is not straightforward. Even if it were possible to evaluate the saving in resources that would need to be devoted to future medical care resulting from the pollution, there are other considerations: quantification of the direct improvements to quality of life; whether or not to take international effects into account when formulating domestic policy; and the appropriate discount rate for evaluating benefits that will be received in the future. Moreover, the environmentalist and the industrialist may well arrive at different evaluations of the benefits of pollution control, reflecting their different viewpoints.

The measurement of costs may also be problematic. For example, it is likely that there will be differences in efficiency between firms. Those using modern technology may face lower costs than those using relatively old capital equipment. Do the authorities try to set a tax that is specific to each firm to take such differences into account? If they do not, but instead set a flat-rate tax, then the incentives may be inappropriate. This would mean that a firm using modern technology would face the same tax as one using old capital. The firm using new capital would then tend to produce too little output relative to those using older, less efficient capital.

## Pollution permits

Another approach is to use a *pollution permit system*, under which the government issues or sells permits to firms, allowing them to pollute up to a certain limit. These permits are then tradable, so that firms that are relatively 'clean' in their production methods and do not need to use their full allocation of permits can sell their polluting rights to other firms, whose production methods produce greater levels of pollution.

One important advantage of such a scheme lies in the incentives for firms. Firms that pollute because of their relatively inefficient production methods will find they are at a disadvantage because they face higher costs. Rather than continuing to purchase permits, they will find that they have an incentive to produce less pollution — which, of course, is what the policy is intended to achieve. In this way, the permit system uses the market to address the externality problem — in contrast to direct regulation of environmental standards, which tries to solve pollution by overriding the market.

A second advantage is that the overall level of pollution can be controlled by this system, as the authorities control the total amount of permits that are issued. After all, the objective of the policy is to control the overall level of pollution, and a mixture of 'clean' and 'dirty' firms may produce the same amount of total emissions as uniformly 'slightly unclean' firms.

*A system of pollution permits could be effective in regulating pollution*

However, the permit system may not be without its problems. In particular, there is the question of enforcement. For the system to be effective, sanctions must be in place for firms that pollute beyond the permitted level, and there must be an operational and cost-effective method for the authorities to check the level of emissions.

Furthermore, it may not be a straightforward exercise for the authorities to decide upon the appropriate number of permits to issue in order to produce the desired reduction in emission levels. Some alternative regulatory systems share this problem, as it is not easy to measure the extent to which marginal private and social costs diverge.

One possible criticism that is unique to a permit form of regulation is that the very different levels of pollution produced by different firms may seem inequitable – as if those firms that can afford to buy permits can pollute as much as they like. On the other hand, it might be argued that those most likely to suffer from this are the polluting firms, whose public image is likely to be tarnished if they acquire a reputation as heavy polluters. This possibility might strengthen the incentives of such firms to clean up their production. Taking the strengths and weaknesses of this approach together, it seems that on balance such a system could be effective in regulating pollution.

### Global warming

Global warming is widely seen to require urgent and concerted action at a worldwide level. The Kyoto summit of 1997 laid the foundations for action, with many of the developed nations agreeing to take action to reduce emissions of carbon dioxide and other 'greenhouse' gases that are seen to be causing climate change. Although the USA withdrew from the agreement in early 2001, apparently

concerned that the US economy might be harmed, in November of that year 178 other countries did reach agreement on how to enforce the Kyoto Accord. The absence of US cooperation is potentially significant, however, as the USA is the world's largest emitter of carbon dioxide, responsible for about a quarter of the world's greenhouse gas emissions.

At the heart of the Kyoto Accord is the decision of countries to reduce their greenhouse gas emissions by an agreed percentage by 2010. The method chosen to achieve these targets was based on a tradable pollution permit system. This was seen to be especially demanding for countries such as Japan, whose industry is already relatively energy-efficient. Japan was thus concerned that there should be sufficient permits available for purchase. More explicitly, it was concerned that sloppy compliance by Russia would limit the amount of permits on offer. The issues of monitoring and compliance are thus seen as critical.

## The NIMBY syndrome

One problem that arises in trying to deal with externalities is that you cannot please all of the people all of the time. For example, it may well be that it is in society's overall interests to relocate unsightly facilities — it may even be that everyone would agree about this; but such facilities have to be located somewhere, and someone is almost bound to object because they are the ones to suffer. This is the **NIMBY** (not in my back yard) syndrome.

For example, many people would agree that it is desirable for the long-run sustainability of the economy that cleaner forms of energy are developed. One possibility is to build wind farms. People may well be happy for these to be constructed — *as long as* they do not happen to be living near them. This may not be the best example, however, as the effectiveness of wind farms is by no means proven, and there is a strong movement against their use on these grounds.

 **term**

**NIMBY (not in my back yard):** a syndrome under which people are happy to support the construction of an unsightly or unsocial facility, so long as it is not in their back yard

### Exercise 6.4

You discover that your local authority has chosen to locate a new landfill site for waste disposal close to your home. What costs and benefits for society would result? Would these differ from your private costs and benefits? Would you object?

## Property rights

The existence of a system of secure property rights is essential as an underpinning for the economy. The legal system exists in part to enforce property rights, and to provide the set of rules under which markets operate. When property rights fail, there is a failure of markets.

One of the reasons underlying the existence of some externalities is that there is a failing in the system of property rights. For example, think about the situation in which a factory is emitting toxic fumes into a residential district. One way of viewing this is that the firm is interfering with local residents' clean air. If those residents could be given property rights over clean air, they could require the firm to compensate them for the costs it was inflicting. However, the problem is that, with such a wide range of people being affected to varying degrees (according to prevailing winds and how close they live to the factory), it is impossible in practical terms to use the assignment of property rights to internalise the pollution externality. This is because the problem of coordination requires high transaction costs in order for property rights to be individually enforced. Therefore, the government effectively takes over the property rights on behalf of the residents, and acts as a collective enforcer.

Nobel prize winner Ronald Coase argued that externality effects could be internalised in conditions where property rights could be enforced, and where the transaction costs of doing so were not too large.

## Summary

➤ In seeking to counter the harmful effects of externalities, governments look for ways of internalising the externality, by bringing external costs and benefits within the market mechanism.

➤ For example, the 'polluter pays' principle argues that the best way of dealing with a pollution externality is to force the polluter to face the full costs of its actions.

➤ Attempts have been made to tackle pollution through taxation, the regulation of environmental standards and the use of pollution permits.

➤ In some cases the allocation of property rights can be effective in curbing the effects of externalities — so long as the transaction costs of implementing it are not too high.

# *Chapter 7*
# Other forms of market failure

Externalities are not the only form of market failure. Problems may arise when firms are in a position to exert undue influence in a market. This chapter examines some of the factors that can encourage the development of large firms, and discusses how this may affect whether markets can operate effectively and in society's best interests. It also looks at how firms may attain and sustain a dominant position in markets, and at how a market works if there are limits on competition. There are also situations where the characteristics of a good or service can affect the effective operation of a market. The chapter explores goods with unusual economic characteristics and markets that may fail as a result of problems with information.

## Learning outcomes

After studying this chapter, you should:
➤ be aware of the relationship between firm size and market concentration
➤ understand what is meant by market dominance
➤ be familiar with factors that may give rise to natural and strategic barriers to entry
➤ be aware of some of the effects on a market if competition is limited
➤ understand the nature of public goods and problems that arise in their provision
➤ be able to identify examples of public goods
➤ be aware of the characteristics of merit and demerit goods
➤ be able to give examples of possible merit and demerit goods
➤ appreciate the significance of asymmetric information as a source of market failure

## Scale and market concentration

An important issue that arises as firms become larger concerns the number of firms that a market can support. Suppose that economies of scale are available right up to the limit of market demand, as in Figure 7.1. If more than one firm were to try to supply this market, each producing at minimum average cost, there would be substantial excess supply, and the situation would not be viable.

In this situation, the largest firm in the market will come to dominate, as it will be able to produce at lower average costs than any potential competitor. This will be reinforced if there are significant learning-by-doing effects, which will further entrench the largest firm as the market leader. Such a market is likely to become a *natural monopoly* (see page 60).

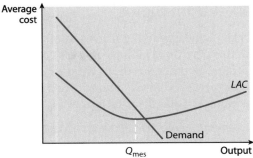

**Figure 7.1**
*How many firms can a market support?*

Such substantial economies of scale are not available in all sectors. It will depend upon the nature of technology and all the other factors that can give rise to economies of scale. In some activities there may be little scope at all for economies of scale. For example, there are no great fixed costs in setting up a restaurant, a hairdressing salon or a dental surgery — at least, compared with those involved in setting up a steel plant or an underground railway. The level of output at which minimum average cost is reached for such activities may thus be relatively small compared with market demand, so there may be room for many firms in the market. This helps to explain the proliferation of bars and take-away restaurants.

There may also be an intermediate position, where the economies of scale are not sufficient to bring about a monopoly situation, but only relatively few firms can operate efficiently. Such markets are known as *oligopolies*, which will be further investigated in Chapter 15.

How does this affect the way in which a market works? Is there any reason to believe that a monopoly or oligopoly will work against society's best interests? If market share is concentrated among a small number of firms, does this *inevitably* mean that consumers will suffer?

The answer to these questions depends upon the behaviour of firms within the market. There may be an incentive for a monopoly firm to use its market power to increase its profits. It can do this by restricting the amount of output that it releases on to the market, and by raising the price to consumers. In Chapter 14 you will see that a monopoly has the incentive to act in this way, since by lowering output and raising price it can increase its overall profits. From the consumer's point of view, the result is a loss of consumer surplus.

If there is an incentive for a single firm to act in this way, there is a similar incentive for firms in an oligopoly to do the same, as they can increase their joint profits — with the same effects on consumers. However, the oligopoly case is more complicated, as there is always the possibility that individual firms will try to increase their own share of the market at the expense of others in the oligopoly.

# Market dominance

A key issue is whether firms actually have the market power to exploit consumers in this way. Do firms have market dominance that can be exploited to bring higher profits? In other words, to what extent do firms have the freedom to set prices at their preferred levels, and to what extent do they have to take into account the actions of other firms or face other constraints?

Even monopoly firms have to accept the constraint of the demand curve. They are not free to set a price at any level they choose, otherwise consumers would simply not buy the product. The question is more one of whether firms are free to choose where to position themselves on their demand curve, rather than having to accept the market equilibrium price.

The fact that most countries have legislation in place to protect consumers from this sort of exploitation by firms recognises that firms might have market power and also have an incentive to use it. In the UK this monitoring is in the hands of the Office of Fair Trading and the Competition Commission. For these purposes, a firm is said to have a dominant position if its market share exceeds 40%. The existence of such bodies helps to act as a restraint on anti-competitive practices by firms.

There may also be natural constraints that limit the extent to which a firm is able to achieve a position of dominance in a market. An important consideration is whether a firm (or firms) in a market needs to be made aware of the possibility of new firms joining the market. Remember that in Chapter 5 a market was seen to tend towards a long-run equilibrium. In response to an increase in consumer demand, a key part of the adjustment involved the entry of new firms, which would be attracted into the market when the incumbent firms were seen to be making abnormal profits. This had the effect of competing away those profits until the incentive for entry was removed. Can firms in a market prevent this from happening?

## Barriers to entry

Another way of thinking about this is to examine what might constitute a barrier to the entry of new firms into a market (see Chapter 4). If such barriers are present, the existing firm or firms may be able to continue to make higher profits.

### *Economies of scale*

One source of entry barriers is the existence of economies of scale, as discussed in Chapter 4. If the largest firm has a significant cost advantage over later entrants, it can adopt a pricing strategy that makes it very difficult for new firms to become established.

This advantage of the existing firm is likely to be reinforced by the learning-by-doing effect; this could produce an even stronger cost advantage that would need to be overcome by new entrants.

### *Ownership of raw materials*

Suppose that the production of a commodity requires the input of a certain raw material, and that a firm in the market controls the supply of that raw material. You can readily see that this would be a substantial barrier to the entry of new firms. Until recently, DeBeers controlled the world's supply of uncut diamonds, and there was no way that new firms could enter the market because of the agreements that DeBeers had with mining companies and governments in those parts of the world where diamonds are mined. This monopoly has lasted for many years and is only now beginning to break down.

*Until recently, DeBeers controlled the world's supply of uncut diamonds*

### The patent system

The patent system exists to provide protection for firms developing new products or processes. The rationale for this is that, unless firms know that they will have ownership over innovative ideas, they will have no incentive to be innovative. The patent system ensures that, at least for a time, firms can be assured of gaining some benefit from their innovations. For the duration of the patent, they will be protected from competition. This therefore constitutes a legal barrier to the entry of new firms.

## Strategic and innocent barriers to entry

In the case of economies of scale, it could be argued that the advantage of the largest firm in the industry is a purely natural barrier to entry that arises from the market position of the firm.

In other cases, it may be that firms can consciously erect barriers to entry in order to make entry into the market more difficult for potential new firms. In other words, firms may make strategic moves to protect their market position behind entry barriers.

One example of this might be the advertising undertaken by firms. Some firms have become (and remain) well known by dint of heavy advertising expenditures. In some cases these expenditures have very little impact on market shares, and merely serve to maintain the status quo. However, for potential entrants they make life very difficult. Any new firm coming into the market has to try to match the advertising levels of existing firms in order to gain a viable market share. Effectively, existing firms have increased the fixed costs of being in the market, making entry more difficult to achieve. For example, when the soft drink Sunny Delight was launched, it had to undertake a large-scale TV advertising campaign to try to break into a market dominated by Coca-Cola and PepsiCo.

An alternative method is for an existing firm to operate with spare capacity, making it clear to potential entrants that entry will trigger a price war. The surplus capacity adds credibility to this threat, as the existing firm is seen to be able to increase output — and thus force down price — very quickly.

# Market failure

How is the market affected if the extent of competition in it is limited? By restricting output and raising price, firms are able to increase their profits, effectively increasing the market price to a level above the marginal cost of production. This implies that there is a loss of allocative efficiency in this situation. From society's point of view, too little of the product is being produced.

To the extent that the monopolist is a member of society, the increase in producer surplus might be regarded as a redistribution from consumers to producers. However, more crucial is the fact that there is a loss of consumer surplus that is not recoverable.

## Extension material

Figure 7.2 shows a market in which a monopoly firm has raised price from $P_0$ to $P_1$. With the price at the original level of $P_0$, consumer surplus is the area of the triangle $AP_0D$. However, if the monopoly firm raises its price to $P_1$, the consumer surplus falls to $AP_1B$. Some of the former consumer surplus becomes profits for the firm (the area $P_0P_1BC$) and the remaining area (the triangle $BCD$) is a net loss to society. This is known as the **deadweight loss** that society incurs as a result of the restriction to competition.

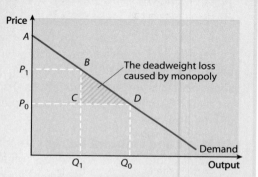

*Figure 7.2  The deadweight loss of monopoly*

This deadweight loss is a measure of the welfare loss imposed on society in a monopoly situation. However, there are two key aspects of efficiency, as was shown in Chapter 5. The loss in *allocative efficiency* shown in Figure 7.2 may be partly offset by improved *productive efficiency*: for example, because a monopoly is able to take advantage of economies of scale that would be sacrificed if it were to be split into many small firms, none of which would be able to reach the minimum average cost level of output.

 **Key term**

**deadweight loss:** loss of consumer surplus that arises when a monopoly raises price and restricts output

## Summary

➤ Cost conditions in a market may affect the number of firms that can operate profitably.

➤ Firms that attain market dominance may be able to harness market power at the expense of consumers, reducing output and raising price.

> This is especially the case where the existing firm(s) is (are) protected by barriers to entry.
> When firms do use such market power, there is a deadweight loss to society that reflects allocative inefficiency.
> However, this may in part be balanced by a gain in productive efficiency.

## Exercise 7.1

Figure 7.3 shows a market in which there are only two firms operating.

a The two firms competing in the market produce at constant marginal cost *OD*, which means that average cost is also constant and equal to marginal cost. Competing intensively, the price is driven down to a level at which no surplus above marginal cost is made. Identify the price charged, the quantity traded and consumer surplus.

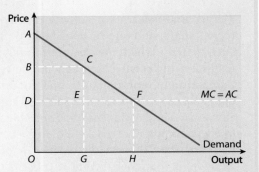

b Suppose the two firms decide to collude to raise price to a level *OB*. Identify the quantity traded and the consumer surplus.

**Figure 7.3 Anticompetitive behaviour**

c You should have found that consumer surplus is much smaller in the second situation than in the first. What has happened to the areas that were formerly part of consumer surplus?

## Regulation of monopoly and mergers

The effectiveness of the market system in allocating resources requires prices to act as signals to producers about consumer demand. Firms will be attracted into activities where consumer demand is buoyant and profitability is high, and will tend to exit from activities in which demand is falling and profitability is low.

This process relies on the existence of healthy competition between firms, and on freedom of entry to and exit from markets. In the absence of these conditions, resources may not be best allocated according to the pattern of consumer demand. For example, if there are barriers to entering a market, the existing firms in the market may have the power to restrict output and raise the price, producing less of the product than is desirable for society. As explained above, such barriers to entry may arise from features such as economies of scale or the patent system. In some situations, existing firms may take strategic action to deter entry.

This is one area of the economy in which governments often choose to intervene to protect consumers. In the UK, the Office of Fair Trading and the Competition Commission are responsible for this part of government policy. These bodies have

the power to investigate markets that appear to be overly concentrated or in which competition appears weak. They can also take action to encourage competition in markets. This is known as **competition policy**.

One of the knotty problems that arises here is that, if firms benefit from economies of scale, it may be more productively efficient to allow large firms to develop than to fragment the industry into lots of small firms in the name of encouraging competition. Thus, the authorities have to find a way of balancing the potential costs of losing allocative efficiency against the potential benefits of productive efficiency.

Merger and acquisition activity has led to the creation of some giant firms in recent years, and one responsibility of the competition authorities is to monitor such activity, which may be seen to have an effect on concentration in markets. Examples of recent cases can be viewed on the websites of the OFT and the Competition Commission. In one enquiry, the Competition Commission investigated takeover bids for the Safeway supermarket chain from Morrisons, Tesco, Sainsbury's and Asda. The Morrisons bid was accepted, as it was least likely to lead to a less competitive market. In an earlier investigation, the Commission blocked a proposed takeover of Manchester United Football Club by BSkyB on the grounds that this would not be beneficial for consumers.

## Contestable markets

It has been argued that in some markets, in order to prevent the entry of new firms, the existing firm would have to charge such a low price that it would be unable to reap any abnormal profits at all.

This theory was developed by William Baumol, and is known as the theory of **contestable markets**. For a market to be contestable, it must have no barriers to entry or exit and no sunk costs. As outlined in Chapter 4, sunk costs are costs that a firm incurs in setting up a business and which cannot be recovered if the firm exits the market. Furthermore, new firms in the market must have no competitive disadvantage compared with the incumbent firm(s): in other words, they must have access to the same technology, and there must be no significant learning-by-doing effects. Entry and exit must be rapid.

Under these conditions, the incumbent firm cannot set a price that is higher than average

**Key terms**

**competition policy:** an area of economic policy designed to promote competition within markets to encourage efficiency and safeguard consumer interests

**contestable market:** a market in which the existing firm makes only normal profit, as it cannot set a higher price without attracting entry, owing to the absence of barriers to entry and sunk costs

www.econ.nyu.edu/user/baumolw

*William Baumol developed the theory of contestable markets*

cost because, as soon as it does, it will open up the possibility of *hit-and-run entry* by new firms, which can enter the market and compete away the supernormal profits.

On the face of it, the conditions for contestability sound pretty stringent. However, suppose a firm has a monopoly on a domestic air route between two destinations. An airline with surplus capacity — that is, a spare aircraft sitting in a hangar — could enter this route and exit again without incurring sunk costs in response to profits being made by the incumbent firm. This is an example of how contestability may limit the ability of the incumbent firm to use its market power.

A moot point is whether the threat of entry will in fact persuade firms that they cannot set a price above average cost. If entry and exit are so rapid, perhaps the firms can risk making some profit above normal profits and then respond to entry very aggressively if and when it happens. After all, it is difficult to think of an example in which there are absolutely no sunk costs. Almost any business is going to have to advertise in order to find customers, and such advertising expenditure cannot be recovered.

## Public goods

### Private goods

Most of the goods that individuals consume are **private goods**. You buy a can of Diet Coke, you drink it, and it's gone. You may choose to share it with a friend, but you do not have to: by drinking it you can prevent anyone else from doing so. Furthermore, once it is gone, it's gone: nobody else can subsequently consume that Coke.

The two features that characterise a private good are:

➤ other people can be excluded from consuming it
➤ once consumed by one person, it cannot be consumed by another

The first feature can be described as *excludability*, whereas the second feature might be described by saying that consumption of a private good is *rivalrous*: the act of consumption uses up the good.

> **Key terms**
>
> **private good:** a good that, once consumed by one person, cannot be consumed by somebody else; such a good has excludability and is rivalrous
>
> **public good:** a good that is non-exclusive and non-rivalrous — consumers cannot be excluded from consuming the good, and consumption by one person does not affect the amount of the good available for others to consume

### Public goods

Not all goods and services have these two characteristics. There are goods that, once provided, are available to all. In other words, people cannot be excluded from consuming such goods. There are other goods that do not diminish through consumption, so they are non-rivalrous in consumption. Goods that have the characteristics of *non-excludability* and *non-rivalry* are known as **public goods**.

Examples of public goods that are often cited include street lighting, a lighthouse and a nuclear deterrent. For example, once street lighting has been provided in a

particular street, anyone who walks along that street at night benefits from the lighting — no one can be excluded from consuming it. So street lighting is non-exclusive. In addition, the fact that one person has walked along the street does not mean that there is less street lighting left for later walkers. So street lighting is also non-rivalrous.

The key feature of such a market is that, once the good has been provided, there is no incentive for anyone to pay for it — so the market will fail, as no firm will have an incentive to supply the good in the first place. This is often referred to as the **free-rider problem**, as individual consumers can free-ride and avoid having to pay for the good if it is provided.

 **term**

**free-rider problem:** when an individual cannot be excluded from consuming a good, and thus has no incentive to pay for its provision

## Extension material

A key question is how well the market for a public good is likely to operate. In particular, will a free market reach a position where there is allocative efficiency, with price equal to marginal social cost?

Think about the supply and demand curves for a public good such as street lighting. To simplify matters, suppose there are just two potential demanders of the good, $a$ and $b$. Consider Figure 7.4. If it is assumed that the supply is provided in a competitive market, $S$ represents the supply curve, reflecting the marginal cost of providing street lighting. The curves $d_a$ and $d_b$ represent the demand curves of the two potential demanders. For a given quantity $Q_1$, $a$ would be prepared to pay $P_a$ and $b$ would pay $P_b$. If these prices are

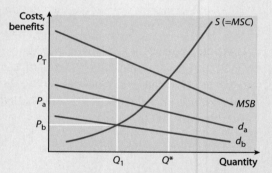

**Figure 7.4** *Demand and supply of a public good*

taken to be the value that each individual places on this amount of the good, then $P_a + P_b = P_T$ represents the social benefit derived from consuming $Q_1$ units of street lighting. Similarly, for any given quantity of street lighting, the marginal social benefit derived from consumption can be calculated as the vertical sum of the two demand curves. This is shown by the curve $MSB$. So the optimal provision of street lighting is given by $Q^*$, at which point the marginal social benefit is equated with the marginal cost of supplying the good.

However, if person $a$ were to agree to pay $P_a$ for the good, person $b$ could then consume $Q_1$ of the good free of charge, but would not be prepared to pay in order for the supply to be expanded beyond this point — as person $b$'s willingness to pay is below the marginal cost of provision beyond this point. So the social optimum at $Q^*$ cannot be reached. Indeed, when there are many potential consumers, the likely outcome is that *none* of this good will be produced: why should any individual agree to pay if he or she can free-ride on others?

The free-rider problem helps to explain why these sorts of goods have typically been provided through state intervention. This begs the question of how the state can identify the optimal quantity of the good to be provided — in other words, how the government determines $Q^*$. The extent to which individuals value a particular good cannot be directly observed. However, by including statements about the provision of public goods in their election manifestos, politicians can collect views about public goods provision via the medium of the ballot box. This is an indirect method, but it provides some mandate for the government to take decisions.

Note that public goods are called 'public goods' not because they are publicly provided, but because of their characteristics.

The free-rider problem makes it difficult to charge for a public good, so the private sector will be reluctant to supply such goods. In fact, pure public goods are relatively rare, but there are many goods that have some but not all of the required characteristics. On the face of it, the lighthouse service seems to be a good example of a public good. Once the lighthouse has been constructed and is sending out its signal, all boats and ships that pass within the range of its light can benefit from the service: that is, it is non-excludable. Moreover, the fact that one ship has seen the lighthouse signal does not reduce the amount of light available to the next ship, so it is also non-rivalrous.

However, this does not mean that ships cannot be charged for their use of lighthouse services. In 2002 an article in the *Guardian* reported that ships were complaining about the high charges to which they were subjected for lighthouse services. Ships of a certain size must pay 'light dues' every time they enter or leave UK ports, and the fees collected are used to fund lighthouses, buoys and beacons around the coast. In principle, it could be argued that this renders lighthouses excludable, as ships can be prevented from sailing if they have not paid their dues, and so could not consume the lighthouse services. At the heart of the complaints from the shipping companies was the fact that leisure craft below a certain threshold did not have to pay the charges, and they made more use of the lighthouses than the larger vessels.

In fact, there are many goods that are either non-rivalrous or non-excludable, but not both. One example of this is a football match. If I go to watch a premiership football match, my 'consumption' of the match does not prevent the person sitting next to me from also consuming it, so it is non-rivalrous. However, if I go along without my season ticket (or do not have a ticket), I can clearly be excluded from consuming the match, so it is *not* non-exclusive.

A stretch of road may be considered non-exclusive, as road users are free to drive along it. However, it is not non-rivalrous, in the sense that as congestion builds up consumption is affected. This example is also imperfect as a public good because, by installing toll barriers, users can be excluded from consuming it.

Where goods have some features of a public good, the free market may fail to

produce an ideal outcome for society. Exercise 7.2 provides some examples of goods: to what extent may each of these be considered to be non-rivalrous or non-excludable?

## Exercise 7.2

For each of the following goods, think about whether they have elements of non-rivalry, non-excludability, both or neither:

| | | | |
|---|---|---|---|
| **a** | a national park | **f** | a firework display |
| **b** | a playground | **g** | police protection |
| **c** | a theatre performance | **h** | a lecture |
| **d** | an apple | **i** | a DVD recording of a film |
| **e** | a television programme | **j** | the national defence |

### Tackling the public goods problem

For some public goods, the failure of the free market to ensure provision may be regarded as a serious problem — for example, in such cases as street lighting or law and order. Some government intervention may thus be needed to make sure that a sufficient quantity of the good or service is provided. Notice that this does not necessarily mean that the government has to provide the good itself. It may be that the government will raise funds through taxation in order to ensure that street lighting is provided, but could still make use of private firms to supply the good through some sort of subcontracting arrangement. In the UK, it may be that the government delegates the responsibility for provision of public goods to local authorities, which in turn may subcontract to private firms.

In some other cases, it may be that changes in technology may alter the economic characteristics of a good. For example, in the case of television programmes, originally provision was entirely through the BBC, funded by the licence fee. Subsequently, ITV set up in competition, using advertising as a way of funding its supply. More recently, the advent of satellite and digital broadcasting has reduced the degree to which television programmes are non-excludable, allowing private firms to charge for transmissions.

## Summary

➤ A private good is one that, once consumed by one person, cannot be consumed by anyone else — it has characteristics of excludability and rivalry.
➤ A public good is non-exclusive and non-rivalrous.
➤ Because of these characteristics, public goods tend to be underprovided by a free market.
➤ One reason for this is the free-rider problem, whereby an individual cannot be excluded from consuming a public good, and thus has no incentive to pay for it.
➤ Public goods, or goods with some of the characteristics of public goods, must be provided with the assistance of the government or its agents.

# Merit goods

There are some goods that the government believes everyone should consume, whether or not they wish to, and whether or not they have the means to do so. The key argument is that individuals do not fully perceive the benefits that they will gain from consuming such goods. These are known as **merit goods**.

**Key term**

**merit good:** a good that brings unanticipated benefits to its consumers, such that society believes that it should be consumed by individuals regardless of whether they have the means or the willingness to do so

Clearly, there is a strong political element involved in identifying the goods that should be regarded as merit goods: indeed, there is a subjective or normative judgement involved, since declaring a good to be a merit good requires the decision-maker to make a paternalistic choice on behalf of the population.

One way of viewing merit goods is that they reflect a divergence between the value that individual members of society place on goods and the decision-maker's views about their value to society as a whole. There is clearly a danger here that the decision-makers will force their views on the rest of society, and again, the ballot box may be the ultimate way of preventing this.

Another aspect of the merit good phenomenon is that the government may be in a better position than individuals to take a long-term view of what is good for society. In particular, governments may need to take decisions on behalf of future generations as well as the present. Resources need to be used wisely in the present in order to protect the interests of tomorrow's citizens. Again, this may require decision-makers to make normative judgements about the appropriate weighting to be given to the present as opposed to the future.

At the heart of the notion of a merit good, therefore, is the decision-maker's perception that there is a divergence between the marginal benefit that individuals perceive to arise from consuming a good, and the social benefit that actually accrues from its consumption. This is reminiscent of the arguments in Chapter 6 about consumption externalities, where a positive consumption externality arises when the marginal social benefit from consuming a good is greater than the marginal private benefit.

Figure 7.5 shows how this situation can be analysed. The example used here is education. In the UK everyone is required to attend school, at least up to age 16. Part of this requirement may be attributed to a merit good argument. It can be argued that education provides benefits to society in excess of those that are perceived by individuals. In other words, society believes that individuals will derive a benefit from education that they will not realise until after they have acquired that education. Thus, the government decrees that everyone must consume education up to the age of 16, whether

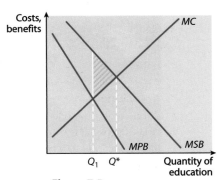

**Figure 7.5**
*A merit good*

they want to or not and whether they have the means to do so or not. This is a merit good argument. In Figure 7.5 marginal social benefit (*MSB*) is shown as being higher than marginal private benefit (*MPB*). Thus, society would like to provide $Q^*$ education, where $MSB = MC$ (marginal social cost), but individuals would choose to consume only $Q_1$ education, where $MPB = MC$, because they do not expect the future benefits to be as high as the government does.

In this case there may be other issues affecting the market for education. Chapter 6 argued that there would also be positive externality effects if educated workers were better able to cooperate with each other. There may be a further argument that individuals may fail to demand sufficient education because of information failure: in other words, they may not perceive the full benefits that will arise from education. The situation may be aggravated if parents have the responsibility of financing their children's education, because they are taking decisions *on behalf of* their children. In the case of tertiary education, there is no guarantee that parents will agree with their children about the benefits of a university education — it could go either way.

Another important issue that arises in the context of education concerns equity in access to higher education. Research has shown that graduates tend to enjoy higher lifetime earnings than non-graduates. However, if some groups have better access to credit markets than others, then those groups may be more able to take advantage of a university education. Specifically, it has been argued that people from low-income households may be discouraged from taking up university places because of failure in credit markets. In other words, the difficulty of raising funds in the present to pay for a university education may prevent people from gaining

© Bryn Colton/Assignments Photographers/Corbis

*Education is often seen as a merit good*

OCR Advanced Economics

the longer-term benefits of having received a university education – hence the launching of student loan schemes, which should help to address this particular form of market failure.

In some societies it has been suggested that the merits of education are better perceived by some groups in society than others. Thus in some less developed countries, individuals in relatively well-off households demand high levels of education, as they realise the long-run benefits that they can receive in terms of higher earnings – and, perhaps, political influence. In contrast, low-income households in remote rural areas may not see the value of education. As a result, drop-out from secondary – and even primary – education tends to be high. This is clearly a merit good argument that may need to be addressed by government, perhaps by making primary education compulsory or free – or both.

Other examples of merit goods are museums, libraries and art galleries. These are goods that are provided or subsidised because someone somewhere thinks that communities should have more of them. Economists are wary of playing the merit good card too often, as it entails such a high normative element. It is also difficult sometimes to disentangle merit good arguments from externality effects.

## Demerit goods

In contrast, there is a category of goods that government thinks should not be consumed even if individuals want to do so. These are known as **demerit goods** – or sometimes as 'merit bads'. Obvious examples are hard drugs and tobacco. Here the argument is that individual consumers overvalue the benefits from consuming such a good.

**Key term**

**demerit good:** a good that brings less benefit to consumers than they expect, such that society believes that it should not be consumed by individuals regardless of whether they wish to do so

Figure 7.6 shows the market for cocaine. Marginal private benefits (*MPB*) are shown as being much higher than marginal social benefits (*MSB*), so that in a free market too much cocaine is consumed. Society would like to be at $Q^*$, but ends up at $Q_1$. In this particular market, the government may see the marginal social benefit from consuming cocaine to be so low (e.g. at $MSB^*$ in the figure) that consumption should be driven to zero.

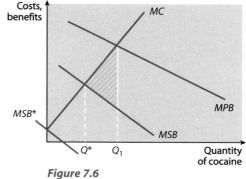

**Figure 7.6**
*A demerit good*

Again, this could be interpreted as partly an information problem, in the sense that individual consumers may not perceive the dangers of addiction and thus may overvalue cocaine. In addition, addiction would have the effect of making an individual's demand for the good highly inelastic in the long run. However, it is paternalistic of the government to intervene directly for

this reason, although it might wish to correct other externalities — for instance, those imposed on others when addicts steal to fund their habit.

An alternative approach is to try to remove the information failure; clearly, the government has adopted this approach in seeking to educate people about the dangers of tobacco smoking.

### Taxing tobacco

This market for tobacco is characterised in Figure 7.7. Demand (*MPB*) represents the marginal private benefit that consumers gain from smoking tobacco. However, the government believes that consumers underestimate the damaging effects of smoking, so that the true benefits are given by *MSB* (marginal social benefit). Given the marginal cost (supply) curve, in an unregulated market consumers will choose to smoke up to $Q_1$ tobacco. The optimum for society, however, is at $Q^*$.

One way of tackling this problem is through taxation. If the government imposes a tax shown by the red line in Figure 7.7, this effectively shifts the supply curve to the market, as shown in the figure. This raises the price in the market, so consumers are persuaded to reduce their consumption to the optimal level at $Q^*$. Notice that because the demand curve (*MPB*) is quite steep (relatively inelastic), a substantial tax is needed in order to reach $Q^*$. Empirical evidence suggests that the demand for tobacco is relatively inelastic — and therefore tobacco taxes have risen to comprise a large portion of the price of a packet of cigarettes.

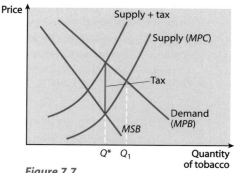

**Figure 7.7**
*Taxing tobacco*

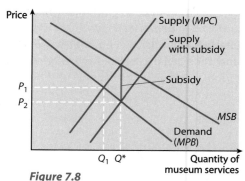

**Figure 7.8**
*Subsidising museum services*

Conversely, if the government wishes to encourage the consumption of a merit good, it may do so through subsidies. Thus, the museum service is subsidised, and the ballet and opera have enjoyed subsidies in the past. Figure 7.8 shows how such a subsidy might be used to affect the quantity of museum services provided. Demand (*MPB*) again shows the demand for museum services from the public, which is below the marginal social benefit (*MSB*) that the authorities perceive to be the true value of museum services. Thus the free market equilibrium position is at $Q_1$, although the government believes that $Q^*$ is the socially optimum position. By providing a subsidy, the supply curve is shifted to the right, and consumers will choose to demand the optimum quantity at the subsidised price $P_2$.

# Information failures

If markets are to be effective in guiding resource allocation, it is important that economic decision-makers receive full and accurate information about market conditions. Consumers need information about the prices at which they can buy and the quality of the products for sale. Producers need to be able to observe how consumers react to prices. Information is thus of crucial significance if markets are to work. However, there are some markets in which not all traders have access to good information, or in which some traders have more or better access to it than others. This is known as a situation of **asymmetric information**, and can be a source of market failure.

**Key** *term*

**asymmetric information:** a situation in which some participants in a market have better information about market conditions than others

### Healthcare

One example of asymmetric information is in healthcare. Suppose you go to your dentist for a check-up. He tells you that you have a filling that needs to be replaced, although you have had no pain or problems with it. In this situation the seller in a market has much better information about the product than the buyer. You as the buyer have no idea whether or not the recommended treatment is needed, and without going to another dentist for a second opinion you have no way of finding out. You might think this is an unsatisfactory situation, as it seems to give a lot of power to the seller relative to the consumer. The situation is even worse where the dentist does not even publish the prices for treatment until after it has been carried out! The Office of Fair Trading criticised private dentists for exactly this sort of practice when they reported on this market in March 2003. Indeed, dentists are now required by law to publish prices for treatment.

The same argument applies in the case of other areas of healthcare, where doctors have better information than their patients about the sort of treatment that is needed.

### Exercise 7.3

Ethel, an old-age pensioner, is sitting quietly at home when the doorbell rings. At the door is a stranger called Frank, who tells her that he has noticed that her roof is in desperate need of repair, and if she does not get something done about it very soon, there will be problems in the next rainstorm. Fortunately, he can help — for a price. Discuss whether there is a market failure in this situation, and what Ethel (or others) can do about it.

### Education

The market for education is similar. Teachers or government inspectors may know more about the subjects and topics that students need to study than the students do themselves. This is partly because teachers are able to take a longer view and

can see education provision in a broader perspective. Students taking economics at university may have to take a course in mathematics and statistics in their first year, and some will always complain that they have come to study economics, not maths. It is only later that they come to realise that competence in maths is crucial these days for the economics that they will study later in their course.

How could this problem be tackled? The answer would seem to be obvious – if the problem arises from an information failure, then the answer should be to improve the information flow, in this case to students. This might be achieved by providing a convincing explanation of why the curriculum has been designed in a particular way. It may also be necessary to provide incentives for students to study particular unpopular subjects, perhaps by making success a requirement for progression to the next stage of the course. By understanding the economic cause of a problem, it is possible to devise a strategy that should go some way towards removing the market failure.

## Second-hand cars

One of the most famous examples of asymmetric information relates to the second-hand (or 'pre-owned', by the latest terminology) car market. This is because the first paper that drew attention to the problem of asymmetric information, by Nobel laureate George Akerlof, focused on this market.

Akerlof argued that there are two types of car. Some cars are good runners and are totally reliable, whereas some are continually breaking down and needing parts and servicing; the latter are known as 'lemons' in the USA (allegedly from fruit machines, where lemons offer the lowest prize). The problem in the second-hand car market arises because the owners of cars (potential sellers) have better information about their cars than the potential buyers. In other words, when a car owner decides to sell a car, he or she knows whether it is a lemon or a good-quality car — but a buyer cannot tell.

*Publishing Pictures*

*The second-hand car market is an example of a market with asymmetric information*

In this sort of market, car dealers can adopt one of two possible strategies. One is to offer a high price and buy up all the cars in the market, knowing that the lemons will be sold on at a loss. The problem is that, if the lemons make up a large proportion of the cars in the market, this could generate overall losses for the dealers. The alternative is to offer a low price, and just buy up all the lemons to sell for scrap. In this situation, the market for good-quality used cars is effectively destroyed — an extreme form of market failure!

Again, the solution may be to tackle the problem at its root, by finding a way to provide information. In the case of second-hand cars, AA inspection schemes or the offering of warranties may be a way of improving the flow of information about the quality of cars for sale.

## Summary

➤ A merit good is one that society believes should be consumed by individuals whether or not they have the means or the willingness to do so.

➤ There is a strong normative element in the identification of merit goods.

➤ Demerit goods (or 'merit bads') are goods that society believes should not be consumed by individuals even if they wish to do so.

➤ In the case of merit and demerit goods, 'society' (as represented by government) believes that it has better information than consumers about these goods, and about what is good (or bad) for consumers.

➤ Information deficiency can lead to market failure in other situations: for example, where some participants in a market have better information about some aspect(s) of the market than others.

➤ Examples of this include healthcare, education and second-hand cars.

## Exercise 7.4

The *Guardian* reported on 27 August 2004 that the pharmaceutical company GlaxoSmithKline had been forced to publish details of a clinical trial of one of its leading antidepressant drugs following a lawsuit that had accused the company of concealing evidence that the drug could be harmful to children. Discuss the extent to which this situation may have led to a market failure because of information problems.

# Chapter 8
# Government intervention and government failure

*Previous chapters have identified various ways in which markets can fail to bring about an efficient allocation of resources in a society. This chapter investigates questions of equity, and discusses whether inequality in the distribution of income requires intervention by government. The chapter also explores how some well-intentioned interventions by government can sometimes produce unintended results.*

## Learning outcomes

After studying this chapter, you should:
- ➤ be aware of global inequality in the distribution of income
- ➤ appreciate that there is also inequality in the distribution of income between different groups within societies
- ➤ be able to identify areas in which government actions may have unintended distortionary effects
- ➤ be aware of some sources of government failure
- ➤ be familiar with the effects of minimum wage legislation and rent controls
- ➤ be able to analyse the effects of sales taxes and subsidies

## Equity

In discussing ways in which markets may fail to lead to an optimal allocation of resources, the focus has been primarily on questions of efficiency. In particular, it has been noted that allocative efficiency will not be attained in circumstances in which there is a divergence between private and social costs or benefits. However, it was noted in Chapter 5 that there is no unique overall equilibrium for a society, and that a different distribution of income between individuals will lead to a different Pareto optimum position.

This highlights the potential importance of issues of *equity*. One aspect of this is whether individuals face equal opportunities, and whether identical people receive

identical treatment in economic terms. However, there is also the unavoidable fact that people are not identical, and that different innate abilities and talents command different rewards. This then raises the question of whether society needs to provide some protection for any of its members who find themselves disadvantaged by the way in which resources are allocated. In other words, do communities need a system whereby resources are transferred from some members of society to others?

This is another area in which normative judgements arise. The government may take the view that everybody in society has the right to some minimum standard of living. This may reflect the government's view of the collective desires of the population. In order to alleviate poverty, therefore, some income may need to be transferred from the relatively rich in society to the relatively poor. The normative judgement arises because of the need to define what constitutes a minimum standard of living, and to determine the extent to which such transfers should be undertaken.

This argument is effectively saying that a free market allocation of resources may produce a distribution of income among individuals that is not acceptable in terms of society's objectives.

The question of income distribution can be explored at a number of levels. You could look at the global distribution — the way in which incomes are distributed between countries. You could also examine income distribution *within* countries — that is, between different groups in society. For example, in the UK the richest 10% of households receive more than ten times the income of the poorest 10% of households.

Some variation in incomes between households is, of course, inevitable. There are good economic reasons for this, which will be discussed later in the book. For example, there may be differences in pay between different occupations, or between people producing goods or services that are more highly valued by consumers. There may also be differences in income that arise because of the pattern of distribution of wealth within a society. The extent to which a society wishes government to intervene to influence the pattern of wealth and income distribution is often a prominent issue during electioneering.

### Global inequality

It is well known that there is substantial inequality in the distribution of incomes worldwide. Figure 8.1 gives some indication of how unequal it is. The World Bank classifies countries according to income. Low-income countries (LICs) are those in which average annual income is less than $825, middle-income countries (MICs) have an average income between $826 and $10,065; high-income countries (HICs) have average incomes

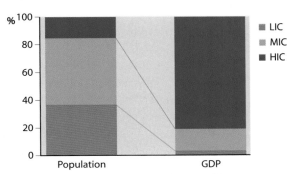

**Figure 8.1** *Distribution of the world population and GDP, 2004*
Source: *World Development Report*, 2006.

**part 2**

above $10,065. Figure 8.1 shows the distribution of income and people between these broad groups of countries. In 2004 about 37% of the world's population lived in low-income countries, but they received only 3% of the world's GDP. In contrast, the 15.8% of people living in the high-income countries received more than 80% of the world's GDP.

There is also substantial inequality *within* many societies. Some inequality is to be expected, as people differ in their innate ability, talents and training. However, it is clear that the degree of inequality varies between countries. In order to examine this more carefully, it is necessary to have a way of measuring inequality.

### Measuring income inequality

Table 8.1 presents data for some selected countries. Such data are not collected every year, as it is quite expensive to gather the statistics needed to describe the distribution of income; hence the variety of survey years for the data. As the pattern of income distribution tends not to change dramatically from one year to the next, however, there is still some justification for comparing across countries.

These data come from surveys conducted on the income levels of individual households. Households are then ranked in ascending order of income levels, and the shares of total income going to groups of households are calculated.

For example, for Ethiopia, the first country listed in the table, it can be seen that the poorest 10% of households receive 3.0% of total household income, and the

| | GNI per capita | | Percentage share of income or consumption | | | | | | |
|---|---|---|---|---|---|---|---|---|---|
| | US$ 2002 | Survey year | Lowest 10% | Lowest 20% | Second 20% | Third 20% | Fourth 20% | Highest 20% | Highest 10% |
| Ethiopia | 100 | 1995 | 3.0 | 7.1 | 10.9 | 14.5 | 19.8 | 47.7 | 33.7 |
| Sierra Leone | 140 | 1983–5 | 0.5 | 1.1 | 2.0 | 9.8 | 23.7 | 63.4 | 43.6 |
| Bangladesh | 360 | 1995–6 | 3.9 | 8.7 | 12.0 | 15.7 | 20.8 | 42.8 | 28.6 |
| Pakistan | 410 | 1996–7 | 4.1 | 9.5 | 12.9 | 16.0 | 20.5 | 41.1 | 27.6 |
| India | 480 | 1997 | 3.5 | 8.1 | 11.6 | 15.0 | 19.3 | 46.1 | 33.5 |
| Zimbabwe | 706 | 1990–1 | 1.8 | 4.0 | 6.3 | 10.0 | 17.4 | 62.3 | 46.9 |
| Indonesia | 710 | 1996 | 3.6 | 8.0 | 11.3 | 15.1 | 20.8 | 44.9 | 30.3 |
| Sri Lanka | 840 | 1995 | 3.5 | 8.0 | 11.8 | 15.8 | 21.5 | 42.8 | 28.0 |
| Bolivia | 900 | 1990 | 2.3 | 5.6 | 9.7 | 14.5 | 22.0 | 48.2 | 31.7 |
| China | 940 | 1998 | 2.4 | 5.9 | 10.2 | 15.1 | 22.2 | 46.6 | 30.4 |
| Belarus | 1,360 | 1998 | 5.1 | 11.4 | 15.2 | 18.2 | 21.9 | 33.3 | 20.0 |
| South Africa | 2,600 | 1993–4 | 1.1 | 2.9 | 5.5 | 9.2 | 17.7 | 64.8 | 45.9 |
| Brazil | 2,850 | 1996 | 0.9 | 2.5 | 5.5 | 10.0 | 18.3 | 63.8 | 47.6 |
| Malaysia | 3,540 | 1995 | 1.8 | 4.5 | 8.3 | 13.0 | 20.4 | 53.8 | 37.9 |
| Hungary | 5,280 | 1996 | 3.9 | 8.8 | 12.5 | 16.6 | 22.3 | 39.9 | 24.8 |
| South Korea | 9,930 | 1993 | 2.9 | 7.5 | 12.9 | 17.4 | 22.9 | 39.3 | 24.3 |
| UK | 25,250 | 1991 | 2.6 | 6.6 | 11.5 | 16.3 | 22.7 | 43.0 | 27.3 |
| USA | 34,870 | 1997 | 1.8 | 5.2 | 10.5 | 15.6 | 22.4 | 46.4 | 30.5 |
| Japan | 35,990 | 1993 | 4.8 | 10.6 | 14.2 | 17.6 | 22.0 | 35.7 | 21.7 |

*Table 8.1 Income distribution in selected countries*     Note: countries are listed in ascending order of average incomes.
Source: *World Development Report.*

OCR Advanced Economics

*Shanty town in a less developed country*

poorest 20% receive just 7.1%. At the top end of the distribution, the richest 10% receive 33.7% of the total income. This contrasts quite markedly with the second country listed (Sierra Leone), where the data suggest greater inequality in distribution, with the poorest 10% receiving only 0.5% of total household income and the richest 10% getting as much as 43.6%.

### Income distribution in the UK

Table 8.1 shows that the UK is neither the most equal nor the most unequal of societies as far as post-tax income is concerned. Inequality in the UK increased between the mid-1970s and the mid-1990s, but has stabilised since then. There is some evidence that measures introduced since 1997 have improved the income distribution, in the sense that inequality would have continued to increase without these measures. For example, some research carried out by the Institute for Fiscal Studies has shown that, in the absence of policies introduced by the government, poverty would have been higher in 2005 than it was in the mid-1990s. The trends in income distribution, and the causes of inequality, will be explored in Chapter 11.

An important issue here is whether the government needs to intervene in order to influence the distribution of income within a society such as the UK — and to what extent such redistribution is desirable for society as a whole. There is a narrow path to be trodden between protecting vulnerable members of society, and giving incentives for people to provide work effort. If richer households are taxed too heavily, it may affect their incentives to work. On the other hand, taxes need to be set at a sufficient level to be able to protect the poor. These issues will be revisited in Chapter 11.

### Regional disparities

One particular aspect of inequality is between regions of the UK. This partly reflects the way in which regions have tended to specialise in different types of economic activity. Then as the pattern of production has changed over time, some areas have gone into decline whilst others have boomed. This leads to inequality in incomes

because of variations in the unemployment rate between regions. One explanation for the persistence of such patterns through time is related to the immobility of factors of production. People are reluctant to move house in search of jobs, and firms may also be reluctant to move to find workers, because of the costs involved with relocation. In other words, disparities may arise because of *geographical immobility*.

In addition, there may be unemployment that arises because people who are unemployed do not have the sorts of skill for which employers are looking. In other words, there may also be disparities in income that arise because of *occupational immobility*. Such immobility may cause disparities within regions as well as between regions.

There may be a number of market-failure explanations for regional inequality. For example, it may be that one reason why people do not move in search of jobs is a lack of information about job opportunities — in other words, an information failure.

## Summary

➤ Allocative efficiency can be achieved in a range of alternative situations, some of which may be more 'equitable' than others.

➤ There may be situations in which the government finds it appropriate to intervene to influence the income distribution within a society.

➤ There is substantial global disparity in the distribution of resources, and significant inequality within countries.

➤ There is also disparity in income levels between regions in the UK.

## Exercise 8.1

Examine the data provided in Table 8.1, and identify the countries with the most and least unequal distribution of income. Discuss whether there is an association between the degree of inequality and the level of average income (as measured by GNI per capita — notice that the countries are ranked in ascending order of GNI per capita).

## Government failure

Most governments see it as their responsibility to try to correct some of the failures of markets to allocate resources efficiently. This has led to a wide variety of policies being devised to address issues of market failure. Some of these have been discussed already. However, some policies have unintended effects that may not culminate in successful elimination of market failure. Indeed, in some cases government intervention may introduce new market distortions, leading to a phenomenon known as **government failure**. The remainder of this chapter examines some examples of such government failure.

OCR Advanced Economics

## The minimum wage

In 1999 the UK National **Minimum Wage** came into force, designed to protect workers on low pay. To illustrate how this works, Figure 8.2 represents the labour market for office cleaners. Employers demand labour according to the wage rate — the lower the wage, the higher the demand for the labour of office cleaners. On the supply side, more workers will offer themselves for work when the wage rate is relatively high. If the market is unregulated, it will reach equilibrium with a wage rate $W^*$ and quantity of labour $L^*$.

Suppose now that the government comes to the view that $W^*$ is not sufficiently high to provide a reasonable wage for cleaners. One response is to impose a minimum wage, below which employers are not permitted to offer employment — say, $W_{min}$ on the figure. This will have two effects on the market situation. First, employers will demand less labour at this higher wage, so employment will fall to $L_d$. Second, more workers will be prepared to offer themselves for employment at the higher wage, so labour supply will rise to $L_s$. However, the net effect of this is that there is an excess supply of labour at this wage and hence unemployment, with more workers offering themselves for work than there are jobs available in the market.

 **terms**

**government failure:** a misallocation of resources arising from government intervention

**minimum wage:** a system designed to protect the low paid by setting a minimum wage rate that employers are permitted to offer workers

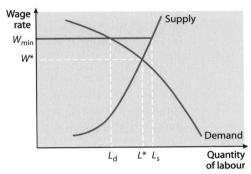

**Figure 8.2**
*A minimum wage*

What is happening here is that, with the minimum wage in effect, *some* workers (those who manage to remain in employment) are better off, and now receive a better wage. However, those who are now unemployed are worse off. It is not then clear whether the effect of the minimum wage is to make society as a whole better off — some people will be better off, but others will be worse off.

Notice that this analysis rests on some assumptions that have not been made explicit. In particular, it rests on the assumption that the labour market is competitive. Where there are labour markets in which the employers have some market power, and are able to offer lower wages to workers than would be obtained in a free market equilibrium situation, it is possible that the imposition of a minimum wage will increase employment. This possibility will be explored in Chapter 19.

## Rent controls

Another market in which governments have been tempted to intervene is the housing market. Figure 8.3 represents the market for rented accommodation. The free market equilibrium would be where demand and supply intersect, with the equilibrium rent being $R^*$ and the quantity of accommodation traded being $Q^*$.

If the government regards the level of rent as excessive, to the point where households on low incomes may be unable to afford rented accommodation, then, given that housing is one of life's necessities, it may regard this as unacceptable.

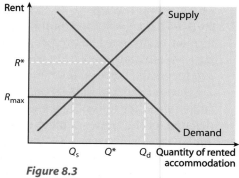

**Figure 8.3**
*Rent controls*

The temptation for the government is to move this market away from its equilibrium by imposing a maximum level of rent that landlords are allowed to charge their tenants. Suppose that this level of rent is denoted by $R_{max}$ in Figure 8.3. Again, there are two effects that follow. First, landlords will no longer find it profitable to supply as much rental accommodation, and so will reduce supply to $Q_s$. Second, at this lower rent there will be more people looking for accommodation, so that demand for rented accommodation will move to $Q_d$. The upshot of the rent controls, therefore, is that there is less accommodation available, and more homeless people.

It can be seen that the well-meaning rent control policy, intended to protect low-income households from being exploited by landlords, merely has the effect of reducing the amount of accommodation available. This is not what was supposed to happen.

### Sales tax

Governments need to raise funds to finance the expenditure that they undertake. One way of doing this is through expenditure taxes such as value added tax (VAT) or excise duties on such items as alcohol or tobacco. You might think that raising money in this way to provide goods and services that would otherwise not be provided would be a benefit to society. But there is a downside to this action, even if all the funds raised by a sales tax are spent wisely.

The effects of a sales tax can be seen in a demand and supply diagram. An **indirect tax** is paid by the seller, so it affects the supply curve for a product. Figure 8.4 illustrates the case of a *fixed rate* or *specific* tax — a tax that is set at a constant amount per pack of cigarettes. Without the tax, the market equilibrium is at the intersection of demand and supply with a price of $P_0$ and a quantity traded of $Q_0$. The effect of the tax is to reduce the quantity that firms are prepared to supply at any given price — or, to put it another way, for any given quantity of cigarettes, firms need to receive the amount of the tax over and above the price at which they would have been prepared to supply that quantity. The effect is thus to move the supply curve upwards by the amount of the tax, as shown in the figure. We get a new equilibrium with a higher price at $P_1$ and a lower quantity traded at $Q_1$.

**Key term**

**indirect tax:** a tax levied on expenditure on goods or services (as opposed to a direct tax, which is a tax charged directly to an individual based on a component of income)

An important question is: who bears the burden of the tax? If you look at the diagram, you will see that the price difference between the with-tax and without-tax situations (i.e. $P_1 - P_0$) is *less* than the amount of the tax, which is the vertical distance between the with-tax and without-tax supply curves. Although the seller may be responsible for the mechanics of paying the tax, part of the tax is effectively passed on to the buyer in the form of the higher price. In Figure 8.4, the **incidence of the tax** falls partly upon the seller, but most of the tax is borne by the buyer.

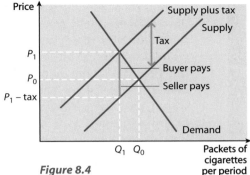

**Figure 8.4**
*The effects of an indirect tax on cigarettes*

The price elasticity of demand determines the incidence of the tax. If demand were perfectly inelastic, then the sellers would be able to pass the whole burden of the tax on to the buyers through an increase in price equal to the value of the tax, knowing that this would not affect demand.

**Key term**

**incidence of a tax:** the way in which the burden of paying a sales tax is divided between buyers and sellers

However, if demand were perfectly elastic, then the sellers would not be able to raise the price at all, so they would have to bear the entire burden of the tax.

## Exercise 8.2

Sketch demand and supply diagrams to confirm that the statements in the previous paragraph are correct — that is, that if demand is perfectly inelastic, then the tax falls entirely on the buyers, whereas if demand is perfectly elastic, it is the sellers who have to bear the burden of the tax.

If the tax is not a constant amount, but a percentage of the price (known as an *ad valorem* tax), the effect is still on the supply curve, but the tax steepens the supply curve, as shown in Figure 8.5. Here, the free market equilibrium would be where demand equals supply, with price at $P_0$ and the quantity traded at $Q_0$. With an *ad valorem* tax in place, the price rises to $P_1$, with quantity falling to $Q_1$.

In some situations, the government may wish to encourage production of a particular good or service, perhaps because it views a good as having strategic significance to the country. One way it can do this is by giving **subsidies**.

Subsidies were discussed in the previous chapter in the context of merit goods. Here, subsidies are used to encourage producers to increase their

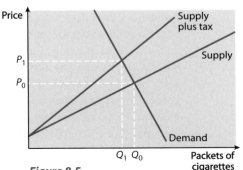

**Figure 8.5**
*The effects of an* ad valorem *tax on cigarettes*

part 2

output of particular goods. Subsidies have been especially common in agriculture, which is often seen as being of strategic significance. In recent years, the USA has come under pressure to reduce the subsidies that it grants to cotton producers. Analytically, we can regard a subsidy as a sort of negative indirect tax that shifts the supply curve down – as shown in Figure 8.6. Without the subsidy, market equilibrium is at a price $P_0$ and the quantity traded is $Q_0$. With the subsidy in place, the equilibrium price falls to $P_1$ and quantity traded increases to $Q_1$.

Again, notice that because the price falls by less than the amount of the subsidy, the benefits of the subsidy are shared between the buyers and sellers –

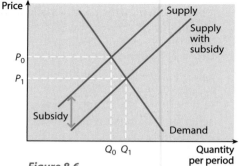

**Figure 8.6**
*The effects of a subsidy*

> **Key term**
>
> **subsidy:** a grant given by the government to producers to encourage production of a good or service

depending on the elasticity of demand. If the aim of the subsidy is to increase production, it is only partially successful; the degree of success also depends upon the elasticity of demand.

## Extension material

An important question is how a sales tax will affect total welfare in society. Consider Figure 8.7, which shows the market for DVDs. Suppose that the government imposes a specific tax on DVDs. This would have the effect of taking market equilibrium from the free market position at $P^*$ with quantity traded at $Q^*$ to a new position, with price now at $P_t$ and quantity traded at $Q_t$. Remember that the price rises by less than the amount of the tax, implying that the incidence of the tax falls partly on buyers and partly on sellers. In Figure 8.7 consumers pay more of the tax (the area $P^*P_tBE$) than the producers (who pay $FP^*EG$). The effect on society's overall welfare will now be examined.

Remember that the total welfare that society receives from consuming a product is the sum of consumer and producer surplus. The situation before and after the sales tax is as follows. Before the tax, consumer surplus is given by the area $AP^*C$ and producer surplus is given by the triangle $P^*CH$. How about afterwards? Consumer surplus is now the smaller triangle $AP_tB$, and producer surplus is $FGH$. The area $P_tBGF$ is the revenue raised by the

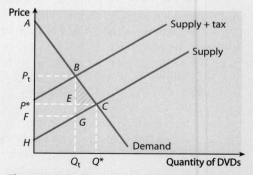

*Figure 8.7 A sales tax and economic welfare*

126

OCR Advanced Economics

government from the tax, which should be included in total welfare on the assumption that the government uses this wisely. The total amount of welfare is now *ABGH*. If you compare these total welfare areas before and after the tax, you will realise that they differ by the area *BCG*. This triangle represents a deadweight loss that arises from the imposition of the tax. It is sometimes referred to as the **excess burden** of the tax.

So, even where the government intervenes to raise funding for its expenditure — and spends wisely — a distortion is introduced to resource allocation, and society must bear a loss of welfare.

 **term**

**excess burden of a sales tax:** the deadweight loss to society following the imposition of a sales tax

## Prohibition

Another example of how government intervention may have unintended effects is when action is taken to prohibit the consumption of a demerit good. Consider the case of a hard drug, such as cocaine. It can be argued that there are substantial social disbenefits arising from the consumption of hard drugs, and that addicts and potential addicts are in no position to make informed decisions about their consumption of them. One response to such a situation is to consider making the drug illegal — that is, to impose **prohibition**.

 **term**

**prohibition:** an attempt to prevent the consumption of a demerit good by declaring it illegal

Figure 8.8 shows how the market for cocaine might look. You may wonder why the demand curve takes on this shape. The argument is that there are two types of cocaine user. There are the recreational users, who will take cocaine if it is available at a reasonable price, but who are not addicts. In addition, there is a hard core of habitual users who are addicts, whose demand for cocaine is highly inelastic. Thus, at low prices demand is relatively elastic because of the presence of the recreational users, who are relatively price-sensitive. At higher prices the recreational users drop away, and demand from the addicts is highly price-inelastic. Suppose that the supply in free market equilibrium is given by $S_0$; the equilibrium will be with price $P_0$ and quantity traded $Q_0$. If the drug is made illegal, this will affect supply. Some dealers will leave the market to trade in something else, and the police will succeed in confiscating a certain proportion of the drugs in the market. However, they are unlikely to be totally successful, so supply could move to, say, $S_1$.

In the new market situation, price rises substantially to $P_1$, and quantity traded falls to $Q_1$. However, what has happened is that the recreational users have dropped

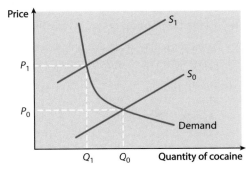

**Figure 8.8** Prohibition

out of the market, leaving a hard core of addicts who will pay any price for the drug, and who may resort to muggings and robberies in order to finance their habit. This behaviour clearly imposes a new sort of externality on society. And the more successful the police are in confiscating supplies, the higher the price will be driven. There may thus be disadvantages in using prohibition as a way of discouraging consumption of a demerit good.

## Costs of intervention

Some roles are critical for a government to perform if a mixed economy is to function effectively. A vital role is the provision by the government of an environment in which markets can operate effectively. There must be stability in the political system if firms and consumers are to take decisions with confidence about the future. And there must be a secure system of property rights, without which markets could not be expected to work.

In addition, there are sources of market failure that require intervention. This does not necessarily mean that governments need to substitute markets with direct action. However, it does mean that they need to be more active in markets that cannot operate effectively, while at the same time performing an enabling role to encourage markets to work well whenever this is feasible.

Such intervention entails costs. There are costs of administering, and costs of monitoring the policy to ensure that it is working as intended. This includes the need to look out for the unintended distortionary effects that some policies can have on resource allocation in a society. It is therefore important to check that the marginal costs of implementing and monitoring policies do not exceed their marginal benefits.

## Summary

➤ Government failure can occur when well-meaning intervention by governments has unintended effects.

➤ In some circumstances a minimum wage intended to protect the low paid may aggravate their situation by increasing unemployment.

➤ Rent controls may have the effect of reducing the amount of accommodation available.

➤ A sales tax imposes an excess burden on society.

➤ Prohibition may also have unintended effects.

# The national and international economy

# Part 3

# Chapter 9
# Measuring economic performance

This part of the book switches attention to macroeconomics. Macroeconomics has much in common with microeconomics, but focuses on the whole economy, rather than on individual markets and how they operate. Although the way of thinking about issues is similar, and although similar tools are used, now it is interactions between economic variables at the level of the whole economy that are studied. This process will introduce some of the major concerns of the media, such as unemployment, inflation and economic growth.

## Learning outcomes

After studying this chapter, you should:

➤ be aware of the main economic aggregates in a modern economy
➤ understand the distinction between real and nominal variables
➤ be familiar with the use of index numbers and the calculation of growth rates
➤ appreciate the significance of alternative measurements of inflation and unemployment in the context of the UK economy
➤ be familiar with the role and importance of the balance of payments
➤ be aware of the circular flow of income, output and expenditure
➤ understand the meaning of GDP and its use as an indicator in international comparisons

## Economic performance

Previous chapters have emphasised the importance of individual markets in achieving allocative and productive efficiency. In a modern economy, there are so many separate markets that it is difficult to get an overall picture of how well the economy is working. When it comes to monitoring its overall performance, the focus thus tends to be on the **macroeconomic** aggregates. 'Aggregate' here means 'totals' — for example, total unemployment in an economy, or total spending on goods and services — rather than, say, unemployed workers in a particular occupation, or spending on a particular good.

There are a number of dimensions in which the economy as a whole can be monitored. One prime focus of economic policy in recent years has been the inflation rate, as it has been argued that maintaining a stable economic environment is crucial to enabling markets to operate effectively. A second focus has been unemployment, which has been seen as an indicator of whether the economy is using its resources to the full — in other words, whether there are factors of production that are not being fully utilised. In addition, of course, there may be concern that the people who are unemployed are being disadvantaged.

**Key term**

**macroeconomics:** the study of the interrelationships between economic variables at an aggregate (macro-economic) level

Perhaps more fundamentally, there is an interest in economic growth. Is the economy expanding its potential capacity as time goes by, thereby making more resources available for members of society? In fact, it might be argued that this is the most fundamental objective for the economy, and the most important indicator of the economy's performance.

Other concerns may also need to be kept in mind. In particular, there is the question of how the economy interacts with the rest of the world. The UK is an 'open' economy — one that actively engages in international trade — and this aspect of UK economic performance needs to be monitored too. This is done through the balance of payments accounts.

## The importance of data

To monitor the performance of the economy, it is crucial to be able to observe how the economy is functioning, and for this you need data. Remember that economics, especially macroeconomics, is a non-experimental discipline. It is not possible to conduct experiments to see how the economy reacts to various stimuli in order to learn how it works. Instead, it is necessary to observe the economy, and to come to a judgement about whether or not its performance is satisfactory, and whether macroeconomic theories about how the economy works are supported by the evidence.

So, a reliable measure is needed for tracking each of the variables mentioned above, in order to observe how the economy is evolving through time. The key indicators of the economy's performance will be introduced as this chapter unfolds.

Most of the economic statistics used by economists are collected and published by various government agencies. Such data in the UK are published mainly by the Office of National Statistics (ONS). Data on other countries are published by the International Monetary Fund (IMF), the World Bank and the United Nations, as well as national sources. There is little alternative to relying on such sources because the accurate collection of data is an expensive and time-consuming business.

Care needs to be taken in the interpretation of economic data. It is important to be aware of how the data are compiled, and the extent to which they are indicators

www.imf.org

*An IMF meeting*

of what economists are trying to measure. It is also important to remember that the economic environment is ever changing, and that single causes can rarely be attributed to the economic events that are observed. This is because the ceteris paribus condition that underlies so much economic analysis is rarely fulfilled in reality. In other words, you cannot rely on 'other things remaining constant' when using data about the real world.

It is also important to realise that even the ONS cannot observe with absolute accuracy. Indeed, some data take so long to be assembled that early estimates are provisional in nature and subject to later revision as more information becomes available. Data used in international comparisons must be treated with even greater caution.

## Real and nominal measurements

The measurement of economic variables poses many dilemmas for statisticians. Not least is the fundamental problem of what to use as units of measurement. Suppose economists wish to measure total output produced in an economy during successive years. In the first place, they cannot use volume measures. They may be able to count how many computers, passenger cars, tins of paint and cauli-flowers the economy produces — but how do they add all these different items together to produce a total?

An obvious solution is to use the money values. Given prices for all the items, it is possible to calculate the money values of all these goods and thus produce a meas-urement of the total output produced in an economy during a year in terms of pounds sterling. However, this is just the beginning of the problem because, in order to monitor changes in total output between 2 years, it is important to be aware that not only do the volumes of goods produced change, but so too do their prices. In effect, this means that, if pounds sterling are used as the unit of measurement, the unit of measurement will change from one year to the next as prices change.

This is a problem that is not faced by most of the physical sciences. After all, the length of a metre does not alter from one year to the next, so if the length of something is being measured, the unit is fixed. Economists, however, have to make allowance for changing prices when measuring in pounds sterling.

OCR Advanced Economics

Measurements made using prices that are current at the time a transaction takes place are known as measurements of **nominal values**. When prices are rising, these nominal measurements will always overstate the extent to which an economic variable is growing through time. Clearly, to analyse performance, economists will be more interested in **'real' values** — that is, the quantities produced after having removed the effects of price changes. One way in which these real measures can be obtained is by taking the volumes produced in each year and valuing these quantities at the prices that prevailed in some base year. This then enables allowance to be made for the changes in prices that take place, permitting a focus on the real values. These can be thought of as being measured at *constant prices.*

For example, suppose that last year you bought a tub of ice cream for £2, but that inflation has been 10%, so that this year you had to pay £2.20 for the same tub. Your *real* consumption of the item has not changed, but your spending has increased. If you were to use the value of your spending to measure changes in consumption through time, it would be misleading, as you know that your *real* consumption has not changed at all (so is still £2), although its *nominal* value has increased to £2.20.

**Key terms**

**nominal value:** value of an economic variable based on current prices, taking no account of changing prices through time

**real value:** value of an economic variable taking account of changing prices through time

**index number:** a device for comparing the value of a variable in one period or location with a base observation (e.g. the retail price index measures the average level of prices relative to a base period)

## Index numbers

In some cases there is no apparent unit of measurement that is meaningful. For example, if you wished to measure the general level of prices in an economy, there is no meaningful unit of measurement that could be used. In such cases the solution is to use **index numbers**, which is a form of ratio that compares the value of a variable with some base point.

For example, suppose the price of a 250g pack of butter last year was 80p, and this year it is 84p. How can the price between the two periods be compared? One way of doing it is to calculate the percentage change:

$$100 \times (84 - 80) \div 80 = 5\%$$

(Note that this is the formula for calculating any growth rate in percentage terms. The change in the variable is always expressed as a percentage of the initial value, not the final value.)

An alternative way of doing this is to calculate an index number. In the above example, the current value of the index could be calculated as $100 \times 84 \div 80 = 105$. In other words, the current value is divided by the base value and multiplied by 100. The resulting number gives the current value relative to the base value. This turns out to be a useful way of expressing a range of economic variables where you want to show the value relative to a base period.

One particular use for this technique is when you want to show the average level of prices at different points in time. For such a general price index, one procedure is to define a typical basket of commodities that reflects the spending pattern of a representative household. The cost of that bundle can be calculated in a base year, and then in subsequent years. The cost in the base year is set to equal 100, and in subsequent years the index is measured relative to that base date, thereby reflecting the change in prices since then. For example, if in the second year the weighted average increase in prices were 2.5%, then the index in year 2 would take on the value 102.5 (based on year 1 = 100). Such a general index of prices could be seen as an index of the *cost of living* for the representative household, as it would give the level of prices faced by the average household relative to the base year.

## Summary

➤ Macroeconomics is the study of the interrelationships between economic variables at the level of the whole economy.

➤ Some variables are of particular interest when monitoring the performance of an economy — for example, inflation, unemployment and economic growth.

➤ As economists cannot easily conduct experiments in order to test economic theory, they rely on the use of economic data: that is, observations of the world around them.

➤ Data measured in money terms need to be handled carefully, as prices change over time, thereby affecting the units in which many economic variables are measured.

➤ Index numbers are helpful in comparing the value of a variable with a base date or unit.

## The consumer price index

The most important general price index in the UK is the **consumer price index** (CPI), which has been used by the government in setting its inflation target since the beginning of 2004. This index is based on the prices of a bundle of about 650 goods and services measured at different points in time. The information is compiled through the *Family Expenditure Survey*, in which data about the prices of goods and services in the bundle are collected on a monthly basis from a sample of 7,000 households across the country. Some prices are observed directly in randomly selected shops; these are then used to create an index based on 1996 = 100. The weights for the items included in the index are set to reflect the typical spending habits of consumers in the economy, based on the share of each component in their total expenditure. These weights are updated each year, as changes in the consumption patterns of households need to be accommodated if the index is to remain representative.

 **terms**

**consumer price index (CPI):** a measure of the general level of prices in the UK, adopted as the government's inflation target since December 2003

**inflation:** the rate of change of the average price level: for example, the percentage annual rate of change of the CPI

It is important to remember that the CPI provides a measurement of the *level* of prices in

the economy. This is not inflation: **inflation** is the *rate of change* of prices, and the percentage change in the CPI provides one estimate of the inflation rate.

Being able to calculate percentage changes is a useful skill. Going back to the example of the ice cream from page 133, remember that you had bought a tub of ice cream for £2 last year, but now have to pay £2.20. The percentage change in the price is obtained by dividing the *change* in price by the original price and multiplying by 100. Thus, the percentage change is $100 \times 0.20/2.00 = 10\%$.

## Alternative measurements of inflation

The traditional measure of inflation in the UK for many years was the **retail price index** (RPI), which was first calculated (under another name) in the early twentieth century to evaluate the extent to which workers were affected by price changes during the First World War. When the Blair government first set an explicit inflation target, it chose the RPIX, which is the RPI excluding mortgage interest payments. This was felt to be a better measure of the effectiveness of macroeconomic policy. It was argued that if interest rates are used to curb inflation, then including mortgage interest payments in the inflation measure will be misleading.

**Key term**

**retail price index (RPI):** a measure of the average level of prices in the UK

The CPI replaced RPIX partly because it is believed to be a more appropriate indicator for evaluating policy effectiveness. In addition, it has the advantage of being calculated using the same methodology as is used in other countries within the European Union, so that it is more useful than the RPIX for making international comparisons of inflation.

The CPI and RPI are based on a similar approach, although there are some significant differences in the detail of the calculation. Both measures set out to calculate the overall price level at different points in time. Each is based on calculating the overall cost of a representative basket of goods and services at different points in time relative to a base period. Both are produced by combining some 120,000 individual prices, which are collected each month for around 650 representative items. The result of these calculations is an index that shows how the general level of prices has changed relative to the base year. The rate of inflation is then calculated as the percentage rate of change of the price index, whether it be the CPI or the RPI.

The indexes share a common failing, arising from the fixed weights used in calculating the overall index. Suppose the price of a particular item rises more rapidly than other prices during the year. One response by consumers is to substitute an alternative, cheaper, product. As the indexes are based on fixed weights, they do not pick up this substitution effect, and therefore tend to overstate the price level in terms of the cost of living. Some attempt is made to overcome this problem by changing the weights on an annual basis in order to limit the impact of major changes. This includes incorporating new items when appropriate — for example, digital cameras were included in the CPI calculations for the first time in 2004, reflecting a change in consumer spending patterns.

The CPI and RPI differ for a number of reasons, partly because of differences in the content of the basket of goods and services that are included, and partly in terms of the population of people who are covered by the index. For example, in calculating the weights, the RPI excludes pensioner households and the highest-income households, whereas the CPI does not. There are also some other differences in the ways that the calculations are carried out.

Figure 9.1 shows data for the rates of change of the RPI and the CPI since March 1997. These rates have been calculated on a monthly basis, computing the percentage rate of change of each index relative to the value 12 months previously.

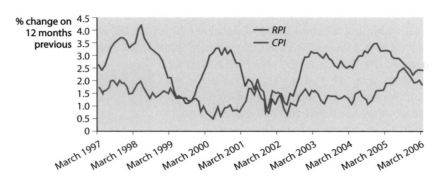

*Figure 9.1*
*Alternative inflation measures in the UK, 1997–2006*

Source: ONS.

A noticeable characteristic of Figure 9.1 is that for much of the period the CPI has shown a lower rate of change than the RPI. In part this reflects the way in which the prices are combined, but it also reflects the fact that different items and households are covered. The National Statistician, Len Cook, said:

> The CPI's fairly recent development as a macroeconomic indicator of inflation means that it has some distinct advantages over RPIX... Its coverage of spending and households better matches other economic data. The way it combines individual prices also has some clear statistical benefits, and helps us to compare UK inflation with inflation in other countries.

Until the end of 2003, the government's target for inflation was set at 2.5% per annum in the RPIX. After that date, the target for CPI was set at 2% per annum. It is noticeable that the CPI accelerated relative to the RPI towards the end of the period shown in Figure 9.1.

## Inflation in the UK and throughout the world

Figure 9.2 shows a time path for the rate of change in price levels since 1949. RPI has been used for this purpose, as the CPI was introduced only in 1997, so there is no consistent long-run series for it. The figure provides the backdrop to understanding the way the UK economy evolved during this period. Apart from the period of the Korean War, which generated inflation in 1951–52, the 1950s and early 1960s were typified by a low rate of inflation, with some acceleration becoming apparent in the early 1970s.

OCR Advanced Economics

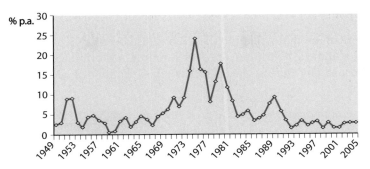

Figure 9.2 RPI inflation, 1949–2005 (% change over previous year)

Source: *Economic Trends Annual Supplement.*

The instability of the 1970s was due to a combination of factors. Oil prices rose dramatically in 1973–74 and again in 1979–80, which certainly contributed to rising prices, not only in the UK but worldwide. However, inflation was further fuelled by the abandonment of the fixed exchange rate system under which sterling had been tied to the US dollar until 1972. Chapter 31 explains the effect on the economy of having a floating exchange rate, but in essence it freed up monetary policy in a way that was perhaps not fully understood by the government of the day. As you can see in Figure 9.2, prices were allowed to rise rapidly — by nearly 25% in 1974/75. The diagram also shows how inflation was gradually reined in during the 1980s, and underlines the relative stability that has now been achieved, with inflation keeping well within the target range set by the Blair government.

Figure 9.3 shows something of the extent to which the UK's experience is typical of the pattern of inflation worldwide. You can see from this how inflation in the industrial countries followed a similar general pattern, with a common acceleration in the early 1970s, and a period of gradual control after 1980. However, you can also see that the developing countries in the world experienced inflation at a much higher average level after 1974 because they proved to be less able to bring prices under control after the oil price shocks. Much of this reflects events in Latin America, which suffered especially high rates of inflation in the 1980s and 1990s. This instability in the macroeconomic environment has almost certainly hindered development in the countries affected, and makes it important to understand how inflation is generated and how to curb it. This topic will be revisited in Chapter 11.

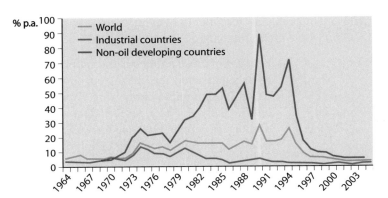

Figure 9.3 World inflation since 1964 (% change in the consumer price index)

Source: IMF.

## Unemployment

The measurement of unemployment in the UK has also been contentious over the years, and the standard definition used to monitor performance has altered several times, especially during the 1980s, when a number of rationalisations were introduced.

Historically, unemployment was measured by the number of people registered as unemployed and claiming unemployment benefit (the Jobseeker's Allowance (JSA)). This measure of employment is known as the **claimant count of unemployment**. People claiming the JSA must declare that they are out of work, capable of, available for and actively seeking work, during the week in which their claim is made.

 **Key term**

**claimant count of unemployment:** the number of people claiming the Jobseeker's Allowance each month

Figure 9.4 shows monthly data on the claimant count since 1971, expressed as a percentage of the workforce. The surge in unemployment in the early 1980s stands out on the graph, when the percentage of the workforce registered as unemployed more than doubled in a relatively short period. Although this seemed to be coming under control towards the end of the 1980s, unemployment rose again in the early 1990s before a steady decline into the new millennium.

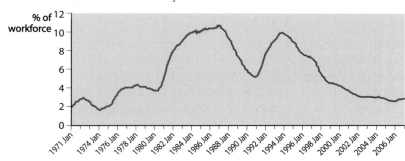

*Figure 9.4*
*Claimant count*
*since 1971*

Source: ONS.

One of the problems with the claimant count is that although people claiming the JSA must declare that they are available for work, it nonetheless includes some people who are claiming benefit, but are not actually available or prepared for work. It also excludes some people who would like to work, and who are looking for work, but who are not eligible for unemployment benefit, such as women returning to the labour force after child birth.

 **Key term**

**ILO unemployment rate:** measure of the percentage of the workforce who are without jobs, but are available for work, willing to work and looking for work

Because of these problems, the claimant count has been superseded for official purposes by the so-called **ILO unemployment rate**, a measure based on the *Labour Force Survey*. This identifies the number of people available for work, and seeking work, but without a job. This definition corresponds to that used by the International Labour Organisation (ILO), and is closer to what economists

would like unemployment to measure. It defines as being unemployed those people who are:

— without a job, want a job, have actively sought work in the last four weeks and are available to start work in the next two weeks; or

— out of work, have found a job and are waiting to start it in the next two weeks

*Labour Market Statistics*, September 2004

However, a major difference between the two alternatives from a measurement perspective is that the claimant count is a full count of all those who register, whereas the ILO measure is based on a sample. Figure 9.5 shows both the claimant and ILO measures for the period since 1984. You can see that the difference between the two measures is narrower when unemployment is relatively high, and wider when unemployment is falling. This may be partly because low unemployment encourages more people who are not eligible for unemployment benefit to look for jobs, whereas they withdraw from the workforce when unemployment rises and they perceive that finding a job will be difficult. This is said to affect women in particular, who may not be eligible for the Jobseeker's Allowance because of their partner's earnings.

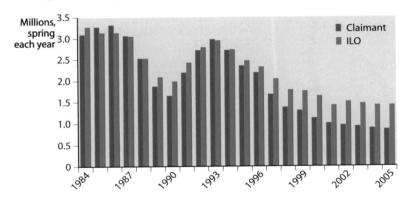

**Figure 9.5**
*Alternative measures of unemployment in the UK, 1984–2005*

Note: numbers unemployed in March–May each year (average).

Source: ONS.

## Summary

➤ The retail price index (RPI) is the best-known measure of the average price level in the UK.

➤ In December 2003 the government adopted the consumer price index (CPI) as its preferred measure of the price level, and inflation is now monitored through the rate of change of CPI.

➤ Unemployment is measured in two ways. The claimant count is based on the number of people claiming Jobseeker's Allowance. However, the ILO measure, based on the *Labour Force Survey*, is more accurate.

## The circular flow of income, expenditure and output

Chapter 1 introduced the notion of *gross domestic product* (GDP), which was described as the total output of an economy. It is now time to examine this concept more closely, and to see how it may be measured.

Consider a simplified model of an economy. Assume for the moment that there are just two types of economic agent in an economy: households and firms. In other words, ignore the government and assume there is no international trade. (These agents will be brought back into the picture soon.) We also assume that all factors of production are owned and supplied to firms by households.

In this simple world, assume that firms produce goods and hire labour and other factor inputs from households. Also assume that they buy investment goods from other firms, for which purpose they need to borrow in a financial market. Households supply their labour (and other factor inputs) and buy consumer goods. In return for supplying factor inputs, households receive income, part of which they spend on consumer goods and part of which they save in the financial market.

If you examine the monetary flows in this economy, you can see how the economy operates. In Figure 9.6 the blue arrow shows the flow of income that goes from firms to households as payment for their factor services (labour, land and capital). The red arrows show what happens to the output produced by firms: part of it goes to house-holds in the form of consumer goods (C); the rest flows back to other firms as investment goods (I). The green arrows show the expenditure flows back to firms, part of which is for consumer goods (C) from households, and part for investment goods (I) from firms. The circle is closed by house-holds' savings, by which part of their income is invested in the financial market; this is then borrowed by firms to finance their purchases of investment goods. These flows are shown by the orange arrows. This model is sometimes known as the circular flow model.

**Figure 9.6**
*The circular flow of income, expenditure and output*

As this is a closed system, these flows must balance. This means that there are three ways in which the total amount of economic activity in this economy can be measured: by the incomes that firms pay out, by the total amount of output that is produced, or by total expenditure. Whichever method is chosen, it should give the same result.

An economy such as the UK's is more complicated than this, so it is also necessary to take into account the economic activities of government and the fact that the UK engages in international trade, so that some of the output produced is sold abroad and some of the expenditure goes on foreign goods and services. However, the principle of measuring total economic activity is the same: GDP can be measured in three ways.

In practice, when the ONS carries out the measurements the three answers are never quite the same, as it is impossible to measure with complete accuracy. The

published data for GDP are therefore calculated as the average of these three measures, each of which gives information about different aspects of a society's total resources.

The expenditure-side estimate describes how those resources are being used, so that it can be seen what proportion of society's resources is being used for consumption and what for investment etc.

The income-side estimate reports on the way in which households earn their income. In other words, it tells something about the balance between rewards to labour (e.g. wages and salaries), capital (profits), land (rents), enterprise (self-employment) and so on.

The output-side estimate focuses on the economic structure of the economy. One way in which countries differ is in the balance between primary production such as agriculture, secondary activity such as manufacturing, and tertiary activity such as services. Service activity has increased in importance in the UK in recent years, with financial services in particular emerging as a strong part of the UK's comparative advantage.

Figure 9.7 traces real GDP in the UK since 1948. In some ways this is an unhelpful way of presenting the data, as the trend component of the series is so strong. In other words, real GDP has been increasing steadily throughout the period. There are one or two periods in which there was a movement away from the trend, but these are relatively rare and not easy to analyse. This reflects the nature of economic variables such as GDP, where the fluctuations around trend are small relative to the trend, but can seem substantial when the economy is experiencing them.

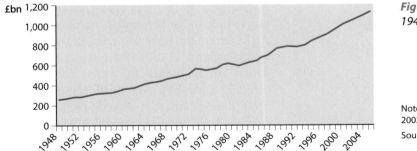

*Figure 9.7 Real GDP, 1948–2005 (£bn)*

Note: reference year is 2002.

Source: ONS.

The ratio of nominal to real GDP is a price index, known as the **GDP deflator**. This is defined as:

$$\text{price index} = 100 \times \frac{\text{GDP at current prices}}{\text{GDP at constant prices}}$$

This provides another measure of the average level of prices in the economy.

It is also sometimes useful to be able to convert nominal measurements into real terms. This can be done by dividing the nominal measurement by the price index, a process known as *deflating* the nominal measure.

Figure 9.8 converts the data into annual growth rates, which in some ways are more revealing. This certainly makes it more straightforward to identify the main periods of fluctuation, in particular periods of negative growth: that is, when the economy contracted. It is also apparent from this graph that the economy has been relatively stable since 1995.

 **Key** term

**GDP deflator:** an implicit price index showing the relationship between real and nominal measures of GDP, providing an alternative measure of the general level of prices in the economy

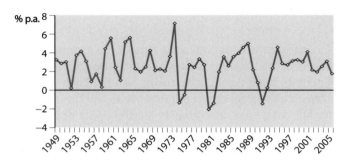

*Figure 9.8* Growth of real GDP, 1949–2005 (% change over previous year)

Source: ONS.

It should be noted that the measure of GDP has not been without its critics. In particular, economists have questioned whether it provides a reasonable measure of the standard of living enjoyed by the residents of a country, and whether its rate of change is therefore informative about economic growth. Chapters 24 and 29 will revisit GDP and evaluate its strengths and weaknesses in this context.

## The business cycle

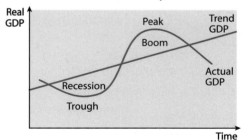

*Figure 9.9* The business cycle

**Key** term

**business cycle:** a phenomenon whereby GDP fluctuates around its underlying trend, following a regular pattern

In the past it has not been uncommon for economies to go through a regular **business cycle**, where the level of economic activity has varied around an underlying trend. Figure 9.9 shows an economy in which real GDP is trending upwards over time but fluctuating around the trend, so that actual GDP follows a regular cycle around the trend. The point of maximum growth is often referred to as the *peak* of the cycle — or a *boom* period — whereas the low point is known as the *trough* of the cycle. If the growth rate is negative for two consecutive quarters, the economy is considered to be in *recession*.

Figure 9.10 illustrates this in a different way, by showing the growth rates of real GDP in the UK over a cycle from 1984 to 1994. There was evidence in Figure 9.8 that the fluctuations have been less marked in the later years shown.

A number of explanations have been advanced to explain the business cycle. One suggestion is that some governments engineer the cycle, taking the economy into a boom in the lead-up to an election, only to slow it down again once elected. This has become known as the *political business cycle*. Another suggestion is that cycles arise because of the lagged impact of policy measures on the economy: in other words, it takes time for policies to take effect — sometimes so long that they can destabilise the economy by having unintended effects.

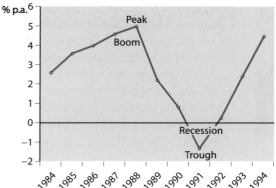

**Figure 9.10** *Profile of a cycle: growth of real GDP, 1984–94 (% change over previous year)*
Source: *Economic Trends Annual Supplement.*

In the past, considerable effort has gone into trying to predict the turning points of the business cycle by looking for *leading indicators* that turn in advance of the cycle — for example, the CBI quarterly survey of business optimism, which is designed to gather firms' views about the cycle. Changes in the number of new dwellings started and changes in consumer borrowing are also seen as leading indicators. In contrast, *coincident indicators* move in step with the current state of the business cycle — for example, real GDP or the volume of retail sales. On the other hand, unemployment tends to be a *lagging indicator*, as firms may not reduce their labour force right at the start of a recession, preferring first to ensure that it is not a temporary blip. In Chapter 12 it will be seen that there are some responses within the economy that tend to dampen the business cycle automatically; these are known as *automatic stabilisers*.

## Summary

➤ The circular flow of income, expenditure and output describes the relationship between these three key variables.

➤ The model suggests that there are three ways in which the total level of economic activity in an economy during a period of time can be measured: by total income, by total expenditure, and by total output produced.

➤ In principle, these should give the same answers, but in practice data measurements are not so accurate.

➤ GDP is a measure of the total economic activity carried out in an economy during a period by residents living on its territory.

➤ Economies tend not to grow according to a constant trend, but to fluctuate around the underlying trend, creating the business cycle.

part **3**

## Exercise 9.1

Table 9.1 provides data on real GDP for the period 1999–2005. Convert the series to an index based on 1998 = 100. Calculate the growth rate of GDP for each year from 1999/2000 to 2004/05. In which year was growth at its highest and in which year was it at its lowest?

| | |
|---|---|
| 1999 | 967 |
| 2000 | 1,005 |
| 2001 | 1,028 |
| 2002 | 1,048 |
| 2003 | 1,075 |
| 2004 | 1,108 |
| 2005 | 1,129 |

*Table 9.1*
*Real GDP in the UK, 1999–2005 (£bn)*

## The balance of payments

Another important dimension over which the macroeconomy needs to be monitored is in relation to a country's transactions with the rest of the world. Such transactions involve exports and imports of goods and services, but also assets, not to mention the flow of factor incomes. All of these transactions are monitored through the **balance of payments**, which is a set of accounts designed to identify international transactions between the UK economy and the rest of the world.

> **Key term**
>
> **balance of payments:** a set of accounts showing the transactions conducted between residents of a country and the rest of the world

The transactions in the balance of payments are separated into three categories. Transactions in goods and services, together with income payments and transfers, comprise the *current account*. The *capital account* reflects transactions in fixed assets, and is relatively small; it refers mainly to transactions involving migrants. The *financial account* records transactions in financial assets.

Commentators often focus on the current account. Three main items appear on this account. First, there is the balance of trade in goods and services — in other words, the balance between UK exports and imports of such goods and services. If UK residents buy German cars, this is an import and counts as a negative entry on the current account; on the other hand, if a German resident buys a British car, this is an export and constitutes a positive entry. The trade in goods is normally negative overall for the UK. However, this is partly balanced by a normally positive flow in trade in services, where the UK earns strong credits from its financial services.

The second item in the current account is income. Part of this represents employment income from abroad, but the major item of income is made up of profits, dividends and interest receipts arising from UK ownership of overseas assets.

Finally, there are international transfers — either transfers through central government or transfers made or received by private individuals. This includes transactions with and grants from international organisations or the EU. The current balance combines these items.

OCR Advanced Economics

Overall, the balance of payments must always be zero, as in some way or other we have to pay for all we consume, and receive payment for all we sell. However, because data can never be entirely accurate, the accounts also incorporate a 'net errors and omissions' item, which ensures that everything balances at the end of the day.

*The import of German cars counts as a negative entry on the current account*

What this really means is that any deficit in the current and capital accounts will always be balanced by a surplus on the financial account. Notice that the financial account incorporates official foreign exchange transactions undertaken by the government. In other words, if UK residents buy more goods and services than they sell (i.e. if there is a current account deficit), then they must pay for them by selling financial assets or foreign exchange (i.e. there must be a financial account surplus).

There are a number of ways in which the overall balance can be achieved. 'Balance' could mean that both current and financial accounts are small, or it could mean that a deficit on one is balanced by a surplus on the other. The media tend to focus on the current balance, and a deficit on the current account is sometimes seen as a matter of concern. Perhaps this harks back to the days of fixed exchange rates, when a current deficit would require authorities to sell foreign exchange reserves in order to balance the accounts. This is no longer the case, as there are other ways of balancing the books. Nonetheless, a persistent deficit on the current account may pose long-term problems that need to be addressed, as it may not be desirable to continue selling UK assets indefinitely.

Table 9.2 presents the components of the balance of payments accounts for 2004. This was a year in which the current account was in deficit, particularly because of a negative balance on trade in goods and services. The financial account was in surplus.

| | |
|---|---|
| Trade in goods and services | −38,425 |
| Income | 26,163 |
| Current transfers | −10,713 |
| **Current balance** | **−22,975** |
| **Capital account** | **1,980** |
| **Financial account** | **12,038** |
| Net errors and omissions | 8,957 |
| **Overall balance of payments** | **0** |

*Table 9.2  The UK balance of payments, 2004 (£m at current prices)*

Suppose the Bank of England holds interest rates high compared with other countries, in order to try to control inflation. High UK interest rates will tend to attract financial inflows from abroad, as investors find the UK attractive as a home for their funds. This implies a surplus on the financial account — and hence a deficit on current account. The downside of such a structure is that UK assets are being sold abroad, which might not be in the best interest of the economy in the long run.

It is this potential long-run difficulty that makes it important to monitor the current balance over time. Figure 9.11 shows the main components of the balance of payments since 1980, in current price terms, which is the form in which the data are published by ONS. This is in the form of a stacked bar chart, and the nature of the balance of payments is that the positive and negative components exactly balance each year. The clear picture that emerges is that the current account has been negative (in deficit) for most of the period since 1980, and that this has been balanced by a positive balance (surplus) on the financial account. In other words, the UK has been importing more goods and services than it has been exporting; but this has been counterbalanced by the surplus on the financial account: that is, of UK assets sold abroad.

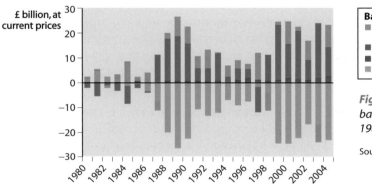

*Figure 9.11* UK balance of payments, 1980–2004

Source: ONS.

The data in Figure 9.11 are measured in current prices, which means that they are *nominal* measurements, which make no attempt to allow for the effects of inflation. It would thus be misleading to infer too much about the magnitude of the quantities shown. A better perspective on this is provided by Figure 9.12, which shows the current account balance expressed as a percentage of nominal GDP. This helps to put the more recent data into perspective.

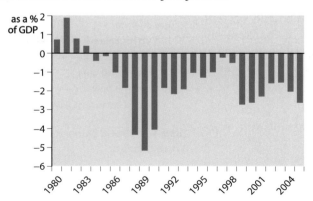

*Figure 9.12* The current account of the UK balance of payments, 1980–2004

Source: ONS.

Closely associated with the balance of payments is the **exchange rate** — the price of domestic goods in terms of foreign currency. Chapter 2 introduced the notion of the demand and supply of foreign currency, shown in Figure 9.13. The demand for pounds arises from overseas residents (e.g. in the euro area) wanting to purchase UK goods, services or assets, whereas the supply of pounds emanates from domestic residents wanting to purchase overseas goods, services or assets. The connection is that the balance of payments accounts itemise these transactions, which entail the demand for and supply of pounds.

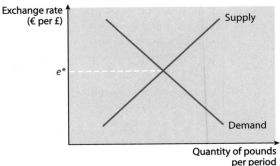

**Figure 9.13**
*The market for pounds sterling*

## Summary

➤ The balance of payments is a set of accounts that itemises transactions taking place between an economy and the rest of the world, including goods, services, income and assets.

➤ The current account sets out transactions in goods, services, investment income and transfers.

➤ The capital account itemises transactions in fixed assets, and is relatively small.

➤ The financial account covers transactions in financial assets, and includes direct investment and official intervention in the foreign exchange market ('official financing').

➤ The overall balance of payments is always zero.

➤ However, this overall balance has often been achieved in the UK through a persistent deficit on the current account, balanced by a corresponding surplus on the financial account.

➤ This may be a matter of concern in the long run.

## Exercise 9.2

Use the data presented in this chapter to evaluate the performance of the UK economy since 1997. If you were the chancellor of the exchequer, which aspects of the economy's performance would you be pleased with, and which ones would concern you?

# Chapter 10
# Aggregate demand, aggregate supply and equilibrium output

*Now that you are familiar with the main macroeconomic aggregates, it is time to start thinking about how economic analysis can be used to explore the way in which these variables interact. This chapter also investigates the notion of macroeconomic equilibrium. As in micro-economics, this relates to the process by which balance can be achieved between the opposing forces of demand and supply. However, there are some important differences in these concepts when applied at the macroeconomic level.*

## Learning outcomes

After studying this chapter, you should:
- understand what is meant by aggregate demand and aggregate supply
- be able to identify the components of aggregate demand and their determinants
- be aware of the possibility of multiplier effects
- be familiar with the notion of the aggregate demand curve
- identify the factors that influence aggregate supply
- be familiar with the notion of the aggregate supply curve
- understand the nature of equilibrium in the macroeconomy
- be able to undertake comparative static analysis of external shocks affecting aggregate demand and aggregate supply

## The components of aggregate demand

Chapter 9 introduced the notion of the circular flow of income, expenditure and output. If aggregate demand were considered in that model, it would comprise the combined spending of households (on consumer goods) and firms (on investment goods). It was noted that in the real world it is also necessary to include international trade (exports and imports) and spending by government in this measure. The full version of aggregate expenditure can be written as:

$$AD = C + I + G + X - M$$

where AD denotes aggregate demand, C is consumption, I is investment, G is government spending, X is exports and M is imports.

Figure 10.1 shows the expenditure-side breakdown of real GDP in the UK in 2005. This highlights the relative size of the components of aggregate demand. Consumption is by far the largest component, amounting to more than 66% of real GDP in 2005. Government current expenditure accounted for about 20%, but notice that this somewhat understates the importance of government in overall spending, as it excludes public spending on investment, which is treated together with private sector investment in the data. Combined public and private sector investment made up almost 17% of total GDP; this includes changes in the inventory holdings of firms. Notice that imports were rather higher than exports, indicating a negative balance of trade in goods and services.

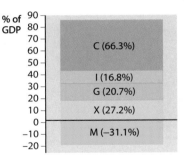

**Figure 10.1**
*The breakdown of real GDP in 2005*

Note: C includes spending by non-profit institutions serving households; I includes changes in inventory holdings; the statistical discrepancy is not shown.

Source: ONS.

In the circular flow model it was noted that total expenditure should be the same as total income and total output if all were measured fully. This seems to suggest that the macroeconomy is always in a sort of equilibrium, in the sense that expenditure and output are always the same. However, this is misleading. Although, when you observe the economy, you should find that expenditure and output are the same *after* the event, this does not mean that equilibrium holds in the sense that all economic agents will have found that their plans were fulfilled. In other words, it is not necessarily the case that planned expenditure equals planned output.

This is the significance of the inclusion of inventory changes as part of investment. If firms find that they have produced more output than is subsequently purchased, their inventory holdings increase. Thus, although after the event expenditure always equals output, this is because any disequilibrium is reflected in unplanned inventory changes.

When you come to consider the conditions under which a macroeconomy will be in equilibrium, you will need to think in terms of the factors that will influence *ex ante* (planned) aggregate demand. The first step is to consider each component in turn.

## Consumption

Consumption is the largest single component of aggregate demand. What factors could be expected to influence the size of total spending by households? John Maynard Keynes, in his influential book *The General Theory of Employment, Interest and Money*, published in 1936, suggested that the most important determinant is **disposable income**. In other words, as real incomes rise, households will tend to

**Key** *term*

**disposable income:** the income that households have to devote to consumption and saving, taking into account payments of direct taxes and transfer payments

spend more. However, he also pointed out that they would not spend all of an increase in income, but would save some of it. Remember that this was important in the circular flow model. Keynes defined the **average propensity to consume** as the *ratio* of consumption to income, and the **marginal propensity to consume** as the proportion of an *increase* in disposable income that households would devote to consumption.

 **Key** *terms*

**average propensity to consume:** the proportion of income that households devote to consumption

**marginal propensity to consume:** the proportion of additional income devoted to consumption

## Extension material

Later writers argued that consumption does not necessarily depend upon current income alone. For example, Milton Friedman put forward the *permanent income hypothesis*, which suggested that consumers take decisions about consumption based on a notion of their permanent, or normal, income levels — that is, the income that they expect to receive over a 5- or 10-year time horizon. This suggests that households do not necessarily vary their consumption patterns in response to changes in income that they perceive to be only transitory. An associated theory is the *life-cycle hypothesis*, developed by Ando Modigliani, who suggested that households smooth their consumption over their lifetimes, on the basis of their expected lifetime incomes. Thus, people tend to borrow in their youth against future income; then in middle age, when earning more strongly, they pay off their debts and save in preparation to fund their consumption in retirement. Consumption thus varies by much less than income, and is based on expected lifetime earnings rather than on current income.

However, income will not be the only influence on consumption. Consumption may also depend partly on the *wealth* of a household. Notice that income and wealth are not the same. Income accrues during a period as a reward for the supply of factor services, such as labour. Wealth, on the other hand, represents the stock of accumulated past savings. If you like, wealth can be thought of in terms of the asset holdings of households. If households experience an increase in their asset holdings, this may influence their spending decisions.

Furthermore, if part of household spending is financed by borrowing, the rate of interest may be significant in influencing the total amount of consumption spending. An increase in the rate of interest that raises the cost of borrowing may deter consumption. At the same time it may encourage saving, as the return on saving is higher when the interest rate is higher. The rate of interest may also have an indirect effect on consumption through its effect on the value of asset holdings. In addition, households may be influenced in their consumption decisions by their expectations about future inflation. Notice that some of these effects may not be instantaneous: that is, consumption may adjust to changes in its determinants only after a time lag.

 **Key** *term*

**consumption function:** the relationship between consumption and disposable income; its position depends upon the other factors that affect how much households spend on consumption

OCR Advanced Economics

This **consumption function** can be portrayed as a relationship between consumption and income. This is shown in Figure 10.2, which focuses on the relationship between consumption and household income, ceteris paribus: in other words, in drawing the relationship between consumption and income, it is assumed that the other determinants of consumption, such as wealth and the interest rate, remain constant. A change in any of these other influences will affect the *position* of the line. Notice that the marginal propensity to consume (*MPC*) is the slope of this line. For example, if the *MPC* is 0.7, this means that for every additional £100 of income received by households, £70 would be spent on consumption and the remaining £30 would be saved.

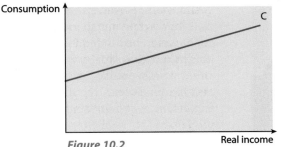

**Figure 10.2**
*The consumption function*

In practice, it is not expected that the empirical relationship between consumption and income will reveal an exact straight line, if only because over a long time period there will be changes in the other influences on consumption, such as interest rates and expected inflation. However, Figure 10.3 shows that the hypothesis is not totally implausible.

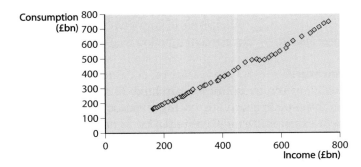

**Figure 10.3**
*Real consumption and disposable income in the UK, 1948–2005*

Source: ONS.

### Investment

The rate of interest is also likely to be influential in affecting firms' decisions about investment spending. Again, this is because the interest rate represents the cost of borrowing; so, if firms need to borrow in order to undertake **investment**, they may be discouraged from spending on investment goods when the rate of interest is relatively high.

Investment leads to an increase in the productive capacity of the economy, by increasing the stock of capital available for production. This capital stock comprises plant and machinery, vehicles and other transport equipment, and buildings, including new dwellings, which provide a supply of housing services over a long period.

**Key** **term**

**investment:** expenditure undertaken by firms to add to the capital stock

Although important, the rate of interest is not likely to be the only factor that determines how much investment firms choose to undertake. First, not all investment has to be funded from borrowing — firms may be able to use past profits for this purpose. However, if firms choose to do this, they face an opportunity cost. In other words, profits can be used to buy financial assets that will provide a rate of return dependent on the rate of interest. The rate of interest is thus still important, as it represents the opportunity cost of an investment project.

In considering an investment project, firms will need to form expectations about the future stream of earnings that will flow from the investment. Their expectations about the future state of the economy (and of the demand for their products) will thus be an important influence on current investment. This is one reason why it is argued that inflation is damaging for an economy, as a high rate of inflation increases uncertainty about the future and may dampen firms' expectations about future demand, thereby discouraging investment.

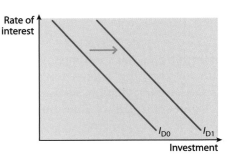

**Figure 10.4**
*Investment and the rate of interest*

Figure 10.4 shows the relationship between investment and the rate of interest. The investment demand function $I_{D0}$ is downward sloping because investment is relatively low when the rate of interest is relatively high. An improvement in business confidence for the future would result in more investment being undertaken at any given interest rate, so the investment function would move from $I_{D0}$ to $I_{D1}$.

## Government expenditure

By and large, you might expect government expenditure to be decided by different criteria from those influencing private sector expenditures. Indeed, some aspects of government expenditure might be regarded as part of macroeconomic policy, as will be seen in Chapter 12. Some other aspects of government expenditure may vary automatically with variations in the overall level of economic activity over time. For example, unemployment benefit payments are likely to increase during recessionary periods. The effects of this will be examined in Chapter 12.

From the point of view of investigating macroeconomic equilibrium, however, government expenditure can be regarded as mainly *autonomous*: that is, independent of the variables in the model that will be constructed in this chapter.

## Trade in goods and services

Finally, there are the factors that may influence the level of exports and imports. One factor that will affect both of these is the exchange rate between sterling and other currencies. This affects the relative prices of UK goods and those produced

overseas. Other things being equal, an increase in the sterling exchange rate makes UK exports less competitive and imports into the UK more competitive.

However, the demand for exports and imports will also depend upon the relative prices of goods produced in the UK and the rest of the world. If UK inflation is high relative to elsewhere, again, this will tend to make UK exports less competitive and imports more competitive. These effects will be examined more carefully in Chapter 30, when it will be shown that movements in the exchange rate tend to counteract changes in relative prices between countries.

In addition, the demand for imports into the UK will depend partly upon the level of domestic aggregate income, and the demand for UK exports will depend partly upon the level of incomes in the rest of the world. Thus, a recession in the European Union will affect the demand for UK exports.

## The multiplier

In his *General Theory*, Keynes pointed out that there may be **multiplier** effects in response to certain types of expenditure. Suppose that the government increases its expenditure by £1 billion, perhaps by increasing its road-building programme. The effect of this is to generate incomes for households — for example, those of the contractors hired to build the road. Those contractors then spend part of the additional income (and save part of it). By spending part of the extra money earned, an additional income stream is generated for shopkeepers and café owners, who in turn spend part of *their* additional income, and so on. Thus, the original increase in government spending sparks off further income generation and spending, causing the multiplier effect. In effect, equilibrium output may change by more than the original increase in expenditure.

> **Key term**
>
> **multiplier:** the ratio of a change in equilibrium real income to the autonomous change that brought it about; it is defined as 1 divided by the marginal propensity to withdraw

*Government spending on road building may increase spending in other areas of the economy due to the multiplier effect*

The size of this multiplier effect depends on a number of factors. Most importantly, it depends upon the size of *withdrawals* or *leakages* from the system. In particular, it depends upon how much of the additional income is saved by households, how much is spent on imported goods, and how much is returned to the government in the form of direct taxes. These items constitute withdrawals from the system, in the sense that they detract from the multiplier effect. For example, if households save a high proportion of their additional income, then this clearly reduces the multiplier effect, as the next round of spending will be that much lower. This seems to go against the traditional view that saving is good for the economy.

However, there are also *injections* into the system in the form of autonomous government expenditure, investment and exports. One condition of macroeconomic equilibrium is that total withdrawals equal total injections. The fact that injections can have this multiplied effect on equilibrium output and income seems to make the government potentially very powerful, as by increasing its expenditure it can have a multiplied effect on the economy.

## Extension point

A numerical value for the multiplier can be calculated with reference to the withdrawals from the circular flow. First, define the *marginal propensity to withdraw* (*MPW*) as the sum of the marginal propensities to save, tax and import. The multiplier formula is then 1 divided by the marginal propensity to withdraw (1/*MPW*). If the value of the multiplier is 2, then for every £100 million injection into the circular flow, there will be a £200 million increase in equilibrium output.

It is worth noting that the size of the leakages may depend in part upon the domestic elasticity of supply. If domestic supply is inflexible, and therefore unable to meet an increase in demand, more of the increase in income will spill over into purchasing imports, and this will dilute the multiplier effect.

## Summary

➤ Aggregate demand is the total demand in an economy, made up of consumption, investment, government spending and net exports.

➤ Consumption is the largest of these components and is determined by income and other influences, such as interest rates, wealth and expectations about the future.

➤ Investment leads to increases in the capital stock and is influenced by interest rates, past profits and expectations about future demand.

➤ Government expenditure may be regarded as largely autonomous.

➤ Trade in goods and services (exports and imports) is determined by the competitiveness of domestic goods and services compared with the rest of the world, which in turn is determined by relative inflation rates and the exchange rate. Imports are also affected by domestic income, and exports are affected by incomes in the rest of the world.

➤ Autonomous spending, such as government expenditure, may give rise to a magnified impact on equilibrium output through the multiplier effect.

## Exercise 10.1

Identify each of the following as an injection or a leakage, and state whether it increases or decreases the impact of the multiplier:

a  saving by households

b  expenditure by central government

c  spending by UK residents on imported goods and services

d  expenditure by firms on investment

e  spending by overseas residents on UK goods and services

f  income tax payments

## The aggregate demand curve

The key relationship to carry forward is the **aggregate demand curve**, which shows the relationship between aggregate demand and the overall price level. Formally, this curve shows the total amount of goods and services demanded in an economy at any given overall level of prices.

It is important to realise that this is a very different sort of demand curve from the microeconomic demand curves that were introduced in Chapter 2, where the focus was on an individual product and its relationship with its own price. Here the relationship is between the *total* demand for goods and services and the overall price level. Thus, aggregate demand is made up of all the components discussed above, and price is an average of all prices of goods and services in the economy.

Figure 10.5 shows an aggregate demand curve. The key question is why it slopes downwards. To answer this, it is necessary to determine the likely influence of the price level on the various components of aggregate demand that have been discussed in this chapter, as prices have not been mentioned explicitly (except for how expectations about inflation might influence consumer spending). First, however, the discussion needs to be cast in terms of the price *level*.

When the overall level of prices is relatively low, the purchasing power of income is relatively high. In other words, low overall prices can be thought of as indicating

**Key term**

**aggregate demand (AD) curve:** the relationship between the level of aggregate demand and the overall price level; it shows planned expenditure at any given possible overall price level

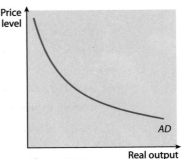

**Figure 10.5**
*An aggregate demand curve*

relatively high real income. Furthermore, when prices are low, this raises the real value of households' wealth. For example, suppose a household holds a financial asset such as a bond with a fixed money value of £100. The relative (real) value of that asset is higher when the overall price level is relatively low. From the above discussion, this suggests that, ceteris paribus, a low overall price level means relatively high consumption.

A second argument relates to interest rates. When prices are relatively low, interest rates also tend to be relatively low, which, it was argued, would encourage both investment and consumption expenditure, as interest rates can be seen as representing the cost of borrowing.

A third argument concerns exports and imports. It has been argued that, ceteris paribus, when UK prices are relatively low compared with the rest of the world, this will increase the competitiveness of UK goods, leading to an increase in foreign demand for UK exports, and a fall in the demand for imports into the UK as people switch to buying UK goods and services.

All of these arguments support the idea that the aggregate demand curve should be downward sloping. In other words, when the overall price level is relatively low, aggregate demand will be relatively high, and when prices are relatively high, aggregate demand will be relatively low.

Other factors discussed above will affect the *position* of the *AD* curve. This point will be explored after the introduction of the other side of the coin — the aggregate supply curve.

*Demand for goods tends to be high when prices are relatively low*

## The aggregate supply curve

In order to analyse the overall macroeconomic equilibrium, it is necessary to derive a second relationship: that between aggregate supply and the price level. Again, remember that the level of aggregate supply covers the output of all sorts of goods and services that are produced within an economy during a period of time. However, it is not simply a question of adding up all the individual supply curves from individual markets. Within an individual market, an increase in price may induce higher supply of a good because firms will switch from other markets in search of higher profits. What you now need to be looking for is a relationship between the *overall* price level and the total amount supplied, which is a different kettle of fish.

The total quantity of output supplied in an economy over a period of time depends upon the quantities of inputs of factors of production employed: that is, the total amounts of labour, capital and other factors used. The ability of firms to vary output in the short run will be influenced by the degree of flexibility the firms have in varying inputs. This suggests that it is necessary to distinguish between short-run and long-run aggregate supply.

In the short run, firms may have relatively little flexibility to vary their inputs. Money wages are likely to be fixed, and if firms wish to vary output, they may need to do so by varying the intensity of utilisation of existing inputs. For example, if a firm wishes to expand output, the only way of doing so in the short run may be by paying its existing workers overtime, and it will be prepared to do this only in response to higher prices. This suggests that in the short run, aggregate supply may be upward sloping, as shown in Figure 10.6, where *SAS* represents **short-run aggregate supply**.

Firms will not want to operate in this way in the long run. It is not good practice to be permanently paying workers overtime. In the long run, therefore, firms will adjust their working practices and hire additional workers to avoid this situation.

What factors influence the position of aggregate supply? Given that aggregate supply arises from the use of inputs of factors of production, one important influence is the availability and effectiveness of factor inputs.

As far as labour is concerned, an increase in the *size* of the workforce will affect the position of aggregate supply. In practice, the size of the labour force tends to change relatively slowly unless substantial international migration is taking place. However, another important factor is the *level of skills* in the workforce. An increase in the skills that workers have will increase the amount of

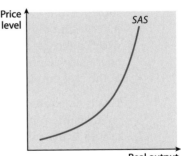

**Figure 10.6**
*Aggregate supply in the short run*

**Key** *term*

**short-run aggregate supply curve:** a curve showing how much output firms would be prepared to supply in the short run at any given overall price level

aggregate output that can be produced and lead to a shift in the aggregate supply curve.

For example, in Figure 10.7 aggregate supply was originally at $SAS_0$. An increase in the skills of the workforce means that firms are prepared to supply more output at any given overall price level, so the aggregate supply curve moves to $SAS_1$.

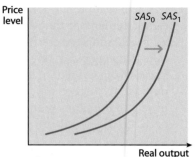

Figure 10.7
A shift in aggregate supply

An increase in the efficiency of capital, perhaps arising from improvements in technology, would have a similar effect, enabling greater aggregate supply at any given overall price level, and raising the productive capacity of the economy.

An increase in the quantity of capital will also have this effect, by increasing the capacity of the economy to produce. However, such an increase requires firms to have undertaken investment activity. In other words, the balance of spending between consumption and investment may affect the position of the aggregate supply curve in future periods.

## Macroeconomic equilibrium

Bringing aggregate demand and aggregate supply together, the overall equilibrium position for the macroeconomy can be identified. In Figure 10.8, with aggregate supply given by *SAS* and aggregate demand by *AD*, equilibrium is reached at the real output level *Y*, with the price level at *P*.

This is an equilibrium, in the sense that if nothing changes then firms and households will have no reason to alter their behaviour in the next period. At the price *P*, aggregate supply is matched by aggregate demand.

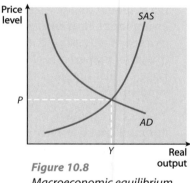

Figure 10.8
Macroeconomic equilibrium

Can it be guaranteed that the macroeconomic equilibrium will occur at the full employment level of output? For example, suppose that in Figure 10.9 the output level $Y^*$ corresponds to the full employment level of output — that is, the level of output that represents productive capacity when all factors of production are fully employed. It may be possible to produce more than this in the short run, but only on a temporary basis, perhaps by the use of overtime. If aggregate demand is at $AD^*$, the macroeconomic equilibrium is at this full

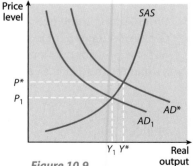

Figure 10.9
Macroeconomic equilibrium at full employment

employment output $Y^*$. However, if the aggregate demand curve is located at $AD_1$ the equilibrium will occur at $Y_1$, which is below the full employment level, so there is surplus capacity in the economy.

## Summary

➤ The aggregate demand ($AD$) curve shows the relationship between aggregate demand in the economy and the overall price level.

➤ The $AD$ curve is downward sloping because of the effect of the price level on real incomes and wealth, interest rate effects, and the effect of the price level on the competitiveness of domestic goods in international markets.

➤ The position of the $AD$ curve depends upon the components of aggregate demand.

➤ The aggregate supply ($SAS$) curve shows the relationship between aggregate supply and the overall price level.

➤ Macroeconomic equilibrium is reached at the intersection of $AD$ and $AS$.

## An increase in aggregate demand

Having identified macroeconomic equilibrium, it is possible to undertake some comparative static analysis. The position of the aggregate demand curve depends on the components of aggregate demand: consumption, investment, government spending and net exports. Factors that affect these components will affect the position of aggregate demand.

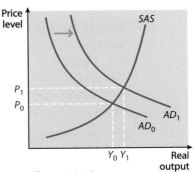

Consider Figure 10.10. Suppose that the economy begins in equilibrium with aggregate demand at $AD_0$. The equilibrium output level is $Y_0$, and the price level is at $P_0$. An increase in government expenditure will affect the position of the aggregate demand curve, shifting it to $AD_1$. The economy will move to a new equilibrium position, with higher output level $Y_1$ and a higher price level $P_1$.

*Figure 10.10*
*A shift in aggregate demand*

This seems to suggest that the government can always reach full employment, simply by increasing its expenditure. However, you should be a little cautious in reaching such a conclusion, as the effect on equilibrium output and the price level will depend upon how close the economy is to the full employment level. Notice that the aggregate supply curve becomes steeper as output and the price level increase. In other words, the closer the economy is to the full employment level, the smaller is the elasticity of supply, so an increase in aggregate demand close to full employment will have more of an effect on the price level (and hence potentially on inflation) than on the level of real output.

Indeed, it might be argued that the aggregate supply curve becomes vertical at some point, as there is a maximum level of output that can be produced given the

availability of factors of production. Such a curve is shown in Figure 10.11, where $Y^*$ represents the full employment level of real output. In this case, the economy has settled into an equilibrium that is below potential capacity output. We may regard this as a longer-run aggregate supply curve ($AS$), since the only way that real output can be beyond $Y^*$ is through the temporary use of overtime, which could not be sustained in the long run.

## The effect of a supply shock

The $AD/AS$ model can also be used to analyse the effects of an external shock that affects aggregate supply. For example, suppose there is an increase in oil prices arising from a disruption to supplies in the Middle East. This raises firms' costs, and leads to a reduction in aggregate supply. Comparative static analysis can again be employed to examine the likely effects on equilibrium.

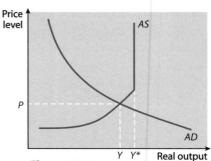

**Figure 10.11**
*Macroeconomic equilibrium in the longer run*

Figure 10.12 analyses the situation. The economy begins in equilibrium with output at $Y_0$ and the overall level of prices at $P_0$. The increase in oil prices causes a movement of the aggregate supply curve from $SAS_0$ to $SAS_1$, with aggregate demand unchanged at $AD$. After the economy returns to equilibrium, the new output level has fallen to $Y_1$ and the overall price level has increased to $P_1$.

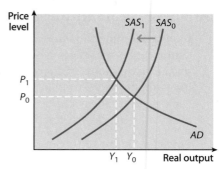

**Figure 10.12** *A supply shock*

*The cost of oil drove up world prices of goods in the 1970s*

At the time of the first oil price crisis back in 1973/74, the UK government of the day tried to maintain the previous level of real output by stimulating aggregate demand. This had the effect of pushing up the price level, but did not have any noticeable effect on real output. Such a result is not unexpected, given the steepness of the aggregate supply curve. Indeed, in Figure 10.12 the previous output level $Y_0$ cannot be reached with aggregate supply in its new position. You can see the effects of the oil shock on the UK economy by looking back at Figures 9.2 and 9.8.

## Exercise 10.2

For each of the following, decide whether the change affects aggregate demand or aggregate supply, and sketch a diagram to illustrate the effects on equilibrium real output and overall price level. Undertake this exercise first for a starting position in the steep part of the $SAS$ curve, and then repeat the exercise for an initial position further to the left, where $SAS$ is more elastic:

**a** an advancement in technology that improves the efficiency of capital

**b** a financial crisis in Asia that reduces the demand for UK exports

**c** an improvement in firms' expectations about future demand, such that investment expenditure increases

**d** the introduction of new health and safety legislation that raises firms' costs

## Movements of and along *AD* and *AS*

It is important to be aware of the distinction between movements *of* the *AD* and *AS* curves, and movements *along* them. Typically, if a shock affects one of the curves, it will lead to a movement *along* the other. For example, if the *AS* curve moves as a result of a supply shock, the response is a movement *along* the *AD* curve, and vice versa. Thus, in trying to analyse the effects of a shock, the first step is to think about whether the shock affects *AD* or *AS*, and the second is to analyse whether the shock is positive or negative: that is, which way the relevant curve will move. The move towards a new equilibrium can then be investigated.

## Summary

➤ Comparative static analysis can be used to analyse the effects of changes in the factors that influence aggregate demand and aggregate supply.

➤ Changes in the components of aggregate demand shift the aggregate demand curve. Within the vertical segment of *AS*, changes in *AD* affect only the overall price level, but below full employment both price and real output will be affected.

➤ Changes in the factors affecting aggregate supply alter the long-run potential productive capacity of the economy.

# Chapter 11
# Macroeconomic policy objectives

*Inevitably, there is a policy dimension to the study of the performance of the macroeconomy. Indeed, in evaluating such performance, it is the success of macroeconomic policy that is under scrutiny. However, the success of macroeconomic policy can be judged only if you are aware of what it is that the policy is trying to achieve. This chapter introduces and analyses the main objectives of policy at the macroeconomic level.*

## Learning outcomes

After studying this chapter, you should:
➤ be familiar with the principal objectives of macroeconomic policy
➤ understand the reasons for setting these policy objectives
➤ be aware of some potential obstacles that may inhibit the achievement of the targets
➤ appreciate that the targets may sometimes conflict with each other

## Targets of policy

Chapter 9 introduced a number of ways in which economists try to monitor and evaluate the performance of the economy at the macroeconomic level. If macroeconomic performance is found to be wanting in some way, then it is reasonable to ask whether some policy intervention might improve the situation. This chapter considers aspects of the macroeconomy that might be regarded as legitimate targets for policy action. Chapter 12 analyses the policy actions that might be introduced, and evaluates their possible effectiveness.

Chapter 9 discussed some key measures of an economy's performance, particularly inflation, unemployment, the balance of payments and GDP. In addition, in Chapter 8 questions were raised about whether governments should be concerned about inequality of income distribution within a society. These areas all raise policy questions that need to be addressed. Furthermore, there is a growing concern about the need to preserve the environment in which we live; Chapter 6 pointed out that an externality element in connection with the environment may be a cause of market failure, and commented that there may be international externalities that need to be considered. As this issue has a macroeconomic dimension to it, it will also need to be analysed in conjunction with the discussion of macroeconomic policy. Each of these objectives will now be considered in turn.

## Price stability

One of the most prominent objectives of macroeconomic policy in recent years has been the need to control inflation. Indeed, this has been at the heart of governments' stated policy objectives since 1976.

### Causes of inflation

As we saw in Chapter 9, inflation occurs when there is a rise in the general price level. However, it is important to distinguish between a one-off increase in the price level and a sustained rise over a long period of time. For example, a one-off rise in the price of oil may have an effect on the price level by shifting aggregate supply, thus affecting the equilibrium price level — as shown in Figure 11.1 (reproducing Figure 10.12 from the previous chapter). However, this takes the economy to a new equilibrium price level, and if nothing else were to change, there would be no reason for prices to continue to rise beyond $P_1$.

Nonetheless, this is one reason why prices may begin to increase. Inflation thus may be initiated on the supply side of the macroeconomy, arising from an increase in the costs faced by firms. This is sometimes referred to as **cost-push inflation**, as the increase in the overall level of prices is cost-driven.

In terms of the $AD/AS$ model, it is clear that an alternative explanation of a rise in the general price level could come from the demand side, where an increase in aggregate demand leads to a rise in prices, especially if the $AS$ curve becomes so steep in the long run as to become vertical, as some macroeconomists believe. This is shown in Figure 11.2, where the increase in aggregate demand from $AD_0$ to $AD_1$ leads to a rise in the overall price level from $P_0$ to $P_1$ with no change at all in real output. An increase in the price level emanating from the demand side of the macroeconomy is sometimes referred to as **demand-pull inflation**.

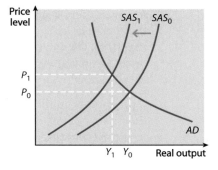

*Figure 11.1  A supply shock*

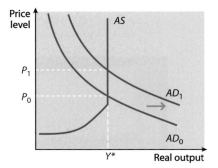

*Figure 11.2  An increase in aggregate demand*

### Key terms

**cost-push inflation:** inflation initiated by an increase in the costs faced by firms, arising on the supply–side of the economy

**demand-pull inflation:** inflation initiated by an increase in aggregate demand

But why should there be *persistent* increases in prices over time? One-off movements in either aggregate demand or aggregate supply may lead to one-off changes in the overall price level, but unless the movements continue in subsequent periods there is no reason to suppose that inflation will continue. One explanation is provided by changes in the supply of money circulating in an economy.

Persistent inflation can take place only when the **money stock** grows more rapidly than real output. This can be shown in terms of aggregate demand and aggregate supply. If the money supply increases, firms and households in the economy find they have excess cash balances: that is, for a given price level they have more purchasing power than they expected to have. Their impulse will thus be to increase their spending, which will cause the aggregate demand curve to move to the right. They will probably also save some of the excess, which will tend to result in lower interest rates — which will then reinforce the increase in aggregate demand. However, as the *AD* curve moves to the right, the equilibrium price level will rise, returning the economy to equilibrium.

**Key term**

**money stock:** the quantity of money in the economy

If the money supply continues to increase, the process repeats itself, with prices then rising persistently. One danger of this is that people will get so accustomed to the process that they speed up their spending decisions, which simply accelerates the whole process.

To summarise, the analysis suggests that, although a price rise can be triggered on either the supply side or the demand side of the macroeconomy, persistent inflation can arise only through persistent excessive growth in the money stock, which can be seen in terms of persistent movements of the aggregate demand curve.

Publishing Pictures

*Prices continually change in every economy, normally upwards*

## Costs of inflation

A crucial question is why it matters if an economy experiences inflation. The answer is that very high inflation gives rise to a number of costs.

The fact that firms have to keep amending their price lists raises the costs of under-taking transactions. These costs are often known as the *menu costs* of inflation; however, this should not be expected to be significant unless inflation really is very high. A second cost of very high inflation is that it discourages people from holding money because, at the very high nominal interest rates that occur when inflation is high, the opportunity cost of holding money becomes great. People therefore try to keep their money in interest-bearing accounts for as long as possible, even if it means making frequent trips to the bank — for which reason these are known as the *shoe leather costs* of inflation.

This reluctance to use money for transactions may inhibit the effectiveness of markets. For example, there was a period in the early 1980s when inflation in Argentina was so high that some city parking fines had to be paid in litres of petrol rather than in cash. Markets will not work effectively when people do not use money and the economy begins to slip back towards a barter economy. The situation may be worsened if taxes or pensions are not properly indexed so that they do not keep up with inflation.

However, these costs are felt mainly when inflation reaches the *hyperinflation* stage. This has been rare in developed countries in recent years, although Latin America was prone to hyperinflation for a period in the 1980s, and some of the transition economies also went through very high inflation periods as they began to introduce market reforms; one example of this was the Ukraine, where inflation reached 10,000% per year in the early 1990s.

However, there may be costs associated with inflation even when it does not reach these heights, especially if inflation is volatile. If the rate of change of prices cannot be confidently predicted by firms, the increase in uncertainty may be damaging, and firms may become reluctant to undertake the investment that would expand the economy's productive capacity.

Furthermore, as Chapter 5 emphasised, prices are very important in allocating resources in a market economy. Inflation may consequently inhibit the ability of prices to act as reliable signals in this process, leading to a wastage of resources and lost business opportunities.

It is these last reasons that have elevated the control of inflation to one of the central planks of UK government macroeconomic policy. However, it should be noticed that the target for inflation has not been set at zero. During the period when the inflation target was set in terms of RPIX (as explained in Chapter 9), the inflation target was 2.5%; from 2004 the target for CPI inflation was 2%. The reasoning here is twofold. One argument is that it has to be accepted that measured inflation will overstate actual inflation, partly because it is so difficult to take account of quality changes in products such as PCs, where it is impossible to distinguish accurately

between a price change and a quality change. Second, wages and prices tend to be sticky in a downward direction: in other words, firms may be reluctant to lower prices and wages. A modest rate of inflation (e.g. 2%) thus allows relative prices to change more readily, with prices in some sectors rising by more than in others. This may help price signals to be more effective in guiding resource allocation.

## Summary

➤ The control of inflation has been the major focus of macroeconomic policy in the UK since about 1976.

➤ Inflation can be initiated on either the supply side of an economy or the demand side.

➤ However, sustained inflation can take place only if there is also a sustained increase in money supply.

➤ High inflation imposes costs on society and reduces the effectiveness with which markets can work.

➤ Low inflation reduces uncertainty, and may encourage investment by firms.

## Exercise 11.1

Suppose that next year inflation in the UK economy suddenly takes off, reaching 60% per annum — in other words, prices rise by 60% — but so do incomes. Discuss how this would affect your daily life. Why would it be damaging for the economy in the future?

## Full employment

For an economy to be operating on the production possibility curve, the factors of production need to be fully employed. From society's point of view, surplus capacity in the economy represents waste. In the macroeconomic policy arena, attention in this context focuses on unemployment. For example, Figure 11.3 shows that it is possible for the economy to be in macroeconomic equilibrium at a level of output $Y_1$ that is below the potential full employment level at $Y^*$. This may be seen as an unnecessary waste of potential output. In addition, there may be a cost suffered by the people who are unemployed in this situation and who could have been productively employed.

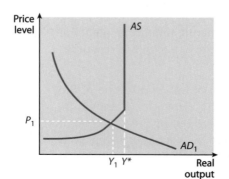

*Figure 11.3* Macroeconomic equilibrium below full employment

### Causes of unemployment

There will always be some unemployment in a dynamic economy. At any point in time, there will be workers transferring between jobs. Indeed, this needs to happen if the pattern of production is to keep up with changing patterns of consumer

OCR Advanced Economics

chapter  *11*

demand and relative opportunity cost. In other words, in a typical period of time there will be some sectors of an economy that are expanding and others that are in decline. It is crucial that workers are able to transfer from those activities that are in decline to those that are booming. Accordingly, there will be some unemployment while this transfer takes place, and this is known as **frictional unemployment**.

In some cases, this transfer of workers between sectors may be quite difficult to accomplish. For example, coal mining may be on the decline in an economy, but international banking may be booming. It is clearly unreasonable to expect coal miners to turn themselves into international bankers overnight. In this sort of situation there may be some longer-term unemployment while workers retrain for new occupations and new sectors of activity.

> **Key terms**
>
> **frictional unemployment:** unemployment associated with job search: that is, people who are between jobs
>
> **structural unemployment:** unemployment arising because of changes in the pattern of economic activity within an economy
>
> **demand-deficient unemployment:** unemployment that arises because of a deficiency of aggregate demand in the economy, so that the equilibrium level of output is below full employment

Indeed, there may be workers who find themselves redundant at a relatively late stage in their career and for whom the retraining is not worthwhile, or who cannot find firms that will be prepared to train them for a relatively short payback time. Such unemployment is known as **structural unemployment**. It arises because of the mismatch between the skills of workers leaving contracting sectors and the skills required by expanding sectors in the economy.

Figure 11.3 showed a different form of unemployment, one that arises because the economy is trapped in an equilibrium position that is below full employment. This is sometimes referred to as **demand-deficient unemployment** — and a solution to it might be to boost aggregate demand. This possibility will be discussed in Chapter 12.

A further reason for unemployment concerns the level of wages. Figure 11.4 shows a labour market in which a free market equilibrium would have wage $W^*$ and quantity of labour $L^*$. If for some reason wages were set at $W_0$, there would be disequilibrium between labour supply (at $L_s$) and labour demand (at $L_d$). Expressing this in a different way, here is a situation in which there are more workers seeking employment at the going wage ($L_s$) than there are firms prepared to hire at that wage ($L_d$). The difference is unemployment.

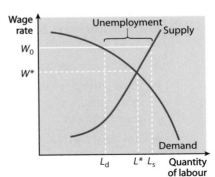

*Figure 11.4*
*Unemployment in a labour market*

There are a number of reasons why this situation might arise. Trade unions may have been able to use their power and influence to raise wages above the equilibrium level, thereby ensuring higher wages for their members who remain in employment, but denying jobs to others. Alternatively, it could be argued that wages

will be inflexible downwards. Thus, a supply shock that reduced firms' demand for labour could leave wages above the equilibrium, and they may adjust downwards only slowly. Chapter 8 mentioned that in some situations the imposition of a minimum wage in a low-wage competitive labour market could also have the effect of institutionally setting the wage rate above its equilibrium level.

Finally, if unemployment benefits are set at a relatively high level compared with wages in low-paid occupations, some people may choose not to work, thereby creating some **voluntary unemployment**. From the point of view of those individuals, they are making a rational choice on the basis of the options open to them. From society's point of view, however, there needs to be a balance between providing appropriate social protection for those unable to obtain jobs and trying to make the best use of available resources for the benefit of society as a whole.

### Costs of unemployment

The costs of unemployment were mentioned earlier. From society's perspective, if the economy is operating below full capacity, then it is operating within the production possibility curve, and therefore is not making the best possible use of society's resources. In other words, if those unemployed workers were in employment, society would be producing more aggregate output; the economy would be operating more efficiently overall.

Furthermore, there may be costs from the perspective of prospective workers, in the sense that **involuntary unemployment** carries a cost to each such individual in terms of forgone earnings and the need to rely on social security support. At the same time, the inability to find work and to contribute to the family budget may impose a cost in terms of personal worth and dignity.

**Key terms**

**voluntary unemployment:** situation arising when an individual chooses not to accept a job at the going wage rate

**involuntary unemployment:** situation arising when an individual who would like to accept a job at the going wage rate is unable to find employment

### Summary

➤ Full employment occurs when an economy is operating on the production possibility curve, with full utilisation of factors of production.

➤ An economy operating below full capacity is characterised by unemployment.

➤ Some unemployment in a dynamic economy is inevitable, as people may have to undergo short spells of unemployment while between jobs — this is known as frictional unemployment.

➤ Structural unemployment occurs when there is a mismatch between the skills that workers have to offer and the skills that employers want. This occurs when the economy is undergoing structural change, with some sectors expanding and some contracting.

➤ Demand-deficient unemployment may occur if the macroeconomy is in equilibrium below full employment.

➤ If wages are held above the equilibrium level — for example, by minimum wage legislation or trade union action — then unemployment may occur.

➤ High levels of unemployment benefit may encourage some workers not to accept jobs as the opportunity cost of not working is low.

## Exercise 11.2

Classify each of the following types of unemployment as arising from frictional, structural, demand-deficient or other causes, and decide whether they are voluntary or involuntary:

a   unemployment arising from a decline of the coal mining sector and the expansion of financial services

b   a worker leaving one job to search for a better one

c   unemployment that arises because the real wage rate is held above the labour market equilibrium

d   unemployment arising from slow adjustment to a fall in aggregate demand

e   unemployment arising because workers find that low-paid jobs are paying less than can be obtained in unemployment benefit

## The balance of payments

Lists of macroeconomic policy objectives invariably include equilibrium on the balance of payments as a key item. Unlike inflation and unemployment, it is not so obvious why disequilibrium in the balance of payments is a problem that warrants policy action.

Figure 11.5 shows the market for pounds relative to euros. Here the demand for pounds arises from residents in the euro area wanting to buy UK goods, services and assets, whereas the supply arises from UK residents wanting to buy goods, services and assets from the euro area. If the exchange rate is at its equilibrium level, this implies that the demand for pounds (i.e. the foreign demand for UK goods, services and assets) is equal to the supply of pounds (i.e. the domestic demand for goods, services and assets from the euro area).

In a free foreign exchange market, the exchange rate can be expected to adjust in order to bring about this equilibrium position. Even under a fixed exchange rate system in which the government pledges to hold the exchange rate at a particular level, any discrepancy between the demand and supply of pounds would have to be met by

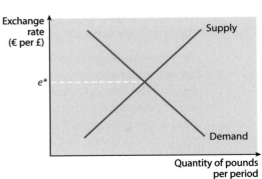

**Figure 11.5**
*The market for pounds sterling*

the monetary authorities buying or selling foreign exchange reserves. Thus, the overall balance of payments is always in equilibrium. So why might there be a problem?

The problem arises not with the *overall* balance of payments, but with an imbalance between components of the balance of payments. In particular, attention focuses on the balance of the current account, which shows the balance in the trade in goods and services together with investment income flows and current transfers.

If the current account is in deficit, UK residents are purchasing more in imports of goods and services than the economy is exporting. In other words, UK earnings from exports are not sufficient to pay for UK imports. This is a bit like a household spending beyond its income, which can be sustained only by selling assets or by borrowing.

The concern for the economy is that a large and sustained deficit on the current account implies that the financial account must be in a large and sustained surplus. This in turn means that the UK is effectively exporting assets. And this means that overseas residents are buying up UK assets, which in turn may mean a leakage of investment income in the future. Alternatively, overall balance could be achieved through the sale of foreign exchange reserves. This soaks up the excess supply of pounds that arises because UK residents are supplying more pounds in order to buy imports than overseas residents are demanding in order to buy UK exports.

However the current account deficit is financed, a large deficit cannot be sustained indefinitely. This begs the question of what is meant by a 'large' deficit. Figure 9.12 showed the current account balance as a percentage of GDP, which gives some idea of the relative magnitude of the deficit. This shows that, although the current account has been in deficit every year since 1984, the deficit has been less than 3% of GDP since 1990. This might be regarded as tolerable.

A critical issue is whether UK assets remain attractive to foreign buyers. Running a sustained deficit on current account requires running a surplus on financial account. If foreign buyers of UK assets become reluctant to buy, UK interest rates might have to rise in order to make UK assets more attractive. A by-product of this would be a curb in spending by UK firms and consumers. Given that part of this reduction in spending would impact on imports, this would begin to reduce the current account deficit.

One way in which the balance of payments is important from a policy perspective occurs when a government wishes to stimulate the economy, perhaps because it regards the level of unemployment as being excessive. An expansionary policy may be intended to increase domestic aggregate demand. However, in designing such a policy it is vital to remember that some of the increased demand will go not on domestic goods, but on imports, which is likely to dilute the effect of the expansion.

A major concern during the early years of the twenty-first century has been the large and persistent current account deficit being run by the US economy.

This has been associated in part with the sizeable government spending of the Bush administration, which was forecast to reach a level that could have global repercussions.

### Causes of a deficit on current account

In Chapter 10 it was argued that the quantity of exports of goods and services from the UK depends partly on income levels in the rest of the world and partly on the competitiveness of UK goods and services, which in turn depends partly on the sterling exchange rate and partly on relative price levels in the UK and elsewhere. Similarly, the level of imports depends partly on domestic income and partly on the international competitiveness of UK and foreign goods and services.

This suggests that a fundamental cause of a deficit on the current account is a lack of competitiveness of UK goods and services, arising from an overvalued exchange rate or from high relative prices of UK goods and services. Alternatively, UK incomes may be rising more rapidly than those in the rest of the world.

## Summary

➤ If the exchange rate is free to reach its equilibrium value, the overall balance of payments will always be zero.

➤ However, a deficit on the current account of the balance of payments must always be balanced by a corresponding surplus on the financial account.

➤ A persistent deficit on current account means that in the long run domestic assets are being sold to overseas buyers, or that foreign exchange reserves are being run down. Neither situation can be sustained in the long run.

➤ A key cause of a deficit on the current account is the lack of competitiveness of domestic goods and services.

## Economic growth

If the ultimate aim of a society is to improve the well-being of its citizens, then in economic terms this means that the resources available within the economy need to expand through time in order to widen people's choices. This requires a process of economic growth, which as we saw in Chapter 1 is an increase in the productive capacity of the economy.

From a theoretical point of view, economic growth can be thought of as an expansion of the productive capacity of an economy. If you like, it is an expansion of the potential output of the economy.

*Wide choice for high street shoppers is a sign of economic growth*

There are two ways in which this has been presented in earlier chapters. The first is in terms of the production possibility curve (*PPC*), which was introduced in Chapter 1. Figure 11.6 is a reminder and reproduces Figure 1.4. Economic growth is characterised as an outward movement of the production possibility curve from $PPC_0$ to $PPC_1$. In other words, economic growth enables a society to produce more goods and services in any given period as a result of an expansion in its resources.

A second way of thinking about economic growth is to use the *AD/AS* model introduced in Chapter 10. In Figure 11.7, an increase in the skills of the workforce will enable firms to produce more output at any given price, so that the aggregate supply curve will shift outwards from $AS_0$ to $AS_1$. This entails an increase in full employment output (or capacity output) from $Y^*$ to $Y^{**}$. This again can be characterised as economic growth.

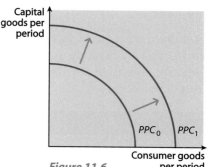

*Figure 11.6*
*Economic growth*

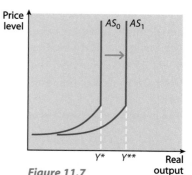

*Figure 11.7*
*A shift in aggregate supply*

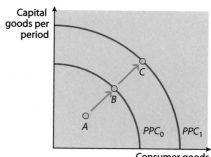

*Figure 11.8*
*Economic growth?*

If economists try to measure economic growth using the rate of change of GDP as an indicator, they are not necessarily measuring what they want to. GDP growth measures the *actual* rate of change of output rather than the growth of the *potential* output capacity of the economy.

In Figure 11.8, a movement from *A* to *B* represents a move to the *PPC*. This is an increase in actual output resulting from using up surplus capacity in the economy, but it is *not* economic growth in our theoretical sense, as moving from *A* to *B* does not entail an increase in productive capacity. On the other hand, a movement of the *PPC* itself, enabling the move from *B* to *C*, *does* represent economic growth. However, when economists observe a change in GDP they cannot easily distinguish between the two sorts of effect, especially if the economy is subject to a business cycle. It is therefore better to think of economic growth in terms of the underlying trend rate of growth of real GDP.

Figure 11.9 helps to illustrate this. It shows the annual growth rate of real GDP in the UK since 1949. You can see that it is quite difficult to determine the underlying trend because the year-to-year movements are so volatile. Figure 11.10 takes 5-yearly average growth rates over the same period, with the horizontal red line showing the underlying trend rate of growth.

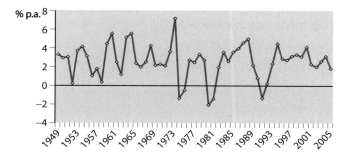

*Figure 11.9*
*Growth of real*
*GDP, 1949–2005*
*(% change over*
*previous year)*

Source: ONS.

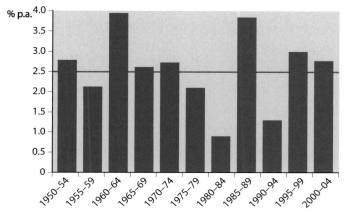

*Figure 11.10*
*Average annual*
*growth rates in the*
*UK since 1950*

## Sources of economic growth

At a basic level, production arises from the use of factors of production — capital, labour, entrepreneurship and so on. Capacity output is reached when all factors of production are fully and efficiently utilised. From this perspective, an increase in capacity output can come either from an increase in the quantity of the factors of production, or from an improvement in their efficiency or productivity. **Productivity** is a measure of the efficiency of a factor of production. For example, **labour productivity** measures output per worker, or output per hour worked. The latter is the more helpful measure, as clearly total output is affected by the number of hours worked, which does vary somewhat across countries. **Capital productivity** measures output per unit of capital. **Total factor productivity** refers to the average productivity of all factors, measured as the total output divided by the total amount of inputs used.

This way of looking at economic growth suggests that investment will be an important source of growth, as it allows an increase in capital. Technological progress may be important in raising the productivity of capital. However, labour is also significant, so investment in

 **terms**

**productivity:** measure of the efficiency of a factor of production

**labour productivity:** measure of output per worker, or output per hour worked

**capital productivity:** measure of output per unit of capital

**total factor productivity:** the average productivity of all factors, measured as the total output divided by the total amount of inputs used

**part 3**

improving the quality of the labour force, through education and training, may be important. This is investment in human capital.

An increase in productivity raises aggregate supply and the potential capacity output of an economy, and thus contributes to economic growth.

## Exercise 11.3

Which of the following represent genuine economic growth, and which may just mean a move to the *PPC*?

**a** an increase in the rate of change of potential output

**b** a fall in the unemployment rate

**c** improved work practices that increase labour productivity

**d** an increase in the proportion of the population joining the labour force

**e** an increase in the utilisation of capital

**f** a rightward shift in the aggregate supply curve

### Benefits of economic growth

Expanding the availability of resources in an economy enables the standard of living of the country's population to increase. For developing countries this may facilitate the easing of poverty, and may allow investment in human capital that will improve standards of living further in the future. In the industrial economies, populations have come to expect steady improvements in incomes and resources. Indeed, we may regard it as being important that a society is able to bring about improvements in the standard of living of its citizens as time goes by. With electorates coming to expect such improvements, governments are likely to be sensitive to the importance of achieving steady economic growth through time.

Thus, for any society, economic growth is likely to be seen as a fundamental objective — perhaps even the most important one. It can be argued that other policy objectives may be regarded as being subsidiary to the growth target. In other words, the control of inflation, the maintenance of full employment and the achievement of stability in the current account of the balance of payments are all seen as important short-run objectives because their achievement facilitates long-run economic growth.

### Costs of economic growth

Economic growth also brings some costs, perhaps most obviously in terms of pollution and degradation of the environment. In designing long-term policy for economic growth, governments need to be careful to maintain a good balance between enabling resources to increase and safeguarding the environment. Pollution reduces the quality of life, so pursuing economic growth without regard to this may be damaging. This means that it is important to consider the long-term

effects of economic growth — it may even be important to consider the effects not only for today's generation of citizens, but also for future generations.

In other words, although economic growth can be seen as an important objective for economic policy, it is nonetheless important to evaluate the benefits and costs to be derived from it.

## Exercise 11.4

Discuss with your fellow students the various benefits and costs associated with economic growth, and evaluate their relative importance.

## Summary

➤ Economic growth is the expansion of an economy's productive capacity.

➤ This can be envisaged as a movement outwards of the production possibility curve, or as a rightward shift of the aggregate supply curve.

➤ Economic growth can be seen as the underlying trend rate of growth in real GDP.

➤ Economic growth can stem from an increase in the inputs of factors of production, or from an improvement in their productivity: that is, the efficiency with which factors of production are utilised.

➤ Investment contributes to growth by increasing the capital stock of an economy, although some investment is to compensate for depreciation.

➤ The contribution of capital is reinforced by the effects of technological progress.

➤ Labour is another critical factor of production that can contribute to economic growth: for instance, education and training can improve labour productivity. This is a form of human capital formation.

➤ Economic growth is seen to be important because it allows an increase in the resources available to contribute to the standard of living of an economy's inhabitants.

➤ However, there may be costs attached to economic growth, particularly in respect of the environment.

➤ Responsible policy must evaluate the benefits and the costs of economic growth to ensure that an appropriate balance is maintained.

## Concern for the environment

International externalities pose problems for policy design because they require coordination across countries. If pollution caused by the UK manufacturing sector causes acid rain elsewhere in Europe, the UK is imposing costs on other countries that are not fully reflected in market prices. Furthermore, there may be effects that cross generations. If the environment today is damaged, it may not be enjoyed by future generations — in other words, there may be intergenerational externality effects.

There is a macroeconomic dimension to these issues. If policy were only designed to achieve economic growth, regardless of the consequences for the environment, these externality effects could be severe, and for this reason they cannot be tackled solely at the microeconomic level of individual markets.

## Income redistribution

The final macroeconomic policy objective to be considered concerns attempts to influence the distribution of income within a society. This may entail transfers of income between groups in society — that is, from richer to poorer — in order to protect the latter. Income redistribution may work through progressive taxation (whereby those on high incomes pay a higher proportion of their income in tax) or through a system of social security benefits such as the Jobseeker's Allowance or Income Support.

### Causes of inequality

Some degree of inequality in the income distribution within a society is inevitable. People have different innate talents and abilities, and choose to undergo different types and levels of education and training, such that they acquire different sets of skills. Market forces imply that different payments will be made to people in different sectors of economic activity and different occupations. Income inequality also arises because of inequality in the ownership of assets. However, people in identical circumstances and with identical skills and abilities *may* receive identical income. This notion is sometimes known as *horizontal equity*, which most people would agree is desirable.

One category of policy measures is designed to encourage horizontal equity. Equal opportunities legislation tries to ensure that members of society do not suffer discrimination that might deny them equal pay for equal work, or equal access to employment. Nonetheless, there remain significant differences in earnings and employment between ethnic groups and between men and women. These issues are explored more fully in Chapter 19.

*Equal opportunities legislation tries to ensure equal pay for equal work*

Setting this aside, the key question remaining is the extent to which the government needs to intervene at the macroeconomic level in order to influence the distribution of income and protect vulnerable groups by redistributing from richer to poorer. Indeed, are there economic effects of inequality suggesting that redistribution of income is needed for reasons other than the purely humanitarian objective of alleviating poverty and protecting the vulnerable?

### The costs of inequality

In a society where there is substantial inequality in the distribution of income, there are likely to be groups of people who are disadvantaged in various ways: for example, they may find it more difficult to obtain education for themselves or for their children. In the UK it remains the case that a lower proportion of students from low-income families go to university. It may also be that some potential entrepreneurs find it more difficult to obtain the credit needed to launch their business ideas.

If this is so, it suggests that there are people in society who are inhibited from developing their productive potential — which in turn implies that economic growth in the future will be lower than it might be. This could provide a justification for redistributing income — or at least for trying to ensure that there is equality of opportunity for all members of society. However, it might be argued that redistribution can be taken too far. If the higher-income groups in society face too high a marginal tax rate on their income — in other words, if additions to income are very heavily taxed for the rich — this could remove their incentive to exploit income-earning opportunities, which could have a damaging impact on economic growth.

Too much inequality may also lead to high crime rates and social discontent, which in turn may lead to political instability in a society. This could affect the security of property rights and inhibit economic growth.

There is some evidence that inequality has been widening in many countries in recent years. In particular, the way that technology has been progressing places a higher premium on skills, so that the gap between the earnings of skilled and unskilled workers has been widening.

## Policy conflicts

In evaluating these policy options, it is important to realise that there may sometimes be potential conflicts and trade-offs between the targets. For example, a policy that pursued full employment, perhaps through increasing government expenditure, might endanger the achievement of price stability. The pursuit of economic growth may need to be tempered by the need to conserve the environment.

### Summary

➤ Economic growth is the most important long-run macroeconomic policy objective, as this enables improvements in the well-being of society's citizens.

➤ However, there may be a need to moderate the pursuit of economic growth in order to protect the environment.

➤ Macroeconomic policy may also encompass the redistribution of income within society, on grounds of equity and also because extreme inequality may inhibit economic growth.

# Chapter 12
# Policy: supply or demand?

*Previous chapters have shown that there may be a range of macroeconomic policy objectives, from economic growth, full employment, the control of inflation and equilibrium on the current account of the balance of payments, to concerns for the environment and for the distribution of income. Attention now turns to the sorts of policy that might be implemented to try to meet these targets. Policies at the macroeconomic level are designed to affect either aggregate demand or aggregate supply, and each will be examined in turn.*

## Learning outcomes

After studying this chapter, you should:
➤ understand and be able to evaluate policies that affect aggregate demand, including fiscal, monetary and exchange rate policies
➤ understand and be able to evaluate policies that affect aggregate supply
➤ be able to appraise the relative merits of policies applied to the demand and supply sides of the macroeconomy
➤ be familiar with how macroeconomic policy has been conducted in the UK in recent years

## Macroeconomic policy objectives revisited

Chapter 11 identified a number of objectives that might be seen as desirable for the macroeconomy. These can be interpreted in terms of Figure 12.1, which shows an economy in macroeconomic equilibrium.

### Price stability

The first objective discussed related to the control of inflation, where it was pointed out that prices can increase because of shifts in either aggregate demand or aggregate supply. However, it was also pointed out that *persistent* inflation would arise only in a situation in which money stock was growing more rapidly than real output. This seems to suggest that one policy response to control persistent inflation would be to control the growth of the money stock.

An increase in money stock affects aggregate demand, shifting the aggregate demand curve to the right and causing prices to rise in an attempt to regain macroeconomic equilibrium. Thus, attempts to control inflation can be interpreted as attempts to create stability in the overall equilibrium price level.

### Full employment

A second macroeconomic policy objective is full employment, which occurs at $Y^*$ in Figure 12.1. If the aggregate demand curve is positioned well to the left in Figure 12.1, macroeconomic equilibrium occurs at less than the full employment level of real output. This suggests that, to restore full employment, policy should be aimed at altering the position of the aggregate demand curve in order to bring the economy back to $Y^*$.

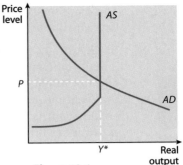

**Figure 12.1**
*Macroeconomic policy objectives*

### Balance of payments

Policy-makers need to be aware of the dangers of a prolonged and substantial deficit on the balance of payments current account, which can have long-run effects on the ownership pattern of UK assets. If these assets are sold to foreigners, their sale will have a long-run effect on the aggregate supply curve. However, the deficit is caused by an imbalance between the components of aggregate demand, so in a sense the current account objective is related to both aggregate supply and aggregate demand. In effect, the need to achieve current account balance acts as a constraint on attempts to meet other policy objectives, so the trade-offs between objectives are of the greatest importance in this case.

### Economic growth

The achievement of economic growth is a long-term objective, the aim of which is to increase the economy's productive capacity. With respect to Figure 12.1, this can be interpreted in terms of policies affecting the *position* of the long-run aggregate supply curve. Economic growth occurs when the aggregate supply curve moves to the right. Thus, in order to influence the economic growth rate of a country, economists need to look for policies that can affect aggregate supply.

## Demand-side policies

Policies that aim to influence an economy's aggregate demand are designed either to stabilise the level of output and employment or to stabilise the price level. The prime focus is thus on the short-run position of the macroeconomy. The two major categories of policy are fiscal policy and monetary policy.

### Fiscal policy

The term **fiscal policy** covers a range of policy measures that affect government expenditures and revenues. For example,

**Key** *term*

**fiscal policy:** decisions made by the government on its expenditure, taxation and borrowing

an expansionary fiscal policy would be seen as an increase in government spending (or reduction in taxes) that shifts the aggregate demand curve to the right.

In Figure 12.2 macroeconomic equilibrium is initially at the intersection of aggregate supply ($AS$) and the initial aggregate demand curve ($AD_0$), so that real output is at $Y_0$, which is below the full employment level of output at $Y^*$. As government expenditure is one of the components of aggregate demand, an increase in such expenditure moves the aggregate demand curve from $AD_0$ to $AD_1$. In response, the economy moves to a new equilibrium, in which the overall price level has risen to $P_1$ but real output has moved to $Y_1$, which is closer to the full employment level $Y^*$.

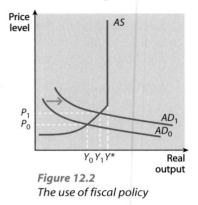

**Figure 12.2**
*The use of fiscal policy*

In this scenario, government expenditure is treated as an injection into the circular flow, and it will be reinforced by a multiplier effect. In the present context, an increase in government expenditure is effective in raising the level of real output in the economy, although some of the increase is dissipated in the form of an increase in the overall level of prices. Notice that such a move cannot be interpreted as 'economic growth' *per se*, as this term is reserved for a situation in which there is an increase in the full employment (potential capacity) level of real output. It is also important to be aware that, if the multiplier is relatively low, the reinforcement of fiscal policy through this route will also be relatively weak.

This kind of policy is effective only if the aggregate demand curve intersects the aggregate supply curve in the upward-sloping segment of $AS$. If the economy is already at the full employment level of output, an increase in aggregate demand merely results in a higher overall level of prices. The effective use of such policy thus requires policy-makers to have good information about the current state of the economy; in particular, they need to know whether the economy is at or below full employment. Otherwise, the results could be damaging for the price stability target. In other words, there is a danger that an expansionary fiscal policy will lead to inflation, but not affect output very much if the $AS$ curve is relatively steep.

The effect on the balance of payments must also be borne in mind. Part of an increase in aggregate demand is likely to be spent on imports, but there is no immediate reason for exports to change, so in the short run there is likely to be an increase in the current account deficit on the balance of payments.

Although the focus of the discussion so far has been on government expenditure, fiscal policy also refers to taxation. In fact, the key issue in considering fiscal policy is the *balance* between government expenditure and government revenue, as it is this balance that affects the position of aggregate demand directly.

An increase in the **government budget deficit** (or a decrease in the **government budget surplus**) moves the aggregate demand curve to the right. The budget deficit

may arise either from an increase in expenditure or from a decrease in taxation, although the two have some differential effects.

To a certain extent, the government budget deficit changes automatically, without active intervention from the government. If the economy goes into a period of recession, unemployment benefit payments will rise, thereby increasing government expenditure. At the same time, tax revenues will decrease, partly because people who lose their jobs no longer pay income tax. In addition, people whose income is reduced — perhaps because they no longer work overtime — also pay less tax. This is reinforced by the progressive nature of the income tax system, which means that people pay lower rates of tax at lower levels of income. Furthermore, VAT receipts will fall if people are spending less on goods and services.

 **terms**

**government budget deficit (surplus):** the balance between government expenditure and revenue

**automatic stabilisers:** effects by which government expenditure adjusts to offset the effects of recession and boom without the need for active intervention

The opposite effects will be evident in a boom period, preventing the economy from overheating. For example, tax revenues will tend to increase during the boom, and the government will need to make fewer payments of social security benefits. By such **automatic stabilisers**, government expenditure automatically rises during a recession and falls during a boom.

In the past there was a tendency for governments to use fiscal policy in a *discretionary* way in order to influence the path of the economy. A government might use its discretion to increase government expenditure to prevent a recession, for example. Indeed, there have been accusations that governments have sometimes, in some countries, used fiscal policy to create a 'feel-good' factor in the run-up to a general election, by allowing the economy to boom as the election approaches, only to impose a clampdown afterwards.

Such intervention has been shown to be damaging to the long-run path of the economy because of its effect on inflation. Furthermore, there are other problems with using fiscal policy in this way. Apart from anything else, it takes time to collect data about the performance of the economy, so its *current* state is never known for certain. Because the economy responds quite sluggishly to policy change, it is often the case that the policy comes into effect just when the economy is already turning around of its own accord. This is potentially destabilising, and can do more harm than good.

*The government budget deficit will change regardless of government intervention*

**part 3**

## Exercise 12.1

Use *AD/AS* analysis to consider the effect of an expansionary fiscal policy on the equilibrium level of real output and the overall price level. Undertake this exercise with different initial positions along the aggregate supply curve, first analysing an economy that begins at full employment and then one in which aggregate demand creates an equilibrium that is below full employment. Discuss the differences in your results.

### Fiscal policy in the UK

If the government spends more than it raises in revenue, the resulting deficit has to be financed in some way. The government deficit is the difference between public sector spending and revenues, and is known as the *public sector net cash requirement* (PSNCR), which until 1999 was known as the *public sector borrowing requirement* (PSBR). Part of the PSNCR is covered by borrowing, and the government closely monitors its *net borrowing.* Over time, such borrowing leads to *net debt*, which is the accumulation of past borrowing. Figure 12.3 shows public sector net debt as a percentage of GDP. The Labour government has aimed to keep this below 40% — and has been successful in achieving this after 1998.

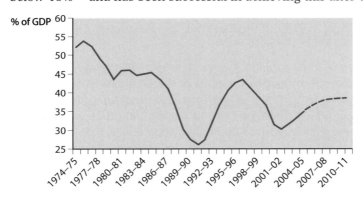

*Figure 12.3*
*Public sector net debt (% of GDP)*

Source: HM Treasury (projections from 2005/06 onwards).

In 1998 the UK government issued its *Code for Fiscal Stability*, which established its objectives for fiscal policy and the rules under which it would operate. The Treasury set these out in the *Budget 2004* statement as follows:

> The Government's fiscal policy objectives are:
> ➤ over the medium term, to ensure sound public finances and that spending and taxation impact fairly within and between generations; and
> ➤ over the short term, to support monetary policy and, in particular, to allow the automatic stabilisers to help smooth the path of the economy

This highlights two major concerns of the government that represent a change in practice. First, there is a concern for the long-run effects of policy on spending and borrowing. It has come to be recognised that sustainable economic growth has to take into account the needs of future generations. The government therefore has taken the view that its current spending should be met out of current revenues, and that only investment for the future should be met through borrowing.

The second important commitment is to use fiscal policy as a *support* to monetary policy. In other words, monetary policy is seen as the most important way of influencing the macroeconomy, and, although the automatic stabilisers are allowed to cut in, there is no intention of using discretionary policy. This clear statement is intended to increase the credibility of government policy by indicating its refusal to take action that could destabilise the macroeconomy.

This suggests that fiscal policy has two kinds of effect. In the first place, the automatic stabilisers help to regulate the economy over the cycle by allowing aggregate demand to be affected by changes in the government budget deficit during the cycle.

The second one is a supply-side effect. By improving the credibility of government policy, and by ensuring that the macroeconomy is not destabilised by inappropriate interventions, it is hoped that the private sector will have more confidence in the future state of the economy. Such confidence may then affect the amount of investment that firms will be prepared to undertake. This would shift aggregate supply in the long run.

## Summary

➤ Fiscal policy is concerned with the decisions made by government about its expenditure, taxation and borrowing.

➤ As government expenditure is an autonomous component of aggregate demand, an increase in expenditure will shift the *AD* curve to the right.

➤ If *AD* intersects *AS* in the vertical segment of *AS*, the effect of the increase in aggregate demand is felt only in prices.

➤ However, if the initial equilibrium is below the full employment level, the shift in *AD* will lead to an increase in both equilibrium real output and the overall price level.

➤ In fact, it is net spending that it is important, so government decisions on taxation are also significant.

➤ The government budget deficit (surplus) is the difference between government expenditure and revenue.

➤ The budget deficit varies automatically through the business cycle because of the action of the automatic stabilisers.

➤ If the government runs a budget deficit, it may need to undertake net borrowing, which over time affects the net debt position.

### Monetary policy

**Monetary policy** is the approach currently favoured by the UK government to stabilise the macroeconomy. It entails the use of monetary variables such as the money supply and interest rates to influence aggregate demand.

The prime instrument of monetary policy in recent years has been the interest rate. Through the interest rate, monetary policy affects aggregate demand. At higher interest

rates, firms undertake less investment expenditure and households undertake less consumption expenditure. This is partly because, when the interest rate is relatively high, the cost of borrowing becomes high and people are discouraged from borrowing for investment or consumption purposes. There are reinforcing effects that operate through the exchange rate if UK interest rates are high relative to elsewhere in the world. If the exchange rate rises because of high interest rates, this will reduce the competitiveness of UK goods.

Suppose the government believes that the economy is close to full employment and is in danger of overheating. Overheating could push prices up without any resulting benefit in terms of higher real output. An increase in the interest rate will lead to a fall in aggregate demand, thereby relieving the pressure on prices. This is illustrated in Figure 12.4, where the initial position has aggregate demand relatively high at $AD_0$, real output at the full employment level $Y_0$ and the overall price level at $P_0$. The increase in interest rates shifts aggregate demand to the left, to $AD_1$. Real output falls slightly to $Y_1$ and the equilibrium price level falls to $P_1$.

**Key** *terms*

**monetary policy:** the decisions made by government regarding monetary variables such as the money supply or the interest rate

**Monetary Policy Committee:** body within the Bank of England responsible for the conduct of monetary policy

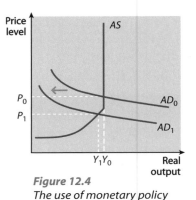

*Figure 12.4*
*The use of monetary policy*

### Monetary policy in the UK

One of the first steps taken by Tony Blair's government after it was first elected in 1997 was to devolve the responsibility for monetary policy to the Bank of England, which was given the task of achieving the government's stated inflation target, initially set at 2.5% for RPIX inflation. As noted in Chapter 9, the target was amended in 2004, when it became 2% per annum as measured by the CPI.

*A meeting of Monetary Policy Committee of the Bank of England*

According to this arrangement, the **Monetary Policy Committee** (MPC) of the Bank of England sets interest rates in such a way as to keep inflation within 1 percentage point (either way) of the 2% target for CPI inflation. If it fails to achieve this, the Bank has to write an open letter to the chancellor of the exchequer to explain why the target has not been met.

OCR Advanced Economics

Operationally, the MPC sets the interest rate at which it makes short-term loans to monetary institutions such as banks. This is known as the **repo rate**, which is short for 'sale and repurchase agreement'. The commercial banks tend to use this rate as their own base rate, from which they calculate the rates of interest that they charge to their borrowers. Thus, if the MPC changes the repo rate, the commercial banks soon adjust the rates they charge to borrowers. These will vary according to the riskiness of the loans; thus credit cards are charged at a higher rate than mortgages, but all the rates are geared to the base rate set by the commercial banks, and hence indirectly to the repo rate set by the Bank of England.

**Key term**

**repo rate:** short for 'sale and repurchase agreement'; the interest rate that is set by the Monetary Policy Committee of the Bank of England in order to influence inflation

Figure 12.5 shows the target rates for RPIX up to December 2003 and for the CPI thereafter, together with the outcomes. The repo rate is also shown. As you can see, inflation has remained within the 1% band throughout the period. The association between the repo rate and movements in the inflation rate does not seem very close. This is partly because the relationship between them is obscured to some extent by other influences; it also reflects the fact that the MPC takes into account a wide range of factors when deciding whether to move the repo rate or to leave it as it was in the previous month.

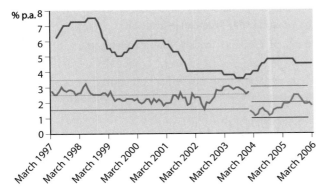

Legend:
— RPIX
— Repo rate
— CPI
— Target 2.5%
— Target 2%
— Upper bound
— Lower bound
— Upper bound
— Lower bound

Source: ONS, Bank of England.

*Figure 12.5*
*UK interest rates and the inflation target, 1997–2006*

For example, at the August 2005 meeting the MPC discussed developments in:
- financial markets
- the international economy
- money and credit
- demand and output
- the labour market
- costs and prices

All these factors were discussed in some detail before taking a decision on what the repo rate should be. In the event, the MPC at this meeting decided to cut the repo rate by 0.25% in spite of the way that inflation seemed to be accelerating — partly due to increases in the price of oil. The MPC took the view that economic activity needed some encouragement, and that the 'slackening in the pressure of demand on supply capacity should lead to some moderation in inflation'.

In the interests of transparency, the minutes of the regular MPC meetings are published on the internet — you can see them at **http://www.bankofengland.co.uk/mpc**.

By influencing the level of aggregate demand, the MPC can affect the rate of inflation so as to keep it within the target range, although the effects of a change in the repo rate are not likely to take immediate effect.

One reason for giving the Bank of England such independence is that it increases the credibility of the policy. If firms and households realise that the government is serious about controlling inflation, they will have more confidence in its actions, and will be better able to form expectations about the future path the economy will take. In particular, firms will be encouraged to undertake more investment, and this will have a supply-side effect, shifting the aggregate supply curve to the right in the long run.

## Summary

➤ Monetary policy is concerned with the decisions made by government on monetary variables such as money supply and the interest rate.

➤ A change in the interest rate influences the level of aggregate demand through the investment expenditure of firms, the consumption behaviour of households and (indirectly) net exports.

➤ Since 1997, the Bank of England has been given independent responsibility to set interest rates in order to meet the government's inflation target.

➤ The Monetary Policy Committee (MPC) of the Bank sets the repo rate, which is then used as a base rate by the commercial banks and other financial institutions.

➤ Giving independence to the Bank of England in this way increases the credibility of monetary policy.

➤ If this encourages investment, there may be a long-run impact on aggregate supply.

## Policies affecting aggregate supply

Demand-side policies have been aimed primarily at stabilising the macroeconomy in the relatively short run, but with the intention of affecting aggregate supply in the long run, by influencing firms' and households' confidence in the future path of the economy. However, there are also a number of policies that can be used to influence the aggregate supply curve directly.

 **Key** *term*

**supply-side policies:**
range of measures
intended to have a
direct impact on
aggregate supply —
and specifically the
potential capacity
output of the economy

Chapter 10 indicated that the position of the aggregate supply curve depends primarily on the quantity of factor inputs available in the economy, and on the efficiency with which those factors are utilised. **Supply-side policies** thus focus on affecting these determinants of aggregate supply in order to shift the *AS* curve to the right.

Investment is one key to this in the long run, and this chapter has already shown how demand-side policies that stabilise the macroeconomy in the short run may also have long-run effects on aggregate supply by encouraging investment.

## Education and training

Investment is also needed in human capital, and one form that this can take is education and training. An important supply-side policy therefore takes the form of encouraging workers (and potential workers) to undertake education and training to improve their productivity.

This takes place partly through education in schools and colleges in preparation for work. It is important, therefore, that the curriculum is designed to provide key skills that will be useful in the workplace. However,

*Investment in human capital can increase productivity*

this does not mean that all education has to be geared directly to providing skills; problem-solving and analytical skills, for example, can be developed through the study of a wide range of disciplines.

Adult education is also important. When the structure of the economy is changing, retraining must be made available to enable workers to move easily between sectors and occupations. This is crucial if structural unemployment is not to become a major problem. For any society — whether industrialised or less economically developed and needing to reduce its dependence on agriculture — education and skills are necessary to enable workers to switch into new activities in response to structural changes in the economy.

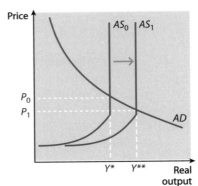

Figure 12.6 shows how such a policy can affect the aggregate supply curve, moving it from $AS_0$ to $AS_1$. This move enables an increase in the potential output capacity of the economy, and it need not be inflationary. Indeed, in the figure the overall price level falls from $P_0$ to $P_1$ following the shift in aggregate supply, with real output increasing from $Y^*$ to $Y^{**}$.

**Figure 12.6**
*A shift in aggregate supply*

## Flexibility of markets

The rationale for including retraining as a supply-side policy rests partly on the argument that this provides for greater flexibility in labour markets, enabling workers to switch between economic activities to improve the overall workings of the economy.

There are other ways of improving market flexibility. One is to limit the power of the trade unions, whose actions can sometimes lead to inflexibility in the labour market, either through resistance to new working practices that could improve

productivity or by pushing up wages so that the level of employment is reduced. This issue will be revisited in Chapter 19.

Indeed, maintaining the flexibility of markets is one way in which the macro-economic stability promoted by disciplined fiscal and monetary policy can improve aggregate supply. Macroeconomic stability enables price signals to work more effectively, as producers are better able to observe changes in relative prices. This can promote allocative efficiency.

### Promotion of competition

Chapter 7 noted that, if firms gain dominance in a market, the pursuit of profits may lead them to use their market position to restrict output and raise prices. Such market dominance arises because of a lack of competition.

In addition, it is possible that in some markets the lack of competition will produce complacency, depriving firms of the incentive to operate at maximum efficiency. This was especially true in the UK for the formerly nationalised industries such as electricity and gas supply, which were widely believed to have operated with wide-spread productive inefficiency.

Policies that promote competition may thus lead to improvements in both alloca-tive and productive efficiency. This was one of the motivations behind the privati-sation drive that began in the 1980s under Margaret Thatcher. However, it should be noted that there is not wholesale agreement on whether privatisation has invariably led to improvements in efficiency in industries such as the railways or water supply. Rail privatisation will be examined in Chapter 21.

### Unemployment benefits

An important influence on labour supply, particularly for low-income workers, is the level of unemployment benefit. If unemployment benefit is provided at too high a level, it may inhibit labour force participation, in that some workers may opt to live on unemployment benefit rather than take up low-skilled (and low-paid) employment. In such a situation, a reduction in unemployment benefit may induce an increase in labour supply, which again will move the aggregate supply curve to the right.

However, such a policy needs to be balanced against the need to provide protec-tion for those who are unable to find employment. It is also important that unem-ployment benefit is not reduced to such a level that workers are unwilling to leave their jobs to search for better ones, as this may inhibit the flexibility of the labour market.

### Incentive effects

Similarly, there are dangers in making the taxation system too progressive. Most people accept that income tax should be progressive — that is, that those on relatively high incomes should pay a higher rate of tax than those on low incomes — as a way of redistributing income within society and preventing inequality from

becoming extreme. However, there may come a point at which marginal tax rates are so high that a large proportion of additional income is taxed away, reducing incentives for individuals to supply additional effort or labour. This could also have an effect on aggregate supply. Again, however, it is important to balance these incentive effects against the distortion caused by having too much inequality in society.

---

### Exercise 12.2

For each of the following policies, identify whether it is an example of fiscal, monetary or supply-side policy. Discuss how each policy affects either aggregate demand or aggregate supply (or both), and examine its effects on equilibrium real output and the overall price level:

**a**  an increase in government expenditure

**b**  a decrease in the rate of unemployment benefit

**c**  a fall in the rate of interest

**d**  legislation limiting the power of trade unions

**e**  encouragement for more students to attend university

**f**  provision of retraining in the form of adult education

**g**  a reduction in the highest rate of income tax

**h**  measures to break up a concentrated market

**i**  an increase in the repo rate

---

## Relative merits

In the context of the aggregate demand/aggregate supply model, it is clear that demand- and supply-side policies are aimed at achieving rather different objectives.

The primary rationale for monetary and fiscal policies is to stabilise the macro-economy. In this, fiscal policy has come to take on a subsidiary role, supporting monetary policy. This was not always the case, and there have been periods in which fiscal policy has been used much more actively to try to stimulate the economy. There are still some countries in which such policies are very much the vogue: for example, it has been suggested that much of Latin America's problem with high inflation has stemmed from fiscal indiscipline, although not all Latin American economists accept this argument. The fact that fiscal policy has not always been well implemented does not mean that such policies cannot be valuable tools — but it does warn against misuse.

In the UK, the use of monetary policy with the support of fiscal policy seems to be working reasonably effectively in the early twenty-first century. Furthermore, it seems to be operating in such a way as to complement the supply-side policies. When a stable macroeconomic environment is created, microeconomic markets

are able to operate effectively and investment is encouraged, thereby leading to a boost in aggregate supply.

Supply-side policies aim to influence aggregate supply directly, either raising the supply of factor inputs or improving productivity and efficiency.

## Summary

➤ Policies to shift the aggregate supply curve may be used to encourage economic growth.

➤ Education and training can be viewed as a form of investment in human capital, which is designed to improve the productivity of workers.

➤ Measures to improve the flexibility of labour and product markets may lead to an overall improvement in productivity and thus may affect aggregate supply.

➤ Promoting competition can also improve the effectiveness of markets in the economy.

➤ Incentive effects are an important influence on aggregate supply. For example, if unemployment benefits are set too high, this may discourage labour force participation. An over-progressive income taxation structure can also have damaging incentive effects.

➤ Demand-side and supply-side policies have different objectives. Demand-side policies such as fiscal and monetary policy are aimed primarily at stabilising the economy. Supply-side policies are geared more towards promoting economic growth.

➤ However, effective stabilisation of the economy may also have long-term effects on aggregate supply.

# Chapter 13
# International transactions

*The world economy is becoming increasingly integrated, and it is no longer possible to think of any single economy in isolation. The UK economy is no exception. It relies on international trade, engaging in exporting and importing activity, and many UK firms are increasingly active in global markets. This situation has created opportunities for UK firms to expand and become global players, and for UK consumers to have access to a wider range of goods and services. However, there is also a downside: global shocks, whether caused by increases in oil prices, financial crises or the emergence of China as a world economic force, can reverberate throughout economies in all parts of the world. It is also apparent that, although economic analysis suggests that there are potential gains to be reaped from international trade, it is still the case that many countries interfere with freedom of trade and try to protect their domestic markets. These are some of the issues that will be explored in this chapter.*

## Learning outcomes

After studying this chapter, you should:
➤ appreciate the importance of trade and exchange between nations
➤ realise how countries may be able to gain from engaging in international trade
➤ be aware of the risks that come from overspecialisation
➤ understand what is meant by globalisation, and be aware of the factors that have given rise to this phenomenon
➤ be familiar with the arguments for trade liberalisation as opposed to protectionism

## Gains from international trade

Chapter 1 highlighted the importance of specialisation, by which, it was argued, workers could become more productive. This same principle can be applied in the context of international trade. Suppose there are two countries — call them Anywhere and Somewhere. Each country can produce combinations of agricultural goods and manufactures. However, Anywhere faces lower opportunity cost in producing manufactured goods, and Somewhere has lower

opportunity cost of agricultural goods. Their respective *PPC*s are shown in Figure 13.1.

The pattern of opportunity cost is reflected in the different slopes of the countries' *PPC*s. If the countries each produce some of each of the goods, one possibility (chosen for simplicity) is that they produce at point *A*, which is the intersection of the two *PPC*s. At this point each country produces 20 units of manufactures and 20 units of agricultural goods. Total world output is thus 40 units of manufactures and 40 units of agricultural goods — this point is marked on the figure.

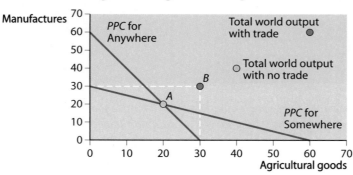

*Figure 13.1*
*PPCs for*
*Anywhere and*
*Somewhere*

However, suppose each country were to specialise. Anywhere could produce 60 units of manufactured products, and Somewhere could produce 60 units of agricultural goods. Then if they were to engage in trade, one possible outcome is point *B*, where they would each now have 30 units of each good, leaving them both unequivocally better off: they would each have more of both commodities. The figure shows that total world output of each type of good has increased by 20 units.

It can be seen that in this situation trade may be mutually beneficial. Notice that this particular result of trading has assumed that the countries exchange the goods on a one-to-one basis. Although this exchange rate makes both better off, it is not the only possibility. It is possible that exchange will take place at different prices for the goods, and clearly, the prices at which exchange takes place will determine which of the countries will gain most from the trade that occurs.

## Exercise 13.1

Next time you go shopping, make a list of the goods that you see on offer that have been imported from elsewhere in the world. See if you can detect any patterns in the sorts of goods that come from different parts of the world.

Figure 13.2 shows production possibility curves for two countries, each of which produces both coats and scooters. The countries are called 'Here' and 'There'.

a   Suppose that Here produces 200 scooters and There produces 100: how many coats are produced in each country?

b   Now suppose that 300 scooters and 200 coats are produced by Here, and that There produces only coats. What has happened to total production of coats and scooters?

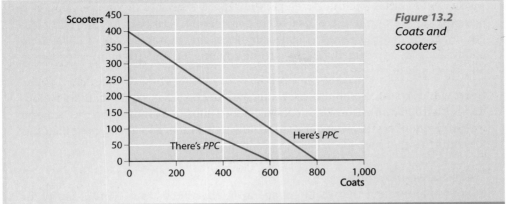

Figure 13.2
Coats and
scooters

In the above examples and exercises, specialisation and trade are seen to lead to higher overall production of goods. Although the examples have related to goods, you should be equally aware that services too may be a source of specialisation and trade. This is potentially important for an economy such as the UK's, where there is a comparative advantage in the provision of financial services.

### Who gains from international trade?

Specialisation can result in an overall increase in total production. However, one of the fundamental questions of economics is 'for whom?' So far nothing has been said about which of the countries will gain from trade. It is possible that exchange can take place between countries in such a way that both countries are better off. But whether this will happen in practice depends on the prices at which exchange takes place. After analysing the way in which prices come to be determined in various markets, this question will be revisited, as the rate at which commodities are exchanged between nations will have important implications for determining who gains from trade.

In particular, specialisation may bring dangers and risks, as well as benefits. One obvious way in which this may be relevant is that, by specialising, a country allows some sectors to run down. For example, suppose a country came to rely on imported food and allowed its agricultural sector to waste away. If the country then became involved in a war, or for some other reason was unable to import its food, there would clearly be serious consequences if it could no longer grow its own foodstuffs. For this reason, many countries have in place measures designed to protect their agricultural

*The extent to which countries trade varies enormously*

sectors — or other sectors that are seen to be strategic in nature. This is a contentious area, and there has been considerable criticism of the European Common Agricultural Policy — especially from the vantage point of developing countries, which argue that they are disadvantaged by the overprotection of European agriculture.

Overreliance on some commodities may also be risky. For example, the development of artificial substitutes for rubber had an enormous impact on the demand for natural rubber; this was reflected in falls in its price, which caused difficulties for countries that had specialised in producing rubber.

### Trade between nations

Countries all around the world engage in international trade. This is partly for obvious reasons: for example, the UK is not a sensible place to grow bananas on a commercial scale, but people living in the UK like to eat bananas. International trade enables individuals to consume goods that cannot be easily produced domestically. It makes sense for bananas to be produced in countries where the relative opportunity cost is low.

The extent to which countries engage in international trade varies enormously, as can be seen in Figure 13.3, which shows total trade (exports plus imports) as a percentage of GDP. In some cases, the extent of dependence on trade reflects the availability of natural resources in a country, but it may also reflect political attitudes towards trade.

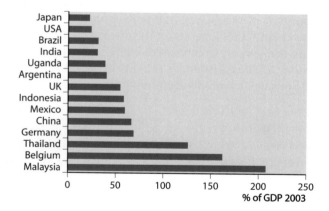

*Figure 13.3 Trade as a % of GDP*

Source: *Human Development Report* 2005.

The USA has a large and diverse economy, with a wealth of natural resources, and does not depend so heavily on trade. Argentina, Brazil and India have a similar level of dependence, but this partly reflects a conscious policy over many years to limit the extent to which their economies have to rely on external trade. At the other extreme, countries such as Malaysia and Thailand have followed policies that promote exports, believing that this will allow more rapid economic growth. China is in a process of transition, having been closed to international trade for a long period and now not only opening up, but also relying heavily on exporting in order to stimulate economic growth.

OCR Advanced Economics

Moves towards closer integration between countries have strongly affected the pattern of world trade. For example, the moves towards European integration have made western Europe a major player in world trade. Something of this can be seen in Figure 13.4, which shows the destination of world exports in 2002 (i.e. the percentage of the world's exports *imported* by each region). You can see that 40% of the world's exports head for western Europe and 22% to North America. Asia has also become an important part of the world trade scene, with China expanding its trading at an unprecedented rate in recent years.

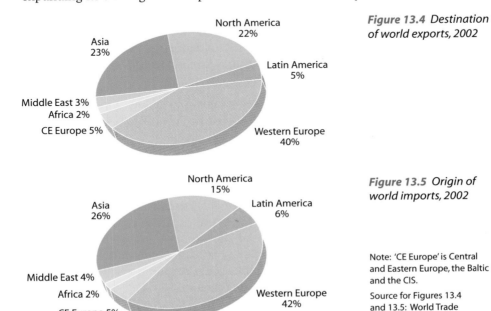

*Figure 13.4* *Destination of world exports, 2002*

*Figure 13.5* *Origin of world imports, 2002*

Note: 'CE Europe' is Central and Eastern Europe, the Baltic and the CIS.

Source for Figures 13.4 and 13.5: World Trade Organization.

Figure 13.5 shows the origin of world imports (i.e. the percentage of the world's imports *exported* by each region). Notice that North America has a much smaller share in this diagram, indicating that it is exporting far less than it is importing. On the other hand, Asia and Western Europe were exporting more than they were importing in 2002. Given the size of its population, Africa contributes very little to world trade.

## Globalisation

The term '**globalisation**' has been much used in recent years, especially by the protest groups that have demonstrated against it. It is therefore important to be clear about what the term means before seeking to evaluate the strengths and weaknesses of the phenomenon.

Ann Krueger, the first deputy managing director of the IMF, defined globalisation as 'a phenomenon by which economic agents in any given part of the world are much

**Key** *term*

**globalisation:** a process by which the world's economies are becoming more closely integrated

more affected by events elsewhere in the world'. Joseph Stiglitz, the Nobel laureate and former chief economist at the World Bank, defined it as follows:

> Fundamentally, [globalization] is the closer integration of countries and peoples of the world which has been brought about by the enormous reduction of costs of transportation and communication, and the breaking down of artificial barriers to the flows of goods, services, capital, knowledge, and (to a lesser extent) people across borders.

> J. Stiglitz, *Globalization and its Discontents* (Penguin, 2004)

On this basis, globalisation is crucially about the closer integration of the world's economies. Critics have focused partly on the environmental effects of rapid global economic growth, and partly on the opportunities that powerful nations and large corporations have for exploiting the weak.

The quotation from the book by Joseph Stiglitz not only defines what is meant by globalisation, but also offers some reasons for its occurrence.

## Transportation costs

One of the contributory factors to the spread of globalisation has undoubtedly been the rapid advances in the technology of transportation and communications.

Improvements in transportation have enabled firms to fragment their production process to take advantage of varying cost conditions in different parts of the world. For example, it is now possible to site labour-intensive parts of a production process in areas of the world where labour is relatively plentiful, and thus relatively cheap. This is one way in which **multinational corporations** (MNCs) arise, in some cases operating across a wide range of countries.

 **terms**

**multinational corporation:** a company whose production activities are carried out in more than one country

**General Agreement on Tariffs and Trade (GATT):** the precursor of the WTO, which organised a series of 'rounds' of tariff reductions

**World Trade Organization (WTO):** a multilateral body now responsible for overseeing the conduct of international trade

Furthermore, communications technology has developed rapidly with the growth of the worldwide web and e-commerce, enabling firms to compete more easily in global markets.

These technological changes have augmented existing economies of scale and scope, enabling firms to grow. If the size of firms were measured by their gross turnover, many of them would be found to be larger in size than a lot of the countries in which they operate (when size is measured by GDP): for instance, on this basis General Motors is bigger than Hong Kong or Norway.

## Reduction of trade barriers

A second factor that has contributed to globalisation has been the successive reductions in trade barriers during the period since the Second World War, first under the auspices of the **General Agreement on Tariffs and Trade (GATT)**, and later under the **World Trade Organization (WTO)**, which replaced it.

In addition to these trade-liberalising measures, there has been a trend towards the establishment of free trade areas and customs unions in various parts of the world, with the European Union being just one example.

By facilitating the process of international trade, such developments have encouraged firms to become more active in trade, and thus have added to the impetus towards globalisation.

### Deregulation of financial markets

Hand in hand with these developments, there have been moves towards removing restrictions on the movement of financial capital between countries. Many countries have removed capital controls, thereby making it much easier for firms to operate globally. This has been reinforced by developments in technology that enable financial transactions to be undertaken more quickly and efficiently.

## The pattern of world trade

In order to provide the context for a discussion of the place of the UK economy in the global economy, it is helpful to examine the pattern of world trade.

Table 13.1 presents some data on this pattern. It shows the size of trade flows between regions. The rows of the table show the exports from each of the regions to each other region, while the columns show the pattern of imports from each region. The numbers on the 'diagonal' of the table (in bold type) show the trade flows *within* regions. One remarkable feature of the table is the high involvement of Western Europe in world trade, accounting for 40.6% of imports and 42.4% of the exports. Of course, this includes substantial flows within Europe. In contrast, Africa shows very little involvement in world trade, in spite of the fact that, in population terms, it is far larger.

Indeed, trade flows between the developed countries — and with the more advanced developing countries — have tended to dominate world trade, with the flows between developing countries being relatively minor. This is not surprising,

| | Destination | | | | | | | |
| Origin | North America | Latin America | Western Europe | C/E Europe/ Baltic/CIS | Africa | Middle East | Asia | World |
|---|---|---|---|---|---|---|---|---|
| North America | **382** | 152 | 170 | 7 | 12 | 20 | 204 | 947 |
| Latin America | 215 | **54** | 44 | 3 | 4 | 5 | 23 | 348 |
| Western Europe | 270 | 55 | **1,787** | 168 | 66 | 68 | 208 | 2,622 |
| C/E Europe, etc. | 14 | 6 | 176 | **80** | 4 | 7 | 24 | 311 |
| Africa | 24 | 5 | 71 | 1 | **11** | 3 | 24 | 139 |
| Middle East | 38 | 3 | 40 | 2 | 9 | **17** | 116 | 225 |
| Asia | 394 | 39 | 260 | 21 | 26 | 48 | **792** | 1580 |
| World | 1,337 | 314 | 2,548 | 282 | 132 | 168 | 1,391 | 6,172 |

*Table 13.1 Intra- and interregional merchandise trade, 2002 (US$bn)*

Note: world totals have been calculated from the table.       Source: World Trade Organization.

given that by definition the richer countries have greater purchasing power. However, the degree of openness to trade of economies around the world varies also as a result of conscious policy decisions. Some countries, especially in East Asia, have adopted very open policies towards trade, promoting exports in order to achieve export-led growth. In contrast, countries such as India and a number of Latin American countries have been much more reluctant to become dependent on international trade, and have adopted a more closed attitude towards trade.

## The pattern of UK trade

Figures 13.6(a) and (b) show the destination of UK exports of goods and services to major regional groupings in the world. The most striking feature of this graph is the extent to which the UK relies on Europe and the USA for more than three-quarters of its exports. Figures 13.7(a) and (b) reveal a similar pattern for the UK's imports of goods and services.

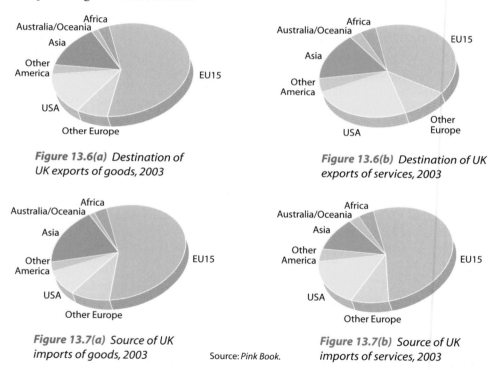

**Figure 13.6(a)** Destination of UK exports of goods, 2003

**Figure 13.6(b)** Destination of UK exports of services, 2003

**Figure 13.7(a)** Source of UK imports of goods, 2003

Source: Pink Book.

**Figure 13.7(b)** Source of UK imports of services, 2003

The proportion of UK trade (both exports and imports) that is with Europe has undergone substantial change over the past 40 years. This can be seen in Figure 13.8. In 1960, when the Commonwealth was still thriving and the UK was ambivalent about the idea of European integration, less than a quarter of UK exports went to other European countries. However, this has changed as the UK has grown closer to Europe, and now more than half of the UK's exports go to other members of the European Union.

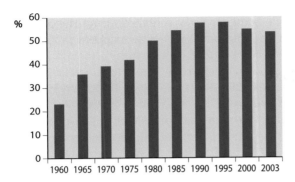

**Figure 13.8** *UK exports of goods to EU 15 (%)*

Note:'EU 15' refers to the 15 countries that were members of the European Union prior to the most recent expansion in May 2004.

Source: calculated from data in Europa: *EU Economy Annual Review 2004.*

Table 13.2 shows the top 10 countries that make up the UK's export markets and import sources, and the top 10 export and import commodities in 2003. This again shows the importance of UK trade with European countries in the twenty-first century, although the USA remains an important trading partner, ranked first among the UK's export markets, and the second largest source of imports into the UK.

A substantial share of exports consists of road vehicles together with machinery and equipment of various types, and pharmaceuticals — and oil, of course. In terms of these commodities, it is noticeable how many commodity groups appear in both top 10 lists: that is, as both exports and imports — most obviously road vehicles, which tops both lists. In part, this reflects the fact that the commodity groups are quite widely defined. In other words, there are many different types of road vehicle or pharmaceutical product, and specialisation may mean that firms

|  | **Export markets** | | **Import sources** | | **Exports** | | **Imports** | |
|---|---|---|---|---|---|---|---|---|
| | Country | % of total UK exports | Country | % of total UK imports | Commodity | % of total UK exports | Commodity | % of total UK imports |
| 1 | USA | 15.4 | Germany | 14.2 | Road vehicles | 9.3 | Road vehicles | 12.7 |
| 2 | Germany | 11.0 | USA | 9.7 | Oil | 7.8 | Office machines | 6.7 |
| 3 | France | 10.0 | France | 8.6 | Pharmaceuticals | 6.3 | Electrical machinery | 6.3 |
| 4 | Netherlands | 7.2 | Netherlands | 7.0 | Power-generating equipment | 6.2 | Misc. manufactures | 5.5 |
| 5 | Irish Republic | 6.5 | Belgium–Lux. | 5.6 | Electrical machinery | 5.7 | Telecomms. equipment | 5.2 |
| 6 | Belgium–Lux. | 6.0 | Italy | 4.8 | Misc. manufactures | 5.7 | Oil | 4.5 |
| 7 | Spain | 4.7 | Irish Republic | 4.2 | Office machines | 5.1 | Clothing | 4.4 |
| 8 | Italy | 4.5 | Spain | 3.9 | Telecomms. equipment | 4.9 | Other transport equipment | 3.7 |
| 9 | Sweden | 2.0 | China | 3.5 | General industrial machinery | 3.9 | General industrial machinery | 3.6 |
| 10 | Japan | 2.0 | Japan | 3.4 | Other transport equipment | 3.9 | Pharmaceuticals | 3.5 |

**Table 13.2** *The UK's top 10 export markets, import sources and export and import commodities, 2003*

in particular countries focus on particular types of vehicle or drug. The only item that appears in the top 10 list of imports that does not also appear in exports is clothing.

## Exercise 13.2

**a** Using the data provided in Table 13.1, calculate the share of each region in world exports and imports. Think about the factors that might influence the contrasting performance of Western Europe and Africa. In addition, for each region calculate the share of exports and imports that are within the region and comment on any significant differences that you find.

**b** Using Table 13.2, calculate the cumulative percentage of exports and imports in the UK's top 10 export markets and import sources. Discuss the extent to which this suggests that the UK concentrates on trading with a relatively small number of partners.

**c** Why should the list of top 10 export commodities contain so many common items with the list of top 10 imports?

**d** Are there any aspects of the pattern of world trade that took you by surprise? Can you find reasons for these?

## Summary

➤ Globalisation has taken place as countries and peoples of the world have become more closely integrated.

➤ Factors contributing to this process have been the rapid advances in the technology of transportation and communications, the reduction of trade barriers and the deregulation of financial markets.

➤ There are substantial differences in the degree to which countries trade: trade with and within Western Europe accounts for an appreciable proportion of world trade, whereas Africa shows very little involvement.

➤ More than three-quarters of UK exports go to Europe and the USA.

➤ The share of UK trade with the rest of Europe has increased substantially since 1960.

## The benefits from specialisation revisited

It has been argued that countries can gain from engaging in international trade by specialising in the production of goods and services in which they have a lower opportunity cost of production. This helps to explain some of the patterns in world trade that are shown in the data.

When you think about the global economy, it should be clear that relative opportunity costs will vary according to the very different balance of conditions around the world, not only in terms of climate (which may be important in agricultural

production), but also in terms of the relative balance of factors of production (labour, capital, land, entrepreneurship etc.) and the skills of the workforce. This helps to explain why MNCs may choose to locate capital-intensive parts of their production process in one location and labour-intensive activities elsewhere, reflecting different relative prices in different countries.

It may also help to explain some of the patterns of trade. At first glance, it may seem curious that the UK both exports and imports cars, as initially this may seem to contradict the notion of specialisation. However, if UK and (say) German cars have different characteristics, then each country may choose to specialise in certain segments of the market, taking advantage of the economies of scale that are so crucial in car production. Consumers benefit from this, as they then have a wider range of products to choose from.

## Trade liberalisation or protectionism?

In spite of the well-known gains from trade, countries often seem reluctant to open their economies fully to international trade, and tend to intervene in various ways to protect their domestic producers.

### Tariffs

A policy instrument commonly used in the past to give protection to domestic producers is the imposition of a **tariff**. Tariff rates in developed countries have been considerably reduced in the period since the Second World War, but nonetheless are still in place.

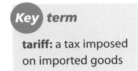
**Key term**

**tariff:** a tax imposed on imported goods

Figure 13.9 shows how a tariff is expected to operate. $D$ represents the domestic demand for a commodity, and $S_{\text{dom}}$ shows how much domestic producers are prepared to supply at any given price. The price at which the good can be imported from world markets is given by $P_{\text{w}}$. If dealing with a global market, it is reasonable to assume that the supply at the world price is perfectly elastic. So, in the absence of a tariff, domestic demand is given by $D_0$, of which $S_0$ is supplied within the domestic economy and the remainder ($D_0 - S_0$) is imported. If the government wishes to protect this industry within the domestic economy, it needs to find a way of restricting imports and encouraging home producers to expand their capacity.

By imposing a tariff, the domestic price rises to $P_{\text{w}} + T$, where $T$ is the amount of the tariff. This has two key effects. One is to reduce the demand for the good from $D_0$ to $D_1$; the second is to encourage domestic producers to expand their output of this good from $S_0$ to $S_1$. As a consequence, imports fall substantially ($D_1 - S_1$).

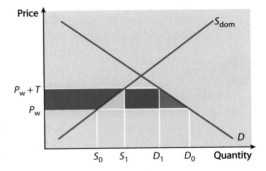

*Figure 13.9*
*The effects of a tariff*

## part 3

On the face of it, the policy has achieved its objective. Furthermore, the government has been able to raise some tax revenue (given by the green rectangle).

However, not all the effects of the tariff are favourable for the economy. Consumers are certainly worse off, as they have to pay a higher price for the good; they therefore consume less, and there is a loss of consumer surplus. Some of what was formerly consumer surplus has been redistributed to others in society. The government has gained the tariff revenue, as mentioned. In addition, producers gain some additional producer surplus, shown by the dark-blue area. There is also a deadweight loss to society, represented by the red and pale-blue triangles. In other words, overall society is worse off as a result of the imposition of the tariff.

Effectively, the government is subsidising inefficient local producers, and forcing domestic consumers to pay a price that is above that of similar goods imported from abroad.

Some would try to defend this policy on the grounds that it allows the country to protect an industry, thus saving jobs that would otherwise be lost. However, this involves sacrificing the benefits of specialisation. In the longer term it may delay structural change. For an economy to develop new specialisations, there needs to be a transitional process in which old industries contract and new ones emerge. Although this process may be painful, it is necessary in the long run if the economy is to remain competitive. Furthermore, the protection that firms enjoy that allows them to reap extra producer surplus from the tariff may foster complacency and an inward-looking attitude. This is likely to lead to X-inefficiency, and an inability to compete in the global market.

Even worse is the situation that develops where nations respond to tariffs raised by competitors by putting up tariffs of their own. This has the effect of further reducing the trade between countries, and everyone ends up worse off, as the gains from trade and specialisation are sacrificed.

### Quotas

An alternative policy that a country may adopt is to limit the imports of a commodity to a given volume. For example, a country may come to an agreement with another country that only a certain quantity of imports will be accepted by the importing country. Such arrangements are sometimes known as **voluntary export restraints** (VERs).

> **Key term**
>
> **voluntary export restraint:** an agreement by a country to limit its exports to another country to a given quantity (quota)

Figure 13.10 illustrates the effects of a quota. $D$ represents the domestic demand for this commodity, and $S_{dom}$ is the quantity that domestic producers are prepared to supply at any given price. Suppose that, without any agreement, producers from country A would be prepared to supply any amount of the product at a price $P_a$. If the product is sold at this price, $D_0$

represents domestic demand, of which $S_0$ is supplied by domestic producers and the remainder $(D_0 - S_0)$ is imported from country A.

By imposing a quota, total supply is now given by $S_{total}$, which is domestic supply plus the quota of imports allowed into the economy from country A. The market equilibrium price rises to $P_1$ and demand falls to $D_1$, of which $S_1$ is supplied by domestic producers and the remainder is the agreed quota of imports.

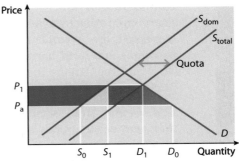

Figure 13.10 The effects of a quota

Figure 13.10 shows who gains and who loses by this policy. Domestic producers gain by being able to sell at the higher price, so (as in the case of the tariff) they receive additional surplus given by the dark-blue area. Furthermore, the producers exporting from country A also gain, receiving the green rectangle (which, in the case of the tariff, was tax revenue received by the government). As in the case of the tariff, the two triangles (red and pale blue) represent the loss of welfare suffered by the importing country.

Such an arrangement effectively subsidises the foreign producers by allowing them to charge a higher price than they would have been prepared to accept. Furthermore, although domestic producers are encouraged to produce more, the protection offered to them is likely to lead to X-inefficiency and weak attitudes towards competition.

There are a number of examples of such agreements, especially in the textile industry. For example, the USA and China have had long-standing agreements on quotas for a range of textile products. Ninety-one such quotas expired at the end of 2004 as part of China's accession to the World Trade Organization. As you might expect, this led to extensive lobbying by producers in the USA, especially during the run-up to the 2004 presidential election. Trade unions in the USA supported the producers, arguing that 350,000 jobs had been lost since the expiry of earlier quota agreements in 2002. In the case of three of these earlier agreements, some restraint had been reinstated for bras, dressing gowns and knitted fabrics. Producers in other countries, such as Sri Lanka, Bangladesh, Nepal, Indonesia, Morocco, Tunisia and Turkey, were lobbying for the quotas to remain, regarding China as a major potential competitor. However, for the USA at least, it can be argued that the removal of the quotas would allow domestic consumers to benefit from lower prices, and would allow US textile workers to be released for employment in higher-productivity sectors, where the USA maintains a competitive advantage.

Similar problems arose in connection with the dismantling of quotas for Chinese textile products being imported into Europe. This led to problems in 2005 when warehouses full of fashion products were prohibited from entry into the EU following a late agreement to delay the dismantling of the quotas.

## Non-tariff barriers

There are other ways in which trade can be hampered, one example being the use of what are known as **non-tariff barriers**. These often comprise rules and regulations that control the standard of products that can be sold in a country.

**Key** *term*

**non-tariff barrier:** an obstacle to free trade other than a tariff — for example, quality standards imposed on imported products

This is a grey area, as some of the rules and regulations may seem entirely sensible and apply equally to domestic and foreign producers. For example, laws that prohibit the sale of refrigerators that contain CFCs are designed to protect the ozone layer, and may be seen to be wholly appropriate. In this case, the regulation is for purposes other than trade restriction.

However, there may be other situations in which a regulation is more clearly designed to limit trade. For example, the USA specifies a larger minimum size for vine-ripened tomatoes than for green tomatoes, thereby raising costs for the former. This has to do with trade because vine-ripened tomatoes are mainly imported from Mexico, but green tomatoes are mainly grown in Florida. Thus, the regulation gives Florida producers an advantage.

Such rules and regulations may operate against producers in less developed countries, who may find it especially difficult to meet demanding standards of production. This applies in particular where such countries are trying to develop new skills and specialisations to enable them to diversify their exports and engage more actively in international trade.

## Summary

➤ Countries can gain from international trade by specialising in the production of goods or services in which they have a lower opportunity cost of production.

➤ In spite of these possible gains, countries have often introduced protectionist measures to restrict trade, including tariffs, quotas and non-tariff barriers.

# Market structure

# Part 4

# Chapter 14
# Perfect competition and monopoly

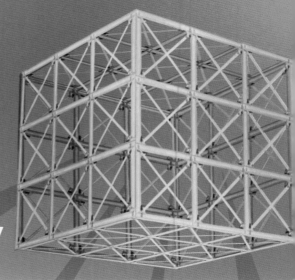

One of the reasons given for market failure in Part 2 of the book concerned what is termed 'imperfect competition'. It was argued that, if firms can achieve market dominance, they may distort the pattern of resource allocation. As a prelude to the modules covering the economics of work and leisure and transport economics, it is now time to look at market structure more closely in order to evaluate the way that markets work, and the significance of this for resource allocation. The fact that firms try to maximise profits is not in itself bad for society. However, the structure of a market has a strong influence on how well the market performs. 'Structure' here is seen in relation to a number of dimensions, but in particular to the number of firms operating in a market and the way in which they interact. The chapter considers two extreme forms of market structure: perfect competition and monopoly.

## Learning outcomes

After studying this chapter, you should:
- ➤ be familiar with the assumptions of the model of perfect competition
- ➤ understand how a firm chooses profit-maximising output under perfect competition
- ➤ appreciate how a perfectly competitive market reaches long-run equilibrium
- ➤ understand how the characteristics of long-run equilibrium affect the performance of the market in terms of productive and allocative efficiency
- ➤ be familiar with the assumptions of the model of monopoly
- ➤ understand how the monopoly firm chooses the level of output and sets its price
- ➤ understand why a monopoly can arise in a market
- ➤ understand how the characteristics of the monopoly equilibrium affect the performance of the market in terms of productive and allocative efficiency
- ➤ be aware of the relative merits of perfect competition and monopoly in terms of market performance
- ➤ understand the significance of concentration in a market and how to measure it

## Perfect competition

### Assumptions
At one end of the spectrum of market structures is **perfect competition**. This model

has a special place in economic analysis because, if all its assumptions were fulfilled, and if all markets operated according to its precepts (including the markets for leisure goods and services, and for transportation services), the best allocation of resources would be ensured for society as a whole. Although it may be argued that this ideal is not often achieved, perfect competition nonetheless provides a yardstick by which all other forms of market structure can be evaluated. The assumptions of this model are as follows:

> Firms aim to maximise profits.
> There are many participants (both buyers and sellers).
> The product is homogeneous.
> There are no barriers to entry to or exit from the market.
> There is perfect knowledge of market conditions.
> There are no externalities.

**Key term**

**perfect competition:** a form of market structure that produces allocative and productive efficiency in long-run equilibrium

### Profit maximisation

The first assumption is that firms act to maximise their profits. You might think that firms acting in their own self-interest are unlikely to do consumers any favours. However, it transpires that this does not interfere with the operation of the market. Indeed, it is the pursuit of self-interest by firms and consumers that ensures that the market works effectively.

### Many participants

This is an important assumption of the model: that there are so many buyers and so many sellers that no individual trader is able to influence the market price. The market price is thus determined by the operation of the market.

On the sellers' side of the market, this assumption is tantamount to saying that there are limited economies of scale in the industry. If the minimum efficient scale (that is, the level of output at which a firm's long-run average costs reach their minimum) is small relative to market demand, then no firm is likely to become so large that it will gain influence in the market.

### A homogeneous product

This assumption means that buyers of the good see all products in the market as being identical, and will not favour one firm's product over another. If there were brand loyalty, such that one firm was more popular than others, then that firm would be able to charge a premium on its price. By ruling out this possibility the previous assumption is reinforced, and no individual seller is able to influence the selling price of the product.

### No barriers to entry or exit

By this assumption, firms are able to join the market if they perceive it to be a profitable step, and they can exit from the market without hindrance. This assumption is important when it comes to considering the long-run equilibrium towards which the market will tend.

### Perfect knowledge

It is assumed that all participants in the market have perfect information about trading conditions in the market. In particular, buyers always know the prices that firms are charging, and thus can buy the good at the cheapest possible price. Firms that try to charge a price above the market price will get no takers. At the same time, traders are aware of the product quality.

### No externalities

Chapter 6 described externalities as a form of market failure that prevents the attainment of allocative efficiency. Here externalities are ruled out in order to explore the characteristics of the perfect competition model.

## Perfect competition in the short run

### The firm under perfect competition

With the above assumptions, it is possible to analyse how a firm will operate in the market. An important implication of these assumptions is that no individual trader can influence the price of the product. In particular, this means that the firm is a **price taker**, and has to accept whatever price is set in the market as a whole.

> **Key term**
>
> **price taker:** a firm that must accept whatever price is set in the market as a whole

As a price taker, the firm faces a perfectly elastic demand curve for its product, as is shown in Figure 14.1. In this figure $P_1$ is the price set in the market, and the firm cannot sell at any other price. If it tries to set a price above $P_1$ it will sell nothing, as buyers are fully aware of the market price and will not buy at a higher price, especially as they know that there is no quality difference between the product produced by different firms in the market. What this also implies is that the firm can sell as much output as it likes at that going-price — which means there is no incentive for any firm to set a price below $P_1$. Thus, all firms charge the same price, $P_1$.

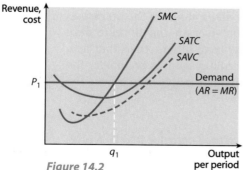

**Figure 14.1**
Costs in the short run

**Figure 14.2**
The firm's short-run supply decision

### The firm's short-run supply decision

If the firm can sell as much as it likes at the market price, how does it decide how much to produce?

Chapter 4 explained that to maximise profits a firm needs to set output at such a level that marginal revenue is equal to marginal cost. Figure 14.2 illustrates this rule by adding the short-run cost curves to the demand curve. (Remember that *SMC* cuts *SAVC* and *SATC* at their minimum points.) As the demand curve is horizontal, the firm faces constant average and marginal revenue and will choose output at $q_1$, where $MR = SMC$.

If the market price were to change, the firm would react by changing output, but always choosing to supply output at the level at which $MR = SMC$. This suggests that the short-run marginal cost curve represents the firm's short-run supply curve: in other words, it shows the quantity of output that the firm would supply at any given price.

However, there is one important proviso to this statement. If the price falls below short-run average variable cost, the firm's best decision will be to exit from the market, as it will be better off just incurring its fixed costs. So the firm's **short-run supply curve** is the $SMC$ curve above the point where it cuts $SAVC$ (at its minimum point).

### Industry equilibrium in the short run

One crucial question not yet examined is how the market price comes to be determined. To answer this, it is necessary to consider the industry as a whole. In this case there is a conventional downward-sloping demand curve, of the sort met in Chapter 2. This is formed according to preferences of consumers in the market and is shown in Figure 14.3.

On the supply side, it has been shown that the individual firm's supply curve is its marginal cost curve above $SAVC$. If you add up the supply curves of each firm operating in the market, the result is the industry supply curve, shown in Figure 14.3 as Supply = $\Sigma SMC$ (where '$\Sigma$' means 'sum of'). The price will then adjust to $P_1$ at the intersection of demand and supply. The firms in the industry between them will supply $Q_1$ output, and the market will be in equilibrium.

### The firm in short-run equilibrium revisited

As this seems to be a well-balanced situation, with price adjusting to equate market demand and supply, the only question is why it is described as just a *short-run equilibrium*. The clue to this is to be found back with the individual firm.

Figure 14.4 illustrates the position facing an individual firm in the market. As before, the firm maximises profits by accepting the price $P_1$ as set in the market and producing up to the point where $MR = SMC$, which is at $q_1$. However, now

**Key** term

short-run supply curve: for a firm operating under perfect competition, the curve given by its short-run marginal cost curve above the price at which $MC = SAVC$; for the industry, the short-run supply curve is the horizontal sum of the supply curves of the individual firms

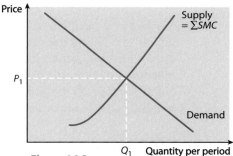

**Figure 14.3**
*A perfectly competitive industry in short-run equilibrium*

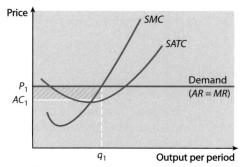

**Figure 14.4**
*The firm in short-run supply equilibrium*

the firm's average revenue (which is equal to price) is greater than its average cost (which is given by $AC_1$ at this level of output). The firm is thus making supernormal profits at this price. (Remember that 'normal profits' are included in average cost.) The total amount of supernormal profits being made is shown as the shaded area on the graph. Notice that average revenue minus average costs equals profit per unit, so multiplying this by the quantity sold determines total profit.

This is where the assumption about freedom of entry becomes important. If firms in this market are making profits above opportunity cost, the market is generating more profits than other markets in the economy. This will prove attractive to other firms, which will seek to enter the market — and the assumption is that there are no barriers to prevent them from doing so.

This process of entry will continue for as long as firms are making supernormal profits. However, as more firms join the market, the *position* of the industry supply curve, which is the sum of the supply curves of an ever-larger number of individual firms, will be affected. As the industry supply curve shifts to the right, the market price will fall. At some point the price will have fallen to such an extent that firms are no longer making supernormal profits, and the market will then stabilise.

If the price were to fall even further, some firms would choose to exit from the market, and the process would go into reverse. Therefore price can be expected to stabilise such that the typical firm in the industry is just making normal profits.

### Perfect competition in long-run equilibrium
Figure 14.5 shows the situation for a typical firm and for the industry as a whole once long-run equilibrium has been reached and firms no longer have any incentive to enter or exit the market. The market is in equilibrium, with demand equal to supply at the going price. The typical firm sets marginal revenue equal to marginal cost to maximise profits, and just makes normal profits.

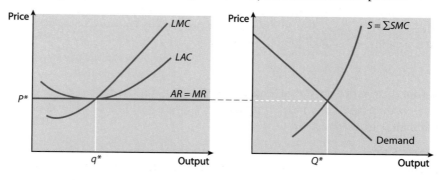

*Figure 14.5*
*Long-run*
*equilibrium*
*under perfect*
*competition*

### *The long-run supply curve*
Comparative static analysis can be used to explore this equilibrium a little more deeply. Suppose there is an increase in the demand for this product. Perhaps, for some reason, everyone becomes convinced that the product is really health promoting, so demand increases at any given price. This disturbs the market equilibrium, and the question then is whether (and how) equilibrium can be restored.

chapter *14*

Figure 14.6 reproduces the long-run equilibrium that was shown in Figure 14.5. Thus, in the initial position market price is at $P^*$, the typical firm is in long-run equilibrium, producing $q^*$, and the industry is producing $Q^*$. Demand was initially at $D_0$, but with the increased popularity of the product it has shifted to $D_1$. In the short run this pushes the market price up to $P_1$ for the industry, because as market price increases, existing firms have the incentive to supply more output: that is, they move along their short-run supply curves. So in the short run a typical firm starts to produce $q_1$ output. The combined supply of the firms then increases to $Q_1$.

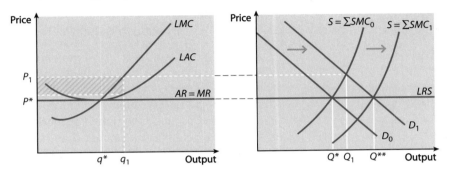

**Figure 14.6**
*Adjusting to an increase in demand under perfect competition*

However, at the higher price the firms start making supernormal profits (shown by the shaded area in Figure 14.6), so in time more firms will be attracted into the market, pushing the short-run industry supply curve to the right. This process will continue until there is no further incentive for new firms to enter the market — which occurs when the price has returned to $P^*$, but with increased industry output at $Q^{**}$. In other words, the adjustment in the short run is borne by existing firms, but the long-run equilibrium is reached through the entry of new firms. This suggests that the **industry long-run supply curve** (LRS) is horizontal at price $P^*$, which is the minimum point of the long-run average cost curve for the typical firm in the industry.

> **Key term**
>
> **industry long-run supply curve:** under perfect competition, a curve that is horizontal at the price which is the minimum point of the long-run average cost curve for the typical firm in the industry

### Efficiency under perfect competition

Having reviewed the characteristics of long-run equilibrium in a perfectly competitive market, you may wonder what is so good about such a market in terms of productive and allocative efficiency.

#### Productive efficiency

For an individual market, productive efficiency is reached when a firm operates at the minimum point of its long-run average cost curve. Under perfect competition, this is indeed a feature of the long-run equilibrium position. So, productive efficiency is achieved in the long run — but not in the short run, when a firm need not be operating at minimum average cost.

#### Allocative efficiency

For an individual market, allocative efficiency is achieved when price is set equal

to marginal cost. Again, the process by which supernormal profits are competed away, through the entry of new firms into the market, ensures that price is equal to marginal cost within a perfectly competitive market in long-run equilibrium. So allocative efficiency is also achieved. Indeed, firms set price equal to marginal cost even in the short run, so allocative efficiency is a feature of perfect competition in both the short run and the long run.

## Exercise 14.1

Figure 14.7 shows the short-run cost curves for a firm that is operating in a perfectly competitive market.

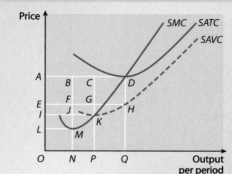

*Figure 14.7*
*A firm operating under perfect competition*

a   At what price would the firm just make 'normal' profits?

b   What area would represent total fixed cost at this price?

c   What is the shutdown price for the firm?

d   Within what range of prices would the firm choose to operate at a loss in the short run?

e   Identify the firm's short-run supply curve.

f   Within what range of prices would the firm be able to make short-run supernormal profits?

g   What conditions must hold for supernormal profits to be competed to zero in the long run?

## Exercise 14.2

Starting from a diagram like Figure 14.5, track the response of a perfectly competitive market to a decrease in market demand for a good — in other words, explain how the market adjusts to a leftward shift of the demand curve.

### Evaluation of perfect competition

A criticism sometimes levelled at the model of perfect competition is that it is merely a theoretical ideal, based on a sequence of assumptions that rarely holds in the real world. Perhaps you have some sympathy with that view.

It could be argued that the model does hold for some agricultural markets. One study in the USA estimated that the elasticity of demand for an individual farmer producing sweetcorn was −31,353, which is pretty close to being perfectly elastic.

However, to argue that the model is useless because it is unrealistic is to miss a very important point. By allowing a glimpse of what the ideal market would look like, at least in terms of resource allocation, the model provides a measure against which alternative market structures can be compared. Furthermore, economic analysis can be used to investigate the effects of relaxing the assumptions of the model, which can be another valuable exercise. For example, it is possible to examine how the market is affected if firms can differentiate their products, or if traders in the market are acting with incomplete information. This scenario was in fact explored in Chapter 7, describing the effects of asymmetric information on a market.

So, although there may be relatively few markets that display all the characteristics of perfect competition, that does not destroy the usefulness of the model in economic theory. It will continue to be a reference point when examining alternative models of market structure.

## Extension material: a word of warning

Some writers, such as Nobel prize winner Friedrich von Hayek, have disputed the idea that perfect competition is the best form of market structure. Hayek argued that supernormal profits can be seen as the basis for investment by firms in new technologies, research and development (R&D) and innovation. If supernormal profits are always competed away, as happens under perfect competition, such activity will not take place. Similarly, Joseph Schumpeter argued that only in monopoly or oligopoly markets can firms afford to undertake R&D. Under this sort of argument, it is not quite so clear that perfect competition is the most desirable market structure.

## Summary

- ➤ The model of perfect competition describes an extreme form of market structure. It rests on a sequence of assumptions.
- ➤ Its key characteristics include the assumption that no individual trader can influence the market price of the good or service being traded, and that there is freedom of entry and exit.
- ➤ In such circumstances each firm faces a perfectly elastic demand curve for its product, and can sell as much as it likes at the going market price.
- ➤ A profit-maximising firm chooses to produce the level of output at which marginal revenue (*MR*) equals marginal cost (*MC*).
- ➤ The firm's short-run marginal cost curve, above its short-run average variable cost curve, represents its short-run supply curve.
- ➤ The industry's short-run supply curve is the horizontal summation of the supply curves of all firms in the market.
- ➤ Firms may make supernormal profits in the short run, but because there is freedom of entry these profits will be competed away in the long run by new firms joining the market.
- ➤ The long-run industry supply curve is horizontal, with price adjusting to the minimum level of the typical firm's long-run average cost curve.
- ➤ Under perfect competition in long-run equilibrium, both productive efficiency and allocative efficiency are achieved.

# Monopoly

At the opposite end of the spectrum of market structures is **monopoly**, which strictly speaking is a market with a single seller of a good. However, there is a bit more to it than that, and economic analysis of monopoly rests on some important assumptions. In the real world, the Competition Commission, the official body in the UK with the responsibility of monitoring monopoly markets, is empowered to investigate a merger if it results in the combined firm having more than 25% of a market. Some discussion of the theory of how monopoly markets operate is necessary in order to understand why such monitoring is required.

 **Key** *term*

**monopoly:** a form of market structure in which there is only one seller of a good or service

## Assumptions

The assumptions of the monopoly model are as follows:
- There is a single seller of a good.
- There are no substitutes for the good, either actual or potential.
- There are barriers to entry into the market.

It is also assumed that the firm aims to maximise profits. These assumptions all have their counterparts in the assumptions of perfect competition, and in one sense this model can be described as being at the opposite end of the market structure spectrum.

If there is a single seller of a good, and if there are no substitutes for the good, the monopoly firm is thereby insulated from competition. Furthermore, any barriers to entry into the market will ensure that the firm can sustain its market position into the future. The assumption that there are no potential substitutes for the good reinforces the situation. (Chapter 15 explores what happens if this assumption does not hold.)

## A monopoly in equilibrium

The first point to note is that a monopoly firm faces the market demand curve directly. Thus, unlike perfect competition, the demand curve slopes downwards. For the monopolist, the demand curve may be regarded as showing average revenue. Unlike a firm under perfect competition, therefore, the monopolist has some influence over price, and can make decisions regarding price as well as output. This is not to say that the monopolist has complete freedom to set the price, as the firm is still constrained by market demand. However, the firm is a *price maker* and can choose a location along the demand curve.

Recall a piece of analysis in Chapter 3, which looked at the relationship between the own-price elasticity of demand along a straight-line demand curve and total revenue. The key graphs are reproduced here as Figure 14.8. The analysis pointed out that the price elasticity of demand is elastic above the mid-point of the demand curve and inelastic in the lower half, with total revenue increasing with a price fall when demand is elastic, and falling with a price fall when demand is inelastic.

The marginal revenue curve (*MR*) has been added to the figure, and it has a fixed relationship with the average revenue curve (*AR*). This is for similar mathematical reasons to those that explained the relationship between marginal and average costs in Chapter 4. *MR* shares the intercept point on the vertical axis (point *A* in Figure 14.8) and has exactly twice the slope of *AR*. Whenever you have to draw this figure, remember that *MR* and *AR* have this relationship — meeting at *A*, and with the distance *BC* being the same as the distance *CD*. *MR* is zero (meets the horizontal axis) at the maximum point of the total revenue curve.

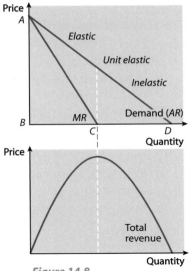

Figure 14.8
*Elasticity and total revenue*

As with the firm under perfect competition, a monopolist aiming to maximise profits will choose to produce at the level of output at which marginal revenue equals marginal cost. This is at $Q_m$ in Figure 14.9. Having selected output, the monopolist will then set the price at the highest level at which all output will be sold — in Figure 14.9 this is $P_m$.

This choice allows the monopolist to make supernormal profits, which can be identified as the shaded area in the figure. As before, this area is average revenue minus average cost, which gives profit per unit, multiplied by the quantity.

It is at this point that barriers to entry become important. Other firms may see that the monopoly firm is making healthy supernormal profits, but the existence of barriers to entry will prevent those profits from being competed away, as would happen in a perfectly competitive market.

It is important to notice that the monopolist cannot be guaranteed always to make such substantial profits as are shown in Figure 14.9. The size of the profits depends upon the relative position of the market demand curve and the position of the cost curves. If the cost curves in the diagram were higher, the monopoly profits would be much smaller, as the distance between average revenue and average costs would be less. It is even possible that the cost curves will be so high as to force the firm to incur losses, in which case it would probably shut down.

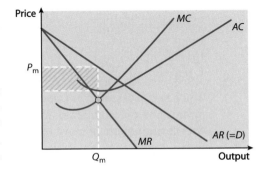

Figure 14.9
*Profit maximisation and monopoly*

## Exercise 14.3

Table 14.1 shows the demand faced by a monopolist at various prices.

**a** Calculate total revenue and marginal revenue for each level of demand.

**b** Plot the demand curve (*AR*) and marginal revenue on a graph.

**c** Plot total revenue on a separate graph.

**d** Identify the level of demand at which total revenue is at a maximum.

**e** At what level of demand is marginal revenue equal to zero?

**f** At what level of demand is there unit price elasticity of demand?

**g** If the monopolist maximises profits, will the chosen level of output be higher or lower than the revenue-maximising level?

**h** What does this imply for the price elasticity of demand when the monopolist maximises profits?

| Demand (000s per week) | Price (£) |
|---|---|
| 0 | 80 |
| 1 | 70 |
| 2 | 60 |
| 3 | 50 |
| 4 | 40 |
| 5 | 30 |
| 6 | 20 |
| 7 | 10 |

*Table 14.1 Monopolist's demand schedule*

## Exercise 14.4

Draw a diagram to analyse the profit-maximising level of output and price for a monopolist, and analyse the effect of an increase in demand.

### How do monopolies arise?

Monopolies may arise in a market for a number of reasons. In a few instances, a monopoly is created by the authorities. For example, for 150 years the UK Post Office held a licence giving it a monopoly on delivering letters. From the beginning of 2006, the service was fully liberalised, although any company wanting to deliver packages weighing less than 350 grams and charging less than £1 can do so only by applying for a licence. The Post Office monopoly formerly covered a much wider range of services, but its coverage was gradually eroded over the years, and competition in delivering larger packages has been permitted for some time. Nonetheless, it remains an example of one way in which a monopoly can be created.

The patent system offers a rather different form of protection for a firm. The patent system was designed to provide an incentive for firms to innovate through the development of new techniques and products. By prohibiting other firms from copying the product for a period of time, a firm is given a temporary monopoly.

In some cases the technology of the industry may create a monopoly situation. In a market characterised by substantial economies of scale, there may not be room for more than one firm in the market. This could happen where there are substantial

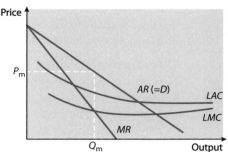

fixed costs of production but low marginal costs: for example, in establishing an underground railway in a city, a firm faces very high fixed costs in building the network of rails and stations and buying the rolling stock. However, once in operation, the marginal cost of carrying an additional passenger is very low.

Figure 14.10 illustrates this point. The firm in this market enjoys economies of scale right up to the limit of market demand. The largest firm operating in the market can always produce at a lower cost than any potential entrant, so will always be able to price such firms out of the market. Here the economies of scale act as an effective barrier to the entry of new firms and the market is a **natural monopoly**. A profit-maximising monopoly would thus set $MR = MC$, produce at quantity $Q_m$ and charge a price $P_m$.

**Figure 14.10**
*A natural monopoly*

**Key term**

**natural monopoly:** monopoly that arises in an industry in which there are such substantial economies of scale that only one firm is viable

Such a market poses particular problems regarding allocative efficiency. Notice in the figure that marginal cost is below average cost over the entire range of output. If the firm were to charge a price equal to marginal cost it would inevitably make a loss, so such a pricing rule would not be viable. Notice, however, that it would clearly not make economic sense to have multiple underground railway systems trying to serve the same routes in a city.

There are markets in which firms have risen to become monopolies by their actions in the market. Such a market structure is sometimes known as a *competitive monopoly*. Firms may get into a monopoly position through effective marketing, through a process of merger and acquisition, or by establishing a new product as a widely accepted standard.

In the first Microsoft trial in 1998, it was claimed that Microsoft had gained 95% of the world market for operating systems for PC computers. The firm claimed that this is because it was simply very good at what it does. However, part of the reason why it was on trial was that other interested parties alleged that Microsoft was guilty of unfair market tactics and predatory behaviour.

## Exercise 14.5

In 2000, AOL merged with Time Warner, bringing together an internet service provider with an extensive network and a firm in the entertainment business.

One product that such a merged company might produce is a digitised music performance that could be distributed through the internet. Think about the sorts of costs entailed in producing and delivering such a product, and categorise them as fixed or variable costs. What does this imply for the economies of scale faced by the merged company?

## Monopoly and efficiency

The characteristics of the monopoly market can be evaluated in relation to productive and allocative efficiency (see Figure 14.9).

### Productive efficiency

A firm is said to be productively efficient if it produces at the minimum point of long-run average cost. It is clear from the figure that this is extremely unlikely for a monopoly. The firm will produce at the minimum point of long-run average cost only if it so happens that the marginal *revenue* curve passes through this exact point — and this would happen only by coincidence.

### Allocative efficiency

For an individual firm, allocative efficiency is achieved when price is set equal to marginal cost. It is clear from Figure 14.9 that this will not be the case for a profit-maximising monopoly firm. The firm chooses output where *MR* equals *MC*; however, given that *MR* is below *AR* (i.e. price), price will always be set above marginal cost.

## Perfect competition and monopoly compared

It is possible to identify the extent to which a monopoly by its behaviour distorts resource allocation, by comparing the monopoly market with the perfectly competitive market. To do this, the situation can be simplified by setting aside the possibility of economies of scale. This is perhaps an artificial assumption to make, but it can be relaxed later.

Suppose that there is an industry with no economies of scale, which can be operated either as a perfectly competitive market with many small firms, or as a monopoly firm running a large number of small plants.

Figure 14.11 shows the market demand curve ($D = AR$), and the long-run supply curve under perfect competition (*LRS*). If the market is operating under perfect competition, the long-run equilibrium will produce a price of $P_{pc}$, and the firms in the industry will together supply $Q_{pc}$ output. Consumer surplus is given by the area $AP_{pc}E$, which represents the surplus that consumers gain from consuming this product. In other words, it is a measure of the welfare that society receives from consuming the good, as was explained in Chapter 3.

Now suppose that the industry is taken over by a profit-maximising monopolist. The firm can close down some of the plants to vary its output over the long run, and the *LRS* can be regarded as the monopolist's long-run marginal cost curve. As the monopoly firm faces the market demand curve directly, it will also face the *MR* curve shown, so will maximise profits at quantity $Q_m$ and charge a price $P_m$.

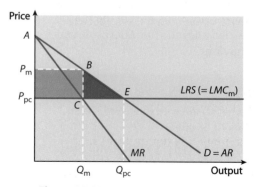

**Figure 14.11** *Comparing perfect competition and monopoly*

OCR Advanced Economics

Thus, the effect of this change in market structure is that the profit-maximising monopolist produces less output than a perfectly competitive industry and charges a higher price.

It is also apparent that consumer surplus is now very different, as in the new situation it is limited to the area $AP_mB$. Looking more carefully at Figure 14.11, you can see that the loss of consumer surplus has occurred for two reasons. First, the monopoly firm is now making profits shown by the shaded area $P_mBCP_{pc}$. This is a redistribution of welfare from consumers to the firm, but, as the monopolist is also a member of society, this does not affect overall welfare. However, there is also a deadweight loss, which represents a loss to society resulting from the monopolisation of the industry. This is measured by the area of the triangle $BCE$. The existence of this deadweight loss provides the rationale for intervention by the Competition Commission and the Office of Fair Trading, which have the responsibility for protecting consumer interests and attempting to promote competition.

## Summary

➤ A monopoly market is one in which there is a single seller of a good.

➤ The model of monopoly used in economic analysis also assumes that there are no substitutes for the goods or services produced by the monopolist, and that there are barriers to the entry of new firms.

➤ The monopoly firm faces the market demand curve, and is able to choose a point along that demand curve in order to maximise profits.

➤ Such a firm may be able to make supernormal profits, and sustain them in the long run because of barriers to entry and the lack of substitutes.

➤ A monopoly may arise because of patent protection or from the nature of economies of scale in the industry (a 'natural monopoly').

➤ A profit-maximising monopolist does not achieve allocative efficiency, and is unlikely to achieve productive efficiency in the sense of producing at the minimum point of the long-run average cost curve.

➤ A comparison of perfect competition with monopoly reveals that a profit-maximising monopoly firm operating under the same cost conditions as a perfectly competitive industry will produce less output, charge a higher price and impose a deadweight loss on society.

## Market concentration

The discussion above has shown that the models of perfect competition and monopoly produce very different outcomes for productive and allocative efficiency. Perfect competition produces a 'good' allocation of resources, but monopoly results in a deadweight loss. In the real-world economy it is not quite so simple. In particular, not every market is readily classified as following either of these extreme models. Indeed, you might think that the majority of markets do not correspond to either of the models, but instead display a mixture of characteristics.

An important question is whether such markets behave more like a competitive market or more like a monopoly. There are many different ways in which markets with just a few firms operating can be modelled, because there are many ways in which the firms may interact. Some of these models are explored in Chapter 15.

It is helpful to have some way of gauging how close a particular market is to being a monopoly. One way of doing this is to examine the degree of concentration in the market. Later it will be seen that this is not all that is required to determine how efficiently a market will operate; but it is a start.

Concentration is normally measured by reference to the **concentration ratio**, which measures the market share of the largest firms in an industry. For example, the three-firm concentration ratio measures the market share of the largest three firms in the market; the five-firm concentration ratio calculates the share of the top five firms, and so on. Concentration can also be viewed in terms of employment, reflected in the proportion of workers in any industry that are employed in the largest firms.

 **Key** *term*

***n*-firm concentration ratio:** a measure of the market share of the largest *n* firms in an industry

Consider the following example. Table 14.2 gives average circulation figures for the firms that publish national newspapers in the UK. In the final column these are converted into market shares. Where one firm produces more than one newspaper, their circulations have been combined (e.g. News International publishes both the *Sun* and *The Times*).

| Firm | Average circulation | Market share (%) |
|---|---|---|
| News International Newspapers Ltd | 3,744,104 | 34.3 |
| Associated Newspapers Ltd | 2,263,414 | 20.8 |
| Trinity Mirror plc | 2,138,901 | 19.6 |
| Express Newspapers Ltd | 1,328,901 | 12.2 |
| Telegraph Group Ltd | 859,258 | 7.9 |
| Guardian Newspapers Ltd | 317,534 | 2.9 |
| Independent Newspapers (UK) Ltd | 225,491 | 2.1 |
| Financial Times Ltd | 27,301 | 0.3 |

*Table 14.2 Concentration in the UK newspaper industry*

The three-firm concentration ratio is calculated as the sum of the market shares of the biggest three firms: that is, 34.3 + 20.8 + 19.6 = 74.7%.

Concentration ratios may be calculated on the basis of either shares in output or shares in employment. In the above example the calculation was on the basis of output (daily circulation). The two measures may give different results because the largest firms in an industry may be more capital-intensive in their production methods, which means that their share of employment in an industry will be smaller than their share of output. For the purposes of examining market structure, however, it is more helpful to base the analysis of market share on output.

This might seem an intuitively simple measure, but it is *too* simple to enable an evaluation of a market. For a start, it is important to define the market appropriately; for instance, in the above example are the *Financial Times* and the *Sun* really part of the same market?

There may be other difficulties too. Table 14.3 gives some hypothetical market shares for two markets. The five-firm concentration ratio is calculated as the sum of the market shares of the largest five firms. For markets A and B, the result is the same. In both cases the market is perceived to be highly concentrated, at 75%. However, the nature of likely interactions between the firms in these two markets is very different because the large relative size of Firm 1 in Market A is likely to give it substantially more market power than any of the largest five firms in Market B. Nonetheless, the concentration ratio is useful for giving a first impression of how the market is likely to function.

| Largest firms in rank order | Market A | Market B |
|---|---|---|
| Firm 1 | 68 | 15 |
| Firm 2 | 3 | 15 |
| Firm 3 | 2 | 15 |
| Firm 4 | 1 | 15 |
| Firm 5 | 1 | 15 |

*Table 14.3 Market shares (% of output)*

Figure 14.12 shows the five-firm concentration ratio for a number of industrial sectors in the UK. Concentration varies from 14.1% in tools and 15.6% in paper, printing and publishing to 96% in iron and steel and 99.2% in tobacco. In part, the difference between sectors might be expected to reflect the extent of economies of scale, and this makes sense for many of the industries shown.

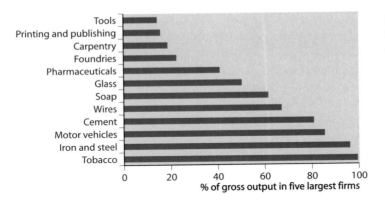

*Figure 14.12 Concentration in UK industry, 1992*

Source: *Census of Production 1992.*

## Summary

➤ Real-world markets do not often conform to the models of perfect competition or monopoly, which are extreme forms of market structure.

➤ It is important to be able to evaluate the degree of concentration in a market.

➤ While not a perfect measure, the concentration ratio is one way of doing this, by calculating the market share of the largest firms.

# Chapter 15
# Monopolistic competition and oligopoly

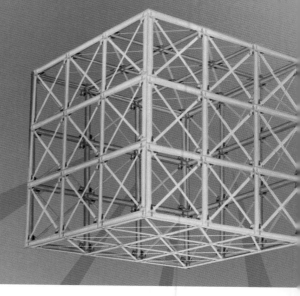

The previous chapter introduced the models of perfect competition and monopoly, and described them as being at the extreme ends of a spectrum of forms of market structure. In between those two extremes are other forms of market structure, which have some but not all of the characteristics of either perfect competition or monopoly. It is in this sense that there is a spectrum of structures. Attention in this chapter is focused on some of these intermediate forms of market structure, including a discussion of the sorts of pricing strategy that firms may adopt, and how they decide which to go for. This chapter also discusses ways in which firms may try to prevent new firms from joining a market, in terms of both pricing and non-price strategies. The theory of contestable markets completes the discussion.

## Learning outcomes

After studying this chapter, you should:

➤ be familiar with the range of market situations that exists between the extremes of perfect competition and monopoly
➤ understand the meaning of product differentiation and its role in the model of monopolistic competition
➤ understand the conditions under which price discrimination is possible and how this affects consumers and producers
➤ understand the notion of oligopoly and be familiar with approaches to modelling firm behaviour in an oligopoly market
➤ understand the benefits that firms may gain from forming a cartel — and the tensions that may result
➤ be aware of the possible pricing rules that can be adopted by firms
➤ understand the notion of cost-plus pricing, and how this may relate to profit maximisation
➤ be familiar with the idea of predatory pricing
➤ be aware of the concept of limit pricing
➤ understand the notion of contestable markets and its implications for firms' behaviour
➤ be familiar with other entry deterrence strategies

OCR Advanced Economics

# Monopolistic competition

If you consider the characteristics of the markets that you frequent on a regular basis, you will find that few of them display all of the characteristics associated with perfect competition. However, there may be some that show a few of these features. In particular, you will find some markets in which there appears to be intense competition among many buyers, but in which the products for sale are not identical. For example, think about restaurants. In many cities, you will find a wide range of restaurants, cafés and pubs that compete with each other for business, but do so by offering slightly different products.

*Indian restaurants operate in monopolistic competition*

The theory of **monopolistic competition** was devised by Edward Chamberlin, writing in the USA in the 1930s, and his name is often attached to the model, although Joan Robinson published her book on imperfect competition in the UK at the same time. The motivation for the analysis was to explain how markets worked when they were operating neither as monopolies nor under perfect competition.

The model describes a market in which there are many firms producing similar, but not identical, products: for example, package holidays, hairdressers and fast-food outlets. In the case of fast-food outlets, the high streets of many cities are characterised by large numbers of different types of takeaway — burgers, fish and chips, Indian, Chinese, fried chicken and so on.

## Model characteristics

Three important characteristics of the model of monopolistic competition distinguish this sort of market from others.

### *Product differentiation*

First, firms produce differentiated products, and face downward-sloping demand curves. In other words, each firm competes with the others by making its product slightly different. This allows the firms to build up brand loyalty among their regular customers, which gives them some influence over price. It is likely that firms will engage in advertising in order to maintain such brand loyalty, and heavy advertising is a common characteristic of a market operating under monopolistic competition.

Because other firms are producing similar goods, there are substitutes for each firm's product, which means that demand is relatively price elastic (although

this does not mean that it is never inelastic). However, it is certainly not perfectly price elastic, as was the case with perfect competition. These features — that the product is not homogeneous and demand is not perfectly price elastic — represent significant differences from the model of perfect competition.

### Freedom of entry

Second, there are no barriers to entry into the market. Firms are able to join the market if they observe that existing firms are making supernormal profits. New entrants will be looking for some way to differentiate their product slightly from the others — perhaps the next fast-food restaurant will be Nepalese, or Peruvian.

This characteristic distinguishes the market from the monopoly model, as does the existence of fairly close substitutes.

### Low concentration

Third, the concentration ratio in the industry tends to be relatively low, as there are many firms operating in the market. For this reason, a price change by one of the firms will have negligible effects on the demand for its rivals' products.

This characteristic means that the market is also different from an oligopoly market, where there are a few firms that interact strategically with each other.

### Overview

Taking these three characteristics together, it can be seen that a market of monopolistic competition has some of the characteristics of perfect competition and some features of monopoly; hence its name.

### Short-run equilibrium

Figure 15.1 represents short-run equilibrium under monopolistic competition. $D_s$ is the demand curve and $MR_s$ is the corresponding marginal revenue curve. $AC$ and $MC$ are the average and marginal cost curves for a representative firm in the industry. If the firm is aiming to maximise profits, it will choose the level of output such that $MR_s = MC$. This occurs at output $Q_s$, and the firm will then choose the price that clears the market at $P_s$.

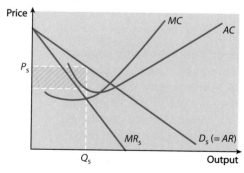

**Figure 15.1** *Short-run equilibrium under monopolistic competition*

This closely resembles the standard monopoly diagram that was introduced in Chapter 14. As with monopoly, a firm under monopolistic competition faces a downward-sloping demand curve, as already noted. The difference is that now it is assumed that there is free entry into the market under monopolistic competition, so that Figure 15.1 represents equilibrium only in the short run. This is because the firm shown in the figure is making supernormal profits, shown by the shaded area (which is $AR - AC$ multiplied by output).

## The importance of free entry

This is where the assumption of free entry into the market becomes important. In Figure 15.1 the supernormal profits being made by the representative firm will attract new firms into the market. The new firms will produce differentiated products, and this will affect the demand curve for the representative firm's product. In particular, the new firms will attract some customers away from this firm, so that its demand curve will tend to shift to the left. Its shape may also change as there are now more substitutes for the original product.

## Long-run equilibrium

This process will continue as long as firms in the market continue to make profits that attract new firms into the activity. It may be accelerated if firms are persuaded to spend money on advertising in an attempt to defend their market shares. The advertising may help to keep the demand curve downward sloping, but it will also affect the position of the average cost curve, by pushing up average cost at all levels of output.

Figure 15.2 shows the final position for the market. The typical firm is now operating in such a way that it maximises profits (by setting output such that $MR = MC$); at the same time, the average cost curve ($AC$) at this level of output is at a tangent to the demand curve. This means that $AC = AR$, and the firm is just making normal profit (i.e. is just covering opportunity cost). There is thus no further incentive for more firms to join the market. In Figure 15.2 this occurs when output is at $Q_1$ and price is set at $P_1$.

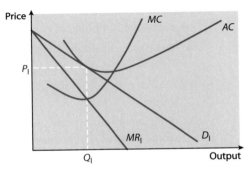

*Figure 15.2 Long-run equilibrium under monopolistic competition*

## Efficiency

One way of evaluating the market outcome under this model is to examine the consequences for productive and allocative efficiency. It is clear from Figure 15.2 that neither of these conditions will be met. The representative firm does not reach the minimum point on the long-run average cost curve, and so does not attain productive efficiency; furthermore, the price charged is above marginal cost, so allocative efficiency is not achieved.

## Evaluation

If the typical firm in the market is not fully exploiting the possible economies of scale that exist, it could be argued that product differentiation is damaging society's total welfare, in the sense that product differentiation allows firms to keep their demand curves downward sloping. In other words, too many different products are being produced. However, this argument could be countered by pointing out that consumers may enjoy having more freedom of choice. The very fact that they are prepared to pay a premium price for their chosen brand indicates that

they have some preference for it. For example, some people may be prepared to pay £50 to watch Chelsea although they could watch 90 minutes of football at Wimbledon AFC for £10.

Another crucial difference between monopolistic competition and perfect competition is that under monopolistic competition firms would like to sell more of their product at the going price, whereas under perfect competition they can sell as much as they like at the going price. This is because price under monopolistic competition is set above marginal cost. The use of advertising to attract more customers and to maintain consumer perception of product differences may be considered a problem with this market. It could be argued that excessive use of advertising to maintain product differentiation is wasteful, as it leads to higher average cost curves than needed. On the other hand, the need to compete in this way may result in less X-inefficiency than under a complacent monopolist.

## Exercise 15.1

Figure 15.3 shows a firm under monopolistic competition.

a  Identify the profit-maximising level of output.

b  At what price would the firm sell its product?

c  What supernormal profits (if any) would be made by the firm?

d  Is this a short-run or a long-run equilibrium? Explain your answer.

e  Describe the subsequent adjustment that might take place in the market (if any).

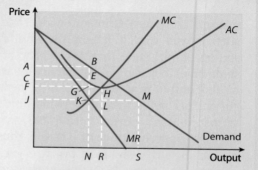

*Figure 15.3*
*A firm under monopolistic competition*

f  At what level of output would productive efficiency be achieved? (Assume that *AC* represents long-run average cost for this part of the question.)

## Summary

➤ The theory of monopolistic competition has its origins in the 1930s, when economists such as Edward Chamberlin and Joan Robinson were writing about markets that did not conform to the models of perfect competition and monopoly.

➤ The model describes a market where there are many firms producing similar, but not identical, products.

➤ By differentiating their product from those of other firms, it is possible for firms to maintain some influence over price.

➤ To do this, firms engage in advertising to build brand loyalty.

➤ There are no barriers to entry into the market, and concentration ratios are low.

➤ Firms in the short run may make supernormal profits.

➤ In response, new entrants join the market, shifting the demand curves of existing firms and affecting their shape.

➤ The process continues until supernormal profits have been competed away, and the typical firm has its average cost curve at a tangent to its demand curve.

➤ Neither productive nor allocative efficiency is achieved in long-run equilibrium.

➤ Consumers may benefit from the increased range of choice on offer in the market.

## Price discrimination

One thing that monopoly and monopolistic competition have in common is that, by setting price above marginal cost, a deadweight loss is imposed on society, with output lower than would be implied by the $P = MC$ outcome. This section examines a special case of monopoly, in which a monopolist will produce the level of output that is allocatively efficient.

Consider Figure 15.4. Suppose this market is operated by a monopolist that faces constant marginal cost $LMC$. (This is to simplify the analysis.) Chapter 14 showed that under perfect competition the market outcome would be a price $P^*$ and quantity $Q^*$. (See Figure 14.11 for an explanation of this if you need a reminder.) What would induce the monopolist to produce at $Q^*$?

One of the assumptions made throughout the analysis so far is that all consumers in a market get to pay the same price for the product. This leads to the notion of consumer surplus. In Figure 15.4, if the market were operating under perfect competition and all consumers were paying the same price, consumer surplus would be given by the area $AP^*B$. If the market were operated by a monopolist, also charging the same price to all buyers, then profits would be maximised where $MC = MR$: that is, at quantity $Q_m$ and price $P_m$.

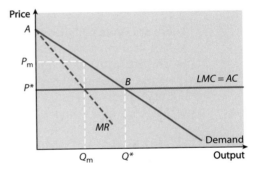

**Figure 15.4**
*Perfect price discrimination*

But suppose this assumption is now relaxed; suppose that the monopolist is able to charge a different price to each individual consumer. A monopolist is then able to charge each consumer a price that is equal to his or her willingness to pay for the good. In other words, the demand curve effectively becomes the marginal revenue curve, as it represents the amount that the monopolist will receive for each unit of the good. It will then maximise profits at point $B$ in Figure 15.4, where $MR$ (i.e. $AR$) is equal to $LMC$. The difference between this situation and that under perfect competition is that the area $AP^*B$ is no longer consumer surplus, but producer surplus: that is, the monopolist's profits. The monopolist has hijacked the whole of the original consumer surplus as its profits.

From society's point of view, total welfare is the same as it is under perfect competition (but more than under monopoly without discrimination). However, now there has been a redistribution, from consumers to the monopoly — and presumably to the shareholders of the firm. This situation is known as **perfect price discrimination** or **first-degree price discrimination**.

> **Key term**
>
> **perfect/first-degree price discrimination:** situation arising in a market whereby a monopoly firm is able to charge each consumer a different price

Perfect price discrimination is fairly rare in the real world, although it might be said to exist in the world of art or fashion, where customers may commission a painting, sculpture or item of designer jewellery and the price is a matter of negotiation between the buyer and supplier.

However, there are situations in which partial price discrimination is possible. For example, students or old-age pensioners may get discounted bus fares, the young and/or old may get cheaper access to sporting events or theatres etc. In these instances, individual consumers are paying different prices for what is in fact the same product.

There are three conditions under which a firm may be able to price discriminate:
➤ The firm must have market power.
➤ The firm must have information about consumers and their willingness to pay — and there must be identifiable differences between consumers (or groups of consumers).
➤ The consumers must have limited ability to resell the product.

### Market power
Clearly, price discrimination is not possible in a perfectly competitive market, where no seller has the power to charge other than the going market price. So price discrimination can take place only where firms have some ability to vary the price.

### Information
From the firm's point of view, it needs to be able to identify different groups of consumers with different willingness to pay. What makes price discrimination profitable for firms is that different consumers display different sensitivities to price: that is, they have different price elasticities of demand.

> **Key term**
>
> **arbitrage:** a process by which prices in two market segments will be equalised by a process of purchase and resale by market participants

### Ability to resell
If consumers could resell the product easily, then price discrimination would not be possible, as consumers would engage in **arbitrage**. In other words, the group of consumers who qualified for the low price could buy up the product and then turn a profit by reselling to consumers in the other segment(s) of the market. This would mean that the firm would no longer be able to sell at the high price, and would no longer try to discriminate in pricing.

In the case of student discounts and old-age concessions, the firm can identify particular groups of consumers; and such 'products' as bus journeys or dental treatment cannot be resold. But why should a firm undertake this practice?

The simple answer is that, by undertaking price discrimination, the firm is able to increase its profits. This is shown in Figure 15.5, which separates two distinct groups of consumers with differing demand curves. Thus, panel (a) shows Market A and panel (b) shows Market B, with the combined demand curve being shown in panel (c), which also shows the firm's marginal cost curve.

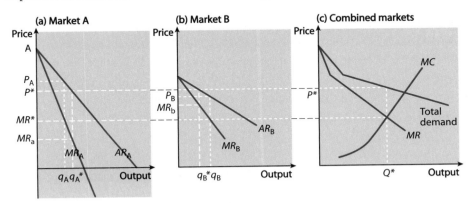

**Figure 15.5** *A price-discriminating monopolist*

If a firm has to charge the same price to all consumers, it sets marginal revenue in the combined market equal to marginal cost, and produces $Q^*$ output, to be sold at a price of $P^*$. This maximises profits when all consumers pay the same price. The firm sells $q_A^*$ in Market A, and $q_B^*$ in Market B.

However, if you look at panels (a) and (b), you will see that marginal revenue in Market A is much lower (at $MR_a$) than that in Market B (at $MR_b$). It is this differ-ence in marginal revenue that opens up a profit-increasing opportunity for the firm. By taking sales away from Market A and selling more in Market B, the firm gains more extra revenue in B than it loses in A. This increases its profit. The optimal position for the firm is where marginal revenue is equalised in the two markets. In Figure 15.5 the firm sells $q_A$ in Market A at the higher price of $P_A$. In Market B sales increase to $q_B$ with price falling to $P_B$. Notice that in both situations the amounts sold in the two sub-markets sum to $Q^*$.

The consumers in Market B seem to do quite well by this practice, as they can now consume more of the good. Indeed, it is possible that with no discrimin-ation the price would be so high that they would not be able to consume the good at all.

An extreme form of price discrimination was used by NAPP Pharmaceutical Holdings, as a result of which the firm was fined £3.2 million by the Office of Fair Trading. NAPP sold sustained-release morphine tablets and capsules in the UK. These are drugs administered to patients with incurable cancer. NAPP realised that

the market was segmented. The drugs were sold partly to the National Health Service for use in hospitals, but were also prescribed by GPs. As these patients were terminally ill, they tended to spend a relatively short time in hospital before being sent home. NAPP realised that GPs tended to prescribe the same drugs as the patients had received in hospital. It therefore reduced its price to hospitals by 90%, thereby forcing all competitors out of the market and gaining a monopoly in that market segment. It was then able to increase the price of these drugs prescribed through GPs, and so maximise profits. The OFT investigated the firm, fined it and instructed it to stop its actions, thus saving the NHS £2 million per year.

## Exercise 15.2

In which of the following products might price discrimination be possible? Explain your answers.

a hairdressing

b peak and off-peak rail travel

c apples

d air tickets

e newspapers

f plastic surgery

g beer

## Summary

➤ In some markets a monopolist may be able to engage in price discrimination by selling its product at different prices to different consumers or groups of consumers.

➤ This enables the firm to increase its profits by absorbing some or all of the consumer surplus.

➤ Under first-degree price discrimination, the firm is able to charge a different price to each customer and absorb all consumer surplus.

➤ The firm can practise price discrimination only where it has market power, where consumers have differing elasticities of demand for the product, and where consumers have limited ability to resell the product.

## Oligopoly

A number of markets seem to be dominated by relatively few firms — think of commercial banking in the UK, cinemas or the newspaper industry. A market with just a few sellers is known as an **oligopoly** market. An important characteristic of such markets is that when making economic decisions each firm must take account of its rivals' behaviour and reactions. The firms are therefore interdependent.

An important characteristic of oligopoly is that each firm has to act strategically, both in reacting to rival firms' decisions and in trying to anticipate their future actions and reactions.

 **Key** *term*

**oligopoly:** a market with a few sellers, in which each firm must take account of the behaviour and likely behaviour of rival firms in the industry

*High-street banking is an oligopoly market*

There are many different ways in which a firm may take such strategic decisions, and this means that there are many ways in which an oligopoly market can be modelled, depending on how the firms are behaving. This chapter reviews just a few such models.

Oligopolies may come about for many reasons, but perhaps the most convincing concerns economies of scale. An oligopoly is likely to develop in a market where there are some economies of scale — economies that are not substantial enough to require a natural monopoly, but which are large enough to make it difficult for too many firms to operate at minimum efficient scale.

Within an oligopoly market, firms may adopt rivalrous behaviour or they may choose to cooperate with each other. The two attitudes have implications for how markets operate. Cooperation will tend to take the market towards the monopoly end of the spectrum, whereas non-cooperation will take it towards the competitive end. In either scenario, it is likely that the market outcome will be somewhere between the two extremes.

### The kinked demand curve model

One model of oligopoly revolves around how a firm *perceives* its demand curve. This is called the kinked demand curve model, and was developed by Paul Sweezy in the USA in the 1930s.

The model relates to an oligopoly in which firms try to anticipate the reactions of rivals to their actions. One problem that arises is that a firm cannot readily observe its demand curve with any degree of certainty, so it must form expectations about how consumers will react to a price change.

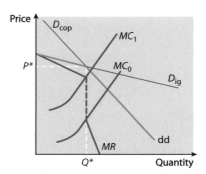

*Figure 15.6*
*The kinked demand curve*

Figure 15.6 shows how this works. Suppose the price is currently set at $P^*$; the firm is selling $Q^*$ and is trying to decide whether to alter price. The problem is that it knows for sure about only one point on the demand curve: that is, when price is $P^*$, the firm sells $Q^*$.

However, the firm is aware that the degree of sensitivity to its price change will depend upon whether or not the other firms in the market will follow its lead. In other words, if its rivals ignore the firm's price change, there will be more sensitivity to this change than if they all follow suit.

Figure 15.6 shows the two extreme possibilities for the demand curve which the firm perceives that it faces. If other firms *ignore* its action, $D_{ig}$ will be the relevant demand curve, which is relatively elastic. On the other hand, if the other firms *copy* the firm's moves, $D_{cop}$ will be the relevant demand curve.

The question then is: under what conditions will the other firms copy the price change, and when will they not? The firm may imagine that if it raises price, there is little likelihood that its rivals will copy. After all, this is a non-threatening move that gives market share to the other firms. So for a price *increase*, $D_{ig}$ is the relevant section.

On the other hand, a price reduction is likely to be seen by the rivals as a threatening move, and they are likely to copy in order to preserve their market positions. For a price *decrease*, then, $D_{cop}$ is relevant.

Putting these together, the firm perceives that it faces a kinked demand curve (*dd*). Furthermore, if the marginal revenue curve is added to the picture, it is seen to have a discontinuity at the kink. It thus transpires that $Q^*$ is the profit-maximising level of output under a wide range of cost conditions from $MC_0$ to $MC_1$; so, even in the face of a change in marginal costs, the firm will not alter its behaviour.

Thus, the model predicts that if the firm perceives its demand curve to be of this shape, it has a strong incentive to do nothing, even in the face of changes in costs. However, it all depends upon the firm's perceptions. If there is a general increase in costs that affects all producers, this may affect the firm's perception of rival reaction, and thus encourage it to raise price. If other firms are reading the market in the same way, they are likely to follow suit. Notice that this model does not explain how the price reaches $P^*$ in the first place.

### Game theory

A more recent development in the economic theory of the firm has been in the application of **game theory**. This began as a branch of mathematics, but it became apparent that it had wide applications in explaining the behaviour of firms in an oligopoly.

**Key term**

**game theory:** a method of modelling the strategic interaction between firms in an oligopoly

Game theory itself has a long history, with some writers tracing it back to correspondence between Pascal and Fermat in the mid-seventeenth century. Early applications in economics were by Antoine

Augustin Cournot in 1838, Francis Edgeworth in 1881 and J. Bertrand in 1883, but the key publication was the book by John von Neumann and Oskar Morgenstern, *Theory of Games and Economic Behaviour*, in 1944. Other famous names in game theory include John Nash (played by Russell Crowe in the film *A Beautiful Mind*), John Harsanyi and Reinhard Selton, who shared the 1994 Nobel prize for their work in this area.

Almost certainly, the most famous game is the **prisoners' dilemma**, introduced in a lecture by Albert Tucker (who taught John Nash at Princeton) in 1950. This simple example of game theory turns out to have a multitude of helpful applications in economics.

Two prisoners, Al Fresco and Des Jardins, are being interrogated about a major crime, and the police know that at least one of the prisoners is guilty. The two are kept in separate cells and cannot communicate with each other. The police have enough evidence to convict them of a minor offence, but not enough to convict them of the major one.

Each prisoner is offered a deal. If he turns state's evidence and provides evidence to convict the other prisoner, he will get off — *unless* the other prisoner also confesses. If both refuse to deal, they will just be charged with the minor offence. Table 15.1 summarises the sentences that each will receive in the various circumstances.

*Russell Crowe playing the part of mathematician and game theorist John Nash in* A Beautiful Mind

**Key term**

**prisoners' dilemma:** an example of game theory with a range of applications in oligopoly theory

|  |  | Des | | | |
|---|---|---|---|---|---|
|  |  | Confess | | Refuse | |
| Al | Confess | 10 | 10 | 0 | 15 |
|  | Refuse | 15 | 0 | 5 | 5 |

*Table 15.1*
*The prisoners' dilemma: possible outcomes (years in jail)*

In each case, Al's sentence (in years) is shown in orange and Des's in blue. In terms of the entries in the table, if both Al and Des refuse to deal, they will be convicted of the minor offence, and each will go down for 5 years. However, if Al confesses and Des refuses to deal, Al will get off completely free, and Des will take the full rap of 15 years. If Des confesses and Al refuses, the reverse happens. However, if both confess, they will each get 10 years.

Think about this situation from Al's point of view, remembering that the prisoners cannot communicate, so Al does not know what Des will choose to do and vice versa. You can see from Table 15.1 that, whatever Des chooses to do, Al will be better off confessing. If Des confesses, Al is better off confessing also, going down for 10 years instead of 15; if Des refuses, Al is still better off confessing, going free instead of getting a 5-year term. John Nash referred to such a situation as a **dominant strategy**.

The dilemma is, of course, symmetric, so for Des too the dominant strategy is to confess. The inevitable result is that, if both prisoners are selfish, they will both confess – and both will then get 10 years in jail. If they had both refused to deal, they would *both* have been better off; but this is too risky a strategy for either of them to adopt. A refusal to deal might have led to 15 years in jail.

> **Key term**
>
> **dominant strategy:** a situation in game theory where a player's best strategy is independent of those chosen by others

What has this to do with economics? Think about the market for DIY products. Suppose there are two firms (Diamond Tools and Better Spades) operating in a duopoly market (i.e. a market with only two firms). Each firm has a choice of producing 'high' output or 'low' output. The profit made by one firm depends upon two things: its own output and the output of the other firm.

Table 15.2 shows the range of possible outcomes for a particular time period. Consider Diamond Tools: if it chooses 'low' when Better Spades also chooses 'low', it will make £2 million profit (and so will Better Spades); but if Diamond Tools chooses 'low' when Better Spades chooses 'high', Diamond Tools will make zero profits and Better Spades will make £3 million.

|  |  | Better Spades | | | |
|---|---|---|---|---|---|
|  |  | High | | Low | |
| Diamond | High | 1 | 1 | 3 | 0 |
| Tools | Low | 0 | 3 | 2 | 2 |

*Table 15.2 Diamond Tools and Better Spades: possible outcomes (profits in £m)*

The situation that maximises joint profits is for both firms to produce low; but suppose you were taking decisions for Diamond Tools — what would you choose?

If Better Spades produces 'low', you will maximise profits by producing 'high', whereas if Better Spades produces 'high', you will still maximise profits by producing high! So Diamond Tools has a dominant strategy to produce high — it is the profit-maximising action whatever Better Spades does, even though it means that joint profits will be lower.

> **Key term**
>
> **Nash equilibrium:** situation occurring within a game when each player's chosen strategy maximises payoffs given the other player's choice, so no player has an incentive to alter behaviour

Given that the table is symmetric, Better Spades faces the same decision process, and also has a dominant strategy to choose high, so they always end up in the northwest corner of the table, even though southeast would be better for each of them. Furthermore, after they have made their choices and seen what the other has chosen, each firm feels justified by its actions, and thinks that it took the right decision, given the rival's move. This is known as a **Nash equilibrium**, which has the characteristic that neither firm needs to amend its behaviour in any future period. This model can be used to investigate a wide range of decisions that firms need to take strategically.

## Exercise 15.3

Suppose there are two cinemas, X and Y, operating in a town; you are taking decisions for Firm X. You cannot communicate with the other firm; both firms are considering only the next period. Each firm is choosing whether to set price 'high' or 'low'. Your expectation is that the payoffs (in terms of profits) to the two firms are as shown in Table 15.3 (Firm X in brown, Firm Y in blue):

| | | Firm Y chooses: | | | |
|---|---|---|---|---|---|
| | | High price | | Low price | |
| Firm X | High price | 0 | 10 | 1 | 15 |
| chooses: | Low price | 15 | 1 | 4 | 4 |

*Table 15.3  Cinemas X and Y: possible outcomes*

**a**  If Firm Y sets price high, what strategy maximises profits for Firm X?

**b**  If Firm Y sets price low, what strategy maximises profits for Firm X?

**c**  So what strategy will Firm X adopt?

**d**  What is the market outcome?

**e**  What outcome would maximise the firms' joint profit?

**f**  How might this outcome be achieved?

**g**  Would the outcome be different if the game were played over repeated periods?

### Cooperative games and cartels

Look back at the prisoners' dilemma game in Table 15.2. It is clear that the requirement that the firms are unable to communicate with each other is a serious impediment from the firms' point of view. If both firms could agree to produce 'low', they would maximise their joint profits, but they will not risk this strategy if they cannot communicate.

If they could join together in a **cartel**, the two firms could come to an agreement to adopt the low–low strategy. However, if they were to agree to this, each firm would have a strong incentive to cheat because, if each now knew that the other firm was going to produce low, they would also know that they could produce high and dominate the market — at least, given the payoffs in the table.

**Key term**

**cartel:** an agreement between firms on price and output with the intention of maximising their joint profits

This is a common feature of cartels. Collusion can bring high joint profits, but there is always the temptation for each of the member-firms to cheat and try to sneak some additional market share at the expense of the other firms in the cartel.

There is another downside to the formation of a cartel. In most countries around the world (with one or two exceptions, such as Hong Kong) they are illegal. For example, in the UK the operation of a cartel is illegal under the UK Competition

Act, under which the Office of Fair Trading is empowered to fine firms up to 10% of their turnover for each year the cartel is found to have been in operation.

This means that overt collusion is rare. The most famous example is not between firms but between nations, in the form of the Organisation of Petroleum Exporting Countries (OPEC), which over a long period of time has operated a cartel to control the price of oil.

Some conditions may favour the formation of cartels — or at least, some form of collusion between firms. The most important of these is the ability of each of the firms involved to monitor the actions of the other firms, and so ensure that they are keeping to the agreement.

### Collusion in practice

Although cartels are illegal, the potential gains from collusion may tempt firms to find ways of working together. In some cases, firms have joined together in rather loose strategic alliances, in which they may work together on part of their business, perhaps in undertaking joint research and development or technology swaps.

For example, in 2000 General Motors (GM) and Fiat took an equity stake in each other's companies, with GM wanting to expand in Europe and needing to find out more about the technology of making smaller cars. Such alliances have not always been a success, and in the GM–Fiat case GM and Fiat separated in 2005.

The airline market is another sector where strategic alliances have been important, with the Star Alliance and the One World Alliance carving up the long-haul routes between them. Such alliances offer benefits to passengers, who can get access to a wider range of destinations and business-class lounges and frequent-flier rewards, and to the airlines, which can economise on airport facilities by pooling their resources. However, the net effect is to reduce competition, and the regulators have interfered with some suggested alliances, such as

*The Star Alliance reduces competition*

that between British Airways and American Airlines in 2001, which was investigated by regulators on both sides of the Atlantic. The conditions under which the alliance would have been permitted were such that British Airways withdrew the proposal.

Alternatively, firms may look for **tacit collusion**, in which the firms in a market observe each other's behaviour very closely and refrain from competing on price, even if they do not actually communicate with each other. Such collusion may emerge gradually over time in a market, as the firms become accustomed to market conditions and to each other's behaviour.

**Key** *term*

**tacit collusion:** situation occurring when firms refrain from competing on price, but without communication or formal agreement between them

One way in which this may happen is through some form of *price leadership*. If one firm is a dominant producer in a market, then it may take the lead in setting the price, with the other firms following its example. It has been suggested that the OPEC cartel operated according to this model in some periods, with Saudi Arabia acting as the dominant country.

An alternative is *barometric price leadership*, in which one firm tries out a price increase and then waits to see whether other firms follow. If they do, a new higher price has been reached without the need for overt discussions between the firms. On the other hand, if the other firms do not feel the time is right for the change, they will keep their prices steady and the first firm will drop back into line or else lose market share. The initiating firm need not be the same one in each round. It has been argued that the domestic air travel market in the USA has operated in this way on some internal routes. The practice is facilitated by the ease with which prices can be checked via computerised ticketing systems, so that each firm knows what the other firms are doing.

The frequency of anti-cartel cases brought by regulators in recent years suggests that firms continue to be tempted by the gains from collusion. The operation of a cartel is now a criminal act in the UK, as it has been in the USA for some time.

## Exercise 15.4

For each of the following markets, identify the model that would most closely describe it (e.g. perfect competition, monopoly, monopolistic competition or oligopoly):

**a** a large number of firms selling branded varieties of toothpaste

**b** a sole supplier of postal services

**c** a large number of farmers producing cauliflowers, sold at a common price

**d** a situation in which a few large banks supply most of the market for retail banking services

**e** a sole supplier of rail transport

## Summary

➤ An oligopoly is a market with a few sellers, each of which takes strategic decisions based on likely rival actions and reactions.

➤ Because there are many ways in which firms may interact, there is no single way of modelling an oligopoly market.

➤ One model is the kinked demand curve model, which argues that firms' perceptions of the demand curve for their products is based on their views about whether or not rival firms will react to their own actions.

➤ This suggests that price is likely to remain stable over a wide range of market conditions.

➤ Game theory is a more recent and more flexible way of modelling interactions between firms.

➤ The prisoners' dilemma can demonstrate the potential benefits of collusion, but also shows that in some market situations each firm may have a dominant strategy to move the market away from the joint profit-maximising position.

➤ If firms could join together in a cartel, they could indeed maximise their joint profits — but there would still be a temptation for firms to cheat, and try to steal market share. Such action would break up the cartel, and move the market away from the joint profit-maximising position.

➤ However, cartels are illegal in most societies.

➤ Firms may thus look for covert ways of colluding in a market: for example, through some form of price leadership.

## Pricing strategies and contestable markets

### Pricing rules

In the analysis of market structure, it was assumed that firms set out to maximise profits. However, Chapter 4 pointed out that sometimes they may set out to achieve other objectives. The price of a firm's product is a key strategic variable that must be manipulated in order to attain whatever objective the firm wishes to achieve.

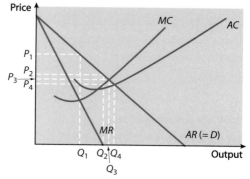

*Figure 15.7*
*Possible pricing rules*

Figure 15.7 illustrates the variety of pricing rules that are possible. The figure shows a firm operating under a form of market structure that is not perfect competition — because the firm faces a downward-sloping demand curve for its product shown by $AR (= D)$.

### *Profit maximisation*
If the firm chooses to maximise profits, it will choose output such that marginal revenue is equal to marginal cost, and will then set the price to clear the market. In terms of the figure, it will set output at $Q_1$ and price at $P_1$.

### Revenue maximisation

The economist William Baumol argued that, if there is a divorce of ownership from control in the organisation of a firm, whereby the shareholders have delegated day-to-day decision making to managers (a principal–agent situation), the managers may find themselves with some freedom to pursue other objectives, such as revenue maximisation. A revenue maximiser in Figure 15.7 would choose to produce at the output level at which marginal revenue is zero. This occurs at $Q_2$ in the figure, with the price set at $P_2$.

### Sales maximisation

If instead managers set out to maximise the volume of sales subject to covering opportunity cost, they will choose to set output at a level such that price equals average cost, which will clear the market. In Figure 15.7 this happens at $Q_4$ (with price at $P_4$).

### Allocative efficiency

It has been argued that allocative efficiency in an individual market occurs at the point where price is equal to marginal cost. In Figure 15.7 this is at $Q_3$ (with price $P_3$). However, from the firm's perspective there is no obvious reason why this should become an objective of the firm, as it confers no particular advantage.

---

## Exercise 15.5

For each of the following situations, identify the pricing rule most appropriate to achieve the firm's objectives, and comment on the implications that this has for efficiency.

a  A firm producing DVD recorders tries to achieve as high a market share as possible, measured in value terms.

b  A local gymnasium tries to make as high a surplus over costs as can be achieved.

c  A national newspaper sets out to maximise circulation (subject to covering its costs), knowing that this will affect advertising revenues.

d  A garden centre producing Christmas trees finds that it cannot influence the price of its product.

---

### Predatory pricing

Perhaps the most common context in which price wars have broken out is where an existing firm or firms have reacted to defend the market against the entry of new firms.

One example occurred in 1996, in the early years of easyJet, the low-cost air carrier, which was then trying to become established. When easyJet started flying the London–Amsterdam route, charging its now well-known low prices, the incumbent firm (KLM) reacted very aggressively, driving its price down to a level just below

 **Key term**

**predatory pricing:** an anti-competitive strategy in which a firm sets price below average variable cost in an attempt to force a rival or rivals out of the market and achieve market dominance

that of easyJet. The response from easyJet was to launch legal action against KLM, claiming it was using unfair market tactics.

So-called predatory pricing is illegal under English, Dutch and EU law. It should be noted that, in order to declare an action illegal, it is necessary to define that action very carefully — otherwise it will not be possible to prove the case in the courts. In the case of predatory pricing, the legal definition is based on economic analysis.

Remember that if a firm fails to cover average variable costs, its strategy should be to close down immediately, as it would be better off doing so. The courts have backed this theory, and state that a pricing strategy should be interpreted as being predatory if the price is set below average variable costs, as the only motive for remaining in business while making such losses must be to drive competitors out of business and achieve market dominance. This is known as the *Areeda–Turner principle* (after the case in which it was first argued in the USA).

On the face of it, consumers have much to gain from such strategies through the resulting lower prices. However, a predator that is successful in driving out the opposition is likely to recoup its losses by putting prices back up to profit-maximising levels thereafter, so the benefit to consumers is short lived.

Having said that, the low-cost airlines survived the attempts of the established airlines to hold on to their market shares. Indeed, in the post-9/11 period, which was a tough one for the airlines for obvious reasons, the low-cost airlines flourished while the more conventional established airlines went through a very difficult period indeed.

In some cases, the very threat of predatory pricing may be sufficient to deter entry by new firms, if the threat is a credible one. In other words, the existing firms need to convince potential entrants that they, the existing firms, will find it in their best interests to fight a price war, otherwise the entrants will not believe the threat. The existing firms could do this by making it known that they have surplus capacity, so that they would be able to increase output very quickly in order to drive down the price.

Whether entry will be deterred by such means may depend in part on the characteristics of the potential entrant. After all, a new firm may reckon that, if the existing firm finds it worth sacrificing profits in the short run, the rewards of dominating the market must be worth fighting for. It may therefore decide to sacrifice short-term profit in order to enter the market — especially if it is diversifying from other markets and has resources at its disposal. The winner will then be the firm that can last the longest; but, clearly, this is potentially very damaging for all concerned.

## Exercise 15.6

Discuss the extent to which consumers benefit from a price war.

## Limit pricing

An associated but less extreme strategy is limit pricing. This assumes that the incumbent firm has some sort of cost advantage over potential entrants: for example, economies of scale.

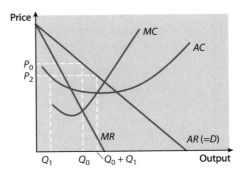

Figure 15.8 shows a firm facing a downward-sloping demand curve, and thus having some influence over the price of its product. If the firm is maximising profits, it is setting output at $Q_0$ and price at $P_0$. As average revenue is comfortably above average cost at this price, the firm is making healthy supernormal profits.

*Figure 15.8 Limit pricing*

Suppose that the natural barriers to entry in this industry are weak. The supernormal profits will be attractive to potential entrants. Given the cost conditions, the incumbent firm is enjoying the benefit of economies of scale, although producing below the minimum efficient scale.

If a new firm joins the market, producing on a relatively small scale, say at $Q_1$, the impact on the market can be analysed as follows. The immediate effect is on price, as now the amount $Q_0 + Q_1$ is being produced, pushing price down to $P_2$. The new firm (producing $Q_1$) is just covering average cost, so is making normal profits and feeling justified in having joined the market. The original firm is still making supernormal profits, but at a lower level than before. The entry of the new firm has competed away part of the original firm's supernormal profits.

One way in which the existing firm could have guarded against entry is by charging a lower price than $P_0$ to begin with. For example, if it had set output at $Q_0 + Q_1$ and price at $P_2$, then a new entrant joining the market would push the price down to a level below $P_2$, and without the benefit of economies of scale would make losses and exit the market. In any case, if the existing firm has been in the market for some time, it will have gone through a process of learning by doing, and therefore will have a lower average cost curve than the potential entrant. This makes it more likely that limit pricing can be used.

Thus, by setting a price below the profit-maximising level, the original firm is able to maintain its market position in the longer run. This could be a reason for avoiding making too high a level of supernormal profits in the short run, in order to make profits in the longer term.

Notice that such a strategy need not be carried out by a monopolist, but could also occur in an oligopoly, where existing firms may jointly seek to protect their market against potential entry.

## Contestable markets

It has been argued that in some markets, in order to prevent the entry of new firms, the existing firm would have to charge such a low price that it would be unable to reap any supernormal profits at all.

This theory was developed by William Baumol and is known as the theory of contestable markets. It was in recognition of this theory that the monopoly model in Chapter 14 included the assumption that there must be no substitutes for the good, *either actual or potential.*

For a market to be contestable, it must have no barriers to entry or exit and no sunk costs. *Sunk costs* refer to costs that a firm incurs in setting up a business and which cannot be recovered if the firm exits the market. Furthermore, new firms in the market must have no competitive disadvantage compared with the incumbent firm(s): in other words, they must have access to the same technology, and there must be no significant learning-by-doing effects. Entry and exit must be rapid.

Under these conditions, the incumbent firm cannot set a price that is higher than average cost because, as soon as it does, it will open up the possibility of *hit-and-run entry* by new firms, which can enter the market and compete away the supernormal profits.

Consider Figure 15.9, which shows a monopoly firm in a market. The argument is that, if the monopolist charges the profit-maximising price, then in a contestable market the firm will be vulnerable to hit-and-run entry – a firm could come into the market, take some of the supernormal profits, then exit again. The only way the monopolist can avoid this happening is to set price equal to average cost, so that there are no supernormal profits to act as an incentive for entry.

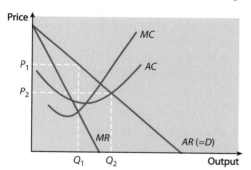

**Figure 15.9**
*Contestability*

On the face of it, the conditions for contestability sound pretty stringent. In particular, the firm in Figure 15.9 enjoys some economies of scale, so you would think that some sunk costs had been incurred.

However, suppose a firm has a monopoly on a domestic air route between two destinations. An airline with surplus capacity (i.e. a spare aircraft sitting in a hangar) could enter this route and exit again without incurring sunk costs in response to profits being made by the incumbent firm. This is an example of how contestability may limit the ability of the incumbent firm to use its market power.

Notice in this example that, although the firm only makes normal profits, neither productive nor allocative efficiency is achieved.

A moot point is whether the threat of entry will in fact persuade firms that they cannot set a price above average cost. Perhaps the firms can risk making some profit above normal profits and then respond to entry very aggressively if and when it happens. After all, it is difficult to think of an example in which there are absolutely no sunk costs. Almost any business is going to have to advertise in order to find customers, and such advertising expenditure cannot be recovered.

### Other entry deterrence strategies

Pricing is not the only strategy that firms adopt in order to deter entry by new firms. Another approach that has been used over a wide range of economic activities is to raise the fixed costs of being in the industry.

#### *Advertising and publicity*

Advertising can be regarded as a component of fixed costs, because expenditure on it does not vary directly with the volume of output. If the firms in an industry typically spend heavily on advertising, it will be more difficult for new firms to become established, as they too will need to advertise widely in order to attract customers.

Similarly, firms may spend heavily on achieving a well-known brand image that will ensure customer loyalty. Hence they may invest a lot in the design and packaging of their merchandise. One example was the high-profile television campaign run by Sunny Delight when trying to gain entry into the soft drinks market in the early part of the twenty-first century.

Notice that such costs are also sunk costs, and cannot be recovered if the new firm fails to gain a foothold. It has sometimes been suggested that the cost of excessive advertising should be included in calculations of the social cost of monopoly.

*Advertising to gain customer loyalty can be expensive*

#### *Research and development*

A characteristic of some industries is the heavy expenditure undertaken on research and development (R&D). A prominent example is the pharmaceutical industry, which spends large amounts on researching new drugs — and new cosmetics.

This is another component of fixed costs, as it does not vary with the volume of production. Again, new firms wanting to break into the market know that they will need to invest heavily in R&D if they are going to keep up with the new and better drugs and cosmetics always coming on to the market.

## Summary

➤ There are many pricing rules that a firm may choose to adopt, depending on the objectives it wishes to achieve.

➤ Although price wars are expected to be damaging for the firms involved, they do break out from time to time.

➤ This may occur when firms wish to increase their market shares, or when existing firms wish to deter the entry of new firms into the market.

➤ Predatory pricing is an extreme strategy that forces all firms to endure losses. It is normally invoked in an attempt to eliminate a competitor, and is illegal in many countries.

➤ Limit pricing occurs when a firm or firms choose to set price below the profit-maximising level in order to prevent entry. The limit price is the highest price that an existing firm can set without allowing entry.

➤ In some cases the limit price may enable the incumbent firm or firms to make only normal profit. Such a market is said to be contestable.

➤ Contestability requires that there are no barriers to entry or exit and no sunk costs — and that the incumbent firm(s) have no cost advantage over hit-and-run entrants.

➤ Firms have adopted other strategies designed to deter entry, such as using advertising or R&D spending to raise the cost of entry by adding to required fixed costs.

## Exercise 15.7

For each of the following, explain under what circumstances the action of the firm constitutes a barrier to entry and discuss whether there is a strategic element to it, or whether it might be regarded as a 'natural' or 'innocent' barrier.

a  A firm takes advantage of economies of scale to reduce its average costs of production.

b  A firm holds a patent on the sale of a product.

c  A firm engages in widespread advertising of its product.

d  A firm installs surplus capacity relative to normal production levels.

e  A firm produces a range of very similar products under different brand names.

f  A firm chooses not to set price at the profit-maximising level.

g  A firm spends extensively on research and development in order to produce a better product.

OCR Advanced Economics

# The economics of work and leisure

# Part 5

# Chapter 16
# Earnings, employment and leisure

*This part of the book considers the economics of work and leisure. It examines the way that labour markets operate, which entails exploring the demand for and supply of labour. In addition, there is discussion of how economic analysis can be applied in order to understand the operation of the leisure industry, which has become an increasingly important sector in the economy. The study of the leisure industry will require some analysis of the markets that have been established to provide leisure opportunities, and the extent to which these operate to ensure an efficient allocation of resources. The present chapter introduces these topics, and provides some background to the labour market and the leisure industry in the UK.*

## Learning outcomes

After studying this chapter, you should:
➤ be aware of the structure of UK employment and earnings
➤ be able to compare the UK labour market situation with that of other countries in the EU and countries elsewhere
➤ be familiar with movements in labour productivity and hence unit labour costs in the UK and elsewhere
➤ understand the distinction between work and leisure and why this is important
➤ appreciate the significance of economic analysis in decisions related to the allocation of time
➤ be familiar with broad trends in leisure industries

## Work and leisure

At first glance, you may wonder why work and leisure should be linked together in this way. However, from an economic point of view, there are close connections between the two things. When an individual takes decisions about participation in the labour force, this also constitutes a decision about leisure. If I decide to occupy my time in writing an economics textbook (which most people would classify as 'work'), I forgo the opportunity of watching television or doing some

gardening. So my leisure time can be regarded as the opportunity cost of writing this textbook. Similarly, if you decide to give up your Saturdays in order to work at a local supermarket or department store, you forgo the chance of going to a football match, or going out with your friends.

In fact, the connections between work and leisure go beyond this simple notion of opportunity cost because another way of looking at this decision is that people work in order to be able to earn the income needed to enjoy their leisure time. The wage rate for an hour's work can be seen as the opportunity cost of an hour's leisure time, but wages are also needed to purchase the means with which to enjoy leisure time. These ideas will be explored in the following discussion, but first it is important to find out about these two important markets — the labour market and the market for leisure.

## Employment and earnings in the UK

The way in which people earn a living is an important aspect of any economy. Indeed, it is a matter of concern to everyone at an individual level, especially those soon to join the labour force.

Looking at the overall situation for labour supply in the UK, in mid-2004 just over 62% of people aged 16 and above were **economically active**. This means that they were in employment, self-employed or unemployed. Unemployment may arise for a number of reasons. It may reflect the fact that some people may not be prepared to accept jobs at the going wage rate. To the extent that this is so, such people may be regarded as being part of *voluntary unemployment.* However, there may also be *involuntary unemployment* — that is, people who would like to work but who are unable to find employment. Chapter 19 examines whether such unemployment arises from market failure in the labour market.

**Key terms**

**economically active:** active in the labour force, including the employed, the self-employed and the unemployed

**ILO unemployment rate:** measure of the percentage of the workforce who are without jobs but are available for work, willing to work and looking for work

The official definition of unemployment was introduced in Chapter 9. In the UK, unemployment is measured by reference to the **ILO unemployment rate**, the data for which are collected in the *Labour Force Survey*.

The overall percentage of the economically active does not vary much from year to year. Since 1992 it has only varied between 62.4% and 63.1%. There has been a slight increase in recent years, as the labour market has been relatively healthy, which may have encouraged some people to believe that it is worth their while to join the workforce. Of the 17.5 million people who were economically inactive in mid-2004, 7.9 million (45%) were above the official retirement age.

Focusing on people aged between 16 and 59 (for women) and 64 (for men), 5.9 million (74%) of the economically inactive in this group did not want jobs. Of those who did want jobs, but had not been looking for work in the previous

4 weeks, a number were long-term sick, or were looking after family members, or were students. There were also small numbers of 'discouraged workers' — that is, people who had withdrawn from the workforce believing that they had no chance of getting a job.

Figure 16.1 shows how the population aged 16 and over have been divided between the various categories in each year since 1992. This shows a gradual rise in the number of employees and a slight fall in the numbers unemployed, although this is easier to see in Figure 16.2, which shows the percentage unemployment rate over this same period.

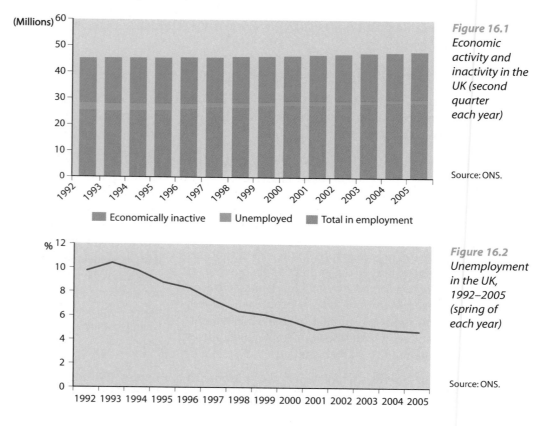

**Figure 16.1**
*Economic activity and inactivity in the UK (second quarter each year)*

Source: ONS.

**Figure 16.2**
*Unemployment in the UK, 1992–2005 (spring of each year)*

Source: ONS.

Over the past 25 years or so, the UK economy has gone through substantial structural change. You can see something of this in Figure 16.3, which shows the changing pattern of employment in the UK since 1978. One of the key features is the change in the balance of employment between manufacturing activity and services. Back in 1978, 26.7% of workforce jobs were in manufacturing activity, and 61.4% were in services. In 2003 only 12.4% of jobs were in manufacturing, and 78.8% were in services. The finance and business services sector grew especially rapidly during this period, more than doubling their number of jobs between 1978 and 2004. Manufacturing employment fell by more than a half in the period.

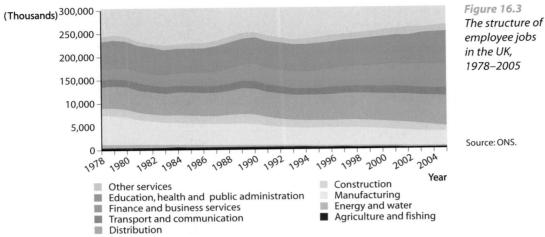

Other services
Education, health and public administration
Finance and business services
Transport and communication
Distribution

Construction
Manufacturing
Energy and water
Agriculture and fishing

**Figure 16.3**
*The structure of employee jobs in the UK, 1978–2005*

Source: ONS.

You should not be too surprised at such changes in the pattern of activity over time. In part they may reflect changes in the pattern of consumer demand as incomes have increased. As real incomes rise, the demand for some goods increases more rapidly than demand for others. For luxury goods, which have an income elasticity of demand greater than 1, the proportion of income spent on them increases as income itself increases. It is worth noting that the demand for many leisure items is likely to be income elastic. So, for example, as real incomes rise, it would be expected that the demand for capital goods associated with leisure activity, such as digital cameras and DVD players, would rise more than proportionately with income. At the same time, the demand for some other goods and services may slacken. If the market economy is working effectively in encouraging the production of those goods and services that people wish to buy, then the structure of economic activity should also change, with some sectors expanding and others contracting.

Patterns of international trade have also changed over time, especially in the context of closer European integration, which may have affected the pattern of specialisation between countries. Figure 16.4 shows the distribution of workforce jobs in the UK in mid-2005. This underlines the importance of service activity in the UK economy, particularly education, health and public administration, distribution, hotels and restaurants, and finance and business services.

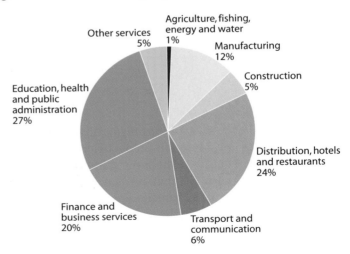

**Figure 16.4** *Workforce jobs in the UK, June 2005*
Source: *Labour Market Statistics.*

# Trends in earnings

Figure 16.5 shows the rate of change of earnings in the UK in the recent past, together with changes in the retail price index. Notice that it is important to look at both earnings and prices because changes in prices (inflation) affect the purchasing power of earnings. An extreme example is 1977, when the earnings index rose by 8.75%, but prices rose by even more (16%), so that the purchasing power of earnings fell. This is seen clearly in Figure 16.6, which shows the annual rate of change of **real earnings**: that is, the rate of change of earnings adjusted for inflation.

 **Key term**

**real earnings:** the level of earnings adjusted for the price level; the rate of change of real earnings is thus the rate of change of earnings adjusted for inflation (the rate of change of prices)

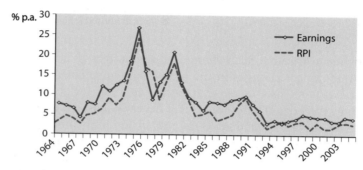

*Figure 16.5*
*Changes in earnings and prices in the UK, 1964–2005*

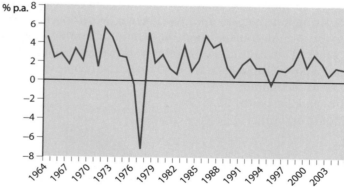

*Figure 16.6*
*Rate of change in real earnings in the UK, 1964–2005*

Note: rate of change of earnings index relative to retail price index.

In most years, earnings can be seen to rise more rapidly than prices. This may reflect rises in the productivity of labour. Whether a rise in real earnings also means an improvement in the standard of living will depend on a number of things. For a start, the fact that average earnings have increased does not mean that all workers share in the benefits, so the distribution of the increases across different groups of workers may be important. Furthermore, it may be argued that the standard of living does not only depend upon income (earnings), but may also reflect other aspects of the quality of life, such as the environment in which people live.

It is also important to be aware that the earnings that people receive differ for a wide variety of reasons. For one thing, it is the case that earnings differ between the various kinds of economic activity that take place within the economy. Figure 16.7 shows something of this. You can readily see that average weekly earnings appear to be lower in the agriculture, fishing and food and the distribution, hotel and restaurant sectors, but higher in energy and water and in banking, finance and insurance.

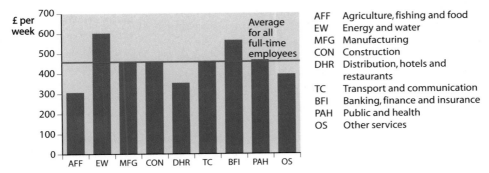

AFF   Agriculture, fishing and food
EW    Energy and water
MFG   Manufacturing
CON   Construction
DHR   Distribution, hotels and restaurants
TC     Transport and communication
BFI    Banking, finance and insurance
PAH   Public and health
OS     Other services

*Figure 16.7* *Average gross weekly earnings in the UK by sector, summer 2005*

Chapters 18 and 19 examine the extent to which this pattern can be explained in terms of economic analysis. One obvious point to notice here is that some of the differences in earnings between economic sectors in the economy may reflect differences in occupational structure, which in turn may be associated with different skills requirements of different jobs. The differences in the wages earned by workers in different occupations can be seen in Figure 16.8, which shows average hourly earnings for various occupational groups. As might be expected, it is clear that managers, senior officials and professionals receive higher hourly earnings that less skilled occupations.

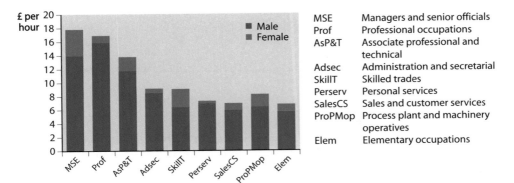

MSE      Managers and senior officials
Prof       Professional occupations
AsP&T   Associate professional and technical
Adsec    Administration and secretarial
SkillT     Skilled trades
Perserv  Personal services
SalesCS  Sales and customer services
ProPMop Process plant and machinery operatives
Elem     Elementary occupations

*Figure 16.8* *Earnings in the UK by occupation, summer 2005*

Figure 16.8 also serves as a reminder that there is a gender gap between earnings of male and female workers — and it would seem that the gap is more significant in some occupations than in others. The reasons for this are examined in Chapter 19. It is also the case that earnings (and employment) show differences between age

and ethnic groups, and one of the important issues to be examined is the extent to which such differences reflect **discrimination** in the labour force, or the extent to which they may be explained by other economic factors at work in the market.

## International differences in productivity

Considering the UK economy in an international context, the relative cost of labour in different countries becomes important because this influences the relative competitiveness of UK goods in both overseas and domestic markets. In other words, the relative costs of production in different countries influences the prices that firms can charge. It thus becomes important to consider changes in **unit labour costs** over time.

If unit labour costs in an economy rise more rapidly than in other countries, there will be a loss of competitiveness. Figure 16.9 compares annual changes in unit labour costs in the UK with changes in the 15 member countries of the EU (EU 15) and with countries in the euro single currency area. This reveals that unit labour costs have grown more rapidly in the UK than elsewhere in the EU in recent years.

**Key** terms

**discrimination:** a situation in a labour market where some people receive lower wages that cannot be explained by economic factors

**unit labour cost:** wages, salaries and other costs of using labour, divided by output per worker

**labour productivity:** a measure of output per worker, or output per hour worked

This in turn partly reflects different levels of productivity across countries. Productivity is a measure of productive efficiency: for example, **labour productivity** is output per unit of labour input. Different countries show appreciable differences in efficiency by this measure.

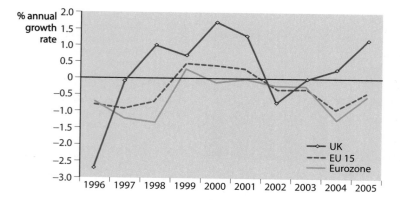

*Figure 16.9*
*Unit labour cost growth in the UK and EU, 1996–2005*

However, international comparisons of productivity are not straightforward, as measurements are subject to differences in data collection and differences in work practices. Figure 16.10 presents data for 2004 on GDP per head of population, expressed as index numbers, with the USA being the reference country and thus set to 100.

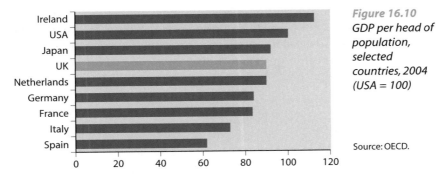

Figure 16.10
GDP per head of
population,
selected
countries, 2004
(USA = 100)

Source: OECD.

On this measure, the UK performs rather better than Germany, France and Italy. As a measure of productivity levels, however, this is a misleading indicator. In particular, working hours are longer in the UK than in many other countries (especially within Europe), so in part, GDP per head reflects differences in the quantity of labour input. For this reason, GDP per hour worked is often seen as a more reliable indicator of relative productivity levels. This measure is graphed in Figure 16.11 and shows quite a different pattern. Indeed, on this basis both Ireland and France show higher productivity than the USA, and the UK's performance is much more modest.

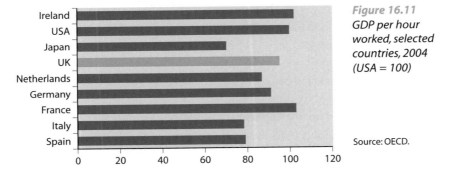

Figure 16.11
GDP per hour
worked, selected
countries, 2004
(USA = 100)

Source: OECD.

Figure 16.12 gives the time path for an index of GDP per hour worked, based this time on 1970 = 100. It shows that European countries have been experiencing stronger productivity growth than the USA over this period.

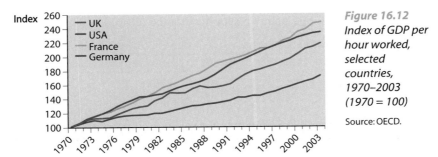

Figure 16.12
Index of GDP per
hour worked,
selected
countries,
1970–2003
(1970 = 100)

Source: OECD.

It is also important to realise that labour productivity is not the only relevant measure, as countries may also differ in their use of capital. Total factor productivity is more difficult to measure, as the measurement of capital stock is especially prone to error and misinterpretation. However, some estimates of multifactor productivity growth are shown in Figure 16.13.

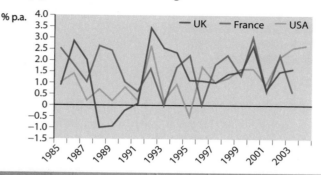

*Figure 16.13*
*Multifactor productivity growth, UK, France and USA, 1985–2004*

Source: OECD.

## Summary

➤ Work and leisure are connected: when an individual takes a decision about how many hours to work, this then also determines how many hours are available for leisure activity.

➤ An additional hour spent at work is the opportunity cost of an hour's leisure — and vice versa.

➤ The overall economic activity rate has not altered very much in the UK in recent years, but there have been changes in the structure of employment between sectors.

➤ Service activity has increased as a proportion of employment, and manufacturing has declined.

➤ This may reflect changes in the pattern of consumer demand, and of specialisation between countries.

➤ Earnings have risen by more than prices in most years.

➤ There have been significant differences in movements of unit labour costs and labour productivity over time between the UK and other countries in the EU.

## Exercise 16.1

Table 16.1 provides data on two labour productivity measures, based on the UK = 100. Discuss whether the UK's position has improved or deteriorated since 1991. Explain your answer, and discuss why this might be important for the UK economy.

| | GDP per worker | | | | | | GDP per hour worked | | | | | |
|---|---|---|---|---|---|---|---|---|---|---|---|---|
| Year | France | Germany | Japan | UK | USA | G7 | France | Germany | Japan | UK | USA | G7 |
| 1991 | 132 | 115 | 108 | 100 | 138 | 124 | 146 | 132 | 95 | 100 | 132 | 121 |
| 1994 | 124 | 111 | 97 | 100 | 131 | 117 | 136 | 125 | 88 | 100 | 122 | 114 |
| 1997 | 121 | 107 | 94 | 100 | 128 | 115 | 135 | 124 | 87 | 100 | 118 | 112 |
| 2000 | 118 | 104 | 90 | 100 | 128 | 113 | 134 | 121 | 85 | 100 | 117 | 111 |
| 2004 | 111 | 100 | 89 | 100 | 127 | 111 | 129 | 116 | 83 | 100 | 116 | 108 |

*Table 16.1*

Source: ONS.

## Hours worked

An important dimension of the labour market is the number of hours that employees work per week. Figure 16.14 shows that this does vary a bit across countries, with full-time workers in the UK putting in more hours per week, on average, than workers in other countries in Europe. Thus in 2005, the average hours worked by full-time employees in the UK was 43.2, which is somewhat above the average for all EU countries, which was 41.8. In 2005, Norway showed the lowest average hours worked (39.4), and Iceland the highest (47.1).

In general, there has been a downward trend in average hours worked across many countries, partly influenced by EU legislation on the number of hours that workers are permitted to work. However, the changes have not been substantial.

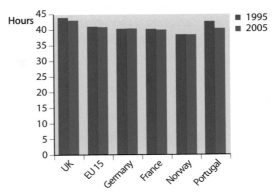

*Figure 16.14  Average hours worked, selected countries, 1995 and 2005 (full-time employees)*

Source: Eurostat.

## Leisure

Although people in the UK are seen to work long hours compared with their European counterparts, it is still the case that the UK leisure industry is thriving. Indeed, it has been estimated that the leisure industry accounts for about 10% of the UK's total employment. Part of this industry caters to visiting tourists from overseas, but clearly the industry has become a key part of the economy.

The ways in which people spend their time outside work have seen some major changes in recent years, partly reflecting changes in technology that have revolutionised how people use their leisure time.

A survey carried out in 2000 under the auspices of the Office for National Statistics looked at how people spend their time. The summary results are shown in Figure 16.15. This reveals that leisure occupies the largest share of people's waking time — although housework and childcare come close for women.

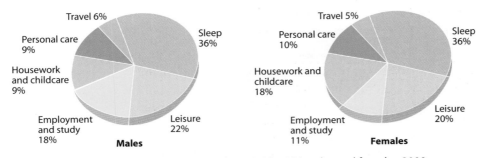

*Figure 16.15  Time spent on main activities, UK males and females, 2000*

Source: *Time Use Survey* (ONS).

Figure 16.16 shows how that leisure time is allocated between different activities, with watching television and video/DVD being the dominant form of leisure activity for both males and females. This accounts for more than half of leisure time. It would seem that social life and entertainment also occupy a large part of leisure time, but hobbies, games and sport between them account for only 10% of leisure time for males, and only 7% for females.

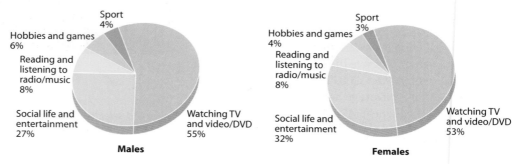

*Figure 16.16* Use of leisure time, UK males and females, 2000
Source: *Time Use Survey* (ONS).

It is helpful to distinguish between different forms of leisure activity. First, there are activities that are *home based*. These include watching television or DVD, but also DIY and cooking for friends. The increased availability of home-based capital goods such as DVD players and computers may have affected the extent to which people spend their leisure time at home — certainly as compared with earlier generations.

A second category of leisure activities are those that are mainly *passive*. This category covers activities that are outside the home, but do not involve active participation. Such activities include going to the cinema or a football match, dining out at a restaurant and what is known as 'leisure shopping'.

Home-based activities take up the most amount of leisure time

Finally, there are *active* leisure activities, which involve active participation in some form of sporting activity, or visiting a theme park. As Figure 16.16 illustrates, such active leisure occupies a relatively small share of people's leisure time. Nonetheless, a majority of the adult population do participate in some form of sport, game or physical activity, according to the *General Household Survey*, as can be seen in Figure16.17. This shows a clear relationship between active leisure participation and age — which is perhaps not surprising. It also shows something of a decline in such participation over time, especially between 1996/97 and 2002/03. This is especially marked among the younger age groups. For both males and females, the most popular activity included in this survey was walking.

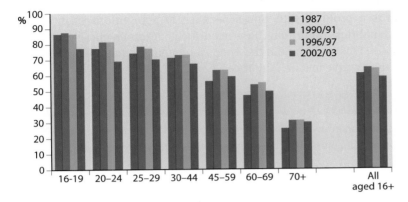

*Figure 16.17*
*Adult participation in a sport, game or physical activity, by age (Great Britain)*

Source: *Social Trends.*

## Leisure choices

Economic analysis provides some important insights into the way in which people take decisions about their leisure activities.

For example, people take decisions about how to allocate their time between work and leisure. This will partly reflect their personal preferences, but even at this level, the decision will depend upon an evaluation of the relative benefits and costs of time spent in work and leisure — a procedure embedded in the economic approach to decision making. Some people are in jobs that give them satisfaction, whereas others may wish to minimise the time spent at work. However, this is not the only influence on the decision about how much time to devote to work as opposed to leisure. The wage that a worker can earn in employment affects the trade-off between work and leisure, and can be seen as the opportunity cost of leisure. At a higher wage, an extra hour of leisure time carries a higher cost in terms of income forgone.

It is also worth noting that an additional hour spent at work provides additional income that can then be used to enhance the enjoyment of the remaining leisure time. This may encourage the use of more capital goods in the enjoyment of leisure. For example, it could be that a worker may choose to work extra hours in order to earn the income needed to buy DVDs that can be watched in the home, as an alternative to taking more time to visit the cinema. This all suggests that, if markets are to be able to allocate resources efficiently within a society, this must include efficiency in the leisure industry, and in the way in which labour markets operate to establish wage rates.

## Health and leisure

A by-product of changing lifestyles is in the effect on a population's health. Recall Figure 16.17. This revealed a fall in participation in active sports and games among

young age groups. To the extent that this reflects the increasing popularity of computer games and other passive activities, there could be implications for the future health of the population. Indeed, there is evidence of an increase in obesity, not only in the UK, but also in many other developed countries. This may have implications for the resources needed to provide healthcare in the future. To the extent that this is a problem that arises because of poor information or the existence of externalities, there may be a need for government intervention to mitigate the effects. This may explain the encouragement given to people to take part in some form of active leisure activity.

## Summary

> The number of hours worked by full-time employees in the UK has fallen since 1995, but average hours worked remains higher than in many other European countries.

> In spite of the long hours worked in the UK, the leisure industry has been thriving, accounting for about 10% of total employment.

> Leisure activity accounts for the largest share of people's waking time.

> Home-based leisure activity comprises a relatively large share of leisure activity undertaken by adults, and there has been something of a decline in participation in active leisure activities — sports and other physical activities.

> Economic analysis can help to explain these changes that have affected the leisure industry.

> A large-scale decline in participation in sporting and other physical activity may contribute to obesity and affect the long-term health of the population.

## Exercise 16.2

The relative price of some leisure activities has changed significantly over the past 10–15 years. For example, the cost of home computers and access to the internet has fallen, as has the cost of DVD players and DVDs. Discuss how this relative price change has changed the pattern of leisure activity in the UK.

# Chapter 17
# Market structure and the leisure sector

*Part 4 of the book introduced the notion of market structure, and outlined its importance in enabling an allocation of resources that is good for society. It is important to see how this works in practice, and this chapter presents an evaluation of how market structure has influenced the efficiency of resource allocation in the leisure sector.*

## Learning outcomes

After studying this chapter, you should:

➤ be familiar with the way in which market structure affects the efficiency of resource allocation in sections of the leisure sector

➤ understand the way in which the package holiday market operates as an oligopoly

➤ appreciate that firms in the package holiday business may face the threat of new entry from firms using the internet, thus affecting the contestability of the market

➤ be familiar with the way in which the market for television broadcasting has evolved over time, from monopoly to duopoly to oligopoly, becoming more competitive as technology has changed

➤ be aware of the importance of market structure in the market for spectator sports

➤ understand developments in the market for air travel, and the impact of the low-cost airlines

➤ appreciate the conditions under which price discrimination can be utilised by a firm in order to increase its profits

➤ be familiar with the way in which the theory of monopolistic competition can help in understanding the leisure sector

## Markets and resource allocation

Chapter 14 showed how a perfectly competitive market allocates resources in such a way that the marginal benefit that consumers receive from consuming the product is equal to the marginal cost of producing that product. This is desirable for society as a whole. If marginal benefit were higher than marginal cost, then consumers

would gain if output were to be increased, as they would gain more benefit from additional units of the good than it would cost society to produce that extra output.

The way in which this outcome is achieved is through the operation of the price mechanism. In a competitive market, firms respond to price signals. If price is at such a level that firms make abnormal profits, this will attract new firms into the market. Industry supply then increases until the price is driven back down to long-run marginal cost. Equally, if price falls below marginal cost, some firms will leave the market, industry supply will contract, and price will drift back up to its equilibrium value at long-run marginal cost. Two vital ingredients of this process are that firms react to price signals and that there is freedom of entry into and exit from the market. It is also important to remember that there are other ways in which markets may fail to deliver a best outcome for society — for example, in the case of externalities, information failure or public goods.

Perfect competition in the real world is rare. There are so many potential sources of market failure that one or other of the stringent assumptions of the perfect competition model always seems to break down. However, this does not nullify the usefulness or power of the model, as it provides us with a standard of comparison for real-world markets. In other words, the existence and characteristics of the model of perfect competition highlight the ways in which real-world markets fall short of or diverge from the ideal. This chapter draws on examples of real-world markets for leisure activities to illustrate ways in which they diverge from perfect competition, and evaluates the extent to which they may be considered to conform to other models of market structure that have been analysed.

## The market for package holidays in the UK

The market for package holidays is big business. In 2004 UK holidaymakers made 64.2 million visits abroad, of which some 20 million were package holidays. To what extent does the market operate efficiently? In order to evaluate efficiency, economic analysis suggests that a starting point is to examine the market structure.

The Association of British Travel Agents (ABTA) is an organisation that acts as a trade association for tour operators and travel agents in the UK. In early 2006, ABTA covered more than 6,000 travel agency offices and more than 1,000 tour operators. According to the ABTA website, between them, these accounted for 85% of UK-sold holidays.

Superficially, the fact that there are more than 6,000 travel agency offices seems to suggest a competitive market, but this is misleading, as it is not only the number of offices that is important, but also the number of firms in the market, and the distribution of the business between them. ABTA's membership comprises about 1,722 individual member companies, but the four largest control a significant part of the market. These are Thomson, Thomas Cook, My Travel and First Choice.

With just four major operators in the market, it would be classified as an *oligopoly*. If the firms were to collude together in order to exploit their market power, this

*Thomas Cook is one of the four big companies that control the travel market*

could have an adverse effect on allocative efficiency. A monopolist attempting to maximise profits would restrict output and raise price, thus pushing the market away from the point at which price is equal to marginal cost. However, the question is whether the firms do collude in this way, or whether there are other forces within the market that constrain or prevent them from exploiting their position.

One way in which firms in a market may be constrained is through the direct effects of regulation. The market for foreign package holidays has been investigated in the past by the Monopoly and Mergers Commission (now the Competition Commission). Investigations took place in the mid-1980s (reporting in 1986), and again in the late 1990s, with a referral to the commission taking place in 1996. The 1986 report investigated allegations of what was, in effect, *resale price maintenance*. Resale price maintenance is where the producer of a good dictates the price at which it should be sold in the retail market — a practice that has been illegal for many years. The commission concluded that this was against the public interest, and outlawed the practice.

In the later investigation, the commission noted that at the time the largest three operators in the market accounted for around 50% of all foreign package holidays sold in 1996. In its report, the commission expressed concern about the degree of *vertical integration* in the market, particularly given that some of the ownership linkages between firms were not made clear to customers. Vertical integration is where a firm is involved in different stages of the production of a good or service. An example is that of First Choice Holidays. The commission pointed out that this firm was not only a tour operator, but also an airline (Air 2000), and for a period was also in a strategic alliance with Thomas Cook (travel agent). Consumers were not always aware that they were dealing with a firm that was involved at these different stages of the production process, which can affect the profit margins on particular holiday packages. However, while recommending greater transparency

in the market, the commission did not condemn the operators outright. It did make a number of recommendations about certain practices, such as tying discounts to the purchase of insurance. But the commission concluded that 'we would characterise the travel trade as at present broadly competitive, and as having served the consumer well'.

The threat of investigation by the competition authorities may be one way of ensuring that operators in a market do not abuse their market position, but are there other forces at work that might influence firms? And how else might a judgement be reached as to the intensity of competition in a market?

One of the problems in evaluating a market is that, in general, it is not possible to observe marginal cost, so that it is not possible to check whether price is being set above marginal cost. An alternative might be to look at profits, and ask whether firms in a market seem to be making excessive profits. In the case of the travel companies, recent experience may not help in this respect. The substantial reduction in demand for foreign holidays following the terrorist attacks of 11 September 2001 in the USA created difficulties for many of the tour operators and travel agents, many of which posted sharp reductions in profits, or even losses. But this is not conclusive evidence that firms were not abusing their market power; it might just be a process of adjustment to lower demand for their products.

Perhaps more relevant is to examine the extent to which the market may be regarded as *contestable.* In other words, to what extent can the existing operators in the market rely on barriers to entry to protect them from hit-and-run entry, or to what extent is it possible for new firms to enter the market? If the market is contestable and open to entry by new firms, then it would not be possible for the existing firms to set prices at a level above average cost, as this would attract new competition.

*Offering specialist advice on skiing packages — a niche market for travel agents*

The growth of the internet may be the key factor that determines the intensity of competition in the travel industry. The growing ability of consumers to by-pass the local travel agent by making their own bookings online suggests that the travel market is highly contestable. It is now possible for a potential holidaymaker to find their flights, hotel accommodation, car rentals or hotel transfers from their PCs. This can be done either by booking direct with airlines and hotels,

or by using one of the growing number of online firms, such as Expedia, the world's largest online travel agent.

The travel agents have thus had to respond to these new online entrants to their market. They have done so partly by themselves going online, and developing their own websites and online sales. They have also responded by looking for niche markets, offering specialist advice on long-haul holidays, adventure trips or skiing packages.

The intensity of this competition is likely to be beneficial for consumers in terms of the prices that can be obtained for package holidays. Inevitably, there may also be dangers. For example, it may be that online purchase of the separate components of a holiday is more risky than buying from a travel agent backed by the code of conduct now issued by ABTA. Or it may be that the online companies themselves will go through a process of merger, acquisition and increasing concentration that may lead at some point to market power.

## Exercise 17.1

Discuss the extent to which the growth of online sales of package holidays is influencing the range of destinations and variety of holidays on offer. Do you think that more regulation of online marketing is needed in order to protect consumer interests?

## Television broadcasting

According to the 2000 Time Use Survey, watching either television or DVD/video occupies more than half of people's leisure time in the UK (see Figure 16.16). It is thus important to ensure that television broadcasting is being provided in an efficient manner. Again, whether this is the case depends partly on the market structure in the television broadcasting sector, which is likely to influence the behaviour of the enterprises engaged in this activity.

There are other aspects of broadcasting that affect the efficiency of the market. Indeed, there are three areas of potential market failure in the sector. A tendency to *concentration* (and hence imperfect competition) is one of these, but in addition, broadcasting has some aspects of a *public good*, and there may also be some *merit good* arguments.

Television broadcasting may be regarded as a public good because there is an extent to which it is non-rivalrous and non-exclusive. When a programme is broadcast, anyone with a television receiver can pick up the signal, so it is difficult to exclude people from consuming the good. Furthermore, if one person watches the programme, this does not reduce the amount of it available for others to watch. You will remember from Chapter 7 that these characteristics mean that public goods are under-provided in the absence of some form of government intervention. Partly for this reason, there has been government intervention in

television broadcasting ever since transmissions first began. The BBC derives much of its income from the licence fee, which is one way of ensuring that people pay for the programmes that they watch. The situation has changed with technology in recent years, making it possible to exclude people from receiving some channels, and enabling firms to charge for particular programmes.

There is a view that television broadcasting has merit good characteristics, as it is believed that viewing habits can influence behaviour. Watching educational programmes may bring beneficial spillover effects, whereas watching violent dramas may have the opposite effect. This argument has been used to justify government intervention to influence the content of programmes that are broadcast.

In terms of market structure, television broadcasting began as a *monopoly* (when only one BBC channel was available). ITV was granted a licence to broadcast in 1955, being funded through advertising revenue, so the market became a *duopoly*. As more terrestrial channels were launched, the market evolved into an *oligopoly*. The cost structure of television broadcasting encourages a relatively high degree of concentration. This is because the ratio of fixed to variable costs is very high, which in turn means that there are substantial economies of scale. The major costs arise in establishing the network of transmitters, and in making the programmes. The marginal cost entailed in transmitting the programmes is very small compared to these fixed costs.

How might the resulting market power be exploited by the firms involved? After all, the BBC does not control the size of its licence fee, and the commercial channels do not charge their customers directly. A danger of lack of competition is that firms may cut their costs, and thus may produce low-quality programmes, or only put out populist programmes that will attract audiences, and thus advertising revenue. But it might not provide the sorts of programme that the authorities would regard as meritorious.

The so-called digital revolution has made it possible for many other channels to become established, some of them available only on a subscription basis. This has affected the barriers to entry, and enabled the market to be more contestable than before. In the UK, there are now more than 300 channels available. Some of these channels cater for

*Liz Barker presenting the BBC's long-standing children's programme,* Blue Peter

niche markets, such as cookery, comedy or home improvement. Issues arising from the merit good argument remain, and clearly the authorities have a greater challenge to face in ensuring that what they see as an appropriate balance of programmes is broadcast, now that there are so many channels to deal with. As with any appeal to a merit good argument, there are bound to be differences between politicians and others about the extent to which the authorities should override consumer preferences.

The way that technology has developed to enable broadcasts to be restricted to subscribers or paying customers has enabled a number of new developments in this market. In particular, there are segments of the market where consumers are clearly prepared to pay a premium in order to view particular programmes. One obvious example of such a market segment is in sporting events, such as Premiership football and test cricket. These examples are discussed in the next section.

## Exercise 17.2

Discuss the extent to which the authorities are justified in intervening to influence the sorts of programme that are being broadcast.

## Spectator sports

Another important form of leisure activity is watching sport. This takes a wide variety of forms. Parents watch their children playing sport at the local sports centre, people attend sporting events, and there is plenty of 'live' sports action on television, both on the terrestrial channels and on specialist subscription channels such as Sky Sports.

As far as professional sporting events are concerned, there is some interlinkage between the markets. Ever since football matches were first televised, it has been argued that matches should not be shown 'live' at the traditional match time of Saturday at 3 p.m., as this was thought to affect attendance at the grounds. For Premiership and Championship clubs, gate receipts remain an important source of income, although television revenues have also become increasingly important in recent years. A lot of attention has been devoted to the earnings that footballers command in the Premiership. This issue is taken up in Chapter 18 (see pages 285–86).

In terms of market structure, the way that the rights to televising events have become concentrated is an especially crucial area. In particular, BSkyB's position in this market has attracted considerable attention in relation to holding rights to televise live sporting events such as football and cricket. An important question is the extent to which BSkyB has monopoly power, and the extent to which it is able to exploit that market power at the expense of the viewers.

There is a specified list of events that are guaranteed to be shown on free-to-air terrestrial channels. This list includes the Olympics, the World Cup (football), the FA Cup Final, the Grand National and Wimbledon.

Test cricket was delisted in 1998 after lobbying from the England and Wales Cricket Board (ECB), which was keen to raise funds for investment. This enabled BSkyB to bid for exclusive rights to domestic test matches, in a deal that would remove cricket from the terrestrial channels from 2006 to 2009. A further review of the list was promised — but not until the switch-over to digital television has been completed.

Premiership football had fallen prey to Sky at a much earlier date. Sky won the rights to live Premiership football in 1992, and maintained its position until an auction that was held in May 2006. The auction was held following intervention by the European Commission, which had ruled that BSkyB's dominance of live Premiership football was acting against consumer interests. In the auction, six packages of matches were sold separately, four of which were bought by BSkyB, and the remaining two by the Irish pay-TV broadcaster Setanta. Within a week of the auction, BSkyB and Setanta reached a deal in respect of the pubs-and-clubs segment of the market. Under this agreement, Sky's corporate customers would get Setanta's sports channels bundled in to their monthly subscription. It would seem that monopoly had been replaced by a duopoly.

BSkyB's moves in these various sports markets were strategic, aiming to build up the number of subscribers by gaining control of these key market segments. From the perspective of BSkyB, this may be seen as an attempt to gain and consolidate entry into the television broadcasting market, which until the advent of satellite broadcasting had been an oligopoly controlled by the terrestrial channels via licensing agreements. Only by reaching a critical mass of subscribers would BSkyB be able to generate sufficient advertising revenue to become profitable.

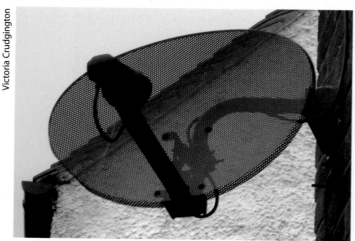
Victoria Crudgington

*The satellite station BSkyB gained a monopoly in the supply of certain televised live football and cricket matches*

Another way of viewing the market situation is that the Premier League was a monopsony seller of the rights to live football — and the ECB of the rights to televise test cricket. By opening up to an auction and selling to the highest bidder, the Premier League gained funds to distribute to the Premiership clubs, and the ECB gained funds to invest in cricket.

The evaluation of the effect of market structure in this situation is tricky. It could be argued that BSkyB has been able to use its market power to charge a high price to consumers for watching live football on television. However, if these matches were to be available on free-to-air television, it could be argued that this would damage match attendance and leave the football clubs struggling for revenue. The monopsony position of the Premier League has enabled it to channel revenue to the clubs, making the Premiership one of the richest leagues in the world. Television revenues and audiences may be even more important in the case of test cricket.

The market situation was the subject of investigation by the UK's Competition Commission, which became involved in 1998 when BSkyB's proposed acquisition of Manchester United was referred by the secretary of state for trade and industry. The acquisition was prohibited on the grounds that it would reinforce the trend towards inequality of wealth between football clubs, and would give BSkyB additional influence over Premier League decisions relating to the organisation of football. However, this did not break the monopoly that BSkyB had over live Premiership broadcasts at that time.

After this, the European Commission became involved, and argued that BSkyB's exclusive right to televise live matches was in violation of European competition rules, as it was 'not in the interest of competition in the broadcasting market or the fans'. At the time, the Premier League agreed that after 2006 the tendering process would ensure that there were at least two television broadcasters of live Premiership matches. The commission intervened again in 2005 when it seemed that the Premier League was delaying matters, and the auction finally took place in April 2006.

## Exercise 17.3

One advantage of the system that allowed BSkyB to gain a monopoly in the supply of televised live football and cricket matches is that this brought money into the respective sports, enabling investment in football clubs and cricket at grass-roots level. Discuss the extent to which consumers have benefited from satellite broadcasting of sporting activities.

## The low-cost airlines

With the growth in the foreign package holiday market, air travel has come to be a key part of the leisure market, as well as being critical in terms of transport. The face of air travel has changed dramatically since the appearance of the low-cost airlines, beginning with Southwestern in the USA (launched as long ago as 1971), followed by Ryanair in 1985 and easyJet in 1995. The model has now been copied by Air Asia and other airlines operating in southeast Asia.

This market provides an illustration of how intensified competition can affect the operation of markets. Before the advent of the low-cost airlines, the market for air travel was dominated by large national carriers, in many cases either state-run or

heavily subsidised by governments. As time went by, these large airlines began to join together in strategic alliances that enabled them to work together yet maintain their individual characters. The market seemed to be consolidating and was effectively becoming more concentrated.

Deregulation provided an opening for changes in the market structure, by reducing the barriers to entry of new firms. However, in order to exploit that opening, the budget airlines needed a good understanding of economic analysis. Their success has been built on a thorough understanding of cost structures and a recognition of the contestability of airlines, together with the judicious use of price discrimination.

Profits depend upon costs as well as revenue. EasyJet (not to mention other budget airlines, such as Ryanair and Flybe) have taken a close look at the structure of costs. Figure 17.1 shows a detailed breakdown of the costs of a typical easyJet flight. By focusing on each individual item of costs and looking for ways of cutting costs to a minimum, the budget airlines have been able to achieve profitability.

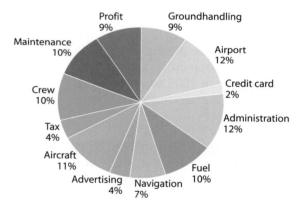

*Figure 17.1* **The cost of an easyJet flight**
Source: *Guardian*, 20 August 2003.

In part, this has been connected with the understanding of demand. The budget airlines offer a 'no frills' approach, doing away with pre-assigned seats and pre-issued tickets, free in-flight catering, a separate business class and so on. They also use more remote airports, where charges are relatively low. But the savings go way beyond these conspicuous items.

In particular, the budget airlines have followed a pattern established by the Texas-based airline Southwestern, which sets out four key rules.

First, only fly one type of plane. This reduces maintenance costs and avoids the need to hold a wide range of spare parts. This is one source of potential economies of scale.

Second, drive down costs every year. This may be achieved while the airline is still expanding if there are economies of scale to be reaped. For example, it may be achieved by negotiating improved deals from suppliers — of fuel, insurance etc.

Third, minimise the time that aircraft spend parked on the tarmac. The no frills and no tickets approach enables a much quicker turn-round of aircraft — which, after all, only earn money for the company when they are in the air. For example, an easyJet plane flying between Luton and Nice can make four round-trips per day — by spending only about half-an-hour on the tarmac at each end.

Fourth, do not try to sell anything except seats. Schemes that offer loyalty bonuses or air miles cost money to administer, and are more complicated than they are worth.

Following these rules, and paying careful attention to the various forms of costs identified in Figure 17.1 has enabled the budget airlines to expand, to make profits (9% in the diagram), and to transform air travel.

As far as price discrimination is concerned, easyJet says on its website that it 'operates a very simple fare structure...based on supply

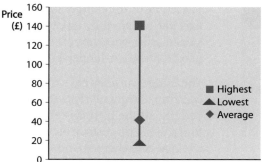

*Figure 17.2*
*Prices paid on an easyJet flight*
Source: *Guardian*, 20 August 2003.

and demand'. The nature of the price structure is that passengers who book early pay the lowest prices, whereas those who book close to their travel time pay the highest prices. Figure 17.2 (based on information in an article in the *Guardian*) shows that on a particular flight from Luton to Nice on 20 August 2003, the prices paid by passengers varied from just £20 to about £140.

You might expect that in a competitive market, the price structure would be the opposite. If prices follow costs, the marginal cost to easyJet of carrying an extra passenger is likely to be pretty low, so the flight could be filled up by offering last-minute deals, with the price being driven close to marginal cost. But this is clearly not happening at easyJet, as the later a passenger books, the higher the price that they face.

This suggests that easyJet understands enough about the nature of demand to use price discrimination on its flights. People who book at the last minute are likely to be business travellers who need to fly urgently, perhaps for a business meeting or to clinch a deal. Such customers are likely to have low elasticity of demand, and thus be prepared to pay a higher price for their ticket. This is in contrast to those who can book well in advance, who are more likely to be people travelling for pleasure — visiting relatives or going on holiday. For these travellers, the choice of when to fly is more flexible. This means there are more possible flights from which they can choose. And we know that when there are substitutes for a commodity, the price elasticity of demand is high. It is for these customers that easyJet can offer the low prices that we see being advertised. After all, at £20, it probably costs some customers more to get to the airport than it costs for the flight!

So, easyJet can make use of this difference in demand elasticity to charge different prices to different customers, even if the product (the flight from London to Nice) is the same for all of them. Thus an understanding of demand is important for easyJet.

The entry of the budget airlines also caused the existing firms to reconsider the way in which they operate. Some reacted by setting up their own budget subsidiaries, with varying degrees of success. Others have had to accept that they need to focus on longer-haul flights.

The budget airlines case therefore provides another example of how competition can transform a market, and how contestability can affect firms' behaviour. Why can the airline business be regarded as contestable? After all, it might be argued that the set-up costs of establishing an airline are likely to be high, so it is difficult to claim that there are no sunk costs faced by firms. However, the key issue is that market conditions on particular routes may well encourage contestability. Once the airline is established, the costs of flying a new route are relatively low. There are bound to be some advertising costs, but otherwise an airline can switch aircraft to new routes quite quickly. It could then switch to other routes if profits were disappointing. In other words, hit-and-run entry is possible on particular routes. This may mean that existing airlines will not set prices at such levels that entry is attracted.

It is also worth noting that the low-cost airlines have flourished not only by taking customers away from the existing airlines, but also by tapping a new customer base. By offering low fares and easy accessibility, they have attracted passengers who would not otherwise have dreamed of flying.

## Price discrimination

From an economic point of view, one interesting aspect of the airline industry is the extensive use of *price discrimination*. This is the process, described in Chapter 15, whereby a firm is able to charge a different price to different customers for the same good. In the context of the airlines, the most obvious example of this is the differences between peak and off-peak fares, as mentioned above.

The practice is made possible because those who have to fly on business need to travel at certain times of day — often at short notice — and have less elastic demand than those who can travel at any time of day, perhaps for leisure trips, shopping etc. A monopoly operator is thus able to charge business travellers a higher price, as they are less sensitive to price — or have less choice about when to travel.

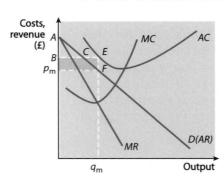

*Figure 17.3*

*A loss-making monopolist using price discrimination*

Passengers who have to pay the higher prices may well see this as exploitative behaviour by the monopolist. However, there may be situations in which a firm would not be able to remain in business without the possibility of price discrimination. For example, consider Figure 17.3. Here, the firm faces average costs that are always above demand (AR). Setting marginal cost equal to marginal revenue suggests

OCR Advanced Economics

that the profit-maximising level of output is at $q_m$, but if the firm chooses to produce this quantity, and sets a price at $p_m$, the result is a loss (given by the shaded area), as average cost exceeds average revenue. Such a situation is not sustainable in the long run. However, if the firm is able to use price discrimination, it may be possible to remain profitable by tapping the consumer surplus of some groups of customers. For example, if the firm can operate perfect price discrimination, it could acquire the area of consumer surplus *ABC* as profit to set against the area of losses, *CEF*.

## Monopolistic competition in the leisure sector

The theory of monopolistic competition describes a market with some features of monopoly and some features of perfect competition. Barriers to entry are low, so the market has many firms. However, firms in the market use product differentiation to influence consumers, and thus face downward-sloping demand curves.

If you look back at the analysis in Chapter 15, you will see that this form of market structure has implications for both productive and allocative efficiency. Firms produce at a level of output that is below that at which long-run average cost would reach the minimum, so there is not productive efficiency. Furthermore, price is set above marginal cost, so allocative efficiency is not achieved either.

A growing section of the leisure sector is food outlets. The number of restaurants and fast-food outlets has mushroomed in recent decades, and on many high streets in UK towns there is a proliferation of eating places and takeaways. This market seems highly contestable, as the set-up costs for starting a new restaurant or takeaway are relatively low. One of the characteristics of a market operating under monopolistic competition is the product differentiation that takes place. Each individual seller sets out to be different from its competitors. This is certainly a characteristic of the fast-food sector, where outlets offer different styles of cuisine — burgers, Indian, Chinese, Thai, Mexican and so on. Before condemning such a market as being damaging to consumers because of the effect on productive and allocative efficiency, it is worth being aware that this market offers consumers a wide range of choice for fast food. If they value this choice, then this should be seen as a benefit that arises because of the market structure.

Another part of the leisure sector that typifies monopolistic competition is local taxi markets. Count the local taxi companies in your local *Yellow Pages*. Again, firms may seek to differentiate their products through having a fleet livery, by advertising pre-booking only or by offering a limousine service. There may also be firms that specialise in longer-distance trips, say to airports.

## Summary

➤ Market structure is important in determining whether allocative efficiency can be achieved.

- However, productive efficiency must also be taken into account.
- The package holiday market has become oligopolistic, with a few large firms dominating the market.
- However, the growth in the internet has meant that the market has become contestable, and the existing firms are facing intense competition from online entrants.
- Television broadcasting has also shown oligopolistic tendencies in the past, and given its characteristics as a public good and a merit good, there has been much government intervention and regulation.
- Again, changing technology has transformed the market and allowed greater competition among broadcasters.
- Spectator sport is another part of the leisure sector where the competition authorities have been active, particularly in relation to the growth of satellite broadcasting, where BSkyB has become a major player with a monopoly in certain areas.
- The low-cost airlines have transformed the market for air travel, making use of a thorough understanding of costs and the use of price discrimination.
- The leisure sector also offers examples of monopolistic competition in food outlets and taxi markets.

# *Chapter 18*
# Labour demand, supply of labour and wage determination

*The economic analysis of labour markets sheds light on a range of topical issues. How are wages determined? Differences in wages between people in different occupations and with different skills can be contentious. For example, why should premiership footballers or pop stars earn such high wages compared with nurses or firefighters? This chapter begins by looking at the labour market as an application of demand and supply analysis.*

## Learning outcomes

After studying this chapter, you should:

- ➤ understand that the demand for labour is a derived demand
- ➤ be aware of the relationship between labour input and total and marginal physical product
- ➤ understand the concept of marginal revenue product
- ➤ be familiar with how a profit-maximising firm chooses the quantity of labour input to use in production
- ➤ be aware of the factors that influence the elasticity of demand for labour
- ➤ understand the decision of an individual worker as regards labour supply
- ➤ be aware of the choice made by the individual worker between work and leisure
- ➤ understand the reasons for earnings differentials between people working in different occupations and with different skills

## Demand for labour

Firms are involved in production. They organise the factors of production in order to produce output. Labour is one of the key factors of production used by firms in this process, but notice that labour is valued not for its own sake, but for the output that it produces. In other words, the fundamental reason for firms to demand labour is for the revenue that can be obtained from selling the output that is produced by using labour. The demand for labour is thus a **derived demand**, and understanding this is crucial for an analysis of the labour market.

To illustrate this, consider a firm that manufactures cricket bats. The firm hires labourers to operate the machinery that is used in production. However, the firm does not hire a labourer because he or she is a nice person. The firm aims to make profit by selling the cricket bats produced, and the labourer is needed because of the labour services that he or she provides. This notion of derived demand underpins the analysis of labour markets.

Chapter 4 introduced the notion of the short-run production function, showing the relationship between the quantity of labour input used and the quantity of output produced. Figure 18.1 should remind you of this. Here $TPP_L$ is the **total physical product of labour**. As this is a short-run production function, capital cannot be varied: remember, this is how the short run is defined in this context.

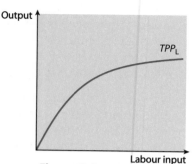

**Figure 18.1**
*A short-run production function*

The curve is drawn to show diminishing returns to labour. In other words, as labour input increases, the amount of additional output that is produced diminishes. This is because capital becomes relatively scarcer as the amount of labour increases without a corresponding increase in capital.

**Key terms**

**derived demand:** demand for a good not for its own sake, but for what it produces — for example, labour is demanded for the output that it produces

**total physical product of labour ($TPP_L$):** in the short run, the total amount of output produced at different levels of labour input with capital held fixed

**marginal physical product of labour ($MPP_L$):** the additional quantity of output produced by an additional unit of labour input

**marginal revenue product of labour ($MRP_L$):** the additional revenue received by a firm as it increases output by using an additional unit of labour input, i.e. the marginal physical product of labour multiplied by the marginal revenue received by the firm

In examining the demand for labour, it is helpful to work with the **marginal physical product of labour**, which is the amount of additional output produced if the firm increases its labour input by 1 unit (e.g. adding 1 more person-hour), holding capital constant. This is in fact given by the slope of $TPP_L$. An example is shown in Figure 18.2. When labour input is relatively low, such as at $L_0$, the additional output produced by an extra unit of labour is relatively high, at $q_0$, since the extra unit of labour has plenty of capital with which to work. However, as more labour is added, the marginal physical product falls, so at $L_1$ labour the marginal physical product is only $q_1$.

What matters to the firm is the revenue that it will receive from selling the additional output produced. In considering the profit-maximising amount of labour to employ, therefore, the firm needs to consider the marginal physical product multiplied by the marginal revenue received from selling the extra output, which is known as the **marginal revenue product of labour** ($MRP_L$).

If the firm is operating under perfect competition, then marginal revenue and price are the same and $MRP_L$ is $MPP_L$ multiplied by the price. However, if the firm faces a downward-sloping demand curve, it has to reduce the price of its product in order to sell the additional output. Marginal revenue is then lower than price, as the firm must lower the price on *all* of the output that it sells, not just on the last unit sold.

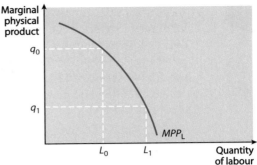

**Figure 18.2**
*The marginal physical product of labour*

Consider a firm operating under perfect competition, and setting out to maximise profits. Figure 18.3 shows the marginal revenue product curve. The question to consider is how the firm chooses how much labour input to use. This decision is based partly on the knowledge of the $MRP_L$, but it also depends on the cost of labour.

The main cost of using labour is the wages paid to the workers. There may be other costs — hiring costs and so on — but these can be set aside for the moment. Assuming that the labour market is perfectly competitive, so that the firm cannot influence the market wage and can obtain as much labour as it wants at the going wage rate, the wage can be regarded as the *marginal cost of labour (MCL)*.

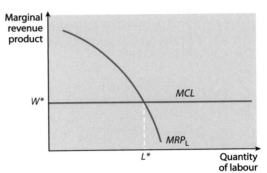

**Figure 18.3**
*The labour input decision of a profit-maximising firm under perfect competition*

If the marginal revenue received by the firm from selling the extra output produced by extra labour (i.e. the $MRP_L$) is higher than the wage, then hiring more labour will add to profits. On the other hand, if the $MRP_L$ is lower than the wage, then the firm is already hiring too much labour. Thus, it pays the firm to hire labour up to the point where the $MRP_L$ is just equal to the wage. On Figure 18.3, if the wage is $W^*$, the firm is maximising profits at $L^*$. The $MRP_L$ curve thus represents the firm's demand for labour curve. This approach is known as *marginal productivity theory*.

This profit-maximising condition can be written as:

wage = marginal revenue × marginal physical product of labour

which is the same as:

marginal revenue = wage/$MPP_L$ [= marginal cost]

Remember that capital input is fixed for the firm in the short run, so the wage divided by the $MPP_L$ is the firm's cost per unit of output at the margin. This shows that the profit-maximising condition is the same as that derived for a profit-maximising firm in Chapter 4: in other words, profit is maximised where marginal revenue equals marginal cost. This is just another way of looking at the firm's decision.

## part 5

### Exercise 18.1

Table 18.1 shows how the total physical product of labour varies with labour input for a firm operating under perfect competition in both product and labour markets. The price of the product is £5 and the wage rate is £30.

| Labour input per period | Output (goods per period) |
|---|---|
| 0 | 0 |
| 1 | 7 |
| 2 | 15 |
| 3 | 22 |
| 4 | 27 |
| 5 | 29 |

*Table 18.1  A profit-maximising firm*

**a** Calculate the marginal physical product of labour at each level of labour input.

**b** Calculate the marginal revenue product of labour at each level of labour input.

**c** Plot the $MRP_L$ on a graph and identify the profit-maximising level of labour input.

**d** Suppose that the firm faces fixed costs of £10. Calculate total revenue and total costs at each level of labour input, and check the profit-maximising level.

### Factors affecting the position of the demand for labour curve

There are a number of factors that determine the *position* of a firm's labour demand curve. First, anything that affects the marginal physical product of labour will also affect the $MRP_L$. For example, if a new technological advance raises the productivity of labour, it will also affect the position of the $MRP_L$. In Figure 18.4 you can see how the demand for labour would change if there were an increase in the marginal productivity of labour as a result of new technology. Initially demand is at $MRP_{L0}$, but the increased technology pushes the curve to $MRP_{L1}$. If the wage remains at $W^*$, the quantity of labour hired by the firm increases from $L_0$ to $L_1$. Similarly, in the long run, if a firm expands the size of its capital stock, this will also affect the demand for labour.

As $MRP_L$ is given by $MPP_L$ multiplied by marginal revenue, any change in marginal revenue will also affect labour demand. In a perfectly competitive product market,

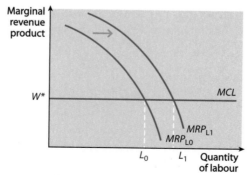

**Figure 18.4**
*The effect of improved technology*

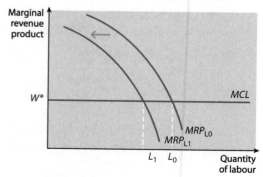

**Figure 18.5**
*The effect of a fall in the demand for a firm's product on the demand for labour*

OCR Advanced Economics

this means that any change in the price of the product will also affect labour demand. For example, suppose there is a fall in demand for a firm's product, so that the equilibrium price falls. This will have a knock-on effect on the firm's demand for labour, as illustrated in Figure 18.5. Initially, the firm was demanding $L_0$ labour at the wage rate $W^*$, but the fall in demand for the product leads to a fall in marginal revenue product (even though the physical productivity of labour has not changed), from $MRP_{L0}$ to $MRP_{L1}$. Only $L_1$ labour is now demanded at the wage rate $W^*$. This serves as a reminder that the demand for labour is a derived demand that is intimately bound up with the demand for the firm's product.

A number of possible reasons could underlie a change in the price of a firm's product — it could reflect changes in the price of other goods, changes in consumer incomes or changes in consumer preferences. All of these indirectly affect the demand for labour.

## Summary

➤ The demand for labour is a derived demand, as the firm wants labour not for its own sake, but for the output that it produces.

➤ In the short run, a firm faces diminishing returns to increases in labour input if capital is held constant.

➤ The marginal physical product of labour is the amount of output produced if the firm employs an additional unit of labour, keeping capital input fixed.

➤ The marginal revenue product of labour is the marginal physical product multiplied by marginal revenue.

➤ With perfect competition in the product market, marginal revenue and price are the same, but if the firm needs to reduce its price in order to sell additional units of output, then marginal revenue is smaller than price.

➤ A profit-maximising firm chooses labour input such that the marginal cost of labour is equal to the marginal revenue product of labour. This is equivalent to setting marginal revenue equal to marginal cost.

➤ The firm has a downward-sloping demand curve for labour, given by the marginal revenue product curve.

➤ The position of the firm's labour demand curve depends on those factors that influence the marginal physical product, such as technology and efficiency, but also on the price of the firm's product.

### Elasticity of the demand for labour

In addition to the factors affecting the *position* of the demand for labour curve, it is also important to examine its *shape*. In particular, what factors affect the firm's elasticity of demand for labour with respect to changes in the wage rate? In other words, how sensitive is a firm's demand for labour to a change in the wage rate (the cost of labour)?

Chapter 3 examined the influences on the price elasticity of demand, and identified the most important as being the availability of substitutes, the relative size of expenditure on a good in the overall budget and the time period over which the elasticity is measured. In looking at the elasticity of demand for labour, similar influences can be seen to be at work.

One significant effect on the elasticity of demand for labour is the extent to which other factors of production, such as capital, can be substituted for labour in the production process. If capital or some other factor can be readily substituted for labour, then an increase in the wage rate (ceteris paribus) will induce the firm to reduce its demand for labour by relatively more than if there were no substitute for labour. The extent to which labour and capital are substitutable varies between economic activities, depending on the technology of production, as there may be some sectors in which it is relatively easy for labour and capital to be substituted, and others in which it is quite difficult.

Second, the share of labour costs in the firm's total costs is important in determining the elasticity of demand for labour. In many service activities, labour is a highly significant share of total costs, so firms tend to be sensitive to changes in the cost of labour. However, in some capital-intensive manufacturing activity, labour may comprise a much smaller share of total production costs.

Third, as was argued above, capital will tend to be inflexible in the short run. Therefore, if a firm faces an increase in wages, it may have little flexibility in substituting towards capital in the short run, so the demand for labour may be relatively inelastic. However, in the longer term, the firm will be able to adjust the factors of production towards a different overall balance. Therefore, the elasticity of demand for labour is likely to be higher in the long run than in the short run.

These three influences closely parallel the analysis of what affects the price elasticity of demand. However, as the demand for labour is a derived demand, there is an additional influence that must be taken into account: the price elasticity of demand for the product. The more price elastic is demand for the product, the more sensitive will the firm be to a change in the wage rate, as high elasticity of demand for the product limits the extent to which an increase in wage costs can be passed on to consumers in the form of higher prices.

In order to derive an industry demand curve for labour, it is necessary to add up the quantities of labour that firms in that industry would want to demand at any wage rate, given the price of the product. As individual firms' demand curves are downward sloping, the industry demand curve will also slope downwards. In other words, more labour will be demanded at a lower wage rate, as shown in Figure 18.6.

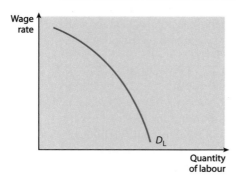

*Figure 18.6*
*An industry demand for labour curve*

## Summary

➤ The elasticity of demand for labour depends upon the degree to which capital may be substituted for labour in the production process.

➤ The share of labour in a firm's total costs will also affect the elasticity of demand for labour.

➤ Labour demand will tend to be more elastic in the long run than in the short run, as the firm needs time to adjust its production process following a change in market conditions.

➤ As the demand for labour is a derived demand, the elasticity of labour demand will also depend on the price elasticity of demand for the firm's product.

## Exercise 18.2

Using diagrams, explain how each of the following will affect a firm's demand for labour:

**a** a fall in the selling price of the firm's product

**b** adoption of improved working practices that improve labour productivity

**c** an increase in the wage (in a situation where the firm must accept the wage as market determined)

**d** an increase in the demand for the firm's product

## Labour supply

So far, labour supply has been considered only as it is perceived by a firm, and the assumption has been that the firm is in a perfectly competitive market for labour, and therefore cannot influence the 'price' of labour. Hence the firm sees the labour supply curve as being perfectly elastic, as drawn in Figure 18.3, where labour supply was described as *MCL*.

However, for the industry as a whole, labour supply is unlikely to be flat. Intuitively, you might expect to see an upward-sloping labour supply curve. The reason for this is that more people will tend to offer themselves for work when the wage is relatively high. However, this is only part of the background to the industry labour supply curve.

An increase in the wage rate paid to workers in an industry will have two effects. On the one hand, it will tend to attract more workers into that industry, thereby increasing labour supply. However, the change may also affect the supply decisions of workers already in that industry, and for existing workers an increase in the wage rate may have ambiguous effects.

### Individual labour supply

Consider an individual worker who is deciding how many hours of labour to supply. As noted in Chapter 16, every choice comes with an *opportunity cost*, so if a worker chooses to take more leisure time, he or she is choosing to forgo income-earning

opportunities. In other words, the wage rate can be seen as the opportunity cost of leisure. It is the income that the worker has to sacrifice in order to enjoy leisure time.

Now think about the likely effects of an increase in the wage rate. Such an increase raises the opportunity cost of leisure. This in turn has two effects. First, as leisure time is now more costly, there will be a substitution effect against leisure. In other words, workers will be motivated to work longer hours.

However, as the higher wage brings the worker a higher level of real income, a second effect comes into play, encouraging the consumption of more goods and services — including leisure, if it is assumed that leisure is a *normal good.*

Notice that these two effects work against each other. The substitution effect encourages workers to offer more labour at a higher wage because of the effect of the change in the opportunity cost of leisure. However, the real income effect encourages the worker to demand more leisure as a result of the increase in income. The net effect could go either way.

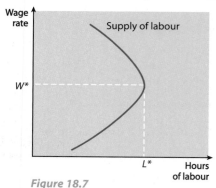

Figure 18.7
A backward-bending individual labour supply curve

It might be argued that at relatively low wages the substitution effect will tend to be the stronger. However, as the wage continues to rise, the income effect may gradually become stronger, so that at some wage level the worker will choose to supply less labour and will demand more leisure. The individual labour supply curve will then be backward bending, as shown in Figure 18.7, where an increase in the wage rate above $W^*$ induces the individual to supply fewer hours of work in order to enjoy more leisure time.

It is important to realise that decisions about labour supply may also be influenced by job satisfaction. A worker who finds his or her work to be satisfying may be prepared to accept a lower wage than a worker who really hates every minute spent at work.

### Industry labour supply

At industry level, the labour supply curve can be expected to be upward sloping. Although individual workers may display backward-bending supply curves, when workers in a market are aggregated, higher wages will induce people to join the market, either from outside the workforce altogether or from other industries where wages have not risen.

## Summary

➤ For an individual worker, a choice needs to be made between income earned from working and leisure.

➤ The wage rate can be seen as the opportunity cost of leisure.

➤ An increase in the wage rate will encourage workers to substitute work for leisure through the substitution effect.

➤ However, there is also an income effect, which may mean that workers will demand more leisure at higher income levels.

➤ If the income effect dominates the substitution effect, then the individual labour supply curve may become backward bending.

➤ However, when aggregated to the industry level, higher wages will encourage more people into the industry such that the industry supply curve is not expected to be backward bending.

## Labour market equilibrium

Bringing demand and supply curves together for an industry shows how the equilibrium wage is determined. Figure 18.8 shows a downward-sloping labour demand curve ($D_L$) based on marginal productivity theory, and an upward-sloping labour supply curve ($S_L$). Equilibrium is found at the intersection of demand and supply. If the wage is lower than $W^*$ employers will not be able to fill all their vacancies, and will have to offer a higher wage to attract more workers. If the wage is higher than $W^*$ there will be an excess supply of labour, and the wage will drift down until $W^*$ is reached and equilibrium obtained.

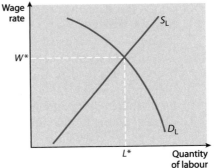

**Figure 18.8**
*Labour market equilibrium*

Comparative static analysis can be used to examine the effects of changes in market conditions. For instance, a change in the factors that determine the position of the labour demand curve will induce a movement of labour demand and an adjustment in the equilibrium wage. Suppose there is an increase in the demand for the firm's product. This will lead to a rightward shift in the demand for labour, say from $D_{L0}$ to $D_{L1}$ in Figure 18.9. This in turn will lead to a new market equilibrium, with the wage rising from $W_0$ to $W_1$.

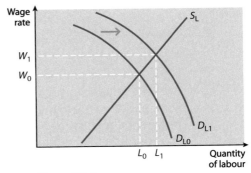

**Figure 18.9**
*An increase in the demand for labour*

This may not be the final equilibrium position, however. If the higher wages in this market now encourage workers to switch from other industries in which wages have not risen, this will lead to a longer-term shift to the right of the labour supply curve. In a free market, the shift will continue until wage differentials are no longer sufficient to encourage workers to transfer.

**part 5**

## Summary

➤ Labour market equilibrium is found at the intersection of labour demand and labour supply.

➤ This determines the equilibrium wage rate for an industry.

➤ Comparative static analysis can be used to analyse the effects of changes in market conditions.

➤ Changes in relative wages between sectors may induce movement of workers between industries.

## Labour markets

So far, the focus has been on the demand and supply of labour, sometimes seen through the eyes of a firm, sometimes through the eyes of a worker and sometimes looking at an industry labour market. It is important to realise that these are separate levels of analysis. In particular, there is no single labour market in an economy like the UK, any more than there is a single market for goods. In reality, there is a complex network of labour markets for people with different skills and for people in different occupations, and there are overlapping markets for labour corresponding to different product markets.

Thus, when in macroeconomics economists talk about *the* labour market, this is a considerable simplification — helpful in its way, but potentially misleading. It is now time to think about some microeconomic issues concerning individual labour markets beginning with the important concepts of transfer earnings and economic rent.

## Transfer earnings and economic rent

### Transfer earnings

Many factors of production have some flexibility about them, in the sense that they can be employed in a variety of alternative uses. A worker may be able to work in different occupations and industries; computers can be put to use in a wide range of activities. The decision to use a factor of production for one particular job rather than another carries an opportunity cost, which can be seen in terms of the next best alternative activity in which that factor could have been employed.

For example, consider a woman who chooses to work as a waitress because the pay is better than she could obtain as a shop assistant. By making this choice, she forgoes the opportunity to work at, say, John Lewis. The opportunity cost is seen in terms of this forgone alternative. If John Lewis were to raise its rates of pay in order to attract more staff, there would come a point where the waitress might reconsider her decision and decide to be a shop assistant after all, as the opportunity cost of being a waitress has risen.

OCR Advanced Economics

The threshold at which this decision is taken leads to the definition of transfer earnings. **Transfer earnings** are defined in terms of the minimum payment that is required in order to keep a factor of production in its present use.

## Economic rent

In a labour market, transfer earnings can be thought of as the minimum payment that will keep the marginal worker in his or her present occupation or sector. This payment will vary from worker to worker; moreover, where there is a market in which all workers receive the same pay for the same job, there will be some workers who receive a wage in excess of their transfer earnings. This excess of payment to a factor over and above what is required to keep it in its present use is known as **economic rent**.

The total payments to a factor can thus be divided between these two — part of the payment is transfer earnings, and the remainder is economic rent.

Probably the best way of explaining how a worker's earnings can be divided between transfer earnings and economic rent is through an appropriate diagram. Figure 18.10 illustrates the two concepts. In the labour market as drawn, firms' demand for labour is a downward-sloping function of the wage rate. Workers' supply of labour also depends on the wage rate, with workers being prepared to supply more labour to the labour market at higher wages. Equilibrium is the point at which demand equals supply, with wage rate $W^*$ and quantity of labour $L^*$.

Think about the nature of the labour supply curve. It reveals how much labour the workers are prepared to supply at any given wage rate. At the equilibrium wage rate $W^*$, there is a worker who is supplying labour at the margin. If the wage rate were to fall even slightly below $W^*$, the worker would withdraw from this labour market, perhaps to take alternative employment in another sector or occupation. In other words, the wage rate can be regarded as the transfer earnings of the marginal worker. A similar argument can be made about any point along the labour supply curve.

This means that the area under the supply curve up to the equilibrium point can be interpreted as the transfer earnings of workers in this labour market. In Figure 18.10 this is given by the area $OBAL^*$.

Total earnings are given by the wage rate multiplied by the quantity of labour supplied (here, area $OW^*AL^*$). Economic rent is thus that part of total earnings that is *not* transfer earnings. In Figure 18.10 this is the triangle

**Key terms**

**transfer earnings:** the minimum payment required to keep a factor of production in its present use

**economic rent:** a payment received by a factor of production over and above what would be needed to keep it in its present use

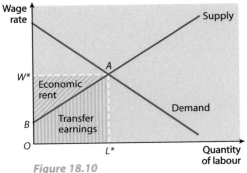

*Figure 18.10*
*Transfer earnings and economic rent*

$BW^*A$. The rationale is that this area represents the total excess that workers receive by being paid a wage ($W^*$) that is above the minimum required to keep them employed in this market.

If you think about it, you will see that this is similar to the notion of producer surplus, which is the difference between the price received by firms for a good or service and the price at which the firms would have been prepared to supply that good or service.

### The balance between transfer earnings and economic rent

What determines the balance between the two aspects of total earnings? In this connection, the elasticity of supply of labour is of critical importance.

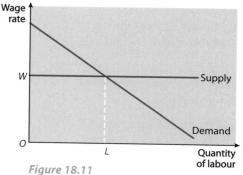

*Figure 18.11*
*Perfectly elastic labour supply*

This can be seen by studying diagrams showing varying degrees of elasticity of supply. First, consider two extreme situations. Figure 18.11 shows a labour market in which supply is perfectly elastic. This implies that there is limitless supply of labour at the wage rate $W$. In this situation there is no economic rent to be gained from labour supply, and all earnings are transfer earnings. Any reduction of the wage below $W$ will mean that all workers leave the market.

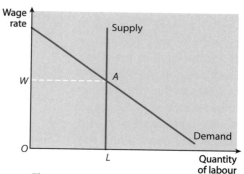

*Figure 18.12*
*Perfectly inelastic labour supply*

Now consider Figure 18.12. Here labour supply is perfectly inelastic. There is a fixed amount of labour being supplied to the market and, whatever the wage rate, that amount of labour remains the same. Another way of looking at this is that there is no minimum payment needed to keep labour in its present use. Now the entire earnings of the factor are made up by economic rent (i.e. the area $OWAL$).

This illustrates how important the elasticity of labour supply is in determining the balance between transfer earnings and economic rent. The more inelastic supply is, the higher the proportion of total earnings that is made up of economic rent.

### Surgeons and butchers: the importance of supply

Consider an example of differential earnings — say, surgeons and butchers. First think about the surgeons. Surgeons are in relatively inelastic supply, at least in the short run. The education required to become a surgeon is long and demanding, and is certainly essential for entry into the occupation. Furthermore, not everyone is cut out to become a surgeon, as this is a field that requires certain innate abilities and talents. This implies that the supply of surgeons is limited and does not vary a great

deal with the wage rate. If this is the case, then the earnings of surgeons are largely made up of economic rent.

The situation may be reinforced by the fact that, once an individual has trained as a surgeon, there may be few alternative occupations to which, if disgruntled, he or she could transfer. There is a natural limit to how many surgeons there are, *and* to their willingness to exit from the market.

How about butchers? The training programme for butchers is less arduous than for surgeons, and a wider range of people is suitable for employment in this occupation. Labour supply for butchers is thus likely to be more elastic than for surgeons, and so economic rent will be relatively less important than in the previous case. If butchers were to receive high enough wages, more people would be attracted to the trade and wage rates would eventually fall.

In addition, there are other occupations into which butchers can transfer when they have had enough of cutting up all that meat: they might look to other sections of the catering sector, for example. This reinforces the relatively high elasticity of supply.

### The importance of demand

Economic rent has been seen to be more important for surgeons than for butchers, but is this the whole story? The discussion so far has centred entirely on the supply side of the market. But demand is also important.

Indeed, it is the position of the demand curve when interacting with supply that determines the equilibrium wage rate in a labour market. It may well be that the supply of workers skilled in underwater basket weaving is strictly limited; but if there is no demand for underwater basket weavers then there is no scope for that skill to earn high economic rents. In the above example, it is the relatively strong demand for surgeons relative to their limited supply that leads to a relatively high equilibrium wage in the market.

### Evaluation

This analysis can be applied to answer some questions that often appear about the labour market. In particular, why should the top footballers and pop stars be paid such high salaries, whereas valued professions such as nurses and firefighters are paid much less?

A footballer such as Wayne Rooney is valued because of the talent that he displays on the

*The talents of Wayne Rooney are in limited supply, which leads to a high equilibrium wage rate*

pitch, and because of his ability to bring in the crowds who want to see him play. This makes him a good revenue earner for his club, and reflects his high marginal productivity. In addition, his skills are rare — some would say unique. Wayne Rooney is thus in extremely limited supply. This combination of high marginal productivity and limited supply leads to a high equilibrium wage rate.

For nurses and firefighters, society may value them highly in one sense — that they carry out a vital, and sometimes dangerous, occupation. However, they are not valued in the sense of displaying high marginal productivity. Furthermore, the supply is by no means as limited as in the case of top-class professional footballers. These factors taken together help to explain why there are such large differences in salaries between occupations. This is one example of how marginal productivity theory helps to explain features of the real world that non-economists often find puzzling.

## Exercise 18.3

Figure 18.13 shows demand and supply in a labour market.

a Identify the area that represents economic rent.

b Which area shows transfer earnings?

c Sketch some diagrams yourself to see how the balance between economic rent and transfer earnings differs if the supply of labour is more or less elastic.

d Sketch some more diagrams to explore the effect of shifts in the demand curve for labour.

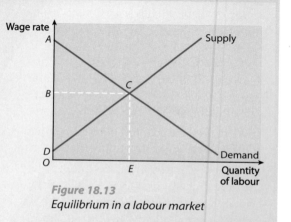

*Figure 18.13*
*Equilibrium in a labour market*

## Summary

➤ In a modern economy, there is a complex network of labour markets for workers with different skills, working in different occupations and industries.

➤ The total payments to a factor of production can be separated into transfer earnings and economic rent.

➤ Transfer earnings represent the minimum payment needed to keep a factor of production in its present use.

➤ Economic rent is a payment received by a factor of production over and above what would be needed to keep it in its present use.

➤ The balance between transfer earnings and economic rent depends critically on the elasticity of supply of a particular kind of labour.

➤ The position of the demand curve is also important.

# Education and the labour market

The above discussion has highlighted the importance of education and training in influencing wage differentials between occupational groups. Education and training might be regarded as a form of *barrier to entry* into a labour market, affecting the elasticity of supply of labour. Because of differences in innate talents and abilities — not to mention personal inclinations — wage differentials can persist even in the long run in certain occupations. However, economists expect there to be some long-run equilibrium level of differential that reflects the preference and natural talent aspects of various occupations.

Changes in the pattern of consumer demand for goods over time will lead to changes in those equilibrium differentials. For example, during the computer revolution, when firms were increasing their use of computers at work and households were increasing their use of home computers, there was a need for more computer programmers to create the software that people wanted, and a need for more computer engineers to fix the computers when they crashed. This meant that the wage differential for these workers increased. This in turn led to a proliferation of courses on offer to train or retrain people in these skills. Then, as the supply of such workers began to increase, so the wage differential narrowed.

*During the computer revolution, firms increased their use of computers*

This is what economists would expect to observe if the labour market is working effectively, with wages acting as signals to workers about what skills are in demand. It is part of the way in which a market system guides the allocation of resources.

## Individual educational choices

In specific cases, such as that of the computer programmers, you can see how individuals may respond to market signals. Word gets around that computer programmers are in high demand, and individual workers and job-seekers respond to that. However, not all education is geared so specifically towards such specific gaps in the market. How do individuals take decisions about education?

Such a decision can be regarded as an example of *cost–benefit analysis.* In trying to decide whether or not to undertake further education, an individual needs to balance the costs of such education against its benefits. One important consideration is that the costs tend to come in the short run, but the benefits only in the long run. Much of the discussion of student university tuition fees centres on this issue. Should students incur high debts now in the expectation of future higher earnings? Work through Exercise 18.4 to take this further.

## Exercise 18.4

Suppose you are considering undertaking a university education. Compile a list of the benefits and the costs that you expect to encounter if you choose to do so. Discuss how you would go about balancing the benefits and costs, remembering that the timing of these needs to be taken into account.

In Exercise 18.4 you will have identified a range of benefits and costs. On the costs side are the direct costs in terms of tuition fees and living expenses, and there are also opportunity costs — the fact that you will have to delay the time when you start earning an income. But there are benefits to set against these costs, which may include the enjoyment you get from undertaking further study and the fact that university can be a great experience — that is, it can be a consumption good as well as an investment good. And, almost certainly, you have considered the fact that you can expect higher future earnings as a university graduate than as a non-graduate.

A recent study by the OECD investigated the relationship between education and earnings in a range of countries. Figure 18.14 presents some of the results, showing the differential in earnings between university graduates and those who left education at the end of secondary schooling. The data are expressed as index numbers, with earnings of secondary school leavers set equal to 100. Thus, for the UK, a male graduate earned 57% more than a secondary school leaver, whereas a female graduate earned 106% more. A study in *Labour Market Trends* in March 2003 also found that those leaving education at age 21 seem to experience around a 50% wage increase compared with those leaving education at 16; however, in that study there was no significant difference between men and women.

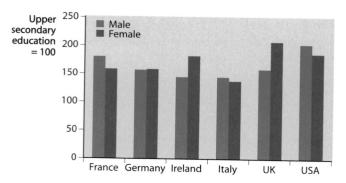

*Figure 18.14*
*Education and earnings*

Note: the graph shows the average employment earnings of people with the equivalent of UK university under-graduate degrees relative to people with only secondary education.

Source: OECD.

These data are a little difficult to interpret. They cannot be taken to mean that a university education increases the *productivity* of workers, because it may be that those who chose to undertake university education were naturally more able. This is the 'signalling' view of education — that the value of the degree is not so much what was learned during the programme of study as an indication that the person was capable of doing it. However, the fact that the returns to education are seen

to vary across degree subjects suggests that employers do look for some value-added to emerge from university education. The evidence suggests that arts degrees have relatively little impact on average wages, whereas degrees in economics, management and law have large effects.

In spite of such evidence that lifetime earnings can be boosted by education, people may still demand too little education for the best interest of society, as was discussed in Chapter 6. This may be because there are *externality effects* associated with education. Although education has been shown to improve productivity, it has also been found that *groups* of educated workers are able to cooperate and work together so that collectively they are even more productive than they are as individuals. From this point of view, an individual worker may not perceive the full social benefit of higher education.

Figure 18.15 is a reminder of this argument. If marginal social benefit (*MSB*) is higher than marginal private benefit (*MPB*), there is a tendency for individuals to demand too little education, choosing to acquire $Q_1$ education rather than the amount $Q^*$, which is the best for society. This argument may be used to suggest that government should encourage people to undertake more education.

*Degrees in law have a large impact on average wages*

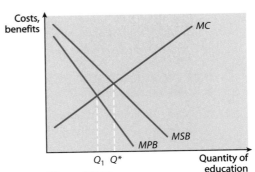

**Figure 18.15**
*Education as a positive consumption externality*

## Summary

➤ Wage differentials may act as signals to guide potential workers in their demand for training and retraining.

➤ People demand education partly for the effect it will have on their future earnings potential.

➤ Externality effects may mean that people choose to demand less education than is desirable for society as a whole.

# *Chapter 19*
# Labour market imperfections and the role of government and the unions

*Product markets do not always work perfectly. For example, a firm (or small group of firms) may come to dominate a market and use its market power to increase its supernormal profits to the detriment of the consumer. It has also been shown that some government interventions in product markets do not always have their intended effects. This chapter explores some of the ways in which imperfections can be manifest in labour markets. It also examines the extent to which legislation has been able to outlaw discrimination on the basis of ethnic origin or gender. The role of trade unions in a modern economy is also discussed.*

## Learning outcomes

After studying this chapter, you should:
➤ understand ways in which labour markets may be imperfect
➤ be aware of the operation of a labour market in which there is a monopsony buyer of labour
➤ be familiar with a bilateral monopoly model in which a monopsony buyer of labour faces a trade union
➤ be aware of ways in which governments may cause imperfections in labour markets through their interventions
➤ understand how unemployment may arise in a market
➤ understand the role of trade unions in the economy
➤ understand the effects of trade union activity on the labour market

## Market failure in labour markets

The previous chapter has described the operation of labour markets and the way in which equilibrium can be achieved. However, as with product markets, there are many ways in which labour markets may fail to achieve the most desirable results for society at large. Such market failure can occur on either the demand or the supply side of the market. On the demand side, it may be that employers — as the buyers of labour — have market power that can be exploited at the expense of

the workers. Alternatively, it may be that some employers act against the interests of some groups of workers relative to others through some form of discrimination in their hiring practices or wage-setting behaviour. On the supply side, there may be restrictions on the supply of some types of labour, or it may be that trade unions find themselves able to bid wages up to a level that is above the free market equilibrium.

On another level, the very existence of unemployment might be interpreted as indicating disequilibrium in the labour market — although there may also be reasons to expect there always to be some unemployment in a modern economy. Finally, there are some forms of government intervention that may have unintended effects on labour markets.

## Monopsony

One type of market failure in a product market occurs when there is a single *seller* of a good: that is, a monopoly market. As you may recall, a firm with this sort of market dominance is able to restrict output, and maximise profits by setting a higher price. A similar form of market power can occur on the other side of the market if there is a single *buyer* of a good, service or factor of production. Such a market is known as a **monopsony**.

**Key** term

**monopsony:** a market in which there is a single buyer of a good, service or factor of production

In Chapter 18 it was assumed that firms in the labour market face perfect competition, and therefore must accept the market wage. However, suppose that one firm is the sole user of a particular type of labour, or is the dominant firm in a city or region, and thus is in a monopsony situation.

Such a monopsonist faces the market supply curve of labour directly, rather than simply accepting the equilibrium market wage. It views this supply curve as its average cost of labour because it shows the average wage rate that it would need to offer to obtain any given quantity of labour input.

Figure 19.1 shows a monopsonist's demand curve for labour, which is the marginal revenue product curve ($MRP_L$), and its supply curve of labour, seen by the firm as its average cost curve of labour ($AC_L$). If the market were perfectly competitive, equilibrium would be where supply equals demand, which would be with the firm using $L^*$ labour at a wage rate $W^*$.

From the perspective of the monopsonist firm facing the supply curve directly, if at any point it wants to hire more labour, it has to offer a higher wage to encourage more workers to join the market — after all, that is what the $AC_L$ curve tells it. However, the firm would then have to pay that higher

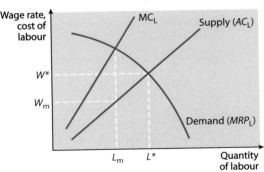

*Figure 19.1*
*A monopsony buyer of labour*

wage to *all* its workers, so the *marginal cost* of hiring the extra worker is not just the wage paid to that worker, but the increased wage paid to all the other workers as well. So the marginal cost of labour curve ($MC_L$) can be added to the diagram.

Remember that, in the diagram for a profit-maximising monopolist in Chapter 14 (Figure 14.9 on page 215), it was pointed out that there was a fixed relationship between the $AR$ and $MR$ curves, with the $MR$ curve having a slope that was exactly twice as steep as $AR$. This diagram depicts the same sort of relationship, with the $MC_L$ having a slope exactly twice as steep as $AC_L$. However, this time they are upward sloping.

If the monopsonist firm wants to maximise profit, it will hire labour up to the point where the marginal cost of labour is equal to the marginal revenue product of labour. Therefore it will use labour up to the level $L_m$, which is where $MC_L = MRP_L$. In order to entice workers to supply this amount of labour, the firm need pay only the wage $W_m$. (Remember that $AC_L$ is the supply curve of labour.) You can see, therefore, that a profit-maximising monopsonist will use less labour, and pay a lower wage, than a firm operating under perfect competition. From society's perspective, this entails a cost, just as was seen in the comparison of monopoly and perfect competition in Chapter 14.

## Exercise 19.1

Figure 19.2 shows a firm in a monopsonistic labour market.

**a** What would the wage rate be if this market were perfectly competitive, and how much labour would be employed?

**b** As a monopsony, what wage would the firm offer to its workers, and how much labour would it employ?

**c** Which area represents the employer's wage bill?

**d** What surplus does this generate for the firm?

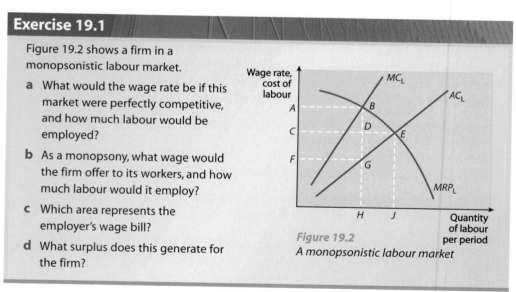

*Figure 19.2*
*A monopsonistic labour market*

## Discrimination

In Chapter 18, it was explained that wage differentials across different labour markets within an economy such as the UK are to be expected because of differences in marginal productivity of different workers, and differences in economic rent and transfer earnings. However, the question often arises as to whether such economic analysis can explain all of the differentials in wages that can be observed. For example, consider Table 19.1.

| | Female/male pay gap (%) | Female/male part-time pay gap (%) | Ethnic employment gap (% points) |
|---|---|---|---|
| 1975 | 36 | 34 | n/a |
| 1979 | 37 | 41 | −1 |
| 1990 | 33 | 41 | −7 |
| 1997 | 26 | 36 | −9 |
| 2000 | 25 | 36 | −9 |
| 2002 | 23 | 36 | −9 |

*Table 19.1*
*Wage differentials in the British economy*

Source: Richard Dickens, Paul Gregg and Jonathan Wadsworth, 'The labour market under New Labour', *Economic Review*, September 2003.

These data point to differentials in pay and employment that require some investigation. There would seem to be a noticeable pay gap between women and men. For full-time workers this has narrowed since 1975, but for part-time workers it has not. It also appears that employment opportunities for ethnic minority groups have worsened since 1975 — in spite of legislation that has increasingly tried to ensure equal opportunities for all. It is important to explore the extent to which these differences can be explained by economic analysis, and the extent to which they reflect discrimination in pay or employment opportunities.

The mere fact that there is inequality does not prove that there is discrimination. You have seen the way in which education and training affects earnings, so differentials between different groups of people may reflect the different educational choices made by those different groups. The gender gap may also reflect the fact that childcare responsibilities interrupt the working lives of many women. This is important in terms of human capital and the build-up of experience and seniority. The increasing introduction of crèche facilities by many firms is reducing the extent of this contribution to the earnings gap, but it has not eliminated it. In addition, there have been changes in social attitudes towards female education beyond the age of 16. When girls were expected to become homemakers,

*The narrowing of the gender pay gap is partly a result of changing social attitudes*

education beyond 16 was not highly valued, so there were generations of women who missed out on education, and consequently found themselves disadvantaged in the labour market. Although attitudes have changed, such effects take a long time to work their way through the system.

## Summary

➤ A market in which there is a single buyer of a good, service or factor of production is known as a monopsony market.

➤ A monopsony buyer of labour will employ less labour at a lower wage than if the market is perfectly competitive.

➤ Wage differentials and employment conditions are seen to vary between males and females and between ethnic groups, and only part of the variance can be explained by economic analysis, suggesting there may be discrimination.

## Unemployment

In Part 3 of the book, unemployment was discussed at a *macroeconomic* level, as one of the key measures of an economy's overall performance. In that context a number of different causes of unemployment were identified.

*Frictional unemployment* was seen as arising when workers switch between jobs. This is a purely transitional phenomenon, and is necessary if the labour market is to be flexible in allowing people to transfer between firms or industries. When retraining is needed to ease the transition, the unemployment may be longer term: for example, when some sectors are declining and others are expanding, workers may need to be re-skilled in order to make the transfer. This is known as *structural unemployment*. It was also pointed out that in the macroeconomic context there may be a state of *demand-deficient unemployment*, in which aggregate demand in the economy is insufficient for the economy to reach full employment.

In a *microeconomic* context, unemployment might be seen from a different angle. While some frictional unemployment cannot be avoided, structural unemployment can be regarded as an indicator of some inflexibility in labour markets, slowing the process by which workers can move from one job to another.

One cause of structural unemployment may be that firms are not providing sufficient training to ensure a smooth transition. On-the-job training is an important way to enable workers to gain the skills that will make them more productive in the future. When firms are taking employment decisions, they are concerned not only with today's marginal revenue product of workers, but with the longer-term perspective.

Providing training is costly to a firm, however, so it will need some assurance that it will be able to reap the benefits at a later date in the form of higher productivity. It may also be aware that firms choosing not to provide training may be able to

poach its newly trained workers without having incurred the costs of the training. In other words, there is a potential *free-rider* problem here.

There may be some skills that are useful only within the firm. Such *firm-specific* skills do not pose quite the same problems. However, for generic transferable skills there is an incentive for firms to underprovide training. Some government intervention may therefore be needed to rectify this situation.

Unemployment could also arise where some people choose not to work simply because unemployment benefit is set at such a level that they are better off on benefits than accepting a low-paid job. This is an area where the government has to maintain a careful balance in policy. On the one hand, it may be seen as important to provide protection for vulnerable people who are unable to obtain employment. On the other hand, if benefits are set at too generous a level, people may opt for unemployment rather than low-paid jobs. This is sometimes known as the **unemployment trap**. Unemployment that results from this is *voluntary unemployment*, in the sense that people are choosing to be unemployed because of the incentives that face them. To counter this, the government needs to ensure that 'work pays'.

**Key term**

**unemployment trap:** a situation in which people choose to be unemployed because the level of unemployment benefit is high relative to the wage available in low-paid occupations

## Disequilibrium unemployment

One important potential cause of unemployment is disequilibrium in a labour market. Some examples of this have already been given. A wage set at a level that is above the equilibrium rate can cause unemployment in a labour market.

This is shown in Figure 19.3 where, given the demand curve $D^*$, the equilibrium wage is at $W^*$, with labour employed up to $L^*$. With the wage held above the equilibrium rate, at $W_1$, the supply of labour ($S_1$) exceeds the quantity of labour that firms are prepared to hire ($D_1$), and the difference ($S_1 - D_1$) is unemployment – the number of workers who would like a job at the going wage rate, but are unable to find a job.

This could occur for a number of reasons. In some circumstances the introduction of a minimum wage could have this effect. Another possibility is that a trade union is able to negotiate a wage that is higher than the equilibrium rate. These will be analysed shortly.

Disequilibrium unemployment could also happen where there is inflexibility in the market. For example, suppose that a firm experiences a fall in the demand for its product. As the price of the product falls, so

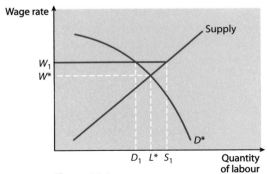

*Figure 19.3*
*Disequilibrium unemployment*

the marginal revenue product of labour falls, and the firm would want to move to a lower employment level and pay lower wages. This is shown in Figure 19.4. If previously the demand for labour was at $D_0$ then $W_0$ would have been the equilibrium wage rate, and employment would have been $L_0$, with no unemployment. When the demand for labour falls to $D_1$, there would be a new potential equilibrium with the wage at $W^*$ and employment

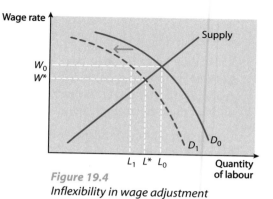

**Figure 19.4**
*Inflexibility in wage adjustment*

$L^*$. However, if the market is sluggish to adjust, perhaps because there is resistance to lowering wages from $W_0$ to $W^*$, then this will cause unemployment. In other words, with the wage remaining at $W_0$, workers continue to try to supply $L_0$ labour, but firms will only demand $L_1$, and the difference is unemployment. This situation of sticky wage adjustment is thus another cause of unemployment.

## Extension material

Chapter 7 introduced the problem of asymmetric information, where market failure can arise because some traders in a market have better information than others. This can happen in labour markets too.

The issue arises from the employer's perspective. When an employer is hiring new workers, a key concern is the quality of the workers applying for jobs. This is partly a question about their innate talents and abilities. It can be overcome to some extent by checking applicants' qualifications; indeed, this is why employers may insist on qualifications, even if they are not directly related to the requirements of the job.

However, there are other differences between workers that are important. Two workers with the same qualifications may show very different productivity. Some workers are naturally hardworking and conscientious, whereas others are always taking rest breaks and getting away with as little effort as possible. At the hiring stage, the employer may not be able to distinguish between the 'workers' and the 'shirkers'.

Suppose a firm pays a wage that is the average warranted by workers and shirkers combined. As time goes by, some workers are likely to quit and go to higher-paid jobs with other firms. The employees who are most likely to leave are the more productive ones, who realise that, if they are paid the average of what is right for the workers and shirkers taken together, they are being paid less than their own value. In the long run, the employer could be left with just the shirkers.

A rational response to this from the employer's perspective is to pay a wage that is higher than the average, in order to encourage the productive workers to stay with the firm. This has the additional benefit of increasing the penalty for being caught shirking (since a worker faces a greater opportunity cost of getting the sack if wages are higher). Thus, paying a higher-than-average wage has an additional incentive effect in that it discourages shirking.

This higher-than-average wage is known as the efficiency wage, and can be seen as a response by firms to the asymmetric information problem. One of the results in the labour market is to raise the level of involuntary unemployment, in the sense that at the higher wage there will be an increase in the number of workers who would be prepared to accept a job, but are unable to find employment.

## Labour mobility

A further reason for labour market inflexibility is that workers are not perfectly mobile. Mobility here can be seen in two important dimensions. First, there may be geographic immobility, where workers may be reluctant to move to a new region in search of appropriate employment. Second, there may be immobility between occupations. Both sorts of immobility can hinder the free operation of labour markets.

### Geographic mobility

There are a number of reasons that help to explain why workers may not be freely mobile between different parts of the country. This will cause problems for the labour market if the available jobs and the available workers are not located in the same area. A key issue involves the costs that are entailed in moving to a new job in a new region. These could be considerable in social terms — people do not like to move away from their friends and relatives, or to leave the area that they know or where their favourite football team plays. Parents may not wish to disrupt their children's education. However, there are also strong economic considerations.

The relatively high rate of owner-occupied housing in the UK means that workers who are owner-occupiers may need a strong inducement to move to another part of the country in search of jobs. For council house tenants, too, it may be quite difficult to relocate to a different area for employment purposes because they will have to return to the bottom of the waiting list for housing. Differences in house prices in different parts of the country further add to the problem of matching workers to jobs.

There may also be information problems, in that it may be more difficult to find out about job availability in other areas. The internet may have reduced the costs of job search to some extent, but it is still easier to find jobs in the local area, where the reputation of firms is better known to locals. Where both partners in a relationship are working, this may also make it more difficult to find jobs further afield, and there is some evidence that females tend to be less mobile geographically than males.

### Occupational mobility

The difficulty that people face in moving between occupations is an important source of labour market inflexibility. This was mentioned earlier in this chapter in the context of structural unemployment. Over time, it is to be expected that the

pattern of consumer demand will change, and if the pattern of economic activity is to change in response, it is important that some sectors of the economy decline to enable others to expand. For example, the demise of coal as a major energy source meant that the coal-mining industry went into decline, and displaced workers needed to find alternative employment. More generally, as the UK economy has moved away from manufacturing towards service sector activities, people have needed to be occupationally mobile to find work.

There are costs involved for workers switching between occupations. A displaced farm worker may not be able to find work as a ballet dancer without some degree of retraining! As explained earlier, firms may be expected to underprovide training to their workers because of the free-rider problem. In other words, firms may be reluctant to provide training for workers who may then choose to leave to work for a competitor, which could afford to pay higher wages because it would not have to pay the costs of the training. There may therefore be a need for some government intervention to ensure that training is provided in order to combat the problem of structural unemployment and to facilitate occupational mobility.

As with geographic mobility, another factor that may impede occupational mobility is the question of information. Workers may not have enough information to enable them to judge the benefits from occupational mobility. For example, they may not be aware of their aptitude for different occupations, or the extent to which they may gain job satisfaction from a job that they have not tried. These arguments do not apply only to workers displaced by structural change in the economy. They are equally valid for workers who are in jobs that may not necessarily be the best ones for them.

## Summary

➤ Unemployment arises for a number of reasons at the microeconomic level.

➤ Structural unemployment, arising from changes in the structure of economic activity within an economy, may reflect inflexibility in a labour market, which slows the process by which workers move from declining into expanding sectors.

➤ Firms may underprovide training in transferable skills because of a possible free-rider effect.

➤ Unemployment in a market may arise if wages are held above the equilibrium level — because of trade union action, a minimum wage or sluggish adjustment to a fall in demand.

➤ Geographic immobility may impede the operations of the labour market, if workers are not readily able to move between different parts of the country.

➤ Occupational immobility may also contribute to the inflexibility of the labour market.

## Effects of government intervention

Labour markets can be a source of politically sensitive issues. Unemployment has been a prominent indicator of the performance of the economy, and there has been an increasing concern in recent years with issues of health and safety and with

ensuring that workers are not exploited by their employers. This has induced governments to introduce a number of measures to provide the institutional setting for the operation of labour markets. However, such measures do not always have their intended effects.

### Minimum wage

In its manifesto published before the 1997 election, the Labour Party committed itself to the establishment of the National **Minimum Wage** (NMW). This would be the first time that such a measure had been used in the UK on a nationwide basis, although minimum wages had sometimes been set in particular industries.

 **term**

**minimum wage:** legislation under which firms are not allowed to pay a wage below some threshold level set by the government

After the election, a Low Pay Commission was set up to oversee the implementation of the policy, which came into force in April 1999. Initially the NMW was set at £3.60 per hour for those aged 22 and over, and £3 for those aged 18–21. From 1 October 2006 the rates were £5.35 for those aged 22 and over and £4.45 for those aged 18–21. A minimum wage of £3.30 per hour applied to 16- and 17-year-olds.

The objectives of the minimum wage policy are threefold. First, it is intended to protect workers against exploitation by the small minority of bad employers. Second, it aims to improve incentives to work by ensuring that 'work pays', thereby tackling the problem of voluntary unemployment. Third, it aims to alleviate poverty by raising the living standards of the poorest groups in society.

The policy has been a contentious one, with critics claiming that it meets none of these objectives. It has been argued that the minority of bad employees can still find ways of exploiting their workers: for example, by paying them on a piecework rate so that there is no set wage per hour. Another criticism is that the policy is too indiscriminate to tackle poverty, and that a more sharply focused policy is needed for this purpose. For example, many of the workers receiving the NMW may not in fact belong to poor households, but may be women working part time whose partners are also in employment. But perhaps most contentious of all is the argument that, far from providing a supply-side solution to some unemployment, a National Minimum Wage is causing an increase in unemployment because of its effects on the demand for labour.

First, consider a firm operating in a perfectly competitive market, so that it has to accept the wage that is set in the overall market of which it is

*McDonald's argued that it was already paying above the minimum wage*

a part. In Figure 19.5 the firm's demand curve is represented by its marginal revenue product curve ($MRP_L$), and in a free market it must accept the equilibrium wage $W^*$. It thus uses labour up to $l^*$.

If the government now steps in and imposes a minimum wage, so that the firm cannot set a wage below $W_{min}$, it will reduce its labour usage to $d_{min}$, since it will not be profitable to employ labour beyond this point.

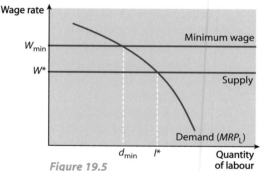

**Figure 19.5**
The effect of a minimum wage on a firm in a perfectly competitive labour market

This effect will be similar for all the other firms in the market, and the results of this can be seen in Figure 19.6. Now the demand curve is the combined demand of all the firms in the market, and the supply curve of labour is shown as upward sloping, as it is the market supply curve. In free market equilibrium the combined demand of firms in the market is $L^*$, and $W^*$ emerges as the equilibrium wage rate.

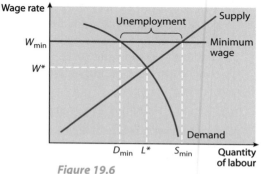

**Figure 19.6**
The effect of a minimum wage in a perfectly competitive labour market

When the government sets the minimum wage at $W_{min}$, all firms react by reducing their demand for labour at the higher wage. Their combined demand is now $D_{min}$, but the supply of labour is $S_{min}$. The difference between these ($S_{min} - D_{min}$) is unemployment. Furthermore, it is involuntary unemployment — these workers would like to work at the going wage rate, but cannot find a job.

Notice that there are two effects at work. Some workers who were formerly employed have lost their jobs — there are $L^* - D_{min}$ of these. In addition, however, the incentive to work is now improved (this was part of the policy objective, remember?), so there are now an additional $S_{min} - L^*$ workers wanting to take employment at the going wage rate. Thus, unemployment has increased for two reasons.

It is not always the case that the introduction of a minimum wage leads to an increase in unemployment. For example, in the market depicted in Figure 19.7 the minimum wage has been set below the equilibrium level, so will have no effect on firms in the market, which will continue to pay $W^*$ and employ $L^*$ workers. At the time of the introduction of the NMW, McDonald's argued that it was in fact already paying a wage above the minimum rate set.

This is not the only situation in which a minimum wage would *not* lead to unemployment. Suppose that the labour market in question has a monopsony buyer of labour. The firm's situation is shown in Figure 19.8. In the absence of a minimum wage, the firm sets its marginal cost of labour equal to its marginal revenue product, hiring $L_0$ labour at a wage $W_0$. A minimum wage introduced at the level $W_{min}$ means that the firm now hires labour up to the point where the wage is equal to the marginal revenue product and, as drawn in Figure 19.8, this takes the market back to the perfectly competitive outcome.

Notice that the authorities would have to be very knowledgeable to set the minimum wage at exactly the right level to produce this outcome. However, any wage between $W_0$ and $W_{min}$ will encourage the firm to increase its employment to some extent as the policy reduces its market power. Of course, setting the minimum wage above the competitive equilibrium level will again lead to some unemployment. Thus, it is critical to set the wage at the right level if the policy is to succeed in its objectives.

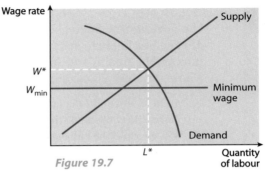

**Figure 19.7**
*A non-binding minimum wage in a perfectly competitive labour market*

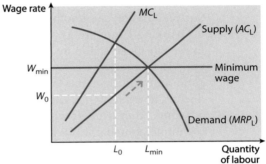

**Figure 19.8**
*A minimum wage with a monopsony buyer of labour*

It is also important to realise that there is not just a single labour market in the UK. In fact, it could be questioned whether a single minimum wage set across the whole country could be effective, as it would 'bite' in different ways in different markets. For example, wage levels vary across the regions of the UK, and it must be questioned whether the same minimum wage could be as effective in, say, London as in Northern Ireland or the north of England.

In a government press release in August 2004, it was revealed that the Low Pay Commission had been asked to prepare a report on the operation of the NMW. The Commission was asked to monitor and evaluate the impact of the NMW and to review the levels of the rates. In reviewing the rates, the Commission was further asked to:

> have regard to the wider social and economic implications; the likely effect on unemployment levels, especially within low-paying sectors and amongst disadvantaged people in the labour market; the impact on the costs and competitiveness of business; and the potential costs to industry and the Exchequer.

This seems to indicate that the government is aware of some of the pitfalls of the National Minimum Wage.

## Health and safety regulation

The government intervenes in the labour market through a range of measures designed to improve safety standards in the workplace. These are administered through the Health and Safety Commission and the Health and Safety Executive, whose responsibilities range:

> from health and safety in nuclear installations and mines, through to factories, farms, hospitals and schools, offshore gas and oil installations, the safety of the gas grid and the movement of dangerous goods and substances, railway safety, and many other aspects of the protection both of workers and the public.

Health and safety inspectors can enter premises without warning, and can issue improvement notices requiring problems to be put right within a specified time; for the most serious failings, they can prosecute.

Such regulation can impinge quite heavily on labour markets. One example is the EU Working Time Directive. This aims to protect the health and safety of workers in the European Union by imposing regulations in relation to working hours, rest periods, annual leave and working arrangements for night workers. The legislation came into effect in the UK in October 1998. Exceptions were made for junior doctors in training, for whom the directive was to be phased in gradually. There are some other workers who have signed contracts opting out of the directive. The UK implemented the 48-hour week later than countries elsewhere in Europe because of a special dispensation. Countries elsewhere complained about this, arguing that it gave UK firms an unfair competitive advantage. This seems to suggest that the directive does indeed have an effect on the labour market.

The effect of these health and safety measures has been to raise the costs to firms of hiring labour. In the case of the Working Time Directive, firms may have to spread the same amount of work over a greater number of workers, and as there are some fixed hiring costs, this raises the cost of labour. Similarly, if the firm has to spend more on ensuring safety, it adds to the firms' costs.

Figure 19.9 illustrates one way of viewing the situation. It shows a perfectly competitive labour market for an industry as a whole rather than an individual firm. Without regulation, the market reaches equilibrium with labour employed up to $L^*$ at a wage of $W^*$. Suppose a health and safety regulation is introduced that adds a constant amount (of £$c$) to firms' cost per unit of labour employed. Firms then find that the average cost of labour is higher by £$c$ — shown as $AC_L$ in the diagram. They will thus employ labour up to the point where the average cost of labour is equal to the marginal revenue product. (Remember that this is a perfectly competitive labour market, so it is the average cost of labour that is significant in the market: each individual firm perceives this as its marginal cost.) This is at the

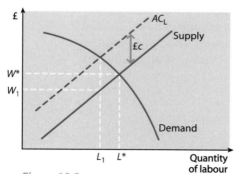

*Figure 19.9*
*The effect of a health and safety regulation in a perfectly competitive market*

quantity of labour $L_1$, and wage is given by $W_1$, which is the wage that attracts $L_1$ workers into the market.

The monopsony market could be analysed in a similar fashion, but the effects are comparable — there is a reduction in the amount of labour employed and a fall in the wage rate.

This sort of intervention can be justified by appealing to a merit good argument (which was discussed in Chapter 7), which claims that the government knows better than workers what is good for them. Thus, individual workers' decisions about labour supply do not take health and safety sufficiently into account, and the regulation that adds to firms' costs is a way of protecting the workers, given that firms have an incentive to skimp on health and safety in order to keep costs down.

As with other policies, the judgement of the degree of regulation that is required is a difficult one to get right. If governments misjudge the amount of protection that workers need and set $c$ too high, this could lead to lower employment than is optimal.

*Health and safety measures increase costs for many industries*

Some health and safety issues arise from externality effects. For example, firms transporting toxic or other dangerous substances may not face the full costs of their activities because they do not have the incentive to control the risk of affecting individuals. Regulation to enforce the appropriate transportation of such substances is a way of internalising such an externality.

## Exercise 19.2

Use Figure 19.10 to explain how the externality effect in the paragraph above comes about.

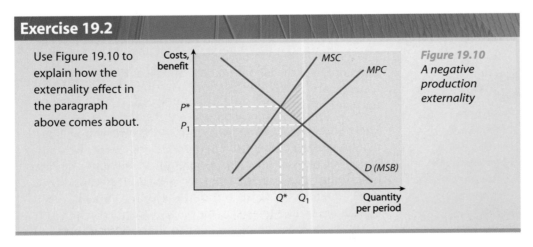

*Figure 19.10 A negative production externality*

## Summary

➤ Governments have intervened in labour markets to protect low-paid workers, but policies need to be implemented with care because of possible unintended side-effects.

➤ The Labour government under Tony Blair introduced the National Minimum Wage in 1999.

➤ In a perfectly competitive labour market, a minimum wage that raises the wage rate above its equilibrium value may lead to an increase in unemployment.

➤ This is partly because firms reduce their demand for labour, but it also reflects an increased labour supply, as the higher wage is an incentive for more workers to join the market.

➤ A minimum wage that is set below the equilibrium wage will not be binding.

➤ A minimum wage established in a monopsony market may have the effect of raising employment.

➤ Health and safety legislation may help to protect workers, and may be interpreted as an example of a merit good.

➤ However, it adds to firms' costs, so may reduce employment.

➤ It is thus important to keep health and safety in perspective, and not overprotect at the expense of lower employment levels.

## Trade unions

**Trade unions** are associations of workers that negotiate with employers on pay and working conditions. Guilds of craftsmen existed in Europe in the Middle Ages, but the formation of workers' trade unions did not become legal in the UK until 1824. In the period following the Second World War, about 40% of the labour force in the UK were members of a trade union. This percentage increased during the 1970s, peaking at about 50%, but since 1980 there has been a steady decline to below 30%.

Trade unions have three major objectives: wage bargaining, the improvement of working conditions, and security of employment for their members. In exploring the effect of the unions on a labour market, it is important to establish whether the unions are in a position to exploit market power and interfere with the proper functioning of the labour market, and also whether they are a necessary balance to the power of employers and thus necessary to protect workers from being exploited.

> **Key term**
>
> **trade union:** an organisation of workers that negotiates with employers on behalf of its members

There are two ways in which a trade union may seek to affect labour market equilibrium. On the one hand, it may limit the supply of workers into an occupation or industry. On the other hand, it may negotiate successfully for higher wages for its members. It turns out that these two possible strategies have similar effects on market equilibrium.

## Restricting labour supply

Figure 19.11 shows the situation facing a firm, with a demand curve for labour based on marginal productivity theory. The average going wage in the economy is given by $W^*$, so if the firm can obtain workers at that wage, it is prepared to employ up to $L_0$ labour.

However, if the firm faces a trade union that is limiting the amount of labour available to just $L_1$, then the union will be able to push the wage up to $W_1$. This might happen where there is a *closed shop*: in other words, where a firm can employ only those workers who are members of the union. A closed shop allows the union to control how many workers are registered members, and therefore eligible to work in the occupation.

In this situation the union is effectively trading off higher wages for its members against a lower level of employment. The union members who are in work are better off — but those who would have been prepared to work at the lower wage of $W^*$ either are unemployed or have to look elsewhere for jobs. If they are unemployed, this imposes a cost on society. If they are working in a second-choice occupation or industry, this may also impose a social cost, in the sense that they may not be working to their full potential.

The extent of the trade-off depends crucially on the elasticity of demand for labour, as you can see in Figure 19.12. When the demand for labour is relatively more elastic, as shown by $D_{L0}$, the wage paid by the firm increases to $W_0$, whereas with the relatively more inelastic demand for labour $D_{L1}$ the wage increases by much more, to $W_1$.

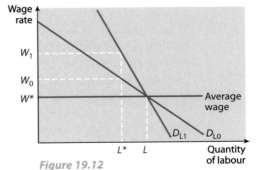

*Figure 19.11*
*A trade union restricts the supply of labour*

This makes good intuitive sense. The previous chapter explained that the elasticity of demand would be low in situations where a firm could not readily substitute capital for labour, where labour formed a small share of total costs, and where the price elasticity of demand for the firm's product was relatively inelastic. If the firm cannot readily substitute capital for labour, the union has a relatively strong bargaining position. If labour costs are a small part of total costs, the firm may be ready to concede a wage increase, as it will have limited overall impact. If the demand for the product is price inelastic, the firm may be able to pass the wage increase on in the form of a higher price for the product without losing large volumes of sales. Thus, these factors improve the union's ability to negotiate a good deal with the employer.

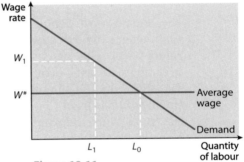

*Figure 19.12*
*The importance of the elasticity of demand for labour*

## Negotiating wages

A trade union's foremost function can be regarded as negotiating higher wages for its members. Figure 19.13 depicts this situation. In the absence of union negotiation, the equilibrium for the firm is where demand and supply intersect, so the firm hires $L_e$ labour at a wage of $W_e$.

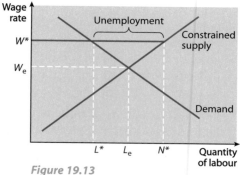

**Figure 19.13**
*A trade union fixes the wage*

If the trade union negotiates a wage of $W^*$, such that the firm cannot hire any labour below that level, this alters the labour supply curve, as shown by the kinked red line. The firm now employs only $L^*$ labour at this wage. So, again, the effect is that the union negotiations result in a trade-off between the amount of labour hired and the wage rate. When the wage is at $W^*$, unemployment is shown on Figure 19.13 as $N^* - L^*$.

The elasticity of demand for labour again affects the outcome, as shown in Figure 19.14. This time, with the relatively more inelastic demand curve $D_{L1}$, the effect on the quantity of labour employed (falls from $L_e$ to $L^{**}$) is much less than when demand is relatively more elastic (falls from $L_e$ to $L^*$).

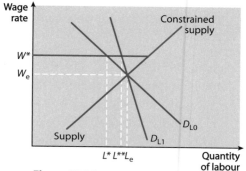

**Figure 19.14**
*The effect of elasticity of demand for labour when the union fixes the wage*

From the point of view of allocative efficiency, the problem is that trade union intervention in the market may prevent wages from acting as reliable signals to workers and firms, and therefore may lead to a sub-optimal allocation of resources.

## Bilateral monopoly

It is important to notice that this analysis has treated the firm as being very passive in the negotiations. Suppose, however, that there is a **bilateral monopoly**, in which the monopoly trade union seller of labour faces a firm that is a monopsony buyer of labour.

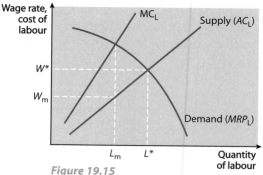

**Figure 19.15**
*A monopsony buyer of labour*

The resulting situation is illustrated in Figure 19.15. If unhindered by the trade union, the firm would offer a

OCR Advanced Economics

wage $W_m$ and use $L_m$ labour. However, if the union now negotiates a higher wage rate, what happens is that, as the wage moves upwards from $W_m$, the firm will take on *more* labour. The market will then move back towards the perfectly competitive level (at wage $W^*$ and quantity $L^*$).

In this situation, the market power of the two protagonists works against both of them to produce an outcome that is closer to perfect competition. It is not possible to predict where the final resting place for the market will be, but it will lie somewhere between $L_m$ and $L^*$, depending upon the relative strengths and negotiating skills of the firm and the union.

### Job security

One possible effect of trade union involvement in a firm is that workers will have more job security: in other words, they may become less likely to lose their jobs with the union there to protect their interests.

From the firm's point of view, there may be a positive side to this. If workers feel secure in their jobs, they may be more productive, or more prepared to accept changes in working practices that enable an improvement in productivity.

For this reason, it can be argued that in some situations the presence of a trade union may be beneficial in terms of a firm's efficiency. Indeed, the union may sometimes take over functions that would otherwise be part of the responsibility of the firm's human resource department.

### Labour market flexibility

One of the most telling criticisms of trade unions has been that they have affected the degree of flexibility of the labour market. The most obvious manifestation of this is that their actions limit the entry of workers into a market.

This may happen in any firm, where existing workers have better access to information about how the firm is operating, or about forthcoming job vacancies, and so can make sure that their own positions can be safeguarded against newcomers. This is sometimes known as the *insider–outsider* phenomenon. Its effect is strengthened and institutionalised by the presence of a trade union, or by professional bodies such as the Royal College of Surgeons.

This and other barriers to entry erected by a trade union can limit the effectiveness and flexibility of labour markets by making it more difficult for firms to adapt to changing market conditions.

## Summary

➤ Trade unions exist to negotiate for their members on pay, working conditions and job security.

> If trade unions restrict labour supply, or negotiate wages that are above the market equilibrium, the net effect is a trade-off between wages and employment.

> Those who remain in work receive higher pay, but at the expense of other workers who either have become unemployed or work in second-choice occupations or industries.

> However, by improving job security, unions may make workers more prepared to accept changes in working practices that lead to productivity gains.

> Barriers to the entry and exit of workers may reduce firms' flexibility to adapt to changing market conditions.

> If a monopsony firm is faced by a trade union acting as a monopoly provider of labour, the firm's ability to reduce employment and lower wages will be limited.

> The final outcome in such a market will depend upon the relative bargaining power of the employer and the union.

## Flexibility and unemployment

Measuring unemployment is a key way of trying to evaluate whether labour markets are operating effectively. Large-scale unemployment suggests that a society is failing to use its resources efficiently, and is operating *within* its production possibility frontier; by reallocating resources within the economy, and thus moving to the frontier, society as a whole can be made better off.

Some of the explanations that have been advanced for unemployment suggest that there is a transitional element: in other words, that unemployment can occur because the market is sluggish in adjusting to equilibrium, or that workers are unemployed because they do not have the right mix of skills that employers are seeking.

*The flexibility of labour markets affects the number of people looking for work and their ability to find jobs*

The more flexible labour markets are, the more rapidly such unemployment will subside as equilibrium is reached. Thus, an important set of policies to examine are those that will improve the flexibility with which labour markets can adjust towards equilibrium. It has been claimed that the degree of flexibility of markets is important in explaining differences in observed unemployment rates between countries, which is an issue that will be discussed later in the chapter.

The benefits of flexibility go beyond the labour market itself. If a labour market does not adjust readily, it will slow the whole process of changing resource allocation, and this in turn will slow the process of economic growth, which may be seen as a prime long-term aim of economic policy.

It may not be straightforward to identify when full employment has been reached. Some unemployment cannot be avoided, and will exist even when the labour market is in equilibrium.

## Unemployment in the UK

The overall unemployment rate in the UK since 1971 is presented in Figure 19.16, using the claimant count measurement method. This counts the number of people claiming unemployment benefit each month. It was briefly introduced in Chapter 9, and provides a useful picture of how unemployment has varied through time. Although the ILO method of measuring unemployment is more useful in many ways, the claimant count data are available over a longer period of time.

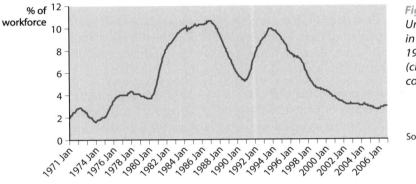

Figure 19.16
Unemployment in the UK, 1971–2006 (claimant count)

Source: ONS.

The large swings in unemployment that are visible on the graph are due to a number of causes. The large increase in the early 1980s reflected in part a change in the emphasis of economic policy. There was a new determination to bring inflation under control using monetary policy whereas in earlier periods the government had been more concerned about achieving full employment. However, other things were happening as well. North Sea Oil came on stream just before the second oil price crisis of 1979–80, a net effect of which was a loss in competitiveness of UK goods, which led to a decline in the manufacturing sector in the 1980s. There were also changes in the demographic structure of the population, which will be taken up at the end of the chapter.

The reduction in unemployment in the late 1980s was associated with what has come to be known as the 'Lawson boom', a period of relatively loose monetary policy that was followed by a severe recession in which unemployment rose again. But perhaps the most striking aspect of Figure 19.16 is the period since 1993, which has seen a steady decline in the unemployment rate and a much steadier pattern.

Figure 19.17 focuses on a different aspect of unemployment. Economists have argued that some unemployment is by its nature transitional, a feature of the adjustment process of the economy. In this context it is useful to examine

the extent to which there is long-term unemployment. Figure 19.17 shows the percentage of the unemployed who have been unemployed for more than a year.

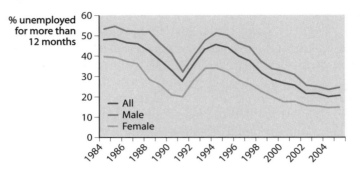

**Figure 19.17** *The long-term unemployed in the UK, 1984–2005*

Notes: data relate to the spring of each year. The long-term unemployed are those who have been without work for a year or more.

Source: ONS.

Notice that the data used here are for the spring quarter of each year. One reason for taking a particular quarter rather than looking at the full set of data for the year is that there tend to be seasonal movements in the unemployment rate that can distract from the underlying trend.

The overall picture shows that there has been a large decline in long-term unemployment, from nearly 50% in 1984 to only just over 20% in the spring of 2005. This might be interpreted as an encouraging sign for the economy, indicating that most unemployment is relatively short term in nature. Indeed, taking this figure together with the previous one, which showed such a large decline in overall unemployment, it might be concluded that the economy is not far from a full-employment position.

Notice that there is a difference between male and female workers in these data, indicating that the majority of long-term unemployed workers are male. There is also an age effect in the data, which is shown in Figure 19.18. This focuses just on the years 1984 and 2005, and shows that long-term unemployment is more prevalent among older workers. There has clearly been a substantial improvement in all age groups, but the decline has been much more marked for younger workers. This may partly reflect the greater difficulty that older workers find in switching occupations, but it may also be associated with the training schemes for younger workers that have been introduced in recent years, which will be discussed shortly.

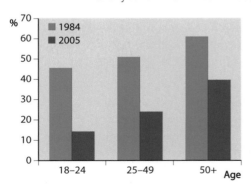

**Figure 19.18**

*Long-term unemployed as a percentage of all unemployed in the UK by age groups, 1984 and 2005*

Source: ONS.

The relatively low proportion of long-term unemployed highlights the fact that unemployment is a dynamic variable. It is easy to fall into the trap of thinking of the unemployed as being a pool of people unable to get work. However, in any period there are always people becoming unemployed, and others obtaining jobs. In a typical year more people get jobs, and more become unemployed, than the average number of people who are unemployed at any one time.

It is also important to remember that there are substantial regional variations in unemployment rates across the UK. Figure 19.19 shows the picture in spring 2005. The percentage rate varies from below 4% in the South West, the South East and the East to 6% or more in Scotland and in London. The data for London may be misleading, however, as there is so much commuting into the London area.

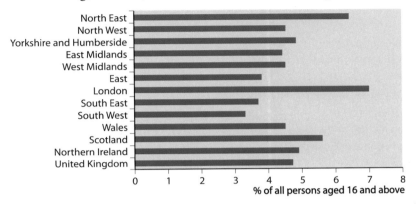

*Figure 19.19*
*Unemployment in regions of the UK, spring 2005*

Source: ONS.

In part, the variation in unemployment rates between regions reflects the differing pattern of economic activity across the country. If a region happens to have a concentration of employment in a declining industry, it will tend to display higher unemployment rates because labour is not perfectly mobile and unemployed workers may find that there are no available jobs in their area, but may still be reluctant to move.

Figure 19.20 compares unemployment in the UK with that of selected other countries. One prominent feature of this graph is that the continuous decline in the unemployment rate that the UK has enjoyed since 1993 has not been shared by the other countries shown — or by the euro area countries as a whole. Indeed, it would appear that France and Germany are converging on a relatively high unemployment rate, whereas the UK has steadied at a lower rate. The pattern is most striking for Germany, which enjoyed a much lower unemployment rate in the 1980s and early 1990s, but has since shown a weaker performance. This may partly reflect the difficulty experienced after the reunification of West and East Germany in the 1990s, beginning with the destruction of the Berlin Wall in 1989, which has undoubtedly affected Germany's unemployment rate.

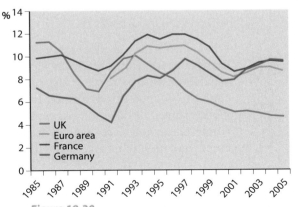

*Figure 19.20*
*Unemployment in selected countries, 1985–2005*
Source: OECD.

## Exercise 19.3

Table 19.2 provides data on unemployment in the regions of the UK in 1992 and 2004.

For each region and each year, calculate an index number for unemployment in the region based on the UK = 100. (If you need to be reminded about how to calculate index numbers, it was discussed in Chapter 9.)

Use your results to identify which regions have experienced the greatest and least changes in the unemployment rate relative to the national average. Discuss the reasons for these results.

| Region | Spring 1992 | Spring 2005 |
|---|---|---|
| UK | 9.7 | 4.7 |
| North East | 11.8 | 6.4 |
| North West | 10.0 | 4.5 |
| Yorkshire & Humberside | 10.1 | 4.8 |
| East Midlands | 8.8 | 4.4 |
| West Midlands | 10.6 | 4.5 |
| East | 7.7 | 3.8 |
| London | 12.0 | 7.0 |
| South East | 7.8 | 3.7 |
| South West | 9.1 | 3.3 |
| Wales | 8.9 | 4.5 |
| Scotland | 9.5 | 5.6 |
| Northern Ireland | 12.1 | 4.9 |

*Table 19.2  Unemployment in UK regions, 1992 and 2005*

Source: ONS.

## Summary

➤ Unemployment has shown quite wide variations through time in the UK, but declined steadily between 1993 and 2005.

➤ The proportion of unemployed workers who have been unemployed for more than a year also showed an appreciable decline.

➤ There are significant variations in unemployment rates across the regions of the UK, but the pattern of the differences altered during the 1990s.

## Policies to promote flexibility

What makes for a flexible labour market? At the microeconomic level, where a prime concern is with achieving a good allocation of resources for society, the issue is whether workers can transfer readily between activities to allow resource allocation to change through time. This requires a number of conditions to be met. Workers need to have information about what jobs are available (and, perhaps, where those jobs are available), and what skills are needed for those jobs. Employers need to be able to identify workers with the skills and talents that they need. If workers cannot find the jobs that are available, or do not have the appropriate skills to undertake those jobs, the market will not function smoothly. Similarly, if employers cannot identify the workers with the skills that they need, that too will impede the working of the market.

Arguably, the problem has become acute in recent years, with a change in the balance of jobs between skilled and unskilled workers. As the economy gears up to more hi-tech activities, and low-skill jobs are outsourced or relocated to other countries, the need for workers to acquire the right skills becomes ever more pressing.

## The New Deal

An important policy launched by the new Labour government in 1997 was a package of policy measures known as the New Deal, which was aimed at reducing long-term unemployment. Figures 19.17 and 19.18 certainly suggest that long-term unemployment has declined, but it cannot be assumed that this reflects the impact of the New Deal alone. After all, other aspects of the economy have improved in the same period, contributing to an overall fall in the unemployment rate.

The New Deal measures were aimed at three age groups — the groups shown in Figure 19.18. Young people aged 18–24 years old who had been unemployed for a period of more than 6 months would be assigned a personal adviser to provide them with information about available jobs and contacts with potential employers. If they were still without a job after a further 4 months, they would either enter a year of full-time education or training, or take up a job with the voluntary sector for 6 months or the environmental task force; or they would go into subsidised employment which would include on-the-job training. Similar targeted programmes were provided for the older age groups.

Notice that such measures are designed to improve the flexibility of the labour market, by providing unemployed workers with information and skills training. Furthermore, employers receive a subsidy to take on workers, who can then be observed in the workplace, which provides a better insight into their potential than any interview or other screening process.

A survey published in *Labour Market Trends* in 2002 indicated that nine out of ten employers in the survey provided at least some of their employees with job-related training. Figure 19.21 indicates that a relatively high percentage of employees received such training, especially in the younger age groups.

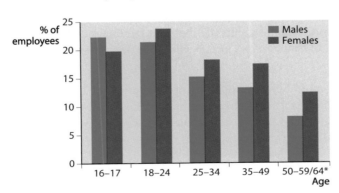

*Figure 19.21*

*Employees receiving job-related training, by age group, 2002*

*59 for women, 64 for men.

Source: *Labour Market Trends.*

## Trade union reform

A further question concerns the extent to which the trade unions have affected the operation of labour markets. By negotiating for a wage that is above the equilibrium level, trade unions may trade off higher wages for lower levels of employment. The potential disruption caused by strike action can also impede the workings of a labour market.

Some indication of this disruption can be seen in Figure 19.22. Clearly, compared with the 1970s and 1980s, the amount of disruption through strikes in recent years has been very low. However, even the 1979 figure pales into insignificance besides the 162 million working days lost in the General Strike of 1926; but, in fact, the 1970s and 1980s were a tempestuous period, in which trade union action severely disrupted UK industry. So why has life become so much quieter?

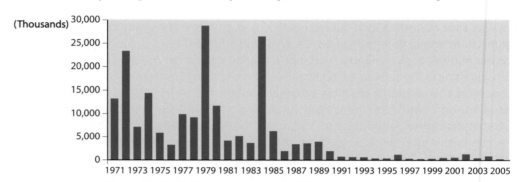

*Figure 19.22* *Working days lost in the UK through industrial action, 1971–2005*
Source: Labour Market Trends.

It was perhaps no surprise that unions should have worked hard to protect their members during the 1980s, when unemployment was soaring and the Thatcher government was determined to control inflation — including inflation of wages. Legislation was introduced in the early 1980s to begin to reform the trade unions, and after the highly disruptive miners' strike ended in 1985, the government introduced a number of further reforms designed to curb the power of the trade unions, making it more difficult for them to call rapid strike action. For example, secret ballots were to be required before strike action could be taken. This may help to explain why trade union membership has been in decline since the 1980s. By weakening the power of trade unions in this way, some labour market inflexibility has been removed.

Another factor may have been changes in the structure of economic activity during this period. Manufacturing employment was falling, whereas the service sectors were expanding. Traditionally, union membership has been higher among workers in the manufacturing sector than in services.

## Regional policy

There have always been differences in average incomes and in unemployment rates between the various regions of the UK. In broad terms, there are two possible responses to this — either persuade workers to move to regions where there are more jobs, or persuade the firms to move to areas where labour is plentiful. Each of these solutions poses problems. Housing markets limit the mobility of workers, and it is costly for firms to relocate their activities.

The regions most affected in the past have been those that specialised in industries that subsequently went into decline: for example, coal mining areas or towns and regions dominated by cotton mills. In a broad context, it is desirable for the economy to undergo structural change as the pattern of international comparative advantage changes, but it is painful during the transition period. Thus, successive governments have implemented regional policies to try to cope with the problems experienced in areas of high unemployment.

*Middlesbrough — one of the areas of the country with a high concentration of heavy industry and manufacturing that has experienced economic decline*

At the same time, the booming regions can be affected because of the opposite problem — a shortage of labour. Thus, measures have been taken to encourage firms to consider relocating to regions where labour is available. This included leading by example, with some civil service functions being moved out of London.

EU funding has helped in this regard, with Scotland, Wales and Northern Ireland all qualifying for grants. Since 1999, the Regional Development Agencies set up by the Labour government have been given responsibility for promoting economic development in their regions. There are eight of these agencies covering the country. Although differentials have narrowed in recent years, it is difficult to know how much of this narrowing can be attributed to the success of regional policy. It has also been pointed out that there are some areas that have been receiving regional aid for more than 70 years, but are still disadvantaged, so it is difficult to argue that regional policy has had outstanding success.

## The Social Chapter

In 1991 the UK signed the Maastricht Treaty. Although concerned primarily with moves towards economic integration and monetary union, the treaty also included a Social Chapter, which aimed to harmonise labour market policies across the member countries.

When the UK signed the treaty, the then prime minister, John Major, negotiated an opt-out from the Social Chapter, arguing that it would damage the competitiveness of UK firms. This raised complaints from other European countries, which were concerned that the UK would become a magnet for foreign investment from inside and outside Europe. When the Blair government came to power, the decision was taken to sign up to the Social Chapter, the government arguing that it would benefit UK workers.

The treaty does not provide for a specific set of policies, but operates through a series of directives that member countries are required to implement. One example of such a directive — the Working Time Directive — was discussed earlier in this chapter. Other directives have covered pregnant worker protection, child labour and redundancy, together with a wide range of health and safety issues. As argued already, the key aim of such directives is to ensure an appropriate balance between protecting workers (and countering information deficiencies and externalities) and enabling flexibility in the labour market.

It has been widely argued that labour markets are highly flexible in the USA and highly inflexible in Europe, with the UK somewhere in between. Figure 19.23 offers some support for this in terms of the general level of unemployment in the USA, the euro area and the UK.

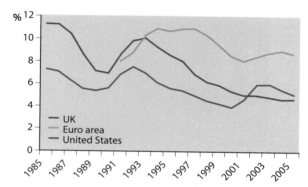

*Figure 19.23* *Unemployment in selected countries, 1985–2005*
Source: OECD.

## Technology and unemployment

One of the greatest fallacies perpetuated by non-economists is that technology destroys jobs. Bands of labourers known as Luddites rioted between 1811 and 1816, destroying textile machines, which they blamed for high unemployment and low wages. In the twenty-first century there is a strong lobbying group in the USA arguing that outsourcing and cheap labour in China are destroying US jobs.

In fact, new technology and an expansion in the capital stock should have beneficial effects — so long as labour markets are sufficiently flexible. Consider a market in which new technology is introduced. If firms in an industry invest in technology and expand the capital stock, this affects the marginal revenue product of labour and hence the demand for labour, as shown in Figure 19.24, where demand shifts from $D_1$ to $D_2$. In this market, the effect is to raise the wage rate from $W_1$ to $W_2$ and the employment level from $L_1$ to $L_2$.

However, it is important to look beyond what happens in a single market, as the argument is that it is all very well expanding employment in the technology sector

— but what about the old industries that are in decline? Suppose the new industries absorb less labour than is discarded by the old declining industries? After all, if the effect of technology is to allow call centres to create jobs in India at the expense of the USA or the UK, does this not harm employment in those countries?

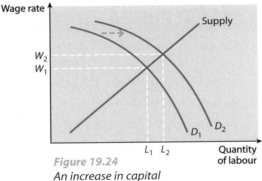

**Figure 19.24**
*An increase in capital*

The counter-argument to this lies in the notion of the gains from specialisation introduced in Chapter 1. This argues that countries can gain from international trade through specialising in certain activities. Setting up call centres in India frees UK workers to work in sectors in which the UK has a comparative advantage, with the result that the UK can import (and thus consume) more labour-intensive goods than before.

There is one proviso, of course. It is important that the workers released from the declining sectors have (or can obtain) the skills that are needed for them to be absorbed into the expanding sectors. This recalls the question of whether the labour market is sufficiently flexible to allow the structure of economic activity to adapt to changes in the pattern of comparative advantage. However, it also serves as a reminder that policy should be aimed at enabling that flexibility, and not at introducing protectionist measures to reduce trade, which would be damaging overall for the economy.

*Technology has often been blamed for taking away jobs*

part 5

## Exercise 19.4

For each of the following situations, sketch a demand and supply diagram for a labour market to analyse the effects on the wage rate and employment level.

a  An increase in the rate of immigration of people into the country.

b  A reduction in the rate of the Jobseekers' Allowance.

c  An improvement in technology that raises labour productivity.

d  A new health and safety regulation to safeguard workers against industrial injury.

e  An increase in the number of old people as a percentage of the population.

## Summary

➤ An important factor influencing the rate of unemployment is the degree of flexibility in labour markets.

➤ The New Deal was a package of measures introduced with the objective of reducing long-term unemployment, through providing information to jobseekers and training.

➤ Trade union reforms were introduced during the 1980s and have contributed to flexibility in labour markets.

➤ Regional policy has attempted to reduce the differentials in unemployment rates between the regions of the UK.

➤ The Social Chapter has attempted to harmonise labour market policies across the EU. In some cases, this may have reduced the flexibility of labour markets in the interest of worker protection.

➤ Adjustment in labour markets is needed in order to cope with the changing international pattern of specialisation.

# Transport economics

# Part 6

# Chapter 20
# Transport, transport trends and the economy

This part of the book examines the economics of transport. This is an important sector in any economy, as the efficiency and coverage of the transport sector is crucial for individuals, who need to move between locations for work and leisure, and for businesses, which need to transport their products — both inputs and outputs. As the economy expands and real incomes rise, it is to be expected that there will be changes in the demand for transport and, perhaps, changes in the pattern of that demand between alternative modes of travel. It is also important to be aware that there has been considerable technological change in recent decades that will inevitably have had an impact on the transport sector. This part of the book examines these aspects of the development of the transport sector, and the role of government in responding to potential areas of market failure.

## Learning outcomes

After studying this chapter, you should:
➤ appreciate the significance of the transport sector in the operation of the economy
➤ understand that the demand for transport is a derived demand
➤ be aware of the nature of the market for transport
➤ be familiar with the characteristics of transport modes
➤ be aware of recent trends in the UK transport sector

## The nature of transport

According to the *Oxford English Dictionary*, to **transport** is to 'take (persons, goods, troops, baggage etc.) from one place to another'. This might be a simple definition, but it provides a context for discussing transport economics, which deals with the economic analysis surrounding transportation, with a particular focus on the transportation of persons and goods. Such transportation is of critical importance for the modern economy. People need to move around as part of everyday life, for shopping, for leisure and for travel to work. Businesses need to move goods around as part of their production process.

**Key terms**

**transport:** process of moving people or goods from one place to another

This includes bringing materials and other production inputs in, and also sending out finished products into the distribution system.

Recent decades have seen the rise of **globalisation** — a process by which firms are increasingly operating in global markets, rather than just functioning within the domestic economy. Transportation becomes even more important in this context, and recent technological change in the transport (and communi-

*Improvements in transport and storage mean fruit and vegetables can be imported into the UK from far afield*

cations) sector has greatly contributed to the process of globalisation. Transport enables the world's economies to become more closely integrated. For example, it makes it possible for multinational corporations to take advantage of differing cost conditions in different parts of the globe. Improvements in transport and storage have enabled even fruit and vegetables to be imported into countries like the UK from far afield. You can see evidence of this in your local supermarket by checking out the country of origin of some of the products on sale.

An important point to notice at the outset is that the demand for transport is a **derived demand**. People and businesses demand transport not for its own sake, but because of the services that it provides. Some people might enjoy travel for its own sake, but in general the demand for transport is indirect. A firm may demand transport in order to deliver its product to the market, or an individual may demand transport in order to get to the office or the shops. This must be borne in mind when undertaking economic analysis of the demand for transport. Another example of derived demand is a firm's demand for labour: firms demand labour not for its own sake, but for the output that it produces.

The supply side of the transport market is also important, of course. Chapter 5 explained that **allocative efficiency** is important for society. In the context of the market for transport, it is important to examine whether the market operates effectively to provide the quantity, range and quality of transport services that people wish to consume. In other words, is the price of transportation services equal to marginal cost across the sector? Chapters 21 and 22 will explore this issue, which depends on the structure of the various markets for transport. Transport offers some interesting examples of how markets operate. We will discuss, in particular, the market

*terms*

**globalisation:** a process by which the world's economies are becoming more closely integrated

**derived demand:** demand for a good or service not for its own sake, but for what it produces

**allocative efficiency:** achieved when society is producing an appropriate bundle of goods relative to consumer preferences

for bus travel and the emergence of low-cost airlines, which seem to have revolutionised air travel.

The role of government has also been important, as the transport sector has been characterised by many examples of externalities. Issues of congestion and the pollution caused by vehicle emissions are well-known examples of externalities, which were the subject of Chapter 6. Issues relating to deregulation and privatisation have also typified the transport sector in recent decades. These will be discussed in Chapters 22 and 23.

The delivery of transportation services occurs in two phases. First, the delivery depends crucially on the availability of infrastructure. In order to provide road transport, there is a need for roads; a rail service requires track, and so on. The second phase is the provision of transport through various modes. For example, road transport can be in the form of private cars, buses and coaches, motor cycles and so on. The distinction between the two phases is significant because the first phase has typically involved government intervention, whereas the second phase has primarily been provided within private markets. The provision of infrastructure poses particular economic problems and requires careful evaluation of direct and indirect costs and benefits. Cost–benefit analysis in the context of transportation will be discussed in Chapter 22.

There is a major coordination problem here. There are many decisions being made by different agents, all of which are interrelated. This is further complicated by the fact that decisions about infrastructure take so long to come into effect. Decisions being taken today will affect the structure and efficiency of the transport system far into the future. An extreme example is the Channel Tunnel. The first recorded suggestion for a tunnel linking England and France was made in 1802, and work actually commenced in 1881, only to be abandoned 2 years later. In more modern times, the English and French governments agreed to have another go at building a tunnel in 1973, but plans were again shelved. More studies were commissioned in the 1980s, work finally commenced in 1987 and the Tunnel was completed in 1994 (2 years late). Thus the period that elapsed between planning the infrastructure and it coming into operation was an extended one. This may be an extreme example, but it illustrates some of the problems in coordinating decisions.

## Modes of transport

The market for transportation services encompasses a variety of modes of transport that need to be considered in any economic analysis of the sector. These modes include rail, road, air and water — and, in addition, there are some categories of goods that can be transported through pipelines. The balance between the various modes of transport has changed over time, partly reflecting changes in technology, but also in response to changes in real incomes and consumer preferences. Within each mode, there may be several forms of transport available. For example, road traffic covers not only cars, but also motor cycles, buses and coaches, light vans, heavy goods vehicles (HGVs) and pedal cycles.

The various modes have different economic characteristics. It might be argued that road transport has more flexibility than some other modes, as it is less constrained by specific infrastructure than the railways or canal network. On the other hand, rail transport has advantages in its ability to carry in bulk at relatively high speed. Air travel is clearly advantageous for long-distance travel, but also requires substantial infrastructure in the form of airports and air traffic control systems. Air travel remains the best way of visiting Australia, but you would not consider flying to the local shops!

## Exercise 20.1

Discuss the relative merits of the major modes of transport (road, rail, air, water and pipeline) in respect of the following characteristics:

a  carrying capacity

b  flexibility of origin and destination

c  the need for infrastructure

d  ability to carry a wide variety of goods

e  the need for security

f  speed of transport

## Passenger traffic

As far as passengers are concerned, road traffic is the most used form of domestic transport, whether measured by the number of journeys undertaken or the average annual distance covered. Figure 20.1 shows index numbers comparing the average annual distance covered by people using various modes of transport relative to the distance covered by car. It shows, for example, that the average distance covered by rail or tube (per person per year) was 6.6% of that covered by car in 1992/94, and just over 7.9% in 2004. Studying these data, you will see that apart from rail all modes fell relative to car travel between 1992/94 and 2004.

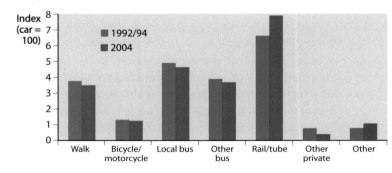

**Figure 20.1**
*Average annual distance travelled in the UK, by transport mode, 1992/94 and 2004*

Source: Department for Transport.

This impression is reinforced by Figure 20.2, which shows the number of 'vehicle kilometres' travelled by car and by other modes of road traffic each year between 1980 and 2005. Note that, to measure the usage of any form of transport, two common methods are used. One is to measure the distance travelled by a vehicle in a year (a vehicle kilometre); an alternative is to measure the distance travelled by vehicle occupants (passenger kilometres, or tonne kilometres in the case of freight). Using passenger kilometres makes a lot of sense if the aim is to compare the efficiency of alternative modes of transport. For example, consider a journey between

London and Newcastle. A train can obviously carry more passengers than a private car, so measuring just in terms of vehicle kilometres would be highly misleading, whereas measuring in terms of passenger kilometres is much more meaningful.

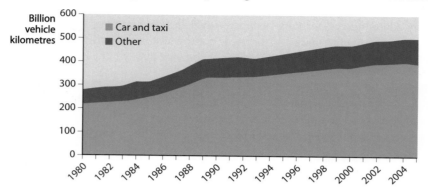

Figure 20.2
Road traffic in the UK by transport mode, 1980–2005

Source: Department for Transport

Figure 20.2 shows a steady expansion in car kilometres throughout the period, but relatively little expansion in the other modes of road transport. This is probably what one would expect from economic analysis. This period was one of generally rising real incomes, and it could be argued that car transport is likely to display a strong positive income elasticity of demand, whereas, for example, bus travel is likely to have a low — and perhaps negative — income elasticity of demand. In other words, bus travel could be seen as an example of an inferior good, so with rising real incomes it would be expected that the pattern of demand would switch away from bus travel towards the use of private cars. On the other hand, it may be that the demand for bus travel depends on other factors as well, such as the reliability of the service provided, and the amount of congestion on the roads.

Figure 20.3 shows the pattern of non-car road traffic by mode over the same period, again measured in vehicle kilometres. The data are shown as index numbers, based on 1980 = 100, in order to demonstrate the changes in the pattern that have been taking place over time. The strongest growth was in the use of light vans, where the number of vehicle kilometres more than doubled between 1980 and 2004. The use of buses and coaches also increased, by a relatively modest 54% over the period. However, there was a fall in the use of pedal cycles (down by 12%) and motorcycles (down by 27% in spite of something of a recovery towards the end of the period).

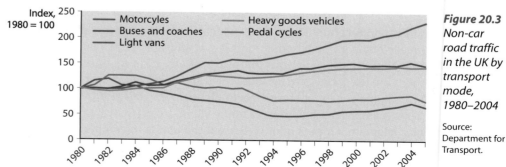

Figure 20.3
Non-car road traffic in the UK by transport mode, 1980–2004

Source: Department for Transport.

To what extent are the trends in road traffic associated with changes in real incomes? One way to explore this question is to look at changes in road traffic relative to changes in real GDP. Figure 20.4 presents some data on this issue. It shows indexes of road traffic and real GDP based on 1980 = 100. Until 1990 it seems that road traffic and real GDP rose together, flattening out in the early 1990s. However, it also seems that after about 1993, real GDP has risen at

*The use of pedal cycles has fallen over the last two decades*

a faster rate than road traffic, especially relative to total passenger kilometres. The fact that the demand for transport has risen with changes in real income could suggest that transport is a normal good, whereas the fall in the usage of motorcycles (especially during the 1980s and early 1990s) might suggest that motorcycle transport could be seen as an inferior good. In other words, as real incomes rise, consumers tend to switch from motor cycles to cars.

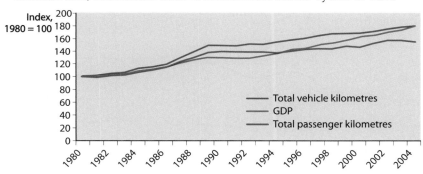

*Figure 20.4 Road traffic and GDP in the UK, 1980–2004*

Source: Department for Transport.

However, the data suggest that the relationship between traffic and income is not a straightforward one. This is what is to be expected, given that in real life it cannot be expected that a ceteris paribus assumption will hold true. In particular, consumers may also respond to changes in the real cost of transport. The theory of demand suggests that the demand for a good depends upon the price of the good and the prices of other goods as well as upon consumer incomes and preferences. This holds for the demand for transport as much as for any other good.

Figure 20.5 provides information about the changes in the costs of various modes of transport between 1980 and 2004, together with an index of real disposable income. This reveals that the real cost of travel has grown relatively slowly. Indeed, in the case of motoring, in spite of increases in the price of petrol/oil (of 10% over this period), the real cost of motoring in 2004 was about 10% *lower* than it had been in 1980. Rail, bus and coach fares had increased during this period, so this may help to explain the dominance of cars, as was shown in Figure 20.2.

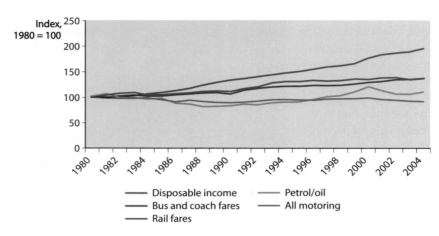

**Figure 20.5**
*Income and the real cost of transport in the UK, 1980–2004*

Source: Department for Transport.

Disposable income — Petrol/oil
Bus and coach fares — All motoring
Rail fares

## Freight traffic

Figure 20.6 summarises the movement of domestic freight according to mode of transport, again showing data between 1980 and 2004. In terms of tonne kilometres, road transport again dominates the scene, although it would appear that shipping of goods is also significant. The data here include both coastal shipping and internal waterways. Rail is seen to carry a relatively small proportion of total freight, with something of an increase since the mid-1990s.

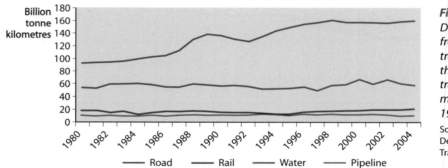

**Figure 20.6**
*Domestic freight transport in the UK, by transport mode, 1980–2004*

Source: Department for Transport.

Road — Rail — Water — Pipeline

In interpreting these data it is important to be aware of the average length of journeys, which varies substantially between the transport modes. Figure 20.7 clearly shows that the average length of domestic haul for freight carried by water was significantly greater than for other modes of transport. This is likely to reflect the cost structure of the mode. It pays to transport freight by sea for long distances because of the relatively high loading costs compared with loading an HGV. In other words, there may be economies of scale (distance) involved here. A similar argument might apply in the case of rail freight transport. The graph reveals that there has been an appreciable increase in the average length of haul by rail, suggesting that rail is competing better for long-haul freight as opposed to short haul, where it would be expected that road transport would have an advantage because of its flexibility.

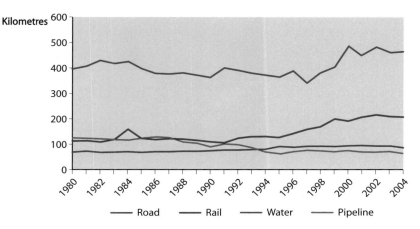

**Figure 20.7**
*Average length of domestic haul in the UK, by transport mode, 1980–2004*

Source: Department for Transport.

For businesses, some use of road transport is inevitable. Rail and water transport may have advantages for long-haul transport, but delivery to individual factories or sales outlets requires an element of road transportation. There are few factories that can have their own rail terminal.

The need to transport raw materials or finished products may have a strong influence on the location decision of firms. If the materials used in the production process are bulky or heavy relative to the output produced by a firm, it may choose to locate where the materials can be conveniently brought in. On the other hand, if the firm's product is fragile or otherwise difficult to transport, the firm may prefer to be located close to its market. Thus the nature of the transportation needs of a firm may have important repercussions for location decisions. Modern industry is less prone to these influences, but location decisions in the past continue to influence the present pattern of activity.

## Forecasting transport needs

The two-phase nature of the delivery of transport services means that it is very important to be able to forecast the future demand for transport. The provision of infrastructure requires careful future planning, given the time that it takes to build new roads or construct new port facilities. The nature of the demand for transport makes such forecasting a difficult undertaking. This is partly because the provision of infrastructure may itself influence demand. For example, there has been considerable debate about the effect of road building and improvement schemes. It has been argued that road improvements have the effect of increasing the amount of traffic on the roads, rather than reducing congestion.

The fact that much of the transport infrastructure is publicly provided means that such forecasting is an integral part of the process — and it also means that the authorities need a way of taking externalities into account when formulating a transport strategy. There also needs to be careful coordination of transport planning, given the interactions between the demands for different modes of transport. For example, decisions taken now about improvements to the rail

network may have implications for the future demand for road transport, and hence for the present need to invest in the road system.

Forecasting of transport needs can only be undertaken with an understanding of the economic processes at work. Such an understanding needs to encompass both the demand and supply sides of the market for transport, and needs to be able to take into account the potential interactions between different transport markets. The demand for transportation services is likely to change over time as real incomes change, and as relative prices move. The supply of transportation services will be influenced by the way that markets evolve through time, and by advances in technology that may bring about changes in the relative importance of different modes of travel.

*Rail transport has advantages for long-haul transport*

As an illustration, Figure 20.8 shows some forecasts of traffic volume made by the Department of Transport in 1997. These relate to billion vehicle kilometres travelled by car (including taxis). The graph shows the actual data up to 1996, and then the forecasts up to 2031. Given that there is considerable uncertainty about the forecasts, three variants are shown. The 'Central' forecast represents the most likely scenario, and the 'High' and 'Low' forecasts represent alternative forecasts based on different assumptions. In producing these forecasts, assumptions had to be made about key influences on traffic, such as the rate of increase of real incomes (GDP), changes in fuel prices and in fuel efficiency, the road network, policies on rail and bus services, and so on. With so many assumptions, you should not be surprised at the range in the forecasts, which naturally becomes wider the further the forecasts extend into the future.

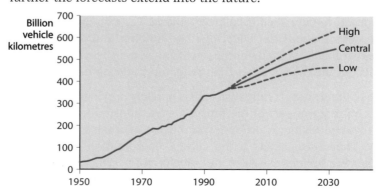

**Figure 20.8**
*Forecasting traffic volume*

Source: Department for Transport.

## Paying for transportation services

A strong reason for public provision of transport services in the past has been that transport infrastructure has some of the characteristics of a public good. Recall from Chapter 7 that a public good is one which is non-rivalrous and non-excludable. In other words, the consumption of a good by one person does not prevent others from also consuming the good, and consumers cannot be excluded from consuming the good. Many roads can be seen to have these characteristics. There is only rivalry in consumption when the road becomes congested, and it is difficult to exclude people from using the road — at least while maintaining a flow of traffic. There are some situations in which it does become possible to charge for road use — as witness the M6 toll road and the London Congestion Charge. However, extending such schemes to a wider range of roads is difficult. In other words, roads may be seen as **quasi-public goods**. Chapter 23 returns to this issue to examine the economic arguments concerning road pricing and the imposition of user charges.

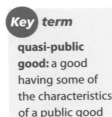

**Key** *term*

**quasi-public good:** a good having some of the characteristics of a public good

## The importance of the transport sector in the economy

The transport sector is a significant sector as far as the overall economy is concerned. In 2005 it accounted for 6% of total employment in the UK. This proportion has remained stable over time, having been 6.5% in 1978. As far as households' budgets are concerned, expenditure on transport in real terms has risen substantially, from £22.33 per week in 1981 to £72 in 2004/05, according to *Social Trends*. This represents 14.4% of total expenditure in 1981, and 16.6% in 2004/05.

The division of this expenditure between categories is dominated by motoring expenditure, as can be seen in Figure 20.9. Motoring accounted for 87% of household expenditure on transport in 2004/05.

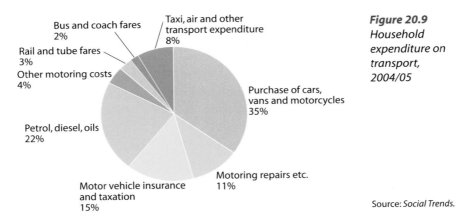

Bus and coach fares 2%
Taxi, air and other transport expenditure 8%
Rail and tube fares 3%
Other motoring costs 4%
Petrol, diesel, oils 22%
Purchase of cars, vans and motorcycles 35%
Motoring repairs etc. 11%
Motor vehicle insurance and taxation 15%

*Figure 20.9*
*Household expenditure on transport, 2004/05*

Source: *Social Trends.*

It might be argued that these data fail to do full justice to the importance of transport in a modern economy. In other words, the importance of transport goes

beyond its ability to employ people and to occupy part of every household's budget. This is because of its pivotal importance to both businesses and households. The economics of transport provision is thus an important area of study. If resources are not well allocated in this sector, it will have repercussions across the whole economy.

The transport sector is seen to be especially critical in the context of international trade. Once countries begin to specialise in the production of certain goods, and want to trade these with other countries, transport becomes of central importance. Such specialisation is important if producers are to reach a sufficiently large market to be able to take full advantage of economies of scale in production. This may be hindered if the transport system is inefficient. Indeed, try to imagine a world in which goods cannot be transported from one country — or from one region — to another. Each country would need to produce all the goods and services that its residents wished to consume. This would be highly inefficient, and would limit the range of commodities that could be consumed.

## Summary

➤ Transport involves the movement of people and goods from one place to another, and is a vital part of a modern economy.

➤ The demand for transport is a derived demand, in the sense that it is demanded not for its own sake, but for the services it provides.

➤ The supply of transportation services in the past has come from a mixture of public and private sector provision.

➤ The provision of appropriate infrastructure for the transport sector may require some government intervention to the extent that it involves public good aspects.

➤ The market for transport covers a range of different modes, each of which may be suitable for particular segments of the market, although the modes may compete with each other in some areas.

➤ Road traffic is the most important mode of passenger transport, whether measured by the number of journeys undertaken or by the distance covered.

➤ There has been a substantial increase in the volume of car traffic in the last 25 years, but relatively little expansion of other modes of road transport.

➤ Road transport is also the most important form of freight transport, although transport by water (coastal shipping and internal waterways) remains important, especially for long hauls.

➤ Economic analysis is an integral part of attempts to forecast future transport needs.

➤ The transport sector is vital to the functioning of a modern economy.

# Chapter 21
# Market structure and the transport sector

*Part 4 of the book introduced the notion of market structure, and outlined its importance in enabling an allocation of resources that is good for society. It is important to see how this works in practice, and this chapter presents an evaluation of how market structure has influenced the allocation of resources in the transport sector.*

## Learning outcomes

After studying this chapter, you should:
➤ be familiar with changes in the market for bus transport in the UK as an example of how market structure can evolve over time
➤ be aware of the issues surrounding the privatisation of the rail industry, and the need to balance efficiency gains against the maintenance of safety standards
➤ understand how contestability may inhibit firms' behaviour in the context of low-cost airlines
➤ be familiar with the notion of a natural monopoly, and appreciate the extent to which the Channel Tunnel may be seen as an example of this

## Markets and resource allocation

Chapter 14 showed how a perfectly competitive market allocates resources in such a way that the marginal benefit that consumers receive from consuming the product is equal to the marginal cost of producing that product. This is desirable for society as a whole. If marginal benefit were higher than marginal cost, then consumers would gain if output were increased, as they would gain more benefit from additional units of the good than it would cost society to produce that extra output.

The way in which this outcome is achieved is through the operation of the price mechanism. In a competitive market, firms respond to price signals. If price is at such a level that firms make abnormal profits, this will attract new firms into the market. Industry supply then increases until the price is driven back down to long-run marginal cost. Equally, if price falls below marginal cost, some firms will leave

the market, industry supply will contract, and price will drift back up to its equilibrium value at long-run marginal cost.

Two vital ingredients of this process are that firms react to price signals and that there is freedom of entry into and exit from the market. It is also important to remember that there are ways in which markets may fail to deliver a best outcome for society — for example, externalities, information failure or in the delivery of public goods.

Perfect competition in the real world is rare. There are so many potential sources of market failure that one or other of the stringent assumptions of the perfect competition model always seems to break down. However, this does not nullify the usefulness or power of the model, as it provides us with a standard of comparison for real-world markets. In other words, the existence and characteristics of the model of perfect competition highlight the ways in which real-world markets fall short or diverge from the ideal. This chapter draws on examples of real-world markets for transport to illustrate ways in which they diverge from perfect competition, and evaluates the extent to which they may be considered to conform to other models of market structure that have been analysed.

## The market for bus transport in the UK

For many years the UK market for bus transport was highly regulated. Local authorities had responsibility for bus transport in their areas, and bus routes between cities in England and Wales were served by a nationalised monopoly company — the National Bus Company, created under the Transport Act of 1968. A second company controlled routes in Scotland. Market forces were thus overridden by local regulation and planning.

During the 1980s, the market was deregulated as part of Margaret Thatcher's privatisation drive, in which many industries that had previously been state operated were sold into private hands. In the case of bus transport, the National Bus Company was broken into 72 separate companies in 1986, with no single buyer being allowed to purchase more than three of these companies, and buyers being prohibited from owning companies that operated in contiguous areas.

*Some bus companies are dominant in certain areas of the country*

The fundamental idea behind this move to withdraw government from direct intervention in these markets was to stimulate competition among firms. It had been argued that one characteristic of state-owned enterprises was X-inefficiency. Managers of such enterprises were seen to be inadequately monitored, and faced no great incentive to improve efficiency. In the absence of competition, complacency would creep in, and production would no longer take place at minimum cost. By allowing and encouraging competition — or by making managers accountable to private shareholders — it was argued that X-inefficiency would be eliminated and productivity improved.

An important effect of deregulation was seen in relation to barriers to entry. With a deregulated market, entry was no longer tightly controlled, and as long as a firm could meet the safety requirements, it could set up in business.

In the case of bus transport, deregulation at first seemed to affect the market in the way that had been expected. During the early part of this period, many small bus companies sprang up, and there was intense competition between them. It seemed that perfect competition could become a reality. In particular, it was argued that barriers to entry were so low that competition would be assured, and that the bus market should be regarded as highly contestable. Prices were being driven down towards marginal cost, and consumers reaped the benefit.

As time went by, however, it became apparent that some bus companies were beginning to grow, and others were going out of business. Gradually the market was becoming more concentrated, as revealed by data published by the Competition Commission (formerly the Monopolies and Mergers Commission). In 1989, the largest firm in the bus industry was Stagecoach, with just 3.9% of the UK industry by turnover. At this time, the largest 9 companies accounted for just 12.8% of the market. This changed rapidly over the following 5 years, by the end of which Stagecoach had increased its share to 13.4%, and the top 9 firms accounted for 56% of the UK market. The process of merger and acquisition continued after that time, and by 2003 the top 4 firms in the market accounted for more than 60% of the market. The shares are shown in Figure 21.1.

However, these data may understate the extent of market power held by the largest firms. This is because not all of the large firms are equally active in the regions. In other words, some firms concentrate their activities in certain areas of the country, and may become dominant in particular

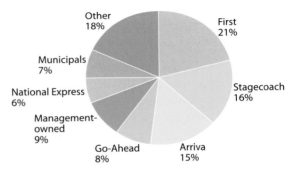

**Figure 21.1** *Bus market shares in the UK, 2003*
Source: Bus Industry Monitor, 2003.

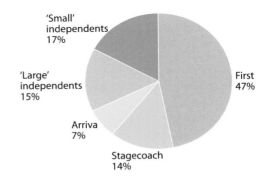

**Figure 21.2** *Bus market shares in west central Scotland, 2003*

Notes: 'large' independents are operators with a market share of 1% or over; 'small' independents are companies with a market share of less than 1%.

Source: Strathclyde Partnership for Transport.

local markets. An example of market shares in a local market is given in Figure 21.2, which shows the situation in the bus market in west central Scotland in 2003. The Office of Fair Trading (OFT) argued that many local markets were likely to be even more concentrated than this, as the 'big four' had tended to focus their strength in particular areas.

One reason for this level of concentration might be the existence of some economies of scale. It might be that bus manufacturers could be persuaded to give discounts on bulk orders for new buses, or perhaps there are economies of scale in servicing and maintaining a large fleet of vehicles. These would enable the larger bus companies to undercut smaller providers.

It seems clear that some of the larger bus companies did indeed achieve economies of scale, since they claimed this as a defence in investigations carried out by the OFT and the Competition Commission. It also seems to be the case that companies were prepared to use their power to increase their market share, and a number of investigations were triggered by accusations of anti-competitive behaviour by bus companies. For example, it was alleged that one large bus company seeking entry into a new market would get hold of competitors' time-tables, and then send along a free bus service to poach all the passengers.

Such *predatory pricing* rarely benefits consumers in the long run. Once competitors have been forced out of the market, the predator firm can then raise price (and restrict output) so as to increase profits. This helps to explain why the OFT has kept a close eye on the bus industry as it has evolved over the last 20 years.

In 1995 the takeover by Stagecoach of Ayrshire Bus prompted an investigation by the Monopolies and Mergers Commission. This case highlighted an important aspect of the influence of market structure on consumer welfare: namely, that there is a potential trade-off between productive and allocative efficiency. By gaining market power, a firm may be able to increase its profits by charging a price above marginal cost, which is damaging in terms of allocative efficiency. On the other hand, by tapping into economies of scale, it improves productive efficiency, which may lead to prices being lower than they would otherwise have been.

Another aspect of Stagecoach's operations (and those of other large bus companies) is an involvement in rail transport. By coordinating its rail and bus services — for example, through timetabling — the company may again be able to make life difficult for competitors. However, it may be argued that, although allocative efficiency may suffer from this practice, productive efficiency improves.

A key question in all of this is the extent to which a bus company on a particular route has sufficient market power to maintain price at such a level as to make supernormal profits. The *sunk costs* involved for another bus company to start serving a new route may be relatively low. This suggests that a bus company that consistently makes supernormal profits on a route is likely to be vulnerable to hit-and-run competition. In other words, if a market for bus transport is contestable, the existing firm may choose not to set price at a level that generates high profits and attracts the entry of new firms. The market would then behave very much as if it were perfectly competitive — at least in terms of pricing. However, it would seem that this has not always been the case.

It is also important to be aware that this is a shrinking market. Figure 21.3 shows how the number of passenger kilometres has declined steadily since 1950, using index numbers based on 1981 = 100. You can see that this decline took place against a backdrop of steadily rising GDP. It might be expected that firms would have less scope for using market power when overall demand is in decline. Figure 21.4 shows that this pattern applied to almost every region after 1982 — but with the notable exception of London, where the number of bus journeys undertaken has seen a steady increase, accelerating towards the end of this period. This may be associated with the policies adopted towards bus travel in the capital, and the introduction of the congestion charge.

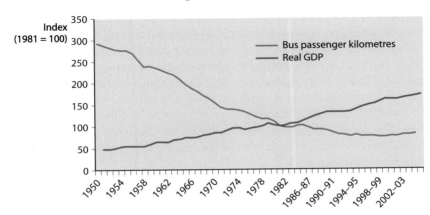

*Figure 21.3*
*Passenger kilometres by bus, 1950–2005*

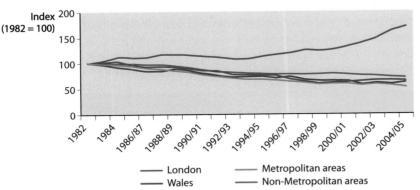

*Figure 21.4*
*Local bus journeys, 1982–2005*

To summarise the situation in the bus industry, it evolved fairly rapidly after deregulation. Having been a tightly regulated sector, it was transformed initially into a state of monopolistic competition, but then went through a process of merger and acquisition, becoming an oligopoly. The monitoring activities of the competition authorities and the potential contestability of markets may have prevented firms from fully exploiting their market positions at the expense of consumers.

However, it is very difficult to come to an overall judgment on the effectiveness of privatisation in this market, as it is impossible to evaluate what the market would have been like had there not been deregulation and privatisation.

## Exercise 21.1

Visit the website of the Office of Fair Trading (www.oft.gov.uk) and find out whether there have been any recent merger cases involving bus transport operators. Discuss the extent to which contestability offers protection to consumers.

## Privatisation and the railways

Another part of the transport sector that went through a process of privatisation is the railways. As with other privatisations, the government hoped to achieve a number of objectives by this process. One objective was to improve efficiency, as it was argued that the managers of state-owned enterprises faced weak incentives to achieve productive efficiency. If an element of competition could be introduced, and if managers could be made accountable to shareholders, it was thought that this should lead to a reduction in X-inefficiency and an overall improvement in welfare. At the time that rail privatisation was being discussed in the early 1990s, there was also a concern about the financing of the rail system, with an escalating need for public subsidies. The Serpell Report, which examined the industry, argued that safety targets had been excessively high, and suggested that there could be some relaxation of maintenance standards.

It was initially envisaged that train operations should be privatised, but that network provision would remain in the hands of the public sector. However, in the event, both train and network operations were privatised in 1996. As far as the network operations were concerned, it was intended that efficiency improvements and maintenance cost reductions would be achieved through a process of contracting out. As far as the train operators were concerned, it was hoped that competition between operators would stimulate efficiency gains.

*It was argued that privatisation of the railways would lead to an improvement in efficiency*

However, for many routes the outcome was that a single operator emerged, so that competition was less intense than had been hoped. Figure 21.5 shows the national market shares among train operators in 2005. By this time, the largest 5 firms were supplying about 83% of the market, so even on a national scale, concentration was high. The fact that some companies have become sole operators on individual routes suggests that competition is likely to be limited. In the context of a broader transport market, it is also potentially significant that some of the large suppliers of rail transport are also significant providers in the bus market.

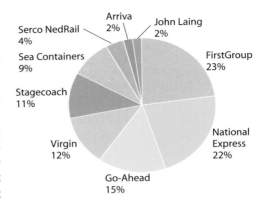

**Figure 21.5**
*Market shares of train operators, 2005*

In terms of carrying freight, the market was even more concentrated, with the largest company (English, Welsh and Scottish Railway, EWS) carrying 11% of all land-hauled freight in the UK in 2005, and with an estimated 80% of the rail freight market in the UK. However, given that there is strong competition from road haulage, the lack of competition in the rail sector may not be a major concern, particularly as substantial economies of scale are available.

One of the most contentious parts of the rail market since privatisation has been the development and maintenance of the network. After privatisation, Railtrack became the monopoly owner of railway infrastructure. This includes track, signalling, stations, depots, bridges, tunnels, level crossings, viaducts and so on. A high-profile fatal train crash at Hatfield in 2000, resulting from a fault in the track, brought Railtrack under the spotlight and in 2002 it was replaced by Network Rail. Network Rail is a company 'limited by guarantee', which means that it is a private organisation operating as a commercial enterprise, but with no shareholders and hence no requirement to pay dividends. Any profits are reinvested to maintain and upgrade the rail infrastructure.

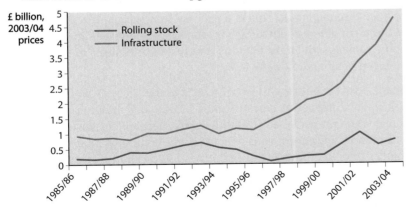

**Figure 21.6**
*Investment in rolling stock and rail infrastructure, 1985–2004*

Figure 21.6 shows the level of investment in rolling stock (vehicles) and rail infrastructure since 1985. This seems to show that investment in infrastructure began

to increase after privatisation, accelerating towards the end of the period shown. Investment in rolling stock seemed to dip after privatisation, but then began to pick up again.

The overall regulation and planning of the rail industry has also gone through a process of change. On privatisation, responsibility for monitoring market structure was given to the Office of the Rail Regulator, whose brief involved 'the regulation of the monopoly and dominant elements of the railways with particular focus on the rail network infrastructure operator'. From the point of view of economic analysis, one danger is that a monopoly operator would choose to maximise profits by setting prices high and restricting output, but equally there is a concern that profits would be increased at the expense of safety or service standards.

The Transport Act of 2000 introduced further changes, launching the Strategic Rail Authority (SRA) to promote better use of the railways within an integrated transport policy. The SRA itself was wound up in 2005, and its functions subsumed into the Department for Transport (Rail Group). Another reorganisation of functions in 2004 saw the establishment of a new Office of Rail Regulation (ORR) as a combined safety and economic regulator.

The need to achieve such a variety of objectives makes it difficult to evaluate the extent to which rail privatisation has been successful. The original aims of privatisation were to achieve efficiency gains and to reduce maintenance costs. However, the fact that privatisation took place in a context where investment in infrastructure had been neglected over a period of years complicates the analysis. There are also clear costs for society if efficiency gains compromise safety standards. In the early part of the twenty-first century it would seem that the industry is beginning to improve. Time alone will tell whether the rail system will be able to play its full part within an integrated transport system in the future. The significance of this will be discussed in Chapter 22.

### Price discrimination

From an economic point of view, one interesting aspect of the rail industry is the extensive use of *price discrimination*. This is a process by which a firm is able to charge a different price to different customers for the same good (see Chapter 15). In the context of the railways, the most obvious example of price discrimination is the difference between peak and off-peak fares.

The practice is made possible because those who need to use the railways in order to travel to work have to travel at certain times of day, and have less elastic demand than those who can travel at any time of day, perhaps for leisure trips, shopping etc. A monopoly operator is thus able to charge commuters travelling in peak periods a higher price, as they are less sensitive to price — or have less choice about when to travel.

Passengers who have to pay the higher prices may well see this as exploitative behaviour by the monopolist. However, there may be situations in which a firm would not be able to remain in business without the possibility of price discrimination. For example, consider Figure 21.7. Here, the firm faces average costs that are always above demand (AR). Setting marginal cost equal to marginal revenue suggests that the profit-maximising level of output is $q_m$, but if the firm chooses to produce this output, and sets a price at $p_m$, the result is a loss (given by the shaded area), as average cost exceeds average revenue. Such a situation is not sustainable in the long run.

However, if the firm is able to use price discrimination, it may be possible to remain profitable by tapping the consumer surplus of some groups of customers. For example, if the firm can operate perfect price discrimination, it could acquire the area of consumer surplus ABC as profit to set against the area CEF of losses. One of the tasks of the regulator may be to make sure that this practice is not over-exploited by the train operators.

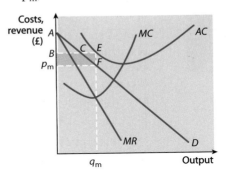

**Figure 21.7** A monopolist using price discrimination

## Exercise 21.2

Discuss the arguments for and against privatisation, and whether you think that rail privatisation has benefited rail passengers.

## The low-cost airlines

The case study of the low-cost airlines is an interesting example of the way in which intensified competition in a market can affect the operation of markets. As this example is also pertinent in examining the leisure sector, this case study appears in Chapter 17. You will find it on pages 267–70.

## The Channel Tunnel — a natural monopoly?

Chapter 14 pointed out that some markets may result in a *natural monopoly*, mainly because of the structure of their costs. The argument is illustrated by Figure 21.8.

Here is a market in which there are substantial economies of scale, such that long-run average cost (LAC) is falling right up to the limit of market demand. In such a situation, it would be expected that the largest firm in the market would always be able to undercut the price of any competitor that tried to enter the market, and thus would come to dominate the market and become a natural monopoly. In this situation, it is the existence of economies of scale that constitute a barrier to the entry of new firms.

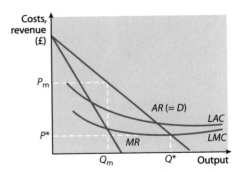

**Figure 21.8** A natural monopoly

This situation may arise where there are large fixed (or set-up) costs, but relatively low variable costs. One example might be an underground railway system in a city. There are large set-up costs involved in building the rail network and buying the rolling stock, but very low variable costs, in the sense that the cost of carrying one additional passenger is very low indeed.

At first glance, it might be thought that the Channel Tunnel is rather similar. The construction and other fixed costs of building the tunnel are very high indeed compared with the marginal cost of transporting one additional passenger through it. Furthermore, there is only one Channel Tunnel (and only likely to be), so is this not a good example of a natural monopoly?

If this were the case, then concern might arise if the tunnel operator was able to charge a monopoly price in order to maximise profits — thus producing at quantity $Q_m$ in Figure 21.10, and setting price at $P_m$. This would entail some allocative inefficiency, as the price would be set above marginal cost.

One response to this could be for the authorities to regulate the market, and require the firm to set a price that was equal to marginal cost — that is, the price that would ensure allocative efficiency. Figure 21.10 shows that this would not be a viable solution. The problem is with the pattern of average costs. At the output level $Q^*$, setting price equal to marginal cost (at $P^*$) causes the firm to make substantial losses, as long-run average cost exceeds average revenue (price) at this point.

*Cross-channel ferry companies operate in an oligopoly market with the Channel Tunnel*

The question that then arises is whether it is likely that the Channel Tunnel operator will have the power to exploit its market position. Strictly speaking, there is no question of contestability here. It is not possible for a second tunnel to be set up to provide hit-and-run entry, especially given the sunk costs that would be involved.

However, this does not mean that the Channel Tunnel does not face competition. The cross-Channel ferry companies provide stiff competition for the tunnel, and may prevent it from exercising its market power. The Channel Tunnel may perhaps never be forced to set a price as low as marginal cost, but setting a price much above average cost would probably invoke a price response from the ferries.

The cross-Channel routes may thus be regarded as an *oligopoly* market, in which the tunnel and the ferry companies will set

OCR Advanced Economics

price having some regard to the actions and likely reactions of the other operators in the market.

Notice that the market interactions work in both directions. In recent years, there has been some consolidation among the ferry operators, through a process of merger and acquisition. This has triggered a number of investigations by the OFT and the Competition Commission. In reaching their judgements, the effect on the ferry companies of competition from the Channel Tunnel has been an influential factor.

## Exercise 21.3

Discuss the extent to which the rail route between London and Edinburgh may be seen as a potential monopoly situation.

## Duopoly — Boeing and Airbus

At first glance, aircraft manufacture seems another potential natural monopoly — again because of its cost structure. The key issue for aircraft manufacture lies in the enormous cost of research and development (R&D), besides which the marginal cost of producing an additional aircraft is relatively minor. And yet, the market is effectively a *duopoly*, with Boeing and Airbus being the only effective global competitors.

This market has triggered much transatlantic debate and contention. Boeing, the US producer, has accused European governments of unfairly subsidising Airbus's R&D programme. In return, Airbus has responded by pointing to the benefits that Boeing has received from the US military research programme.

Without being drawn into this debate, the net effect of the interventions has been to create a duopoly situation in which Boeing and Airbus appear to compete aggressively for market share. This probably means better allocative efficiency than if one of the firms were able to dominate the global market. Ultimately, air travellers benefit from this.

## Monopolistic competition in road transport

The theory of monopolistic competition describes a market with some features of monopoly and some features of perfect competition. Entry barriers are low, so the market has many firms. However, firms in the market use product differentiation to influence consumers, and thus face downward-sloping demand curves.

If you look back at the analysis in Chapter 15, you will see that this form of market structure has implications for both productive and allocative efficiency. Firms produce at a level of output below that at which long-run average cost would reach the minimum, so there is not productive efficiency. Furthermore, price is set above marginal cost, so allocative efficiency is not achieved either.

Take a drive along a motorway or trunk road in the UK, and observe the heavy goods vehicles (HGVs) and smaller vans that you pass. You will see HGVs and vans in a wide variety of liveries, from a wide range of countries and carrying a wide diversity of loads.

This is a market characterised by many competing firms, many of which operate in niche markets. Firms try to differentiate their offering by carrying particular categories of products — building materials, perhaps, or electronic goods. Some may trade between certain destinations. They advertise by broadcasting these specialisms on their vehicles, in the *Yellow Pages* or on the internet.

Another part of the road transport market that may typify monopolistic competition is local taxi markets. Count the local taxi companies in your local *Yellow Pages*. Again, firms may seek to differentiate their products through having a fleet livery, by advertising pre-booking only or by offering a limousine service. There may also be firms that specialise in longer-distance trips, say to airports.

## Summary

➤ Market structure is important in determining whether allocative efficiency can be achieved.

➤ However, productive efficiency must also be taken into account.

➤ After deregulation, the market for bus transport in the UK went through a process of evolution from monopolistic competition to oligopoly.

➤ Rail privatisation was introduced to promote greater productive efficiency, but it has taken many years for the industry to settle down.

➤ The low-cost airlines have transformed the market for air travel, using price discrimination and a thorough understanding of costs.

➤ The Channel Tunnel offers an example of a natural monopoly, but it cannot ignore competition from the ferry companies.

➤ The transport sector also offers examples of duopoly (Boeing and Airbus) and monopolistic competition in road haulage.

# *Chapter 22*
# Resource allocation issues in transport

*The transport sector is critical to the operation of the economy, and it is important to analyse the way in which resources are allocated within the transport sector, as well as between transport and the rest of the economy. This analysis goes beyond the issues of market structure that were raised in the previous chapter.*

## Learning outcomes

After studying this chapter, you should:
➤ understand and be able to evaluate the objectives of transport policy
➤ appreciate why markets may not always ensure the 'best' allocation of resources within the transport sector
➤ understand the nature and features of an integrated transport policy
➤ be familiar with the Private Finance Initiative as one way in which private funding of transport projects can be encouraged
➤ be aware of the importance of cost–benefit analysis as a method of appraising capital projects in the transport sector
➤ be able to discuss the uses and limitations of the cost–benefit approach to transport decision making

## The importance of transport policy

Chapters 20 and 21 emphasised the importance of the transport sector for the economy. Transport is important for businesses because both inputs and outputs need to be transported, and workers need to travel to work. Transport is important for consumers because they have a derived demand for transport in connection with their employment (travel to work), and also in relation to their consumption of leisure (travel to holiday destinations or for other leisure activities) and their consumption of goods and services, whereby the goods consumed need to be transported to the consumer. From the point of view of firms operating in the economy, transport may be seen as an important input, and in many cases a

significant item of costs. For firms competing internationally, an efficient transport system can be vital in maintaining competitiveness, by keeping down firms' costs relative to their foreign competitors. Equally, an inefficient transport system can be an obstacle to competing successfully in overseas markets.

Can the provision of the required transport services be left to the market? Would a good allocation of resources be achieved in the transport sector if the authorities allowed the free market to hold sway? Or is there a need for a transport policy by which the government can direct and guide the allocation of resources towards a better balance for consumers and businesses? This is tantamount to asking whether there is some sort of market failure present in the transport sector that would prevent the achievement of allocative and productive efficiency.

The previous chapter explored some ways in which market failure may be present, by looking at the influence of market structure on the transport sector. It showed that there are several markets within the transport sector that would not be expected to operate according to the perfectly competitive ideal, but could incline towards monopoly, or at least towards imperfect competition. To some extent this was likely to be mitigated by the contestability of many transport markets. Where a market is contestable, the firm or firms within the market have limited power to influence the selling price of their product. Contestability in transport markets arises partly because of conditions within particular markets, but also because of the interconnections between modes. For example, a railway operating company faces competition from long-distance coaches and low-cost airlines on particular routes.

Market structure is not the only source of market failure. There are other aspects of the transport sector which might suggest that some form of state intervention — or at least state monitoring — would be desirable. Externalities are especially significant in the transport sector: for example, in relation to the environment and traffic congestion. To some extent, such problems can be tackled through taxation, regulation and measures such as road pricing. Some specific examples

*Transport involves the movement of people and goods from one place to another, and is a vital part of a modern economy*

of the treatment of negative externalities will be explored and evaluated in Chapter 23.

However, there is also reason to argue that transport is sufficiently important to the economy for the government to take a long view of the market. Indeed, one reason for this is that the market for transport is not really a single market, but a series of interconnected markets. It then becomes important to have a coordinated view, rather than allowing markets for rail, air, road and water transport to operate independently. This may be especially important because different modes of transport have differing effects in the long run: for example, in terms of their impact on the environment. Thus there may be reasons for the government to intervene to influence the future balance of the transport system. This is discussed later in this chapter.

Many transport investment projects have long gestation lags. In other words, the decision to build a new road, Channel Tunnel or airport takes a long time to bear fruit. It may be many years after the original decision to proceed before such schemes come into operation and generate benefits for users. Such long-term planning is best undertaken by the government, which may be able to afford to take a longer-term view of investment decisions. Furthermore, the government may be in a better position to take appropriate account of externality effects in reaching such decisions.

A further complication is that, in many cases, aspects of transport infrastructure have some characteristics of public goods. This may create a free-rider problem and make it difficult for private firms to charge users. Again, this suggests that some form of government intervention may be needed in order to ensure the appropriate provision of such infrastructure.

Putting all of these arguments together, it would seem that there is a pressing need for a transport policy that is carefully integrated, so as to be able to take all of these various issues fully into account.

## Summary

➤ Transport involves the movement of people and goods from one place to another, and is a vital part of a modern economy.

➤ It is therefore important to ensure good allocation of resources in the transport sector.

➤ This requires an integrated approach to transport policy to ensure an appropriate balance of resources across the various transport modes.

➤ Transport policy is also important because of the need to take a long-term view of the provision of transportation services.

## The objectives of transport policy

The provision of infrastructure is of central importance in the transport sector. The major modes of transport all require investment in infrastructure, whether it be

roads, a rail network, or airport or port facilities. As has been mentioned, such projects have long planning horizons in the case of new ventures, and typically also entail high maintenance costs. One key objective for transport policy is thus to have a coherent overview of what constitutes a desirable long-term pattern of transportation.

This aspect of an integrated transport policy requires coordination across the various modes of travel as a result of their interconnectedness. For example, consider someone who needs to travel from, say, London to Edinburgh. The options are to drive, to take a train or coach, or to fly. The choice of mode will depend upon a range of factors, such as the relative travel times, relative prices, preferences and convenience. Perceptions of the relative safety of different modes of travel may also be a concern. A choice of one mode will be based on considerations of opportunity cost relative to the next best alternative mode of transport. This has implications for the supply side, as decisions taken now about investment in different parts of the transport sector will affect future comparisons between the modes.

This issue was recognised in the government White Paper, *A New Deal for Transport: Better for Everyone*, issued in 1998. This was followed in July 2000 by the publication of a Ten-Year Plan for transport, which the government claimed was 'the beginning of a more strategic approach' to the transport sector. A further White Paper, *The Future of Transport*, was issued in July 2004. This document updated the Ten-Year Plan and set out a strategy for a coherent transport network for 2030, covering the following aspects:

'the **road** network providing a more reliable and freer-flowing service for both personal travel and freight, with people able to make informed choices about how and when they travel;

the **rail** network providing a fast, reliable and efficient service, particularly for interurban journeys and commuting into large urban areas;

**bus** services that are reliable, flexible, convenient and tailored to local needs;

making **walking** and **cycling** a real alternative for local trips; and

**ports** and **airports** providing improved international and domestic links'.

It should be noted that there may be interactions with other markets as well. Traditionally, the government has taken an active role in planning land use across the nation. The establishment of a 'green belt' of protected rural landscape may have indirect effects on the transportation system, as land-use planning affects the location of industrial activity and housing. This has an impact on transport because of the need for people to travel to work, and for business to transport freight — that is, inputs and outputs. Decisions on housing developments or the location of industrial estates thus need to be coordinated with decisions on the provision of transport infrastructure.

The design of transport policy must also keep in mind the importance of achieving an *efficient* system. This is important from the commercial point of view.

If UK firms face higher transportation costs than firms operating elsewhere in Europe, this could potentially put them at a considerable disadvantage. In other words, the transport system can be seen as essential in enabling markets to operate, and in facilitating economic growth. Indeed, the development of a functional transport system may be seen as an essential ingredient of economic development: the lack of such a system has hindered progress in many less developed countries and in the transition economies. Of course, there are many other factors as well, but the importance of transportation should not be underplayed.

From an economics point of view, a key question is: why can't markets be relied upon to deliver a coherent vision of the future transport network? In other words, why is it necessary for the government to intervene?

## Public goods

Chapter 7 discussed the problems entailed in ensuring the provision of **public goods** — that is, goods which are non-excludable and non-rivalrous. Street lighting was the example used. It is not possible to exclude one person from enjoying the benefits of street lighting in a road (it is non-excludable). Furthermore, one person's consumption of street lighting does not leave less lighting for the next passer-by (it is non-rivalrous). In the absence of state intervention, the market will fail to provide the socially desirable amount of street lighting because of the **free-rider problem**. No individual consumer has an incentive to pay for the good in this situation.

In the transport sector, it can be argued that there are aspects of transport infrastructure that have partial characteristics of a public good. It is not impossible to charge road users for making use of a particular stretch of road, but it would be difficult (given present technology) to extend charging to all roads in the country. This suggests that some government involvement in the provision of infrastructure is essential. This does not necessarily mean that the government has to provide the roads, but it may need to enable the private sector to be adequately rewarded for that provision in some way. The objectives of transport policy should thus include taking steps to ensure the provision of appropriate infrastructure in the presence of the free-rider problem.

 **Key terms**

**public good:** a good that is non-exclusive and non-rivalrous; consumers cannot be excluded from consuming the good, and consumption by one person does not affect the amount of the good available for others to consume

**free-rider problem:** when an individual cannot be excluded from consuming a good, and thus has no incentive to pay for its provision

## Meeting demand?

Another argument that has been put forward is that the government should intervene to ensure that the demands for transportation in the future can be met. The need for intervention here may arise if the government is better able to evaluate the strength and nature of future demand than private firms. The need to coordinate with other aspects of government policy might help to reinforce this argument.

Even more important is the question of whether the transport system should be solely designed to meet future demand, or whether the future demand for transport should itself be managed. For example, it may be that the government has some vision of the future transport system in the UK, and may need to plan carefully in order to move towards that vision. This may be seen as a **merit good** argument, in which the government has better information about what is desirable than the population at large.

An important aspect of this issue arises in the context of road transport. Forecasts of the future demand for car journeys suggest a steady increase in the demand for road transport. One response to this might be to embark on a road-building programme in order to ensure that the increase in demand can be accom-modated. But is this the best way forward?

This is a complex area. For one thing, there is some evidence that increasing the quantity of road space available does not simply help to accommodate existing traffic, but may actually lead to an increase in the number of journeys undertaken. If this is the case, then the road-building programme could never catch up with actual demand.

Furthermore, if there are negative externalities involved in car journeys, then private motorists will always choose to undertake more journeys than is desirable for society as a whole. In Chapter 23, the possibility of using road pricing to influence the demand for journeys will be examined. However, in the longer term, it is important to ensure that the programme for road construction and improve-ment is in line with the overall objectives of transport policy and with the plans for other modes of transport.

## Exercise 22.1

Table 22.1 presents some data about the relative safety record of different modes of transport. Discuss the extent to which these data should influence transport policy.

*Table 22.1  Passenger death rates by mode of transport, 1993 and 2002 (rate per billion passenger kilometres)*

Note: data are for Great Britain, except water and air, which relate to the UK.

Source: *Social Trends.*

| Mode | 1993 | 2002 |
|---|---|---|
| Motor cycle | 106.0 | 111.3 |
| Walking | 70.1 | 44.8 |
| Bicycle | 46.5 | 29.5 |
| Car | 3.2 | 2.8 |
| Van | 1.6 | 1.0 |
| Bus or coach | 0.7 | 0.4 |
| Rail | 0.4 | 0.3 |
| Water | 0.0 | 0.0 |
| Air | 0.0 | 0.0 |

### Environmental sustainability

In designing an integrated transport policy that attempts to manage the pattern and level of demand for the various transport modes, an important consideration is environmental **sustainability**. Concern for the environment has become a prominent and contentious issue in recent decades, nowhere more than in relation to transport. Safeguarding the environment has been seen as critical, partly because of its direct impact on the quality of life. People gain utility from living in or visiting a pleasant environment — or even just from knowing that such areas exist. However, concern for the environment goes beyond these direct effects. The threat of global warming raises issues about the importance of safeguarding the environment for the benefit of future generations as well as people living today. In terms of economic analysis, this is tantamount to arguing that there are externality effects that may cross national borders, or that may cross generations. Decisions taken today that affect the environment may have repercussions for other nations, or for future generations, which are not reflected in market prices.

**Key** term

**sustainable transport development:** an approach to planning the transport system which ensures that present needs can be met without compromising the ability of future generations to meet their transport needs

These effects must be taken into account in an integrated transport policy, as different modes of transport have different implications for the environment. For example, this helps to explain why the 2004 White Paper included a clause about the need to encourage walking and cycling for local trips. The use of cars for short journeys is seen as especially damaging from an environmental perspective. Yet another spin-off is that walking and cycling are seen to be beneficial from a health perspective, and with a growing problem of obesity affecting people in the UK, a transport system that discourages people from taking physical activity may have long-term effects on the health service.

The difference in greenhouse gas emissions between the various types of transport is seen clearly in Figure 22.1. The implications of this for policy also seem clear. Rail transport is responsible for the smallest quantity of emissions, and has shown a decrease in emissions since 1990. Buses and coaches have also shown some decrease in emissions in this period. However, emissions from all other modes have increased, with an especially large increase in emissions from air travel and road freight. However, private vehicles remain the greatest source of $CO_2$ emissions. From a policy perspective, then, it would seem that the authorities need to be aware of these differences, and to design policy that will achieve an

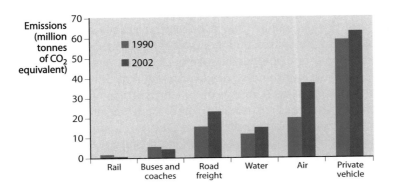

*Figure 22.1*
*Greenhouse gas emissions from different types of UK transport, 1990 and 2002*

Source: Economic and Social Research Council.

appropriate balance between private and public transport — that is, between the use of private vehicles and the use of rail, bus and coach travel.

In order to achieve a sustainable transport policy, there must be two themes. First, it is important to use policy to influence the future demand for transport overall. Second, it is important for policy to shape the pattern of transportation between the modes, by encouraging less use of road transport as well as encouraging more sustainable modes of transport, such as rail, bus, cycling and walking.

## Summary

➤ Transport policy aims to coordinate the planning of transport across the different modes: road, rail, bus, walking and cycling, water and air.

➤ Policy also needs to be coordinated with other aspects of economic policy, such as the location of housing and industrial developments.

➤ Transport infrastructure has some of the characteristics of a public good, so some state intervention is needed to ensure its provision.

➤ Policy cannot be purely reactive in trying to meet demand, but must also be proactive in managing the demand for transport services.

➤ Environmental sustainability must be an integral part of policy for transport.

## Financing transport policy

If the government is to be active in influencing the future of the transport sector in the UK, especially if it is to be involved in the provision of transport infrastructure, the question arises as to how to raise the necessary finance — both for investment and for maintenance. Chapter 23 will examine the possible use of taxation to finance transport projects, and to combat the impact of negative externalities. However, there have been some other initiatives in recent years to provide funding for transport projects, most importantly the Private Finance Initiative, launched in 1992.

### The Private Finance Initiative (PFI)

PFI was launched in 1992 as a way of trying to increase the involvement of the private sector in the provision of public services. This established a partnership between the public and private sectors. The public sector specifies, perhaps in broad terms, the services that it requires, and then invites tenders from the private sector to design, build, finance and operate the scheme. In some cases, the project might be entirely freestanding: for example, the government may initiate a project such as a new bridge that is then taken up by a private firm, which will recover its costs entirely through user charges such as tolls. In other cases, the project may be a joint venture between the public and private sectors. The public sector could get involved with such a venture in order to secure wider social benefits, perhaps through reductions in traffic congestion that would not be reflected in market prices, and thus would not be fully taken into account by the private sector. In other cases, it may be that the private sector undertakes a project and then sells the services to the public sector.

Figure 22.2 shows the range of PFI deals that were signed during the first 10 years of the scheme: you can see that a sizeable proportion of these were in transport, involving road construction, street lighting, bridges and rail projects. The largest project in this period was the Channel Tunnel Rail Link (£4,178 million), signed in 2000. Subsequently, projects involving the London Underground totalling £10,695 million were signed in 2003.

The aim of PFI is to improve the financing of public sector projects. This is partly achieved by introducing a competitive element into the tendering process, but in addition it enables the risk of a project to be shared between the public and private sectors. This should enable efficiency gains to be made.

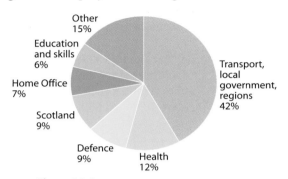

**Figure 22.2**
*PFI signed deals as at 1 September 2001*

However, PFI has been much debated — and much criticised. One effect of PFI is to reduce the pressures on public finances by enabling greater private sector involvement in funding. But it might be argued that this may in fact raise the cost of borrowing, if the public sector would have been able to borrow on more favourable terms than commercial firms. The introduction of a competitive element in the tendering process may be beneficial, but on the other hand, it could be argued that the private sector may have less incentive than the public sector to give due attention to health and safety issues. In other words, there may be a concern that private firms will be tempted to sacrifice safety or service-standards in the quest for profit. Achieving the appropriate balance between efficiency and quality of service is an inevitable problem to be faced in whatever way transport is financed and provided, but it becomes a more critical issue to the extent that use of PFI switches the focus more towards efficiency and lower costs.

## Cost–benefit analysis

The importance of externalities in regard to environmental issues means that it is especially important to be aware of externalities when taking decisions that are likely to affect the environment. One area in which this has been especially contentious in recent years is road-building programmes. If decisions to build new roads, or to expand existing ones such as the M25, are taken only by reference to commercial considerations, there could be serious implications for resource allocation.

In taking such decisions, it is desirable to weigh up the costs and benefits of a scheme. If it turns out that the benefits exceed the costs, it might be thought appropriate to go ahead. However, in valuing the costs and the benefits, it is clearly important to include some estimate for the externalities involved in order that the

decision can be based on all relevant factors. A further complication is that, with many such schemes, the costs and benefits will be spread out over a long period of time, and it is important to come to a reasonable balance between the interests of present and future generations.

It is therefore very important to have a framework within which the costs and benefits can be evaluated, whether or not they have a market value attached to them. *Social cost–benefit analysis* offers just such a framework. The Department for Transport (DfT) routinely applies cost–benefit analysis to major road schemes using a standard approach. This is based on computer software that has been in use since the 1970s: the COBA (**Co**st–**B**enefit **A**nalysis) programme. In evaluating transport projects, the DfT appraises on the basis of five key objectives: environment, safety, economy, accessibility and integration.

Suppose that a new section of trunk road is proposed. What are the steps that COBA goes through in order to reach an evaluation of the project? There are three key procedures to invoke. First, the expected construction cost needs to be measured. Second, the benefits to users must be evaluated. These costs and benefits should ideally incorporate all of the costs and benefits that will be associated with the scheme, including some that would not normally be given a monetary value. Third, it is important to be aware that the scheme is likely to provide a stream of costs and benefits over a period of time. In taking decisions in the present period, analysts need to be careful not to give too much weight to benefits (or costs) that will only accrue in the very long term. It would not be sensible to regard benefits that will appear in 30 years' time as highly as benefits that will flow after only 5 years. Future costs and benefits thus need to be converted into their 'present values' through a process of discounting future values.

Figure 22.3 shows the process adopted within the COBA system, reproduced from the DfT's *COBA Manual.* Notice that the first step is to identify user costs on the existing road network (A1 in the diagram), so that the benefits from the scheme can be evaluated as the reduction in user costs. In other words, first check the existing scenario, and then see how this will improve as a result of the new project. The costs of the project are then deducted to give an estimate of the net present value of the project. If this is positive, the scheme may be viewed favourably, although, of course, there may be other schemes under consideration and these might come out with a higher net present value. In this case, the process enables the DfT to set priorities among a range of projects, remembering

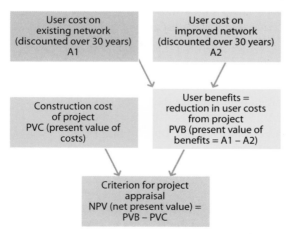

**Figure 22.3** *The COBA appraisal process*
Source: Department for Transport, *COBA Manual*, 2003.

that the opportunity cost of a project can be seen in terms of the net present value of the next best alternative. If funds are committed to a particular project, this may have to be at the expense of another scheme, given the limits of the overall budget.

In many ways, the difficult part of applying such a system comes in the way in which the user costs are evaluated. In order for the process to be carried out, it is vital that a monetary value is placed on the various user costs involved, both with the existing road network and under the new proposal. Under the COBA process, the user costs include changes in time, operating costs and the cost of accidents. In other words, the question is whether the new scheme will allow more speedy travel, cheaper travel and safer travel. The costs of the scheme are appraised in terms of the capital costs (including the preparation and supervision costs), and any changes in the capital cost of maintaining the proposed new network as compared to the existing one.

The need to assign monetary values is both the strength and the weakness of COBA. It is a strength because it enables external benefits and costs to be brought into consideration. It is a weakness because such valuations may be contentious, although the process is now so well established that at least some of the issues are now familiar to analysts. It might also be argued that, as long as similar methods are applied consistently across a range of projects, then at least the ranking procedure should be reliable.

It is important to appreciate that the focus of COBA is on user benefits. Although this is important, it is a partial approach that crucially neglects many of the externalities that are seen to be relevant to most transport projects. COBA thus needs to be augmented by consideration of other pertinent issues. This is done through the completion of an Appraisal Summary Table (AST), which covers the five main categories of issues: environment, safety, economy, accessibility and integration. The sub-categories explored under each of these headings are set out in Figure 22.4. This approach does at least provide a focus for appraisal by identifying

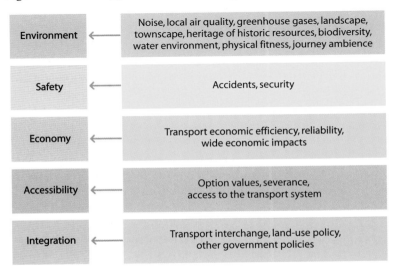

**Figure 22.4**
*The AST approach*

the issues that need to be considered. However, such items will not be fully taken into account until a way is found of giving them a monetary valuation. Some attempt is made to move towards a measurement by rating a project under each heading on a seven-point scale, from 'large negative' to 'large positive'.

So, the procedure is first to undertake a COBA and to calculate the ratio of benefits to costs — which might produce a value of, say, 2.80. This suggests that the project is generating benefits almost three times the costs. The AST would then be used to summarise other non-monetised impacts. A particular road scheme might be found to have beneficial impacts in terms of noise, journey ambience and security; neutral impacts on water environment, wider economic impacts and physical fitness; but adverse impacts on local air quality, greenhouse gases and biodiversity. The appraisal would then need to weigh up the relative strength of these impacts to determine whether the scheme would be good value for money.

## Summary

➤ An important part of transport policy relates to the way that investment in and mainte-nance of transport projects are financed.

➤ The Private Finance Initiative was devised to provide greater encouragement of the private sector in the provision of public services; this has been used extensively in the transport sector.

➤ Cost–benefit analysis has been widely used as a framework for evaluating the net present value of transport projects.

➤ This entails evaluating the benefits and costs of a project, including some external benefits and costs.

➤ The Department of Transport routinely uses this method (using computer software COBA) for all road projects.

## Exercise 22.2

Suppose there is a proposal to construct a new stretch of motorway close to where you live. Identify the costs and benefits of the scheme, including direct costs and benefits and not forgetting externalities. Discuss how you would seek to evaluate the proposal. Make sure you take into account the most important issues listed in the AST approach.

# Chapter 23
# Market failure and the role of government in transport

*The previous chapter discussed the need for an integrated transport policy in order to deal with a range of problems arising from various forms of market failure. The policy instruments devised to deal with these issues come under consideration in this chapter. Some policy measures introduced have been contentious, and an understanding of the economic analysis underlying transport policy helps to explain why this might be the case.*

## Learning outcomes

After studying this chapter, you should:

➤ be aware of the importance of externalities in the transport sector and be able to discuss how these may be tackled through regulation and taxation
➤ understand the meaning and rationale of the hypothecation of taxation
➤ appreciate the importance of environmental issues in the transport sector
➤ be able to evaluate transport policy in its treatment of environmental issues
➤ understand how market failure is relevant to the problem of traffic congestion and evaluate the policy options for tackling this issue
➤ understand what is meant by user-charging and road pricing, and analyse and evaluate their economic basis
➤ be able to compare the experience of the UK with that of other countries

## Market failure and transport

Earlier chapters have highlighted the fact that market failure is significant in the transport sector, arising in a number of guises. A problem when the government attempts to rectify market failure is that there are some situations in which the remedy is worse than the disease. Well-intended government intervention can sometimes have distortionary effects on resource allocation that leave society no better off — or even worse off. It is important to be aware of this and to try to guard against it when designing policy measures. This chapter begins with a reminder of the key areas of market failure that can affect the transport sector.

## Imperfect competition

One source of market failure is imperfect competition in a market, whether this be monopoly, oligopoly or some other form of market structure besides perfect competition. In such a market, it is likely that price will be set at a level that is above marginal cost, thus imposing some cost on society as a whole through a loss of allocative efficiency. In the transport sector, one common reason for the appearance of imperfect competition arises from the cost structure, such that a potential natural monopoly situation may arise.

The frequency with which firms operating in the transport sector have been referred to the competition authorities suggests that there is a real danger of such situations arising. However, as discussed earlier, there is also a growing awareness that contestability is relatively strong in many transport markets. This is partly because of the competition that arises between alternative modes of transport. The low-cost airlines are a good example of such contestability.

Contestability weakens the pressure on government to intervene, and the competitive pressures within a contestable market act as a natural constraint on the actions of firms. If a firm knows that the market in which it is operating is contestable, it will not set a price above average cost, for fear of attracting hit-and-run entry by new competitors. However, it is wise for the competition authorities (the OFT and the Competition Commission) to maintain a watching brief on the transport sector, and to be ready to intervene if necessary.

## Externalities

Another form of market failure that is prevalent in transport markets is externalities. Externalities arise in situations where there are costs or benefits associated with a transaction that are not fully reflected in market prices. This could lead to a situation in which, for example, social costs exceed private costs. This causes allocative inefficiency, as the decisions made by private firms or individuals will not correspond to what is best for society as a whole. For example, if a firm uses a fleet of trucks to transport freight around the country and these trucks have been poorly maintained, so they give off noxious fumes, this imposes costs on other road users — or people who live close to the roads. However, the firm will not need to face up to the full cost of its activities unless forced to do so by policy.

Another example of externalities in the transport sector is where new infrastructure, such as a new road or rail link, entails damage to the environment. Such damage must be factored into the cost–benefit appraisal of any major scheme for transport infrastructure, as was discussed in Chapter 22. The policy issue here is to achieve balance in the long-term operations of the transport sector.

## Information and health and safety

Information failure can be a significant source of market failure, especially where some participants in a market have better information than others. One area in which this is relevant in the transport sector is in relation to the merit good argument mentioned in Chapter 22. It was argued that the government is more

able to take a long-term view of the transport market, and has better information about how the future balance of transport could be shaped than enterprises in the private sector, or those responsible for managing public enterprises in a particular part of the transport sector. It could also be argued that the government has broader information, so is able to undertake a coordinating role between the competing transport modes.

Another merit good argument relates to health and safety regulations. Individual workers may take decisions about their supply of labour that do not adequately recognise health and safety issues. The authorities have better information about health and safety and thus impose regulations on firms to safeguard workers' interests. This imposes costs on firms, and may have the effect of reducing the demand for labour — but in the best interests of the workers who *are* employed. However, it is clearly important to reach an appropriate balance between ensuring the health and safety of workers and maintaining employment.

In the transport sector, health and safety issues also arise in the context of passenger health and safety. This has been contentious for the railways since privatisation. The privatised rail sector was given productivity targets to meet. The danger then was that those targets would be met at the expense of safety. Again, some form of regulation to avoid this danger is important.

*The rail crash at Ladbroke Grove, October 1999; safety on the railways remains a contentious issue*

## Public goods

Transport infrastructure may be seen to have some of the characteristics of a public good, which means that some form of public intervention will be needed to ensure that sufficient infrastructure is provided. This was discussed in the previous

chapter. The provision and maintenance of roads, street lighting and road signage all come into this category. In the absence of intervention, too little of such goods would be provided, as the free-rider problem makes it impossible to charge users for their consumption of street lighting or road signs. For some stretches of road, or some sections of the road network, some form of user charging may be possible. This will be discussed later in the chapter.

## Exercise 23.1

Identify the form of market failure that is potentially present in each of the following situations, and comment on the likely consequences for society in the absence of intervention by the authorities.

**a** a motorway services area

**b** the provision of road signs

**c** spillage from an oil tanker close to a tourist beach

**d** the provision of safety belts in coaches

**e** motorway maintenance

## Taxation and regulation of transport

Given that these various forms of market failure are likely to distort the pattern of resource allocation in the transport sector, how can the authorities seek to improve matters? In a particular market, there are usually two main possibilities. First, taxes can be used to influence the price of a good or service, and thus influence the market equilibrium. Second, some form of direct regulation or control can be used to influence the market outcome.

Consider the case of externalities. Externalities arise in situations where there are items of cost or benefit associated with transactions that are not reflected in market prices. In these circumstances, a free market will not lead to an optimum allocation of resources. In order to deal with such market situations, one approach is to bring those externalities into the market mechanism — a process known as **internalising an externality**. For example, in the case of pollution, this principle would entail forcing polluting firms to face the full social cost of their production activities. This is sometimes known as the **polluter pays principle**.

 **Key terms**

**internalising an externality:** an attempt to deal with an externality by bringing an external cost or benefit into the price system

**polluter pays principle:** the principle that the cost of pollution should be borne by whoever is responsible for that pollution

### Pollution

Figure 23.1 illustrates a negative production externality such as pollution. It shows a market for freight transportation by road. Let us suppose that firms in this market

use trucks that emit fumes, thus imposing costs on society that the firms do not face. In other words, the marginal private costs faced by the firms are less than the marginal social costs that are inflicted on society. Firms in this market would choose to transport freight up to the point $Q_1$ and charge a price of $P_1$. At this point, marginal social benefit is below the marginal cost of transporting goods, and it can be claimed that 'too much' freight is being transported. Society would be better off at $Q^*$, with a price charged at $P^*$.

One point to notice here is that this optimum position is not characterised by *zero* pollution. In other words, from society's point of view, it pays to abate pollution only up to the level where the marginal benefit of reducing pollution is matched by the marginal cost of doing so. Reducing pollution to zero would be too costly.

However, how could society reach the optimum position at $Q^*$? In line with the principle that the polluter should pay, one approach would be to impose a tax on firms such that they faced the full cost of their actions. In Figure 23.1, if firms are required to pay a tax equivalent to the vertical distance between marginal private cost (*MPC*) and marginal social cost (*MSC*), they would choose to produce at $Q^*$, paying a tax equal to the green line on the diagram.

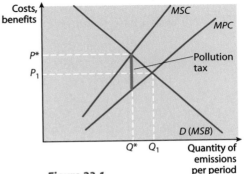

**Figure 23.1**
*Tackling pollution using taxation*

An alternative way of looking at this question is to draw a diagram that shows the marginal benefit and marginal cost of emissions reduction. This is done in Figure 23.2. Here, *MB* represents the marginal social benefits from reducing emissions, and *MC* the marginal costs of reducing emissions. The optimum amount of reduction is found where marginal benefit equals marginal cost, at $e^*$. Up to this point, the marginal benefit to society of reducing emissions exceeds the marginal cost of so doing, so it is in the interest of society to reduce pollution. However, beyond that point the marginal cost of reducing the amount of pollution exceeds the benefits that accrue, so society would be worse off. Setting a tax equal to $t^*$ in Figure 23.2 will induce firms to undertake the appropriate amount of emission reduction.

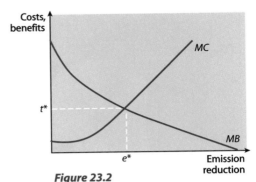

**Figure 23.2**
*Reducing emission of toxic fumes*

However, this is not the only way of reaching the objective. Figure 23.2 suggests that there is another possibility: namely, to set environmental standards and to prohibit emissions beyond $e^*$. This amounts to the control of quantity rather than price. If the government has full information about marginal costs and marginal benefits, the two policies will produce the equivalent result.

Either of the approaches outlined above is fine, *if* the authorities have full information about marginal costs and benefits. But how likely is this? In fact, the measurement of both marginal benefits and marginal costs is fraught with difficulties.

We cannot measure the marginal social benefits of reducing pollution with any degree of precision. There are many different factors to be taken into consideration. It may be argued that there are significant gains to be made in terms of improved health and lower death rates if pollution can be reduced. Quantifying this is not straightforward, however, even if we could come to a valuation of the saving in resources devoted to future healthcare. There may also be considerations in terms of direct improvements to the quality of life of members of society. In addition, there is the question of whether to take into account international effects when formulating domestic policy, and of choosing an appropriate discount rate for evaluating benefits that will be received in the future. The environmentalist and the industrialist may well arrive at different evaluations of the benefits of controlling pollution.

The measurement of costs may also be problematic. For example, it is likely that there will be differences in efficiency between firms. Those using modern trucks may face lower costs than those using relatively old vehicles. Do the authorities try to set a tax that is specific to each firm to take such differences into account? If they do not and set a flat-rate tax, then the incentives may be inappropriate. This would mean that a firm using modern trucks would face the same tax as one using old vehicles. The firm using new capital would then tend to produce too little output relative to those using older, less efficient capital.

*Pollution by motor vehicles is regulated by the government*

In practice, the government has chosen to address this problem of traffic fumes through regulation rather than taxation. Part of the annual MoT test of all vehicles entails measuring the fumes emitted, which must come within certain limits set by legislation. Otherwise the vehicle will fail its MoT test and not be permitted on the roads.

### Evaluation

For any intervention by the government, care is needed to ensure that taxes or regulations have their intended effects. In other words, it is important to guard against the possibility of government failure. If taxes are set at too high (or too low) a level, or if regulations are too stringent (or too loose), the best result for society in terms of resource allocation will not be achieved. Furthermore, it is important to remember that markets are interconnected, so intervention in one market may have knock-on effects on resource allocation elsewhere.

## Hypothecation

Within the transport sector, a contentious issue has been the level of duties levied on petrol and diesel, and road taxes. Motorists have claimed that they are being unfairly treated by heavy duties and high road taxes — not to mention the fines imposed when drivers are caught on speed cameras. Such arguments lead towards the notion of **hypothecation**.

**Key term**

**hypothecation:** in the context of the transport sector, the principle that revenues raised from taxing transport should be used to improve the transport system

Literally speaking, 'hypothecation' comes from the phrase 'hypothetical dedication'. In the transport arena, what this means is that revenues raised from the taxation of transport should be dedicated to expenditures that are concerned with transportation. For example, the revenues from gasoline tax in the USA are dedicated to the funding of transportation infrastructure.

Another example of hypothecation is the London Congestion Charge, where it was agreed that any net revenues raised by the scheme would be ploughed back into improving London's transport network. This is seen as one way of enabling improvements to public transport systems and traffic management, with private road users footing the bill. As a way of making charges politically acceptable to those who pay them, hypothecation may be an effective device. However, does it make sense in terms of economic analysis? If there are significant externalities associated with private motoring that affect other aspects of the economy, then there is a case for taxing motorists more heavily, and for using some of the revenues to correct for other distortions of resource allocation: for example, in remedying environmental damage.

## Transport and the environment

In formulating a vision of the future pattern of transport in the UK, the environment is seen to be a central concern. For example, there is a major concern about the emission of greenhouse gases from private motoring, which suggests that car usage needs to be managed, rather than being allowed to continue to expand in line with demand. This requires greater encouragement to use public transport, or a shift towards more fuel-efficient cars. However, individual consumers will not switch towards public transport unless its quality can be improved — which then requires investment to bring about those improvements and make public transport a more attractive alternative.

The keynote in this is to secure *sustainable transport development*. As discussed in Chapter 22, this means moving towards a future pattern of transportation that will not damage prospects for future generations. In the light of the data presented in the previous chapter (see Figure 22.1 on page 349), it could be argued that a sustainable transport system would see more freight being shifted from road towards rail, given its lower rate of $CO_2$ emissions as compared with road transport. The data also suggest that gains could be made by switching individual

journeys away from private cars, which remain the most polluting mode of transport.

One way of encouraging more use of public transport might be through a subsidy. Figure 23.3 shows how this might work. Here, $S_0$ represents the supply curve in the absence of a subsidy, so that with demand at $D$, the market equilibrium is with price $P_0$ and quantity of bus journeys $Q_0$. If the authorities introduce a subsidy of an amount $BC$, this encourages the bus companies to supply more bus journeys at any given price, so the effective supply curve is now $S_1$, and the equilibrium moves to a lower price $P_1$ and higher quantity $Q_1$.

How effective is such a policy likely to be? Figure 23.3 was drawn with the demand curve relatively steep. This is probably realistic to some degree, as the demand for bus journeys is probably not too sensitive to price, so a subsidy has relatively little impact on the number of bus journeys undertaken. In addition, the cost to the authorities is relatively high. It is shown by the shaded area ($ABCP_1$) in Figure 23.3. This seems to suggest that the use of subsidies will be expensive and ineffective. This will be reinforced if increases in the real income of consumers cause the demand curve to shift to the left over time — in other words, if bus journeys can be regarded as an inferior good — which again seems a reasonable assumption.

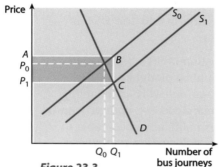

**Figure 23.3**
*A subsidy to bus companies*

In evaluating such a policy measure, it is important to realise that the benefits from encouraging more bus travel may go beyond the individual market. If the demand for bus journeys is inelastic, this makes subsidies relatively expensive. Nonetheless, in combination with measures to discourage private motor vehicles (reducing the number of city-centre parking spaces, introducing bus lanes and so on), subsidies can be an effective way of changing people's attitudes towards transport modes.

There may also be a case for subsidising rural bus travel, where there are communities that would otherwise be isolated. In other words, subsidies for bus travel may contribute to social inclusion of rural communities where bus routes might prove unprofitable for the private sector in the absence of some form of subsidy. The Rural Bus Subsidy Grant and Rural Bus Challenge policies were introduced in 1998. An evaluation undertaken for the Department for Transport after 5 years of operation suggested that these measures had been successful in meeting their objectives.

The rural subsidies apart, subsidies have not been widely used as a way of encouraging more usage of buses and coaches. Such subsidies as have been provided tend to be aimed at rather different targets — for example, bus passes for the elderly, which are intended to provide protection for vulnerable individuals, rather than as part of a transport policy.

## Congestion and road pricing

With the introduction of the congestion charge in parts of central London, the London authorities have been attempting to tackle congestion. When traffic on the roads reaches a certain volume, congestion imposes heavy costs on road users. This is another example of an externality.

Figure 23.4 illustrates the situation. Suppose that $D$ ($MSB$) represents the demand curve for car journeys along a particular stretch of road. When deciding whether to undertake a journey, a driver will balance the marginal benefit gained from making the journey against the marginal cost that he or she faces. This is given by $MPC$ — the marginal private cost of undertaking journeys. When the road is congested, a motorist who decides to undertake the journey adds to the congestion and slows the traffic. The $MPC$ curve incorporates the cost to the motorist of joining a congested road, and the chosen number of journeys will be at $Q_1$.

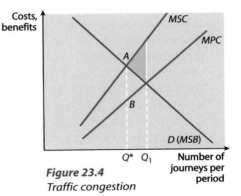

**Figure 23.4**
*Traffic congestion*

However, in adding to the congestion, the motorist not only suffers the costs of congestion, but also imposes some marginal increase in costs on all other users of the road, as everyone suffers from slower journeys as a result of the extra congestion. Thus the marginal social cost ($MSC$) of undertaking journeys is higher than the cost faced by any individual motorist. $MSC$ is therefore shown to be higher than $MPC$. Society would be better off with lower congestion if the number of journeys were limited to $Q^*$, where marginal social benefit equals marginal social cost.

The extent of the welfare loss that society endures as a direct result of the congestion is given by the shaded area in Figure 23.4. This measures the extent to which marginal social cost exceeds marginal private cost between $Q^*$ and $Q_1$. One possible remedy is to impose a tax on journeys undertaken. Such a tax would need to be set at a level that reflected the difference between marginal social cost and marginal private cost — at $Q^*$, this is the distance $AB$. This policy forces motorists to face the social cost of their actions, so that they will choose to be at $Q^*$.

It could be argued that the full social cost of congestion goes beyond the direct effects arising from the externality. There are broader issues to be considered that cannot readily be quantified as part of the social cost of congestion. This comes back to the issue raised earlier that the existence of an efficient and well-functioning transport system is important to ensuring the smooth functioning of other markets, and for maintaining the competitiveness of domestic firms that are competing in international markets. If the transport system grinds to a halt because of congestion, it is not just the people stuck in the traffic jam who bear the costs. The economy at large may also suffer.

An important issue here concerns the practicality of road taxes. The first attempt at road pricing was in Singapore in the mid-1970s. The Singapore government was concerned to prevent the build-up of traffic congestion in the central business district (CBD). It thus introduced a charge that had to be paid by all vehicles entering the CBD during peak periods. This was quite costly to implement given the technology available, as the only way of monitoring the policy was to have individuals located at all entry points into the CBD watching for cars not displaying a current ticket entitling them to enter the district. As technology has improved, so Singapore has switched to a system of electronic road pricing, whereby all cars have to be fitted with an electronic device that is triggered every time a vehicle enters a restricted section of road. The

*The congestion charge helps to keep an efficient flow of traffic in Central London*

driver is then automatically charged. Such a system can be made very flexible, allowing charges to be varied according to the degree of congestion that is currently occurring.

The London Congestion Charge operates on a similar basis, with motorists having to pay a fixed charge for entering a specified area within Central London. When Singapore began its scheme, it had an important advantage — it is relatively compact, with relatively few entry points into the CBD. (Singapore is approximately the size of the Isle of Wight and in 2004 had a population of about 4.3 million, so you can understand why it should be worried about the possible effects of congestion.)

It is also possible to levy charges for specific stretches of road in the form of tolls. The Severn Bridge and the M6 Toll Road are examples of this. Such charges tend to be used quite sparingly, as there is a danger of slowing the traffic so much in order to collect the fees that nothing is gained in terms of easing congestion — although tolls may allow private companies to recoup the construction and maintenance costs of the road. Technology has again made life a bit easier, at least for regular users, who can be charged automatically using an electronic device. For example, such a system is in place for the tunnels that join Hong Kong Island to Kowloon, which carry enormous traffic flows every day.

### Evaluation

In addition to its charge for entering the CBD, Singapore has for many years operated a scheme whereby anyone wanting to buy a car must obtain a Certificate of Entitlement (CoE). These CoEs are auctioned every month, and for many years were being sold at prices that far exceeded the price of a car. The policy enabled the Singapore authorities to regulate strictly the number of cars that were allowed in the country. However, such a policy is not well targeted, as it is not car ownership that needs to be controlled, but car usage. A road-pricing scheme is thus superior to a tax on car ownership for tackling road congestion. A tax on petrol or diesel is also relatively ineffective, as duty on petrol has to be paid whether the motorist is going to drive on a congested street in the city centre or a crowded motorway – or whether that motorist is using uncongested rural roads, where the issue of congestion does not arise.

This is an important aspect of the congestion issue. Not all drivers impose the same congestion costs on others. The extent to which this happens depends upon which roads a motorist uses, and at what time of day. This makes policy design tricky. For example, consider Figure 23.5, which shows the demand for journeys on an urban road. For much of the time, demand is relatively low, at $D_{low}$. In this situation, there is no congestion, and marginal private and social costs coincide, so there is no need for any intervention. However, at other times of day, demand may be higher so that traffic begins to build up. When demand reaches $D_{medium}$, there is some congestion, and a small tax is needed in order that motorists face the social cost of their journeys – this is given by the distance $XY$. However, in peak times, when traffic becomes heavy (demand is $D_{peak}$), congestion becomes greater, and the difference between marginal social costs and marginal private costs requires a much larger tax ($AB$).

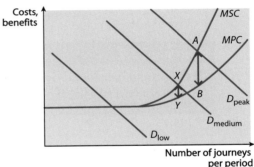

**Figure 23.5**
*Finding the right tax when demand varies*

Similarly, the demand for journeys in different parts of the national road network varies substantially. There are roads in rural areas that never experience congestion, and there are roads in some urban areas that never seem to be free of it. The nature of traffic flows on the inter-urban motorways – or on the M25 – may be different again.

Thus road pricing needs to be a very flexible tool if it is truly to target congestion when and where it happens. However, it is clearly more targeted than a general tax on petrol, which treats every mile travelled as being equivalent – except insofar as congestion affects fuel consumption.

In general, user charges tend to be favoured by economic analysis because if people do not have to take account of both private and social costs when taking decisions, they will tend to make decisions that are not in the best interests of society as a whole. Transport policy provides many good examples of how this works out in the real world.

part 6

## Summary

➤ Market failure affects the transport sector in various ways, including imperfect competition, externalities, information failure and public goods provision.

➤ In order to deal with market failure, the government can intervene by using taxation and/or regulation to achieve a better outcome for society.

➤ Pollution is an example of an externality, and can be tackled through taxation or through direct control of emissions.

➤ It has been argued that the revenues raised through the taxation of transport should be dedicated to transport-related expenditures. This principle is known as hypothecation.

➤ In formulating a vision of the future of the transport sector, it is important to aim for sustainable transport development, particularly in terms of safeguarding the environment for future generations.

➤ Congestion on the roads is another example of externalities. This may be tackled through the use of road pricing or by imposing tolls for the use of certain stretches of road.

## Exercise 23.2

Discuss the arguments for and against the London Congestion Charge. Use the internet to find out how effective the policy has been to date.

# Economics of development

# Part 7

# Chapter 24
# The concept of development

One of the gravest economic challenges facing the world today is the global inequity in the distribution of resources. Worldwide, it is estimated that at the beginning of the twenty-first century more than a billion people were living in what the United Nations regards as absolute poverty. Furthermore, there were 114 million primary-age children who were not enrolled for school, more than a billion people without access to safe water, and 2.4 billion without access to sanitation. Progress since then has been slow. Part 7 considers how to come to terms with such facts, and applies economic analysis in an attempt to understand what has gone wrong, and what could be done to improve matters.

## Learning outcomes

After studying this chapter, you should:
- understand what is meant by economic and human development
- be familiar with the most important economic and social indicators that can help to evaluate the standard of living in different societies
- recognise the strengths and limitations of such indicators in providing a profile of a country's stage of development
- be familiar with ways of measuring and monitoring inequality and poverty in the context of less developed countries
- be aware of the importance of political and cultural factors in influencing a country's path of development

## Defining development

The first step is to define what is meant by 'development'. You might think that it is about economic growth — if a society can expand its productive capacity, surely that is development? But development means much more than this. Economic growth may well be a necessary ingredient, since development cannot take place without an expansion of the resources available in a society; however, it is not a *sufficient* ingredient, because those additional resources must be used wisely, and the growth that results must be the 'right' sort of growth.

Wrapped up with development are issues concerning the alleviation of poverty — no country can be considered 'developed' if a substantial portion of its population is living in absolute poverty. Development also requires structural change, and possibly changes in institutions and, in some cases, cultural and political attitudes.

## The Millennium Development Goals

In September 2000, the 189 member states of the United Nations met at what became known as the *Millennium Summit.* They agreed the following declaration:

**Key term**

**Millennium Development Goals (MDGs):** targets set for each less developed country, reflecting a range of development objectives to be monitored each year to evaluate progress

> We will spare no effort to free our fellow men, women and children from the abject and dehumanising conditions of extreme poverty to which more than a billion of them are currently subjected.

This was a global recognition of the extreme inequality that is a feature of the world distribution of resources. Development economics sets out to explain why it is that some countries have gone through a prolonged process of economic growth and development, while others have not. It also seeks to propose ways in which less developed countries can begin to narrow the existing gap in living standards.

Before beginning to analyse these important questions, it is important to identify what is meant by 'development', and to recognise the symptoms of under-development. Once the symptoms have been identified, explanations can be sought.

As part of the Millennium Summit, it was agreed to set quantifiable targets for a number of dimensions of development, in order to monitor progress. These are known as the **Millennium Development Goals (MDGs)**, and will be the starting point for learning to recognise the symptoms of underdevelopment.

There are eight goals, each of which has specific targets associated with it.

### Goal 1: Eradicate extreme poverty and hunger

The target for goal 1 is to halve the proportion of people whose income is less than $1 per day, and to halve the proportion of people suffering from hunger, between 1990 and 2015. This level of income is the official poverty line set by the United Nations Development Programme (UNDP), below which people are regarded as being in absolute poverty. The alleviation of such extreme poverty is essential for development to take place. This will be monitored through the following indicators:

➤ proportion of population living on less than $1 per day
➤ poverty gap ratio (incidence × depth of poverty)
➤ share of poorest quintile in national consumption
➤ prevalence of underweight children under 5 years of age
➤ proportion of population below the minimum level of dietary energy consumption

Most of these measures are self-explanatory. However, the poverty gap ratio may need some explanation. The idea is that it is not only the number of people living below $1 per day that is important. It is also relevant to know how far below $1 per day they live. The poverty gap ratio measures the average percentage distance that people live below the poverty line.

### Goal 2: Achieve universal primary education

The target here is to ensure that by 2015 all children everywhere will be able to complete a full course of primary schooling. Education is seen as an essential feature of the process of development, as it provides the knowledge that is needed for people to use resources effectively. The indicators are:

- net enrolment ratio in primary education
- proportion of pupils starting grade 1 who reach grade 5
- literacy rate of 15- to 24-year-olds

### Goal 3: Promote gender equality and empower women

This target aims to eliminate gender disparity in primary and secondary education, preferably by 2005, and in all levels of education no later than 2015. Gender inequality is widespread in less developed countries, and means that large numbers of women are disadvantaged. Indicators are:

- ratio of girls to boys in primary, secondary and tertiary education
- ratio of literate females to males among 15- to 24-year-olds
- share of women in waged employment in the non-agricultural sector
- proportion of seats held by women in national parliament

*The first of the UN's Millennium Development Goals is to eradicate extreme poverty and hunger*

### Goal 4: Reduce child mortality

The target here is to reduce the under-5 mortality rate by two-thirds between 1990 and 2015. The indicators are:

- under-5 mortality rate
- infant mortality rate (defined as the probability of dying between birth and exactly one year of age, expressed per 1,000 live births)
- proportion of 1-year-old children immunised against measles

### Goal 5: Improve maternal health

The target is to reduce the maternal mortality ratio by three-quarters between 1990 and 2015. The indicators specified to monitor this target are:

- maternal mortality ratio
- proportion of births attended by skilled health personnel

### Goal 6: Combat HIV/AIDS, malaria and other diseases

The target is to have halted, and begun to reverse, the spread of HIV/AIDS and the incidence of malaria and

OCR Advanced Economics

other major diseases by 2015. The impact of HIV/AIDS and other diseases has been felt especially in sub-Saharan Africa, and is having adverse effects on the age structure of the population in many less developed countries. Indicators will cover:

➤ HIV prevalence among 15- to 24-year-old pregnant women
➤ contraceptive prevalence rate
➤ number of children orphaned by HIV/AIDS
➤ prevalence and death rates associated with malaria
➤ proportion of population in malaria-risk areas
➤ prevalence and death rates associated with tuberculosis (TB)
➤ proportion of TB cases detected and cured under DOTS (directly observed treatment short course)

## Goal 7: Ensure environmental sustainability

The targets here are to integrate the principles of sustainable development into national policies and programmes and to reverse the loss of environmental resources; to halve the proportion of people without sustainable access to safe drinking water by 2015; and to have achieved a significant improvement in the lives of at least 100 million slum dwellers by 2020. Development must be *sustainable*, in the sense that the foundations for future development need to be laid in such a way that they do not endanger the resources available for future generations. The indicators are:

➤ change in land area covered by forest
➤ extent of land area protected to maintain biological diversity
➤ GDP per unit of energy use
➤ carbon dioxide emissions (per capita)
➤ proportion of population with sustainable access to an improved water source
➤ proportion of population with access to improved sanitation
➤ proportion of population with access to secure tenure

## Goal 8: Develop a global partnership for development

The target here is to develop further an open, rule-based, predictable, non-discriminatory trading and financial system, including a commitment to good governance, development and poverty reduction, both nationally and internationally. A wide range of indicators will be used to monitor this in relation to *official development assistance* (ODA), *market access*, *debt sustainability* and some other targets. The need for international cooperation in ensuring development is pressing and will be a recurring theme in the following chapters.

This final goal is less focused than the other seven, but no less important. There is a widespread view that less developed countries have been disadvantaged by the international trading system, and that richer countries have been insufficiently cooperative — partly in terms of the amount of overseas aid (ODA) that has been provided, but also in terms of a reluctance of some more developed countries to open their markets to products from less developed countries.

**part 7**

ODA was the subject of a UN summit in the 1970s, at which the more developed countries promised to provide overseas assistance. Indeed, there was a specific commitment that 0.7% of developed countries' GDP would be devoted to this purpose. But progress has fallen well short of this goal, as will be seen in Chapter 28.

'Market access' refers to the difficulty experienced by developing countries seeking to increase exports to the developed world in order to earn more foreign exchange. This target is aimed especially at landlocked and small island developing states, but market access is not a problem for these countries alone.

'Debt sustainability' refers to the difficulties that many countries have experienced in paying off their accumulated debt. This has been a major problem in recent years, especially in sub-Saharan Africa, where some countries have been devoting more resources to paying off debts than to providing education and healthcare for their people. The issue is being addressed by the Heavily Indebted Poor Countries (HIPC) initiative, but progress was relatively slow in the early years of the scheme.

Other targets relate to youth unemployment, access to affordable essential medical drugs and access to new technology, especially in the fields of information and communications.

 **term**

**development:** a process by which real per capita incomes are increased and the inhabitants of a country are able to benefit from improved living conditions: that is, lower poverty and enhanced standards of education, health, nutrition and other essentials of life

These eight goals represent key facets of **development** that need to be addressed. They constitute an enormous challenge for the period up to 2015, especially as progress in the early years has been slow and uneven. In thinking about these goals, you can begin to understand the various dimensions of development, and realise that it is about much more than economic growth — although growth may be seen as a prerequisite for the achievement of the goals. At the same time, failure to achieve these goals will retard economic growth.

*Overseas aid is a focus of UN summits*

To summarise, development is about more than just economic growth. Achieving higher real income per capita is a necessary part of development, but it is not all there is to it. A country will not be recognised as achieving development unless it is also able to alleviate poverty, improve education levels and health standards, and provide an enhanced physical and cultural environment. Furthermore, such improvements must reach all inhabitants of the country, and not be confined to certain groups within society. In other words, economic growth may be *necessary* for development to take place, but it is not *sufficient*. Expanding the resources available within a society is the first step, but those resources also need to be used well.

## Summary

➤ Economic growth is one aspect of economic development, in that it provides an increase in the resources available to members of society in less developed countries.

➤ However, in addition, development requires that the resources made available through economic growth are used appropriately to meet development objectives.

➤ The Millennium Development Goals were set by the Millennium Summit of the United Nations in September 2000.

➤ These eight goals comprise a set of targets for each less developed country, to be achieved by 2015.

## Exercise 24.1

Select two or three less developed countries in different regions of the world. Visit the Millennium Development Goals website at **http://www.developmentgoals.org**. Discuss the extent to which progress is being made towards the goals in your chosen countries.

## Which are the less developed countries?

In its *Human Development Report 2005*, the UNDP identified 137 countries or areas as 'developing'. In addition, there are 27 'transition' economies in Central and Eastern Europe and the Commonwealth of Independent States (CIS). However, the range of countries that fall under this definition of developing countries is very wide, including countries such as Singapore and South Korea, which were also classified as being in the 'high-income' bracket. In the discussion that follows, this wide range of countries will be referred to as *less developed countries* (*LDCs*), and the discussion will be illustrated by examples from a selection of countries from different regions of the world.

A variety of other terms have been coined to try to describe this group of countries. The term 'developing countries', referred to above, might be seen as an over-optimistic description of some countries, where very little progress seems to have been made in the last 40 years or so. In the past, it was quite common to refer to the 'Third World', but this term has been made redundant by the demise of the Soviet bloc, formerly regarded as the 'Second World'. The *Brandt Commission* in the

early 1980s referred to the more developed countries as the 'North' (including Australia!) and the rest of the world as the 'South', but this did not really catch on.

In broad terms, the countries regarded as LDCs are concentrated in four major regions: sub-Saharan Africa, Latin America, South Asia and Southeast Asia. This excludes some countries in the 'less developed' range, but relatively few. For some purposes it may be necessary to treat China separately, rather than including it as part of Southeast Asia, partly because of its sheer size, and partly because it has followed a rather different development path. Figure 24.1 shows average income levels in countries around the world.

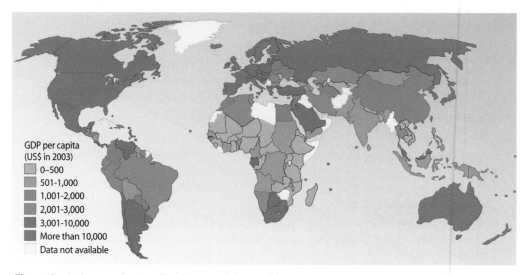

GDP per capita
(US$ in 2003)
- 0–500
- 501-1,000
- 1,001-2,000
- 2,001-3,000
- 3,001-10,000
- More than 10,000
- Data not available

*Figure 24.1  Average income levels around the world*

It is very important when discussing economic development to remember that there is wide diversity among the countries that are classified as LDCs, and although it is tempting to generalise, you need to be a little wary of doing so. Different countries have different characteristics, and face different configurations of problems and opportunities. Therefore, a policy that works for one country might fail totally in a different part of the world.

## Indicators of development

### GDP per capita

The first step is to be able to measure 'development'. One possible measure is GDP per capita — the average level of income per person in the population. GDP does have some advantages as a measure. First, it is relatively straightforward and thus is widely understood. Second, it is a well-established indicator and one that is available for almost every country in the world, so it can be used to compare income levels across countries. For this purpose, it naturally helps to adjust for population size by calculating GDP per person (GDP *per capita*, as it is known). This then provides a measure of average income per head.

Figure 24.2 provides data on GDP per capita for a selection of countries from each of the four major groupings. These countries will be used as examples throughout this section of the book: they are colour-coded by region. Because of the diversity of countries in each of the regions, such a selection must be treated with a little caution. Singapore, South Korea and China have been chosen to represent East Asia and the Pacific, in order to highlight three of the countries that have achieved rapid economic growth over a sustained period.

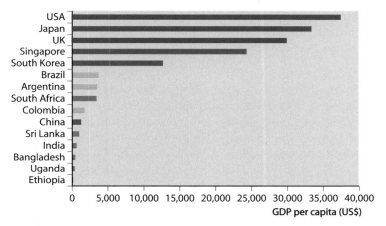

*Figure 24.2*
*GDP per capita,*
*selected*
*countries, 2003*
*(US$)*

Source: *Human Development Report,* 2005.

The extreme differences that exist around the globe are immediately apparent from the data. GDP per capita in Ethiopia is just $97, whereas in the USA the figure is $37,648. (Luxembourg heads this particular league table, with average income of $59,143 in 2003.)

In trying to interpret these data, a number of issues need to be borne in mind, as the comparison is not as straightforward as it looks.

### Exchange rate problems

The data presented in Figure 24.2 are expressed in terms of US dollars. This allows economists to compare average incomes using a common unit of measurement. At the same time, however, it may create some problems.

It is important to compare average income levels in order to evaluate the standard of living, and compare standards across countries. In other words, the aim is to assess people's command over resources in different societies, and to be able to compare the purchasing power of income in different countries.

GDP is calculated initially in terms of local currencies, and subsequently converted into US dollars using official exchange rates. Will this provide information about the relative local purchasing power of incomes? Not necessarily.

One reason for this is that official exchange rates are sometimes affected by government intervention. Indeed, in many of the less developed countries, exchange rates are pegged to an international currency – usually the US dollar. In these circumstances, exchange rates are more likely to reflect the government's

policy and actions than the relative purchasing power of incomes in the country under scrutiny. For example, a government may choose to maintain an overvalued currency in order to try to maximise the earnings from its exports. In the case of China, the government has been tempted into the opposite situation, maintaining an undervalued currency in order to maximise export volume.

Where exchange rates are free to find their own equilibrium level, they are likely to be influenced strongly by the price of internationally traded goods, which is likely to be a very different combination of goods than that typically consumed by residents in these countries. Again, it can be argued that official exchange rates may not be a good reflection of the relative purchasing power of incomes across countries.

The United Nations International Comparison Project has been working on this problem for many years. It now produces an alternative set of international estimates of GDP based on *purchasing power parity* (PPP) exchange rates, which are designed to reflect the relative purchasing power of incomes in different societies more accurately. Figure 24.3 shows estimates for the same set of countries that were given in Figure 24.2.

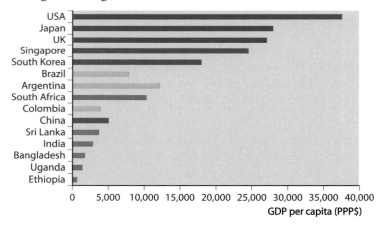

*Figure 24.3*
*GDP per capita,*
*selected*
*countries, 2003*
*(PPP$)*

Source: *Human Development Report,* 2005.

Comparing the two graphs, you will notice that the gap between the low-income and high-income countries seems less marked when PPP dollars (PPP$) are used as the unit of measurement. In other words, the US dollar estimates exaggerate the gap in living standards between rich and poor countries. This is a general feature of these measurements — that measurements in US dollars tend to understate real incomes for low-income countries and overstate them for high-income countries compared with PPP$ data. Put another way, people in the lower-income countries have a stronger command over goods and services than is suggested by US-dollar comparisons of GDP per capita. You will also see that in some cases, using PPP$ alters the rankings of the countries — for example, compare Brazil and Argentina in the two figures.

Figure 24.4 shows the relative size of GDP per capita in PPP$ for the regional groupings of countries around the world in 2003. The gap in income levels

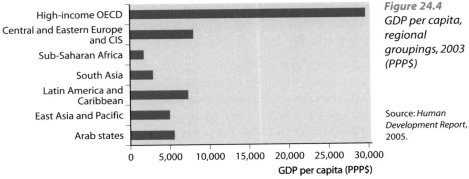

*Figure 24.4*
*GDP per capita,*
*regional*
*groupings, 2003*
*(PPP$)*

Source: *Human Development Report,* 2005.

between the LDCs and the high-income OECD countries shows very clearly in the graph; equally, the gap between the countries of sub-Saharan Africa and South Asia, on the one hand, and those in East Asia and Latin America, on the other, is apparent. The graph also puts into context the position of the transition economies of Central and Eastern Europe and the CIS, and the Arab states. The Arab states are rather different in character because their oil resources have enabled them to increase their average income levels.

### The informal sector and the accuracy of data

Even when measured in PPP$, GDP has limitations as a measure of living standards. One limitation that is especially important when considering low-income countries is that in many LDCs there is considerable *informal economic activity*, which may not be captured by a measure like GDP, based on monetary transactions. Such activity includes subsistence agriculture, which remains important in many countries, especially in sub-Saharan Africa. In other words, GDP may not capture production that is directly used for consumption. Remember that GDP is measured by adding up the total transactions that take place in an economy. In the case of barter or production for consumption, there are no transactions to be measured, so they will not be captured in GDP.

The informal sector also encompasses many other forms of activity in both rural and urban areas, from petty traders, shoe-shiners and wayside barbers to small-scale enterprises operating in a wide range of activities. In 1999 the ILO estimated that the informal sector accounted for 50.2% of total employment in Ethiopia; in 2000 it was thought to account for 45.8% of total employment in India. This suggests the need for some caution in the use of GDP per capita data, which in these cases would underestimate real living standards.

### Income distribution

Another important limitation of GDP per capita as a measure of living standards is that it is an *average* measure, and so does not reveal information about how income is distributed among groups in society.

In Brazil, the poorest 10% of households received less than 1% of total income in 1996, whereas the richest 10% received nearly half. In Belarus, on the other hand, the poorest 10% received 5% of income and the richest 10% received 20%. These

are extreme examples of the degree of inequality in the distribution of income within countries. Table 8.1 on page 120 provides similar data for a range of countries around the world.

These data are produced by first ranking the households in order of household income, and then calculating the share of household income going to the poorest 10%, the poorest 20% and so on. The groups of 10% of the population are referred to as *deciles*; thus, the poorest 10% is the first decile, the next 10% is the second decile, and so on. Similarly, the poorest 20% is the first *quintile*.

The data are not very easy to assimilate, especially for a large number of countries. In order to explore the question of income inequality, it is important to find a way of summarising the data to make it easier to interpret. Table 24.1 provides some summary data for a range of countries.

| Country | GDP per capita 2003 (PPP$) | Ratio of top decile to poorest decile | Ratio of top quintile to poorest quintile | Gini index (%) |
|---|---|---|---|---|
| Sierra Leone | 548 | 87.2 | 57.6 | 62.9 |
| Ethiopia | 711 | 6.6 | 4.3 | 30.0 |
| Uganda | 1,457 | 14.9 | 8.4 | 43.0 |
| Bangladesh | 1,770 | 6.8 | 4.6 | 31.8 |
| Zimbabwe | 2,443 | 22.0 | 12.0 | 56.8 |
| India | 2,892 | 7.3 | 4.9 | 32.5 |
| Indonesia | 3,361 | 7.8 | 5.2 | 34.3 |
| China | 5,003 | 18.4 | 10.7 | 44.7 |
| Belarus | 6,052 | 6.9 | 4.6 | 30.4 |
| Brazil | 7,790 | 68.0 | 26.4 | 59.3 |
| Malaysia | 9,230 | 22.1 | 12.4 | 49.2 |
| South Africa | 10,346 | 33.1 | 17.9 | 57.8 |
| Hungary | 14,584 | 5.5 | 3.8 | 26.9 |
| Singapore | 24,481 | 17.7 | 9.7 | 42.5 |
| United Kingdom | 27,147 | 13.8 | 7.2 | 36.0 |
| Japan | 27,967 | 4.5 | 3.4 | 24.9 |
| United States | 37,562 | 15.9 | 8.4 | 40.8 |

*Table 24.1 Inequality measures for selected countries*
Source: *Human Development Report*, 2005.

By looking at the ratio of the richest decile or quintile to the poorest, it is possible to get some impression of the gap between the poorest and richest households. For example, in Sierra Leone the richest 10% of households receive 87.2 times more income than the poorest 10%, whereas in Hungary the gap is less than six-fold.

One thing to notice about this table is that the countries are listed in ascending order of average income. If you cast your eye down the columns of the table, you will see that there is no very strong relationship between average income and the decile and quintile ratios. The contrast in the pattern of the income shares between Sierra Leone and Ethiopia is striking, but average income levels are not too different.

### The Lorenz curve

It would be useful to have a way of presenting such data visually. Although conventional types of graph are not well suited to this purpose, an alternative graphical technique is the **Lorenz curve**. Some of these are shown in Figure 24.5.

**Key term**

**Lorenz curve:** a graphical means of depicting the distribution of income within a country

| Country | Lowest 10% | Lowest 20% | Second 20% | Third 20% | Fourth 20% | Highest 20% | Highest 10% |
|---|---|---|---|---|---|---|---|
| Ethiopia | 3.0 | 7.1 | 10.9 | 14.5 | 19.8 | 47.7 | 33.7 |
| Bangladesh | 3.9 | 8.7 | 12.0 | 15.7 | 20.8 | 42.8 | 28.6 |
| Brazil | 0.9 | 2.5 | 5.5 | 10.0 | 18.3 | 63.8 | 47.6 |

**Table 24.2** *Income distribution in Ethiopia, Bangladesh and Brazil, various years*

Source: World Development Report, 2000/2001.

Lorenz curves are constructed as follows. Using data provided in Table 24.2, the first step is to convert the numbers in the table into *cumulative* percentages. Using Brazil as an example, the poorest 20% receive 2.5% of total household income, the poorest 40% receive 2.5% + 5.5% = 8%, the poorest 60% receives 8% + 10% = 18%, and so on. These cumulative percentages are then plotted to produce the Lorenz curve, as in Figure 24.5.

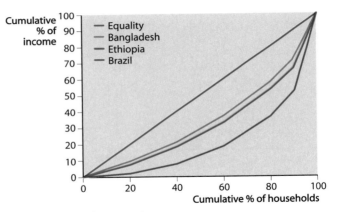

**Figure 24.5**
*Lorenz curves, various years*

Suppose that income is perfectly equally distributed between households — in other words, suppose the poorest 10% of households receive exactly 10% of income, the poorest 20% receive 20% and so on. The Lorenz curve would then be a straight line going diagonally across the figure.

This is a help in interpreting the countries' curves. The closer a country's Lorenz curve is to the diagonal equality line, the more equal is the distribution of income. You can see on the figure how unequal the income distribution is in Brazil compared with that in Bangladesh or Ethiopia.

### The Gini index

The Lorenz curve is fine for comparing income distribution in just a few countries. However, it would also be helpful to have an index that can summarise the relationship in a numerical way. The Gini index does just this. It is a way of quantifying the degree of equality of income distribution, and is obtained by calculating the

ratio of the area between the equality line and a country's Lorenz curve to the whole area under the equality line. This is normally expressed as a percentage, although sometimes you may find data that treat it as a proportion (i.e. with values between 0 and 1). The closer the Gini index is to 100 (or to 1), the further the Lorenz curve is from equality, and thus the more unequal the income distribution. The values for the Gini index are shown in the final column of Table 24.1.

### The Kuznets hypothesis

The economist Simon Kuznets argued that there is expected to be a relationship between the degree of inequality in income distribution and the level of development that a country has achieved. He claimed that in the early stages of economic development income is fairly equally distributed, with everyone living at a relatively low income level. However, as development begins to take off there will be some individuals at the forefront of enterprise and development, and their incomes will rise more rapidly. So in this middle phase the income distribution will tend to worsen. At a later stage of development, a high proportion of the population will be absorbed into the modern sector, and society may be able to afford to redistribute income to protect the poor. All will then begin to share in the benefits of development.

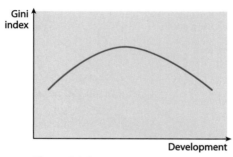

**Figure 24.6**
*The Kuznets curve*

This can be portrayed as the relationship between the Gini index and the level of development. The thrust of the Kuznets hypothesis is that this should reveal an inverted U-shaped relationship, as shown in Figure 24.6. Although the data in Table 24.1 do not strongly support this hypothesis, there is some evidence to suggest that the relationship does hold in some regions of the world.

### Social indicators

A further question that arises is whether GDP can be regarded as a reasonable indicator of a country's *standard of living*. GDP provides an indicator of the total resources available within an economy in a given period, calculated from data about total output, total incomes or total expenditure. This focus on summing the transactions that take place in an economy over a period can be seen as a rather narrow view of what constitutes a country's standard of living. After all, it may be argued that the quality of people's lives depends on more things than simply the material resources that are available.

For one thing, people need to have knowledge if they are to make good use of the resources that are available. Two societies with similar income levels may nonetheless provide very different quality of life for their inhabitants, depending on the education levels of the population. Furthermore, if people are to benefit from consuming or using the available resources, they need a reasonable lifespan coupled with good health. So, good standards of health are also crucial to a good quality of life.

It is important to remember that different societies tend to set different priorities for the pursuit of growth and the promotion of education and health. Some countries have higher levels of health and education than other countries with similar levels of GDP per capita. This needs to be taken into account when judging relative living standards by comparing GDP per capita. For a given level of real GDP per capita, there may be substantial differences in living standards between a country that places a high priority on providing education and healthcare, and one that devotes resources to military expenditure. In the longer term, there may also be significant differences between a society that spends its resources on present consumption, and one that engages in investment in order to increase consumption in the future.

A reasonable environment in which to live may be seen as another important factor in one's quality of life. There are some environmental issues that can distort the GDP measure of resources. Suppose there is an environmental disaster — perhaps an oil tanker breaks up close to a beautiful beach. This reduces the overall quality of life by degrading the landscape and preventing enjoyment of the beach. However, it does not have a negative effect on GDP; on the contrary, the money spent on clearing up the damage actually adds to GDP, so that the net effect of an environmental disaster may be to *increase* the measured level of GDP!

### The Human Development Index

To deal with the criticism that GDP per capita fails to take account of other dimensions of the quality of life, in 1990 UNDP devised an alternative indicator, known as the **Human Development Index** (HDI). This was designed to provide a broader measure of the stage of development that a country had reached.

**Key** *term*

**Human Development Index:** a composite indicator of the level of a country's development, varying between 0 and 1

The basis for the HDI is that there are three key aspects of human development: resources, knowledge of how to make good use of those resources, and a reasonable life span in which to make use of those resources (see Figure 24.7). The three components are measured by, respectively, GDP per capita in PPP$, indicators of education (adult literacy and school enrolment) and life expectancy. The measurements are then combined to produce a composite index ranging between 0 and 1, with higher values reflecting higher human development.

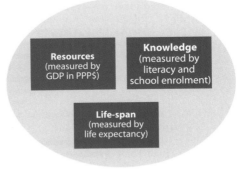

*Figure 24.7 Components of the Human Development Index*

Values of the HDI for 2003 are charted in Figure 24.8 for the selected countries. You can see that the broad ranking of the countries is preserved, but the gap between low and high human development is less marked. The exception is South Africa, which is ranked much lower on the basis of the HDI than on GDP per capita: in other words, South Africa has achieved relatively high income, but other aspects of human development have not kept pace. There are other countries in the world

that share this feature. If you compare the data here with those for Figure 24.3, you will see that there are also countries that seem to perform better on HDI grounds than on GDP per capita — for example, China and Sri Lanka.

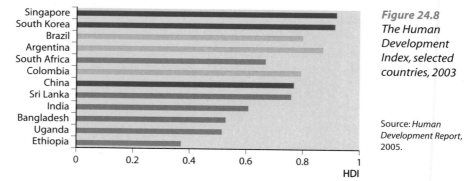

*Figure 24.8*
*The Human Development Index, selected countries, 2003*

Source: *Human Development Report,* 2005.

Figure 24.9 shows the relative contribution of the three components of the HDI for the set of countries, and Figures 24.10 and 24.11 show the actual levels of two of the measures that enter into the HDI: life expectancy and adult literacy rates. It is clear that life expectancy is primarily responsible for the low ranking of South Africa in the HDI, as its level of life expectancy is not very different from that of the other sub-Saharan African countries in the sample, even though its average income level is much higher. In contrast, Bangladesh performs quite well in terms of lifespan, but relatively poorly in terms of education. By comparing these data, you can get some idea of the diversity between countries that was mentioned earlier.

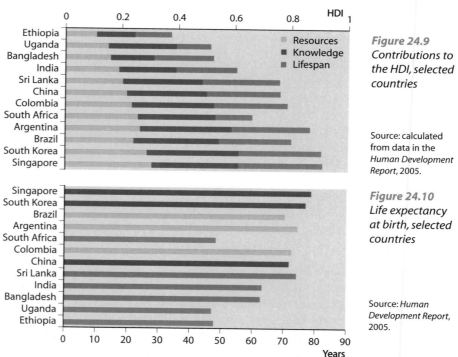

*Figure 24.9*
*Contributions to the HDI, selected countries*

Source: calculated from data in the *Human Development Report,* 2005.

*Figure 24.10*
*Life expectancy at birth, selected countries*

Source: *Human Development Report,* 2005.

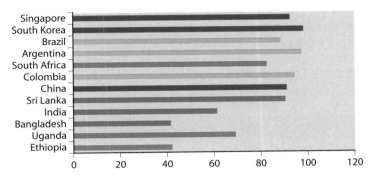

*Figure 24.11*
*Adult literacy, selected countries (% of people aged 15 and over)*

Source: *Human Development Report, 2005.*

In part, this diversity reflects differing priorities that governments have given to different aspects of development. Countries such as Brazil have aimed primarily at achieving economic growth, while those such as Sri Lanka have given greater priority to promoting education and healthcare.

Another way of putting a country into perspective is to construct a *development diamond*. An example is shown in Figure 24.12. This compares Ghana's perform-ance with the average for countries in its region, i.e. sub-Saharan Africa. On each axis, the value of the variable achieved by Ghana is expressed as a proportion of the value for sub-Saharan Africa. In this instance, Ghana is seen to have lower GNI per capita and adult literacy, but higher life expectancy and better access to improved water.

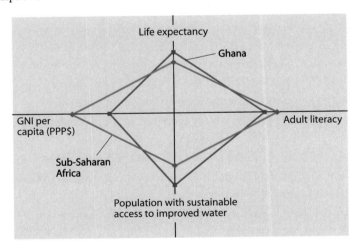

*Figure 24.12*
*Development diamond for Ghana compared with all countries in sub-Saharan Africa*

There is a view that growth should be the prime objective for development, since by expanding the resources available the benefits can begin to trickle down through the population. An opposing view claims that by providing first for basic needs, more rapid economic growth can be facilitated. The problem in some cases is that growth has not resulted in the trickle-down effect, and inequality remains. It may be significant that countries such as Brazil and South Africa, where the GDP per capita ranking is high relative to the HDI ranking, are countries in which there remain high levels of inequality in the distribution of income.

The HDI may be preferred to GDP per capita as a measure of development on the grounds that it reflects the key dimensions of development as opposed to growth. However, it will always be difficult to reduce a complex concept such as development to a single statistic. The diverse characteristics of LDCs demand the use of a range of alternative measures in order to identify the configuration of circumstances and problems facing a particular country.

## Exercise 24.2

Table 24.3 presents some indicators for two countries, A and B.

| | Country A | Country B |
|---|---|---|
| GDP per capita (PPP$) | 12,106 | 13,346 |
| Life expectancy (in years at birth) | 74.5 | 48.4 |
| Adult literacy rate (%) | 97.2 | 82.4 |
| People living with HIV/AIDS (% of adults aged 15–49) | 0.7 | 21.5 |
| Infant mortality rate (per 1,000 live births) | 17 | 53 |

*Table 24.3* Selected standard of living indicators for two countries, 2003
Source: *Human Development Report*, 2005.

a Discuss the extent to which GDP (here measured in PPP$) provides a good indication of relative living standards in the two countries.

b Discuss what other indicators might be useful in this evaluation.

## Summary

➤ Less developed countries (LDCs) are largely located in four major regions: sub-Saharan Africa, Latin America, South Asia and Southeast Asia.

➤ These regions have shown contrasting patterns of growth and development.

➤ GDP is a widely used measure of the total amount of economic activity in an economy over a period of time.

➤ The trend rate of change of GDP may thus be an indicator of economic growth.

➤ However, converting from a local currency into US dollars may distort the use of GDP as a measure of the purchasing power of local incomes.

➤ There may be variation in the effectiveness of data collection agencies in different countries, and variation in the size of the informal sector.

➤ Average GDP per person also neglects the important issue of income distribution.

➤ GDP may neglect some important aspects of the quality of life.

➤ The Human Development Index (HDI) recognises that human development depends upon resources, knowledge and health, and therefore combines indicators of these key aspects.

➤ Different countries have different characteristics, and face different configurations of problems and opportunities.

# Chapter 25
# Economies at different stages of development

*Development has been seen to entail a variety of dimensions. It is partly about economic growth, but it is also about how different societies make use of the resources at their disposal. Countries in different parts of the world have followed different paths to development — with varying degrees of success. Differences partly reflect the different characteristics of each country. Less developed countries (LDCs) do seem to share some characteristics, but each country also faces its own configuration of problems and opportunities. This chapter explores some of the common characteristics that LDCs display, but also examines some of the key differences between them.*

## Learning outcomes

After studying this chapter, you should:
➤ be familiar with the common characteristics of less developed countries
➤ be aware of the diversity of experience of less developed countries
➤ be aware of significant differences between regions of the world in terms of their level and pace of development
➤ understand the importance of the structure of economic activity in an economy
➤ be familiar with the relative importance of different forms of economic activity in the process of development

## Characteristics of less developed countries

It was seen in Chapter 24 that different countries are at different stages of development, as measured either by GDP per capita or by the Human Development Index (HDI). You will also realise that there is substantial diversity among these countries, and across regions of the world. It seems clear too that some countries have been much more successful than others in pursuing economic and human development. There are some countries in East Asia that have achieved rapid economic growth, and have been able to close the gap in living standards between them and the more developed countries. There are others, especially in sub-

Saharan Africa, which seem to have stagnated, making little or no progress in growth terms since the 1960s. This chapter will examine some of the characteristics that less developed countries have in common, and seek to explain why different combinations of these characteristics may have joined with cultural, political and social influences to result in different experiences of growth and development.

### The Human Development Index (HDI)

In considering the HDI in Chapter 24, some very important characteristics of LDCs were examined. We saw that the HDI is intended to capture the key components that the United Nations Development Programme (UNDP) perceives to be crucial for human development: namely, resources, the knowledge to make good use of those resources, and a sufficient general level of health that people can live long enough to enjoy consuming the resources.

 **term**

**human capital:** the stock of skills and expertise and other characteristics that contribute to a worker's productivity; can be increased through education and training, and improved nutrition and healthcare

These indicators provide the first clues to the key characteristics of LDCs. LDCs have relatively low incomes, low levels of education in the population, and low levels of health. Education and health are important for many reasons. They are included in the HDI because they are seen as essential components of the quality of life, contributing directly to human development. However, they are also important because they are aspects of what is often called **human capital**. If an individual undertakes education, this can be viewed as an investment, gathering skills that can be later used to generate a flow of income. Health is also a form of human capital that influences a worker's productivity.

The fact that many people in LDCs tend to have low levels of human capital has major implications for productivity in those countries, and has also been seen as a critical factor in the adoption of new technology, which typically demands high levels of skills from workers.

### Demographic issues

Some other characteristics of LDCs are important in setting the scene for analysing development. It is widely believed that population growth is of special significance, and Figure 25.1 shows the past experience of population growth in the selected countries that were highlighted in Chapter 24. The irregular pattern of this graph, which is in descending order of GDP per capita, suggests that there is no strong correlation between income levels and population growth. However, in part this may reflect individual characteristics of some of the countries selected. For example, Singapore is a very small country with a population of only 4.3 million in 2004. (But imagine 4.3 million people living on the Isle of Wight!) Singapore has been concerned that its population is too small, and has put in place policies to encourage people to have more children. This may help to explain its relatively rapid population growth. China, on the other hand, faces the opposite problem and has imposed policies to discourage large families.

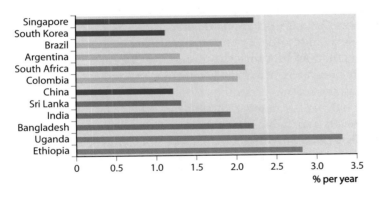

*Figure 25.1*
*Population*
*growth, selected*
*countries,*
*1975–2003*

Source: *Human*
*Development Report,*
2005.

The prime concern about rapid population growth is felt by countries like Ethiopia, Uganda and Bangladesh, where it has been suggested that the population has been growing too fast for education and healthcare services to keep up. Chapter 27 will return to this topic. However, Figure 25.2 shows one aspect of the problem: namely, the percentage of the population below 15 years of age in selected countries. In Uganda it amounts to more than half of the population, and in Ethiopia it is well over 40%. These children need to be supported by the working population, and in countries where HIV/AIDS is widespread this is particularly difficult because the disease is especially prevalent among those of working age. This is one example of dependency. People who are too young or too old to be part of the working population are in a state of dependency on those in work. If the proportion of dependants increases because of shrinkage of the working population, this places added pressure on those remaining.

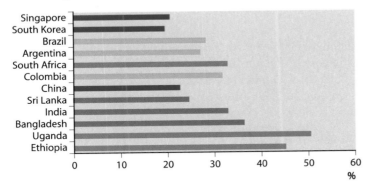

*Figure 25.2*
*Population below*
*15 years of age*
*(%), selected*
*countries*

Source: *Human*
*Development Report,*
2005.

### Poverty

A further characteristic of LDCs is the prevalence of poverty. One approach to measuring poverty is to define a basket of goods and services that is regarded as the minimum required to support human life: households that have incomes too low to allow them to purchase that basic bundle of goods are regarded as being in **absolute poverty**.

 **Key** term

**absolute poverty:** the situation describing a household if its income is insufficient to allow it to purchase the minimum bundle of goods and services needed for survival

The UNDP regards households in which income is below $1 per day per person as being in absolute poverty, as this is its declared *poverty line*. For a country like the UK, the absolute poverty line is not very significant because so few people fall below it. However, for LDCs absolute poverty is widespread. Figure 25.3 shows the prevalence of absolute poverty in the selected countries. This indicates the extent of the challenge facing some of these countries if they are to meet the Millennium Development Goal of halving the number of people in poverty by 2015. For sub-Saharan Africa, this would entail reducing the number of people below the poverty line from 44.6% of the population in 1990 to 22.3% by 2015. However, by 2001, it was reported that the percentage of people below the poverty line in this region had actually *increased* to 46.4%, which amounts to some 313 million people.

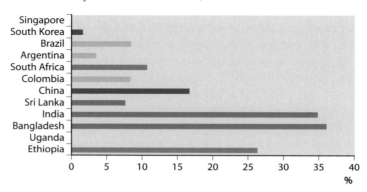

**Figure 25.3**
*Population (%) living on less than $1 per day, selected countries*

Note: no data are available for Uganda or Singapore.

Source: *Human Development Report*, 2005.

The number of people living below the poverty line is not a perfect measure. In particular, it would also be useful to know *how far* below the poverty line people are living, which would indicate the intensity of poverty. However, this is not easy to measure.

Poverty can also be defined in relative terms. If a household has insufficient income for its members to participate in the normal social life of the country, it is said to be in **relative poverty**. This too is defined in terms of a poverty line, this time it is 50% of the median (middle-ranked) household disposable income. Relative poverty can occur in any society.

Absolutely poverty and relative poverty reflect different things. Absolute poverty is about whether people have enough to survive, whereas relative poverty is more about inequality than about poverty. This is not to say that relative poverty should not be of concern to policy makers, but people in absolute poverty clearly require urgent action.

 **Key term**

**relative poverty:** the situation applying to a household whose income falls below 50% of the median household disposable income

One aspect of poverty is the problem of accessing essential services such as healthcare and improved water and sanitation. Figure 24.4 shows one aspect of this — the percentage of the population with no access to improved water. This is another of the Millennium Development Goals introduced at the beginning of Chapter 24 (Goal 7).

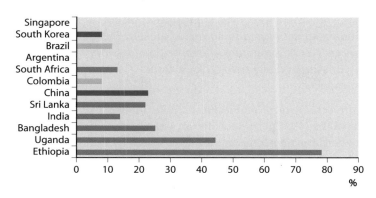

*Figure 25.4*
*Population (%) with*
*no access to improved*
*water, selected*
*countries*

Note: no data are available
for Argentina or Singapore.

Source: *Human*
*Development Report*, 2005.

An important part of development is the provision of *infrastructure.* In part this is necessary to help to alleviate poverty by providing essential services. But there are other vital aspects of infrastructure that are essential for markets to operate effectively. This is particularly true of transport and communications and market facilities. Many areas of infrastructure display characteristics of public goods, so that government intervention is essential to ensure adequate provision. (Public goods were discussed in Chapter 7.) A problem for many LDCs, however, is that the government does not have the resources to provide the necessary infrastructure.

## Summary

➤ One common characteristic of LDCs is the relatively low levels of human capital in the population.

➤ Improvements in education, healthcare and nutrition are all needed in order to raise the skills and productivity of labour.

➤ Demographic factors are also important for LDCs, many of which have shown a more rapid rate of population growth than can readily be resourced.

➤ One result of the demographic situation is that many LDCs have a high proportion of the population who are aged below 15 years — in some cases, more than half of the people are young.

➤ Poverty is widespread, and its alleviation is a key part of the development process.

## The structure of economic activity in LDCs

### Dependence on the primary sector

In evaluating the characteristics of LDCs, it is helpful to consider the structure of economic activity. One way of viewing this is to consider the separation between primary, secondary and tertiary production activities. The *primary sector* involves the extraction of raw materials and the growing of crops. It includes agriculture, the extraction of minerals (and oil), forestry, fishing and so on. The *secondary sector* is where these raw materials or crops are processed or transformed into goods. It includes various forms of manufacturing activity, ranging from the processing of food to the manufacture of motor vehicles or computer equipment. The *tertiary*

*sector* is concerned with the provision of services. It includes transport and communication, hairdressing, financial services and so on. A subset of tertiary activity involves intellectual services. This is sometimes known as the *quaternary sector* and includes hi-tech industry, information technology, some forms of scientific research and other 'information products'.

Figure 25.5 contrasts the structure of economic activity in two very different economies — Ethiopia and the UK. These data do not exactly correspond to the primary, secondary and tertiary divisions, as 'Industry' here includes not only manufacturing activity but also mining, construction, electricity, water and gas. Nonetheless, the contrast is striking. In the UK, the agricultural sector has dwindled almost to nothing, and services have become the dominant form of activity, although industry still accounts for more than a quarter of GDP. In Ethiopia, industry takes up only 10% of GDP — and remember this includes not only manufacturing but some other forms of activity as well. Agriculture, on the other hand, is the largest single sector.

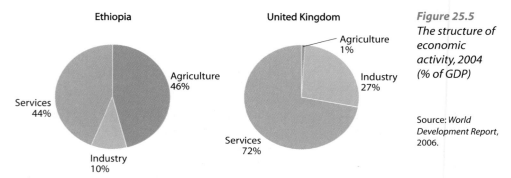

**Figure 25.5**
*The structure of economic activity, 2004 (% of GDP)*

Source: *World Development Report,* 2006.

Indeed, many LDCs have an economic structure that is strongly biased towards agriculture. The evidence of this for the selected countries is presented in Figures 25.6 and 25.7. Figure 25.6 shows the percentage of GDP coming from the agricultural sector. In interpreting these data, it is important to be aware that labour productivity tends to be lower in agriculture than in other sectors. The data therefore understate the importance of agriculture in the structure of the economy, as the percentage of the labour force engaged in agriculture is higher than the agricultural share of output. This is further reinforced by the importance of unrecorded agricultural production in the subsistence sector. In other words, if farmers produce food for their own consumption, this will not be included in GDP.

Figure 25.7 underlines the situation by showing the percentage of the population living in urban areas. It would appear that, for many of the low-income countries in the group, the majority of their people are relying on rural economic activities. In many LDCs, there is a stark contrast between the urban and the rural areas. This shows up partly in terms of income differences, as you might expect from the different kinds of employment opportunities available in the urban areas. However, it shows up in other ways too — for example, in terms of access to

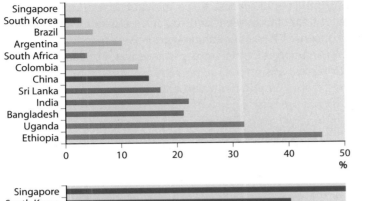

*Figure 25.6*
*Agriculture as a %*
*of GDP, selected*
*countries, 2004*

Source: *World Development Report, 2006.*

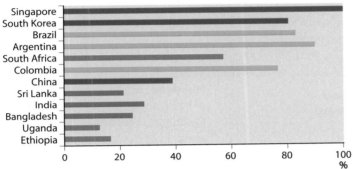

*Figure 25.7*
*Population living*
*in urban areas*
*(%), selected*
*countries*

Source: *Human Development Report, 2005.*

education and healthcare, which tend to be better provided in the urban areas, partly because many teachers and doctors prefer to live there. In some countries, the inequality between different regions is tantamount to there being a *dual economy*. The economic activity in the country takes place in two quite different styles, and a traditional rural sector may co-exist with a burgeoning modern sector in the urban areas.

This inequality between regions in a country may have the effect of encouraging migration towards the cities. There might be many reasons for this. It may be that workers head for the cities because they are attracted by the chance of obtaining higher wages or better living conditions. Alternatively, households might decide to send some members to earn in the city while the rest remain in the rural area. This might be seen as a way of diversifying risk rather than having all household members active in the same (rural) labour market. Figure 25.8 shows something of this trend in a range of countries: it plots the percentage of the country's population living in urban areas at three points in time: 1975, 2003 and a projection to 2015.

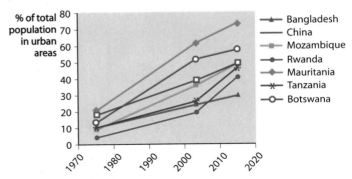

*Figure 25.8 Urbanisation in selected LDCs, 1975, 2003 and 2015*
Source: *Human Development Report, 2005.*

Such movements of people are likely to pose severe problems. Consider Rwanda, for example. In 1975 just 4% of its population lived in the urban areas. By 2015 this is predicted to rise to just over 40%. Rwanda may not have a massively large population (a projected 11.3 million in 2015), but for a government needing to provide public goods, such urban expansion puts significant pressure on urban infrastructure — roads, housing, water supply, sanitation and so on. Just as important, such migration puts enormous pressure on urban labour markets, so the provision of jobs for all these additional workers becomes a major challenge. The net result is that many rural workers exchange poor living conditions in the rural areas for unemployment in an urban environment.

### The informal sector

Furthermore, as employment in the newer sectors cannot expand at such a rate, the result is an expansion of the informal sector. Migrants to the city who cannot find work are forced to find other forms of employment, as most LDCs do not have well-developed social security protection. The cities of many LDCs are therefore characterised by substantial amounts of informal activity, as was mentioned in Chapter 24. The scale of the informal sector can be seen in Figure 25.9: for example, in Ghana nearly 80% of employment in the urban areas is made up of informal activity.

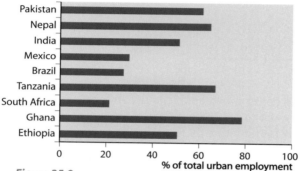

**Figure 25.9**
*Urban informal employment as a % of total urban employment, selected countries*
Note: the data are for national definitions and various years.
Source: International Labour Organization.

Such informal activity covers a multitude of economic activities. If you were to visit a city in an LDC, you might see many examples, such as hawkers selling food at the kerbside, roadside barbers and rickshaw drivers. However, in some cities, the informal sector has developed beyond such activities, and you might find small manufacturing concerns recycling old car tyres as shoes, or packing cases as furniture.

The growth of the urban informal sector may have externality effects on living standards in the urban areas. If there is rapid growth of the urban population, it is unlikely that the

*For many migrants to cities in LDCs informal employment may be the only form of work they can find*

authorities will be able to ensure adequate infrastructure to cope with the growing numbers of residents: for example, in terms of housing, water supply or sanitation. This may lead to the growth of shanty towns — informal settlements in which new arrivals congregate, often in very poor conditions.

In some ways the existence of the informal sector may be seen as beneficial for an LDC, as it offers a coping strategy for the poor, and may even provide some training and skills that might later help workers to find employment in the modern or formal sector. These benefits need to be weighed against the potential costs arising from the externalities mentioned earlier. Furthermore, if the informal sector acts as a cushion for migrant workers, it is possible that it will be seen as reducing the opportunity cost of unemployment, which in turn could increase the flow of migrants.

## Summary

- ➤ Economic activity can be classified into primary, secondary and tertiary production activities.
- ➤ Primary activity centres around agriculture and mineral extraction; secondary activity focuses mainly on manufacturing activity; tertiary activity is concerned with the provision of services.
- ➤ Many LDCs have an economic structure that is biased towards the primary sector.
- ➤ Agriculture is often characterised by low productivity.
- ➤ The importance of agriculture is also reflected in the high proportion of the population of many LDCs that live in rural areas.
- ➤ Inequality between rural and urban areas has led to rapid internal migration in some LDCs, and to the growth of the urban informal sector.
- ➤ Migration puts pressure on urban infrastructure.

## The diversity of less developed countries

Although this chapter has identified a number of characteristics that many LDCs seem to have in common, it is difficult — and dangerous — to generalise too much when trying to analyse LDCs or to devise a policy to foster development. This is because every country has its own configuration of characteristics, strengths and weaknesses. To some extent, regional groupings of countries display some common features, but even here there remains an inherent diversity.

### The East Asian experience

The rapid growth achieved by the East Asian **tiger economies**, as they came to be known, was undoubtedly impressive, and held out hope that other less developed countries could begin to close the gap in

 **Key term**

**tiger economies:** a group of newly industrialised economies in the East Asian region, including Hong Kong, Singapore, South Korea and Taiwan

living standards. Indeed, the term 'East Asian miracle' was coined to describe how quickly these **newly industrialised economies** had been able to develop. At the heart of the success were four countries: Hong Kong, Singapore, South Korea and Taiwan; others, such as Malaysia and Thailand, were not far behind.

**newly industrialised economies:** economies that have experienced rapid economic growth from the 1960s to the present

### How was their success achieved?

None of these countries enjoys a rich supply of natural resources. Indeed, Hong Kong and Singapore are small city-states whose only natural resources are their excellent harbours and good positions — but with small populations.

The tigers soon realised that to develop manufacturing industry it would be crucial to tap into economies of scale. This meant producing on a scale that would far outstrip the size of their domestic markets — which meant that they would have to rely on international trade. Only in this way would they be able to gain the benefits of specialisation.

By being very open to international trade and focusing on exports, the tigers were able to sell to a larger market, and thereby improve their efficiency through economies of scale. This enabled them to enjoy a period of **export-led growth**. In other words, the tiger economies expanded by selling their exports to the rest of the world, and building a reputation for high-quality merchandise. This was helped by their judicious choice of markets on which to focus: they chose to move into areas of economic activity that were being vacated by the more developed nations, which were producing new sorts of product.

**export-led growth:** a situation in which economic growth is achieved through the exploitation of economies of scale, made possible by focusing on exports, and so reaching a wider market than would be available within the domestic economy

The export-led growth hypothesis explains part of the success of the tiger economies, but there were other contributing factors. The tiger economies nurtured their human capital and attracted foreign investment. Their governments intervened to influence the direction of the economy, but also encouraged markets to operate effectively, fostering macroeconomic and political stability and developing good infrastructure. Moreover, these countries embarked on their growth period at a time when world trade overall was buoyant.

## Sub-Saharan Africa

The experience of countries in sub-Saharan Africa is in total contrast to the success story of the tiger economies. Even accepting the limitations of the GDP per capita measure, the fact that it was lower in 2000 than it had been in 1975 (or even earlier) paints a depressing picture. Can sub-Saharan Africa learn from the experience of the tiger economies?

OCR Advanced Economics

Part of the explanation for the failure of growth in this region lies in the fact that sub-Saharan Africa lacks many of the positive features that enabled the tiger economies to grow. Export-led growth is more difficult for countries that have specialised in the production of goods for which demand is not buoyant. Furthermore, it is not straightforward to develop new specialisations if human and physical capital levels are low, the skills for new activities are lacking and poverty is rife. On the other hand, continuing to rely on specialisation in agriculture when many of the potential export markets are characterised by strong protectionism is also fraught with difficulty. Encouraging development when there is political instability, and when markets do not operate effectively, is a major challenge. Chapter 27 considers some of the obstacles to development that are faced by LDCs.

### Latin America

Countries in Latin America followed yet another path. There was a period in which the economies of Argentina, Brazil and Mexico, among others, were able to grow rapidly, enabling them to qualify as 'newly industrialised economies'. However, such growth could not be sustained in the face of the high rates of inflation that afflicted many of the countries in this region, especially during the 1980s. Indeed, many of them experienced bouts of hyperinflation, inhibiting economic growth.

In part this reflected fiscal indiscipline, with governments undertaking high levels of expenditure which they financed by printing money. In many cases, countries in this region have tended to be relatively closed to international trade. International debt reached unsustainable levels, and continues to haunt countries such as Argentina which, in 2005, wrote off its debt by offering its creditors about 33% of the value of its outstanding debt. Around three-quarters of the creditors accepted the deal, knowing that otherwise they would probably get nothing at all. However, whether anyone will be prepared to lend to Argentina in the future remains to be seen. Latin American economies also tend to be characterised by high levels of income inequality, and poverty remains a major problem.

*Latin American countries, including Mexico, have run into economic difficulties after a period of rapid growth*

## Exercise 25.1

Table 25.1 provides a selection of indicators for three countries. One of these is in sub-Saharan Africa, one is in Southeast Asia and the other is in Latin America. See if you can identify which is which.

| | Country A | Country B | Country C |
|---|---|---|---|
| Life expectancy at birth (years) | 68.9 | 73.1 | 46.4 |
| Adult literacy (%) | 95.7 | 91.4 | 83.3 |
| Population growth, 1975–2001 (% p.a.) | 1.5 | 2.0 | 3.2 |
| Urban population (% of total) | 20.0 | 74.6 | 34.3 |
| % of population under 15 years | 25.9 | 33.3 | 42.7 |
| % of population with access to safe water, 2000 | 84.0 | 88.0 | 57.0 |
| % of adults aged 15–49 living with HIV/AIDS | 1.79 | 0.28 | 15.01 |
| Growth of GDP per capita, 1975–2001 (% p.a.) | 5.4 | 0.9 | 0.3 |
| Gini index (%) | 43.2 | 51.9 | 44.5 |
| Exports of primary goods (% of all merchandise exports) | 22.0 | 15.0 | 79.0 |

*Table 25.1 Indicators for three countries*
Note: data are for 2001 unless otherwise stated.
Source: *Human Development Report*, 2003.

## Summary

➤ A small group of countries in Southeast Asia, known as the East Asian tiger economies, underwent a period of rapid economic growth, closing the gap on the more developed countries.

➤ This success arose from a combination of circumstances, including a high degree of openness to international trade, which was seen as crucial if economies of scale were to be reaped.

➤ However, the tigers are also characterised by high levels of human capital and political and macroeconomic stability.

➤ In contrast, countries in sub-Saharan Africa have stagnated; in some cases, real per capita incomes were lower in 2000 than they had been in 1975.

➤ Countries in Latin America began well, experiencing growth for a period, but then ran into economic difficulties.

# Chapter 26
# Theories and models of development

*In the last 50 years or so, thinking about the process of development has evolved. This evolution partly arose from growing experience of the way in which different countries were developing — or, indeed, failing to develop. Improvements in data collection and increasing knowledge of conditions in different regions of the world emphasised the gap in living standards that was opening up between the industrial nations and less developed countries. However, the evolution of thinking also reflected changes in economic thinking and new developments in economic analysis as applied to the problems of less developed countries. The models that were developed during this period continue to shape the way that development is viewed, and the way in which policy is designed to encourage development.*

## Learning outcomes

After studying this chapter, you should:
➤ understand the importance of and potential gains from international trade
➤ be familiar with the stages of development identified by Walt Rostow as being critical for economic development
➤ understand the process of development flowing from the Harrod–Domar model of economic growth and its implications for less developed countries
➤ be familiar with the findings and limitations of the model of development first proposed by Arthur Lewis
➤ be aware of the arguments put forward in dependency theory
➤ understand the arguments for and against balanced and unbalanced growth

## The importance of international trade

The central importance of international trade for growth and development has been recognised since the days of Adam Smith and David Ricardo. For example, during the Industrial Revolution a key factor was that Britain could bring in raw materials from its colonies for use in manufacturing activity. Today, consumers in the UK are able to buy and consume many goods that simply could not be produced within the

part 7

domestic economy. From the point of view of economic analysis, Ricardo showed that countries could gain from trade through a process of *specialisation*.

### Absolute and comparative advantage

The notion of specialisation was discussed in Chapter 1, where you were introduced to Colin and Debbie, who produced pots and bracelets with varying levels of effectiveness. Colin and Debbie's relative skill levels in producing these two goods can now be extended. Table 26.1 reminds you of Colin and Debbie's production possibilities.

| Colin | | Debbie | |
|---|---|---|---|
| Pots | Bracelets | Pots | Bracelets |
| 12 | 0 | 18 | 0 |
| 9 | 3 | 12 | 12 |
| 6 | 6 | 6 | 24 |
| 3 | 9 | 3 | 30 |
| 0 | 12 | 0 | 36 |

*Table 26.1*
*Colin and Debbie's production*

You may remember that Debbie is much better at both activities than Colin. If they each devote all their time to producing pots, Colin produces only 12 to Debbie's 18. If they each produce only bracelets, Colin produces 12 and Debbie, 36.

This illustrates **absolute advantage**. Debbie is simply better than Colin at both activities. Another way of looking at this is that, in order to produce a given quantity of a good, Debbie needs less labour time than Colin.

### Key terms

**absolute advantage:** the ability to produce a good more efficiently (e.g. with less labour)

**comparative advantage:** the ability to produce a good *relatively* more efficiently (i.e. at lower opportunity cost)

**law of comparative advantage:** a theory arguing that there may be gains from trade arising when countries (or individuals) specialise in the production of goods or services in which they have a comparative advantage

There is another significant feature of this table. Although Debbie is better at producing both goods, the difference is much more marked in the case of bracelet production than for pot production. So Debbie is relatively more proficient in bracelet production: in other words, she has a **comparative advantage** in making bracelets. This is reflected in differences in opportunity cost. If Debbie switches from producing pots to producing bracelets, she gives up 6 pots for every 12 additional bracelets that she makes. The opportunity cost of an additional bracelet is thus $6/12 = 0.5$ pots. For Colin, there is a one-to-one trade-off between the two, so his opportunity cost of a bracelet is 1 pot.

More interesting is what happens if the same calculation is made for Colin and pot making. Although Debbie is absolutely better at making pots, if Colin increases his production of pots, his opportunity cost in terms of bracelets is still 1. But for Debbie the opportunity cost of making pots in terms of bracelets is $12/6 = 2$, so Colin has the lower opportunity cost. Although Debbie has an *absolute* advantage in pot making, Colin has a *comparative*

OCR Advanced Economics

advantage. It was this difference in comparative advantage that gave rise to the gains from specialisation that were set out in Chapter 1.

The **law of comparative advantage** states that overall output can be increased if all individuals specialise in producing the goods in which they have a comparative advantage.

## Gains from international trade

This same principle can be applied in the context of international trade. This was seen in Chapter 13 in respect of two hypothetical countries called Anywhere and Somewhere that produced combinations of agricultural goods and manufactures. Figure 26.1 reproduces the earlier diagram showing the production possibility curves for the two countries. Notice that because Somewhere's *PPC* lies entirely within Anywhere's, Anywhere has an absolute advantage in the production of both goods.

The pattern of comparative advantage is reflected in the different slopes of the countries' *PPC*s. If each country specialises in producing the product in which it has a comparative advantage, then total world output of each type of good can be increased, as was shown in Chapter 13. Potentially, each country could then be made better off by engaging in trade.

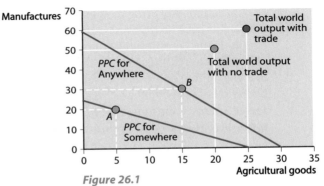

*Figure 26.1*
*PPCs for Anywhere and Somewhere*

This demonstrates the fact that there are potential gains from specialisation. However, it does not guarantee that both countries will benefit equally. The way that the gains from trade are divided between the countries depends on the conditions under which trade takes place, which in turn is governed by the rate of exchange between the two countries. In the example above, in the absence of trade, Anywhere can produce 2 units of manufactured goods for 1 unit of agricultural goods, so will only gain from trade if it can get a better deal than this. For example, if it could get 1 unit of agricultural goods in exchange for 1.5 units of manufactured goods, it will be better off. Similarly, in the domestic economy, Somewhere can produce 1 unit of agricultural goods for 1 unit of manufactures, so it will be better off if it can exchange on more favourable terms than this — that is, if it can get more than 1 unit of manufactures for 1 unit of agricultural goods.

Thus the terms under which trade takes place are extremely important in determining whether trade will be beneficial, and to which country. In the real world, the situation is more complicated, as different countries use different currencies and therefore the exchange rate is also important. In addition, activities are

characterised by economies of scale, so *PPCs* become curved. There are also multiple countries, each with different sources of comparative advantage, and multiple products as well. In particular, differences in transport costs and uncertainty about exchange rates mean that a greater difference in opportunity cost is needed to ensure that there are gains from trade. The way in which transport costs have fallen in recent years with technological change in the transport sector has given new impetus to international trade.

Nonetheless, the principles are the same. There are potential gains to be made from trade if countries specialise in producing goods or services in which they have a comparative advantage. The way that the gains from trade are divided will depend on the terms of trade, and on exchange rates. It may be that countries with relatively strong market power can influence the terms of trade in their favour, and thus gain more from trade than those in a relatively weak position.

Specialisation can result in an overall increase in total production. However, specialisation may bring dangers and risks, as well as benefits. One obvious way in which this may be relevant is that, by specialising, a country allows some sectors to run down. For example, suppose a country came to rely on imported food, and allowed its agricultural sector to waste away. If the country then became involved in a war, or for some other reason was unable to import its food, there would clearly be serious consequences if it could no longer grow its own foodstuffs. For this reason, many countries have in place measures designed to protect their agricultural sectors — or other sectors that are seen to be strategic in nature.

Chapter 13 pointed out that specialisation may bring dangers and risks, as well as benefits. For example, there may be activities that a country may regard as being of strategic importance, so that it decides to maintain an activity even when it lacks comparative advantage in it. This might apply to the case of food production or military capability. Over-reliance on a narrow range of commodities may also carry risks, as is discussed in Chapter 27.

## Exercise 26.1

Figure 26.2 shows production possibility curves for two countries, each of which produces both wheat and tools. The countries are called North and South.

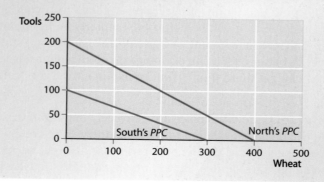

*Figure 26.2*
*PPCs for North and South*

a   Which country has an absolute advantage in the production of both commodities?

b   Which country has a comparative advantage in the production of wheat?

c   Which country has a comparative advantage in the production of tools?

d   Suppose that North produces 100 tools and South produces 50. How much wheat is produced in each country?

e   Now suppose that North produces 150 units of tools and 100 of wheat, and that South produces only wheat. What has happened to total production of tools and wheat?

## Summary

➤ Specialisation opens up the possibility of trade.

➤ The theory of comparative advantage states that, even if one country has an absolute advantage in the production of goods and services, trade may still increase total output if each country specialises in the production of goods and services in which it has a comparative advantage.

➤ Who gains from specialisation and trade depends crucially on the prices at which exchange takes place.

## Economic growth

Although development is about more than **economic growth**, growth is a crucial part of any process of economic and human development. It provides the necessary increase in resources to enable a country to provide for the basic needs of its citizens and to expand its choices in the future, and it lays the foundations for future development.

**Key term**

**economic growth:** an increase in the productive capacity of the economy

Chapter 1 interpreted economic growth in terms of a movement of the production possibility curve (*PPC*). Figure 26.3 serves as a reminder. Here it is assumed that the country has a choice between producing capital goods (for investment) and producing consumer goods. In the initial period, the country begins with the production possibility frontier at $PPC_0$ and can produce at point $A$, producing $C_1$ consumer goods and $I_1$ capital goods. The increase in capital goods enables an increase in the productive capacity of the economy, so that in the following period the *PPC* shifts to $PPC_1$ and the country is able to produce at point $B$, with $C_2$ consumer goods and $I_2$ capital goods. This in turn allows a further shift of the *PPC*, and so the process of economic growth has begun.

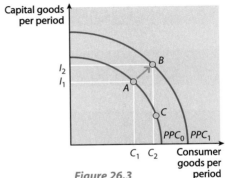

Figure 26.3
*Economic growth*

There are some important points to notice about this process. First, in order to produce more consumer goods in the future, current consumption

has to be sacrificed. In other words, the country could instead have chosen to be at point *C* and enjoy more consumption in the initial period; however, had it done so, the opportunity cost would have been less investment, and therefore the *PPC* would not have moved so far in the second period. This is shown in Figure 26.4, where the choice to be at point *C* means producing only $I_0$ capital goods, and the *PPC* shifts by a very small amount in the following period. Thus, a society that chooses to use its resources for consumption in the present achieves a slower rate of economic growth.

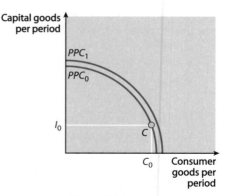

Figure 26.4
Less economic growth

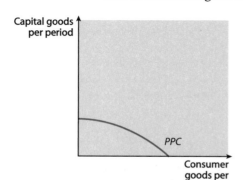

Figure 26.5
A limited capacity to produce capital goods

Second, if the country has a limited capacity to produce investment goods, the PPC will take on a much flatter shape, as in Figure 26.5. In this case a sacrifice of current consumption will not appreciably increase the amount of capital goods that is produced, and again, the rate of economic growth will tend to be modest.

For a less developed country (LDC) this may well be the case. In many LDCs the capacity to produce capital goods is limited because the countries lack the technical knowledge and resources needed to produce them. Furthermore, a country in which there are high levels of poverty, and in which many households face low income-earning opportunities, needs to devote a large proportion of its resources to consumption. The question for LDCs is thus how to overcome this problem in order to kick-start a process of economic growth.

Figure 26.6 illustrates the difficulties. A shortage of capital means low per capita incomes, which means low savings, which in turn means low investment, limited capital, and hence low per capita incomes. In this way a country can get trapped in a *low-level equilibrium* situation.

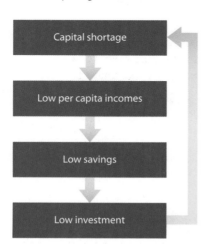

Figure 26.6
A low-level equilibrium trap

Another view of economic growth was presented in Chapter 11, where it was characterised in terms of a shift in the aggregate supply curve. Again, it was argued that investment is critical to the process of expanding the productive capacity of the economy. This is illustrated in Figure 26.7, where the aggregate supply curve shifts from $AS_0$ to $AS_1$. It was argued in Chapter 11 that the aggregate supply curve could move to the right either following invest-ment, which would expand the stock of capital, or following an improvement in the effectiveness of markets. All of this suggests that the first focus for LDCs must be on savings and investment.

## Stages of economic growth

The economic historian Walt Rostow examined the pattern of development that had been followed in history. He argued in 1960 that all of the more developed countries could be seen to have passed through five **stages of economic growth**. Figure 26.8 gives a general impression of how income per capita changes through these stages.

In the first stage — the *traditional society* — land is the basis of wealth, most of the production that takes place is in agriculture, and investment is low. Some societies can remain in this stage or get trapped in it. This may correspond to the low-level equilibrium trap that was referred to above. Income per capita is static in this phase.

In order to escape from this situation, Rostow argued that a country must establish the *preconditions* for economic growth. In this period, agricultural productivity begins to increase. This enables resources to be released from the agricultural sector so that some diversification can take place: for example, into some manufacturing activity. Such changes are typically accompanied by a range of social and political changes. It is also important in this stage that some resources are devoted to the provision of the infrastructure that is needed for industrialisation to take place, especially in terms of transport and communications and market facilities.

In the *take-off* stage the economy passes through a 20–30-year period of acceler-ated growth, with investment rising relative to GDP. Barriers that held back economic growth are overcome. The process of growth in this period tends to be driven by a few leading sectors. A key element of this period is the emergence of entrepreneurs — people who are able to recognise opportuni-ties for productive investment, and who are willing to accept the risk of carrying out that investment. A flow of funds for investment is also needed. Such funds may come from domestic savings, but it may also be necessary to draw in funds from external sources.

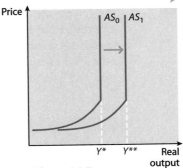

**Figure 26.7**
*Economic growth as a shift in aggregate supply*

**Key** *term*

**stages of economic growth:** a process described by economic historian Walt Rostow, which set out five stages through which he claimed that all developing countries would pass

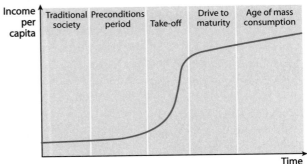

**Figure 26.8**
*The stages of economic growth*

The *drive to maturity* stage is a period of self-sustaining growth. New sectors begin to emerge to complement the leading sectors that emerged during the take-off, so that the economy becomes more diversified and balanced. In this period, investment continues to take a relatively high proportion of GDP.

The final period is the *age of mass consumption*, in which the economy is now fully diversified, output per head continues to rise, but consumption now takes a higher proportion of GDP. Countries in this stage have effectively become developed.

Rostow's discussion has been much criticised. For example, it has been suggested that, as an economic historian, Rostow was more concerned with describing the way in which economies had developed in the past than with providing an explanation of *why* they had developed in this way. Nor does his approach provide much helpful guidance for designing policy that would stimulate development in those countries that are still stuck in the 'traditional society' stage, except insofar as countries could study the preconditions and try to replicate them. For example, he offers no explanation of how the barriers to growth disappear in the take-off stage, although it is helpful to be aware that there may be such barriers, and that they need to be overcome.

## Dependency theory

A group of writers in the 1950s and 1960s put forward a very different view of economic history. This came to be known as **dependency theory**. The essence of the approach was to deny that the developed countries achieved success purely by internal mechanisms or by domestic saving and investment. Instead, it was argued that the countries that first went through the process of industrialisation did so by exploiting the resources of countries elsewhere in the world.

These writers argued that the world could be seen as being divided into the *core* of countries that had developed, located in North America and Western Europe, and a *periphery* of countries in Asia, Africa and Latin America that remained reliant on primary production, and which were controlled by the countries in the core. The core used the countries in the periphery as a source of raw materials and a market for their goods, thus perpetuating the divide between them.

 **Key** *term*

**dependency theory:** the notion that the countries of the world can be divided into the core and the periphery, and that the countries in the core developed by exploiting those in the periphery

The triangular slave trade could be construed as an example of this. It worked as follows: a slave ship would sail from England, France or colonial North America with a cargo of manufactured goods. These would be exchanged (at a profit) in Africa for slaves, who would then be traded on the sugar or tobacco plantations in North America and the Caribbean (at another profit) in exchange for raw materials (sugar, tobacco etc.). These raw materials would then be transported back to the factories. The British treatment of manufacturing industry in India has also come in for criticism, where (for example) the Indian cotton industry was suppressed in order to protect the cotton mills of Lancashire.

*The triangular slave trade illustrates how periphery countries were exploited*

However, there is a limit to how far these arguments can be pressed. It is clear that colonial influence was not all bad, and colonies benefited from physical and social infrastructure — such as railways, roads and educational structures — provided by the colonising nations. It is also the case that a number of countries that were never colonised, such as Afghanistan, Ethiopia and Thailand, failed to develop.

In today's increasingly integrated world, the question of interdependence between countries is of great significance. It remains to be seen whether globalisation will offer further opportunities for exploitation of the poor by the rich (as some critics maintain), or whether it will offer the basis for new mutually beneficial partnerships between the countries of the world. However, it remains the case that many LDCs continue to be heavily reliant on primary production, and it is important to explore the extent to which this is an obstacle to development. Dependency theorists suggest that one possible route forward for countries in the periphery is to begin forging trading links with each other, rather than continuing to depend upon countries in the core. Indeed, some attempts have been made to establish trading agreements between LDCs, but this process has a long way to go.

## Industrialisation

So what are the prospects for a country wanting to move towards **industrialisation**, and to reduce its reliance on primary production?

In an influential paper in 1954, Sir Arthur Lewis argued that agriculture in many LDCs was characterised by surplus labour. Perhaps farms were operated on a household basis, with the work and the crop being shared out between members of the household. If there was not enough work to be done by all the members of the household, then, although all seemed to be employed, there would in fact be *hidden unemployment*, or *underemployment*. Given the size of the rural population and its rapid growth, there could be almost unlimited *surplus labour* existing in this way.

**Key term**

**industrialisation:** a process of transforming an economy by expanding manufacturing and other industrial activity

*Sir Arthur Lewis argued that surplus labour in the rural economy was the key to the industrialisation of less developed countries*

Lewis then pointed out that it would be possible to transfer such surplus labour into the industrial sector without a loss of agricultural output, as the remaining labour would be able to take up the slack. All that would be necessary is for the industrial sector to set a wage sufficiently higher than the rural wage to persuade workers to transfer. Industry could then reap profits that could be re-invested to allow industry to expand, without any need for the industrial wage to be pulled upwards to cause inflation.

Unfortunately, the process did not prove to be as smooth as Lewis suggested. One reason relates to *human capital* levels. Agricultural workers do not have the skills or training that prepares them for employment in the industrial sector, so it is not so straightforward to transfer them from agricultural to industrial work.

Furthermore, to the extent that they were able to transfer, the expanding industry did not always reinvest the surplus in order to enable continuous expansion of the industrial sector. Foreign firms tended to repatriate the profits (as will be seen in Chapter 27), and in any case tended to use modern, relatively capital-intensive technology that did not require a large pool of unskilled labour.

**Key term**

**Lewis model:** a model developed by Sir Arthur Lewis that argued that less developed countries could be seen as being typified by two sectors, traditional and modern, and that labour could be transferred from the traditional to the modern sector in order to bring about economic growth and development

Perhaps more seriously, the **Lewis model** encouraged governments to think in terms of industry-led growth, and to neglect the rural sector. This meant that agricultural productivity often remained low, and inequality between urban and rural areas grew.

## The Harrod–Domar model

Returning to the issue of economic growth, if it is seen in terms of a shift in aggregate supply, then the focus must be on investment, which enables an

increase in productive capacity, as Rostow emphasised. This idea is also supported by the **Harrod–Domar model** of economic growth, which first appeared in separate articles by Roy Harrod in the UK and Evsey Domar in the USA in 1939. This model was to become significant in influencing LDCs' attitudes towards the process of economic growth. It was developed in an attempt to determine how equilibrium could be achieved in a growing economy.

**Key term**

**Harrod–Domar model:** a model of economic growth that emphasises the importance of savings and investment

The basic finding of the model was that an economy can remain in equilibrium through time only if it grows at a particular rate. This unique *stable growth path* depends on the *savings ratio* and the *productivity of capital.* Any deviation from this path will cause the economy to become unstable. This finding emphasised the importance of savings in the process of economic growth, and led to the conclusion that a country seeking economic growth must first increase its flow of savings.

Figure 26.9 illustrates the process that leads to growth in a Harrod–Domar world. Savings are crucial in enabling investment to be undertaken — always remembering that some investment will have to be used to replace existing capital that has worn out. Investment then enables capital to accumulate and technology to be improved. The accumulation of capital leads to an increase in output and incomes, which leads to a further flow of savings, and the cycle begins again.

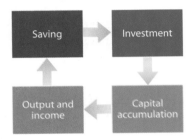

The key question is whether this process can allow an LDC to break out of the low-level equilibrium trap. Figure 26.9 can be used to identify a number of problems that may prevent the Harrod–Domar process from being effective for LDCs.

*Figure 26.9*
*The Harrod–Domar process of economic development*

Generating a flow of savings in an LDC may be problematic. When incomes are low, households may have to devote most of their resources to consumption, and so there may be a lack of savings. Nonetheless, some savings have proved possible. For example, in the early 1960s South Korea had an average income level that was not too different from that of countries like Sudan or Afghanistan, but it managed to build up the savings rate during that decade.

Setting aside the problem of low savings for the moment, what happens next?

### Will savings lead to investment and the accumulation of capital?
If a flow of savings can be generated, the next important step is to transform the savings into investment. This is the process by which the sacrifice of current consumption leads to an increase in productive capacity in the future.

Some important preconditions must be met if savings are to be transformed into investment. First, there must be a way for potential borrowers to get access to the funds. In developed countries this takes place through the medium of financial

markets. For example, it may be that households save by putting their money into a savings account at the bank; then with this money the bank can make loans to entrepreneurs, enabling them to undertake investment.

In many LDCs, however, financial markets are undeveloped, so it is much more difficult for funds to be recycled in this way. For example, a study conducted in 1997 by the Bank of Uganda found that almost 30% of households interviewed in rural Ugandan villages had undertaken savings at some time. However, almost none of these had done so through formal financial institutions, which did not reach into the rural areas. Instead, the saving that took place tended to be in the form of fixed assets, or money kept under the bed. Such savings cannot readily be transformed into productive investment.

In addition, governments in some periods have made matters worse by holding down interest rates in the hope of encouraging firms to borrow. The idea here is that a low interest rate means a low cost of borrowing, which should make borrowing more attractive. However, this ignores the fact that, if interest rates are very low, there is little incentive to save because the return on saving is so low. In this case, firms may wish to invest but may not be able to obtain the funds to do so.

The other prerequisite for savings to be converted into investment is that there must be entrepreneurs with the ability to identify investment possibilities, the skill to carry them through and the willingness to bear the risk. Such entrepreneurs are in limited supply in many LDCs.

During the 1950s, Hong Kong, one of the so-called *tiger economies*, benefited from a wave of immigrant entrepreneurs, especially from Shanghai, who provided the impetus for rapid development. In Singapore the entrepreneurship came primarily from the government, and from multinational corporations which were encouraged to become established in the country. Singapore and South Korea also adopted policies that ensured a steady flow of savings, so that, for example, in Singapore gross domestic savings amounted to 52% of GDP in 1999.

*Singapore skyline — can saving lead to investment and economic development?*

OCR Advanced Economics

## Will investment lead to higher output and income?

For investment to be productive in terms of raising output and incomes in the economy, some further conditions need to be met. In particular, it is crucial for firms to have access to physical capital, which will raise production capacity. Given their limited capability of producing capital goods, many LDCs have to rely on capital imported from the more developed countries. This may be beneficial in terms of upgrading home technology, but such equipment can be imported only if the country has earned the foreign exchange to pay for it. A shortage of foreign exchange may therefore make it difficult for the country to accumulate capital.

The tiger economies were all very open to international trade, and focused on promoting exports in order to earn the foreign exchange needed to import capital goods. This strategy worked very effectively, and the economies were able to widen their access to capital and move to higher value-added activities as they developed their capabilities.

## The importance of human capital

If the capital *can* be obtained, there is then a need for the skilled labour with which to operate the capital goods. Human capital, in the form of skilled, healthy and well-trained workers, is as important as physical capital if investment is to be productive.

In principle, it might be thought that today's LDCs have an advantage over the countries that developed in earlier periods. In particular, they can learn from earlier mistakes, and import technology that has already been developed, rather than having to develop it anew. This suggests that a *convergence* process should be going on, whereby LDCs are able to adopt technology that has already been produced, and thereby grow more rapidly and begin to close the gap with the more developed countries.

However, by and large this has not been happening, and a lack of human capital has been suggested as one of the key reasons for the failure. This underlines the importance of education in laying the foundations for economic growth as well as contributing directly to the quality of life.

The education systems of the tiger economies had been well established, either through the British colonial legacy (in the case of Singapore and Hong Kong) or through past Japanese occupation periods (in Taiwan and South Korea). In all of these countries, education received high priority, and cultural influences encouraged a high demand for education. The tiger economies thus benefited from having highly skilled and well-disciplined labour forces that were able to make effective use of the capital goods that had been acquired.

## Harrod–Domar and external resources

Figure 26.10 extends the earlier schematic presentation of the process underlying the Harrod–Domar model of economic growth. This has been amended to underline the importance of access to technology and human capital.

The discussion above has emphasised the difficulty of mobilising domestic savings, both in generating a sufficient flow of savings and in translating such savings into productive investment.

The question arises as to whether an LDC could supplement its domestic savings with a flow of funds from abroad. Figure 26.10 identifies three possible injections into the Harrod–Domar process. First, it might be possible to attract flows of overseas assistance from higher-income countries. Second, perhaps the amount of investment could be augmented directly by persuading multinational corporations to engage in foreign direct investment. Third, the LDC might be able to borrow on international capital markets to finance its domestic investment. It is worth noting that the tiger economies took full advantage of these external sources of funds.

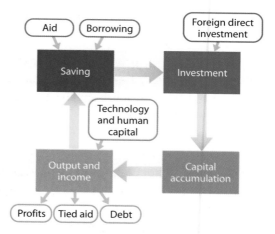

**Figure 26.10** *The Harrod–Domar process of economic development augmented*

These three possibilities are explored more fully in Chapter 27. However, it is worth noting that each of these ways of attracting external resources has a downside associated with it. As far as overseas assistance is concerned, in the past such flows have been seen by some donor countries as part of trade policy, and have brought less benefit to LDCs than had been hoped. In the case of the multinational corporations, there is a tendency for the profits to be repatriated out of the LDC, rather than recycled into the economy. Finally, international borrowing has to be repaid at some future date, and many LDCs have found themselves burdened by debt that they can ill afford to repay.

## Extension material

The algebra of the Harrod–Domar model can be revealing.

Suppose there is a closed economy with no government. If there is equilibrium in the goods market, then planned saving ($S$) equals planned investment ($I$):

$$S = I$$

Assume that there is no depreciation, so investment results in capital accumulation ($\Delta K$):

$$I = \Delta K$$

Assume also that the capital–output ratio ($k$) remains constant over time. Then:

$$k = \frac{\Delta K}{\Delta Y}$$

where $Y$ is income and/or output.

If savings are a proportion (*s*) of income, then for equilibrium to be maintained:

$$sY = \Delta K = k\Delta Y$$

Rearranging, this implies that the growth rate of output ($\Delta Y/Y$) must be equal to $s/k$.

This then provides a simple rule. If a government wishes to achieve a growth rate of, say, 5%, and knows that the capital–output ratio is 3, then the saving ratio needs to be $3 \times 5 = 15\%$. This is a simple rule, but deceptive, for the reasons that have been outlined.

## Summary

➤ Although development is a broader concept than economic growth, growth is a key ingredient of development.

➤ Economic growth can be seen in terms of a shift in the production possibility curve, or a shift in long-run aggregate supply.

➤ Walt Rostow identified a sequence of stages of economic growth through which all developed countries have passed.

➤ Dependency theory argued that countries in the periphery have been exploited by countries in the core, and that they should reduce reliance on the core by trading with each other.

➤ Lewis argued that surplus labour could be transferred from the traditional into the modern sector, thus enabling a harmonious process of growth and transformation. But it did not turn out to be so straightforward.

➤ The Harrod–Domar model of economic growth highlights the importance of savings, and of transforming savings into productive investment.

➤ However, where markets are underdeveloped, this transformation may be impeded.

➤ Human capital is also a critical ingredient of economic growth.

➤ If resources cannot be generated within the domestic economy, a country may need to have recourse to external sources of funding.

## Balanced and unbalanced growth

Another important debate has been about whether governments should be proactive in promoting growth — and whether they should be proactive in promoting particular *types* of growth. One particular issue that came under scrutiny in this context concerned **balanced** and **unbalanced growth**. This comes down to a question of whether the government should try to synchronise growth across a range of different sectors (balanced growth), or whether growth should initially be concentrated in a small number of sectors (unbalanced growth). Advocates of a balanced growth approach, such as Ragnar Nurkse and Paul Rosenstein-Rodan, argued that coordination was essential.

An example often used to illustrate the need for balanced growth concerns a shoe factory. At first glance, this is the sort of activity that should be able to contribute

to the growth process in a less developed country. It is labour intensive, so makes use of the labour resources available. It uses materials that can be produced in a mainly agrarian society, and does not rely on expensive imports of materials or capital. So suppose a shoe factory sets up in an LDC. The factory is built and starts to produce shoes. Who is going to buy the shoes that are produced? The firm's workers will be one source of demand, but if nothing else has changed in the economy, they will not provide sufficient demand to make the factory profitable, and the workers who are still in the subsistence economy will not have money with which to buy shoes.

**Key terms**

**balanced growth:**
economic growth achieved by a coordinated expansion across many different economic activities

**unbalanced growth:**
economic growth achieved by selective expansion of a limited number of interlinked activities

But suppose that a shoe factory, a bicycle manufacturer, a textile factory, a flour mill and other activities are all started up at the same time? Then there will be sufficient demand from the workers employed to make all of these activities profitable. If the government can at the same time provide the infrastructure needed in the economy — for transport, communications and so on — then this will be even more effective, as all of the activities can share (and will need) the infrastructure.

For this balanced route to development to be effective, it is crucial for all of these activities to be initiated at the same time — there is a need for a 'big push' across a range of activities. This sounds plausible, but is it operationally feasible? The problem is that for many LDCs the resources available are likely to be insufficient to provide the initial impetus or funding. Furthermore, the organisational problems in providing the coordination function are likely to be beyond many LDC governments or their bureaucratic structures.

*Shoes produced by LDCs could be sold overseas if there is not sufficient demand at home*

As a result, writers such as Albert Hirschman have argued for unbalanced growth, whereby the available resources are focused on a narrow range of activities. These activities, or sectors, should be chosen with care to maximise the forward and backward linkages present. Industries should be encouraged that can use local materials, or which complement other existing activities. For example, this might entail processing some raw material already being produced before exporting it, rather than leaving the processing to be done elsewhere in the world. Should they arise, problems of over-supply (as in the shoes case) could be overcome by tapping into world markets as a source of demand.

The coordination problems facing LDC governments may render planned (balanced) development growth infeasible. The intricacies of trying to operate central planning entail so many decisions, and require such an elaborate bureaucracy, that it is beyond the capabilities of many LDC governments. More recently, attention has switched to examine the extent to which the market can be invoked to assist with the allocation of resources and the initiation of a process of economic growth.

## Market-friendly growth

This alternative way of viewing the process of economic growth has been put forward by the World Bank. The core argument is that markets should be allowed to work without government intervention wherever possible, and that the government should intervene only where markets cannot operate effectively. This is called a **market-friendly growth** strategy. The World Bank has argued that four areas should be of high priority to LDCs looking to stimulate development: *people*, *microeconomic markets*, *macroeconomic stability* and *global linkages*.

 **term**

**market-friendly growth:** economic growth in which governments intervene less where markets can operate effectively, but more strongly where markets are seen to fail

At the core of this approach is the argument that, if markets can be made to work effectively, this will lead to more efficient resource allocation. Furthermore, governments should intervene only where markets themselves cannot operate effectively because of some sort of market failure. If the four components can be made to work together, it will lay the foundations for economic growth and development.

### People

The importance of human capital formation has already been stressed. The need for skilled and disciplined labour to complement capital accumulation is critical for development. However, this is an area in which market failure is widespread.

If people do not fully perceive the future benefits to be gained from educating their children, they will demand less education than is desirable for society. In the rural areas of many LDCs, it is common for education to be undervalued in this way and for drop-out rates from schooling to be high. This may arise both from a failure to perceive the potential future benefits that children will derive from

education, and from the high opportunity cost of education in villages where child labour is widespread.

The situation in many LDCs has been worsened in the past by poor curriculum design, whereby the legacy of colonial rule was a school system and curriculum not well directed at providing the sort of education likely to be of most benefit in the context of an LDC. Furthermore, there tended to be a bias towards providing funds to the further and higher education sectors, which benefit mainly the rich elites within society, rather than trying to ensure that all children received at least primary education.

The benefits from developing people as resources may overflow into other component areas: for example, through an increase in labour productivity — if healthy and educated people are able to work better — or by ensuring that products are better able to meet international standards, thereby reinforcing linkages with the rest of the world.

## Microeconomic markets

The World Bank has also argued that LDCs need to encourage competitive and effective microeconomic markets in order to ensure that their resources are well allocated.

It is important that prices can act as signals to guide resource allocation. This can then create a climate for enterprise, enabling people to exploit their capabilities. In the past, many governments in LDCs have tended to intervene strongly in markets, distorting prices away from market equilibrium values — especially food prices, which were kept artificially low in urban areas, thus damaging farmers' incentives. In addition, it is important to encourage the development of financial markets that will act to channel savings into productive investment.

Again, there are likely to be overflow effects from this. First, if microeconomic markets can be made to operate effectively, this will ensure that people get a good

return on the education that they undertake, which will encourage a greater demand for education in the future. Second, foreign direct investment is more likely to be attracted into a country in which there are effective operational domestic markets. And the existence of effective financial markets creates a financial discipline that encourages stability at the macroeconomic level.

*World Bank headquarters in Washington DC*

# chapter 16

## Macroeconomic stability

It is argued that stability in the macroeconomy is important in order to encourage investment. If the macroeconomic environment is unstable, firms will not be sufficiently confident of the future to want to risk investing in projects. In addition, if the government becomes overactive in the economy, this may starve the private sector of resources.

A key aim for an LDC should be to ensure that prices can act as effective signals in guiding resource allocation. If overall inflation is allowed to get out of hand, then clearly allocative efficiency cannot be expected. In contrast, a stable macroeconomy should serve to improve the operation of microeconomic markets. An economy that is stable should also be better able to withstand external shocks.

## Global linkages

The domestic markets of most LDCs are limited in terms of effective demand. For LDC producers to be able to benefit from economies of scale, they need to be exporting in sufficient quantities — which clearly means being involved in and committed to international trade. Global linkages thus become important. Furthermore, LDCs can gain access to technology only from abroad, as they do not have the capacity to produce it themselves.

Again, there are likely to be spillover effects. The availability of physical and financial capital may help the stability of the macroeconomy; participation in world markets may help domestic markets to operate; and global linkages can provide the knowledge and technology that will improve human capital in the domestic economy.

It is important to notice that establishing global links is a two-way process. On the one hand, it is important for an LDC to be in a strong enough position to form links with more developed countries without creating a vulnerability to outside influence that may damage it: for example, in reaching trade agreements. On the other hand, the more developed countries need to be willing to accept such linkages. This has not always been the case in the past, as witness the protectionist response of the USA in the early part of the twenty-first century to the incursions of goods from China into the US market.

So there is an interdependent system in which the four aspects of potential intervention interact. The self-reinforcing aspect of these four components not only provides a focus for analysis, but also highlights the fact that if any one of the elements is lacking, there may be problems.

Whether these aspects are sufficient to encourage development is an important issue. In most LDCs two additional issues will need to be tackled. First, there is the question of infrastructure. The *public good* aspects of some types of infrastructure need to be borne in mind. The provision of transport and communications systems, and the improvement of market facilities to enable trading to take place, may be crucial for the smooth development of an LDC.

Second, it is important that LDC governments maintain an appropriate balance in their spending priorities. Civil and international conflict has all too often diverted resources away from development priorities. Something of this can be seen in Figure 26.11, which shows military expenditure relative to expenditure on health and education in our selection of LDCs.

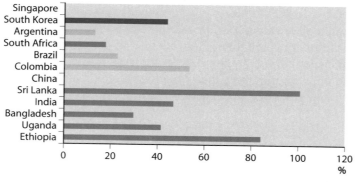

*Figure 26.11*
*Military expenditure as a percentage of combined public expenditure on education and health, selected countries, 2001*

Note: data are not available for China and Singapore.

Source: *Human Development Report,* 2004.

The tiger economies offer a good illustration of how markets can be enabled to bring about rapid growth and development. Indeed, the World Bank model is based partly on its observation of the experience of these and some other economies. Although in some cases (especially Singapore and South Korea) the governments played an active role in encouraging economic growth and influencing the pattern of economic activity, markets were nonetheless nurtured and encouraged to play a role in resource allocation.

## Summary

➤ An important issue is the extent to which governments should try to plan the process of development, or whether markets should be encouraged to drive resource allocation.

➤ Some writers have argued that a planned expansion across a wide range of economic activities (balanced growth) is the way forward for many LDCs.

➤ However, many LDCs lack the resources to be able to coordinate such an expansion.

➤ An alternative is to focus resources on a narrow range of activities through a process of unbalanced growth.

➤ The World Bank has advocated a market-friendly approach to economic growth and development.

➤ Four key elements are seen as crucial to the process: investment in people, properly functioning microeconomic markets, macroeconomic stability and global linkages.

➤ These elements reinforce one another.

## Exercise 26.2

Think back over the models that were introduced in this chapter. Discuss the extent to which the models offer practical policy advice for LDCs.

part **7**

# *Chapter 27*
# Obstacles to growth and development

*This chapter focuses on some of the obstacles that have hindered development in less developed countries, especially in sub-Saharan Africa, where very little progress seems to have been made after several decades of development efforts. This is in contrast to some countries in East Asia, which have experienced such rapid growth since the 1960s that they have successfully closed the income gap with countries that developed in earlier periods.*

## Learning outcomes

After studying this chapter, you should:
- ➤ be aware of important obstacles to economic growth and development
- ➤ understand the causes and significance of rapid population growth
- ➤ understand the dangers of continued dependence on primary production, especially on low-productivity agriculture
- ➤ appreciate the importance of missing markets, especially financial markets
- ➤ be aware of the importance of social capital in promoting long-term development
- ➤ appreciate the significance of relationships with more developed countries

## Problems facing less developed countries

Previous chapters have highlighted some of the characteristics of less developed countries (LDCs), and have examined some of the models that have attempted to explain how the economic growth process works. The models may help to identify which of the characteristics of LDCs have been significant in inhibiting growth and development. In other words, there may be some inherent characteristics of LDCs that have created obstacles to development. These may be regarded as *internal* problems — problems that arise because of domestic issues. However, it is apparent that LDCs have also faced obstacles from outside. Such *external* problems arise in an international context because of the interactions between countries in global markets, and through political ties. Such international linkages have become more important with the spread of globalisation.

This chapter investigates some of these internal and external obstacles to development. Internally, one group of issues arises in relation to the balance of factors of production available in LDCs, which tend to be characterised by a relative abundance of labour resources and a lack of capital. A second group of issues relates to the underdevelopment of markets — especially financial markets, which may be of particular importance given the stress on saving and investment in many of the models. There are also issues arising from government failure. Externally, issues arise from trade interactions and from the trend towards globalisation.

## Population growth

Early writers on development were pessimists. For example, Thomas Malthus argued in the late eighteenth century that real wages would never rise above a bare subsistence level. This was based on his ideas about the relationship between population growth and real incomes.

Malthus, having come under the influence of David Ricardo, believed that there would always be *diminishing returns to labour.* This led him to believe that, as the population of a country increased, the average wage would fall, since a larger labour force would be inherently less productive. Furthermore, Malthus argued that the birth rate would rise with the real wage, because if families had more resources they would have more children; at the same time, the death rate would fall with an increase in the real wage, as people would be better fed and therefore healthier.

### Extension material

Figure 27.1 shows one way of looking at the relationship between population growth and real wages. The left-hand panel illustrates the relationship between population size and the real wage rate, reflecting diminishing returns to labour in agriculture. The right-hand panel shows the birth rate ($B$) and death rate ($D$) functions. When the wage is relatively high, say at $W_1$, the birth rate ($B_1$) exceeds the death rate ($D_1$), which in turn means that the population will grow. However, as population grows, the real wage must fall (as shown in the left-hand panel), so eventually the wage converges on $W^*$, which is an equilibrium situation.

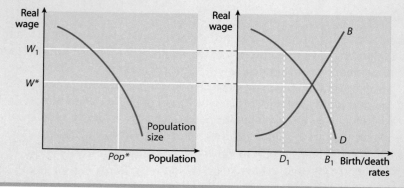

Figure 27.1
Malthus's theory of population

For these reasons, Malthus believed that it was not possible for a society to experience sustained increases in real wages, basically because the population was capable of exponential growth, while the food supply was capable of only arithmetic growth as a result of diminishing returns.

Although he was proved wrong (he had not anticipated the improvements in agricultural productivity that were to come), the question of whether population growth constitutes an obstacle to growth and development remains. At the heart of this is the debate about whether people should be regarded as key contributors to development, in their role as a factor of production, or as a drain on resources, consuming food, shelter, education and so on. Ultimately, the answer depends upon the quantity of resources available relative to the population size.

*Thomas Malthus*

In global terms, world population is growing at a rapid rate: by more than 80 million people per year. In November 1999, global population went through the 6 billion mark — that is, about six times as many people as there were in 1800. But the growth is very unevenly distributed: countries such as Italy, Spain, Germany and Switzerland are projected to experience declining populations in the period 2000–15, while the population of sub-Saharan Africa continues to grow by 2.4% per annum, and that of 'low human development' countries (according to the UNDP definition) by 2.5%. A country whose population is growing at 2.5% per annum will see a doubling in just 28 years, so the growing pressure on resources to provide education and healthcare is considerable. The proportion of the population aged below 15 is very high for much of sub-Saharan Africa, as noted in Chapter 25.

> **Key** *term*
>
> **demographic transition:** a process through which many countries have been observed to pass, whereby improved health lowers the death rate, and the birth rate subsequently also falls, leaving low and stable population growth

It has been observed that developed countries seem to have gone through a common pattern of population growth as their development progressed. This pattern has become known as the **demographic transition**, and is illustrated in Figure 27.2 for England and Wales between 1750 and 2000. This shows the birth rate and death rate for various years over this period. Remember that the natural rate of increase in population is given by the birth rate minus the death rate (ignoring net migration).

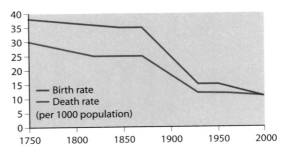

*Figure 27.2 The demographic transition in England and Wales, 1750–2000*

Source: D. Perkins et al., *The Economics of Development* (Norton, 2001, updated with data from the World Bank).

Notice that between 1750 and 1820 the death rate fell more steeply than the birth rate, which means that the population growth rate accelerated in this period. This was the time when Britain was embarking on the Industrial Revolution, and corresponds to the early 'take-off' period of economic growth. At this stage the birth rate remains high. However, after 1870 there is a further fall in the death rate, accompanied by an even steeper fall in the birth rate, such that population growth slows down. You can see that by 2000 the natural population growth has shrunk to zero.

This demographic transition process has been displayed in most of the developed countries. The supporting story is that when the development process begins, death rates tend to fall as incomes begin to rise. In time, families adapt to the change and new social norms emerge in which the typical family size tends to get smaller. For example, as more women join the workforce, the opportunity cost of having children rises — by taking time out from careers to have children, their forgone earnings are now higher. This process has led to stability in population growth.

However, for countries that have undergone the demographic transition in a later period, things have not been so smooth. Figure 27.3 shows the demographic transition for Sri Lanka, which is one of the countries that have achieved some stability in the rate of population growth. Here, it is not until after about 1920 that the death rate begins to fall — and it falls more steeply than it did in the early stages of economic growth in England and Wales.

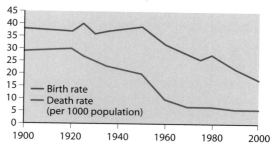

**Figure 27.3** *The demographic transition in Sri Lanka, 1750–2000*

Source: D. Perkins et al., *The Economics of Development* (Norton/World Bank).

of economic growth in England and Wales. After 1950 it falls even more steeply, partly because methods of hygiene and modern medicine were able to bring the death rate down more rapidly.

Perhaps more crucially, the birth rate in Sri Lanka has remained high for much longer — in other words, households' decisions about family size do not seem to have adjusted as rapidly as they did in England and Wales. This has led to a period of relatively rapid population growth.

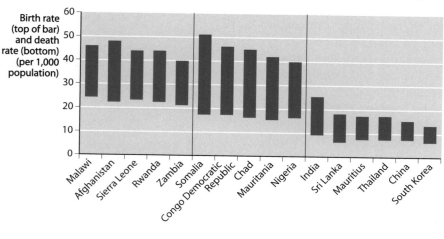

**Figure 27.4**
*Birth and death rates in selected countries, 1999*

Source: World Bank.

OCR Advanced Economics

In Figure 27.4, presenting data for a range of countries around the world, the top point of each bar represents the birth rate and the bottom point the death rate; the length of each bar thus represents the rate of natural population increase. You will see that there are three important groupings. The first is of five countries that do not yet seem to have entered the demographic transition, and for which both birth rates and death rates have remained relatively high. These are mainly low-income countries.

The second group represents countries in which death rates have begun to fall, but birth rates have remained high. As a result, these are currently going through a period of rapid population growth.

The final group represents countries that have seen falls in both birth and death rates, so that population growth has now been reduced. Notice that this includes Sri Lanka, which was discussed earlier.

## Extension material

To some extent, a household's choice of family size might be viewed as an *externality* issue. Figure 27.5 illustrates this. *MPB* (= *MSB*) represents the marginal benefit that the household receives from having different numbers of children (which is assumed to equal the marginal social benefit), and *MPC* represents the marginal private costs that are incurred. If education is subsidised, or if the household does not perceive the costs inflicted on society by having many children, then the marginal social cost of children (*MSC*) is higher than the marginal private cost.

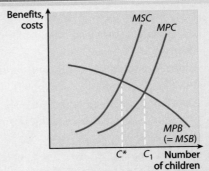

**Figure 27.5**
*The microeconomics of fertility*

Households will thus choose to have $C_1$ children, rather than the $C^*$ number that is optimal for society. In other words, a choice of large family size might be interpreted as a market failure. Note that this discussion assumes that the household has the ability to choose its desired family size by having access to, and knowledge of, methods of contraception.

Figure 27.6 shows fertility rates for the group of countries selected in previous chapters. The fertility rate records the average number of births per woman. Thus, in Uganda the average number of births per woman is more than 7. Of course, this does not mean that the average number of *children* per family is so high, as not all the babies survive.

This pattern of high fertility has implications for the age structure of the population, leading to a high proportion of young dependants. It puts a strain on an LDC's limited resources because of the need to provide education for so many children, and in this sense high population growth can prove an obstacle to development.

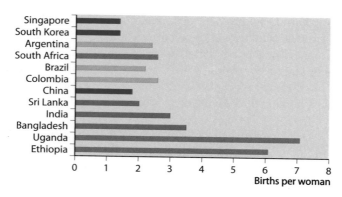

*Figure 27.6*
*Total fertility rates, selected countries, 2000–05*

Source: *Human Development Report,* 2004.

This argument might be countered by pointing out that people themselves are a resource for the country. However, it is a question of the balance between population and the availability of resources.

## Summary

➤ Early writers such as Malthus were pessimistic about the prospects for sustained development, believing that diminishing returns to labour would constrain economic growth.

➤ Globally, population is growing rapidly, with most of the increase taking place in less developed countries.

➤ Developed countries and some LDCs have been seen to pass through a demographic transition, such that population growth stabilises following decreases in death and birth rates.

➤ However, many LDCs have not completed the transition, remaining in the rapid population growth phase.

➤ Coupled with the age structure of the population, rapid population growth can create difficulties for LDCs because of the pressure on resources.

## Exercise 27.1

Discuss the way in which the age structure of a population may influence its rate of economic growth and development.

## Dependence on primary production

Chapter 25 mentioned that many LDCs, especially in sub-Saharan Africa, continue to rely heavily on the agricultural sector to provide employment and incomes. Because labour productivity in agriculture tends to be relatively low, this may keep rural incomes low. The pressures of population growth tend to reinforce this dependence.

It is worth being aware that one of the driving forces behind the Industrial Revolution in Britain was an increase in agricultural productivity, enabling more workers to shift into manufacturing activity. In an LDC context, this transition may run into a number of problems. In some LDCs, the problem stems from the form of land tenancy agreements, which can lead to inefficiency. In other cases, problems arise because of insecure property rights and the inheritance laws that pertain.

### Land tenancy

One characteristic of many LDCs is that land is unequally distributed. If a landowner has more land than can be farmed as a single unit, it is likely that he will hire out parcels of land to small farmers. The way in which this is done turns out to be important for productivity and incentives.

One common form of land tenancy agreement in LDCs is **sharecropping.** In this system a tenant-farmer and a landlord of a piece of land have an agreement to share the resulting crop. The tenant-farmers in this case act as *agents*, farming the land on behalf of the landlord (the *principal*). The landlord would like the farmers to maximise returns from the land. However, the tenants will set out to balance the return received with the cost of producing the crop in terms of work effort. A *principal–agent problem* arises here, since if tenants receive only a portion of the crop, their incentive will be to supply less effort than is optimal for the landlord. There is also an asymmetric information problem, in the sense that the landlord cannot easily monitor the amount of effort being provided by a tenant. The tenants know how much of the low output results from low effort, and how much from unfavourable weather conditions — but the landlord does not. The problems that can arise from *asymmetric information* are discussed in Chapter 7.

**Key** *term*

**sharecropping:** a form of land tenure system in which the landlord and tenant share the crop

Notice that, under a sharecropping contract, tenants have little incentive to invest in improving the land or production methods, because part of the reward for

*The efficiency of agricultural production in many LDCs is hampered by the form of land tenancy agreements*

innovation goes to the landlord. On the other hand, the risk of the venture is shared between the landlord and the tenant, as well as the returns.

An alternative would be for the landlord to charge the tenants a fixed rent for farming the land. This would provide better incentives for them to work hard, as they would now receive all of the returns. However, it would also mean that they carried all the risk involved — if the harvest is poor, it is the tenants who will suffer, having paid a fixed rent for the land.

Yet another possibility would be for the landlord to hire tenants on a wage contract, and pay a fixed wage for their farming the land. This again would provide little incentive for the tenants to supply effort, as the wage would be paid regardless. As the landlord may not be able to monitor the supply of effort, this would create a problem. Moreover, the landlord would now face all of the risk.

Thus, for these forms of tenancy, careful consideration needs to be given to the incentives for work effort, the incentives for innovation and investment, and the sharing of risk.

**Land ownership**

In other circumstances, inheritance laws can damage agricultural productivity: for example, where land is divided between sons on the death of the head of household, which means that the average plot size declines in successive generations. In some societies, property rights are inadequate: for example, women may not be permitted to own land, which can bring problems given that much of the agricultural labour is provided by women. Furthermore, in an attempt to make the best of adverse circumstances, over-farming and a lack of crop rotation practices can mean that soil becomes less productive over time. All of this makes it more difficult to achieve improvements in productivity in the agricultural sector.

Poverty is thus perpetuated over time; and with limited resources available for survival, farmers have no chance to adopt innovative farming practices. The very fact that people are struggling to make the best of the resources and arrangements available may make it difficult for them to step back and look for broader improvements that would allow the reform of economic and social institutions.

Although these are important issues, it may be difficult for governments to devise policies to promote more efficient contracts, or changes in land ownership. The question of land ownership and land tenure is an example of how the legal and cultural framework may sometimes inhibit development, and land reform may be regarded as an important aspect of development.

# Unemployment and underemployment

With the rural areas experiencing low incomes and high population growth, it is perhaps natural that people should want to migrate to the urban areas in search of higher incomes and an escape from poverty — a process known as **urbanisation**.

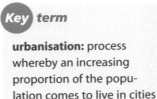

Migration occurs in response to a number of factors. One is the attraction of the 'bright lights' of the cities — people in rural areas often perceive urban areas as offering better access to education and healthcare facilities, and better recreational opportunities. Perhaps more important are the economic gains to be made from migrating to the cities, in terms of the wage differential between urban and rural areas.

**Key** term

**urbanisation:** process whereby an increasing proportion of the population comes to live in cities

Urban wages tend to be higher for a number of reasons. Employment in the manufacturing or service sectors typically offers higher wages, in contrast to the low productivity and wages in the agricultural sector. In addition, labour in the urban areas tends to be better organised, and governments have often introduced minimum wage legislation and social protection for workers in the urban areas — especially where they rely on them for electoral support.

Such wage differentials attract a flow of migrants to the cities. However, in practice there may not be sufficient jobs available, as the new and growing sectors typically do not expand quickly enough to absorb all the migrating workers. The net result is that rural workers exchange poor living conditions in the rural areas for unemployment in the urban environment.

This can be partly regarded as an *externality* effect. Consider Figure 27.7. Here *MPB* represents the marginal private benefit that migrants expect to gain from moving to the cities. *MPC* represents the marginal private costs that migrants face in relocating. Thus, people will migrate up to the point $Q_0$. However, migrants impose costs on other urban dwellers, in terms of congestion, pollution, noise and perhaps in the rise of shanty towns that allow disease to spread. In other words, there are externality effects on other urban residents, and marginal social costs (*MSC*) are higher than the private costs perceived by migrants. As a result, society would prefer to be at $Q^*$ in terms of city size.

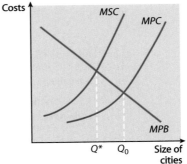

**Figure 27.7**
*The externality effect of migration*

Figure 27.8 shows the rate of migration since 1975, and projected to 2015, in a range of countries. For example, in Tanzania the percentage of the population living in the urban areas was just 10.1% in 1975, but is projected to rise to 46.8% in 2015. The pressure on urban infrastructure from such a change is substantial. An offshoot of this is the growth of the informal sector, as was mentioned in Chapter 25. New migrants are likely to become involved in the informal sector while searching for a formal job, and some of them may remain in the informal sector, given the shortage of formal sector job opportunities.

One way of viewing this process is that rural poverty has encouraged people to exchange rural underemployment and poverty for urban unemployment, or underemployment in the informal sector.

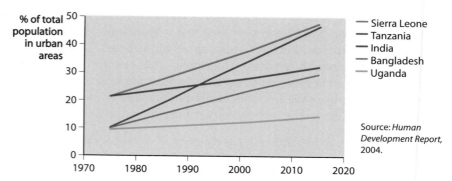

Figure 27.8 *Urbanisation in LDCs, selected countries, 1975–2015 (projected)*

Source: *Human Development Report, 2004.*

# The impact of HIV/AIDS

The HIV/AIDS epidemic has had a major impact on LDCs, especially in sub-Saharan Africa. The relative incidence of the disease across regions is illustrated in Figure 27.9. The high prevalence in sub-Saharan Africa is clearly visible. However, this conceals large differences between countries. There are countries in sub-Saharan Africa where the prevalence is unimaginably high: for example, in Botswana it was estimated that in 2003 some 37.3% of the population aged 15–49 was affected; and in Swaziland the prevalence rate was 38.8%.

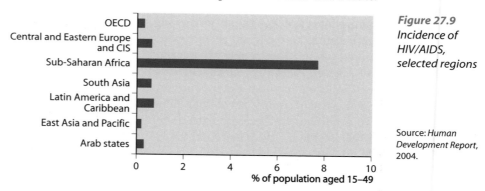

Figure 27.9 *Incidence of HIV/AIDS, selected regions*

Source: *Human Development Report, 2004.*

The repercussions of the disease are especially marked because of its impact on people of working age. This has affected the size of the labour force and left many orphans with little hope of receiving an education, which in turn has implications for the productivity of future generations.

Governments have reacted to the disease in very different ways. In countries where the government has been open about the onset of the disease and has striven to promote safe sex, the chances of keeping the disease under control are much higher. For example, in 1990 the incidence of HIV/AIDS amongst adults in Thailand and South Africa was similar, at about 1%. Thailand confronted the problem through a widespread public campaign such that, by 2001, the incidence was still about 1%. South Africa did little to stop the spread of the disease, with the

president choosing to downplay the problem. In 2001 the incidence of the disease in South Africa was estimated to be about 25%. Some other governments have also kept silent, perhaps not wanting to admit that it is a problem, and in their countries the disease has run rampant. There may also be problems in measuring the incidence of HIV/AIDS accurately, as individuals may be hesitant to seek treatment or to report that they have the disease for fear of social stigma.

## The need for structural change

Given the difficulties caused by overreliance on primary production and the burgeoning urban informal sector, a key question concerns structural change. A transformation of the structure of economic activity seems crucial for growth and development to take place, but how can this be initiated? A major problem is that the rate of growth that would be needed in the industrial sector to absorb the number of workers looking for employment is far in excess of what has been — or could be — achieved. This poses a substantial challenge for LDCs.

Models such as the Harrod–Domar model highlight the importance of saving and investment for the growth process, as it is only through this channel that the productive capacity of the economy can be raised in the long run. This applies particularly to a situation in which an LDC is looking for structural change through the expansion of manufacturing activity. In order for a flow of funds for investment to be mobilised, and in order for those funds to be appropriately channelled into productive investment, fully functioning financial markets are needed.

## Lack of financial markets

Chapter 26 identified some of the problems that may arise in an LDC in terms of generating a flow of savings, and in channelling those funds into productive investment. The undeveloped nature of financial markets is especially problematic in the rural areas, where the lack of formal financial markets makes borrowing to invest in agricultural improvements almost impossible.

One of the problems is that the cost of establishing rural branches of financial institutions in remote areas is high; the fixed costs of making loans for relatively small-scale projects are similarly high. This is intensified by the difficulty that banks have in obtaining information about the creditworthiness of small borrowers, who typically may have no collateral to offer.

Attempts have been made to remedy this situation through *microfinance* schemes. This approach was pioneered by the Grameen Bank, which was founded in Bangladesh in 1976. The bank made small-scale loans to groups of women who otherwise would have had no access to credit, and each group was made corporately responsible for paying back the loan. The scheme has claimed great success, both in terms of the constructive use of the funds in getting small-scale projects off the ground and in terms of high payback rates.

## Case study  The Grameen Bank

In 1974 a severe famine afflicted Bangladesh, and a flood of starving people converged on the capital city, Dhaka. Muhammad Yunus was an economics professor at Chittagong University. He tells how he was struck by the extreme contrast between the neat and abstract economic theories that he was teaching, and the plight and suffering of those surviving in bare poverty, and suffering and dying in the famine.

He also tells how he decided to study the problem at first hand, taking his students on field trips into villages near to the campus. On one of these visits they interviewed a woman who was struggling to make a living by making bamboo stools. For each stool that she made, she had to borrow the equivalent of 15 pence for the raw materials. Once she had paid back the loan, at interest rates of up to 10% per week, her profit margin was just 1p. The woman was never able to escape from her situation because she was trapped by the need to borrow, and the need to pay back at such punitive rates of interest. Her story was by no means unique, and Yunus was keen to find a way of enabling women like her to have access to credit on conditions that would allow them to escape from poverty. He began experimenting by lending out some of his own money to groups in need.

Muhammad Yunus launched the Grameen Bank experiment in 1976. The idea was to provide credit for small-scale income-generating activities. Loans would be provided without the need for collateral, with borrowers being required to form themselves into groups of five with joint responsibility for the repayments. The acceptance of this joint responsibility and the lack of collateral helped to minimise the transaction costs of making and monitoring the loans.

On any criteria, the project proved an enormous success. The repayment record has been impressive, although the Grameen Bank charges interest rates close to those in the formal commercial sector — which are much lower than the informal money-lenders. After the initial launch of the Bank, lending has been channelled primarily to women borrowers, who are seen to invest more carefully and to repay more reliably — and to be most in need. Table 27.1 offers some information about the scale and scope of the Grameen Bank by the late 1990s.

| | |
|---|---:|
| No. of villages where Grameen operates | 38,551 |
| No. of Grameen centres | 65,960 |
| No. of branches | 1,112 |
| No. of staff | 12,589 |
| No. of Grameen members | |
|    Female | 2,210,160 |
|    Male | 124,620 |
|    Total | 2,334,780 |
| Cumulative no. of houses built with | |
|    Grameen housing loans | 438,764 |

*Table 27.1 The Grameen Bank as of 31 May 1998*

Source: *Muhammad Yunus, Banker to the Poor*, Aurum Press, London, 1998.

By the end of May 1998 more than $2.4 billion had been loaned by the Grameen Bank, including more than 2 million loans for milch cows, nearly 100,000 for rickshaws, 57,000 for sewing machines and many more for processing, agriculture, trading, shopkeeping, peddling and other activities. Grameen-type credit programmes are now operating in 59 countries in Africa, Asia, the Americas, Europe and Papua New Guinea.

As for the impact of Grameen loans in economic terms, the loans are seen to have generated new employment, to have reduced the number of days workers are inactive, and to have raised income, food consumption and living conditions of Grameen Bank members — not to mention their social impact on the lives of millions of women.

Other schemes have involved groups of households pooling their savings in order to accumulate enough funds to launch small projects. Members of the group take

it in turns to use these joint savings, paying the loan back in order for the next person to have a turn. These are known as *rotating savings and credit schemes (ROSCAs)*, and they have had some success in providing credit for small schemes. In spite of some successful enterprises, however, such schemes have been found to be less sustainable than Grameen-style arrangements, and have tended to be used to obtain consumer durable goods rather than for productive investment and innovation.

## Case study  Example of a ROSCA

Suppose that 12 individuals are saving for a bicycle (a key form of transport in many developing countries). A bicycle costs $130, and each individual saves $10 per month. Simple arithmetic indicates that it would take 13 months for enough funds to have accumulated for the 12 individuals to buy their bicycles. Suppose that the 12 people agree to work together. First, they explain to the bicycle dealer that there is a guaranteed order for 12 bicycles, and they negotiate a discount of $10 per bicycle. They then meet at the end of each month, and each pays $10 into the fund. At the end of the first month,

there are sufficient funds for one person to buy a bicycle — usually chosen by a lottery. As a result, even the last person in turn gets the bicycle earlier because of the discount they negotiated. Of course, without the discount, one unfortunate person would have to wait the full period, but clearly this is a very efficient way of making use of small amounts of savings. With more people, or higher contributions, the funds can be used for more substantial projects. Administration costs are minimal, but the schemes do rely on trust, such that the first person to win the lottery does not then stop making payments.

In the absence of such schemes, households may be forced to borrow from local moneylenders, often at very high rates of interest. For example, a survey by the Bank of Uganda found that households were paying rates between 0% (when borrowing from family members) and 500%. In part this may reflect a high risk of the borrower's defaulting, but it may also reflect the ability of local moneylenders to use market power. The absence of insurance markets may also deter borrowing for productive investment, especially in rural areas.

## Macroeconomic instability

In the World Bank's market-friendly view of the growth process, macroeconomic stability is highlighted as one of the key conditions that enable markets to work effectively. There are two aspects to this argument. One is that firms will be reluctant to undertake investment if they find it difficult to predict future market conditions. If inflation is high and volatile, it will not be easy for firms to form expectations about the future, so this will discourage investment. Second, it is argued that prices will fail to act as reliable signals to guide resource allocation when inflation is either high or unstable. This may then distort the pattern of resource allocation, which may be especially important for LDCs that are trying to improve the allocation of resources, and to encourage a process of structural change.

Inflation has been a feature of some — but not all — LDCs. It was a prominent feature of many Latin American economies, peaking during the 1980s at annual rates above 1,000%. However, the relationship between inflation and economic growth is a complex one. It is true that few countries that have experienced very high inflation rates have been successful in terms of economic growth. It is also the case that countries that have experienced rapid growth have maintained relatively low inflation rates. Nonetheless, there are countries that have maintained low inflation rates, but have then experienced slow (or even negative) growth rates. A tentative conclusion might be that low inflation is necessary for rapid growth to take place, but not sufficient. In other words, low inflation may be a crucial part of a growth strategy, but achieving it does not guarantee rapid growth.

## Government failure

Such periods of hyperinflation partly reflected government failure. Many Latin American economies ran large fiscal deficits in this period, financing these through money creation, which led inexorably to galloping inflation. It was claimed by some (mainly Latin American) writers that inflation could be of benefit to economic growth, by redistributing income towards those in the economy with a high marginal propensity to save — namely, the government and the rich. However, there is no conclusive evidence that this does lead to higher growth, as governments cannot always be relied upon to use the funds wisely, and the rich have a tendency to indulge in luxury consumption, rather than undertaking productive investment.

Government failure has been important in many LDCs, and not only in relation to fiscal indiscipline. Governments that depend upon being re-elected may be tempted to introduce policies that are more designed to keep them in power than to foster long-term economic development. One common manifestation of this has been observed in relation to food prices. In a number of cases, governments depend primarily on the urban population to vote them back into office. Governments then may be tempted to introduce policies that are pro-urban. This might mean, for example, imposing low prices for food in order to combat urban poverty. This has undesirable effects as it affects the incentives for farmers and may thus inhibit growth. Similarly, minimum wage legislation may have the effect of leading to higher unemployment — again, mainly in the urban areas, where such legislation is likely to bite more strongly.

## Sustainability

Economic growth may have important effects on the environment, and in pursuing growth, countries must bear in mind the need for **sustainable development**, safeguarding the needs of future generations as well as the needs of the present.

 **term**

**sustainable development:** 'development which meets the needs of the present without compromising the ability of future generations to meet their own needs' (Brundtland Commission, 1987)

430

OCR Advanced Economics

These issues have been widely discussed in the context of the more developed countries. However, the issue is equally important for LDCs. Deforestation has been a problem for many LDCs that have areas of rainforest. In some cases, logging for timber has destroyed large areas of valuable land; in other cases, land has been cleared for unsuitable agricultural use. This sort of activity creates relatively little present value, and leaves a poorer environment for future generations.

Another aspect of environmental degradation concerns *biodiversity*. This refers to the way in which misuse of the environment is contributing to the loss of plant species — not to mention those of birds, insects and mammals — which are becoming extinct as their natural habitat is destroyed. Some of the lost species may not even have been discovered yet. Given the natural healing properties of many plants, this could mean the destruction of plants that might provide significant new drugs for use in medicine. But how can something be valued when its very existence is as yet unknown?

One way of viewing the environment is as a factor of production that needs to be used effectively, just like any other factor of production. In other words, each country has a stock of *environmental* capital that needs to be utilised in the best possible way.

However, if the environmental capital is to be used appropriately, it must be given an appropriate value and this can be problematic. If property rights are not firmly established — as they are not in many LDCs — it is difficult to enforce legislation to protect the environment. Furthermore, if the environment (as a factor of production) is underpriced, then 'too much' of it will be used by firms.

There are externality effects at work here too, in the sense that the loss of biodiversity is a global loss, and not just something affecting the local economy. In some cases there have been international externality effects of a more direct kind, such as when forest fires in Indonesia caused the airport in Singapore to close down because of the resulting smoke haze.

China has been one of the fastest-growing economies in the world since 1978. To have averaged almost 8% growth per annum over such a long period is extraordinary. In 2004 the *Asian Development Bank* reported that China's GDP had grown by 9.1% in 2003, and it predicted that in 2004 the country's growth would account for 15% of the expected expansion in the *world* economy. Exports from the rest of the world to China grew by 34.6% in 2003.

In August 2004, *The Economist* reported that 16 of the world's most polluted cities are now located in China, and that around half of China's population (i.e. some 600 million people) have water supplies that are contaminated by animal and human waste. River systems are heavily polluted, and air pollution is becoming a serious issue, partly as a result of the country's heavy reliance on coal-fired electricity generation. Shanghai's environmental protection bureau estimated that 70% of the 1 million cars in Shanghai do not reach even the oldest European emission standard.

This illustrates the trade-off between rapid economic growth and protection of the environment. The other factor in the equation is the desire to alleviate poverty. The

World Bank estimated that in 2003, some 216 million people in China were living in poverty — defined as living on less than $1 per day. The need to bring so many people out of extreme poverty lends urgency to the drive for economic growth. However, this needs to be balanced against the need to ensure sustainable development. In other words, economic growth must be achieved in such a way that it does not destroy the environment for future generations.

*In 2003, some 216 million people in China were living in poverty*

There are many aspects to this issue, of which protecting the environment is just one. Sustainable development also entails taking account of the depletion rates of non-renewable resources, and ensuring that renewable resources *are* renewed in the process of economic growth.

So, although economic growth is important to a society, the drive for growth must be tempered by an awareness of the possible trade-offs with other important objectives.

## External obstacles to growth and development

Not all of the obstacles facing LDCs in their quest for growth and development arise from domestic factors. The law of comparative advantage highlights the fact that countries can gain through specialisation. It is not necessary to have an *absolute* advantage to benefit from specialisation and trade, so long as there is some source of *comparative* advantage. In the case of most LDCs, it may be crucial to be able to import some goods that cannot be produced domestically. For example, there are few LDCs that are capable of producing capital goods, although these are extremely important if a process of industrialisation is to be initiated.

However, although the law of comparative advantage identifies the potential gains from international trade, it does not guarantee that those gains can actually be made, and the terms under which trade takes place may place limits on the extent to which LDCs can benefit. There may thus be external obstacles that will affect LDCs.

## Trade in primary goods

The law of comparative advantage argues that countries may gain from trade by specialising in the production of goods and services in which they have a comparative advantage. For LDCs such comparative advantage almost inevitably lies in the production of labour- and/or land-intensive goods. LDCs tend to have relatively abundant natural resources and labour, but scarce capital. This pattern determines the nature of their comparative advantage. Figure 27.10 shows the extent to which some LDCs depend upon primary exports. You can see that this varies substantially between countries.

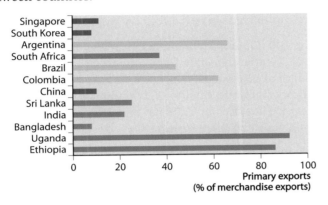

*Figure 27.10*
*Dependence on primary exports, selected countries*

Source: *Human Development Report*, 2004.

However, it is now being argued that LDCs should try to reduce their reliance on primary production and develop new activities. It is clearly important to investigate how these two different arguments can be reconciled: in other words, to explore why it is that LDCs cannot continue to rely on their existing comparative advantage.

It is worth noting that some countries are heavily dependent not just on primary products in general, but on a very narrow range of primary products — in some cases, a single commodity. Figure 27.11 shows the extent to which some countries rely on a narrow range of commodities. This dependence creates a situation of great vulnerability if the markets for those commodities are not stable. It must be remembered that most LDCs are relatively small players in international markets, so may have little or no influence over price.

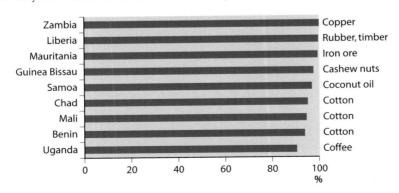

*Figure 27.11*
*Dependence on non-fuel primary commodity exports (as a percentage of total merchandise exports)*

Source: World Trade Organization, *World Trade Report*, 2003.

There are two ways in which LDCs have been affected by the pattern of their comparative advantage in the conduct of international trade. These relate to the short-run and long-run movements in relative prices – the **terms of trade**.

**Key** *term*

**terms of trade:** the ratio of export prices to import prices

Suppose that both export and import prices are rising through time, but import prices are rising more rapidly than export prices. This means that the ratio of export to import prices will fall – which in turn means that a country must export a greater volume of its goods in order to acquire the same volume of imports. In other words, a fall in the terms of trade makes a country worse off.

Suppose a country imports 100,000 units of a manufactured good each year and that the price in year 1 is £1. In order to pay for these imported goods, the country exports 100,000 units of agricultural goods, which are also priced at £1 per unit in year 1. In year 2 the country still wants to buy 100,000 units of imported manufactures, but finds that the price has risen to £1.08 per unit. Furthermore, the price of its exported agricultural goods has fallen to 90p.

The terms of trade are calculated as the ratio of export prices to import prices. In year 1 this is $100 \times 1/1 = 100$. However, in year 2 the calculation is $100 \times 0.90/1.08 = 83.3$. There has thus been an appreciable deterioration in the terms of trade.

The effects of this can be seen in the volume of exports that are now needed for the country to maintain its volume of imports. In order to buy its 100,000 units of imports, the country now needs to export $100,000 \times 1.08/0.9 = 120,000$ units of exports.

One problem faced by LDCs that export primary products is that they are each too small as individual exporters to be able to influence the world price of their products. They must accept the prices that are set in world commodity markets.

### Short-run volatility

In the case of agricultural goods, demand tends to be relatively stable over time, but supply can be volatile, varying with weather and climatic conditions from season to season. Figure 27.12 shows a typical market in two periods. In period 1 the global harvest of this commodity is poor, with supply given by $S_1$: equilibrium is achieved with price at $P_1$ and quantity traded at $Q_1$. In period 2 the global harvest is high at $S_2$, so that prices plummet to $P_2$ and quantity traded rises to $Q_2$.

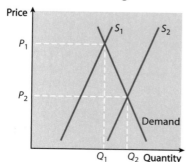

**Figure 27.12**
*Volatility in supply*

Notice that in this case the movement of prices is relatively strong compared with the variation in quantity. This reflects the price elasticity of demand, which is expected to be relatively inelastic for many primary products. From the consumers' point of view, the demand for foodstuffs and other agricultural goods will tend to be inelastic, as demand will not be expected to respond strongly to changes in prices.

For many minerals and raw materials, however, the picture is different. For such commodities, supply tends to be stable over time, but demand fluctuates with the business cycle in developed countries, which are the importers of raw materials. Figure 27.13 illustrates this. At the trough of the business cycle, demand is low, at $D_1$, and so the equilibrium price will also be low, at $P_1$. At the peak of the cycle, demand is more buoyant, at $D_2$, and price is relatively high, at $P_2$.

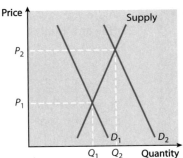

*Figure 27.13*
*Volatility in demand*

From an individual LDC's point of view, the result is the same: the country faces volatility in the prices of its exports. From this perspective it does not matter whether the instability arises from the supply side of the market or from the demand side. The problem is that prices can rise and fall quite independently of conditions within the domestic economy.

Instability of prices also means instability of export revenues, so if the country is relying on export earnings to fund its development path, to import capital equipment or to meet its debt repayments, such volatility in earnings can constitute a severe problem, e.g. if export earnings fall such that a country is unable to meet its commitments to repaying debt.

### Long-run deterioration
The nature of the demand for primary products may be expected to influence the long-run path of relative prices. In particular, the income elasticity of demand is an important consideration. As real incomes rise in the developed countries, the demand for agricultural goods can be expected to rise relatively slowly. Ernst Engel pointed out that at relatively high income levels, the proportion of expenditure devoted to foodstuffs tends to fall and the demand for luxury goods rises. This suggests that the demand for agricultural goods shifts relatively slowly through time.

In the case of raw materials, there have been advances in the development of artificial substitutes for many commodities used in manufacturing. Furthermore, technology has changed over time, improving the efficiency with which inputs can be converted into outputs. This has weakened the demand for raw materials produced by LDCs.

Furthermore, if some LDCs are successful in boosting output of these goods, there will be an increase in supply over time. Figure 27.14 shows the result of such an increase. Suppose that the market begins with demand at $D_0$ and supply at $S_0$. Market equilibrium results in a price of $P_0$ and quantity of $Q_0$. As time goes by, demand moves

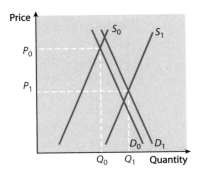

*Figure 27.14*
*Long-term movements of demand and supply*

to the right a little to $D_1$, and supply shifts to $S_1$. The result is a fall in the price of the commodity to $P_1$.

It is thus clear that, not only may LDCs experience short-run volatility in prices, but the terms of trade may also deteriorate in the long run. Some of these arguments were advanced by Raul Prebisch and Hans Singer in the early 1950s. They produced some empirical evidence to support their case, suggesting that the terms of trade had moved in favour of manufactured goods over a long period of time. Figure 27.15 provides some more recent evidence on this situation, showing the relative price of non-fuel primary commodities (compared with manufactured goods) during the twentieth century. You can see that the long-run trend is downwards.

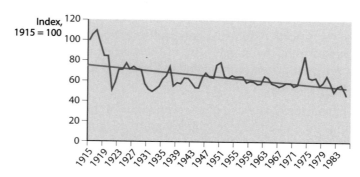

**Figure 27.15**
*Index of the price of non-fuel primary commodities relative to manufactured goods, 1915–85*

Source: Enzo Grilli and Maw Cheng Yang, *World Bank Economic Review*, January 1988.

In the light of the twin problems of short-run volatility and long-run deterioration in the terms of trade, it is perhaps no surprise that many LDCs see themselves as trapped by their pattern of comparative advantage, rather than being in a position to exploit it. They are therefore reluctant to continue in such a state of dependency on primary products, but the process of diversification into a wide range of products has been difficult to achieve.

## International debt

For some LDCs, these problems have been compounded by strategies adopted to cope with balance of payments problems. The origins of this date back to the time of the first oil price crisis in 1973/74, when oil prices were suddenly raised by a substantial percentage. For many oil-importing countries, this posed a major problem, as the demand for oil was relatively inelastic, so the increase in the price of oil led immediately to a deficit on the current account of the balance of payments. Borrowing from the International Monetary Fund (IMF) was one solution, as offering help with short-run balance of payments problems is exactly the role that the IMF was designed to fulfil. However, IMF loans come with strings attached, so many LDCs in the late 1970s looked elsewhere for funds, borrowing from commercial sources. Such loans were often on variable interest rate terms. In the 1980s, oil prices rose again. Furthermore, interest rates rose worldwide when governments in North America and Western Europe adopted strict monetary policies. This created problems for many LDCs that had borrowed heavily —

especially those that had not perhaps used the funds as wisely as they might have. Some countries in Latin America threatened to default on their loans, and various plans had to be devised to salvage the financial system.

The problems of debt have proved a major obstacle to development in many countries. Latin American countries were affected strongly, as they had borrowed large amounts in US dollar terms. Countries in sub-Saharan Africa had borrowed less in money terms, but accumulated debts that were substantial relative to GDP or exports. They thus found that a high share of their export revenues were being used to make payments on past debts, and were thus not available for promoting development at home. The problem reached a point at which it was clear that the debt burdens of many LDCs were unsustainable, and the World Bank launched an initiative to tackle the problem. This is discussed in Chapter 28.

## Diversity in development

With all these obstacles to growth and development, from both internal and external sources, it would be easy to despair of ever being able to tackle poverty in the world. However, it is important to remember that not all countries face all of the obstacles. Countries face different configurations of characteristics and problems, and such diversity needs to be matched by diversity in the design of policies to promote growth and development. Policy issues are the subject of the next chapter.

## Summary

➤ The pattern of existing comparative advantage suggests that LDCs should specialise in the production of primary commodities such as agricultural goods, minerals or other raw materials.

➤ However, the prices of such goods tend to be volatile in the short run, varying from year to year as a result of instability arising from either the supply side or the demand side.

➤ Furthermore, the nature of demand for such products and the development of artificial substitutes for some raw materials may be expected to lead to a long-run deterioration in the terms of trade for primary producers.

➤ These factors will limit the extent to which LDCs benefit from international trade in primary commodities.

➤ International debt also grew to be a major obstacle to development for many countries.

## Exercise 27.2

Looking back over the nature of the economic growth process and the obstacles to growth that have been outlined, discuss the extent to which countries in sub-Saharan Africa may be able to use the pattern of development that was so successful in East Asia to promote growth.

# Chapter 28
# Policies to promote development

*The previous chapters in this part of the book have identified a range of problems faced by less developed countries (LDCs). The governments of LDCs that wish to stimulate development need to devise policies that will make the best possible use of the resources available to them domestically. However, in many cases, domestic resources are lacking, so it is important to consider the alternative possibility of mobilising resources from outside the country. This can be done by attracting foreign direct investment, accepting overseas assistance or borrowing on international capital markets. This chapter reviews policy possibilities from both domestic and international perspectives, and also considers the role of the World Bank, the International Monetary Fund (IMF) and the World Trade Organization (WTO).*

## Learning outcomes

After studying this chapter, you should:
➤ be aware of the need for less developed countries to mobilise external resources for development
➤ understand the benefits and costs associated with foreign direct investment
➤ be familiar with the potential use of overseas assistance for promoting development, and the effectiveness of such flows of funds in the past
➤ be aware of the possible use and dangers of borrowing to obtain funds for development
➤ understand the role of the Bretton Woods institutions in international development
➤ be familiar with Structural Adjustment Programmes and the HIPC initiative

## Institutions and development

The design of economic policy must be considered in the context of the economic and institutional environment within which policy measures are implemented. The role of institutions in the development process has increasingly been seen as an important one in recent years. LDC governments, multilateral institutions such as the World Bank, non-governmental organisations and major trade groupings like the European Union all contribute to the policy environment. The interactions between them are also extremely important.

chapter 28

## LDC governments

The governments of LDCs have the ultimate responsibility for designing their domestic economic and development policy, but it has often been argued that many are ill-equipped to devise and implement the sorts of policies that are required to stimulate the process of development. This is partly related to the level of development of the political and cultural systems in LDCs, and may also depend upon the existence (or absence) of a reliable and non-corrupt bureaucracy that would enable policies to be set in motion. Another major factor to remember is the constraint that LDC governments face in terms of resources. Where average incomes are low and tax collection systems are undeveloped, governments have difficulty in generating a flow of revenue domestically, which is needed in order to launch policies encouraging growth and development.

In some cases, governments have tended to rely on taxes on international trade, which are relatively easy to administer, rather than on domestic direct or indirect taxes. Naturally, this has not helped to stimulate international trade.

Some LDC governments have responded to the problem by borrowing funds from abroad. However, in many cases such funds have not been best used. They have sometimes been used for prestige projects, which impress lenders (or donors) but do little to further development. Other funds have been diverted into private use by government officials, and there are well-documented examples of politicians, officials and civil servants accumulating personal fortunes at the expense of their countries' development. Figure 28.1 presents a Corruption Perception Index, produced regularly by the non-governmental organisation Transparency International. Notice how Singapore and South Korea, the tiger economies, are rated as 'highly clean' — indeed, on this index Singapore was the fifth least corrupt nation in the world.

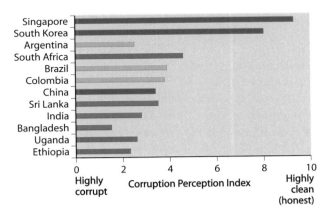

**Figure 28.1**
*Perceptions of corruption, selected countries, 2004*

Source: Transparency International (**www.transparency.org**).

We need to be careful with such indicators, for by its nature corruption is difficult to identify and to measure. It may be disguised more successfully in some countries than in others. Nonetheless, the way in which firms and governments perceive the relative state of corruption in different countries may affect their decisions about where to locate foreign direct investment or provide overseas assistance.

Tendencies towards corruption are likely to be more significant in countries where there is relatively little political stability, so that the government knows it will not remain in power for long. In this situation, it is not only corruption that may be problematic, as in general the incentives for such governments are weak. There is little reason to expect a government to take a long-term view of the development process, and to introduce policies that will only bring benefits in the distant future, if it only faces a short period in office, or if it perceives that it needs to bring in populist policies to ensure re-election. In other words, even in the absence of corruption, there may be little incentive for governments to take a long-term perspective.

## The Bretton Woods institutions

The conduct of international trade is overseen by a number of multilateral institutions. These institutions have been influential in policy design for many LDCs. At the end of the Second World War in 1945, a conference was held at Bretton Woods, New Hampshire, USA, to establish a system of fixed exchange rates. This became known as the *dollar standard*, as countries agreed to fix their currencies relative to the US dollar. John Maynard Keynes was an influential delegate at the conference. In addition to establishing the exchange rate system (which operated until the early 1970s), the conference set up three key institutions with prescribed roles in support of the international financial system.

### International Monetary Fund

The **International Monetary Fund (IMF)** was set up with a specific brief to offer short-term assistance to countries experiencing balance of payments problems. Thus, if a country were running a deficit on the current account, it could borrow from the IMF in order to finance the deficit. However, the IMF would insist that, as a condition of granting the loan, the country needed to put in place policies to deal with the deficit — typically, restrictive monetary and fiscal policies.

### World Bank

The International Bank for Reconstruction and Development was the second institution established under the Bretton Woods agreement. It soon became known as the **World Bank**. The role of the World Bank is to provide longer-term funding for projects that will promote development. Much of this funding is provided at commercial interest rates, as the role of the bank was seen to be the channelling of finance to projects that normal commercial banks would perceive as being too risky. However, some concessional lending is also made through the International Development Association (IDA), which is part of the World Bank.

**Key terms**

**International Monetary Fund (IMF):** multilateral institution that provides short-term financing for countries experiencing balance of payments problems

**World Bank:** multilateral organisation that provides financing for long-term development projects

**General Agreement on Tariffs and Trade (GATT):** the precursor of the WTO, it organised a series of 'rounds' of tariff reductions

**World Trade Organization (WTO):** multilateral body responsible for overseeing the conduct of international trade

## World Trade Organization

Initially, Bretton Woods set up the **General Agreement on Tariffs and Trade (GATT)**, with a brief to oversee international trade. This entailed encouraging countries to reduce tariffs, but GATT also provided a forum for trade negotiations and for settling disputes between countries.

GATT was replaced by the **World Trade Organization (WTO)** in 1995. Between them, these organisations have presided over a significant reduction in the barriers to trade between countries — not only tariffs, but other forms of protection too.

## Non-governmental organisations

There are many non-governmental organisations (NGOs) that have been active in the development field. Many of these are non-profit-making charities, sometimes known as private voluntary organisations. They operate in the private sector, although they often act as channels for official development funds. NGOs have been active in providing and channelling emergency humanitarian aid to countries that have experienced some form of natural catastrophe, but have also been active in providing funds for long-term development projects.

NGOs have played an important role in areas where governments and official organisations may find difficulty. For example, they have been able to operate at the very local level, funding and overseeing small-scale projects in rural areas of many LDCs. Among the better-known NGOs are Oxfam, CAFOD and Save the Children Fund.

A further way in which NGOs have played a valuable role in promoting development is through *advocacy*. NGOs have acted as pressure groups, trying to persuade governments and the Bretton Woods institutions to adopt policies that are more favourable towards LDCs. In this, they have acted as the voice of the poor on an international stage. Perhaps the most public — and successful — example of such advocacy was the *Jubilee 2000* campaign, in which pressure was put on the World Bank and the IMF to alter their stance towards debt relief. This is discussed later in the chapter.

## Trade groupings

For many LDCs, the process of development has been strongly influenced by the operations of major trade groupings and trading nations. LDCs need to engage in international trade in order to exploit comparative advantage, and to obtain goods (especially capital goods) that they are unable to produce domestically. However, the power of the USA and Japan, and of trade groupings such as the EU, is such that they are able to influence the terms under which trade takes place. This does not always work in favour of the LDCs. When the EU acts to protect its farmers, or the USA tries to protect its cotton producers, this places obstacles in the way of LDCs which are keen to be able to export their own crops. Thus it may be that, on the one hand, the World Bank encourages LDCs to focus on expanding their export activity, whilst on the other hand, the major potential importing nations set up protectionist barriers in order to protect their own markets. This naturally creates tension in international

relations, and gives weight to the arguments of the dependency theorists (see Chapter 26).

## Summary

➤ Governments in LDCs have limited resources with which to encourage a more rapid rate of economic growth and development.

➤ Corruption and poor governance have meant that some of the resources that have been available have not been used wisely in some LDCs.

➤ The Bretton Woods conference in 1945 set up three major multilateral organisations: the IMF, the World Bank and GATT (which later became the WTO).

➤ The IMF has the role of providing short-term finance for countries experiencing balance of payments problems.

➤ The World Bank provides longer-term financing for development projects.

➤ The WTO oversees the conduct of international trade.

➤ Non-governmental organisations (NGOs) have been active in promoting development and providing a voice for the poor on an international stage.

➤ For LDCs to develop, more cooperation is needed from the more developed countries. However, many of them have tried to protect their domestic producers, thus making it more difficult for LDCs to engage in international trade.

## Markets or state planning?

Chapter 26 outlined the World Bank's view of *market-friendly growth*. The idea is that countries wishing to promote development need to do so in a market-friendly way. This may entail governments doing less in those parts of the economy where markets can be relied upon, but intervening more where market failure is inevitable. The fundamental premise is that economic development should be market led.

An alternative to this approach is to rely on *central planning*. This view of the development process was attractive to many countries, with the Soviet Union being seen as a role model for many years. The breakdown of the Soviet bloc has discredited this approach to some extent, although there are still a few countries that adhere to central planning, such as Cuba and North Korea. Elsewhere, governments have come to see the benefits that derive from allowing market forces to play at least some role in resource allocation. For example, market reforms in China have contributed to that country's outstanding success in achieving rapid economic growth.

Allowing market forces to lead resource allocation has some key advantages over central planning for many LDCs. These arise from the problems mentioned above relating to the lack of reliable bureaucracy in many LDCs and the temptations to corruption. Central planning relies very heavily on bureaucratic structures in order to manage the process of development. It also relies on reliable and detailed

information about the economy. Without these, central planning cannot operate effectively. In contrast, a market system is efficient because it devolves decision making to individuals, and uses prices to provide signals and to coordinate the allocation of resources.

Problems arise where institutions do not enable the free operation of markets, and an early priority in seeking to promote development is to ensure that measures are in place that will allow markets to work. These measures would include such things as secure property rights and the provision of appropriate infrastructure. Indeed, intervention may be needed in various parts of the economy in order to counter problems arising from *market failure.*

It is important to note that views on the extent to which governments need to intervene, and the sort of intervention that may be justified, will depend upon the view taken of the theories of development discussed earlier. For example, if it is believed that an *unbalanced* growth strategy is desirable, then one role for the government could be to identify and encourage the key sectors that will drive the process of growth. A similar strategy might fit Rostow's notion of the take-off. On the other hand, commitment to a *balanced* growth strategy would be more likely to entail government intervention to ensure that the infrastructure needed for the development process was in place.

## Domestic policies for development

The objective of domestic policy is to make the best use of the resources that are available within a society. Policy must also try to balance the need to tackle short-term problems with devising a strategy that will cater for the long run.

A strategy for the long run needs to bear in mind the need for balance in the *structure* of economic activity. This means reducing the dependence on primary production, and moving towards a more diversified economy. A precondition for this is to bring about improvements in agricultural productivity. This enables food production to be secured and may then permit some release of surplus labour into new types of economic activity.

As we saw in the previous section, it is important to be aware of areas of potential market failure that may inhibit development, growth and structural transformation. Of particular importance may be the provision of *infrastructure.* Intervention here is justified because of the public goods characteristics of much infrastructure, which means that there will be insufficient provision if it is left to the private sector. Improved roads and communication links, and market facilities, are examples of public goods that are essential for economic development.

Another area of potential market failure relates to aspects of *human capital.* The presence of information failures and externality effects may combine to prevent efficient provision of education and healthcare. However, these are of vital importance, not only for short-run purposes of alleviating poverty, but also because the improvement of human resources contributes to productivity improvements, and

© Jeremy Horner/ Corbis

*The provision of infrastructure is important to the development of LDCs*

hence to economic growth. To the extent that households make inappropriate decisions on family size, there may also be a need to try to influence the rate of population growth.

LDC governments should also take steps to ensure a *stable macroeconomic environment* in order to enable the private sector to take good decisions. Only in a stable macroeconomic environment will firms be able to form reliable expectations about the future, and thus take good decisions about investment.

If you look back at the section in Chapter 26 that deals with market-friendly growth, you will see that these aspects of domestic policy are the key elements advocated by the World Bank.

Given the parlous state of many LDC economies, such domestic measures are unlikely to be sufficient to stimulate self-sustained development. This partly reflects the severe scarcity of resources faced by many LDC governments. An implication of this is that LDCs must also attempt to mobilise resources from external sources.

## The role of external resources in development

The shortage of resources in many LDCs has been a severe obstacle to their economic growth and development. This was emphasised by the Harrod–Domar model of economic growth which was introduced in Chapter 26. Figure 28.2 offers a reminder.

The underlying process by which growth can take place requires the generation of a flow of savings that can be transformed into investment in order to generate an increase in capital, which in turn enlarges the productive capacity of the economy. This then enables output and incomes to grow, which in turn feeds back into savings and allows the process to become self-sustaining.

However, the process will break down if savings are inadequate, or if markets do not operate sufficiently well to maintain the chain. In considering the possibility that the process could be initiated by an inflow of resources from outside the economy, there are three possible routes to be examined: foreign direct investment, overseas aid and international borrowing. As Figure 28.2 indicates, associated with each of these inflows there are likely to be some costs, and potential leakages from the system.

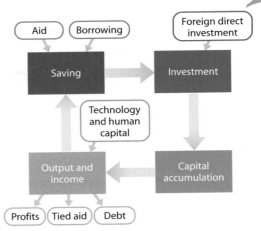

**Figure 28.2** *The Harrod–Domar process of economic development*

### Foreign direct investment

One possible source of external funding that has been attractive to many LDCs is **foreign direct investment (FDI)**. This entails encouraging foreign **multinational corporations (MNCs)** to set up part of their production in an LDC.

In evaluating the potential impact of MNCs operating in LDCs, it is important to consider the characteristics of such companies. Many operate on a large scale, often having an

**Key terms**

**foreign direct investment (FDI):** investment undertaken by foreign companies

**multinational corporation (MNC):** a company whose production activities are carried out in more than one country

annual turnover that exceeds the less developed country's GDP. They tend to have their origins in the developed countries, although some LDCs are now beginning to develop their own MNCs.

MNCs are in business to make profits, and it can be assumed that their motivation is to maximise global after-tax profits. While they may operate in globally oligopolistic markets, they may have monopoly power within the LDCs in which they locate. They operate in a wide variety of different product markets — some are in primary production (Geest, Del Monte, BP), some are in manufacturing (General Motors, Mitsubishi) and some are in tertiary activity (WalMart, McDonald's). These characteristics are important in shaping the analysis of the likely benefits and costs of attracting FDI into an LDC.

MNCs have three basic motivations for locating in another country:
➤ market seeking
➤ resource seeking
➤ efficiency seeking

Some MNCs may engage in FDI because they want to sell their products in a particular market, and find it preferable to produce within the market rather than elsewhere: such FDI is *market seeking*. Other MNCs may undertake investment in a country in order to take advantage of some key resource — say, a natural

resource such as oil or natural gas, or a labour force with certain skills, or simply cheap unskilled labour: such FDI is *resource seeking*. Still other MNCs may simply review their options globally and decide that they can produce most efficiently in a particular location, which might entail locating a part of their production chain in a certain country: such FDI is *efficiency seeking*.

To set a context for the discussion, Figure 28.3 shows the relative size of net FDI inflows for the set of countries selected previously. This reveals a very uneven pattern, with Bangladesh receiving only 0.1% of GDP as inflows of FDI and Singapore receiving 7%.

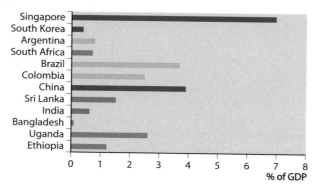

*Figure 28.3*
*Net foreign direct investment flows, selected countries, 2002*

Source: *Human Development Report,* 2004.

In some ways this chart is misleading, as it conceals the true size of FDI inflows into China. Remember that China's GDP is very large, so almost 4% of China's GDP represents a very substantial flow of investment. Some of this is market seeking, as the opening up of China's market of 1.3 billion people is a major attraction. However, it may also be partly resource seeking, with MNCs wanting to take advantage of China's resource of labour.

### Potential benefits

Perhaps the prime motivation for LDCs in attracting FDI inflows is the injection they provide into the Harrod–Domar chain of development. In addition to providing *investment*, MNCs are likely to supply *capital* and *technology*, thereby helping to remedy the LDC's limited capacity to produce capital goods. They may also assist with the development of the country's human capital, by providing training and skills development for the workers they employ, together with management expertise and entrepreneurial skills, all of which may be lacking in the LDC.

LDCs may also hope that the MNC will provide much needed modern-sector *jobs for local workers*. Given the rate of migration to urban areas, such employment could be invaluable to the LDC, where employment cannot keep up with the rapid growth of the labour force.

The LDC government may also expect to be able to collect *tax revenues*, both directly from the MNC in the form of a tax on profits, and indirectly from taxes on the workers' employment incomes. Moreover, the MNC will export its products, and thus generate a flow of foreign exchange for the LDC.

In time, there may also be *spillover effects.* As local workers learn new skills and gain management expertise and knowledge about technology, they may be able to benefit local firms if at some stage they leave the MNC and take up jobs with local companies — or use their new-found knowledge to start their own businesses. These externality effects can be significant in some cases.

### Potential costs

In evaluating the potential benefits of FDI, however, LDCs may need to temper their enthusiasm a little, as there may be costs associated with attracting MNCs to locate within their borders. This would certainly be the case if the anti-glob-alisation protesters are to be believed, as they have accused the MNCs of exploiting their strength and market power, the effect of which can be to damage the LDCs in various ways.

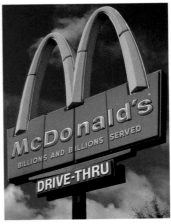

*Some MNCs locate in other countries to seek new markets*

In examining such costs, it is important to be objective and to try to reach a balanced view of the matter. Some of the accusations made by the critics of glob-alisation may have been overstated; on the other hand, it is also important to remember that MNCs are profit-making firms and not humanitarian organisations seeking to promote justice and equality.

A first point to note is that, because most MNCs originate in more developed countries, they tend to use technology that suits the conditions with which they are familiar. In many cases, these will tend to be relatively *capital intensive*, which may not be wholly appropriate for LDC factor endowments. One upshot of this is that the employment effects may not be substantial, or may be limited to relatively low-skilled jobs.

It is dangerous to generalise here. The sort of technology that MNCs tend to use may be entirely suitable for a country like Singapore, which has progressed to the stage where it needs hi-tech capital-intensive activity to match its well-trained and disciplined workforce. However, such technology would not be appropriate in much of sub-Saharan Africa. MNCs are surely aware of such considerations when taking decisions about where to locate. A decision to set up production in China may be partly market oriented, but efficiency considerations will also affect the choice of technology.

An important consideration is whether the MNC will make use of local labour. It might hire local unskilled labour, but use expatriate skilled workers and managers. This would tend to reduce the employment and spillover effects of the MNC presence. Another possibility is that the MNC may pay wages that are higher than necessary in order to maintain a good public image, and to attract the best local workers. (You might like to reread the extension material on pages 296–97 on the *efficiency wage.* The argument for firms paying a higher wage than needed is an efficiency wage argument.) This is fine for the workers lucky enough to be

employed at a high wage, but it can make life difficult for local firms if they cannot hold on to their best workers.

In addition, the LDC government's desire for *tax revenue* may not be fully met. In seeking to attract MNCs to locate within their borders, LDCs may find that they need to offer tax holidays or concessions as a 'carrot'. This will clearly limit the tax revenue benefits that the LDC will receive. It is also possible that MNCs can manipulate their balance sheets in order to minimise their tax liability. A high proportion of the transactions undertaken by an MNC are internal to the firm. Thus, it may be possible to set prices for internal transactions which ensure that profits are taken in the locations with the lowest tax. This process is known as *transfer pricing*. It is not strictly legal, but is difficult to monitor.

As far as the *foreign exchange earnings* are concerned, a key issue is whether the MNC will recycle its surplus within the LDC or repatriate its profits to its shareholders elsewhere in the world. If the latter is the case, this will limit the extent to which the LDC will benefit from the increase in exports. However, at least the MNC will be able to market its products internationally, and if the country becomes better known as a result then, again, there may be spillovers for local firms. Gaining credibility and the knowledge to sell in the global market is problematic for LDCs, and this is one area in which there may be definite benefits from the MNC presence.

The LDC should also be aware that the MNC may use its *market power* within the country to maximise profits. Local competitors will find it difficult to compete, and the MNC may be able to restrict output and raise price. In addition, some MNCs have been accused of taking advantage of more lax environmental regulations, polluting the environment to keep their costs low. The actions of the anti-globalisation protesters in this area may have influenced MNCs to clean up their act somewhat.

Finally, MNCs tend to locate in urban areas in LDCs — unless they are purely resource seeking, in which case they may be forced to locate near the supply of whatever natural resource they are seeking. Locating in the urban areas may increase the *rural–urban inequality* discussed earlier, and encourage an even greater rate of migration.

## Exercise 28.1

Draw up a list of the benefits and costs of MNC involvement in an LDC, and evaluate the benefits relative to the costs. Remember that many LDCs are enthusiastic about attracting MNCs to locate in their countries. Try to identify which are the most important benefits that they are looking for.

Given the need to evaluate the benefits and costs of FDI flows, it is important that LDC governments can negotiate good deals with the MNCs. For example, countries such as Indonesia have negotiated conditions on the share of local

workers that will be employed by the MNC after a period of, say, 5 years. This helps to ensure that the benefits are not entirely dissipated. Of course, it helps if the LDC has some key resource that the MNC cannot readily acquire elsewhere. There is some recent evidence that high levels of human capital help to attract FDI flows, which may help to explain why East Asia and China have been recipients of more FDI inflows than countries in sub-Saharan Africa.

## Summary

➤ Multinational corporations (MNCs) are companies whose production activities are carried out in more than one country.

➤ Foreign direct investment (FDI) by MNCs is one way in which an LDC may be able to attract external resources.

➤ MNCs may be motivated by markets, resources or cost effectiveness.

➤ LDCs hope to benefit from FDI in a wide range of ways, including capital, technology, employment, human capital, tax revenues and foreign exchange. There may also be spillover effects.

➤ However, MNCs may operate in ways that do not maximise these benefits for the LDCs.

### Overseas assistance

If LDCs could enter a phase of economic growth and rising incomes, one result would be an increase in world trade. This would benefit nations around the world, and the more developed industrial countries would be likely to see an increase in the market for their products. This might be a reason for the governments of more developed countries to help LDCs with the growth and development of their economies. Of course, there may also be a humanitarian motive for providing assistance — that is, to reduce global inequality.

Indeed, there may be market failure arguments for providing aid. For example, it may be that governments have better information about the riskiness of projects in LDCs than private firms have. In relation to the provision of education and healthcare, it was argued earlier that externality effects may be involved. However, LDC governments may not have the resources needed to provide sufficient education for their citizens. Similarly, it was argued that some infrastructure may have public good characteristics that require intervention.

Official aid is known as **overseas development assistance (ODA)**, and is provided through the Development Assistance Committee of the OECD. Notice that the

discussion here focuses not on short-run aid to deal with an emergency, such as a drought or tsunami, but rather on funds that are provided to foster long-term development. Figure 28.4 shows the relationship between the amount of ODA received per capita and GDP per capita of recipient LDCs in 2000. It suggests

 **term**

**overseas development assistance (ODA):** aid provided to LDCs by countries in the OECD

part **7**

that humanitarian motives are not always paramount in determining the recipients of aid. In particular, the fact that Israel received more ODA per person than any other country in 2000, in spite of being a high-income country, suggests a political motivation. Israel (labelled 'x' in Figure 28.4) actually received more ODA as a percentage of GDP than India. There has been considerable criticism of the USA over many years for the way in which it has used aid to favour countries that have been important in US foreign policy.

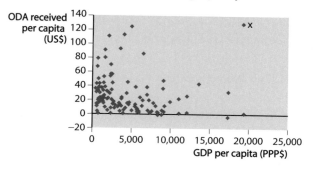

ODA received per capita (US$)

GDP per capita (PPP$)

**Figure 28.4**
*ODA and GDP per capita of recipient countries, 2000*

A contentious issue is whether ODA should be channelled to those countries most in need of it, or focused on those countries best equipped to make good use of the funding. If humanitarian motives are uppermost, then you would expect there to be a strong relationship between flows of overseas assistance and average income levels. However, if other motives are important, this relationship might be less apparent.

Figure 28.5 shows the top 15 recipients of ODA as a percentage of the total aid disbursed in 2004. The fact that Iraq heads the list, and that Afghanistan and Pakistan come high up the list may reflect the importance of these countries in terms of US foreign policy in the aftermath of 9/11 and the Iraq war. Countries that fall in the UNDP's 'low human development' category are coloured green in this graph. You need to be careful in interpreting these data, because looking at the overall size of the flows does not take account of differing country sizes. For this reason Figure 28.6 may be more useful. This chart shows the extent to which some countries are dependent on overseas assistance by expressing receipts of ODA relative to the recipient country's gross national income. This gives a different picture, and emphasises the extent to which some LDCs rely on flows of overseas assistance.

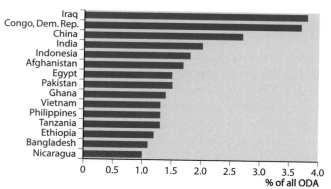

% of all ODA

**Figure 28.5**
*Top 15 recipients of aid, 2003/04 (% of total)*

Source: OECD.

chapter 28

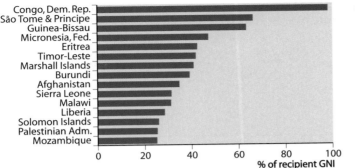

**Figure 28.6**
*Top 15 recipients of aid, 2003/04 (% of recipient GNI)*

Source: OECD.

At a meeting of the United Nations in 1974, the industrial countries agreed that they would each devote 0.7% of their GNP to ODA. This goal was reiterated at the Millennium Summit as part of the commitment to achieving the Millennium Development Goals. Progress towards this target has not been impressive. Figure 28.7 shows the performance of donor countries relative to this target, and you can see that only five countries had achieved the 0.7% UN target by 2004. The amount of ODA provided by the UK as a percentage of GNI increased after 1997, but the USA's share has fallen. However, it should be borne in mind that in terms of US$, the USA is by far the largest contributor.

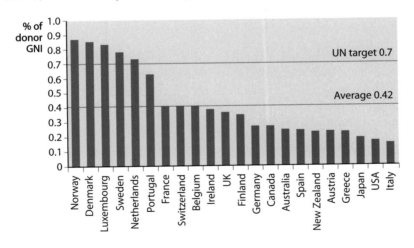

**Figure 28.7**
*Overseas Development Assistance in 2004*

Source: OECD.

An encouraging sign is that total ODA flows increased in the late 1990s and the early years of the new millennium, as can be seen in Figure 28.8. This seemed to represent an enhanced awareness of the importance of such flows for many LDCs. Indeed, at the summit meeting of G8 at Gleneagles in July 2005 the commitment to the UN target for ODA was reiterated.

A World Bank study of the effectiveness of aid, published in 1997, reported that 'foreign aid to developing countries since 1970 has had no net impact on either the recipients' growth rate or the quality of their economic policies'. Some evidence was found to suggest that aid was more effective in countries where 'sound economic

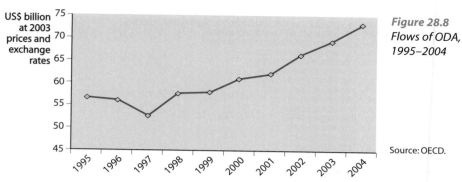

Figure 28.8
Flows of ODA,
1995–2004

Source: OECD.

management' was being practised. In other words, it was argued that aid might prove effective in stimulating growth only if the country were also implementing 'good' economic policies — particularly in terms of openness to trade, low inflation and disciplined fiscal policy.

There are many possible reasons for the ineffectiveness of aid. It may simply be that providing aid to the poorest countries reduces its effectiveness, in the sense that the resources of such countries are so limited that the funding cannot be efficiently utilised. In some cases it may be related to the fact that aid flows are received by LDC governments, which can be inefficient or corrupt, so there are no guarantees that the funds are used wisely by these governments. Or it might simply be that the flows of aid have not been substantial enough to have made a difference.

There are other explanations, however. For example, some donor countries in the past have regarded aid as part of their own trade policy. By tying aid to trade deals, the net value of the aid to the recipient country is much reduced: for instance, offering aid in this way may commit the recipient country to buying goods from the donor country at inflated prices.

In other cases, aid has been tied to use in specific projects. This may help to assure the donor that the funds are being used for the purpose for which they were intended. However, it is helpful only if appropriate projects were selected in the first place. There may be a temptation for donors to select prestige projects that will be favourably regarded by others, rather than going for the LDC's top-priority development projects.

Such deals are becoming less common, as now more ODA is being channelled through multilateral organisations than bilaterally between donor and recipient directly. This may mean that aid flows will be more effective in the future. In 1994, 66.1% of total aid was untied (45.8% in the case of aid from the UK), but by 1999 this proportion had increased to 83.8% (91.8% from the UK).

An important issue for all sorts of aid is that it should be provided in a way that does not damage incentives for local producers. For example, dumping cheap grain into LDC markets on a regular basis would be likely to damage the incentives for local farmers by depressing prices.

## Summary

➤ Overseas development assistance (ODA) comprises grants and concessional funding provided from the OECD countries to LDCs.

➤ The countries most in need of ODA may not be in a position to use it effectively.

➤ In some cases, the direction of ODA flows is influenced by the political interests of the donor countries.

➤ The more developed countries have pledged to devote 0.7% of their GNPs to ODA, but few have reached this target so far.

➤ Some evidence suggests that aid has been ineffective except in countries that have pursued 'good' economic policies.

➤ The tying of aid to trade deals or to specific projects can limit the aid's benefits to recipient LDCs.

## Exercise 28.2

Discuss the view that it is only worthwhile providing long-term development aid to countries that have the infrastructure and human capital to make good use of it, even if these are not the countries in most need of assistance.

### International borrowing

The final option for LDCs is to borrow the funds needed for development. This may be on concessional terms from the World Bank or the IMF, or on a commercial basis from international financial markets.

It is important to notice that, when countries borrow from the World Bank or the IMF, the loans come with strings attached. In other words, these bodies impose conditions on countries wanting to borrow, typically in relation to the sorts of economic policy that should be adopted. Such policy programmes will be considered below.

As with other forms of external finance, problems have arisen for some LDCs that have tried to borrow internationally. These problems first became apparent in the early 1980s, when Mexico announced that it could not meet its debt repayment commitments. But the stock of outstanding debt has been a major issue for many LDCs, especially in sub-Saharan Africa.

Figure 28.9 presents some data about this. It can be seen that in 1990 the debt position

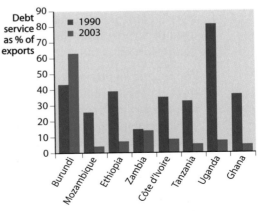

**Figure 28.9** *Debt servicing in sub-Saharan Africa, 1990 and 2003*

Sources: *Human Development Report*, 2005.

for many of these countries was serious indeed. In the case of Uganda, in 1990 more than 80% of the value of exports of goods and services was needed just to service the outstanding debt. For a country with limited resources, this leaves little surplus to use for promoting development. The encouraging aspect of Figure 28.9 is that for most of these countries the situation was much improved in 2003.

Figure 28.10 shows the relationship between stocks of external debt and the growth of GNP per capita in the late 1990s. Nicaragua is excluded because its debt level at that time was way off the scale. The striking aspect of this figure is that the countries with the highest levels of debt experienced low or negative growth, supporting the contention that debt is a constraint on growth.

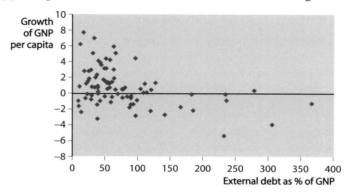

**Figure 28.10**
*Debt and growth in LDCs in the late 1990s*

Sources: *Human Development Report,* 1999.

But how did this situation arise? The story begins in the mid-1970s with the first oil price crisis. In 1973–74 oil prices quadrupled. Countries that were not oil producers were suddenly faced with a deficit on the current account of the balance of payments, as the demand for oil in the short run was highly inelastic.

For LDCs, this was a major problem. They knew that if they went to the IMF for a loan they would be forced to accept onerous conditions, so they were reluctant to do this. On the other hand, the commercial banks were keen to lend because they were holding the windfall gains of the oil producers. LDCs were therefore encouraged to borrow from the banks rather than the IMF, and they took out loans at variable interest rates.

The second oil price crisis came in 1979–80, when prices tripled. Many LDCs were now in deep trouble, carrying a legacy of past debts and needing to borrow still more to pay for their oil imports. Furthermore, countries such as the USA and the UK were adopting macroeconomic policies that were pushing interest rates to high levels, making it more difficult for LDCs to meet their existing commitments.

This resulted in the debt crisis of the 1980s, when a number of countries were threatening to default on their debts. A number of plans (including the Baker and Brady Plans) were introduced to safeguard the international financial system, but from the LDCs' viewpoint these entailed mainly a *rescheduling* of existing debt: in other words, they were given longer to pay. A consequence was that debt levels continued to grow.

The problems were made worse because in some countries the borrowed funds were not used wisely. Development through borrowing is sustainable only if the funds are used to enable exports to grow, so that the funds can be repaid. When they do not lead to increased export earnings, repayment problems will inevitably result.

## Summary

➤ A third way for LDCs to obtain external funds is through borrowing.

➤ Loans provided by the World Bank and the IMF have conditions attached that are not always palatable for LDCs.

➤ Many LDCs have borrowed in the past, but have then been unable to meet the repayments.

➤ In some cases this was because the funds were not well used.

## Exercise 28.3

Discuss the extent to which good government within a developing country is a necessary condition for the successful mobilisation of internal and external resources.

## The Heavily Indebted Poor Countries (HIPC) Initiative

In the run-up to the new millennium it was clear that many countries' international debt burdens had become unsustainable. Pressure was put on the World Bank and the UN to offer *debt forgiveness* to LDCs. This pressure came in particular from non-government organisations under the banner of *Jubilee 2000*.

The World Bank was reluctant to consider this route. One of the reasons for its reluctance concerns *moral hazard*. It is argued that if a country expects to be forgiven its debt, it will have no incentive to behave responsibly — and other countries too will have less of an incentive to pay off their debts.

The response was the **HIPC Initiative**, which allows for debt forgiveness on condition that the country demonstrates a commitment to 'good' policies over a period of time. The HIPC Initiative was first launched in 1995, but the conditions were then so restrictive that few countries were able to benefit — in particular, countries were required to follow the policy package for a period of 6 years before they would qualify for any debt relief. Consequently, a number of pressure groups, including Jubilee 2000, lobbied the World Bank to allow the initiative to be more accessible.

The policies concerned overlap with a previous package of measures, which came to be known as a

 **Key** *terms*

**HIPC Initiative:** initiative launched in 1995 to provide debt relief for heavily indebted poor countries

**Structural Adjustment Programme:** package of economic policy measures recommended by the World Bank

**Structural Adjustment Programme (SAP)**. SAPs have been on the World Bank agenda for many years, and comprise a package of policies designed to help a country initiate a process of growth and development. Under the HIPC Initiative, a new set of measures was added to encourage countries to devote funds to poverty alleviation programmes.

The HIPC policy package incorporates four main steps:
1  successful implementation of policies to enhance economic growth (the World Bank's model of market-friendly growth was discussed in Chapter 26)
2  development of a Poverty Reduction Strategy Paper (PRSP)
3  encouragement of private enterprise
4  diversification of the export base

Uganda was the first country to qualify for debt relief under HIPC, and Figure 28.8 suggests that this has had an effect, with debt service having been reduced substantially. Indeed, there is some evidence that debt levels for low-income countries are coming under control, as can be seen in Figure 28.11, which shows that the ratio of total debt service to exports has fallen for all low-income countries from 27% in 1990 to 13.5% in 2002. Indeed, for the least developed countries the ratio is down to 7.5% in 2003, from 16.2% in 1990. However, the regional pattern shown in Figure 28.11 indicates that debt levels continue to grow in Latin America and the Caribbean, and in Central and Eastern Europe (CEE) and the Commonwealth of Independent States (CIS).

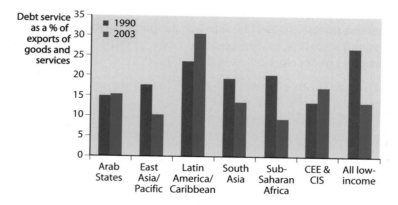

*Figure 28.11*
*Debt service,*
*selected regions,*
*1990 and 2003*

Source: *Human Development Report,* 2005.

In July 2005 government leaders from the G8 countries met at a summit meeting in Gleneagles. At this meeting the countries present pledged to cancel the debt of the world's most indebted countries – which effectively meant those countries that had qualified under the HIPC initiative. It remains to be seen as to how this recommitment will work out in practice. Jubilee 2000 has continued to argue that HIPC remains overly restrictive, and has pointed out that there are countries that face heavy debt burdens that have been excluded from HIPC, and are therefore also excluded from the Gleneagles statement. This includes such countries as Bangladesh, Cambodia, the Philippines, Nigeria and Peru.

## Case Study  Uganda

Uganda was the first country to qualify for debt relief under the HIPC Initiative and illustrates some of the key issues.

Uganda is a landlocked country in East Africa, bordering a range of countries and with ongoing civil conflict in the north.

The country gained independence from the UK in 1962, and was governed initially by Milton Obote. There was some political instability in the early years, although GDP per capita remained fairly constant. Obote stayed in power partly by using the army to carry out a coup against his own government. Then in 1971 he was overthrown by Idi Amin, who ruled through military power. During this period the Ugandan economy essentially collapsed, as you can see in Figure 28.12, which shows the time-path of Uganda's real GDP per capita. This was partly the result of Amin's expulsion of all Asian Ugandans, who had run the country's limited manufacturing industry and distribution sector. He also killed an estimated 300,000 people during his time in power.

Amin was illiterate and allowed no written instructions, which impeded the bureaucracy. In 1978 he invaded Tanzania, but the Tanzanian army, with the help of exiled Ugandans, fought back and took Kampala in 1979. Elections were held in 1980, and Milton Obote came back to power, albeit under allegations of election fixing. Obote's second period was characterised by civil war and lasted until a coup by Tito Okello in 1985. The Okello regime lasted only until 1986 when the current president, Yoweri Museveni, took over, bringing some stability and economic recovery. Indeed, the introduction of a SAP followed soon after Museveni came to power.

In terms of the HIPC requirements, Uganda has done everything expected of it. It has established a strong record of sound macroeconomic policies and structural adjustment reforms. It has produced its Poverty Reduction Strategy Paper (PRSP) and tried to implement it. The plan included a drive for universal primary education initiated in 1997, supported by $75 million from the World Bank.

I visited Uganda in November 1997 to undertake a survey in the rural areas. Even at this early stage in the new policy, some of the effects of the HIPC Initiative were evident. In some cases, children had been held back from attending school in anticipation of the new measures. In other cases, some older children had returned to school — there were several 13-year-olds in the first year of primary education, and 'children' of up to 19 years old enrolled in primary education.

However, although the debt burden has lessened (see Figure 28.9), and in spite of rapid growth during the 1990s (Uganda was one of the fastest-growing economies in the world in this period), the country remains poor. However, in terms of the HDI, Uganda moved out of the 'low human development' group of countries in 2003.

A number of factors seem to have affected Uganda's situation. First, the international price of coffee has fallen to unanticipated low levels. With

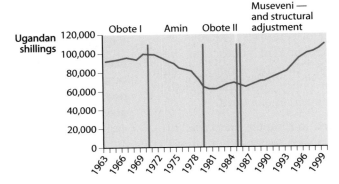

**Figure 28.12**
*Real GDP per capita in Uganda, 1963–99*

**part 7**

Uganda continuing to rely heavily on coffee for export earnings, this is a major setback. Efforts have been made to bring about greater diversification, and this is beginning to show results. However, the IMF also concedes that 'further cooperation of the international community is needed to help remove the barriers to trade'. There is a major issue lurking here: it is all very well persuading LDCs to stimulate and diversify their exports, but if they cannot find buyers, the impact will be limited.

In addition, some countries have not conceded the debt relief that is due under the agreements —

another indication that international cooperation is crucial in enabling the HIPC measures to become effective.

There is some further evidence that one of the reasons for the persistence of poverty in the rural areas, in spite of Uganda's macroeconomic success, was the lack of integration of these rural areas into national markets. In part this is a result of poor infrastructure — poor roads, lack of market facilities and poor information about national trading conditions.

*Peter Smith*

## Summary

➤ The HIPC Initiative was designed to address the problems of debt in the poorest countries.

➤ Under the HIPC Initiative, debt relief is provided to countries that have shown a commitment to World Bank-approved policies and have implemented a Poverty Reduction Strategy Paper (PRSP).

## Trade policy

Another area in which policy may be important in contributing to economic development is in the area of trade policy. If a country is short of foreign exchange, there are two broad approaches that it can take in drawing up its trade policy to deal with the problem. One is to reduce its reliance on imports in order to economise on the need for foreign currency — in other words, to produce goods at home that it previously imported. This is known as an **import substitution** policy.

An alternative possibility is to try to earn more foreign exchange through **export promotion**.

### Import substitution

The import substitution strategy has had some appeal for a number of countries. The idea is to boost domestic production of goods that were previously imported, thereby saving foreign exchange. A typical policy instrument used to achieve this is the imposition of a **tariff**.

Tariffs were discussed in Chapter 13 (pages 191–204), when it was pointed out that not all of the results of a tariff are favourable for an economy. Effectively, the government subsidises inefficient

**Key terms**

**import substitution:** policy encouraging domestic production of goods previously imported in order to reduce the need for foreign exchange

**export promotion:** policy entailing encouraging domestic firms to export more goods in order to earn foreign exchange

**tariff:** a tax imposed on imported goods

local producers, and forces domestic consumers to pay a price that is above that of the good if imported from abroad.

Some would defend this policy on the grounds that it allows the LDC to protect an *infant industry*. In other words, through such encouragement and protection, the new industry will eventually become efficient enough to compete in world markets.

There are two key problems with this argument. First, unless the domestic market is sufficiently large for the industry to reap economies of scale, local producers will never be in a position to compete globally. Second, because of such protection, domestic firms are never exposed to international competition, and so will not have an incentive to improve their efficiency to world levels. In other words, tariff protection fosters an inward-looking attitude among local producers that discourages them from trying to compete in world markets. They remain happy with the protection that allows them to reap extra profits.

## Export promotion

Export promotion requires a more dynamic and outward-looking approach, as domestic producers need to be able to compete with producers already established in world markets. The choice of which products to promote is critical, as it is important that the LDC develops a new pattern of comparative advantage if it is to benefit from an export promotion strategy.

For primary producers, a tempting strategy is one that begins with existing products and tries to move along the production chain. For example, in 1997 (under encouragement from the World Bank) Mozambique launched a project whereby, instead of exporting raw cashew nuts, it would establish processing plants that would then allow it to export roasted cashew nuts. In the early 1970s Mozambique was the largest producer of cashew nuts in the world, but by the late 1990s the activity had stagnated, and the country had been overtaken by producers in Brazil and India.

This would seem to have been a good idea because it makes use of existing products and moves the industry into higher value-added activity. However, the project ran into a series of problems. On the one hand, there were internal constraints: processing the nuts requires capital equipment and skilled labour, neither of which was in plentiful supply in Mozambique. In addition, tariff rates on processed commodities are higher than on raw materials, so the producers faced more barriers to trade. They also found that they were trying to break into a

*By the late 1990s Brazil and India had overtaken Mozambique in cashew nut production*

market that was dominated by a few large existing producers, which were reluctant to share the market. Furthermore, the technical standards required to sell processed cashew nuts were beyond the capability of the newly established local firms. Indeed, the setting of high technical specifications for imported products is one way in which countries have tried to protect their own domestic producers — it is an example of a **non-tariff barrier**.

**Key term**

**non-tariff barrier:** an obstacle to free trade other than a tariff (e.g. quality standards imposed on imported products)

These are just some of the difficulties that face new producers from LDCs wanting to compete in world markets. The East Asian tiger economies pursued export promotion strategies, making sure that their exchange rates supported the competitiveness of their products and that their labour was appropriately priced. However, it must be remembered that the tiger economies expanded into export-led growth at a time when world trade itself was booming, and when the developed countries were beginning to move out of labour-intensive activities, thereby creating a niche to be filled by the tigers. If many other countries had expanded their exports at the same time, it is not at all certain that they could all have been successful.

As time goes by, it becomes more difficult for other countries to follow this policy. It is particularly difficult for countries that originally chose import substitution, because the inward-looking attitudes fostered by such policies become so deeply entrenched.

It should also be remembered that there will always be dangers in trying to develop new kinds of economic activity that may entail sacrificing comparative advantage. This is not to say that LDCs should remain primary producers for ever, but it does suggest that it is important to select the new forms of activity with care in order to exploit a *potential* comparative advantage.

## Summary

➤ In designing a trade policy, an LDC may choose to go for import substitution, nurturing infant industries behind protectionist barriers in order to allow them to produce domestically goods that were formerly imported.

➤ However, such infant industries rarely seem to grow up, leaving the LDC with inefficient producers, which are unable to compete effectively with world producers.

➤ Export promotion requires a more dynamic and outward-looking approach, and a careful choice of new activities.

## Exercise 28.4

Discuss the relative merits of import substitution and export promotion as trade strategies. Under what conditions might import substitution have a chance of success?

# The UK economy

# Part 8

# Chapter 29
# The performance of the UK economy

This part of the book examines the performance of the UK economy in more depth than was possible in the AS section of the course. Analysis of the multiple objectives of macroeconomic policy reveals some important sources of conflict, as policies designed to meet one objective can be seen to jeopardise the meeting of other targets. The multiplicity of objectives also means that there are multiple dimensions over which the performance of the economy has to be monitored and measured. Given the trade-offs that exist between some objectives, it is also important to prioritise them appropriately. All this must be set in the context of recent economic history, which provides the backdrop to analysing the performance of the UK economy.

## Learning outcomes

After studying this chapter, you should:
➤ be familiar with the prime aims of macroeconomic policy
➤ be aware of key measures of economic performance
➤ be able to analyse and evaluate the performance of the UK economy in relation to the main policy objectives
➤ understand, in broad terms, measures of the distribution of income and wealth using concepts such as deciles and Lorenz curves
➤ be familiar with alternative measures of the standard of living, and be able to evaluate their strengths and weaknesses
➤ appreciate the limitations of statistical measures of economic performance
➤ be able to compare and analyse UK economic performance relative to that of other countries

## Measuring performance

What is meant by the 'performance' of an economy? A simple response would be to say that performance is an indication of how well the economy is doing — but this only has meaning in relation to some notion of what represents 'good' and

'bad' performance. It is also crucial to know in what dimensions the economy's performance is important.

Chapter 11 set out a number of objectives of macroeconomic policy, and it seems sensible to regard these as defining the areas in which the economy's performance needs to be measured and monitored. After all, if policy is used to influence the economy in certain ways, this must be because that policy is intended to lead to desirable outcomes. According to this argument, the performance of an economy must be judged against the objectives that have been set. This is important to remember when comparing the performance of different countries that may have set out to achieve different objectives or set different priorities. Here is a brief reminder of the objectives discussed in Chapter 11.

### Price stability

The control of inflation has been the prime target of macroeconomic policy in the UK since the mid-1970s. Figure 29.1 shows inflation, as measured by the annual rate of change of the consumer price index, in the UK since 1997. The present target for the CPI inflation rate is 2% per annum. You can see from the graph that inflation has been consistently below the target rate except for an interlude in late 2005, when it crept over the 2% target. The Bank of England's Monetary Policy Committee ascribed this primarily to the increase in the price of energy, oil prices having increased at that time.

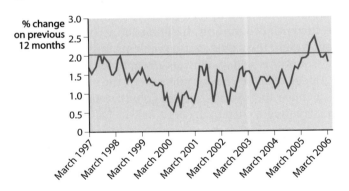

**Figure 29.1**
*Inflation in the UK, 1997–2006*

Source: ONS.

Prices play a key role in an economy, acting as signals that guide the allocation of resources. When prices are unstable, firms may find it difficult to interpret these price signals, which may lead to a misallocation of resources. Furthermore, instability of prices creates difficulties for firms trying to forecast future expected demand for their products, which may discourage them from undertaking investment. This in turn means that the economy's capacity to produce may expand by less than it could otherwise have done — in other words, high or unstable inflation may dampen economic growth through its effect on investment. (Chapter 11 identified some other costs of inflation, and you might wish to look back to remind yourself of them. However, the effects on resource allocation and investment are widely accepted to be the most important damaging effects of inflation.)

## Full employment

A second key policy objective is full employment. Unemployment imposes costs on society and on the individuals who are unemployed. From society's point of view, the existence of substantial unemployment represents a waste of resources and indicates that the economy is working below full capacity. Unemployment in the UK in the early part of the twenty-first century is at a relatively low level, having fallen from the peak reached in the mid-1980s. This is shown in Figure 29.2.

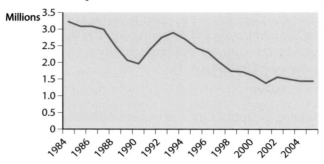

*Figure 29.2*
*Unemployment in the UK, 1984–2005 (ILO definition)*

Note: numbers unemployed in March–May each year (average).

Source: ONS.

## Balance of payments

Under a flexible exchange rate system, the overall balance of payments will always be zero because the exchange rate adjusts to ensure that this is so (as was explained in Chapter 11). Nevertheless, the balance of payments remains an objective, not so much to ensure overall balance as to maintain an appropriate balance between the current account and the financial account. If the current account is in persistent deficit, this could cause problems in the long run, as the implication is that the country is selling off its assets in order to obtain goods for present consumption. Under a fixed exchange rate system, the need to maintain the exchange rate acts as a constraint upon economic growth, which tends to lead to an increase in imports, creating a current account deficit. This is what happened in the UK economy in the period after the Second World War, as is discussed in Chapter 31.

## Economic growth

It is through economic growth that the productive capacity of the economy is raised, and this in turn allows the living standards of the country's citizens to be progressively improved over time. This can be represented as a rightward shift of the aggregate supply curve, as in Figure 29.3, where capacity output increases from $Y^*$ to $Y^{**}$ as a result of an increase in aggregate supply from $AS_0$ to $AS_1$. In a sense, therefore, this is the most fundamental of the policy objectives. However, attaining other policy objectives may be a prerequisite for success in achieving growth.

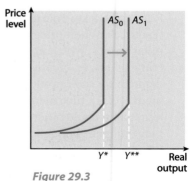

*Figure 29.3*
*A shift in aggregate supply*

### Environmental considerations

It must be recognised that it is not only resources that contribute to living standards: conserving a good environment is also important. Sustainable growth and development means growth that does not prejudice the consumption possibilities of future generations, and this consideration may act as a constraint on the rate of economic growth.

### Income redistribution

The final macroeconomic policy objective considered in Chapter 11 concerned attempts to influence the distribution of income within a society. This may entail transfers of income between groups — that is, from the rich to the poor — in order to protect the vulnerable. Such transfers may take place through progressive taxation (whereby those on higher incomes pay a greater proportion of their income in tax) or through a system of social security benefits such as the Jobseeker's Allowance or Income Support.

### Correcting market failure

At the *microeconomic* level there are policy measures designed to deal with various forms of market failure. Competition policy is one example of this; it is designed to prevent firms from abusing monopoly power, and to improve the allocation of resources. Although such policies operate at the microeconomic level, they have consequences for macroeconomic objectives such as economic growth.

### Productivity

A further measure of the performance of the economy is productivity, which may be regarded as a measure of the efficiency with which factors of production are being utilised in the economy. This is important if the economy's performance is to be judged relative to that of other countries. For example, if the UK's trading competitors were all experiencing greater improvements in productivity, this would have potentially damaging effects on the competitiveness of UK goods and services in international markets.

## Measurement and analysis

Accepting these policy objectives as representing the criteria by which an economy should be judged, what indicators or measurements can be used to monitor performance? And what level of performance would be evidence of 'success'? These questions may be more straightforward for some of the policy objectives than for others, but in each case it is important to consider carefully how performance is to be monitored and judged.

### Inflation

In the case of **inflation**, the government since 1997 has provided a clear target by which policy should be judged. The Bank of England's Monetary Policy Committee (MPC) is charged with the responsibility of ensuring that the government's inflation target of

 **Key term**

**inflation:** a rise in the general price level

2% per year is achieved. The way in which this is done is discussed in Chapter 30. The MPC's brief is to keep inflation within one percentage point (either way) of the target.

Figure 29.4 shows the extent to which this has been achieved. Until the end of 2003, the target was expressed in terms of the **retail price index** (RPIX), with the target being 2.5%. Since the beginning of 2004 the target has been defined relative to the **consumer price index** (CPI), with the target being 2%. The graph shows that the MPC was successful in keeping within the target band throughout the period shown.

 **terms**

**consumer price index:** a measure of the average level of prices in the UK; the government's inflation target is set in terms of the percentage rate of change of this index

**retail price index:** an alternative measure of the general level of prices in the UK

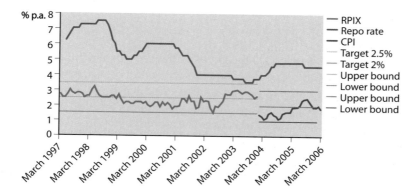

Figure 29.4
UK interest rates and the UK inflation target, 1997–2006

Source: ONS, Bank of England.

Why should the target be 2%? Why not 5%, or 0%? The fundamental rationale for having low inflation is that it can help to foster long-run sustainable economic growth. The argument is that when inflation is low and predictable, firms will be more confident in forming expectations about the future, so will be prepared to undertake the investment that is needed to expand the productive capacity of the economy and shift the aggregate supply curve to the right, as in Figure 29.3.

However, it is argued that a modest rate of inflation is preferable to zero inflation. This is because prices need to act as signals to firms and thus guide resource allocation. In other words, relative prices need to adjust if resources are to be used in the best way for society as a whole. It is thought that relative prices can adjust more easily when there is a little bit of inflation than if the overall price level is completely stable — that is, if the inflation target were to be zero.

The change of inflation target from RPI to CPI reflected concerns that it is important to measure inflation as accurately as possible to ensure that the indicator is appropriate, given what it is intended to represent. The CPI has some advantages in this respect (see Chapter 9). The difficulties of measuring with precision is another reason for setting a non-zero target and for allowing a range of acceptable values either side of that target. The difficulty of allowing for quality

changes is one complication here. In other words, part of the observed price change (especially for products such as computers and mobile phones) represents improvements in the quality of products. This means that observed inflation is likely to overstate the actual (quality-adjusted) change in prices over time.

### Unemployment

Figure 29.2 showed the numbers unemployed in the UK using the ILO definition. This is the accepted definition of unemployment for official purposes. As was explained in Chapter 9, the **ILO unemployment rate** identifies the number of people available for work, and seeking work, but without a job.

 **term**

**ILO unemployment rate:** measure of the percentage of the workforce who are without jobs but are available for work, willing to work and looking for work

Unemployment is regarded as an important policy target because the existence of high levels of unemployment implies that the country's resources are not being used efficiently. If the labour that is underutilised could be brought into productive activity, this would increase the real output being produced, and thus enhance average incomes. This is the equivalent of observing an economy that is operating within its production possibility curve (PPC) at point *A* on Figure 29.5. A reduction in unemployment would enable the economy to move to a point on the *PPC*, say, at *B*. Of course, unemployment that is involuntary may also be costly for those individuals who are unemployed but would prefer to be working.

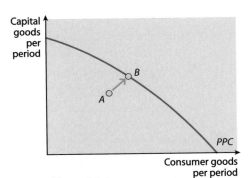

**Figure 29.5**
*A reduction in unemployment enables a move to the production possibility curve*

In evaluating the level of unemployment in an economy, it is important to be aware that unemployment can never be zero. There will always be some people who are unable to find jobs, or are unemployed for a period between jobs, while searching for a job. It is not possible to put a precise number on this irreducible minimum unemployed, but it has been argued that the UK economy was close to this in the first few years of the twenty-first century.

It should also be remembered that it may be desirable to have some unemployment present, as the process of job search is crucial in the evolution of an economy through time. At any particular moment, there will be some forms of economic activity that are in decline in an economy, and some which are expanding. This is how the economy adjusts to changing patterns of consumer demand, and changing patterns of international specialisation. Having said that, it is also desirable to have labour markets operating as efficiently and flexibly as possible, in order to minimise the time that people need to devote to job search or retraining. Chapter 32 examines some policies designed on the supply side of the economy to improve the flexibility with which the labour market can operate.

At the heart of the discussion of unemployment is the notion that resources should be allocated as efficiently as possible to keep the economy as close to the full employment level of output as possible. Recognising that the economy operates within an international context, it is also important to strive for efficiency in order to maintain the competitiveness of UK goods and services relative to the country's trading partners. This leads to the question of the balance of payments.

## Summary

➤ The control of inflation has been regarded as the prime target for macroeconomic policy in recent years.

➤ The target is set at 2% per annum change in the consumer price index (CPI).

➤ The Bank of England's Monetary Policy Committee has the responsibility of conducting monetary policy in such a way as to meet the target.

➤ The percentage change in the CPI is as good a measure of inflation as any available, but it still overestimates the true rate of inflation because of the difficulty in identifying quality changes.

➤ Another key objective of policy is to maintain low unemployment, so that the economy's resources are being fully utilised.

➤ Some unemployment will always be present to allow the structure of economic activity to change over time, which requires people to be able to engage in retraining and job search.

### The balance of payments

Chapter 9 introduced the balance of payments, a set of accounts that monitors the transactions that take place between UK residents and the rest of the world. For an individual household it is important to monitor incomings and outgoings, as items purchased must be paid for in some way — either by using income or savings, or by borrowing. In a similar way, a country has to pay for goods, services or assets that are bought from other countries. The balance of payments accounts enable the analysis of such international transactions.

As with the household, transactions can be categorised as either incoming or outgoing items. For example, if a car made in the UK is exported (i.e. purchased by a non-resident of the UK), this is an 'incoming' item, as the payment for the car is a credit to the UK. On the other hand, the purchase of a bottle of Italian wine (an import) is a debit item.

**Key term**

**balance of payments:** set of accounts that identifies transactions between the residents of a country and the rest of the world

Similarly, all other transactions entered into the balance of payments accounts can be identified as credit or debit items, depending upon the direction of the payment. In other words, when money flows into the country as the result of a transaction, that is a credit; if money flows out, it is a debit. As all items have to be paid for in some way, the overall balance of payments when everything is added together must be zero. However, individual components can be positive or negative.

In line with international standards, the accounts are divided into three categories. The **current account** identifies transactions in goods and services, together with income payments and international transfers. Income payments here include the earnings of UK nationals from employment abroad and payments of investment income. Transfers are mainly transactions between governments — for example, between the UK government and EU institutions — which make up the largest component. Flows of bilateral aid and social security payments abroad are also included here.

The **financial account** measures transactions in financial assets, including investment flows and central government transactions in foreign exchange reserves.

The **capital account** is relatively small. It contains capital transfers, the largest item of which is associated with migrants. When a person changes status from a non-resident to resident of the UK, any assets owned by that person are transferred to being UK-owned.

 **Key terms**

**current account of the balance of payments:** account identifying transactions in goods and services between the residents of a country and the rest of the world

**financial account of the balance of payments:** account identifying transactions in financial assets between the residents of a country and the rest of the world

**capital account of the balance of payments:** account identifying transactions in (physical) capital between the residents of a country and the rest of the world

Figure 29.6 shows the relative size of the main accounts since 1970. Notice that these data are in current prices, so no account has been taken of changing prices during the period. This has the effect of compressing the apparent magnitude of the variables in the early part of the period (when prices were relatively low), and exaggerating the size towards the end of the period. Expressing these nominal values as a percentage of nominal GDP (as in Figure 29.7 for a longer period) provides a less misleading picture.

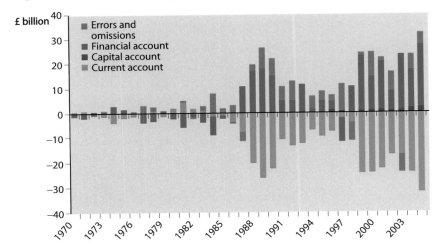

**Figure 29.6**
*The UK balance of payments, 1970–2005 (at current prices)*

Source: ONS.

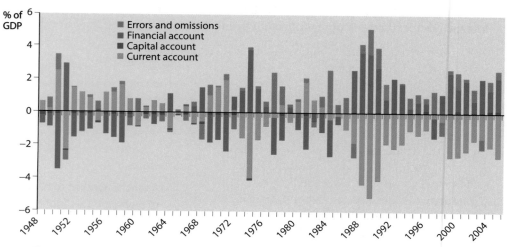

*Figure 29.7* The UK balance of payments, 1948–2005 (% of GDP)     Source: ONS.

As the total balance of payments must always be zero, the surplus (positive) components above the line must always exactly match the deficit (negative) items below the line. However, both graphs indicate that the magnitudes of the three major accounts vary through time.

## The current account

The current account has been in deficit every year since 1984. The recorded current account surpluses in 1980–83 were associated with North Sea oil, which was then just coming on stream. There followed a phase in which the deficit grew to record levels, peaking in 1989. During the 1990s, the deficit fell until 1999, at which time the UK economy entered a period in which the current account was consistently in substantial deficit, and the financial account in surplus.

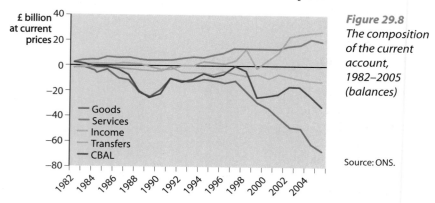

*Figure 29.8*
*The composition of the current account, 1982–2005 (balances)*

Source: ONS.

Figure 29.8 shows the components of the current account. You can see that until the early 1990s the overall balance on the current account (CBAL) tracked closely the trade in goods. More recently, however, the trade in goods has moved further into deficit, although this has been partially offset by a gradual increase in the

OCR Advanced Economics

trade in services and (except in 1999) by an increase in income — which is made up mainly of investment income.

Trade in goods (sometimes known as **visible trade**) has traditionally shown a deficit for the UK — it has shown a surplus in only 6 years since 1900. As reserves of oil in the North Sea run down, the UK is likely to become a net importer of oil, but up to 2004 it continued to be a net exporter of oil: in other words, the oil part of the trade in goods was in surplus. However, imports of cars and other consumer goods have persistently exceeded exports. A summary for 2004 is presented in Table 29.1. You should be aware that these data are in current prices, so you need to focus on the relative sizes rather than the absolute values.

In contrast, trade in services has recorded a surplus in every year since 1966. This is sometimes referred to as **invisible trade**. Table 29.2 shows the component items in 1994 and 2004 — again, measured in current prices, so that no allowance has been made for the effects of inflation.

As you can see, the largest deficit items in trade in services are transportation (especially air transport services, which has shown a deficit every year since the mid-1980s) and travel, where again the deficit has grown significantly since the late 1980s. The main reason for this is the increasing number of UK residents travelling abroad. However, these negative items are more than compensated by the surplus components, especially financial services, which have grown steadily, as have computer and information services. You can see that 'other business' also makes a significant contribution. This category comprises trade-related services such as merchanting and consultancy services, which includes advertising, engineering and legal services, and operational leasing.

An important item on the current account is investment income, which represents earnings on past investment abroad. This

**Key terms**

**visible trade:** trade in goods

**invisible trade:** trade in services

| Item | 1994 | 2004 |
|---|---|---|
| Food, beverages and tobacco | –3,849 | –11,601 |
| Basic materials | –2,971 | –2,599 |
| Oil | 3,937 | 1,869 |
| Coal, gas and electricity | –787 | –336 |
| Semi-manufactured goods: | | |
|    Chemicals | 4,650 | 4,087 |
|    Precious stones and silver | 207 | 238 |
|    Other | –4,477 | –8,068 |
| Finished manufactured goods | | |
|    Motor cars | –3,534 | –6,636 |
|    Other consumer goods | –5,208 | –19,307 |
|    Intermediate goods | –1,054 | –5,181 |
|    Capital goods | 1,248 | –9,902 |
|    Ships and aircraft | 397 | –251 |
| Commodities not classified | 315 | –927 |
| **Total** | **–11,126** | **–58,684** |

*Table 29.1* Trade in goods (balances) £ million in current prices, 1994 and 2004
Source: ONS *Pink Book.*

| Item | 1994 | 2004 |
|---|---|---|
| Transportation | –836 | –3,163 |
| Travel | –3,846 | –15,458 |
| Communications | –272 | 94 |
| Construction | 32 | 96 |
| Insurance | 1,492 | 5,556 |
| Financial | 4,615 | 12,242 |
| Computer and information | 517 | 3,811 |
| Royalties and licence fees | 550 | 1,997 |
| Other business | 4,762 | 14,332 |
| Personal, cultural and recreational | 185 | 1,045 |
| Government | –820 | –363 |
| **Total** | **6,379** | **20,189** |

*Table 29.2* Trade in services (balances), £ million in current prices, 1994 and 2004
Source: ONS *Pink Book.*

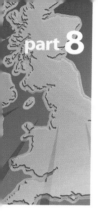

*Financial services are one of the largest credit items on the UK balance of payments*

item has shown strong growth since 1999 (when there was a deficit). The largest item in this part of the account is earnings from direct investment, although there is also an element of portfolio investment — earnings from holdings of bonds and other securities. The final category is current transfers. This includes taxes and social contributions received from non-resident workers and businesses, bilateral aid flows and military grants. However, the largest item is transfers with EU institutions, which has been in persistent deficit.

## The financial account

The trend towards globalisation means that both inward and outward investment increased substantially during the 1990s, although there was a dip after 2000. However, Figure 29.7 shows that the financial account has been in strong surplus in the early part of the twenty-first century. This is in part forced by the deficit on the current account. In other words, if an economy runs a current account deficit, it can do so only by running a surplus on the financial account. Effectively, what is happening is that, in order to fund the current account deficit, the UK is selling assets to foreign investors and borrowing abroad.

An important question is whether this practice is sustainable in the long run. Selling assets or borrowing abroad has future implications for the current account, as there will be outflows of investment income, and debt repayments in the future following today's financial surplus. It also has implications for interest rate policy. If the authorities hold interest rates high relative to the rest of the world, this will tend to attract inflows of investment, again with future implications for the current account.

## The capital account

The capital account is relatively small. The largest item relates to the flows of capital associated with migration. If someone migrates to the UK, that person's status changes from being a non-resident to being a resident. His or her property

then becomes part of the UK's assets, and a transaction has to be entered in the balance of payments accounts. There are also some items relating to various EU transactions. This account has been in surplus for 20 years.

## Summary

➤ The balance of payments is a set of accounts that contains details of the transactions that take place between the residents of an economy and the rest of the world.

➤ The accounts are divided into three sections: the current, financial and capital accounts.

➤ The current account identifies transactions in goods and services, together with some income payments and international transfers.

➤ The financial account measures transactions in financial assets, including investment flows and central government transactions in foreign reserves.

➤ The capital account, which is relatively small, contains capital transfers.

➤ The overall balance of payments must always be zero.

➤ The current account has been in persistent deficit since 1984, reflecting a deficit in trade in goods that is partly offset by a surplus in invisible trade.

➤ The financial account has been in strong surplus — as is required to balance the current account deficit.

## Exercise 29.1

Allocate each of the following items to the current, financial or capital account, and calculate the balances for each account. Check that (together with errors and omissions) the total is zero. All data refer to 2002, at current prices in £ billion.

| | | | | |
|---|---|---|---|---|
| a Trade in goods | −46.68 | g Trade in services | +15.58 |
| b Migrants' transfers | +1.28 | h Other capital transfers | −0.41 |
| c Total net direct investment | −5.11 | I Compensation of employees | +0.07 |
| d Investment income | +21.41 | j Total net portfolio investment | +50.09 |
| e Current transfers | −8.60 | k Other transactions in financial assets | −36.59 |
| f Transactions in reserve assets | +0.46 | l Errors and omissions | +8.50 |

### Economic growth

**Economic growth** is defined as an increase in the productive capacity of the economy. It is the process by which the total resources available to inhabitants of a country expand as time goes by. The measurement of economic growth is normally based on changes in real GDP over time, but it is important to recall that GDP is subject to the fluctuations of the business cycle. This means that to measure economic growth, the underlying trend growth of real GDP needs to be identified. Figure 29.9 shows the extent to which the growth rate of real GDP varies from one year to the next. The graph also includes the long-run

**Key term**

**economic growth:** an increase in the productive capacity of the economy

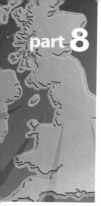

average growth rate of 2.4%, which has been regarded as the trend rate of growth of the UK economy in recent years.

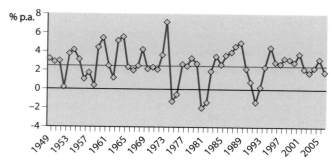

*Figure 29.9*
*Growth of real*
*GDP, 1949–2005*
*(% change over*
*previous year)*

Source: *Economic Trends Annual Supplement.*

In some ways, economic growth may be seen as the most fundamental policy objective for an economy. It is economic growth that enables a country to improve the standard of living of its inhabitants, which is ultimately what most societies wish to achieve. However, care needs to be taken in this respect, as the standard of living of people in a country does not only depend upon the *quantity* of resources that are available, as will be discussed later in the chapter. The standard of living also depends upon the *quality* of those resources, and on the way in which they are divided up among members of a society. For this purpose, the members of a society may need to include future generations as well as the present one, in the sense that economic growth that is achieved at the expense of the environment may leave future generations worse off. In other words, the unremitting pursuit of economic growth without regard to the costs may not be the best policy.

Nonetheless, economic growth is a central target of economic policy, as without it the well-being of a country's inhabitants is likely to stagnate. Indeed, a policy objective such as low inflation may be regarded as a target because achieving it is expected to encourage investment in order to enable a higher rate of economic growth. Thus other targets may be seen as subservient to economic growth.

## Productivity

Closely associated with economic growth is the notion of productive efficiency. Efficiency (and competitiveness) depends upon the relative costs of production in different countries, which influence the prices that firms can charge. This in turn partly reflects different levels of **productivity** across countries. Productivity is a measure of productive efficiency: for example, labour productivity is output per unit of labour input. Different countries show appreciable differences in efficiency by this measure.

**Key** *term*

**productivity:**
a measure of
productive efficiency

However, international comparisons of productivity are not straightforward, as measurements are subject to differences in data collection and differences in work practices. Figure 29.10 presents data for 2003 on GDP per head of population, expressed as index numbers; the USA is the reference country and is therefore set to 100. On this measure, the UK performs rather better than Japan,

France, Germany, Italy and Spain. As a measure of productivity levels, however, this is a misleading indicator. In particular, working hours are longer in the UK than in many other countries (especially within Europe), so in part GDP per head reflects differences in the quantity of labour input.

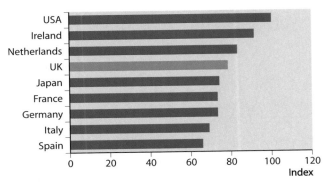

*Figure 29.10*
*GDP per head of population, selected countries, 2004 (USA = 100)*

Source: OECD.

For this reason, GDP per hour worked is often seen as a more reliable indicator of relative productivity levels. This measure is shown in Figure 29.11, and demonstrates quite a different pattern. Indeed, on this basis both Ireland and France show higher productivity than the USA, and the UK's performance is much more modest.

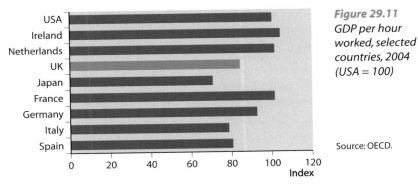

*Figure 29.11*
*GDP per hour worked, selected countries, 2004 (USA = 100)*

Source: OECD.

Figure 29.12 gives the time path for an index of GDP per hour worked, based on 1970 = 100. It shows that European countries have been experiencing stronger productivity growth than the USA over this period.

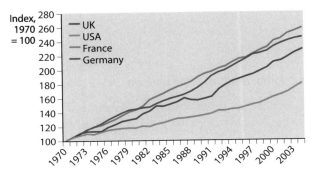

*Figure 29.12 Index of GDP per hour worked, 1970–2004*

Source: OECD.

It is also important to realise that labour productivity is not the only relevant measure, as countries may also differ in their use of capital. Total factor productivity is more difficult to measure, as the measurement of capital stock is especially prone to error and misinterpretation. However, some estimates of multifactor productivity growth are shown in Figure 29.13.

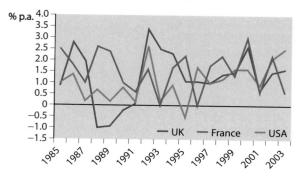

**Figure 29.13**
*Multifactor productivity growth, 1985–2003*

Source: OECD.

## Summary

➤ Economic growth is an increase in the productive capacity of an economy.

➤ It may be seen as the ultimate target of macroeconomic policy, as it allows an improvement in the well-being of a country's inhabitants.

➤ It is important to distinguish between the underlying trend growth rate and temporary changes in GDP due to the business cycle.

➤ Productivity is important as a measure of the productive efficiency being achieved in an economy.

### Evaluating inequality

Inequality is present in all societies, and always will be. However, the degree of inequality varies from one country to another; and before exploring the causes of inequality, and the policies that might be used to influence how income and wealth are distributed within society, it is necessary to be able to characterise and measure inequality. This is important in order to be able to judge relative standards of living in different countries or different periods.

One way of presenting data on this topic is to rank households in order of their incomes, and then calculate the share of total household income that goes to the poorest 10%, the poorest 20% and so on. When the groups are divided into tenths they are referred to as *deciles*; thus, the poorest 10% is the first decile, the next 10% is the second decile and so on. Similarly, the poorest 20% is the first *quintile*.

Table 29.3 presents some data for three countries. Notice that the unit of measurement is normally the household rather than the individual, on the presumption that members of a household tend to share their resources — a millionaire's life-partner may not earn any income, but he or she is not usually poor.

| | UK, 1991 | USA, 1997 | Japan, 1993 |
|---|---|---|---|
| First decile | 2.6 | 1.8 | 4.8 |
| First quintile | 6.6 | 5.2 | 10.6 |
| Second quintile | 11.5 | 10.5 | 14.2 |
| Third quintile | 16.3 | 15.6 | 17.6 |
| Fourth quintile | 22.7 | 22.4 | 22.0 |
| Top quintile | 43.0 | 46.4 | 35.7 |
| Top decile | 27.3 | 30.5 | 21.7 |

*Table 29.3*
*Distribution of income in the USA, the UK and Japan, by quintiles (%)*

Source: *World Development Report*, 2000/2001.

These data are not very easy to assimilate, especially for large numbers of countries, and to explore the question of income inequality, some summary measures need to be developed.

By calculating the ratio of the income accruing to the richest decile or quintile to the income of the poorest, some impression can be gained of the gap between the poorest and richest households. Table 29.4 summarises the results of such calculations for the three countries.

| Country | Ratio of top decile to poorest decile | Ratio of top quintile to poorest quintile |
|---|---|---|
| United States | 16.9 | 8.9 |
| United Kingdom | 10.5 | 6.5 |
| Japan | 4.5 | 3.4 |

*Table 29.4 Ratio of income of richest to poorest households*

It can be seen that in the UK households in the top decile receive ten and a half times more income than those in the poorest decile. On the basis of these data, inequality in the UK is lower than that in the USA, but higher than that in Japan.

## The Lorenz curve

There is a method of presenting these data visually, via the Lorenz curve. Some Lorenz curves are shown in Figure 29.14.

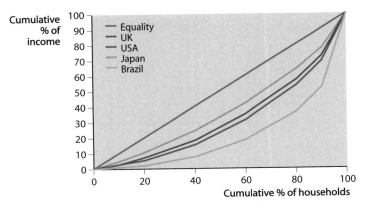

*Figure 29.14*
*Lorenz curves*

Source: *World Development Report*, 2000/2001.

Lorenz curves are constructed as follows. Using the data in Table 29.3, the first step is to convert the numbers in the table into *cumulative* percentages. In other

words (using the UK as an example), the data show that the poorest 20% receive 6.6% of total household income, the poorest 40% receive 6.6% + 11.5% = 18.1%, the poorest 60% receive 18.1% + 16.3% = 34.4%, and so on. It is these cumulative percentages that are plotted to produce the Lorenz curve, as in Figure 29.14. (The figure also plots the lowest and highest deciles.)

> **Key term**
>
> **Lorenz curve:** a graphical way of depicting the distribution of income within an economy

Suppose that income were perfectly equally distributed between households. In other words, suppose the poorest 10% of households received exactly 10% of income, the poorest 20% received 20%, and so on. The Lorenz curve would then be a straight line going diagonally across the figure.

To interpret the country curves, the closer a country's Lorenz curve is to the diagonal equality line, the more equal is the distribution. You can see from the figure that Japan comes closest to the equality line, bearing out the earlier conclusion that income is more equally distributed in that country. The UK and the US curves are closer together, but there seems to be slightly more inequality in the USA, as its Lorenz curve is further from the equality line. Brazil has also been included on the diagram, as an example of a society in which there is substantial inequality.

## Exercise 29.2

Use the data provided in Table 29.5 to calculate the ratios of the highest decile income to the lowest decile income, and of the highest quintile income to the lowest quintile income. Then draw Lorenz curves for the two countries, and compare the inequalities shown for Belarus and South Africa with each other and with the countries already discussed.

| | Percentage share of income or consumption: | |
| | South Africa | Belarus |
| --- | --- | --- |
| Lowest decile | 1.1 | 5.1 |
| Lowest quintile | 2.9 | 11.4 |
| Second quintile | 5.5 | 15.2 |
| Third quintile | 9.2 | 18.2 |
| Fourth quintile | 17.7 | 21.9 |
| Highest quintile | 64.8 | 33.3 |
| Highest decile | 45.9 | 20.0 |

Table 29.5 *Income distribution in Belarus and South Africa*

Source: *World Development Report,* 2000/2001.

## The Gini index

The Lorenz curve is fine for comparing income distribution in just a few countries. However, it would also be helpful to have an index that could summarise the relationship in a numerical way. The **Gini index** does just this. It is a way of trying to quantify the equality of income distribution in a country, and is obtained by calculating

> **Key term**
>
> **Gini index:** a measure of the degree of inequality of income in a society

the ratio of the area between the equality line and the country's Lorenz curve to the whole area under the equality line. This is often expressed as a percentage. With reference to Figure 29.15, the Gini index is calculated by the following formula:

$$\text{Gini index} = \frac{(\text{Area A}) \times 100}{\text{Area (A + B)}}$$

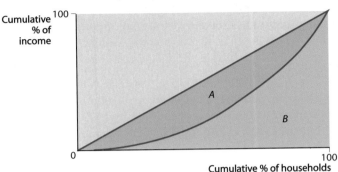

*Figure 29.15*
*The Gini index and the Lorenz curve*

The closer the Gini index is to 100, the further the Lorenz curve is from equality, and thus the more unequal is the income distribution. The Gini index values for the countries in Figure 29.14 are shown in Table 29.6.

| Country | Gini index |
|---|---|
| United Kingdom | 36.0 |
| United States | 40.8 |
| Japan | 24.9 |
| Brazil | 59.3 |

*Table 29.6*
*The Gini index*

Source: *Human Development Report,* 2005.

When measuring income inequality, some important measurement issues need to be borne in mind. For example, in talking about the 'poorest' and 'richest' households, you need to be aware that absolute income levels per household may be a misleading indicator, given that households are of different sizes and compositions. Thus, when looking at the income distribution in the UK, it is important to make adjustments for this.

The way this is done is by the use of *equivalence scales.* These allow a household to be judged relative to a 'reference household' made up of a childless couple. It can then be decided that a household with a husband, wife and two young children rates as 1.18 relative to the childless couple with a rating of 1. So if the couple with two children had an income of, say, £40,000 per year, this would be the equivalent of 40,000/1.18 = £33,898. In order to examine the inequality of income, it is these equivalised incomes that need to be considered.

A further question is whether income is the most appropriate indicator. People tend to smooth their consumption over their lifetimes, and it has been argued that it is more important to look at consumption (expenditure) than income when considering inequality.

Then there is the question of housing costs. In the short run, households have no control over their spending on housing. Some measures of inequality therefore choose to exclude housing costs from the calculations in order to focus on the income that households have at their disposal for other expenditures. As housing

tends to constitute a higher proportion of the budgets of poor households, measures of inequality that exclude housing costs tend to show greater levels of inequality.

It is also important to bear in mind that the standard of living that households can achieve depends partly on government-provided services, such as health and education. Remember that rich as well as poor households may benefit from these.

Finally, in considering inequality in a society, it may be important to examine inequalities in the distribution of wealth as well as income. Wealth can be regarded as the accumulated stock of assets that households own, and in the UK wealth is more unequally distributed than income.

It is interesting to note that many people remain unaware of where they fit into the income distribution of their country. A survey in the USA in 2000 found that 19% of Americans believed that they were in the top 1% of earners.

## Measuring poverty

One aspect of inequality is poverty. If there is a wide gap between the richest and poorest households, it is important to evaluate just how poor those poorest households are, and whether they should be regarded as being 'in poverty'. This requires a definition of poverty.

One way of defining poverty is to specify a basket of goods and services that is regarded as the minimum required to support human life. Households that are seen to have too low an income to allow them to purchase everything in that basic bundle of goods would be regarded as being in **absolute poverty**.

Globally, the UN Development Programme regards households in which income is below $1 per day per person as being in absolute poverty, as this is their declared *poverty line*.

*Below the poverty line — in the UK, poverty is measured in relative terms*

For a country like the UK, this absolute poverty line is not helpful, as so few people fall below it. Thus poverty in the UK is defined in *relative* terms. If a household has insufficient income for its members to participate in the normal social life of the country, it is said to be in **relative poverty**. This too is defined in terms of a poverty line, set at 50% of the median household disposable income. (The median is the income of the middle-ranked household.)

Figure 29.16 presents some data for a range of developed countries. The proportion of people below the relative poverty line varies substantially across these countries, from 7% in Slovakia to 18.8% in the Russian Federation.

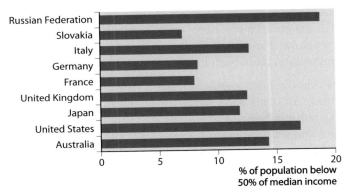

**Key terms**

**absolute poverty:** situation describing a household if its income is insufficient to allow it to purchase the minimum bundle of goods and services needed for survival

**relative poverty:** situation applying to a household whose income falls below 50% of adjusted household disposable income

*Figure 29.16 Poverty in developed nations, 1999–2000*

Source: *Human Development Report*, 2005.

The percentage falling below the poverty line is not a totally reliable measure on its own: it is also important to know *how far* below the poverty line households are falling. The *income gap* (the distance between household income and the poverty line) is a useful measure of the intensity of poverty as well as of its incidence.

## Exercise 29.3

Imagine that you are the Minister for Poverty Alleviation in a country in which the (absolute) poverty line is set at $500. Of the people living below the poverty line, you know that there are two distinct groups, each made up of 50 individuals. The people in group 1 have an income of $450, whereas those in group 2 have only $250. Suppose that your budget for poverty alleviation is $2,500.

a   Your prime concern is with the most needy: how would you use your budget?

b   Suppose instead that your prime minister instructs you to reduce the percentage of people living below the poverty line: do you adopt the same strategy for using the funds?

c   How helpful is the poverty line as a strategic target of policy action?

## Changes in inequality and poverty over time

Although the distribution of income does not change rapidly from one year to the next, there have been changes over time. Figure 29.17 plots the Gini index, calculated for both income and expenditure, in the UK over the period 1974–99.

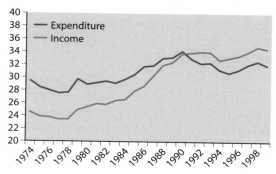

*Figure 29.17 Gini index for income and expenditure, 1974–99*

Source: Institute for Fiscal Studies in *Economic Review*, November 2003

Because people can be expected to smooth their consumption through time, expenditure inequality is seen to have been a little steadier than income inequality. However, both show a noticeable increase in inequality during the 1980s, since when there seems to have been no discernible trend.

It is worth noting that this has not been a general trend across all of the developed countries. A study by the OECD in 2002 found no generalised trend in the distribution of household incomes since the mid-1970s, although about half of the countries studied did show an increase between the mid-1980s and mid-1990s.[1]

Another study, undertaken by the Institute for Fiscal Studies, analysed trends and noted that there were very different trends identifiable over some 'periods of political interest'.[2] In particular, between 1979 and 1990, with Margaret Thatcher as prime minister, income growth was higher for each successive quintile.

The richest quintile saw income growth that was more than eight times that of the poorest. In other words, inequality increased during this period. Under John Major, from 1990 to 1997, growth was sluggish, but the poorest quintile gained relative to higher quintile groups. Under Tony Blair, from 1997 to 2001 income growth was more or less equally divided over the quintile groups.

*Inequality increased from 1979 to 1990 when Margaret Thatcher was prime minister*

[1] Michael Förster and Mark Pearson, 'Income distribution and poverty in the OECD area: trends and driving forces', *OECD Economic Studies*, no. 23, 2002.

[2] Alissa Goodman and Andrew Shephard, 'Inequality and living standards in Great Britain: some facts', *IFS Briefing Notes*, no. 19, updated December 2002.

However, you should not read too much into these differences. The causes of change in income distribution reflect not only the political stance of the government in power, but other changes occurring in society, and in the pattern of employment over time.

## Summary

➤ Some degree of inequality in income and wealth is present in every society.

➤ Inequality is measured by ranking households in order of income, then comparing the income received by the richest decile (or quintile) with that received by the poorest.

➤ The Lorenz curve gives a visual impression of the income distribution; this can be quantified into the Gini index as a single statistic representing the degree of income inequality.

➤ Calculations of the income distribution are normally undertaken using equivalised incomes, taking into account the size and composition of households.

➤ In some cases, consumption (expenditure) provides a more reliable measure of inequality, as people tend to smooth their consumption over time.

➤ Absolute poverty measures whether individuals or households have sufficient resources to maintain a reasonable life.

➤ Relative poverty measures whether individuals or households are able to participate in the life of the country in which they live: this is calculated as 50% of median adjusted household disposable income.

➤ Income distribution and poverty levels change relatively slowly over time.

➤ In the UK there has been little change since the mid-1990s, following a decade of increasing inequality.

## Evaluating the standard of living

GDP is a way of measuring the total output of an economy over a period of time. Although this measure can provide an indicator of the quantity of resources available to citizens of a country in a given period, as an assessment of the standard of living it has its critics.

GDP does have some things going for it. First, it is relatively straightforward and thus is widely understood. Second, it is a well-established indicator and one that is available for almost every country in the world, so it can be used to compare income levels across countries. For this purpose, it naturally helps to adjust for population size by calculating GDP per person (GDP *per capita*, as it is known). This then provides a measure of average income per head.

Figure 29.18 provides data on GDP per capita for selected countries. The extreme differences that exist around the globe are immediately apparent from the data. GDP per capita in Burundi was just $83 in 2003, whereas in the USA the figure was $37,648. Luxembourg heads this particular league table, with average income of $62,298 in 2003, which is off the scale of the figure.

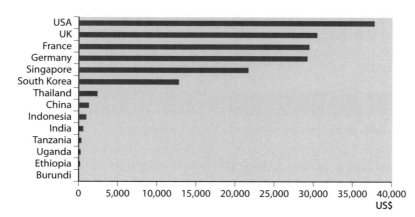

**Figure 29.18**
*GDP per capita,*
*selected*
*countries, 2003*

Source: *Human*
*Development Report,*
2005

In trying to interpret these data, a number of issues need to be borne in mind, as the comparison is not as straightforward as it looks.

### Inequality in income distribution

One important point to notice is that looking at the average level of income per person may be misleading if there are wide differences in the way in which income is distributed within countries. In other words, it cannot be assumed that every Burundian receives $83, or that every Luxembourgian receives $62,298. If income is more unequally distributed in some countries, this will affect one's perception of what the term 'average' means.

It is also important to be aware of differences in the overall level of taxation, which may vary between countries. In other words, in trying to compare average income levels across countries, it is household *disposable* income that is pertinent, as there may be differing degrees to which income is taxed away by governments.

### The informal sector and the accuracy of data

A further problem with undertaking international comparisons is that it is never absolutely certain that the accuracy with which data are collected is consistent across countries. Definitions of GDP and other variables are now set out in a clear, internationally agreed form, but even when countries are working to the same definitions, some data collection agencies may be more reliable than others.

One particular area in which this is pertinent relates to the informal sector. In every economy there are some transactions that go unrecorded. In most economies, there are economic activities that take place that cannot be closely monitored because of their informal nature. These are especially prevalent in many developing countries, where often substantial amounts of economic activity take place without an exchange of money. For example, in many countries subsistence agriculture remains an important facet of economic life.

However, this phenomenon is not confined to the developing countries. In every country, there is a certain amount of economic activity that takes place in the informal economy (or the 'cash economy' as it is sometimes known). The extent of this informal economy varies substantially between countries. Figure 29.19 shows some data for a range of European countries. You can see that even within Europe, the size of the informal economy varies from just 8.8% of GDP in Switzerland up to 28.6% in Greece. The UK has one of the smaller informal economies in this data set, which is based on calculations from World Bank data.

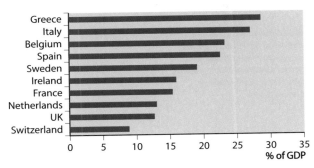

**Figure 29.19**
*The informal economy, selected countries, 2000*

Source: Friedrich Schneider, 'Size and measurement of the informal economy in 110 countries', University of Linz, 2002

Where such activity varies in importance between countries, comparing incomes on the basis of measured GDP may be misleading, as GDP will be a closer indicator of the amount of real economic activity in some countries than in others.

### Exchange rate problems

The data presented in Figure 29.18 were expressed in terms of US dollars. This allows a comparison of average incomes using a common unit of measurement. At the same time, however, it may create some problems.

It is important to compare average income levels in order to evaluate the standard of living, and compare standards across countries. In other words, the aim is to be able to assess people's command over resources in different societies, and to be able to compare the purchasing power of income in different countries.

GDP is calculated initially in terms of local currencies, and subsequently converted into US dollars using official exchange rates. Will this provide information about the relative local purchasing power of incomes? Not necessarily.

One reason for this is that official exchange rates are sometimes affected by government intervention. Indeed, in many of the less developed countries, exchange rates are pegged to an international currency — usually the US dollar. In these circumstances, exchange rates are more likely to reflect the government's policy and actions than the relative purchasing power of incomes in the countries under scrutiny.

Where exchange rates are free to find their own equilibrium level, they are likely to be influenced strongly by the price of internationally traded goods — which is likely to be a very different combination of goods than that typically consumed by residents in these countries. Again, it can be argued that the official exchange rates may not be a good reflection of the relative purchasing power of incomes across countries.

The United Nations International Comparison Project has been working on this problem for many years. It now produces an alternative set of international estimates of GDP based on purchasing power parity (PPP) exchange rates, which are designed to reflect the relative purchasing power of incomes in different societies more accurately. Figure 29.20 shows estimates for the same set of countries that were given in Figure 29.18.

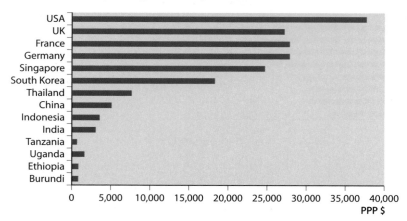

*Figure 29.20*
*GDP per capita,*
*selected*
*countries, 2003*
*(PPP$)*

Source: *Human Development Report*, 2005.

Comparing the two graphs, you will notice that the gap between the low-income and high-income countries seems less marked when PPP dollars are used as the unit of measurement. In other words, the US dollar estimates exaggerate the gap in living standards between rich and poor countries. Measurements in US dollars tend to understate real incomes for low-income countries and overstate them for high-income countries compared with PPP-dollar data. Put another way, people in the lower-income countries have a stronger command over goods and services than is suggested by US-dollar comparisons of GDP per capita.

### Social indicators

A final question that arises is whether GDP can be regarded as a reasonable indicator of a country's standard of living. You have seen that GDP provides an indicator of the total resources available within an economy in a given period, calculated from data about total output, total incomes or total expenditure. This focus on summing the transactions that take place in an economy over a period can be seen as a rather narrow view of what constitutes the 'standard of living'. After all, it may be argued that the quality of people's lives depends on more things than simply the material resources that are available.

For one thing, people need to have knowledge if they are to make good use of resources. Two societies with similar income levels may nonetheless provide a very different quality of life for their inhabitants, depending on the education levels of their population. Furthermore, if people are to benefit from consuming or using the available resources, they need a reasonable lifespan coupled with good health. So, good standards of health are also crucial to a good quality of life.

It is important to remember that different societies tend to set different priorities for the pursuit of growth and the promotion of education and health. This needs to be taken into account when judging relative living standards through a comparison of GDP per capita, as some countries have higher levels of healthcare and education than other countries with similar levels of GDP per capita.

A reasonable environment in which to live may be seen as another important factor in one's quality of life. Some environmental issues can distort the GDP measure of resources. Suppose there is an environmental disaster — perhaps an oil tanker breaks up close to a beautiful beach. This reduces the overall quality of life by degrading the landscape and preventing enjoyment of the beach. However, it does not have a negative effect on GDP; on the contrary, the money spent on clearing up the damage actually adds to GDP, so that the net effect of an environmental disaster may be to *increase* the measured level of GDP!

It is also important to be aware that GDP is an aggregate measure that does not reveal the sorts of goods being produced. For example, there may be substantial differences in the priorities of national governments between such items as healthcare, education and military expenditure. In countries where military expenditure takes a high proportion of GDP, there may be fewer resources left to be devoted to consumer durables or other goods.

From time to time, economists have proposed alternative measures to provide a more realistic estimate of the level of economic welfare enjoyed by the inhabitants of a country. One example is the **Measure of Economic Welfare (MEW)**, which was first proposed by William Nordhaus and James Tobin in 1972. This began with GNP, and then made various adjustments so that it only included the consumption and investment items that

 **Key** *term*

**Measure of Economic Welfare (MEW):** indicator that amends GDP per capita so that it only reflects items that contribute directly to economic well-being

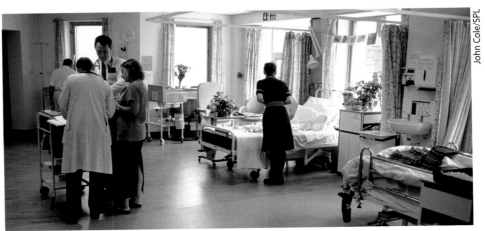

John Cole/SPL

*The standard of healthcare in a country may be seen as an important indicator of the standard of living*

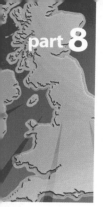
contribute directly to economic well-being. For example, they argued that the value of production in the informal sector of the economy should be included, but that deductions should be made for such things as environmental damage. In addition, they made adjustments (upward) for leisure time and (downward) for travel-to-work time. Although this measure did not really catch on, it led to considerable debate on the measurement of the standard of living in the presence of environmental and other external effects.

One of the problems with the Nordhaus–Tobin approach is the difficulty of arriving at objective measures of the externalities that they were trying to recognise in the calculations. This led to mistrust of any precise estimates that were produced. Nonetheless, it is widely recognised that the use of GDP per capita needs to be augmented by other indicators in order to arrive at a reasonable valuation of the standard of living. In the UK, for example, the Office for National Statistics publishes a series of environmental accounts that enable the monitoring of greenhouse gas and other emissions, and energy usage.

## Summary

➤ GDP is a widely used measure of the total amount of economic activity in an economy over a period of time.

➤ The trend rate of change of GDP may thus be an indicator of economic growth.

➤ Although GDP is a widely understood and widely available measure, it does have some drawbacks.

➤ Average GDP per person neglects the important issue of income distribution.

➤ There may be variation in the effectiveness of data collection agencies in different countries, and variation in the size of the informal sector.

➤ Converting from a local currency into US dollars may distort the use of GDP as a measure of the purchasing power of local incomes.

➤ GDP may neglect some important aspects of the quality of life.

# Chapter 30
# Controlling the performance of the UK economy

*The setting of objectives for macroeconomic policy implies that there are ways in which the authorities can seek to influence the course of the economy at the macroeconomic level. This chapter explores the main policy instruments that the authorities can use in seeking to control the performance of the UK economy, and evaluates the extent to which such methods of control are likely to be effective. A main focus will be on the tools of monetary policy, which has been the favoured method of influencing the economy in recent years. In addition, the role of the exchange rate will be explained, and the tools of fiscal policy outlined. The possibilities of imposing direct controls on markets and of using supply-side policies will also be investigated.*

## Learning outcomes

After studying this chapter, you should:

➤ be familiar with the prime tools of macroeconomic policy: in particular, monetary and fiscal policy and the foreign exchange rate

➤ be aware of the functions and measures of money, and the importance of interest rates in the economy

➤ understand the alternative types of fiscal policy instrument, including the use of alternative tax instruments and government spending

➤ be able to analyse the impact of changing fiscal instruments on the distribution of income

➤ understand the consequences of a fiscal budget deficit or surplus

➤ appreciate the difference between direct and indirect taxation as means of raising revenue

➤ be aware of alternative tools for influencing the performance of the economy, including minimum wage legislation and other direct controls such as tariffs and quotas

## Policy instruments

The government has four main types of policy instrument with which to attempt to meet its macroeconomic objectives. These policies were introduced in Chapter 12.

part **8**

### Monetary policy

This entails the use of monetary variables such as money supply and interest rates to influence aggregate demand. It will be shown that, under a fixed exchange rate system, monetary policy becomes wholly impotent, as it has to be devoted to maintaining the exchange rate. So, the effectiveness of monetary policy depends upon the policy environment in which it is used.

### Fiscal policy

The term 'fiscal policy' covers a range of policy measures that affect government expenditures and revenues through the decisions made by the government on its expenditure, taxation and borrowing. Fiscal policy is used to influence the level and structure of aggregate demand in an economy. As this chapter unfolds, you will see that the effectiveness of fiscal policy also depends crucially on the whole policy environment in which it is utilised.

### Direct controls

These are policies used by government to intervene directly in some markets — for example, in the form of minimum wage legislation, or tariffs and quotas, intended to influence international trade.

### Supply-side policies

Such policies comprise a range of measures intended to have a direct impact on aggregate supply — specifically, on the potential capacity output of the economy. These measures are often microeconomic in character and are designed to increase output and hence economic growth.

## Monetary policy

**Monetary policy** has become the prime instrument of government macroeconomic policy, with the interest rate acting as the key control variable. Monetary policy involves the manipulation of monetary variables in order to influence aggregate demand in the economy.

### Key terms

**monetary policy:** decisions made by the government regarding monetary variables such as money supply and interest rates

**money stock:** the quantity of money that is in circulation in the economy

In order to understand how monetary policy can influence the level of aggregate demand, it is important to examine the characteristics of key monetary variables — the money supply, interest rates and the exchange rate.

### Money supply

The **money stock** is the quantity of money that is in circulation in the economy. In a modern economy, money performs four important functions. First, it is a *medium of exchange*. In other words, money is what is used when people undertake transactions — for example, when you buy a sandwich for lunch. Second, money is a *store of value*: people (or firms) may choose to hold money in order to undertake transactions in the future. If this

490

were not the case, there would be no reason for people to accept money in exchange for goods or services. Money is also a *unit of account*: it is a way of setting prices so that the value of different goods and services can be compared. Finally, money is a *standard of deferred payment*. Firms signing contracts for future transactions need to be able to set prices for those transactions.

*The notes and coins in circulation in the UK are known as the monetary base*

Firms and households choose to hold some money. They may do this in order to undertake transactions, or as a precaution against the possible need to undertake transactions at short notice. In other words, there is a *demand for money*. However, in choosing to hold money they incur an opportunity cost, in the sense that they forgo the possibility of earning interest by purchasing some form of financial asset.

This means that the interest rate can be regarded as the opportunity cost of holding money; put another way, it is the price of holding money. At high rates of interest, people can be expected to choose to hold less money, as the opportunity cost of holding money is high. *MD* in Figure 30.1 represents such a money demand curve. It is downward sloping.

Suppose the government wants to set the money supply (*MS*) at *M\** in Figure 30.1. This can be achieved in two ways. If the government controls the supply of money at *M\**, equilibrium will be achieved only if the interest rate is allowed to adjust to *r\**. An alternative way of reaching the same point is to set the interest rate at *r\** and then allow the money supply to adjust to *M\**. The government can do one or the other — but it cannot set money supply at *M\** and hold the interest rate at any value *other than r\** without causing disequilibrium. In other words, it is not possible to control both money supply and interest rates simultaneously and independently.

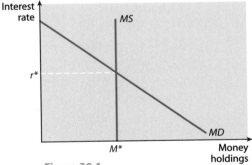

*Figure 30.1*
*The demand for money*

### Measuring money stock

An important characteristic of money is **liquidity**. This refers to the ease with which an asset can be spent. Cash is the most liquid asset, as it can be used for transactions. However, if you are holding funds in a savings account whereby you must either give notice of withdrawal or forfeit some return to withdraw it instantly, then such funds are regarded as being less liquid, as they cannot costlessly or instantly be used for transactions.

 **term**

**liquidity:** the extent to which an asset can be converted to cash without the holder incurring a cost

part **8**

One way of measuring the money stock is from the *monetary base*, which comprises all notes and coins in circulation. Together with the commercial banks' deposits at the Bank of England, this is known as **M0** or **narrow money**. This aims to measure the amount of money held for transactions purposes.

However, there are many assets that are 'near-money', such as interest-bearing current account deposits at banks. These are highly liquid and can readily be converted into cash for transactions. **M4** or **broad money** is a measure of the money stock that includes M0 together with sterling wholesale and retail deposits with monetary financial institutions such as banks. In other words, it includes all bank deposits that can be used for transactions, even though some of these deposits may require a period of notice for withdrawal. However, M4 is held not only for transactions purposes, but also partly as a store of wealth.

 **terms**

**narrow money (M0):** notes and coins in circulation and as commercial banks' deposits at the Bank of England

**broad money (M4):** M0 plus sterling wholesale and retail deposits with monetary financial institutions such as banks and building societies

Figure 30.2 presents the annual percentage rate of change of M0 and M4 since 1990, together with the annual inflation rate (measured by the RPI). This shows the extent to which it is possible for M0 and M4 to follow different paths through time — in 1999, for instance, M4 accelerated while M0 decelerated (and inflation fell). Over the years, the Bank of England has introduced various changes in the way the money definitions are measured, and there have been changes in the categories of institutions that are recognised for the purposes of calculating M4.

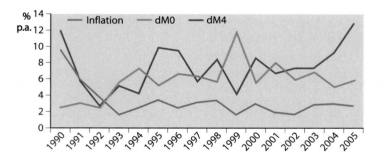

*Figure 30.2*
*Money supply and inflation in the UK, 1990–2005*

Note: d = annualised change in M0 or M4.

Source: ONS.

 **term**

**monetary transmission mechanism:** the channel by which monetary policy affects aggregate demand

A problem with attempting to control the money supply directly is that the complexity of the modern financial system makes it quite difficult to pin down a precise definition or measurement of money. For this and other reasons, the chosen instrument of monetary policy is the interest rate. By setting the interest rate, monetary policy affects aggregate demand through the so-called **monetary transmission mechanism**.

OCR Advanced Economics

## Interest rates

Although in the previous section we talked about 'the interest rate', this is a simplification. In the real-world economy, there are many different interest rates. For example, if you borrow from a bank, you will pay a higher interest rate than would be paid to you on your savings. Indeed, it is this difference between the rates for savers and borrowers that enables the banks to make a profit. This is shown in Figure 30.3, which shows interest rates set by the retail banks since 1995. You can see that the rates tend to move together through time, but that the rate charged on mortgage lending is consistently higher than the rates paid to savers on instant access accounts and time deposits. There is also a differential between these two types of savings account, reflecting the fact that savers can get a higher return by forgoing the right to withdraw their funds without notice (hence the term 'time deposits').

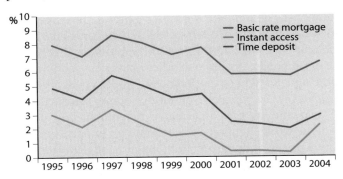

*Figure 30.3* Interest rates (retail banks)

Similarly, interest rates on financial assets differ depending on the nature of the asset. In part, these differences reflect different degrees of risk associated with the assets. A risky asset pays a higher interest rate than a relatively safe asset. A long-term asset tends to pay a higher interest rate than a short-term asset, although the differences have been quite small in the first few years of the twenty-first century.

## The exchange rate

In considering the tools of monetary policy, it is also important to consider the **exchange rate** — that is, the rate at which one currency exchanges against another. This is because the exchange rate, the interest rate and the money supply are all intimately related. If UK interest rates are high relative to elsewhere in the world, they will attract overseas investors, increasing the demand for pounds. This will tend to lead to an appreciation in the exchange rate — which in turn will reduce the competitiveness of UK goods and services, reducing the foreign demand for UK exports and encouraging UK residents to reduce their demand for domestic goods and buy imports instead.

 *term*

**exchange rate:** the price of one currency in terms of another

Indeed, under a fixed exchange rate regime, the monetary authorities are committed to maintaining the exchange rate at a particular level, so could not allow an appreciation to take place. In this situation, monetary policy is powerless to

influence the real economy, as it must be devoted to maintaining the exchange rate. Under a floating exchange rate system, monetary policy is freed from this role, but even so it must be used in such a way that the current account deficit of the balance of payments does not become unsustainable in the long run. In other words, the use of interest rates to target inflation has implications for the magnitude of the current and financial accounts of the balance of payments.

## The exchange rate and international competitiveness

In analysing the balance of payments, the relative competitiveness of UK goods and services is an important issue. If the UK persistently shows a deficit on the current account, does that imply that UK goods are uncompetitive in international markets?

The demand for UK exports in world markets depends upon a number of factors. In some ways, it is similar to the demand for a good. In general, the demand for a good depends on its price, on the prices of other goods, and on consumer incomes and preferences. In a similar way, you can think of the demand for UK exports as depending on the price of UK goods, the price of other countries' goods, incomes in the rest of the world and foreigners' preferences for UK goods over those produced elsewhere. However, in the case of international transactions the exchange rate is also relevant, as this determines the purchasing power of UK incomes in the rest of the world. Similarly, the demand for imports into the UK depends upon the relative prices of domestic and foreign goods, incomes in the UK, preferences for foreign and domestically produced goods and the exchange rate. These factors will all come together to determine the balance of demand for exports and imports.

The exchange rate plays a key role in influencing the levels of both imports and exports. Figure 30.4 shows the time path of the US$/£ exchange rate since 1971. It shows some fluctuations between 1971 and the late 1980s, around a declining trend. Since then the exchange rate seems to have remained fairly steady.

Nonetheless, there was a fall from a peak of $2.50 to the pound in 1972 to $1.50 some 30 years later. Other things being equal, this suggests an improvement in the competitiveness of UK products. In other words, Americans wanting to buy UK goods got more pounds for their dollars in 2002 than in 1972, and thus would have tended to find UK goods more attractive.

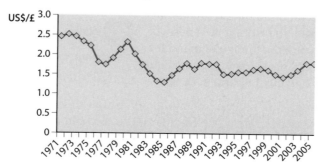

*Figure 30.4*
*The nominal exchange rate, US$/£, 1971–2005*

Source: ONS.

OCR Advanced Economics

*The exchange rate influences the demand for imports and exports*

However, some care is needed because other things do not remain equal. In particular, remember that the competitiveness of UK goods in the US market depends not only on the exchange rate, but also on movements in the prices of goods over time, so this needs to be taken into account — which is why Figure 30.4 refers to the *nominal exchange rate.* In other words, if the prices of UK goods have risen more rapidly than prices in the USA, this will have partly offset the downward movement in the exchange rate.

Figure 30.5 shows the nominal exchange rate again, but also the ratio of UK/US consumer prices (plotted using the righthand scale). This reveals that between 1971 and 1977 UK prices rose much more steeply than those in the USA, and continued to rise relative to the USA until the 1990s. Thus, the early decline in the nominal exchange rate was offset by the movement in relative prices.

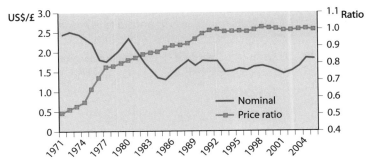

*Figure 30.5*
*The nominal exchange rate, US$/£, and the ratio of UK/US prices, 1971–2005*

Source: ONS, IMF.

In order to assess the overall competitiveness of UK goods compared with the USA, it is necessary to calculate the **real exchange rate**, which is defined as the nominal exchange rate multiplied by the ratio of relative prices.

The real exchange rate is shown in Figure 30.6. The real exchange rate also shows some fluctuations, especially between about 1977 and 1989. However, there does

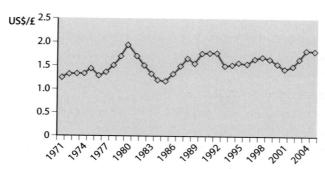

Figure 30.6 *The real exchange rate, US$/£, 1971–2005*
Source: calculated from data shown in Figure 30.5.

not seem to be any strong trend to the series, although the real rate was higher at the end of the period than at the beginning.

Notice that the series in Figure 30.6 relates only to competitiveness relative to the USA, as it is the real US$/£ exchange rate. An alternative measure is the sterling **effective exchange rate**, shown in Figure 30.7. This shows the strength of sterling relative to a weighted average of exchange rates of the UK's trading partners.

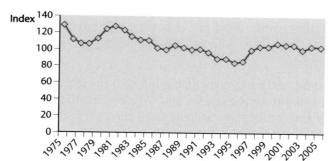

Figure 30.7
*The sterling effective exchange rate, 1975–2005 (1990 = 100)*

Source: ONS.

## Exercise 30.1

Table 30.1 provides data for the €/£ exchange rate, together with the consumer price index for the euro area and for the UK. Use these data to calculate the real exchange rate for the period, and comment on the effect that any movement will have had on the competitiveness of UK goods and services relative to the euro area.

*Table 30.1 Competitiveness of the UK compared to the euro area*

Sources: OECD, IFS.

| | Nominal exchange rate (€/£) | Consumer price index (2000 = 100) | |
|---|---|---|---|
| | | UK | Euro area |
| 1998 | 1.4796 | 97.9 | 96.6 |
| 1999 | 1.5189 | 99.2 | 97.7 |
| 2000 | 1.6456 | 100.0 | 100.0 |
| 2001 | 1.6087 | 101.8 | 102.1 |
| 2002 | 1.5909 | 103.5 | 104.4 |
| 2003 | 1.4456 | 106.5 | 106.6 |
| 2004 | 1.4739 | 109.7 | 108.9 |
| 2005 | 1.4629 | 112.8 | 111.2 |

## Summary

➤ Monetary policy entails the manipulation of monetary variables in order to influence aggregate demand in the economy.

➤ The prime instrument of monetary policy is the interest rate.

➤ People hold money in order to undertake transactions (among other reasons), and the interest rate can be regarded as the opportunity cost of holding money.

➤ There are several alternative definitions of money, depending upon how wide or narrow is the focus.

➤ There is not a single interest rate in the economy, but a variety of rates associated with the wide range of financial assets available.

➤ The monetary authorities can control either the money supply or interest rates, but not both independently.

➤ The exchange rate is also closely associated with money supply and the interest rate, and cannot be ignored in policy design.

➤ The real exchange rate is a measure of the international competitiveness of an economy's goods.

## Fiscal policy

What is the role of **fiscal policy** in a modern economy? Traditionally fiscal policy was used to affect the level of aggregate demand in the economy. The overall balance between government receipts and outlays affects the position of the aggregate demand curve, which is reinforced by multiplier effects. When government outlays exceed government receipts, the result is a *fiscal deficit*. This occurs when the revenues raised through taxation are not sufficient to cover the government's various types of expenditure.

The overall size of the budget deficit may limit the government's actions in terms of fiscal policy. In addition, the overall pattern of revenue and expenditure has a strong effect on the overall balance of activity in the economy. A neutral government budget can be attained either with high expenditure and high revenues, or with relatively low expenditure and revenues. Such decisions affect the overall size of the public sector relative to the private sector. Over the years, different governments in the UK have taken different decisions on this issue — and different countries throughout the world have certainly adopted different approaches.

In part, such issues are determined through the ballot box. In the run-up to an election, each political party presents its overall plans for taxation and spending, and typically they adopt different positions as to the overall balance. It is then up to those voting to give a mandate to whichever party offers a package that most closely resembles their preferences.

**Key** **term**

**fiscal policy:** decisions made by the government on its expenditure, taxation and borrowing

Figure 30.8 shows the time path of government consumption as a share of GDP from 1948 to 2005; it shows fluctuations around a downward trend, suggesting that the public sector has been gradually reducing its share of the economy. Notice that this does not give the full picture, as public sector investment is not taken into account in these data. There are one or two periods in the figure where the decline seems to have been especially rapid. In the early 1950s, this partly reflects the winding down of government activity after the rebuilding that followed the Second World War. The steep decline in the 1980s reflects the privatisation drive of that period, when the government was withdrawing from some parts of the economy.

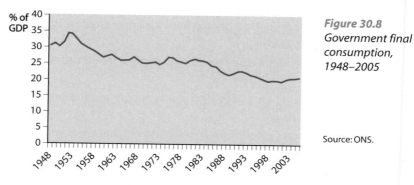

*Figure 30.8*
*Government final consumption, 1948–2005*

Source: ONS.

Figure 30.9 provides an international perspective, showing the share of current and capital expenditure by governments in a range of countries. This reveals something of a contrast between, on the one hand, North America, Australia and Japan, and on the other, many European countries, where governments have been more active in the economy. In part this reflects the greater role that government plays in some countries in providing services such as education and healthcare, whereas in other countries the private sector takes a greater role, often through the insurance market.

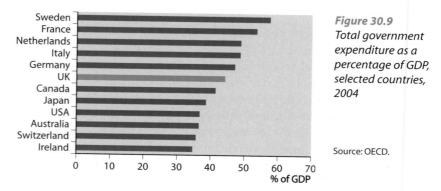

*Figure 30.9*
*Total government expenditure as a percentage of GDP, selected countries, 2004*

Source: OECD.

## Direct and indirect taxes

Fiscal policy, and taxation in particular, has not only been used to establish a balance between the public and private sectors of an economy. In addition, taxation remains an important weapon against some forms of market failure, and it also influences the

distribution of income. In this context, the choice of using direct or indirect taxes is important.

**Direct taxes** are taxes levied on income of various kinds, such as personal income tax. Such taxes are designed to be progressive and so can be effective in redistributing income: for example, a higher income tax rate can be charged to those earning high incomes. In contrast, **indirect taxes** — taxes on expenditure, such as VAT and excise duties — tend to be regressive. As poorer households tend to spend a higher proportion of their income on items that are subject to excise duties, a greater share of their income is taken up by indirect taxes. Even VAT can be regressive if higher-income households save a greater proportion of their incomes.

 **terms**

**direct tax:** a tax levied directly on income

**indirect tax:** a tax levied on expenditure on goods or services

When Margaret Thatcher came to power in 1979, one of her first actions was to introduce a switch away from direct taxation towards indirect taxes. VAT was increased and the rate of personal income tax was reduced. In support of this move, it was pointed out that if an income tax scheme becomes too progressive, it can provide a disincentive towards effort. If people feel that a high proportion of their income is being taken in tax, their incentives to provide work effort are weak. Indeed, a switch from direct to indirect taxation is regarded as a sort of supply-side policy intended to influence the position of aggregate supply.

Indirect taxes can be targeted at specific instances of market failure; hence the high excise duties on such goods as tobacco (seen as a demerit good) and petrol (seen as damaging to the environment because of the externality of greenhouse gas emissions).

### Sustainability of fiscal policy

Another important issue that came to the fore during the 1990s concerned the sustainability of fiscal policy. This is wrapped up with the notion that current taxpayers should have to fund only expenditure that benefits their own generation, and that the taxpayers of the future should make their own decisions, and not have to pay for past government expenditure that has been incurred for the benefit of earlier generations.

In this context, what is significant is the overall balance between receipts and outlays through time. If outlays were always larger than receipts, the spending programme could be sustained only through government borrowing, thereby shifting the burden of funding the deficit to future generations. This could also be a problem if it made it more difficult for the private sector to obtain funds for investment, or if it added to the national debt. At the time of writing, the Chancellor of the Exchequer, Gordon Brown, is committed to following a **Golden Rule of fiscal policy**, which states that, on average over the economic cycle, the government should borrow only to invest and not to fund current expenditure. This is intended to help achieve equity between present and future

 **term**

**Golden Rule of fiscal policy:** rule stating that, over the economic cycle, net government borrowing will be for investment only, and not for current spending

generations. It should perhaps be noted that this is a self-imposed guideline, so there would be no penalty for breaking the rule other than political credibility.

Figure 30.10 shows total public sector receipts and outlays since 1986. Outlays here include investment, but you can see how the two series tend to move in opposite directions over the cycle. To some extent this is to be expected, because of the operation of *automatic stabilisers* (see Chapter 12).

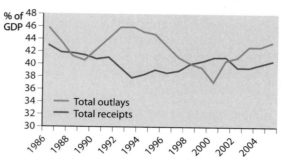

**Figure 30.10**
*UK public sector receipts and outlays, 1986–2005*

Source: OECD

If receipts and outlays more or less balance over the economic cycle, the economy is not in a position whereby the current generation is forcing future generations to pay for its consumption. However, it is not practical to impose this rule at every part of the cycle, so the Golden Rule applies over the economic cycle as a whole. There is also a commitment to keep public sector net debt below 40% of GDP — again, on average over the economic cycle. Figure 30.11 shows data for this on a quarterly basis since 1997.

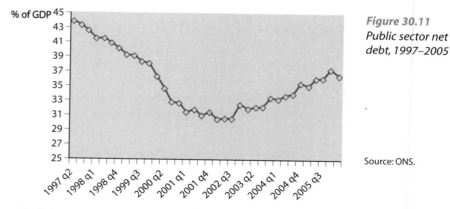

**Figure 30.11**
*Public sector net debt, 1997–2005*

Source: ONS.

## Summary

➤ Fiscal policy concerns the use of government expenditure and taxation to influence aggregate demand in the economy.

➤ The overall balance between private and public sectors varies through time and across countries.

➤ Direct taxes help to redistribute income between groups in society, but if too progressive they may dampen incentives to provide effort.

➤ Indirect taxes tend to be regressive.

➤ The Golden Rule for fiscal policy is that the government should aim to borrow only for investment, and not for current expenditure (averaged over the economic cycle).

➤ There is also a commitment to keep the national debt below 40% of GDP.

---

### Exercise 30.2

Discuss the extent to which the major British political parties adopt differing stances towards establishing a balance between the private and public sectors: in other words, the extent to which each is 'high tax/high public spending' or 'low tax/low public spending'. Analyse the economic arguments favouring each of the approaches.

## Other policy instruments

Monetary and fiscal policy operate by seeking to influence the decisions made by individual economic agents — mainly by manipulating the components of aggregate demand. The economic analysis on which this approach is based is explored in Chapter 31. However, there are also some other instruments of economic policy that the authorities can bring to bear. These may take the form of direct interventions in markets, such as minimum wage legislation, or the imposition of tariffs. They may also take the form of measures intended to affect the supply side of markets: for example, attempts to improve the flexibility with which markets behave.

### Minimum wage

In its manifesto published before the 1997 election, the Labour Party committed itself to the establishment of the National Minimum Wage (NMW). This would be the first time that such a measure had been used in the UK on a nationwide basis, although **minimum wages** had sometimes been set in particular industries.

After the election, a Low Pay Commission was set up to oversee the implementation of the policy, which came into force in April 1999. Initially the NMW was set at £3.60 per hour for those aged 22 and over, and £3 for those aged 18–21. From 1 October 2006 the rates were £5.35 for those aged 22 and over and £4.45 for those aged 18–21. A minimum wage of £3.30 per hour applied to 16- and 17-year-olds.

 **Key** *term*

**minimum wage:** legislation under which firms are not allowed to pay a wage below some threshold level set by the government

*A minimum wage ensures that 'work pays'*

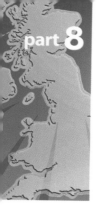

The objectives of the minimum wage policy are threefold. First, it is intended to protect workers against exploitation by the small minority of bad employers. Second, it aims to improve incentives to work by ensuring that 'work pays', thereby tackling the problem of voluntary unemployment. Third, it aims to alleviate poverty by raising the living standards of the poorest groups in society.

The policy has been a contentious one, with critics claiming that it meets none of these objectives. It has been argued that the minority of bad employers can still find ways of exploiting their workers: for example, by paying them on a piecework rate so that there is no set wage per hour. Another criticism is that the policy is too indiscriminate to tackle poverty, and that a more sharply focused policy is needed for this purpose. For example, many of the workers receiving the NMW may not in fact belong to poor households, but may be women working part time whose partners are also in employment. But perhaps most contentious of all is the argument that, far from providing a supply-side solution to some unemployment, the National Minimum Wage causes unemployment because of its effects on the demand for labour.

Figure 30.12 shows a labour market in which firms are operating under perfect competition. This means that no individual firm can influence the wage rate. The demand for labour curve is the combined demand of all the firms in the market, and the supply curve of labour is shown as upward sloping, as it is the market supply curve. In other words, at a higher wage rate, more workers will offer themselves for work. In free market equilibrium, the combined demand of firms in the market is $L^*$, and $W^*$ emerges as the equilibrium wage rate.

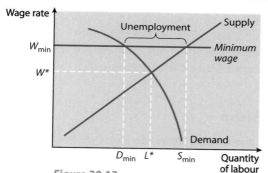

**Figure 30.12**
*The effect of a minimum wage in a perfectly competitive labour market*

When the government sets the minimum wage at $W_{min}$, all firms react by reducing their demand for labour at the higher wage. Their combined demand is now $D_{min}$, but the supply of labour is $S_{min}$. The difference between these $(S_{min} - D_{min})$ is unemployment. Furthermore, it is involuntary unemployment — these workers would like to work at the going wage rate, but cannot find a job.

Notice that there are two effects at work. Some workers who were formerly employed have lost their jobs — there are $L^* - D_{min}$ of these. In addition, however, the incentive to work is now improved (this was part of the policy objective, remember?). So there are

**Figure 30.13**
*A non-binding minimum wage in a perfectly competitive labour market*

now an additional $S_{min} - L^*$ workers wanting to take employment at the going wage rate. Thus, unemployment has increased for two reasons.

It is not always the case that the introduction of a minimum wage leads to an increase in unemployment. For example, in the market depicted in Figure 30.13 the minimum wage has been set below the equilibrium level, so will have no effect on firms in the market, which will continue to pay $W^*$ and employ $L^*$ workers.

It is also possible that, in the absence of the policy, firms had some market power over wages, so were able to pay a wage lower than the free market level. In such cases, the imposition of a minimum wage that forces firms to increase the wage paid may also lead to an *increase* in employment.

It is important to realise that there is not just a single labour market in the UK: for example, wage levels vary across the regions of the UK. Consequently, a single minimum wage set across the whole country 'bites' in different ways in different markets. It must therefore be questioned whether the same minimum wage can be as effective in, say, London as in Northern Ireland or the north of England.

In a government press release in August 2004, it was revealed that the Low Pay Commission had been asked to prepare a report on the operation of the National Minimum Wage. The commission was asked to monitor and evaluate the impact of the NMW and to review the wage rates. In reviewing the rates, the commission was further asked to:

> have regard to the wider social and economic implications; the likely effect on employment levels, especially within low-paying sectors and amongst disadvantaged people in the labour market; the impact on the costs and competitiveness of business; and the potential costs to industry and the Exchequer.

This seems to indicate that the government is aware of some of the pitfalls of the National Minimum Wage.

### Health and safety regulation

The government intervenes in the labour market through a range of measures designed to improve safety standards in the workplace. These are administered through the Health and Safety Commission and the Health and Safety Executive, whose responsibilities range:

> from health and safety in nuclear installations and mines, through to factories, farms, hospitals and schools, offshore gas and oil installations, the safety of the gas grid and the movement of dangerous goods and substances, railway safety, and many other aspects of the protection both of workers and the public.

Health and safety inspectors can enter premises without warning, and can issue improvement notices requiring problems to be put right within a specified time; for the most serious failings, they can prosecute.

Such regulation can impinge quite heavily on labour markets. One example is the EU Working Time Directive. This aims to protect the health and safety of workers

in the European Union by imposing regulations in relation to working hours, rest periods, annual leave and working arrangements for night workers. The legislation came into effect in the UK in October 1998 (except for junior doctors in training, for whom the directive was to be phased in gradually). The UK implemented the 48-hour week later than countries elsewhere in Europe because of a special dispensation. Countries elsewhere complained about this, arguing that it gave UK firms an unfair competitive advantage. This seems to suggest that the directive does indeed have an effect on the labour market.

The effect of these health and safety measures has been to raise the costs to firms of hiring labour. In the case of the Working Time Directive, firms may have to spread the same amount of work over a greater number of workers, and as there are some fixed hiring costs, this raises the cost of labour. Similarly, if the firm has to spend more on ensuring safety, it adds to the firms' costs.

Figure 30.14 illustrates one way of viewing the situation. It shows a perfectly competitive labour market for the market as a whole. Without regulation, the profit-maximising position is with labour employed up to $L^*$ at a wage of $W^*$. Suppose a health and safety regulation is introduced that adds a constant amount (of £$c$) to firm's cost per unit of labour employed. Firms then find that the average cost of labour is higher by £$c$ — shown as $AC_L$ in the diagram. They will perceive this as their marginal cost, and will employ labour up to the profit-maximising point, which is now at the quantity of labour $L_1$ with the wage given by $W_1$, which is the wage that attracts $L_1$ workers into the market.

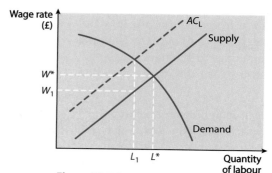

**Figure 30.14**
*The effect of a health and safety regulation in a perfectly competitive market*

## Tariffs

A policy instrument commonly used in the past to give protection to domestic producers is a **tariff**. Tariff rates in the developed countries have been considerably reduced in the period since the Second World War, but nonetheless are still in place.

Tariffs were discussed in Chapter 13 (pages 201–02), when it was pointed out that not all of the results of a tariff are favourable for an economy. Effectively, the government is subsidising inefficient local producers, and forcing domestic consumers to pay a price that is above that of similar goods imported from abroad.

**Key term**

**tariff:** a tax imposed on imported goods

Some would try to defend this policy on the grounds that it allows the country to protect an industry, thus saving jobs that would otherwise be lost. However, this goes against the theory of comparative advantage, and forces society to incur the deadweight loss. In the longer term it may delay structural change. For an economy to develop new specialisations and new sources of comparative advantage, there needs to be a transitional process in which old industries contract and new ones emerge. Although this process may be painful, it is necessary in the long run if the economy is to remain competitive. Furthermore, the protection that firms enjoy that allows them to reap economic rents from the tariff may foster complacency and an inward-looking attitude. This is likely to lead to X-inefficiency, and an inability to compete in the global market.

Even worse is the situation that develops where nations respond to tariffs raised by competitors by putting up tariffs of their own. This has the effect of further reducing the trade between countries, and everyone ends up worse off, as the gains from trade are sacrificed.

## Exercise 30.3

Figure 30.15 illustrates the impact of a tariff. $S_{dom}$ represents the quantity supplied by domestic producers, and $D_{dom}$ shows the demand curve of domestic consumers. The world price is $OE$, and the country can import as much of the good at that price as it wishes.

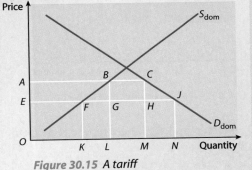

Figure 30.15 A tariff

a   In the absence of government inter-vention, identify domestic demand and supply, and the quantity of imports.

b   Suppose now that a tariff is imposed on imports of this product. Identify the price that will be charged in the domestic market.

c   What will be the quantity demanded, the quantity supplied by home producers, and the quantity imported?

d   Which area represents government revenue from the tariff?

e   Identify the additional economic rent received by domestic producers.

f   Identify and explain the deadweight loss of the tariff.

g   Discuss whether a tariff can be beneficial for society.

h   Suppose that a tariff has been in place on this commodity, but that the government proposes to remove it. Discuss the effects that the removal of the tariff will have, and the difficulties a government might face in removing it.

### Quotas
An alternative policy that a country may adopt is to limit the imports of a commodity to a given volume. For example, a country may come to an agreement with another country that only a certain quantity of imports will be accepted by the importing country. Such arrangements are sometimes known as **voluntary export restraints (VERs)**.

Figure 30.16 illustrates the effects of a quota. $D$ represents the domestic demand for this commodity, and $S_{dom}$ is the quantity that domestic producers are prepared to supply at any given price. Suppose that, without any agreement, producers from country A would be prepared to supply any amount of the product at a price $P_a$. If the product is sold at this price, $D_0$ represents domestic demand, of which $S_0$ is supplied by domestic producers and the remainder $(D_0 - S_0)$ is imported from country A.

**Key term**

**voluntary export restraint:** an agreement by a country to limit its exports to another country to a given quantity (quota)

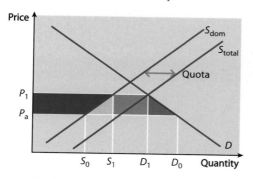

**Figure 30.16** *The effects of a quota*

By imposing a quota, total supply is now given by $S_{total}$, which is domestic supply plus the quota of imports allowed into the economy from country A. The market equilibrium price rises to $P_1$ and demand falls to $D_1$, of which $S_1$ is supplied by domestic producers and the remainder $(D_1 - S_1)$ is the agreed quota of imports.

Figure 30.16 shows who gains and who loses by this policy. Domestic producers gain by being able to sell at the higher price, so (as in the case of the tariff) they receive additional economic rent given by the dark-blue area. Furthermore, the producers exporting from country A also gain, receiving the green rectangle (which, in the case of the tariff, was tax revenue received by the government). As in the case of the tariff, the two triangles (red and pale blue) represent the dead-weight loss of welfare suffered by the importing country.

Such an arrangement effectively subsidises the foreign producers by allowing them to charge a higher price than the price at which they would have been willing to supply the goods. Furthermore, although domestic producers are encouraged to produce more, the protection offered to them is likely to lead to X-inefficiency and weak attitudes towards competition.

There are a number of examples of such agreements, especially in the textile industry. For example, the USA and China have had long-standing agreements on quotas for a range of textile products. Ninety-one such quotas expired at the end of 2004 as part of China's accession to the World Trade Organization. As you might expect, this led to extensive lobbying by producers in the USA, especially during the run-up to the 2004 presidential election. Trade unions in the USA supported the producers, arguing that 350,000 jobs had been lost since the expiry of earlier quota agreements in 2002. In the case of three of these earlier agreements, some restraint had been reinstated for bras, dressing gowns and knitted fabrics. Producers in other countries, such as Sri Lanka, Bangladesh, Nepal, Indonesia, Morocco, Tunisia and Turkey, were lobbying for the quotas to remain, regarding China as a major potential competitor. However, for the USA at least, it can be

*The output of Chinese textile workers is perceived as a threat by producers in the USA and other countries*

argued that the removal of the quotas would allow domestic consumers to benefit from lower prices, and would allow US textile workers to be released for employment in higher-productivity sectors, where the USA maintains a competitive advantage.

There was also a dispute between China and the EU over clothing imports, when quotas on clothing were reintroduced after substantial stocks of goods had already been dispatched to Europe. Italy, in particular, was concerned that its fashion industry would be damaged by unregulated imports of clothing from China.

### Non-tariff barriers

There are other ways in which trade can be hampered, one example being the use of what are known as **non-tariff barriers**. These often comprise rules and regulations that control the standard of products that can be sold in a country.

 **Key term**

**non-tariff barrier:** an obstacle to free trade other than a tariff — for example, quality standards imposed on imported products

This is a grey area, as some of the rules and regulations may seem entirely sensible and apply equally to domestic and foreign producers. For example, laws that prohibit the sale of refrigerators that contain CFCs are designed to protect the ozone layer, and may be seen to be wholly appropriate. In this case, the regulation is for purposes other than trade restriction.

However, there may be other situations in which a regulation is more clearly designed to limit trade. For example, the USA specifies a larger minimum size for vine-ripened tomatoes than for green tomatoes, thereby raising costs for the former. This has to do with trade because vine-ripened tomatoes are mainly imported from Mexico, but green tomatoes are mainly grown in Florida. Thus, the regulation gives Florida producers an advantage.

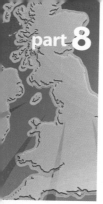

Such rules and regulations may operate especially against producers in less developed countries, who may find it especially difficult to meet demanding standards of production. This applies in particular where such countries are trying to develop new skills and specialisations to enable them to diversify their exports and engage more actively in international trade.

### Supply-side policies

In addition to the instruments discussed in this chapter, governments have looked for ways of influencing aggregate supply. This has encompassed a wide

*US regulations for sizes of tomatoes give green tomato producers in Florida an advantage over vine-ripened tomato producers in Mexico*

range of policies aimed mainly at improving the efficiency with which markets work to allocate resources. These are discussed in Chapter 32. This chapter has examined the instruments of macroeconomic policy and the next will provide a framework of economic analysis that shows how these instruments are expected to affect the performance of the economy.

## Summary

➤ In addition to the instruments of monetary and fiscal policy, governments try to influence the economy through direct controls.

➤ Minimum wage legislation is intended to protect the low paid by ensuring that employers must pay at least a specified minimum wage.

➤ This might improve the pay of those in work, but there may be side effects on the level of employment in some labour markets.

➤ Regulations to safeguard the health and safety of workers may also affect employment levels by raising the costs of hiring labour.

➤ Tariffs, quotas and non-tariff barriers have sometimes been used by governments in order to inhibit international trade and provide protection for domestic jobs.

➤ Such policies may impose welfare costs on society.

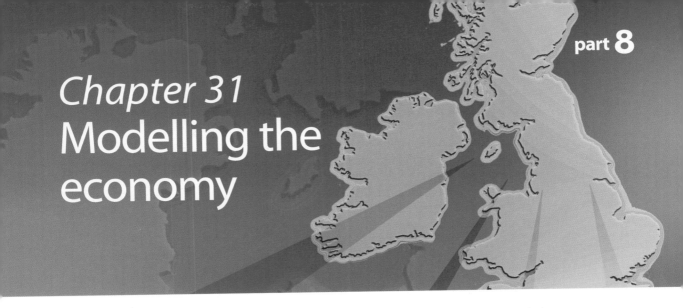

# Chapter 31
# Modelling the economy

The previous chapter outlined the various instruments of policy that governments have at their disposal. In order to understand how these policy instruments are expected to influence the economy, it is important to be able to understand the operation of the economy. This chapter presents some models that can be used for this purpose. The AD/AS model that was introduced in Chapter 10 is at the heart of much of this analysis, and it is now time to look more carefully at the assumptions of that model, and at how different economists have interpreted the model in different ways. In explaining the UK's trading position, it is also important to understand something about the potential gains that can be made from international trade.

## Learning outcomes

After studying this chapter, you should:
➤ be able to understand the assumptions and operations of the *AD/AS* model
➤ be familiar with the concepts of the national income and credit creation multipliers and be able to comment on their usefulness
➤ be able to explain the way in which interest rates are determined using the liquidity preference and loanable funds theories
➤ understand the potential gains to be made from international trade through the concepts of absolute and comparative advantage
➤ be able to analyse the causes and consequences of changes in exchange rates

## The *AD/AS* model — a reminder

To analyse the impact of macroeconomic policy instruments, return to the model of aggregate supply and aggregate demand (*AS/AD*), first introduced in Chapter 10. Figure 31.1 shows an economy in full employment equilibrium. *AD* is the **aggregate demand curve**, with the chief components of aggregate demand being consumption, investment, government spending and net exports. *AS* is the **aggregate supply curve**, which becomes vertical at the full capacity level of output. In other words, $Y^*$ represents the maximum amount of output that the economy

can produce in a period if all its resources are being fully utilised. This can be described as the full employment level of output. The intersection of *AD* and *AS* provides the equilibrium position for the economy, with *P* in Figure 31.1 being the equilibrium price level. Remember that the *AD* curve is very different in nature from the individual demand curve for a commodity. Here the relationship is between the *total* demand for goods and services and the *overall* price level. You might find it helpful to refresh your memory about this model by looking back at Chapter 10.

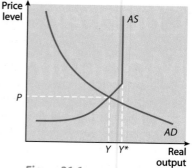

**Figure 31.1**
*Macroeconomic equilibrium revisited*

Notice that it is important to be aware of a debate that developed over the shape of the aggregate supply curve. This is important because it has implications for the conduct and effectiveness of policy options.

During the 1970s, an influential school of macroeconomists, which became known as the **monetarist school**, argued that the economy would always converge on an equilibrium level of output that they referred to as the *natural rate of output*. They also argued that the adjustment to this natural rate would be rapid, perhaps almost instantaneous. Associated with this long-run equilibrium was a **natural rate of unemployment**.

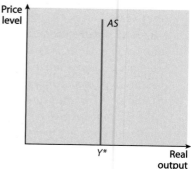

**Figure 31.2**
*Aggregate supply in the long run: the 'monetarist' view*

In this case, the long-run relationship between aggregate supply and the price level would be vertical, as shown in Figure 31.2. Here $Y^*$ is the full employment level of aggregate output — the natural rate of output. In this view of the world, a change in the overall price level does not affect aggregate output because the

## Key terms

**aggregate demand (AD) curve:** curve showing the relationship between the level of aggregate demand and the overall price level; it shows planned expenditure at any given overall price level

**aggregate supply (AS) curve:** curve showing the quantity of output that firms are prepared to supply at any given overall price level

**monetarist school:** group of economists who believed that the macro economy

always adjusts rapidly to the full employment level of output; they also argued that monetary policy should be the prime instrument for stabilising the economy

**natural rate of unemployment:** equilibrium full employment level of unemployment

**Keynesian school:** group of economists who believed that the macro economy could settle in an equilibrium that was below the full employment level

economy always readjusts rapidly back to full employment. Indeed, no change in aggregate demand can affect aggregate output, as it is only the price level that will adjust to restore equilibrium.

An opposing school of thought (often known as the **Keynesian school**) held that the macro economy was not sufficiently flexible to enable continuous full employment. They argued that the economy could settle at an equilibrium position below full employment, at least in the medium term. In particular, inflexibilities in labour markets would prevent adjustment. For example, if firms had pessimistic expectations about aggregate demand, and thus reduced their supply of output, this would lead to lower incomes because of workers being laid off. This would then mean that aggregate demand was indeed deficient, so firms' pessimism was self-fulfilling. Pessimistic expectations would also affect investment, and thus have an impact on the long-run productive capacity of the economy.

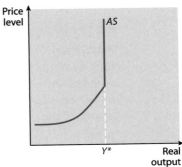

**Figure 31.3**
*Aggregate supply in the long run: the 'Keynesian' view*

Keynesian arguments led to a belief that there would be a range of outputs over which aggregate supply would be upward sloping. Figure 31.3 illustrates such an aggregate supply curve, and will be familiar from Chapter 10. In this diagram, $Y^*$ still represents full employment; however, when the economy is operating below this level of output, aggregate supply is somewhat sensitive to the price level, becoming steeper as full employment is approached.

The policy implications of the monetarist $AS$ curve are strong. If the economy always converges rapidly on the full employment level of output, no manipulation of aggregate demand can have any effect except on the price level. This is readily seen in Figure 31.4, where, regardless of the position of the aggregate demand curve, the level of real output remains at $Y^*$. If aggregate demand is low at $AD_0$, then the price level is also relatively low, at $P_0$. An increase in aggregate demand to $AD_1$ raises the price level to $P_1$ but leaves real output at $Y^*$. In such a world, only supply-side policy (which affects the position of the aggregate supply curve) has any effect on real output.

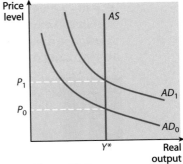

**Figure 31.4**
*Demand-side policy with a vertical AS curve*

## Summary

➤ In using the *AD/AS* model to analyse policy options, it is useful to distinguish between monetarist and Keynesian views about the shape of aggregate supply.

➤ Monetarist economists have argued that the economy always converges rapidly on equilibrium at the natural rate of output, implying that policies affecting aggregate demand have an impact only on prices, leaving real output unaffected. The aggregate supply curve in this world is vertical.

> The Keynesian view is that the economy may settle in an equilibrium that is below full employment, and that there is a range over which the aggregate supply curve slopes upwards.

## Monetary policy

In evaluating the tools of monetary policy, it is important to understand the route by which a change in a monetary variable can have an effect on the real economy. In other words, how can a change in money supply, or the interest rate, affect the level of equilibrium output in the economy?

### The credit creation multiplier

Think, first of all, about the way in which the money supply is created. You might think that this is simply a question of controlling the amount of notes and coins issued by the central bank. However, because there are many different assets that act as near-money in a modern economy, the real picture is more complicated. The actions of the commercial banks also have implications for the size of the money supply.

Consider the way that commercial banks operate. They accept deposits from customers, and supply them with banking services. However, they also provide loans — and this is how they make profits. Suppose that the government undertakes a piece of expenditure, and finances it by issuing money. The firms receiving the payment from the government are likely to bank the money they receive, so bank deposits increase. From the perspective of the commercial banks, they know that it is unlikely that all their customers will want to withdraw their money simultaneously, so they will lend out some of the additional deposits to borrowers who are likely to undertake expenditure on goods or services. As their expenditures work

*The actions of commercial banks have an effect on the money supply*

their way back into the banking system, the commercial banks will find that they can lend out even more, and so the process continues. In other words, an increase in the amount of money in the economy has a multiplied effect on the amount of credit created by the banks. This process is known as the **credit creation multiplier**.

Consider an arithmetic example, illustrated in Figure 31.5. Suppose that the commercial banks always act such as to hold 10% of their assets in liquid form – that is, as cash in the tills. If an extra £100 is lodged as deposits, the commercial banks will add £10 to the cash in tills, and lend out the remaining £90, as in the diagram. When that £90 finds its way back into the hands of the bank, it will keep £9 as cash, and lend out the remaining £81. And so on. The process will stop when the bank is back to a cash ratio of 10%. The original extra £100 will have been converted into £100 in cash, and £900 in loans!

The value of the multiplier is 1 divided by the cash ratio that the commercial banks decide to hold. The smaller this ratio, the larger is the credit multiplier. If the commercial banks want to hold only 5% of their assets in the form of cash, then the credit multiplier will be 1/0.05 = 20.

The significance of this relationship is that changes in the supply of cash have a multiplied impact on the amount of credit in the economy. This makes monetary control through money supply a highly imprecise business, especially if the central bank does not know exactly what the commercial banks' desired liquidity ratio is. In the past, one way that the monetary authorities tried to control money supply was to impose requirements on the proportion of assets that banks held in liquid form. However, this is also imprecise, as banks need not hold exactly the proportion required, in order to give themselves some leeway in the short run. This method of control was abandoned long ago, although the commercial banks are required to keep a small portion of their assets as cash at the Bank of England. This is purely for operational reasons.

> **Key term**
>
> **credit creation multiplier:** process by which an increase in money supply can have a multiplied effect on the amount of credit in an economy

Figure 31.5 *Credit creation*

### The quantity theory of money

Why should the quantity of money or credit in circulation be so important? In order to explain this, it is helpful to outline the so-called quantity theory of money. This in turn requires a new concept, that of the velocity of circulation. If the **money stock** is defined as the quantity of money (notes and coins) in circulation in the economy, the **velocity of circulation** is defined as the speed with which that money

stock changes hands. It is calculated as the volume of transactions divided by the money stock.

In practice, the volume of transactions is represented by nominal income, which is the level of real income ($Y$) multiplied by the average price level ($P$). If $V$ is the velocity of circulation, and $M$ is the size of the money stock, then the following equation holds:

$$V = \frac{PY}{M}$$

**Key terms**

**money stock:** the quantity of money in the economy

**velocity of circulation:** the rate at which money changes hands: the volume of transactions divided by the money stock

Notice that this is just a definition. Multiplying both sides of the equation by $M$ gives:

$$MV = PY$$

This is still based on a definition, so is not a theory. However, the monetarists argued that the velocity of circulation ($V$) would be constant – or at least would be stable over time. They also argued that real output would always tend rapidly towards a natural rate. These assumptions, together with the $MV = PY$ equation, provide us with a direct link between money ($M$) and the overall price level ($P$). This relationship suggests that prices can only increase persistently if money stock itself increases persistently.

Even if we allow real output to vary through time, the equation still shows that persistent inflation can only arise when money stock persistently grows more rapidly than real output.

How can we interpret this in terms of aggregate demand and aggregate supply? If the money supply increases, then firms and households in the economy find they have excess cash balances – that is, for the given price level, they have stronger purchasing power than they had anticipated. Their impulse will thus be to increase spending, which will cause the aggregate demand curve to move to the right. They will probably also save some of the excess, which will tend to result in lower interest rates – which then reinforces the increase in aggregate demand. However, as the $AD$ curve moves to the right, the equilibrium price level will rise, and return the economy to equilibrium.

If money supply continues to increase, the process repeats itself, with price then rising persistently. One danger of this is that people get so accustomed to the process that they speed up their spending decisions, and this accelerates the whole process.

To summarise, the analysis suggests that although a price rise can be triggered on either the supply side or the demand side of the macro economy, persistent inflation can only arise through persistent excessive growth in the money stock, which can be seen in terms of persistent movements of the aggregate demand curve.

## Liquidity preference

The discussion of the tools of monetary policy in Chapter 30 referred to the way in which the interest rate may be regarded as the opportunity cost of holding money.

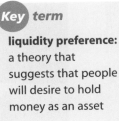
It was argued that economic agents, whether households or firms, will display a demand for money, arising from the functions that money fulfils in a modern economy. This theory of **liquidity preference**, as it is known, was noted by Keynes in his *General Theory*.

**Key term**

**liquidity preference:** a theory that suggests that people will desire to hold money as an asset

Three main motives for holding money have been identified. First, people demand money to hold for *transactions* purposes. People need money in order to buy goods and services and make other transactions. Second, people hold money for *precautionary* reasons. This is so that they have money available in case they need to spend because of an emergency, or because a good opportunity for a bargain arises. Third, Keynes argued that there may be a *speculative* demand for money. If people expect bond prices to fall, then they may hold money to avoid the capital loss that they would otherwise incur.

Figure 31.6 offers a reminder of what is implied for the money market. If the rate of interest is the opportunity cost of money, it is expected that the demand for money (*L*) will be lower when the rate of interest is relatively high, as the opportunity cost of holding money is high. People will be more reluctant to forgo the rate of return that has to be sacrificed by holding money. When the rate of interest is relatively low, this will be less of a concern, so the demand for money will be relatively high.

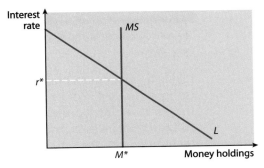

*Figure 31.6 The money market*

The existence of this relationship between the interest rate and the demand for money means that the monetary authorities have to be aware of the need to maintain (or allow) equilibrium in the money market. Interest rates and money supply cannot be fixed independently — the authorities can either fix the interest rate and allow money supply to adjust, or vice versa (see page 491). This is a clear constraint on the use of monetary policy.

An important question is the extent to which the demand for money is stable. If money demand were to be volatile, moving around from one time period to the next, then it would be virtually impossible for the monetary authorities to have any precise control over the market. The situation is further complicated by the way that interest rates influence behaviour.

### The market for loanable funds

Although the rate of interest can be interpreted as the opportunity cost of holding money, this is not the only way of viewing it. From a firm's point of view, it may be seen as the cost of borrowing. For example, suppose that a firm is considering under-

**Key term**

**market for loanable funds:** the notion that households will be influenced by the rate of interest in making saving decisions, which will then determine the quantity of loanable funds available for firms to borrow for investment

*The rate of interest is one of the factors influencing a firm's decision on whether to invest in new capital*

taking an investment project. The rate of interest represents the cost of borrowing the funds needed in order to finance the investment. The higher the rate of interest, the less investment projects will be seen as being profitable. If the firm is intending to finance its investment from past profits, the interest rate is still pertinent, as it then represents the return that the firm could obtain by purchasing a financial asset instead of undertaking the investment. Either way, the rate of interest is important in the decision-making process.

The rate of interest is also important to households, to whom it may represent the return on saving. Households may be encouraged to save more if the return on their saving is relatively high, whereas when the rate of interest is low, the incentive to save is correspondingly low. Within the circular flow of income, expenditure and output, which was explained in Chapter 9, it is the flow of saving from households that enables firms to find the funds needed to fund their investment expenditure. It is now apparent that the rate of interest may play an important role in bringing together these flows.

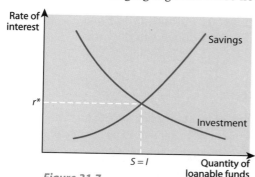

**Figure 31.7**
*The market for loanable funds*

This is illustrated in Figure 31.7. The investment schedule is shown as downward sloping because firms will find more investment projects to be worthwhile when the rate of interest is low. The savings schedule is shown as upward sloping because a higher rate of interest will encourage households to supply more saving. In other words, the supply of loanable funds will be higher when the rate of interest is relatively high.

Keynes believed that this could lead to instability in financial markets. He argued that investment and saving would be relatively insensitive to the rate of interest, such that the schedules in Figure 31.7 would be relatively steep. Investment would depend more crucially on firms' expectations about the future demand for their products, which could be volatile, moving the investment schedule around and thus leading to instability in the rate of interest. He thus came to the conclusion that governments should manage aggregate demand in order to stabilise the economy.

### The rate of interest and aggregate demand

In drawing this analysis together, an important issue concerns the relationship between the rate of interest and the level of aggregate demand. This is critical for the conduct of monetary policy. Indeed, the interest rate has been seen as the prime instrument of monetary policy in recent years — and monetary policy is seen as the prime instrument of macroeconomic policy. By setting the interest rate, monetary policy is intended to affect aggregate demand through the so-called **monetary transmission mechanism**.

**Key** *term*

**transmission mechanism of monetary policy:** the route by which changes in the interest rate feed through into the real economy

At a higher interest rate, firms undertake less investment expenditure because fewer projects are worthwhile. In addition, a higher interest rate may encourage higher saving, which also means that households undertake less consumption expenditure. This may then reinforce the impact on investment because if firms perceive consumption to be falling, this will affect their expectations about future demand, and further dampen their desire to undertake investment. Furthermore, if UK interest rates are high relative to elsewhere in the world, they will attract overseas investors, increasing the demand for pounds. This will tend to lead to an appreciation in the exchange rate, which in turn will reduce the competitiveness of UK goods and services, reducing the foreign demand for UK exports and encouraging UK residents to reduce their demand for domestic goods and buy imports instead. All these factors lower the level of aggregate demand, shifting the $AD$ curve to the left.

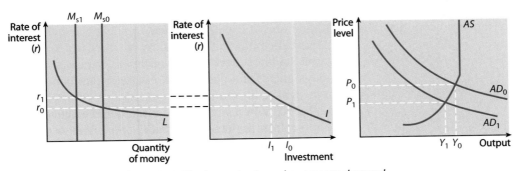

*Figure 31.8 The interest rate and aggregate demand*

This can be seen by looking at Figure 31.8. The initial equilibrium is with real output at $Y_0$, the price level at $P_0$ and the rate of interest at $r_0$. An increase in the rate of interest to $r_1$ will need to be balanced by a decrease in money supply to

maintain money market equilibrium. However, more significant is the effect on investment, which is shown in the middle panel of the figure. The increase in the rate of interest leads to a fall in investment from $I_0$ to $I_1$. This will cause the aggregate demand curve to move from $AD_0$ to $AD_1$, resulting in a lower overall price level $P_1$ and a lower real output level at $Y_1$. The lower level of real output arises because the $AS$ curve was drawn with an upward-sloping segment.

Notice that this may not be the end of the story. If one of the effects of the higher interest rate is to discourage investment, this will also have long-term consequences. Investment allows the productive capacity of the economy to increase, leading to a rightward drift in the $AS$ curve. With lower investment, this process will slow down, leaving the economy with lower productive capacity than it otherwise would have had.

The $AD/AS$ graph is drawn in terms of the overall price level. However, in a dynamic context, such a policy stance may be needed in order to maintain control of inflation. A reduction in interest rates would, of course, have the reverse effect. However, notice that the interaction of the money supply, interest rates and the exchange rate makes policy design a complicated business.

In creating a stable macroeconomic environment, the ultimate aim of monetary policy is not simply to keep inflation low, but to improve the confidence of decision-makers, and thereby encourage firms to invest in order to generate an increase in production capacity. This will stimulate economic growth and create an opportunity to improve living standards.

## Exercise 31.1

Outline the mechanism by which an increase in the rate of interest affects aggregate demand in an economy.

## Fiscal policy

Given the workings of the $AD/AS$ model, what is the role of fiscal policy in a modern economy? The traditional aim of fiscal policy was to affect the level of aggregate demand in the economy. In other words, the overall balance between government receipts and outlays affects the position of the aggregate demand curve, which is reinforced by multiplier effects (see Chapter 10). When government outlays exceed government receipts, the result is a *fiscal deficit*. This occurs when the revenues raised through taxation are not sufficient to cover the government's various types of expenditure.

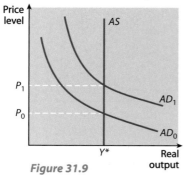

**Figure 31.9**
*Demand-side policy with a vertical AS curve*

Figure 31.9 shows that shifting the aggregate demand curve affects only the overall price level in the economy when the aggregate supply curve is vertical — remember that the monetarist school of thought argued that it would always be vertical. Hence a key issue for a government considering the use of fiscal policy is knowing whether there is spare capacity in the economy, because otherwise an expansion in aggregate demand from increased government spending will push up prices, but leave real output unchanged.

Chapter 10 introduced the concept of the **multiplier**, which suggested that for any increase in autonomous spending, there would be a multiplied increase in equilibrium output. The idea of the multiplier is that, if there is an increase in (say) government expenditure, this provides income for workers, who will then spend that income and create further expenditure streams. The size of these induced effects will depend upon the marginal propensity to withdraw.

> **Key** term
>
> **multiplier:** the ratio of a change in equilibrium real income to the autonomous change that brought it about; it is calculated as 1 divided by the marginal propensity to withdraw

Notice that it is the act of spending that allows these effects to be perpetuated. If the workers who receive additional income do not spend some of that income, the effects are diluted. The amounts that are not spent are referred to as 'withdrawals'. There are three ways in which these withdrawals take place. First, it may be that households decide to save some of the extra income that they receive instead of spending it. The amount of additional income that is saved is known as the *marginal propensity to save* ($s$). Second, some of the extra income will be spent on imports, and the *marginal propensity to import* ($m$) represents the fraction of extra income spent on imported goods or services. Third, a proportion of the extra income ($t$) is taken back by the government as taxes on income. The marginal propensity to withdraw ($mpw$) is thus the sum of these three effects ($s + m + t$).

The size of the multiplier can then be calculated. For example, suppose that households save 5% of extra income ($s = 0.05$) and spend 10% of the extra income on imports ($m = 0.1$), and that 25% goes in tax ($t = 0.25$). The $mpw$ is then $0.05 + 0.1 + 0.25 = 0.4$, and the multiplier is 2.5. An increase in the savings rate to 15% would increase the $mpw$ to 0.5 and reduce the multiplier to 2.

## Exercise 31.2

Calculate the multiplier if households save 20% of any additional income that they receive and spend 10% on imports. Assume that the marginal tax rate is 10%. Check how the multiplier changes if the marginal tax rate increases to 20%.

In terms of the $AD/AS$ diagram, the existence of the multiplier means that if there is an increase in government expenditure, the $AD$ curve moves further to the right than it otherwise would have done, because of the multiplier effects. However, this does not mean that equilibrium income will increase by the full multiplier amount. Looking more closely at what is happening, you can see that there are some forces at work that are acting to weaken the multiplier effect of an increase in government expenditure.

One way in which this happens is through interest rates. If the government finances its deficit through borrowing, a side effect is to put upward pressure on interest rates, which then may cause private sector spending — by households on consumption and by firms on investment — to decline, as the cost of borrowing has been increased. This process is known as the **crowding out** of private sector activity by the public sector. It limits the extent to which a government budget deficit can shift the aggregate demand curve, especially if the public sector activity is less productive than the private sector activity that it replaces.

### Automatic and discretionary fiscal policies

It is important to distinguish between automatic and discretionary changes in government expenditure. Some items of government expenditure and receipts vary automatically with the business cycle. They are known as **automatic stabilisers**. For example, if the economy enters a period of recession, government expenditure will rise because of the increased payments of unemployment and other social security benefits, and revenues will fall because fewer people are paying income tax, and because receipts from VAT are falling. This helps to offset the recession without any active intervention from the government.

**crowding out:** process by which an increase in government expenditure 'crowds out' private sector activity by raising the cost of borrowing

**automatic stabilisers:** process by which government expenditure and revenue vary with the business cycle, thereby helping to stabilise the economy without any conscious intervention from government

More important, however, is the question of whether the government can or should make use of discretionary fiscal policy in a deliberate attempt to influence the course of the economy. As already mentioned, the key issue is whether or not the economy has spare capacity, because attempts to stimulate an economy that is already at full employment will merely push up the price level. The feasibility of using fiscal policy is evaluated in Chapter 32.

### Exercise 31.3

Draw a diagram to show how the effects of an increase in aggregate demand will vary with different shapes of the aggregate supply curve and with different starting positions.

## The importance of international trade

The central importance of international trade for growth and development has been recognised since the days of Adam Smith and David Ricardo. For example, during the Industrial Revolution a key factor was that Britain could bring in raw materials from its colonies for use in manufacturing activity. Today, consumers in the UK are able to buy and consume many goods that simply could not be produced within the domestic economy. From the point of view of economic analysis, Ricardo showed that countries could gain from trade through a process of *specialisation.*

chapter

## Absolute and comparative advantage

The notion of specialisation was introduced in Chapter 1 of the book, where you were introduced to Colin and Debbie, who produced pots and bracelets with varying levels of effectiveness. Colin and Debbie's relative skill levels in producing these two goods can now be extended. Table 31.1 reminds you of Colin and Debbie's production possibilities.

| Colin | | Debbie | |
|---|---|---|---|
| Pots | Bracelets | Pots | Bracelets |
| 12 | 0 | 18 | 0 |
| 9 | 3 | 12 | 12 |
| 6 | 6 | 6 | 24 |
| 3 | 9 | 3 | 30 |
| 0 | 12 | 0 | 36 |

*Table 31.1*
*Colin and Debbie's production*

You may remember that Debbie was much better at both activities than Colin. If they each devote all their time to producing pots, Colin produces only 12 to Debbie's 18. If they each produce only bracelets, Colin produces 12 and Debbie, 36.

This illustrates **absolute advantage**. Debbie is simply better than Colin at both activities. Another way of looking at this is that, in order to produce a given quantity of a good, Debbie needs less labour time than Colin.

There is another significant feature of this table. Although Debbie is better at producing both goods, the difference is much more marked in the case of bracelet production than for pot production. So Debbie is relatively more proficient in bracelet production: in other words, she has a **comparative advantage** in making bracelets. This is reflected in differences in opportunity cost. If Debbie switches from producing pots to producing bracelets, she gives up 6 pots for every 12 additional bracelets that she makes. The opportunity cost of an additional bracelet is thus 6/12 = 0.5 pots. For Colin, there is a one-to-one trade-off between the two, so his opportunity cost of a bracelet is 1 pot.

More interesting is what happens if the same calculation is made for Colin and pot making. Although Debbie is absolutely better at making pots, if Colin increases his production of pots, his opportunity cost in terms of bracelets is still 1. But for Debbie the opportunity cost of making pots in terms of bracelets is 12/6 = 2, so Colin has the lower opportunity cost. Although Debbie has an *absolute* advantage in pot making, Colin has a *comparative* advantage. It was this difference in comparative advantage that gave rise to the gains from specialisation that were set out in Chapter 1.

**Key terms**

**absolute advantage:** the ability to produce a good more efficiently (e.g. with less labour)

**comparative advantage:** the ability to produce a good *relatively* more efficiently (i.e. at a lower opportunity cost)

**law of comparative advantage:** the theory that there may be gains from trade arising when countries (or individuals) specialise in the production of goods or services in which they have a comparative advantage

The **law of comparative advantage** states that overall output can be increased if all individuals specialise in producing the goods in which they have a comparative advantage.

### Gains from international trade

This same principle can be applied in the context of international trade. Suppose there are two countries — call them Overthere and Elsewhere. Each country can produce combinations of agricultural goods and manufactures. However, Overthere has a comparative advantage in producing manufactured goods, and Elsewhere has comparative advantage in agricultural goods. Their respective *PPC*s are shown in Figure 31.10.

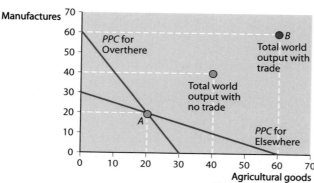

*Figure 31.10*
*PPCs for Overthere and Elsewhere*

You can see the pattern of comparative advantage reflected in the different slopes of the countries' *PPC*s. If the countries each produce some of each of the goods, one possibility (chosen for simplicity) is that they produce at point A, which is the inter-section of the two *PPC*s. At this point each country produces 20 units of manu-factures and 20 units of agricultural goods. Total world output is thus 40 units of manufactures and 40 units of agricultural goods — this point is marked on the figure.

However, suppose each country were to specialise in the product in which it has a comparative advantage. Overthere could produce 60 units of manufactured products, and Elsewhere could produce 60 units of agricultural goods. This would produce total world output at point B. Trade could take place such that each country had 30 units of each good, leaving them both unequivocally better off: they would each have more of both commodities. The figure shows that total world output of each type of good has increased by 20 units.

It can be seen that in this situation trade may be mutually beneficial. Notice that this particular result of trading has assumed that the countries exchange the goods on a one-to-one basis. Although this exchange rate makes both better off, it is not the only possibility. It is possible that exchange will take place at different prices for the goods, and clearly, the prices at which exchange takes place will determine which of the countries gains most from the trade that occurs.

## Exercise 31.4

Figure 31.11 shows production possibility curves for two countries, each of which produces both bales of cotton and cars. The countries are called 'West' and 'East'.

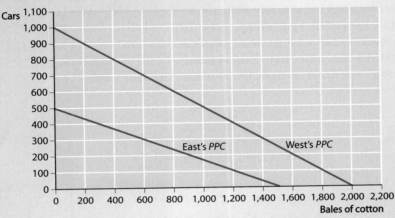

*Figure 31.11* PPCs for East and West

a Which country has an absolute advantage in the production of both commodities?

b Which country has a comparative advantage in the production of bales of cotton?

c Which country has a comparative advantage in the production of cars?

d Suppose that West produces 500 cars and East produces 300. How many bales of cotton are produced in each country?

e Now suppose that 800 cars and 400 bales of cotton are produced by West, and that East produces only bales of cotton. What has happened to total production of bales of cotton and cars?

In the above examples and exercises, specialisation and trade are seen to lead to higher overall production of goods. Although the examples have related to goods, you should be equally aware that services too may be a source of specialisation and trade. This is potentially important for an economy like that of the UK, where there is a comparative advantage in the provision of financial services.

### Who gains from international trade?

Specialisation can result in an overall increase in total production. However, one of the fundamental questions of economics in Chapter 1 was 'for whom?' So far nothing has been said about which of the countries will gain from trade. It is possible that exchange can take place between countries in such a way that both countries are better off. But whether this will actually happen in practice depends on the prices at which exchange takes place.

In particular, specialisation may bring dangers and risks, as well as benefits. One obvious way in which this may be relevant is that, by specialising, a country allows some sectors to run down. For example, suppose a country came to rely on imported food, and allowed its agricultural sector to waste away. If the country then became involved in a war, or for some other reason was unable to import its food, there would clearly be serious consequences if it could no longer grow its own foodstuffs. For this reason, many countries have in place measures designed to protect their agricultural sectors — or other sectors that are seen to be strategic in nature.

Over-reliance on some commodities may also be risky. For example, the development of artificial substitutes for rubber had an enormous impact on the demand for natural rubber; this was reflected in falls in its price and caused difficulties for countries that had specialised in producing rubber.

*This Second World War poster called on people in Britain to keep allotments as declining food imports became a serious issue*

## Summary

➤ Specialisation opens up the possibility of trade.

➤ The theory of comparative advantage shows that even if one country has an absolute advantage in the production of goods and services, trade may still increase total output if each country specialises in the production of goods and services in which it has a comparative advantage.

➤ Who gains from specialisation and trade depends crucially on the prices at which exchange takes place.

## The balance of payments

For an economy that is open to international trade, it is important to be able to monitor the transactions that take place. The balance of payments accounts enable this by itemising all the transactions in goods, services and financial assets that take place between one country and the rest of the world. The exchange rate is also critical in this respect, as it has a strong influence on the relative competitiveness of domestic goods in international markets, and on which countries gain from specialisation and international trade. The way in which the exchange rate is determined thus plays a crucial role in modelling the macro economy and in policy design and effectiveness.

## The foreign exchange market

The foreign exchange market involves demand and supply, just like any normal market. A foreign exchange transaction is needed whenever trade takes place. If, as a UK resident, you buy goods from abroad, you need to purchase foreign exchange — say, euros — and you will have to supply pounds in order to buy euros. Similarly, if a French tourist in the UK buys UK goods or services, the transaction needs to be carried out in pounds, so there is a demand for pounds.

This market is shown in Figure 31.12. The demand curve is downward sloping because when the €/£ rate is low, UK goods, services and assets are relatively cheap in terms of euros, so demand is relatively high. On the other hand, when the €/£ rate is relatively high, people in the Eurozone receive fewer euros for their pounds, so the demand will be relatively low.

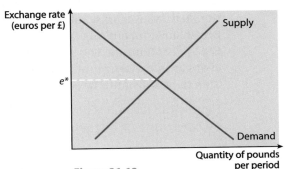

**Figure 31.12**
*The market for pounds*

The supply curve of pounds is upward sloping. When the €/£ rate is relatively high, the supply of pounds will be relatively strong, as UK residents will get plenty of euros for their pounds and thus will demand goods, services and assets from the Eurozone, supplying pounds in order to buy the foreign exchange needed for the transactions. When the €/£ rate is low, Eurozone goods, services and assets will be relatively expensive for UK residents, so fewer pounds will be supplied.

The market is in equilibrium at $e^*$, where the demand for pounds is just matched by the supply of pounds. This position has a direct connection with the balance of payments. If the demand for pounds exactly matches the supply of pounds, this implies that there is a balance between the demand from Eurozone residents for UK goods, services and assets, and the demand by UK residents for Eurozone goods, services and assets. In other words, the balance of payments is in overall balance. The key question for consideration is how the market reaches $e^*$ — in particular, do the authorities allow the exchange rate to find its own way to $e^*$, or do they intervene to ensure that it gets there?

## Summary

➤ The foreign exchange market can be seen as operating according to the laws of demand and supply.

➤ The demand for pounds arises when non-residents want to buy UK goods, services or assets.

➤ The supply of pounds arises when UK residents wish to buy foreign goods, services or assets.

➤ When the exchange rate is at its equilibrium level, this automatically ensures that the overall balance of payments is zero.

**part 8**

## A fixed exchange rate system

**Key term**

**fixed exchange rate system:** a system in which the government of a country agrees to fix the value of its currency in terms of that of another country

In the Bretton Woods conference at the end of the Second World War, it was agreed to establish a fixed exchange rate system, under which countries would commit to maintaining the price of their currencies in terms of the US dollar. This system remained in place until the early 1970s. For example, from 1950 until 1967 the sterling exchange rate was set at $2.80, and the British government was committed to making sure that it stayed at this rate. This system became known as the *dollar standard*. Occasional changes in exchange rates were permitted after consultation if a currency was seen to be substantially out of line — as happened for the UK in 1967.

Figure 31.13 illustrates how this works. Suppose the authorities announce that the exchange rate will be set at $e_f$. Given that this level is set independently by the government, it cannot be guaranteed to correspond to the market equilibrium, and in Figure 31.13 it is set above the equilibrium level. At this exchange rate, the supply of pounds exceeds the demand for pounds. This can be interpreted in terms of the overall balance of payments. If there is an excess supply of pounds, the implication is that UK residents are trying to buy more US goods, services and assets than Americans are trying to buy British: in other words, there is an overall deficit on the balance of payments.

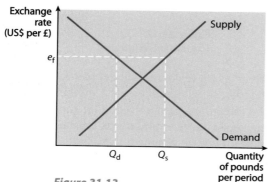

**Figure 31.13**
*Maintaining a fixed exchange rate*

In a free market, you would expect the exchange rate to adjust until the demand and supply of pounds came back into equilibrium. However, with the authorities committed to maintaining the exchange rate at $e_f$, such an adjustment cannot take place. As the UK owes the USA for the excess goods, services and assets that its residents have purchased, the authorities then have to sell **foreign exchange reserves** in order to make the books balance.

**Key term**

**foreign exchange reserves:** stocks of foreign currency and gold owned by the central bank of a country to enable it to meet any mismatch between the demand and supply of the country's currency

In terms of Figure 31.13, $Q_d$ represents the demand for pounds at $e_f$ and $Q_s$ represents the supply. The difference represents the amount of foreign exchange reserves that the authorities have to sell to preserve the balance of payments. Such transactions used to be known as 'official financing', and are now incorporated into the financial account of the balance of payments.

Notice that the *position* of the demand and supply curves depends on factors other than the exchange rate that can

526

OCR Advanced Economics

affect the demand for UK and US goods, services and assets in the respective countries. It is likely that through time these will shift in position. For example, if the preference of Americans for UK goods changes through time, this will affect the demand for pounds.

Consider Figure 31.14. For simplicity, suppose that the supply curve remains fixed, but demand shifts through time. Let $e_f$ be the value of the exchange rate that the UK monetary authorities have undertaken to maintain. If the demand for pounds is at $D_1$, the chosen exchange rate corresponds to the market equilibrium, and no action by the authorities is needed. If demand is at $D_0$, then with the exchange rate at $e_f$ there is an excess supply of pounds (as was the case in Figure 31.13). The monetary authorities in the UK need to buy up the excess supply by selling foreign exchange reserves. Conversely, if the demand for pounds is strong, say because Americans have developed a preference for Scotch whisky, then demand could be at $D_2$. There is now excess demand for pounds, and the UK monetary authorities supply additional pounds in return for US dollars. Foreign exchange reserves thus accumulate.

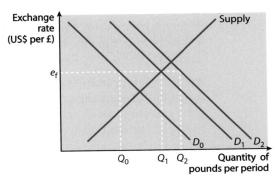

*Figure 31.14*
*Maintaining a fixed exchange rate in the face of changing demand for pounds*

In the long term, the system will operate successfully for the country as long as the chosen exchange rate is close to the average equilibrium value over time, so that the central bank is neither running down its foreign exchange reserves nor accumulating them.

A country that tries to hold its currency away from equilibrium indefinitely will find this problematic in the long run. For example, in the first few years of the twenty-first century, China and some other Asian economies were pegging their currencies against the US dollar at such a low level that they were accumulating reserves. In the case of China, it was accumulating substantial amounts of US government stock. The low exchange rate had the effect of keeping the exports of these countries highly competitive in world markets. However, such a strategy relies on being able to continue to expand domestic production to meet the high demand; otherwise inflationary pressure will begin to build.

During the period of the dollar standard, the pound was probably set at too high a level, which meant that UK exports were relatively uncompetitive, and in 1967 the UK government announced a **devaluation** of the pound from $2.80 to $2.40.

 **terms**

**devaluation:** a process whereby a country in a fixed exchange rate system reduces the price of its currency relative to an agreed rate in terms of a foreign currency

**revaluation:** a process whereby a country in a fixed exchange rate system raises the price of the domestic currency in terms of a foreign currency

During the period of the dollar standard, the UK economy went through what became known as a 'stop–go' cycle of growth. When the government tried to stimulate economic growth, the effect was to suck in imports, as the marginal propensity to import was high. The effect of this was to generate a deficit on the current account of the balance of payments, which then needed to be financed by selling foreign exchange reserves.

This process has two effects. First of all, in selling foreign exchange reserves, domestic money supply increases, which then puts upward pressure on prices, threatening inflation. In addition, the Bank of England has finite foreign exchange reserves, and cannot allow them to be run down indefinitely. This meant that the government had to rein in the economy, thereby slowing the rate of growth again; hence the label 'stop–go'.

An important point emerges from this discussion. The fact that intervention to maintain the exchange rate affects domestic money supply means that, under a fixed exchange rate regime, the monetary authorities are unable to pursue an independent monetary policy. In other words, money supply and the exchange rate cannot be controlled independently of one another. Effectively, the money supply has to be targeted to maintain the value of the currency. Governments may be tempted to use tariffs or non-tariff barriers to reduce a current account deficit, but this has been shown to be distortionary.

### The effects of devaluation

During the stop–go period there were many debates about whether there should be a devaluation. The effect of devaluation is to improve competitiveness. At a lower value of the pound, you would expect an increase in the demand for exports and a fall in the demand for imports, ceteris paribus.

However, this does not necessarily mean that there will be an improvement in the current account. One reason for this concerns the elasticity of supply of exports and import substitutes. If domestic producers do not have spare capacity, or if there are time lags before production for export can be increased, then exports will not expand quickly in the short run, and so the impact of this action on exports will be limited. Similar arguments apply to producers of goods that are potential substitutes for imported products, which reinforces the sluggishness of adjustment. In the short run, therefore, it may be that the current account will worsen rather than improve, in spite of the change in the competitiveness of domestic firms.

This is known as the *J-curve effect*, and is shown in Figure 31.15. Time is measured on the horizontal axis, and the current account is initially in deficit. A devaluation at time *A* initially pushes the current account further

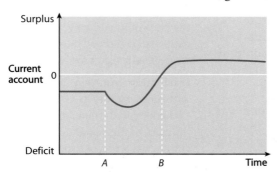

*Figure 31.15 The J-curve effect of a devaluation*

*In order to finance the Vietnam War, the USA had to increase the supply of dollars*

into deficit because of the inelasticity of domestic supply. Only after time *B*, when domestic firms have had time to expand their output to meet the demand for exports, does the current account move into surplus.

A second consideration relates to the elasticity of demand for exports and imports. Again, if competitiveness improves but demand does not respond strongly, there may be a negative impact on the current account. If the demand for exports is price-inelastic, a fall in price will lead to a fall in revenue. Indeed, the *Marshall–Lerner condition* states that a devaluation will have a positive effect on the current account only if the sum of the elasticities of demand for exports and imports is negative and numerically greater than 1.

The Bretton Woods dollar standard broke down in the early 1970s. Part of the reason for this was that such a system depends critically on the stability of the base currency (i.e. the US dollar). During the 1960s the US need to finance the Vietnam War meant that the supply of dollars began to expand, one result of which was accelerating inflation in the countries that were fixing their currency in terms of the US dollar. It then became increasingly difficult to sustain exchange rates at fixed levels. The UK withdrew from the dollar standard in June 1972. Following this, the pound fell steadily for the next 5 years or so.

## Summary

➤ After the Bretton Woods conference at the end of the Second World War, the dollar standard was established, under which countries agreed to maintain the value of their currencies in terms of US dollars.

➤ In order to achieve this, the monetary authorities engaged in foreign currency transactions to ensure that the exchange rate was maintained at the agreed level, accumulating foreign exchange reserves to accommodate a balance of payments surplus and running down the reserves to fund a deficit.

➤ Occasional realignments were permitted, such as the devaluation of sterling in 1967.

➤ Under a fixed exchange rate system, monetary policy can only be used to achieve the exchange rate target.

➤ A devaluation has the effect of improving international competitiveness, but the effect on the current account depends upon the elasticity of demand for exports and imports.

➤ The current account may deteriorate in the short run if the supply response is sluggish.

➤ The Bretton Woods system broke down in the early 1970s.

## Exercise 31.5

A firm wants to purchase a machine tool which is obtainable in the UK for a price of £125,000, or from a US supplier for $300,000. Suppose that the exchange rate is fixed at £1 = $3.

**a** What is the sterling price of the machine tool if the firm chooses to buy in the USA?

**b** From which supplier would the firm be likely to purchase?

**c** Suppose that between ordering the machine tool and its delivery the UK government announces a devaluation of sterling, so that when the time comes for the firm to pay up the exchange rate is £1 = $2. What is the sterling price of the machine tool bought from the USA?

**d** Comment on how the competitiveness of UK goods has been affected.

**e** Discuss the effects that the devaluation is likely to have on the economy as a whole. (Use the *AD/AS* model to help you to analyse these changes.)

## Floating exchange rates

Under a **floating exchange rate system**, the value of the currency is allowed to find its own way to equilibrium. This means that the overall balance of payments is automatically assured, and the monetary authorities do not need to intervene to make sure it happens. In practice, however, governments have tended to be wary of leaving the exchange rate entirely to market forces, and there have been occasional periods in which intervention has been used to affect the market rate.

An example of this was the **Exchange Rate Mechanism (ERM),** which was set up by a group of European countries in 1979 with the objective of keeping member countries' currencies relatively stable against each other. This was part of the European Monetary System (EMS). Each member nation agreed to keep its currency within 2.25% of a weighted average of the members' currencies (known as the European Currency Unit, or ECU). This was an *adjustable peg* system. Eleven realignments were permitted between 1979 and 1987.

OCR Advanced Economics

The UK opted not to join the ERM when it was first set up, but started shadowing the Deutschmark in the mid-1980s, aiming to keep the rate at around DM3 to the pound, as you can see in Figure 31.16. The UK finally decided to become a full member of the ERM in September 1990, agreeing to operate within a 6% band. However, the rate at which sterling had been set against the Deutschmark was relatively high, and the situation was worsened by the effects of German reunification,

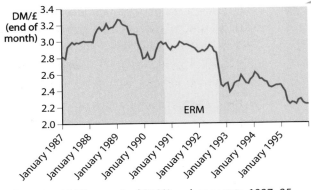

Figure 31.16 *The nominal DM/£ exchange rate, 1987–95*
Source: Bank of England.

which led to substantial capital flows into Germany, reinforcing the overvaluation of sterling. Once it became apparent that sterling was overvalued, speculative attacks began, and the Bank of England's foreign exchange reserves were depleted; in 1992 the pound left the ERM. You can see in Figure 31.16 that the value of the pound fell rapidly after exit.

## What determines exchange rates?

If the foreign exchange market is left free to find its own way to equilibrium, it becomes important to consider what factors will influence the level of the exchange rate. In particular, will the exchange rate resulting from market equilibrium be consistent with the government's domestic policy objectives?

Exchange rate equilibrium also implies a zero overall balance of payments. If the exchange rate always adjusts to the level that ensures this, it might be argued that the long-run state of the economy is one in which the competitiveness of domestic firms remains constant over time. In other words, you would expect the exchange rate to adjust through time to offset any differences in inflation rates between countries. The **purchasing power parity theory of exchange rates** argues that this is exactly what should be expected in the long run. If you look back at Figure 30.6 on p. 496, you will see that, aside from some fluctuations, the real exchange rate has remained fairly constant through time and shows no underlying trend. This is what would be expected if the nominal exchange rate was adjusting to offset changes in relative prices between countries.

However, in the short run the exchange rate may diverge from its long-run equilibrium. An important influence on the exchange rate in the short run is speculation. So far, the discussion of the exchange rate has stressed mainly the current account of the balance of payments. However, the financial account is also significant, especially since regulation of the

**Key terms**

**purchasing power parity theory of exchange rates:** theory stating that, in the long run, exchange rates (in a floating rate system) are determined by relative inflation rates in different countries

**hot money:** stocks of funds that are moved around the globe from country to country in search of the best return

movement of financial capital was removed. Some of these capital movements are associated with direct investment. However, sometimes there are also substantial movements of what has come to be known as **hot money**: that is, stocks of funds that are moved around the globe from country to country in search of the best return. The size of the stocks of hot money is enormous, and can significantly affect exchange rates in the short run. The precise amount of such funds is not known with any precision, but some have claimed that the daily foreign exchange market turnover can reach up to $1.5 trillion.

Such movements can influence the exchange rate in the short run. The returns to be gained from such capital flows depend on the relative interest rate in the country targeted, and on the expected exchange rate in the future, which in turn may depend on expectations about inflation.

Suppose you are an investor holding assets denominated in US dollars, and the UK interest rate is 2% higher than that in the USA. You may be tempted to shift the funds into the UK in order to take advantage of the higher interest rate. However, if you believe that the exchange rate is above its long-run equilibrium, and therefore is likely to fall, this will affect your expected return on holding a UK asset. Indeed, if investors holding UK assets expect the exchange rate to fall, they are likely to shift their funds out of the country as soon as possible, which may then have the effect of pushing down the exchange rate. In other words, this may be a self-fulfilling prophecy. However, speculators may also react to news in an unpredictable way, so not all speculative capital movements act to influence the exchange rate towards its long-run equilibrium value.

Speculation was a key contributing factor in the unfolding of the Asian financial crisis of 1997. Substantial flows of capital had moved into Thailand in search of high returns, and speculators came to believe that the Thai currency (the baht) was overvalued. Outward capital flows put pressure on the exchange rate, and although the Thai central bank tried to resist, it eventually ran down its reserves to the point where it had to devalue. This then sparked off capital flows from other countries in the region, including South Korea.

## Summary

➤ Under a floating exchange rate system, the value of a currency is allowed to find its own way to equilibrium without government intervention.

➤ This means that an overall balance of payments of zero is automatically achieved.

➤ The purchasing power parity theory argues that the exchange rate will adjust in the long run to maintain international competitiveness, by offsetting differences in inflation rates between countries.

➤ In the short run, the exchange rate may diverge from this long-run level, particularly because of speculation.

➤ The exchange rate is thus influenced by relative interest rates and expected inflation, as well as by news about the economic environment.

OCR Advanced Economics

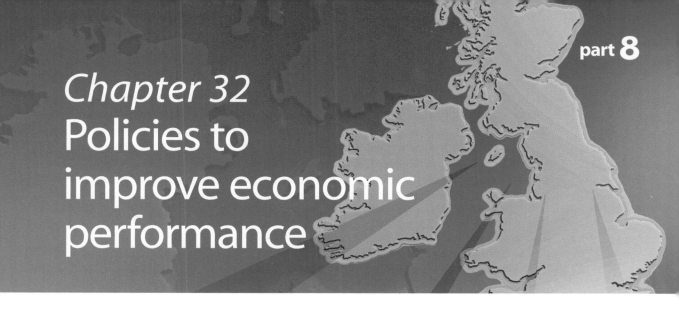

# Chapter 32
# Policies to improve economic performance

*How does macroeconomic policy operate in practice? Having described the range of policy instruments available to a government, and the economic models that help to explain how the economy works, it is now time to see how policies are conducted in practice, and to evaluate their relative effectiveness in seeking to achieve the policy objectives. The discussion will cover domestic policy, including fiscal, monetary and exchange rate policy, as well as other policies designed to affect the trading position of the economy or to improve resource allocation through the supply side of the economy. However, it is also important to realise that domestic policy cannot be implemented in isolation from the global market in which an open economy functions, so domestic policy may sometimes be constrained by the international situation — or may at least have to take it into account.*

## Learning outcomes

After studying this chapter, you should:
➤ be able to understand the role of domestic and international institutions in setting the context for the operation of policy
➤ be familiar with the way in which policies can be implemented in a modern economy
➤ be able to analyse the impact of different policy changes in terms of their effectiveness in achieving the key policy objectives
➤ be able to evaluate the contribution of supply-side policies to the improvement of economic performance
➤ be aware of the way that the performance of the UK economy — and the effectiveness of domestic policy — may be influenced by the international environment
➤ be able to discuss the relative effectiveness of alternative policies in meeting the macroeconomic policy objectives

## Institutions and economic policy

A first step in analysing the way in which economic policy is implemented is to consider the environment within which policy is set, and the institutions that are responsible for putting policy into practice.

In a democratic society, the process begins with the electoral system. For example, in the UK each of the political parties puts together a manifesto that sets out its intentions regarding the way it will govern – including its attitudes towards and intentions for economic policy. The party that is voted into power then has a mandate to carry out those policies on which it was elected. This can be seen as an example of the principal–agent scenario introduced in Chapter 4. In this case, the government acts as the agent of the electorate (the principal). As with other instances of the principal–agent situation, there may sometimes be problems where a government does not perceive itself to be fully accountable to the electorate.

The government has the responsibility of ensuring that the policies desired by the electorate are put into effect. Part of this responsibility lies in ensuring that markets are free to operate effectively. In particular, this entails ensuring there are secure property rights, without which a market system cannot work. The issues of accountability and security of property rights are taken for granted in countries like the UK, but constitute major problems in some countries elsewhere in the world.

In the UK, the government takes decisions on how the economy should operate, but delegates day-to-day decisions to some key institutions. In the case of fiscal policy, the chancellor of the exchequer is responsible for drawing up the annual budget. This sets the parameters for fiscal policy in terms of taxation and government expenditure. The chancellor is assisted in this by the Treasury, which is the UK's economics and finance ministry, and has responsibility for 'formulating and implementing the government's economic and financial policy' (**www.hm-treasury.gov.uk**).

*Treasury building, Whitehall, London*

The framework for monetary policy was set in 1997, when the Bank of England (the UK's central bank) was given responsibility for the conduct of monetary policy. This responsibility rests with the bank's Monetary Policy Committee (MPC), which sets the interest rate in such a way as to meet the inflation target set by the government. An important step taken in 1997 was not only to delegate the responsibility for monetary policy to the Bank of England, but at the same time to make the bank independent of the Treasury and the government. An important reason for this was to demonstrate that the government was committed to the inflation target, and would not compromise that target by excessive borrowing from the central bank, in order to induce a feel-good factor in the run-up to an election.

In the opening years of the twenty-first century, the UK economy operates in a global

environment, and there are other institutions set up to oversee aspects of that global economy.

As discussed in Chapter 31, at the end of the Second World War a conference was held at Bretton Woods in the USA to agree on a set of rules under which international trade would be conducted. This conference established an exchange rate system under which countries agreed to set the price of their currencies relative to the US dollar. In addition, the conference set up three institutions to oversee matters. The *International Monetary Fund* (IMF) would provide assistance (and advice) to countries experiencing balance of payments difficulties, and the World Bank would provide assistance (and advice) on long-term development issues. However, it was also recognised that the conduct of trade would need some oversight. Initially, this role was fulfilled by the *General Agreement on Tariffs and Trade* (GATT), under the auspices of which there was a sequence of 'rounds' of reductions in tariffs, together with a significant reduction in quotas and voluntary export restraints. The last of these was the Uruguay Round, which covered the period 1986–94 and led to the formation of the *World Trade Organization* (WTO), which replaced the GATT in 1995.

While continuing to pursue reductions in barriers to trade, the WTO has also taken on the role of providing a framework for the settlement of trade disputes. You will appreciate that, with all the moves towards regional integration and protectionism, such a role is very important. Indeed, the WTO reports that around 300 cases for settlement of disputes were brought to the WTO in its first 8 years — about the same number that were dealt with over the entire life of the GATT from 1947 to 1994.

## Summary

➤ Proposals for economic policy constitute an important part of the political parties' manifestos prepared in the run-up to elections.

➤ This provides an opportunity for the electorate to express preferences on the role of government during its term in office.

➤ The UK government delegates day-to-day responsibility for economic policy to the Treasury (for fiscal policy) and to the Bank of England (for monetary and exchange rate policy).

➤ The international environment for economic policy is overseen by the World Bank, the International Monetary Fund and the World Trade Organization.

## Fiscal policy

Having discussed the policy environment, the next step is to see how different types of policy are conducted, and how the effectiveness of policy is determined by the economic models that have been introduced, and by the assumptions made. We will begin with fiscal policy.

Fiscal policy is the manipulation of the government's taxation and expenditure in order to influence the economy. For a period after the Second World War the prime aim of economic policy was to maintain full employment, and the main way of trying to achieve this was through an active fiscal policy. It was thought that by manipulating aggregate demand through changes in the government's fiscal balance, the economy could be stabilised close to full employment.

Figure 32.1 shows how this is intended to work. The figure shows an economy with AS being the aggregate supply curve, becoming vertical at the full employment level of output $Y^*$. Suppose that the economy is initially operating with the aggregate demand curve $AD_0$, such that short-run equilibrium is with real output at $Y_0$ and an overall price level at $P_0$. The intention of fiscal policy is to raise the real output level in order to take the economy closer to full employment. An increase in government spending would shift the AD curve to $AD_1$, and real output would increase to $Y_1$ in the new equilibrium. The overall price level would also rise, to $P_1$.

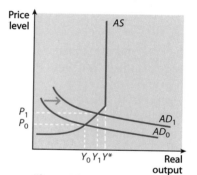

**Figure 32.1**
*The use of fiscal policy*

The active use of fiscal policy to influence the economy in this way went out of fashion under the influence of the monetarist school of macroeconomists. They argued that the aggregate supply curve is vertical, such that the economy will return of its own accord to full employment relatively quickly. If this is the case, then active fiscal policy is damaging to the economy. Figure 32.2 shows an expansionary fiscal policy under the assumption of a vertical aggregate supply curve. The increase in government spending again has the effect of shifting the aggregate demand curve to the right, from $AD_0$ to $AD_1$, but now the impact is *only* on the overall price level, which increases from $P_0$ to $P_1$.

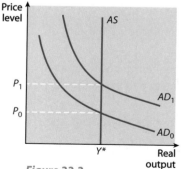

**Figure 32.2**
*Fiscal policy with a vertical AS curve*

Therefore, according to monetarist economists, if the government continues trying to simulate the economy by increasing spending, the result will be that the price level will keep rising, but that real output will remain unchanged. Some countries in Latin America acted in this way during the 1980s, and the result was hyperinflation. Eventually, the continuing inflation acts to discourage investment, and causes the economy to have a lower productive capacity than it otherwise could have reached.

Both economic analysis and the UK experience support the view that fiscal policy should not be used as an active stabilisation device. However, this does not mean that there is no role for fiscal policy in a modern economy. Chapter 30 introduced the so-called *Golden Rule* of fiscal policy adopted under Gordon Brown's chancellorship. This sets the overall constraints within which fiscal policy is to be conducted, to ensure that it is not destabilising and to try to achieve equity between the generations. This Golden Rule states that over the economic cycle, the government should borrow only to invest, and not to fund current expenditure. In addition, public sector net debt is to average less than 40% of GDP over the economic cycle.

## Balance between the public and private sectors

The previous chapter pointed out that decisions about the size of government expenditure and revenue influence the overall balance between the public and private sectors. The balance that is achieved can have an important influence on the overall level of economic activity, and upon economic growth, so the importance of designing an appropriate fiscal policy should not be underestimated. An important theme that runs through much economic analysis is that governments may be justified in intervening in the economy in order to correct market failure. Some of this intervention requires the use of fiscal policy: for example, taxes to correct for the effects of externalities, or expenditure to ensure the provision of public goods. In other words, fiscal policy can be an instrument that operates at the microeconomic level, as well as having macroeconomic implications.

Take infrastructure as an example. Infrastructure covers a range of goods that are crucial for the efficient operation of a market economy. Businesses need good transport links and good communication facilities. Households need good healthcare, education and sanitation facilities, not only in order to enjoy a good standard of life, but also to be productive members of the labour force. Both public goods and externality arguments come into play in the provision of infrastructure, so there needs to be appropriate government intervention to ensure that such goods

*Different governments have taken different approaches regarding which industries should remain part of the public sector*

are adequately provided. The consequence of failing to do this will be to lower the productive capacity of the economy below what would otherwise have been possible. In other words, the aggregate supply curve will be further to the left than it need be.

On the other hand, too much government intervention may also be damaging. One of the most compelling arguments in favour of privatisation was that when the managers of public enterprises are insufficiently accountable for their actions, X-inefficiency becomes a major issue, so public sector activity tends to be less efficient than private sector enterprise. On this argument, too large a public sector may have the effect of lowering aggregate productive capacity below its potential level.

These arguments suggest that an important role for fiscal policy is in affecting the supply side of the economy, ensuring that markets operate effectively to make the best possible use of the economy's resources. Some further aspects of this will be discussed in the context of supply-side policies later in the chapter.

### Income distribution

The other key role for fiscal policy is in affecting the distribution of income within society. Taxes and transfers can have a large effect on income distribution. For example, in 2002/03 the 'original income' of the top quintile of households in the UK was about 15 times greater than that of the bottom quintile. ('Original income' is income before any adjustment is made for the effect of taxation or benefits.) After adjusting for benefits and taxes, the ratio of top to bottom quintile fell to about fourfold. Figure 32.3 shows these data in the form of Lorenz curves. Again, you can see the extent to which tax and benefit measures bring the Lorenz curve closer to the equality line.

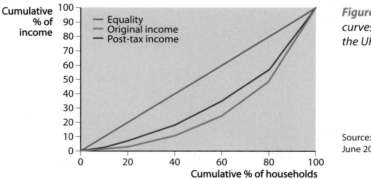

**Figure 32.3** *Lorenz curves for income in the UK, 2002/03*

Source: *Economic Trends,* June 2004.

### Benefits

There are two forms of benefit that households can receive to help equalise the income distribution. First, there are various types of *cash benefit,* such as income support, child benefit, incapacity benefit and working families' tax credit. These are designed to protect families whose income in certain circumstances would otherwise be very low. Second, there are *benefits in kind,* such as health and

education. These accrue to individual households depending on the number of members of the household and their age and gender.

Of these, the cash benefits are far more important in influencing the distribution of income. For the lowest quintile in 2002/03, such benefits made up about three-fifths of the growth in income; they were also significant for the second quintile.

### Taxation

**Direct taxes** (taxes on incomes) tend to be progressive. In other words, higher income groups pay tax at a higher rate. In 2002/03 the top quintile paid 24% of its gross income in tax, compared with only 9% paid in the bottom quintile.

In the UK, the main direct taxes are income tax, corporation tax (paid by firms on profits), capital gains tax (paid by individuals who sell assets at a profit), inheritance tax and petroleum revenue tax (paid by firms operating in the North Sea). There is also the council tax, collected by local authorities. National Insurance contributions are another form of direct taxation.

With a tax such as income tax, its progressive nature is reflected in the way the tax rate increases as an individual moves into a higher income range. In other words, the **marginal tax rate** increases as income increases. The **progressive** nature of the tax ensures that it does indeed help to reduce inequality in income distribution – although its effects are less than the cash benefits discussed earlier.

Table 32.1 shows average tax rates for taxpayers in different income bands in 2005/06. Notice that the table shows *average* rather than *marginal* tax rates. When average rates are rising, marginal tax rates are higher than the average. Exercise 32.1 illustrates this.

**Key terms**

**direct tax:** a tax levied directly on income

**marginal tax rate:** tax on additional income, defined as the change in tax payments due divided by the change in taxable income

**progressive tax:** a tax in which the marginal tax rate rises with income, i.e. a tax bearing most heavily on the relatively well-off members of society

| Income band | Number of taxpayers (m) | Average rate of tax payable (%) | Average amount of tax payable (£) |
|---|---|---|---|
| £4,895–£4,999 | 0.1 | 0.1 | 5 |
| £5,000–£7,499 | 2.9 | 2.0 | 126 |
| £7,500–£9,999 | 3.5 | 5.1 | 445 |
| £10,000–£14,999 | 6.1 | 9.8 | 1,220 |
| £15,000–£19,999 | 5.1 | 13.0 | 2,260 |
| £20,000–£29,999 | 6.4 | 15.4 | 3,760 |
| £30,000–£49,999 | 4.3 | 17.9 | 6,690 |
| £50,000–£99,999 | 1.5 | 25.7 | 17,000 |
| £100,000 and over | 0.5 | 33.4 | 71,100 |
| All incomes | 30.5 | 18.2 | 4,390 |

*Table 32.1 Income tax payable in the UK by annual income 2005/06*

Source: *Social Trends*, no. 36.

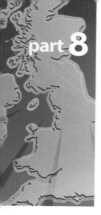

## Exercise 32.1

Table 32.1 shows the amount of tax paid by an individual as income increases. Calculate the average and marginal tax rates at each of the income levels. (*Remember the definition of the marginal tax rate provided above.*)

The effect of **indirect taxes**, on the other hand, can sometimes be **regressive**: in other words, indirect taxes may impinge more heavily on lower-income households. Indirect taxes are taxes that are paid on items of expenditure, rather than on income.

**Key terms**

**indirect tax:** a tax on expenditure, e.g. VAT

**regressive tax:** a tax bearing more heavily on the relatively poorer members of society

Examples of indirect taxes are value added tax (VAT), which is charged on most goods and services sold in the UK at a rate of 17.5%, tobacco taxes, excise duties on alcohol and oil duties. These specific taxes are levied per unit sold. Chapter 8 analysed how the incidence of a tax is related to the price elasticity of demand of a good or service. It explained how, where demand is price-inelastic, producers are able to pass much of an increase in the tax rate on to consumers, whereas if demand is price-elastic, producers have to absorb most of the increase as part of their costs.

Why are some of these taxes regressive? Take the tobacco tax. In the first place, the number of smokers is higher among lower-income groups than among the relatively rich — research has shown that only about 10% of people in professional groups now smoke compared with nearly 40% of those in unskilled manual groups. Second, expenditure on tobacco tends to take a lower proportion of income of the rich compared with that of the poor, even for those in the former group who do smoke. Thus, the tobacco tax falls more heavily on lower-income groups than on the better-off.

As pointed out in Chapter 30, achieving a balance of taxation between direct and indirect taxes is an important aspect of the government's redistributive policy. A switch in the balance from direct to indirect taxes will tend to increase inequality in a society. The incentive effects must also be kept in mind. High marginal tax rates on income can have a disincentive effect; if people know that a large proportion of any additional work they undertake will be taxed away, they may be discouraged from providing more work. In other words, cutting income tax can encourage work effort by reducing marginal tax rates. This is yet another reminder of the need for a balanced policy — one that recognises that, while some income redistribution is needed to protect the vulnerable, disincentive effects may arise if the better-off are over-taxed.

## Exercise 32.2

Using appropriate economic analysis, discuss the various policy measures available to a government wishing to ensure an equitable distribution of income without damaging incentives to work.

## Summary

➤ Fiscal policy entails changes in taxation and in the government's expenditure to influence the level or pattern of aggregate demand.

➤ Fiscal policy has gone out of fashion as a short-run stabilisation device, and now operates under the Golden Rule, which aims to ensure fiscal responsibility and equity between generations.

➤ Fiscal policy retains a key role in ensuring an appropriate balance between private and public sectors, and ensuring the provision of public goods and tackling externality effects.

➤ It also plays a key role in influencing the distribution of income between groups within society.

➤ In doing this, an appropriate balance needs to be found between achieving a desired level of equity between individuals, and providing incentives to work.

## Monetary policy

Monetary policy is the use of monetary variables such as money supply or interest rates in order to influence aggregate demand. However, the previous chapter explained that with a variety of assets acting as near-money in a modern economy, controlling aggregate demand through the money supply has become more difficult. The control of the money supply is also imprecise in its effects because of the operation of the credit multiplier, by which an increase in money supply has a multiplied effect on the amount of credit in the economy. Thus the main instrument of monetary policy in the first few years of the twenty-first century has been the interest rate.

The monetary transmission mechanism explains the way in which a change in the interest rate affects aggregate demand in the economy. Suppose there is a reduction in the interest rate. From firms' point of view, this lowers the cost of borrowing, and would be expected to encourage higher investment spending. Furthermore, consumers may also respond to a fall in the interest rate by increasing their expenditure, both because this lowers the cost of borrowing – so there may be an increase in the demand for consumer durable goods – and because households may perceive that saving now pays a lower return, so may decide to spend more. Thus a fall in the interest rate is expected to have an expansionary effect on aggregate demand. In terms of the *AD/AS* model, this has a similar effect to the impact of an expansionary fiscal policy. The effects of this were shown in Figures 32.1 and 32.2, under alternative assumptions about the shape of the aggregate supply curve.

The discussion of fiscal policy ended by concluding that an expansionary fiscal policy intended to stimulate aggregate demand would be damaging if the economy were close to (or at) full employment, as the main impact would be on the overall price level rather than real output. The same argument applies here, and the analysis therefore suggests that monetary policy should also

not be used to stimulate aggregate demand. However, monetary policy can still play an important role in managing the economy. This arises through its influence on the price level and hence the rate of change of prices — that is, inflation.

As has been explained, monetary policy in the UK is the responsibility of the Bank of England. The Bank's Monetary Policy Committee (MPC) meets each month to decide whether or not the interest rate needs to be altered. The objective of this exercise is to ensure that the government's inflation target is met. If the rate of inflation threatens to accelerate beyond the target rate, the Bank of England can intervene by raising interest rates, thereby having a dampening effect on aggregate demand and reducing the inflationary pressure. In reaching its decisions, the MPC takes a long-term view, projecting inflation ahead over the next 2 years.

However, decisions to change the rate of interest are not taken solely in the light of expected inflation. In its deliberations about the interest rate, the MPC takes a wide variety of factors into account, including developments in:
- financial markets
- the international economy
- money and credit
- demand and output
- the labour market
- costs and prices (e.g. changes in oil prices)

It is also important to realise that the transmission mechanism has a third channel in addition to the effects of the change in interest rate on consumption and investment. This third channel arises through the exchange rate, so that monetary policy cannot be considered in isolation from exchange rate policy. The channels of the transmission mechanism are summarised in Figure 32.4.

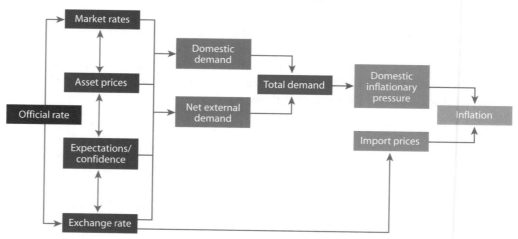

*Figure 32.4  The transmission of monetary policy*

Note: for simplicity, this figure does not show all interactions between variables, but these can be important.

chapter 32

## Summary

➤ Monetary policy is the use of financial variables, such as money supply or the rate of interest, to influence the performance of the economy.

➤ Money supply does not provide a reliable control mechanism, so the prime instrument of monetary policy is the interest rate.

➤ The transmission mechanism from the interest rate to aggregate demand works through investment and consumption and indirectly via the exchange rate.

➤ The Bank of England's Monetary Policy Committee has the responsibility for setting the interest rate at such a level as to achieve the government's inflation target, taking account of the general domestic and international economic environment.

## Exchange rate policy: fixed or floating?

The previous chapter set out the characteristics of fixed and floating exchange rate systems, but did not analyse which of these might be preferred. In evaluating this question, there are many factors to be taken into account; this section will consider three of them. First, it is important to examine the extent to which the respective systems can accommodate and adjust to external shocks that push the economy out of equilibrium. Second, it is important to consider the stability of each of the systems. Finally, there is the question of which system best encourages governments to adopt sound macroeconomic policies.

### Adjustment to shocks

Every economy has to cope with external shocks that occur for reasons outside the control of the country. A key question in evaluating exchange rate systems is whether there is an effective mechanism that allows the economy to return to equilibrium after an external shock.

Under a *floating exchange rate* system, much of the burden of adjustment is taken up by changes in the exchange rate. For example, if an economy finds itself experiencing faster inflation than other countries, perhaps because those other countries have introduced policies to reduce inflation, then the exchange rate will adjust automatically to restore competitiveness.

However, if the country is operating a *fixed exchange rate* system, the authorities are committed to maintaining the exchange rate, and this has to take precedence. Thus, the only way to restore competitiveness is by deflating the economy in order to bring inflation into line with other countries. This is likely to bring with it a transitional cost in terms of higher unemployment and slower economic growth. In other words, the burden of adjustment is on the real economy, rather than on allowing the exchange rate to adjust.

The Bretton Woods system operated for more than 20 years in a period in which many economies enjoyed steady economic growth. However, in the UK the system

brought about a stop–go cycle, in which the need to maintain the exchange rate hampered economic growth because of the tendency for growth to lead to an increase in imports and thus to a current account deficit. The increasing differences between inflation rates in different countries led to the final collapse of the system, suggesting that it was unable to cope with such variation.

Furthermore, a flexible exchange rate system allows the authorities to utilise monetary policy in order to stabilise the economy — remember that under a fixed exchange rate system, monetary policy has to be devoted to the exchange rate target.

### Stability

When it comes to stability, a fixed exchange rate system has much to commend it. After all, if firms know that the government is committed to maintaining the exchange rate at a given level, they can agree future contracts with some confidence. Under a floating exchange rate system, trading takes place in an environment in which the future exchange rate has to be predicted. If the exchange rate moves adversely, firms then face potential losses from trading. This foreign exchange risk is reduced under a fixed rate regime.

 **Key term**

**futures market:** a market in which it is possible to buy a commodity at a fixed price for delivery at a specified future date; such a market exists for foreign exchange

In a climate where speculative activity creates volatility in exchange rates, international trade may be discouraged because of the exchange rate risk. The effects of such volatility can be mitigated to some extent by the existence of **futures markets**. In such a market, it is possible to buy foreign exchange at a fixed price for delivery at a specified future date.

For example, suppose a firm is negotiating a deal to buy component parts for a manufacturing process that will be delivered in 3 months' time. The firm can buy the foreign exchange needed to close the deal in the futures market, and then knows that the contract will be viable, having negotiated a price for the components based on the known exchange rate, rather than on the unpredictable rate that will apply at that future date. The firm might, of course, have to pay a price for the foreign currency that is above the current (*spot*) exchange rate, but as the future rate has been built into the terms of the contract, that will not affect the viability of the deal. The process by which a firm avoids losses by buying forward is known as *hedging*.

However, even with the use of hedging to reduce the risk, it is costly to engage in international trade when exchange rates are potentially volatile, so world trade is unlikely to be encouraged under such a system. Of course, it might be argued that the risk to firms is still present under a fixed exchange rate system, since a government may choose to realign its currency, with even greater costs to firms that are tied into contracts. However, such realignments were rare under Bretton Woods and were more predictable than the volatility that can occur on a day-to-day basis in today's foreign exchange market.

## Macroeconomic policy

Critics of the flexible exchange rate system argue that it is too flexible for its own good. If governments know that the exchange rate will always adjust to maintain international competitiveness, they may have no incentive to behave responsibly in designing macroeconomic policy. Thus, they may be tempted to adopt an inflationary domestic policy, secure in the knowledge that the exchange rate will bear the burden of adjustment. In other words, a flexible exchange rate system does not impose financial discipline on individual countries.

An example of this was seen in the UK in the early 1970s when the UK first moved to a floating exchange rate regime. Money supply was allowed to expand rapidly, and inflation increased to almost 25%, aided by the oil price shock. Other examples are evident in Latin America, where hyperinflation affected many countries during the 1980s and early 1990s. For the country itself, such policies are costly in the long run, as reducing inflation under flexible exchange rates is costly. If interest rates are increased in order to reduce domestic aggregate demand and thus reduce inflationary pressure, the high return on domestic assets encourages an inflow of hot money, thereby putting upward pressure on the exchange rate. This reduces the international competitiveness of domestic goods and services, and deepens the recession.

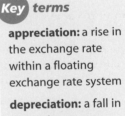

**Key terms**

**appreciation:** a rise in the exchange rate within a floating exchange rate system

**depreciation:** a fall in the exchange rate within a floating exchange rate system

There may also be spillover effects on other countries. Suppose that two countries have been experiencing rapid inflation, and one of them decides to tackle the problem. It raises interest rates to dampen domestic aggregate demand, which leads to an **appreciation** of its currency. For the other country, the effect is a **depreciation** of the currency. (If one currency appreciates, the other must depreciate.) The other country thus finds that its competitive position has improved, and it faces inflationary pressure in the short run. It may then also choose to tackle inflation, which in turn will affect the other country. These spillover effects could be minimised if the countries were to harmonise their policy action.

### The exchange rate and macroeconomic policy

The discussion above has shown that the relationship between the exchange rate and macroeconomic policy is an important one. Under a fixed exchange rate system, the need to maintain the value of the currency is a constraint on macroeconomic policy, and forces adjustment to disequilibrium through the real economy. On the other hand, it does have the benefit of imposing financial discipline on governments.

Under floating exchange rates, the relationship with policy is less obvious. With a flexible exchange rate, the authorities can use monetary policy to stabilise the economy, knowing that there will be overall balance on the balance of payments. Nonetheless, the government needs to monitor the structure of the balance of payments. When interest rates are set at a relatively high level compared with

other countries, the financial account will tend to be in surplus because of capital inflows, with a corresponding deficit on the current account. This may not be sustainable in the long run.

## Summary

➤ There are strengths and weaknesses with both fixed and floating exchange rate systems. A floating exchange rate system is more robust in enabling economies to adjust following external shocks, but it can lead to volatility and thus discourage international trade. A fixed rate system has the added advantage of imposing financial discipline on governments, and may allow policy harmonisation.

➤ The move towards a fixed exchange rate system within the European Union is partly in recognition that international trade is encouraged by stability in trading arrangements. This development is discussed in the next chapter.

➤ Under a floating exchange rate system, much of the burden of adjustment to external shocks is borne by changes in the exchange rate. Under a fixed exchange rate system, adjustment is more likely to take place through variations in the level of economic activity.

## Exercise 32.3

Critically evaluate the following statements, and discuss whether you regard fixed or floating exchange rates as the better system.

**a**  A flexible exchange rate regime is better able to cope with external shocks.

**b**  A fixed exchange rate system provides a more stable trading environment and minimises risk.

**c**  Floating exchange rates enable individual countries to follow independent policies.

**d**  A fixed exchange rate system may encourage governments to adopt distortionary policies such as tariffs and non-tariff barriers in order to control imports.

## Managing the balance of payments

It was argued earlier that, although in the short run it may be possible to balance a deficit on the current account of the balance of payments by a surplus on the financial account, in the long run this might not be sustainable. The main reason for this is that there may be a limit on foreign exchange reserves and on the extent to which it is desirable to fund the current account by borrowing or by selling UK assets.

The question then is how the government could manage the balance of payments: in other words, how is it possible to alter the structure of transactions by reducing the size of the current account deficit? There are two basic routes that could be followed if the government decided that it needed to do so: demand management policies and exchange rate adjustments. A third possibility would be to use supply-side policies, which will be discussed later in the chapter.

*The high income elasticity of demand for imported goods has led to a deficit on the UK current account*

## Demand management

One reason for a current account deficit is that, as real incomes rise in the economy, there is a tendency for UK residents to buy more imported goods or services, because the income elasticity of demand for imports tends to be relatively high. One possibility, therefore, would be to control the level of aggregate demand in order to limit the demand for imports: for example, the government could raise taxes, or reduce government expenditure. Whether the government wants to do this might depend upon whether such a policy would damage other aspects of the economy. For example, a reduction in aggregate demand might cause an increase in unemployment, and if the government gave a higher priority to achieving full employment, it might prefer to live with the current account deficit. It is also possible that long-run economic growth could be inhibited. (The question of conflict between government policy objectives is discussed in Chapter 33.)

The alternative would be to introduce a policy that was targeted more towards reducing the demand for imports. For example, the use of tariffs or quotas would raise the price of imports, and so reduce demand for them, and at the same time would encourage domestic producers to increase their production. However, within the context of the EU it is not realistic to imagine that the UK could set its own independent tariff rates, even if it wanted to do so. In any case, as has already been explained, the use of tariffs entails a misallocation of resources in society, and a deadweight loss.

## Exchange rate adjustment

The competitiveness of UK exports and of domestic goods and services relative to imports both depend crucially on the exchange rate: in particular, the exchange rate influences the size of the current account deficit. Under current policy procedures, the prime target of monetary policy is to keep inflation at a low level. This is achieved by the Bank of England setting interest rates at the level needed to hit the inflation target. However, if the interest rate required for this purpose is high relative to elsewhere in the world, there will tend to be flows of financial capital into the UK. In turn, this suggests that the equilibrium for the exchange rate will be relatively high, which limits the competitiveness of UK goods and services, and results

in a balance of payments that is achieved through a current account deficit and a financial account surplus.

In this way, the government may be restricted in the extent to which it can manipulate the exchange rate to reduce the current account deficit, unless it is prepared to give a higher priority to this than to other targets of macroeconomic policy. This helps to explain why supply-side policies, as described in the next section, have been at the forefront in ensuring the competitiveness of UK firms in international markets.

## Summary

➤ Trade and competitiveness are affected by government policy, both directly and indirectly.

➤ Demand management could be used to reduce a deficit on the current account of the balance of payments, but governments might be reluctant to use this approach if it damages targets for full employment or economic growth.

➤ In principle, exchange rate adjustments could be used to influence the balance of payments, but careful attention needs to be paid to the effects on other targets of macroeconomic policy.

## Supply-side policies

Supply-side policies are directed at influencing the position of the aggregate supply curve. In Figure 32.5, $Y^*$ represents full employment output before the policy,

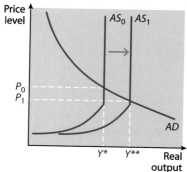

*Figure 32.5*
*A shift in aggregate supply (with a monetarist effect)*

with the equilibrium overall price level at $P_0$. Supply-side policies, which lead to an increase in the economy's productive capacity, shift equilibrium output to $Y^{**}$ and the overall price level to $P_1$.

Notice that the effect on real output is achieved from supply-side policies whether the equilibrium is in the vertical segment of the Keynesian $AS$ curve (or with a monetarist $AS$ curve), as shown in Figure 32.5, or in the upward-sloping segment of the Keynesian $AS$ curve, as in Figure 32.6. Here the shift in aggregate supply raises equilibrium real output from $Y_0$ to $Y_1$.

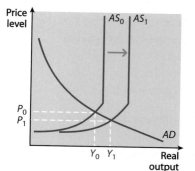

*Figure 32.6*
*A shift in aggregate supply (with a Keynesian effect)*

Supply-side policies include encouraging education and training, improving the flexibility with which markets operate and promoting competition. These policies were discussed in Chapter 12, so you might want to remind yourself of how they operate.

Notice that it is quite difficult to quantify the effects of these supply-side policies. In the case of education and training, some of the effects of increased spending become evident only after very long time lags. In the case of competition policy, again, it is not easy to identify the effects on productive capacity. It is particularly difficult to isolate the impact of these policies when so much else in the economy is changing through time. Nonetheless, these policies do have the effect of stimulating economic growth without inflationary pressure.

Another example that is important to examine is the effect of changing the rate of income tax. When people face high marginal rates of income tax, there is a disincentive to offer additional labour hours, or even to participate in the labour force at all. A reduction in income tax rates would therefore provide an incentive for people to work more hours or to participate in the labour force. This would then lead to higher employment, and a higher potential capacity output for the economy as a whole.

Such high marginal tax rates are normally found at the high end of the income distribution, but there may also be disincentive effects to consider at low incomes. These effects may arise where unemployment benefits are set at such a level that individuals would be little better off if they accepted a low-paid job — a situation sometimes known as the 'unemployment trap'. This effect may be reinforced if the search costs for jobs are relatively high — for example, if the jobs available are not in areas where unemployment is high. There may then be people who do not find it worth their while undertaking a costly search for jobs, especially if the wage they could command would be only marginally better than the benefits that they can receive.

In this situation, a reduction in the rate of unemployment benefits or social security benefits could have the effect of increasing people's willingness to accept jobs. This would reduce unemployment and again lead to an expansion of the economy's potential productive capacity. However, there is a need to keep an appropriate balance between providing incentives to work and protecting the vulnerable.

Supply-side policies may also have an effect on the balance of payments current account. Policies that affect trade and competitiveness fall into this category: for example, supply-side policies to improve the flexibility of the labour market could be seen to improve the competitiveness of UK firms, and thus to improve the current account deficit. In addition, it might be argued that steps taken to increase the productive capacity of the economy would allow an increase in exports that would (ceteris paribus) reduce the current account deficit.

## Summary

➤ Supply-side policies are directed at influencing the position of the aggregate supply curve by increasing the potential productive capacity of the economy.

➤ Such policies include policies to affect the flexibility of labour markets, including education and training.

➤ Policies that promote competition may also lead to efficiency improvements.

➤ Changes in income tax rates, or in social security benefits, can also have an effect on potential capacity by affecting incentives to work.

➤ Improvements in efficiency may have spillover effects on the balance of payments if they improve the international competitiveness of UK goods in world markets.

## Policy in an international context

In practice, the design of domestic economic policy has to be undertaken with due regard for the international environment within which the UK economy operates. This is because the UK is an open economy. It depends upon international trade, and thus needs to interact with other economies.

Part of the interaction comes through financial markets and the balance of payments. If interest rates within Europe or the USA change relative to those in the UK, this will have an effect on the UK economy through the flows of financial capital that will be initiated by the change, with investors looking to move their funds in order to obtain the highest return.

Interaction also comes through trade agreements and the operations of the World Trade Organization. The WTO administers the international trading environment, and has a brief to encourage countries to reduce tariffs and to open their markets more freely to trade. This may also affect the way that the UK frames its domestic policy. For instance, the UK would not be free to raise tariffs to try to protect its domestic manufacturing industry — although economic arguments would suggest that this is not a sensible policy in any case, as was argued in Chapter 30.

Another important issue concerns the UK's relations with the rest of Europe. Although the UK chose not to join the single currency area when it was established, it remains part of Europe. Figure 32.7 shows that an increasing share of UK trade is with other European countries, and as part of the European single market, the UK needs to adopt policies that are consistent with its EU membership. The relationships between the UK and the EU will be examined more thoroughly in Part 9 of the book.

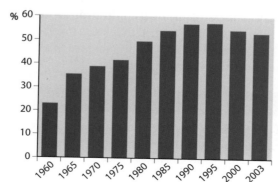

**Figure 32.7**

*Proportion of UK exports going to the EU15, 1960–2003*

Note: EU15 refers to the 15 countries that were members of the European Union prior to the enlargement in May 2004.

Source: calculated from the data in *Europa: EU Economy Annual Review 2004.*

## Foreign direct investment

An important aspect of the UK's interaction with the rest of the world is the spread of foreign direct investment (FDI) by multinational corporations (MNCs). The United Nations Conference on Trade and Development (UNCTAD) has identified three main reasons for such activity:

➤ market seeking     ➤ resource seeking     ➤ efficiency seeking

Some MNCs may engage in FDI because they want to sell their products in a particular market, and find it preferable to produce within the market rather than elsewhere: such FDI is *market seeking*. Second, MNCs might undertake investment in a country in order to take advantage of some key resource. This might be a natural resource such as oil or natural gas, or a labour force with certain skills, or simply cheap unskilled labour: such FDI is *resource seeking*. Third, MNCs might simply review their options globally, and decide that they can produce most efficiently in a particular location. This might entail locating just part of their production chain in a certain country: such FDI is *efficiency seeking*.

Market-seeking FDI has been important in some regions in particular. The opening up of China to foreign investment has proved a magnet for MNCs wanting to gain access to this large and growing market. In addition, non-European firms have been keen to gain entry to the EU's single market, which has encouraged substantial flows of FDI into Europe.

For the UK, there has been a two-way flow of direct investment. In other words, foreign investors have invested in the UK, and UK investors have invested abroad. Figure 32.8 shows the inward and outward flows, expressed as a percentage of GDP. Both inward and outward flows peaked in 2000 — a year in which outward direct investment reached more than 16% of GDP. This reflected intense merger and acquisition activity at that time. The largest outward acquisitions were by Vodafone Airtouch, which invested in Mannesmann AG to the tune of £100 billion, and BP Amoco plc, which purchased Atlantic Richfield Company for a reported £18 billion. After 2000, merger and acquisition activity slowed down, partly following the terrorist attacks in September 2001.

FDI may be perceived as beneficial for an economy such as the UK, supplementing domestic investment by an inflow of foreign funds, and potentially bringing new technologies and business practices that may spread to UK firms. Foreign firms

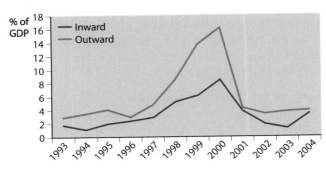

**Figure 32.8**
*UK foreign direct investment, 1993–2004*

Source: ONS.

locating in the UK also have the effect of increasing the amount of competition faced by domestic firms, which may then respond by looking for productivity improvements. The foreign firms may also establish linkages with local firms, and thus have a multiplier effect on the UK economy. Such spillovers may make FDI look attractive. In terms of the *AD/AS* model, FDI may have long-term beneficial effects on aggregate supply.

## Summary

➤ The international economic environment is a strong influence on the design of economic policy, given that the UK is an open economy.

➤ The UK interacts with other countries through its network of international trade, and through the operation of financial markets.

➤ In particular, the role of the UK within the European Union is an important part of policy design.

➤ An important development of recent years has been the spread of foreign direct investment (FDI) by multinational corporations.

➤ Motivations for FDI include market-seeking, resource-seeking and efficiency-seeking reasons.

➤ Cross-border mergers and acquisitions have tended to follow a cyclical pattern over time, with a peak in 2000.

## The policy environment — a summary

In the early years of the twentieth century, it seemed that the policy environment had become relatively stable. Accepting that the ultimate policy objective is to ensure a good standard of living for the UK population, the prime aim of policy must be to achieve economic growth — and to achieve it in a sustainable manner.

Macroeconomic stability is seen as a key prerequisite for economic growth to take place because firms need a stable environment if they are to feel confident about the future, and thus undertake investment. Monetary policy is therefore dedicated to achieving low inflation in line with the government's target. Fiscal policy needs to support monetary policy by maintaining a stable pattern over time, while at the same time dealing with key areas of market failure and producing an acceptable distribution of income between groups within society. Supply-side policies can then be implemented in order to ensure that markets operate effectively and that efficiency gains can be made. At the same time, the UK must operate within an international environment, observing the rules set down for international trade and providing some stability of the exchange rate.

This is the overall context within which policy is implemented. However, there is still one further complication to take into account, namely that some of these policy measures can be seen to come into conflict with each other. There are also many controversial aspects to the place of the UK economy in an increasingly global economy. These are the subject matter of Chapter 33.

part **8**

# *Chapter 33*
# Conflicts and controversies

*Economic policy has often been controversial. As economics is not a precise science, there is plenty of scope for economists to hold differing views about the likely effects of policy. The differences arise because people hold different views about the strength of the relationships between some economic variables. For example, there may be differences of opinion about how sensitive economic variables are to changes in key policy tools, such as the interest rate. Furthermore, closer examination reveals that some policy objectives may conflict with each other, such that a policy that may lead to an improvement in one sphere may lead to deterioration regarding some other policy objective. Such trade-offs need to be considered carefully, and priorities set amongst the key objectives.*

*The world economy is becoming increasingly integrated, and it is no longer possible to think of any single economy in isolation. The UK economy is no exception. It relies on international trade, engaging in exporting and importing activity, and many UK firms are increasingly active in global markets. This situation has created opportunities for UK firms to expand and become global players, and for UK consumers to have access to a wider range of goods and services. However, there is also a downside: global shocks, whether caused by oil prices, financial crises or the emergence of China as a world economic force, can reverberate throughout economies in all parts of the world.*

## Learning outcomes

After studying this chapter, you should:
➤ be familiar with the potential trade-offs and conflicts that exist between various dimensions of the UK's economic performance
➤ understand the potential trade-offs and conflicts that may arise between policy instruments
➤ be able to apply appropriate knowledge and theory to current policy issues
➤ be able to evaluate the relative effectiveness of alternative policies
➤ be aware of the political, economic and social constraints on economic policy
➤ be able to explain the importance of globalisation and indicate how this has affected the UK economy
➤ be aware of the impact that external shocks can have within the global economy

# Conflicts between policy objectives

The design of economic policy is likely to be something of a juggling act. There have been hints of this in the previous chapters. For example, it was pointed out that setting the interest rate in order to influence inflation in the domestic economy may have spin-off effects on the exchange rate. This is just one instance of the way in which macroeconomic variables are interconnected. This is especially so because there may be conflict between some of the targets and the instruments of policy.

Another obvious example is that there may be a conflict between economic growth and the environment, so that the pursuit of economic growth may need to be tempered by concern for the environment. Policy must therefore be designed bearing in mind that there may be a trade-off between these two objectives — at some point, it could be that more economic growth is possible only by sacrificing environmental objectives.

## Unemployment and inflation

This notion of trade-off between conflicting objectives applies in other areas too. One important trade-off was discovered by the Australian economist Bill Phillips. In 1958 Phillips claimed that he had found an 'empirical regularity' that had existed for almost a century and that traced out a relationship between the rate of unemployment and the rate of change of money wages. This was rapidly generalised into a relationship between unemployment and inflation (by arguing that firms pass on increased wages in the form of higher prices).

Figure 33.1 shows what became known as the **Phillips curve**. Although Phillips began with data, he also came up with an explanation of why such a relationship should exist. At the heart of his argument was the idea that when the demand for labour is high firms will be prepared to bid up wages in order to attract labour. To the extent that higher wages are then passed on in the form of higher prices, this would imply a relationship between unemployment and inflation: when unemployment is low inflation will tend to be higher, and vice versa.

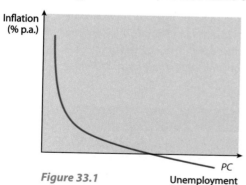

**Figure 33.1**
*The Phillips curve*

**Key term**

**Phillips curve:** a trade-off relationship between unemployment and inflation

From a policy perspective — at least within the Keynesian tradition — this suggests a trade-off between unemployment and inflation objectives. If the Phillips curve relationship holds, attempts to reduce the rate of unemployment are likely to raise inflation. On the other hand, a reduction in inflation is likely to result in higher unemployment. This suggests that it might be difficult to maintain full employment and low inflation at the same time. For example, Figure 33.2 shows a Phillips curve that is drawn such that to achieve an unemployment rate of 5%, inflation would need to rise to 15% per annum; this would not be acceptable these days, when people have become accustomed to much lower inflation rates. Furthermore, to bring inflation down to zero would require an unemployment rate of 15%. Having said that, as recently as 1990 the UK economy was experiencing inflation of nearly 10% and unemployment of 7%, which is not far from this example.

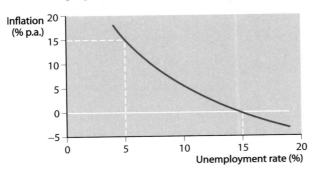

Figure 33.2
The Phillips
curve inflation–
unemployment
trade-off

Nonetheless, the Phillips curve trade-off offers a tempting prospect to policy-makers. For example, if an election is imminent, it should be possible to reduce unemployment by allowing a bit more inflation, thereby creating a feel-good factor. After the election, the process can be reversed. This suggests that there could be a political business cycle induced by governments seeking re-election. In other words, the conflict between policy objectives could be exploited by politicians who see that in the short run an electorate is concerned more about unemployment than inflation.

The 1970s provided something of a setback to this theory, when suddenly the UK economy started to experience both high unemployment and high inflation simultaneously, suggesting that the Phillips curve had disappeared. This combination of stagnation and inflation became known as **stagflation**.

 **term**

**stagflation:** a situation in which an economy simultaneously experiences stagnation (high unemployment) and high inflation

## Extension material

One possibility is that the Phillips curve had not in fact disappeared, but had moved. Suppose that wage bargaining takes place on the basis of *expectations* about future rises in retail prices. As inflation becomes embedded in an economy, and people come to expect it to continue, those expectations will be built into wage negotiations. Another way of viewing this is that expectations about price inflation will influence the *position* of the Phillips curve.

Figure 33.3 shows how this might work. $PC_0$ represents the initial Phillips curve. Suppose we start with the economy at the *natural rate of unemployment*, $U_{nat}$. If the economy is at point

A, with inflation at $\pi_0$ and unemployment at $U_{nat}$, the economy is in equilibrium. If the government then tries to exploit the Phillips curve by allowing inflation to rise to $\pi_1$, the economy moves in the short run to point B. However, as people realise that inflation is now higher, they adjust their expectations. This eventually begins to affect wage negotiations; the Phillips curve then moves to $PC_1$, and unemployment returns to the natural rate. The economy settles at C and is again in equilibrium,

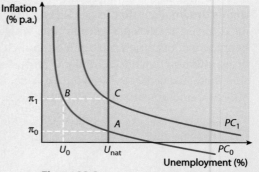

*Figure 33.3*
*An expectations-augmented Phillips curve*

but now with higher inflation than before — and the same initial rate of unemployment. For this reason, the natural rate of unemployment is sometimes known as the non-accelerating-inflation rate of unemployment (NAIRU).

The problem that arises with this is how to get back to the original position with a lower inflation rate. This can happen only if people's expectations adjust so that lower inflation is expected. This means that the economy has to move down along $PC_1$, pushing up unemployment in order to reduce inflation. Then, once expectations adjust, the Phillips curve will move back again until the natural rate of unemployment is restored. If this takes a long time, the cost in terms of unemployment will be high.

Figure 33.4 shows some empirical data for the UK since 1986. From 1986 until 1993 (or even until 1995), the pattern seems consistent with a Phillips curve relationship. However, after that time inflation seems to have stabilised, and unemployment is gradually falling — as if, with stable inflation, people's expectations have kept adjusting and allowed unemployment to fall.

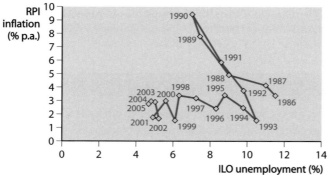

*Figure 33.4*
*Unemployment and inflation in the UK, 1986–2005*

Source: Labour Market Trends.

Figures 33.5 and 33.6 show the pattern of the relationship between unemployment and inflation for two other countries, Sweden and France. Sweden shows a classic Phillips curve pattern; France has experienced less variation in the unemployment rate.

OCR Advanced Economics

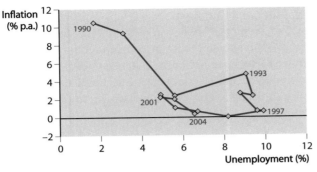

*Figure 33.5*
*Unemployment and inflation in Sweden, 1990–2004*

Source: OECD.

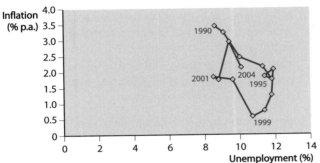

*Figure 33.6*
*Unemployment and inflation in France, 1990–2004*

Source: OECD.

### Economic growth and the current account

In some circumstances, conflict can also arise between achieving economic growth and attaining equilibrium on the current account of the balance of payments. An increase in economic growth resulting in higher real incomes could lead to an increase in imports of goods and services, if UK residents spend a high proportion of their additional income abroad. This was seen as a major problem during the fixed exchange rate era of the 1950s and 1960s, when any deficit on the current account had to be met by running down foreign exchange reserves. This led to a 'stop–go' cycle of macroeconomic policy, where every time growth began to accelerate, the current account went into deficit, and policy then had to be adjusted to slow down the growth rate to deal with the deficit. This arose partly from the nature of the fixed exchange rate system, as the authorities were committed to intervening in order to maintain the value of the pound.

### Exercise 33.1

Given the following list of policy objectives, discuss the possible conflicts that may arise between them, and discuss how these might be resolved:

➤ low inflation
➤ low unemployment
➤ high economic growth
➤ a low deficit on the current account of the balance of payments
➤ maintenance of a high-quality environment
➤ equity in the distribution of income

## Designing the policy mix

The design and conduct of economic policy needs to take account of these conflicts. Differing policy objectives need to be prioritised where there is conflict between them. Choices have to be made about the balance to be achieved between fiscal, monetary and supply-side policies — not forgetting the exchange rate, as the choice of fixed or floating exchange rates will have strong implications for the conduct of domestic policy.

The consensus view in the early part of the twenty-first century is that fiscal policy should be used to achieve the desired balance between the public and private sectors.

Monetary policy should be devoted to meeting the inflation target in order to create a stable macroeconomic environment; this will then encourage growth and enable improvements in the standard of living. Supply-side policies are perhaps the most important, as these contribute to raising efficiency and increasing the productive capacity of the economy.

The keynote in policy design lies in enabling markets to operate as effectively as possible. If the UK were to join the single currency area, this would create a new policy environment, in which responsibility for monetary policy would be delegated to the European Central Bank. This would leave fiscal policy and supply-side policies as the sole instruments available to a UK government. However, these would be subject to the Stability and Growth Pact, which would restrict fiscal policy by capping the permitted size of the budget deficit.

*The European Central Bank, Frankfurt*

## Summary

➤ The achievement of the various policy objectives is complicated by the fact that some are in conflict with one another, so that the achievement of one target may endanger another.

➤ The Phillips curve claims a trade-off relationship between unemployment and inflation, although the appearance of stagflation in the 1970s cast doubt on the hypothesis.

➤ The position of the Phillips curve may be seen to depend on people's expectations about future inflation, so that in the long run the Phillips curve may be vertical at the natural rate of unemployment (or the non-accelerating-inflation rate of unemployment — the NAIRU).

➤ Fiscal policy in a modern economy tends to be confined to determining the balance between the public and private sectors.

➤ Monetary policy tends to be devoted to meeting the inflation target in order to encourage economic growth.

➤ Supply-side policies are of greatest importance, influencing the efficiency with which markets work, and thus affecting the long-run capacity of the economy to produce.

# Globalisation and comparative advantage revisited

Chapter 13 introduced the notion of globalisation — a process by which the world's economies are becoming more closely integrated. The process of globalisation accelerated due to a number of factors. This was partly due to the advances in the technology of transport and communication, which enabled firms to begin to fragment their production process across different locations around the world. It was also partly due to the reduction of trade barriers and the deregulation of financial markets.

This whole process has led to changes in the pattern of trade between countries — for example, as the UK has become more closely integrated with the rest of Europe, there has been an increase in the share of UK trade that is with the rest of Europe, although the USA also remains a significant trading partner. You might find it helpful to look back at Chapter 13 to remind yourself of these changes.

The law of comparative advantage, which was introduced in Chapter 31, helps to explain these changes in the pattern of trade. Indeed, globalisation may be seen as a process that enables countries to enhance the way in which their comparative advantage can be exploited. In some cases, it may enable some countries to develop new specialisations, and thus alter the pattern of their comparative advantage.

From the point of view of economic analysis, it would seem that this process of globalisation, and the increasing use of comparative advantage, would be welcomed by countries around the world. However, it seems that this is not a universal view. Countries often seem reluctant to open their economies fully to international trade, and have tended to intervene to try to protect their domestic producers from what is perceived as excessive competition from foreign firms. In evaluating the benefits and costs of globalisation, there are other issues to be taken into consideration.

## External shocks

One of the issues concerning a more closely integrated global economy is the question of how robust the global economy will be to shocks. In other words, globalisation may be fine when the world economy is booming, as all nations may be able to share in the success. But if the global economy goes into recession, will all nations suffer the consequences? There are a number of situations that might cause the global economy to take a downturn.

### Oil prices

Oil prices seem to provide one possible threat. In the past, sudden changes in oil prices have caused widespread disruption — for example, in 1973/74 and in 1979/80.

Figure 33.7 shows the historical time path of the price of oil, measured in US dollars. In 1973/74 the sudden increase in the price of oil took most people by surprise. Oil prices had been steady for several years, and many economies had become dependent upon oil as an energy source, not only for running cars but for

other uses such as domestic central heating. The sudden increases in the price in 1973/74 and again in 1979/80 caused widespread problems because demand in the short run was highly inelastic, and oil-importing countries faced sudden deficits on their balance of payments current accounts. However, in time people switched away from oil for heating, firms developed more energy-efficient cars, and demand was able to adjust. Arguably, national economies in the 2000s are less vulnerable to changes in the price of oil than they were in 1973. This is not to say that the rise in oil prices to over $60 a barrel in 2006 did not cause problems, but economies were better equipped to withstand the increase. The UK was partly able to weather the storm because of its position as an oil producer.

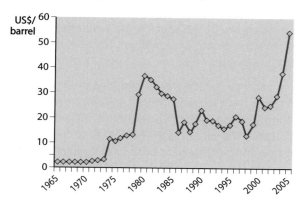

**Figure 33.7**
*The price of oil, 1965–2005*

Source: IMF.

Another difference was that the price rises in 1973–74 and 1979–80 had been primarily supply-side changes, caused by disruptions to supply following the actions of the OPEC cartel. In the 2000s, part of the upward pressure on price that is visible in the figure came from demand, with China's demand for oil being especially strong. There were also fears about the security of supplies from parts of the Middle East in the aftermath of the Iraq war, and with instability in Iran.

### Financial crises

Given the increasing integration of financial markets, a further concern is whether globalisation increases the chances that a financial crisis will spread rapidly between countries, rather than being contained within a country or region. The 1997 Asian financial crisis provides some evidence on this issue.

This crisis began in Thailand and South Korea. Both countries had been the recipients of large flows of FDI. In the case of Thailand, a significant part of this had been investment in property, rather than in productive investment. The Thai currency (the baht) came under speculative pressure early in 1997, and eventually the authorities had to allow a devaluation. This sparked a crisis of confidence in the region, and foreign investors began to withdraw funds, not only from Thailand but from other countries too. As far as globalisation was concerned, the key questions were how far the crisis would spread, and how long it would last.

In the event, five countries bore the main burden of the crisis: Indonesia, Malaysia, the Philippines, South Korea and Thailand. Beyond this grouping there were some knock-on effects because of the trade linkages, but arguably these were not too severe, and were probably dominated by other events taking place in the period. At the time of the crisis, Indonesia and the Philippines had been at a somewhat lower stage of development than the other countries involved, and thus suffered more deeply in terms of recession. However, with the benefit of hindsight, it seems that the region showed resilience in recovering from the crisis. Indeed, it can be argued that South Korea and Thailand in particular emerged as stronger economies after the crisis, through the weeding out of some relatively inefficient firms and institutions, and through a heightened awareness of the importance of sound financial regulation.

### China and the USA

An important question in the early to mid-2000s was how the global economy would cope with two seemingly distant, but related phenomena: the rapid growth of the Chinese economy and the deficit on the US current account of the balance of payments. The US current account deficit arose partly from the heavy public expenditure programme of the Bush administration. However, the deficit grew to unprecedented levels partly through the actions of China and other East Asian economies that had chosen to peg their currencies to the US dollar. Effectively, this meant that those economies were buying US government securities as a way of maintaining their currencies against the dollar, thereby keeping US interest rates relatively low and allowing the US public to borrow to finance high consumer spending.

Who gains from this situation? The USA is able to spend, and China is able to sell, fuelling its rapid rate of economic growth. For how long the situation can be sustained remains to be seen.

## Globalisation evaluated

The economic arguments in favour of allowing freer trade are strong, in the sense that there are potential gains to be made from countries specialising in the production of goods and services in which they have a comparative advantage. Globalisation facilitates and accelerates this process. And yet, there have sometimes been violent protests against globalisation, directed in particular at the WTO, whose meeting at Seattle in 1999 ended in chaos following demonstrations in the streets.

Tension has always been present during moves towards freer trade. Even if the economic arguments appear to be compelling, nations are cautious about opening up to free trade. In particular, there has been concern about jobs in the domestic economy. This is partly because there are transitional costs involved in liberalising trade, as some economic activities must contract to allow others to expand. Vested interests can then lead to lobbying and political pressure, as was apparent in the USA in the early part of the twenty-first century. There is also the question of whether globalisation will allow recession to spread more quickly between countries — but this is not proven.

In many ways, the WTO gets caught in the middle. It has responsibility for encouraging moves towards free trade, and thus comes under pressure from nations that

want to keep some degree of protection because they are unwilling to undergo the transitional costs of structural change. The WTO thus has the unpalatable job of protecting countries from themselves, enforcing short-term costs in the interests of long-term gains.

However, the anti-globalisation protests are based on rather different arguments. One concern is that economic growth can proceed only at some cost to the environment. It has been argued that, by fragmenting the production process, the cost to the environment is high. This is partly because the need to transport goods around the world uses up valuable resources. It is also argued that nations have an incentive to lower their environmental standards in order to attract MNCs by enabling low-cost production. This is not so much an argument against globalisation as an argument that an international agency is required to monitor global environmental standards.

It has also been suggested that it is the rich countries of the world that stand to gain most from increasing global trade, as they have the market power to ensure that trading conditions work in their favour. Again, the WTO may have a role here in monitoring the conditions under which trade takes place. At the end of the day, trade allows an overall increase in global production and more choice for consumers. The challenge is to ensure that these gains are equitably distributed, and that the environment can be conserved.

## Summary

➤ Globalisation is a process by which the world's economies have become more closely integrated.

➤ This has enabled greater exploitation of comparative advantage.

➤ Although closer integration may bring benefits in terms of increased global production and trade, it may also create a vulnerability by allowing adverse shocks to spread more rapidly between countries.

➤ Such shocks would include oil price changes or financial crises. However, the integrated global economy may turn out to be more resilient in reacting to adverse circumstances.

➤ Globalisation facilitates and accelerates the process by which gains from trade may be tapped.

➤ However, the transitional costs for individual economies in terms of the need for structural change have encouraged politicians to turn to protectionist measures.

➤ Critics of globalisation have pointed to the environmental costs of rapid global economic growth and the expansion of trade, and have argued that it is rich countries and multinational corporations that gain the most, rather than less developed countries.

## Exercise 33.2

Examine the economic arguments for and against globalisation.

# Economics in a European context

# Part 9

# Chapter 34
# Synopsis: markets and resource allocation

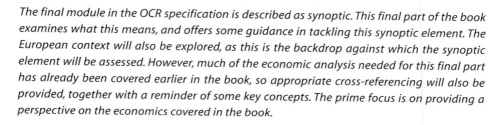

*The final module in the OCR specification is described as synoptic. This final part of the book examines what this means, and offers some guidance in tackling this synoptic element. The European context will also be explored, as this is the backdrop against which the synoptic element will be assessed. However, much of the economic analysis needed for this final part has already been covered earlier in the book, so appropriate cross-referencing will also be provided, together with a reminder of some key concepts. The prime focus is on providing a perspective on the economics covered in the book.*

## Learning outcomes

After studying this chapter, you should:
- ➤ be aware of the nature of the synoptic module
- ➤ recognise the connections between the various strands of economic analysis that were explored earlier in the book
- ➤ appreciate the distinction between microeconomic and macroeconomic analysis
- ➤ understand the significance of key economic concepts in taking a synoptic approach
- ➤ be aware of the need to be able to apply economic analysis to a variety of situations
- ➤ appreciate what it is to think like an economist

## The synoptic approach

Think back over the AS and A2 material that has been presented so far. The discussion has covered a wide variety of topics, and has introduced a range of economic models looking at issues in both microeconomics and macroeconomics. Underlying this variety are some common themes, and a common approach to tackling economic problems and explaining economic events. Economics offers a way of thinking about the world, and provides a range of tools that can help in understanding how individual markets and whole economies operate.

This ability to apply economic analysis in a wide range of situations is a vital part of thinking as an economist. This is what the 'synoptic' module is all about, and what it attempts to assess. The emphasis is therefore not so much on specific knowledge (although this may be important), but on the ability to identify relevant tools and forms of analysis, and bring these to bear on a particular situation. In order to demonstrate the ability to think like an economist, it is thus important to be able to draw on models and concepts from across the whole course of study, and to apply these appropriately in context.

To accomplish this successfully requires an awareness of the key models, and of which model can be applied in which situation. This requires not only a good knowledge of those models, but also an understanding of how those models can be applied in various circumstances. It is also important to be aware that the coverage will encompass both microeconomic and macroeconomic issues, as the assessment will cover both. You need to develop the skill of recognising which model or concept fits which situation.

This is a challenging assignment, and requires a rather different preparation strategy than the other exams that are encountered during the economics course. The key is to be aware of the three Rs — reading, researching and rehearsing.

## Reading

Reading is a key part of preparation. Read a quality daily or weekly newspaper, and watch for economic issues, and the way in which these are analysed and interpreted. Try to develop a critical eye. Do not accept everything that appears in print, but evaluate the arguments against economic analysis. Think about economic issues that are reported and discussed on television, and see whether you agree with the conclusions reached. Get into the habit of asking yourself whether the arguments presented are in line with what you know about economics.

*The quality daily newspapers are full of economic issues, but you may not always agree with the arguments given*

## Researching

Keep up to date with recent developments in the economy. Be familiar with the performance of the UK economy, and how this compares with other countries in Europe. Make use of key sites on the internet, such as Eurostat (**epp.eurostat.ec. europa.eu**) and the Office for National Statistics (**www.statistics.gov.uk**). Do not try to memorise lots of statistics — that is not what is needed. Rather, familiarise yourself with the key issues.

## Rehearsing

Practise using and applying economic ideas. Become aware of how economic analysis is used in formulating policy, interpreting economic events or in helping

in the decision-making process. Practise interpreting data that appear in the press or on websites. Be aware of how economic thinking can improve everyday decision making. Economic thinking can become part of the way you live. The more practice you get, the more you will begin to think like an economist.

## The assessment

The assessment is based on some pre-released stimulus material, so your practice should stand you in good stead during the final preparations for the exam. The way to approach this is not to spend time trying to guess the questions that you will face. Instead, study the material carefully and think about how the economic analysis with which you are familiar would help in seeking to understand that material. You will be able to identify a number of topics that relate to different parts of the course content. This should help you to focus your mind during the preparation period.

It is also helpful to be aware of the kinds of question that you will face. The specification for the module sets these out clearly, as follows:

> The typical structure of the assessment is:
> ➤ a question based on data-handling skills, worth 6 marks
> ➤ a question requiring economic analysis only, worth 9 marks
> ➤ a question requiring commentary (supported by economic analysis), worth 10 marks
> ➤ a question requiring extended commentary (supported by economic analysis), worth 15 marks
> ➤ a final question, usually based around the theme of extracts or one that integrates the stimulus material, which requires discussion, worth 20 marks
>
> The stimulus material will be focused on a contemporary European theme or issue and will relate to both microeconomic and macroeconomic concepts.

(Specification contents at **www.ocr.org.uk**)

Make sure that you are familiar with this pattern so that you are not surprised when you reach the exam room. Be aware that these questions set out to assess different sorts of skill, and make sure that you answer each question explicitly.

## A review of some key concepts

This section offers a brief review of some key concepts encountered in previous chapters. It is not exhaustive; nor does it provide detailed analysis. Where necessary, you should turn back the pages of this book to refresh your memory of concepts that seem less familiar to you. Remember that this synoptic chapter draws on material from the AS modules and from the common themes in the A2 options — the theory of the firm, GDP and living standards, comparative advantage and trade. The economic analysis from those earlier chapters is now set in the European context presented in this part of the book.

## Opportunity cost

Almost the first concept introduced in the book was that of *opportunity cost*. This is such a fundamental concept that you should not need to be reminded of it here. The opportunity cost of a decision is seen in terms of the benefits from the next-best alternative forgone. By choosing to undertake a particular investment project, a firm sacrifices the opportunity to undertake some other project. By choosing to consume one food, a consumer forgoes the possibility of consuming something else. This simple concept has many applications, and you will have seen many examples occurring in the book.

Opportunity cost was first introduced in Chapter 1.

## Competitive markets

Leading on from the concept of opportunity cost is the notion of *scarcity*. Indeed, opportunity cost becomes relevant because scarcity forces economic decision-makers to make choices. Scarcity is important for any society, as it is in the interests of society to ensure that resources are used in the best possible way. This leads to the notion of *allocative efficiency*, under which goods are produced and consumed up to the point where the marginal benefit from consuming a good (or service) is equated to the marginal cost of producing that good (or service). This is also the point at which price is equal to marginal cost.

The demand and supply model was first introduced in Chapters 2 and 3; the role of prices in resource allocation was discussed in Chapter 5.

A fundamental idea is that where there are competitive markets, *prices* play a crucial role in acting as signals to guide the allocation of resources in such a way that allocative efficiency can be achieved. This is because consumers take decisions on the basis of the prices for goods and services on offer, which they can assess in terms of their willingness to pay. From a firm's perspective, prices determine profitability, and hence willingness to supply.

*Competitive markets are important for allocative efficiency*

## Market structure and efficiency

The structure of markets may have an important influence on whether the price mechanism is able to operate effectively. For example, if firms have market power because the market is a *monopoly* or an *oligopoly*, then price may be held above the level at which marginal social benefit is equal to marginal cost. This takes society away from the position of allocative efficiency.

> Notions of market structure were analysed in Chapters 14 and 15.

In evaluating the effects of market structure, it is important to be aware that there is a second dimension to efficiency, namely *productive efficiency*. In many economic activities, there are *economies of scale*. This can mean that average production costs decrease with the volume of production. There are therefore many situations in which there are benefits from large-scale production. In some cases, this may mean a trade-off between allocative and productive efficiency. If firms are kept so small that they cannot take advantage of economies of scale, there may be a gain in allocative efficiency, but a sacrifice of productive efficiency. This is an example of a situation in which the economist has to balance conflicting forces against each other in seeking to evaluate a particular market situation.

> Economies of scale were first introduced in Chapter 4.

## Market failure

The existence of imperfect competition in a market may be seen as one instance of *market failure*. Market failure describes a situation in which the free operation of markets fails to lead to allocative efficiency. This is an important aspect of economic analysis.

> Market failure was introduced in Chapters 6 and 7, and appeared many times subsequently.

A common form of market failure is where there are *externalities* present in a market situation. This occurs when there are items of either costs or benefits associated with a market transaction that are not reflected in market prices. Obvious examples are pollution and traffic congestion, but there are many others.

Market failure can also occur when there is an *information failure*. If participants in a market do not have full information about market conditions, they will be unable to take optimal decisions. This may be especially important when some participants in a market have more, or better, information than others — a situation known as *asymmetric information*. They may then be able to make use of that information in order to introduce a market distortion. This again can lead to market failure. Indeed, in some cases, it may lead to some markets failing to exist at all.

Problems of market failure may also arise from the characteristics of some goods. This is especially important in the case of *public goods*, which are goods having the twin characteristics of non-rivalry and non-exclusivity. The upshot of these characteristics is that goods such as street lighting and law and order will not be adequately supplied (if at all) by the market.

*Maintaining law and order is an example of a public good that would not be adequately supplied by the market*

An important objective of microeconomic policy is to enable an increase in the productive capacity of the economy. This aspect of microeconomic intervention interacts with macroeconomics, as an increase in the overall productive capacity of the economy may be interpreted as economic growth, which is a prime macroeconomic objective. This encompasses measures that ensure there are good incentives for producers and workers, and measures that can improve the flexibility with which markets operate — especially the labour market, which can affect the level of unemployment in the economy.

Supply-side policies were first outlined in Chapter 12.

## Government intervention

In the presence of market failure, governments may be tempted to intervene in order to correct the market failure. The economic analysis of market failure is useful in allowing policy to be designed to correct for market failure at the microeconomic level. The use of *taxation* or *regulation* can be seen to tackle some important market imperfections. For example, pollution (an externality) can be tackled either by imposing taxes (the taxation solution) or by imposing restrictions on emissions (the regulation solution).

Government intervention was first discussed in Chapter 8 and has been widely analysed since then.

It is also important to be aware that there may be limitations on the extent to which government is able to deal with market failures. For example, making use of indirect taxes in order to raise revenue for public expenditure may itself introduce a form of market failure. *Government failure* occurs when government intervention intended to deal with one problem introduces a problem of a different kind.

## Macroeconomic performance

Macroeconomics uses many of the same tools as microeconomics, and employs a similar way of thinking about economic issues. However, the focus of the analysis is different. In macroeconomics, the focus is on the overall level of economic activity, and the performance of the economy in terms of key variables such as economic growth, inflation, unemployment and the balance of payments. By monitoring the performance of such variables, it is possible to gauge how well an economy is working, either relative to its own past performance or relative to other countries. In this connection, it is important to be able to measure those key macroeconomic variables. In particular, it is important to be able to evaluate the standard of living that a country's inhabitants are able to enjoy. Performance is evaluated in relation to the objectives set out by the government.

> Macroeconomic performance was first discussed in Chapter 9; measures of the standard of living were evaluated in Chapters 24 and 29.

Economists use macroeconomic models to evaluate an economy's performance and to understand the important interactions between variables at the macroeconomic level. In particular, the *AD/AS* model helps to provide an understanding of a macro economy, and to analyse how it may be made to operate more effectively.

> The *AD/AS* model made its first appearance in Chapter 10, and has been widely used during later chapters.

## Policy objectives at the macroeconomic level

Governments are seen to have a range of objectives at the macroeconomic level, the most important being to achieve sustainable economic growth. Other objectives, such as the control of inflation to ensure a stable economic environment, or the maintenance of full employment, are seen as important because they may assist in the pursuit of economic growth. However, the *sustainability* of economic growth is also important, as is the need to achieve an acceptable distribution of income between different groups within a society.

> Policy objectives were discussed in Chapters 11 and 12, and more closely analysed in Chapters 28 and 32.

There may, at times, be conflicts between policy instruments in the pursuit of the policy objectives, so that a policy designed to meet one target may endanger other objectives of policy. The authorities thus need to be careful in designing policy and in setting appropriate priorities amongst the objectives.

> Conflicts in macroeconomic policy were discussed in Chapter 33.

The main instrument of policy in the UK in recent years has been *monetary policy*, where a balance has to be maintained between money supply, interest rates and the foreign exchange rate. *Fiscal policy* has taken a subsidiary role, being used to establish a stable environment within which monetary policy can operate, maintaining a balance between public and private sectors, and being used to influence the distribution of income within society.

chapter 34

## International trade

*Globalisation* has had a major impact on economies around the world. This is a process whereby changes in the technology of transport and communications have led to an increasingly integrated global market. One feature of this process is the way in which multinational corporations have grown to an enormous size in the pursuit of economies of scale — and of new markets.

Globalisation was the subject of debate in Chapters 27 and 33.

The potential gains from international trade have been well known to economists for many years, based on the *law of comparative advantage*, which highlights the benefits that can be gained from countries specialising in the production of goods and services in which they have a comparative advantage.

In spite of these potential gains, countries have always been tempted to interfere with free trade, using protectionist measures such as *tariffs* and other *non-tariff barriers* to trade in order to try to protect domestic economic activities. Such measures are known to impose welfare losses, but this has not deterred countries from making use of them.

Comparative advantage was discussed in Chapters 26 and 31.

## The international policy environment

The conduct of international trade and international relations is overseen by three important multilateral organisations. The International Monetary Fund (IMF) oversees international financial markets and has a specific brief to provide assistance to countries that find themselves in difficulties with their balance of payments. The IMF influences domestic policy of countries that ask for help by imposing conditions in exchange for loans. The World Bank has responsibility for encouraging long-term development. The World Trade Organization (WTO) oversees international trade, encouraging countries to reduce tariffs and other restraints on trade, and acting as arbitrator in disputes between countries.

These organisations were discussed in Chapters 28 and 32.

*World Trade Organization meeting, December 2005*

## A European context

Having followed your economics course and reached this point, you have a battery of theories, models and concepts at your disposal, ready to be applied and used. 'Europe' provides the context — the raw material on which to operate with your tools of analysis.

Some topics stand out as being of special relevance. For example, international trade is clearly of central importance in the context of the Single European Market, and exchange rate policy is crucial in the context of European Monetary Union. Theories and models of growth and development may be particularly relevant for the transition economies of Eastern Europe.

However, it is important to realise and remember that 'Europe' is just the playground for your economic tools. The focus is not on how much you know about Europe, but on how well you can apply economics in a European context. Countries in Europe adopt different approaches to many economic issues. They may use different policies for dealing with externalities such as pollution, or demerit goods such as drugs and tobacco. They may have different attitudes towards poverty and inequality. They may simply have different priorities between policy objectives, or different preferences between using taxation as opposed to regulation. They may face different conditions and problems. The scope for asking you to show how well you can apply economic analysis to such issues seems almost endless.

It is therefore important to adopt an economics-centred approach to this module. Be ready for anything, but be ready to apply your economic analysis. Think like an economist, and be prepared to evaluate the issues and the evidence presented to you.

'Europe' is a rich field in which to work, and the following chapters provide a brief background to some key topic areas, and some examples of how economic analysis can be applied to help understand and interpret a range of issues.

part **9**

# Chapter 35
# Economic integration

*The economic landscape of Europe since the Second World War has been shaped by the move towards ever-closer economic integration. The UK has been part of this, although at times a seemingly reluctant participant. The economic arguments in favour of closer economic integration are partly based on notions of comparative advantage and the potential gains of allowing freer trade. However, there are other pertinent issues to be taken into consideration in evaluating the costs and benefits of closer integration. Such integration also has political ramifications that can affect an individual country's attitude towards its potential partners. In this chapter, the history of economic integration in Europe is set out, and the nature of alternative forms of integration is highlighted. You do not need to have a detailed knowledge of the early history of economic integration in Europe. However, it is helpful to be aware of how the relationships between countries in Europe have evolved over time.*

## Learning outcomes

After studying this chapter, you should:
- ➤ be familiar with the chronology of moves towards closer European integration
- ➤ appreciate the position of Europe in the global economy
- ➤ be aware of the different forms that economic integration may take: free trade areas, customs unions, common markets and economic and monetary union
- ➤ know the features of these alternative forms of integration and understand the distinction between them
- ➤ be able to explain why integration does not always operate as economic analysis suggests

## Evolution of the European Union

More than 50 years ago, Robert Schuman (French foreign minister at the time) proposed that France and West Germany should pool their coal and steel resources. That was the beginning of the long road towards European integration. Although integration has been primarily a question of economics, the political

background cannot be ignored. To some people, integration of the countries within Europe was an attempt to avoid the conflict and wars that had afflicted Europe in the past.

The European Coal and Steel Community was established in 1951, with six participating countries: Belgium, France, West Germany, Italy, Luxembourg and the Netherlands. These same countries then formed the European Economic Community (EEC) in 1957. This became known as the *Common Market*. Since then the Community has evolved, drawing in more countries and expanding the scope of its operations. Table 35.1 sets out a chronology of the key events in the development of the present European Union (EU).

| | |
|---|---|
| 9 May 1950 | Robert Schuman proposes that France and West Germany pool their coal and steel resources |
| 1951 | Treaty of Paris: European Coal and Steel Community (ECSC) is established by Belgium, France, West Germany, Italy, Luxembourg and the Netherlands |
| 1957 | Treaties of Rome: European Economic Community (EEC/Common Market) and European Atomic Energy Community (EURATOM) are established by the six ECSC countries |
| 1967 | Institutions of the EEC merge: a single Commission, a single Council of Ministers and a European Parliament; now known as the European Community (EC) |
| 1970 | Werner Plan proposes European monetary unity |
| 1973 | Denmark, Ireland and the UK join the EC |
| 1979 | The European Monetary System (EMS) is launched, including the Exchange Rate Mechanism (ERM), a precursor of the single currency |
| 1981 | Greece joins the EC |
| 1985 | Single European Market Act contains plans for completing the internal market within Europe |
| 1986 | Spain and Portugal join the EC |
| 1989 | The Delors Plan sets out a proposal for creating European economic and monetary union (EMU), including a single currency and the European Central Bank |
| September 1990 | The UK joins the ERM |
| September 1992 | The UK leaves the ERM |
| 1 January 1993 | The Single European Market (SEM) comes into effect |
| November 1993 | Treaty of Maastricht comes into force, creating the European Union (EU) |
| 1995 | Austria, Finland and Sweden join the EU |
| 1 January 2002 | 12 EU countries adopt the euro as their currency; Denmark, Sweden and the UK are not part of this group |
| 2004 | Cyprus, the Czech Republic, Estonia, Hungary, Latvia, Lithuania, Malta, Poland, Slovakia and Slovenia join the EU |

*Table 35.1 Chronology of European integration*

The 10 countries that joined in May 2004 brought the membership of the EU to 25 countries in all (the 'EU25'). Figure 35.1 shows the population size of these 25 countries in 2004, and the years in which they joined. Bulgaria and Romania were judged not to be ready to join in 2004, but were in the queue; negotiations with Turkey began in 2005, but quickly ran into problems. If Turkey were to join, this would add a massive 71.7 million citizens to the EU.

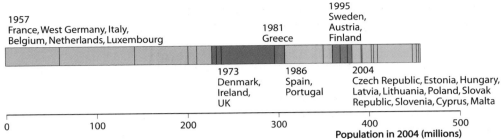

**Figure 35.1** *Population of EU countries, 2004*

Source: data from the *World Development Report*, 2006.

Figure 35.2 shows how the enlarged EU would stand in the world rankings of big countries. This underlines the fact that the 15 pre-2004 member countries of the EU (the 'EU15') already contained more people than the USA; the combined population of the EU25 member states in 2004 was 455 million, compared with 293.5 million in the USA. With Bulgaria, Romania and Turkey (the EU28), the total population would be 556.8 million.

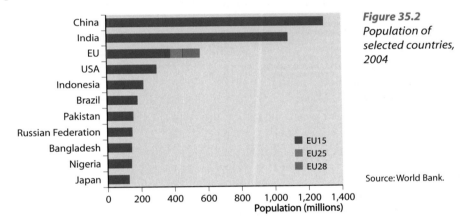

**Figure 35.2**
*Population of selected countries, 2004*

Source: World Bank.

But how important is sheer size of population? After all, what matters in a market is the *effective* demand for goods and services — in other words, demand backed up by real purchasing power. So it is important to look not only at population size, but also at purchasing power. For example, average levels of gross national income (GNI) per capita in US dollars could be a way of trying to judge purchasing power. There will be substantial variation here, with the poorest EU acceding country, Latvia, having a GNI per capita of US$3,480 in 2002, compared with an estimated US$12,320 for Cyprus.

However, comparisons of GNI in US dollars can be quite misleading. Such measurements do not necessarily reflect local purchasing power because they are based on a conversion from local currency into US dollars using official exchange rates. This can give a distorted view of the comparison of income between countries, especially if the US dollar itself is away from its equilibrium level.

Figure 35.3 presents an alternative way of looking at the relative average income levels of the new member countries. The data here relate to GDP per capita measured in purchasing power parity dollars (PPP$), which helps to avoid the distortionary effects of official exchange rates. The data have then been converted into index number form, so that for each country the index shows GDP per capita relative to the EU15 average. For example, the index for the UK is 108.7, showing that the UK enjoys GDP per capita that is 8.7% higher than the average level in the first 15 EU member countries. For Latvia the index is 36.6, meaning that its average income is 36.6% of the EU15 average. Notice that there is some overlap between the average income levels of the countries that joined in 2004 and some of the lower-income previous members: Cyprus has higher average income than Greece, whereas Slovenia and Malta have about the same level as Portugal.

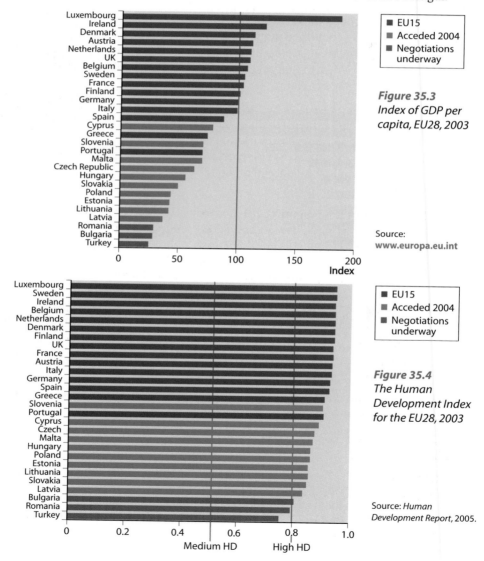

*Figure 35.3*
*Index of GDP per capita, EU28, 2003*

Source:
**www.europa.eu.int**

*Figure 35.4*
*The Human Development Index for the EU28, 2003*

Source: *Human Development Report*, 2005.

Another way of comparing living standards across countries is by using the Human Development Index (HDI), which was introduced in Chapter 24. This takes into account not only GDP per capita, but also education and life expectancy. It takes on values between 0 and 1, with the higher values indicating higher human development. Figure 35.4 shows the values for 2002. All except Romania and Turkey have reached the 'high human development' category.

Nonetheless, it is clear that average income levels are lower in the member nations that joined in 2004 than in the incumbent members. This has implications for the size of effective demand coming from the additional consumers in the single European market, and also implications for the *pattern* of consumer demand in terms of the sorts of goods and services that are in demand.

Figure 35.5 compares the overall structure of economic activity in the EU15 and New13 in 2001, as measured by the contribution of the major sectors to gross value added. The left-hand column shows how important the service sector has become in the structure of economic activity, contributing some 71% of GDP of the EU15 on the value-added measure in 2001. In the acceding countries, agriculture, industry and construction are relatively more important than in the EU15. Thus there may be scope for gains from trade.

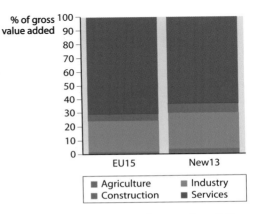

**Figure 35.5** *The structure of economic activity in the EU, 2001*

Note: data include Bulgaria, Romania and Turkey as well as those that joined the EU in May 2004.

Source: Eurostat.

In analysing European integration, there are two tiers to be considered: the evolution of the Single European Market (SEM), and the development of the euro single currency area. We will return to these in Chapters 36 and 37.

## Summary

➤ Practical steps towards economic integration in Europe began with the formation of the European Coal and Steel Community in 1951, whereby six countries agreed to pool their coal and steel resources.

➤ This was so successful that it was replaced by the more wide-ranging European Economic Community (EEC), established in 1957.

➤ Over the following years, the EEC expanded the scope of its operations and the number of participating nations.

➤ By 2004, when ten more countries were granted membership, the combined membership in population terms represented some 455 million people.

➤ There was substantial diversity in the member countries in both living standards and the structure of economic activity.

# Forms of economic integration

Economic integration takes a variety of forms, reflecting different degrees of closeness. The underlying motivation for integration is to allow trading partners to take advantage of the potential gains from international trade, as illustrated by the law of comparative advantage. This states that countries can gain from specialising in the production of goods and services in which they hold a comparative advantage, and by engaging in trade. For example, if one country has a comparative advantage in producing wine, and another has a comparative advantage in producing cars, then both countries can be made better off if they each specialise in producing what they are good at making, and then trade with each other. By reducing the barriers to trade, this specialisation can be encouraged, so there should be potential gains from the process. In practice, there may be other economic and political forces at work that affect the nature of the gains, and the extent to which integration will be possible — and beneficial.

## Free trade areas

The first level of integration is the formation of a so-called **free trade area**. Before the UK joined the European Community in 1973, it was part of the European Free Trade Area (EFTA), together with other countries in Europe that had not joined the Community. The original countries were Austria, Denmark, Norway, Portugal, Sweden, Switzerland and the UK. Finland, Iceland and Liechtenstein joined later, but some EFTA members left in order to join the EU, leaving just Iceland, Liechtenstein, Norway and Switzerland as members of EFTA in the first years of the twenty-first century.

**free trade area:** a group of countries that agree to remove tariffs, quotas and other restrictions on trade between the member countries, but have no agreement on a common barrier against non-members

The notion of a free trade area is that countries within the area agree to remove internal tariff and quota restrictions on trade between them, while still allowing member countries to impose their own pattern of tariffs and quotas on non-members. The lack of a common external tariff wall may cause problems within the member countries. If one country has lower tariffs than the rest, the natural tendency will be for imports into the area to be channelled through that country, with goods then being resold to other member countries. This may distort the pattern of trade and cause unnecessary transaction costs associated with trading activity. It is worth noting that free trade areas are normally concerned with enabling free trade in goods and do not cover the movement of labour.

In spite of these problems, a free trade area does allow member countries to increase their degree of specialisation, and may bring gains. EFTA is not the only example of such an arrangement. In South East Asia, the Association of South-East Asian Nations (ASEAN) began to create a free trade area in 1993. This involved six nations (Brunei, Indonesia, Malaysia, the Philippines, Singapore and Thailand). The group was later expanded to include Cambodia, Laos, Myanmar and

*The signing of the North American Free Trade Agreement in 1992*

Vietnam. Progress towards eliminating tariffs in this group has been relatively slow, but intense competition from the rapidly growing Chinese economy provides a strong motivation for accelerating the process.

Another major trading group operating a free trade area is the North American Free Trade Association (NAFTA), which covers the USA, Canada and Mexico. The agreement was signed in 1992 and launched in 1994, and has led to an expansion of trade between those countries. Unlike in Europe, there is as yet no stated intention that NAFTA should evolve into anything more than a free trade area.

## Exercise 35.1

Figure 35.6 shows the effects of a tariff (reproduced from Chapter 13).

If a country decides to *remove* the tariff, identify the effects on:

**a** consumers of the good

**b** producers of the good

**c** the government

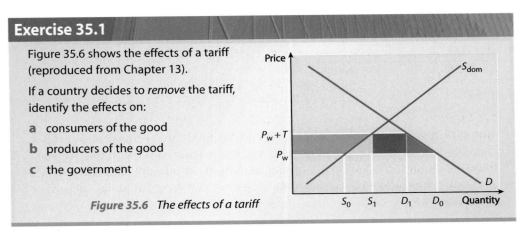

*Figure 35.6  The effects of a tariff*

## Customs unions

A **customs union** is one notch up from a free trade area, in the sense that in addition to eliminating tariffs and quotas between the member nations, a common external tariff wall is set up against non-member nations. Again, the prime reason for establishing a customs union is to encourage trade between the member nations.

part 9

Such increased trade is beneficial when there is **trade creation**. This is where the formation of the customs union allows countries to specialise more, and thus to exploit their comparative advantage. The larger market for the goods means that more economies of scale may be available, and the lower prices that result generate additional trade between the member nations. These lower prices arise partly from the exploitation of comparative advantage, but also from the removal of tariffs between the member nations.

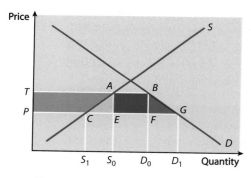

**Figure 35.7**
*The effects of trade creation*

> **Key terms**
>
> **customs union:** a group of countries that agree to remove restrictions on trade between the member countries, and set a common set of restrictions (including tariffs) against non-member states
>
> **trade creation:** the replacement of more expensive domestic production or imports with cheaper output from a partner within the trading bloc

Figure 35.7 illustrates the effects of trade creation. It shows the demand and supply of a good in a certain country that joins a customs union. Before joining the union, the price of the good is $T$, which includes a tariff element. Domestic demand is $D_0$, of which $S_0$ comes from domestic producers, and the remainder is imported. When the country joins the customs union, the tariff is removed and the domestic price falls to $P$. Consumers benefit from additional consumer surplus, given by the area $PTBG$. However, notice that not all of this is pure gain to the country. The area $PTAC$ was formerly part of producer surplus, so there has been a redistribution from domestic firms to consumers. $ABFE$ was formerly tariff revenue collected by the government, so this represents effectively a redistribution from government to consumers. The area $ACE$ is a net gain for the country, as this represents resources that were previously used up in the production of the good, but which can now be used for other purposes. The area $BFG$ also represents a welfare gain to the country.

However, it is also important to be aware that becoming a member of a customs union may alter the pattern of trading relationships. A country that is part of a customs union will be more inclined to trade with other members of the union because of the agreement between them, and because of the absence of internal tariffs. However, given the common external tariff, it is quite possible that members of the union are not the most efficient producers on the global stage. So there may be a situation of **trade diversion**. This occurs where a member country of a customs union imports goods from other members *instead* of from more efficient producers elsewhere in the world. This may mean that there is no net increase in trade,

> **Key term**
>
> **trade diversion:** the replacement of cheaper imported goods by goods from a less efficient trading partner within a bloc

but simply a diversion from an external source to a new source within the union. In this situation, there are not necessarily the same gains from trade to be made.

Figure 35.8 helps to show the effects of trade diversion. Here, $D$ represents the demand curve for a commodity that is initially imported from a country outside the customs union. It is assumed that the supply of the good from the non-member is perfectly elastic, as shown by $S_n$. However, the importing country imposes a tariff of the amount $T$, so the quantity imported is given by $Q_n$, and the price charged is $P_n + T$.

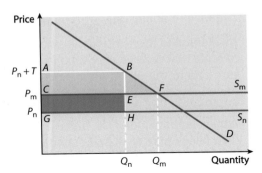

**Figure 35.8**
*The effects of trade diversion*

After the importing country joins the customs union, the tariff is removed, but the good is now imported from a less efficient producer within the union. The supply from this member country is assumed to be elastic at $S_m$, so the new price is $P_m$ and the quantity is $Q_m$.

In examining the welfare effects, there are two issues to consider. First, notice that consumer surplus has increased by the area $ABFC$. However, this is not pure gain to the economy because, in the original position, the government was collecting tariff revenue of the amount $ABHG$. In other words, the increase in consumer surplus comes partly as a pure gain (the triangle $BFE$), but partly at the expense of the government ($ABEC$). This is not all, because the area $CEHG$ was also formerly part of tariff revenue, but now is a payment by domestic consumers to producers in the other (member) country. This means that whether the country is better or worse off depends upon the relative size of the areas $BFE$ (which is a gain) and $CEHG$ (which is a loss).

There are some further disadvantages of customs unions. Certainly, the transactions costs involved in administering the union cannot be ignored, and where there are traditional rivalries between nations there may be political sensitivities to overcome. This may impede the free working of the union, especially if some member nations are more committed to the union than others, or if some countries have close ties with non-member states.

It is also possible that a geographical concentration of economic activity will emerge over time within the union. This may result where firms want to locate near the centre of the area in order to minimise transportation costs. Alternatively, it may be that all firms will want to locate near the richest part of the market. Over time, this could mean that firms tend to concentrate in certain geographical areas, while the countries that are more remote, or which have smaller populations or lower average incomes, become peripheral to the centre of activity. In other words, over time, there may be growing inequality between regions within the union.

These disadvantages must be balanced against the benefits. For example, it may be that it is the smaller countries in the union that have the most to gain from tapping economies of scale that would not be accessible to them if they were confined to selling only within their domestic markets.

In addition to these internal economies of scale, there may be external economies of scale that emerge over time as the transport and communications infrastructure within the union improves. Furthermore, opening up domestic markets to more intense competition may induce efficiency gains, as firms will only be able to survive in the face of international competition by adopting best practice techniques and technologies. Indeed, another advantage of a customs union is that technology may be disseminated amongst firms operating within the union.

## Common markets

It may be that the countries within a customs union wish to move to the next stage of integration, by extending the degree of cooperation between the member nations. A **common market** adds to the features of a customs union by harmonising some aspects of the economic environment between them. In a pure common market, this would entail adopting common tax rates across the member states, and a common framework for the laws and regulations that provide the environment for production, employment and trade. A common market would also allow for the free movement of factors of production between the member nations, especially in terms of labour and capital (land is less mobile by its nature!). Given the importance of the public sector in a modern economy, a common market would also set common procurement policies across member governments, so that individual governments did not favour their own domestic firms when purchasing goods and services.

 **Key term**

**common market:** a set of trading arrangements in which a group of countries remove barriers to trade among them, adopt a common set of barriers against external trade, establish common tax rates and laws regulating economic activity, allow free movement of factors of production between members and have common public sector procurement policies

You will see in the next chapter that the SEM has encompassed most of these features, although tax rates have not been harmonised across the countries that are included.

## Economic and monetary union

Moving beyond a common market, there is the prospect of full **economic and monetary union**. This entails taking the additional step of adopting fixed exchange rates between the member states. This in turn requires member states to follow a common monetary policy, and it is also seen as desirable to harmonise other aspects of macroeconomic policy across the union.

The adoption of fixed exchange rates is a contentious aspect of proposals for economic and monetary union. With fixed exchange rates, governments are no longer able to use monetary policy for internal domestic purposes. This is because

monetary variables become subservient to the need to maintain the exchange rate, and it is not possible to set independent targets for the rate of interest or money supply if the government has to maintain the value of the currency on the foreign exchange market. This is all very well if all countries in the union are following a similar business cycle, but if one country becomes poorly synchronised with the others, there may be major problems.

For example, it could be that the union as a whole is enjoying a boom, and setting interest rates accordingly. For an individual member country suffering a recession, this could mean deepening and prolonging the recession, as it would not be possible to relax interest rates in order to allow aggregate demand to recover.

 **Key** *term*

**economic and monetary union:** a set of trading arrangements the same as for a common market, but in addition having fixed exchange rates between the member countries and a common monetary policy

A successful economic and monetary union therefore requires careful policy coordination across the member nations. Notice that economic and monetary union involves fixed exchange rates between the member countries, but does not necessarily entail the adoption of a common currency, although this may follow at some stage.

## Structural change

A feature that all of these forms of integration have in common is that they involve the removal of barriers to trade amongst member countries. It is important to be aware that this will not be perceived as a good thing by all the parties involved. In order to benefit from increased specialisation and trade, countries need to allow the pattern of their production to change. The benefits to the expanding sectors are apparent, but it is also the case that industries that formerly enjoyed protection from competition will become exposed to competition, and will need to decline in order to allow resources to be transferred into the expanding sectors. This can be a painful process for firms that need to close down, or move into new markets, and for workers who may need to undergo retraining before they are ready for employment in the newly expanding parts of the economy.

An especially contentious area of debate in the UK concerns the structural change that has taken place in recent decades, in which manufacturing activity has declined and financial services have expanded. This seems to reflect the changing pattern of the UK's comparative advantage, in which banking, finance and insurance have become a major strength of the economy, whereas the manufacturing sector has found it more difficult to compete with the host of new entrants into this market from elsewhere in the world.

### Exercise 35.2

Find out how the structure of employment in the UK has changed in the last 15–20 years. Discuss whether the process of deindustrialisation that has taken place will benefit the economy in the long run.

**part 9**

## Summary

➤ Economic integration can take a variety of forms, of differing degrees of closeness.

➤ A free trade area is where a group of countries agree to remove restrictions on trade between them, but without having a common external tariff.

➤ A customs union is a free trade area with an agreed common set of restrictions on trade with non-members.

➤ A customs union can entail trade creation, in which member countries benefit from increased trade and specialisation.

➤ However, there may also be trade diversion, in which countries divert their trading activity from external trade partners to countries within the union.

➤ Trade diversion does not always bring gains, as the producers within the union are not necessarily more efficient than external producers.

➤ A common market is a customs union in which the member countries also agree to harmonise their policies in a number of key respects.

➤ Economic and monetary union entails fixed exchange rates between member countries, but not necessarily agreement to adopt a common currency.

# Chapter 36
# The Single European Market and economic and monetary union

Two major steps towards economic integration have taken place in the period since 1990. On 1 January 1993, the Single European Market (SEM) came into operation. Then, on 1 January 2002, 12 European countries adopted the euro as their common currency. The expansion of the SEM in 2004 to incorporate ten new members was a further significant development. This chapter highlights these developments and assesses their impact on the economic performance of the UK, referring to relevant areas of economic analysis that help in analysing the costs and benefits of closer economic integration.

## Learning outcomes

After studying this chapter, you should:
- ➤ understand the significance of the SEM
- ➤ evaluate the costs and benefits of membership of a single currency area
- ➤ be aware of the role and effectiveness of monetary and fiscal policy within a single currency area
- ➤ be able to evaluate the arguments for and against the UK joining the Eurozone

## The Single European Market (SEM)

From the moment of formation of the European Economic Community (EEC) in 1957, the member countries began working towards the creation of a single market in which there would be free movement of goods, services, people and capital. In other words, the idea was to create a *common market* in which there would be no barriers to trade. The EEC was a *customs union* in which internal tariffs and non-tariff barriers were to be removed and a common tariff was to be set against the rest of the world.

The main focus in the early years of the EEC was on coal and steel, together with the introduction of the Common Agricultural Policy (CAP). Initially, the objective of the CAP was to produce as much food as cheaply as possible, but the focus has changed in more recent years, especially since the reforms introduced in 2003.

A package of measures that came into effect in January 1993 might be seen as the final stages in the evolution of the SEM. The key measures were the removal (or reduction) of border controls and the winding down of non-tariff barriers to trade within the EU. In this way, physical, technical and fiscal barriers were removed. It has also become increasingly easy for people to move around within the EU, with passport and customs checks being abolished at most internal borders. Associated with these measures were a number of expected benefits.

### Transaction costs

Tariff barriers between EU countries were abolished under the Treaty of Rome, but a range of non-tariff barriers had built up over the years as countries sought to protect domestic employment. It was expected that the removal of these obstacles to trade, combined with the removal of border controls, would reduce the costs of trade within the EU. However, it is difficult to gauge the significance of these transaction cost savings, as it is not easy to quantify them.

### Economies of scale

By now, you should be familiar with the notion of economies of scale, and its importance in respect of reaching productive efficiency. As trade increases, firms will find that they are operating in a larger market. This should allow them to exploit more fully the economies of large-scale production. From society's point of view, this should lead to a more efficient use of resources, as long as the resulting trade creation effects are stronger than any trade diversion that may take place.

It seems that the nature of technological change in recent years has favoured the growth of large-scale enterprises. Improved transport and communications have

*The Common Agricultural Policy led to the creation of huge reserves of grain as well as of other agricultural commodities*

contributed to this process. The SEM has enabled firms in Europe to take advantage of these developments.

### Intensified competition

Firms will find that they are facing more intense competition within that larger market from firms in other parts of the EU. This then brings up the same arguments that are used to justify privatisation — that intensified competition will cause firms or their managers to seek more efficient production techniques, perhaps through the elimination of X-inefficiencies. This again is beneficial for society as a whole.

However, a note of caution needs to be sounded here. The argument that economies of scale are there to be tapped has led to the growth of some giant firms, formed through a process of merger and acquisition, often involving cross-border deals. For example, Vodafone Airtouch acquired Mannesmann AG in 2000 for a reported £100 billion, and became one of Britain's largest companies. There is a danger that these large firms will gain sufficient market power as to be in a position to make monopoly profits — at the expense of the consumer. This could occur either through a firm reaching a monopoly position, or through cooperation between a few large firms in an oligopoly market. The regulation of such large firms could be problematic, especially where they are operating on a European scale, rather than just within a domestic market. It is in this context that the European Commission has developed its own competition authority, which has the power to operate competition policy across the EU as a whole.

From the perspective of individual countries, there has been a divergence of views concerning these large firms. In some countries, large firms have been seen as 'national champions'. These have been protected (or even subsidised) by domestic governments, based on the argument that they will then be better prepared to compete in the broader European market. Elsewhere, governments have taken the view that the only way to ensure that domestic firms are lean enough to be competitive in overseas markets is to face intense competition at home, as an inducement to efficiency.

### Who gains most from the SEM?

As trade within Europe becomes freer, two groups of countries stand to gain the most. First, the pattern of comparative advantage between countries will be important. Many EU countries are advanced industrial nations, where labour is expensive relative to capital. These countries tend to specialise in manufacturing or capital-intensive service activities, and already have fairly similar structures. It is thus possible that the relatively labour-abundant countries of southern Europe may gain more from closer integration and an expansion of trade. This is because they have a pattern of comparative advantage that is significantly different from existing members. This diversity was reinforced by the new entrants who joined in May 2004.

Second, if the main effect of integration is to remove barriers to trade, the countries with the most to gain may be those that begin with relatively high barriers.

Figure 36.1 shows growth rates in the countries in 2001–02, just before the enlargement of 2004. This shows that the joining members were, on the whole, enjoying more rapid economic growth than the EU15 countries. The enlargement thus may have the effect of introducing new *dynamic economies*, and this may have spillover effects for the other member nations.

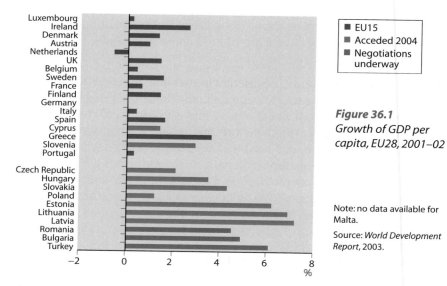

*Figure 36.1*
*Growth of GDP per capita, EU28, 2001–02*

Note: no data available for Malta.

Source: *World Development Report*, 2003.

### How important is this to the UK?

An important piece of background information is that, over the years, UK trade has become increasingly focused on Europe. This was seen in Figure 32.7, which showed the percentage of UK exports going to the EU15 countries: it has increased steadily, from about 23% in 1960 to about 53% in 2003. This means that the UK depends heavily on trade with other countries in the EU, so successful economic performance cannot be seen in isolation from events in the broader market.

## Summary

➤ The prime objective of the EEC was to create a single market in Europe, in which there would be free movement of goods, services, people and capital.

➤ The EEC was a customs union, in which internal tariffs and non-tariff barriers were to be removed and a common tariff was set against the rest of the world.

➤ The EEC also established the Common Agricultural Policy to protect agriculture and to produce as much food as cheaply as possible.

➤ The Single Market package came into effect at the beginning of 1993, freeing up trade between participating countries and winding down non-tariff barriers.

➤ This was expected to encourage trade by lowering transaction costs, enabling firms to reap economies of scale, and enhancing efficiency by stimulating competition between European firms.

## Exercise 36.1

Explain why it might be the relatively labour-intensive countries of southern Europe — and the countries of Eastern Europe and the Baltic that joined in 2004 — that stand to gain most from the SEM.

# The single currency

The establishment of the SEM was seen by some as an end in itself, but others regarded it as a step towards full monetary integration, in which all member states would adopt a single currency, thereby reducing the transaction costs of international trade even more. However, full monetary union and the adoption of a common currency is about much more than transaction costs and has raised considerable debate, not least because of the political dimension. Critics of closer integration are concerned about the loss of sovereignty by individual countries. This concern is partly an economic one, focusing on the loss of separate currencies and (perhaps more significantly) the loss of control over national economic policy.

### The European Monetary System

The foundations for monetary union began to be laid down in 1979, with the launch of the European Monetary System (EMS). One aspect of the EMS was the Exchange Rate Mechanism (ERM), which can be seen as a precursor of the single currency. As discussed in Chapter 31, those countries that chose to opt into the ERM agreed to maintain their exchange rates within a band of plus or minus 2.25% against the average of their currencies — known as the European Currency Unit (ECU). The UK remained outside the ERM except for a brief flirtation between September 1990 and September 1992. During this period, the UK was operating within a slightly wider (6%) band.

During the period of the EMS/ERM, it was recognised that occasional realignment of currencies might be needed, and in fact there were 11 realignments between 1979 and 1987. However, the conditions under which such realignments were permitted were gradually tightened, so that they became less frequent as time went by.

Another key feature of the EMS period was the removal of capital controls. During the early part of this period, most of the member nations restricted the movement of financial capital across borders. This gave them some scope for using monetary policy independently of other countries. However, it was agreed that such capital controls would be phased out.

The Delors Plan, issued in 1989, set out proposals for creating European economic and monetary union (EMU), together with plans for a single currency and a European central bank. It was crucial to establish a European central bank because, with a single currency, a central bank is needed to administer monetary policy throughout the EU.

*The signing of the Maastricht Treaty on the European Union*

### Treaty of Maastricht

The next major step was the Maastricht Treaty, which created the European Union (EU). This treaty encompassed not only economic issues, such as the introduction of the single currency, but also aspects of social policy, steps towards creating a common foreign, security and defence policy, and the development of a notion of European 'citizenship'.

It was considered that, if a single currency was to be established, the participating nations would need to have converged in their economic characteristics. If the countries were too diverse in their economic conditions, the transition to a single currency would be costly. For example, if they had very different inflation rates, interest rates or levels of outstanding government debt, the tensions of union might be too great to sustain. Strong countries would be dragged down, and weak countries would be unable to cope. The Maastricht Treaty therefore set out the *convergence criteria* by which countries would be eligible to join the single currency area. These criteria covered aspects of both monetary and fiscal policy.

### Monetary policy

This is obviously important, as monetary union entails the centralisation of monetary policy within the EU. If there is to be a single currency and a single central bank to control interest rates or money supply, the monetary conditions of the economies concerned need to be reasonably close before union takes place. It was thus important to evaluate whether countries were sufficiently close to be able to join with minimal tension.

#### *Inflation*

Could countries with widely different inflation rates successfully join in a monetary union? One view is that it would be unreasonable to expect a country with 10% or 20% inflation to join a monetary union along with a country experiencing inflation at just 1%. An alternative view is that it is equally unreasonable to expect a country to cure its inflation before joining a union when one of the alleged benefits of joining is that it will cure inflation by enforcing financial discipline and removing discretion over monetary policy from individual states. However, the first criterion specified by the treaty was that countries joining the union should be experiencing low and similar inflation rates – defined as inflation no more than 1.5% above the average of the three countries in the EMS with the lowest rate.

### Interest and exchange rates

Given that financial capital tends to follow high interest rates, it is argued that diversity of interest rates before union may be undesirable, as this would imply instability of capital movements. Similarly, it has been argued that a period of exchange rate stability before union would be some indication that countries have been following mutually consistent policies, and would indicate that union is plausible.

The criteria set out in the treaty required that long-term interest rates be no more than 2% above the average of the three EMS countries with the lowest rate, and that each joining country should have been in the narrow band of the ERM for a period of 2 years without the need for realignment.

### Fiscal policy

Should there also be conformity in fiscal stance between countries? Would there be severe problems if countries embarked upon union and policy coordination in conditions in which unemployment rates differed markedly? These are separate but related questions. If unemployment is high, this will be connected (via social security payments) with the fiscal stance adopted by the government – as judged in terms of the government budget deficit.

The reason why unemployment rates are relevant is that there may need to be fiscal transfers between member states in order to reduce the differentials. This will clearly be politically significant in the context of a monetary union, and is an issue that will affect the long-term viability of the union. However, although unemployment rates are potentially important for this reason, the convergence criteria did not refer to unemployment directly. Instead, the criteria included a reference to fiscal policy. In practice, the divergence in unemployment rates was substantial.

Two areas are critical in judging the distance between countries in terms of fiscal policy. First, there is the question of the short-term fiscal stance, which can be measured by the budget deficit. Second, it is important to consider some indication of a longer-term commitment to stability in fiscal policy, in terms of achieving sustainable levels of outstanding government debt. Thus, the treaty required that the budget deficit be no larger than 3% of GDP, and that the national debt be no more than 60% of GDP.

### Economic and monetary union

The final stage of the transition towards the single currency was European Economic and Monetary Union (EMU). Under EMU, exchange rates between participating countries were permanently locked together: in other words, no further realignments were allowed. Furthermore, the financial markets of the

countries were integrated, with the European Central Bank setting a common interest rate across the union. This was achieved in 1999.

## Formation of the euro area

In the event, 11 countries were judged to have met the Maastricht criteria (Belgium, Germany, Spain, France, Ireland, Italy, Luxembourg, the Netherlands, Austria, Portugal and Finland). Together with Greece, these countries formed the single currency area, which came into operation on 1 January 2002.

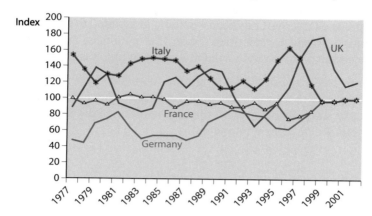

**Figure 36.2**
*Interest rates in Europe, 1977–2002 (EU12 = 100)*

Source: European Commission.

Figure 36.2 shows how interest rates in some of the Eurozone countries moved from 1977 (2 years before the formation of the EMS) until the first year of the euro. The graph shows interest rates in each country as an index, with the average of the Eurozone countries at 100. You can see that, although there is some evidence that some of the countries were converging in the run-up to monetary union, there seems to have been little historical tendency for interest rates to move together. This is especially the case for Italy, which at times seemed to have followed opposite paths to the others. Germany showed consistently lower interest rates than most other countries. From 1999, however, convergence was forced under EMU, which meant an especially rapid adjustment for Italy. The graph also reveals how a different time path of interest rates was followed by the UK.

## Costs and benefits of a single currency

Chapter 31 discussed alternative exchange rate regimes and evaluated the relative merits of fixed and floating exchange rate systems. Some of the arguments for and against a single currency area such as the Eurozone are similar, since a common currency is effectively creating an area in which exchange rates between member nations are fixed for ever, even if that common currency varies relative to the rest of the world. The question of whether such an arrangement is beneficial overall for the member states rests on an evaluation of the benefits and costs of joining together. An *optimal currency area* occurs when a group of countries are better off with a single currency.

## Benefits

The main benefits of a single currency area come in the form of a *monetary efficiency gain*, which has the effect of encouraging more trade between member countries. The hope is that this will bring further gains from exploiting comparative advantage between countries and enabling firms to reap the benefits of economies of scale.

The efficiency gain comes from two main sources. First, there are gains from reducing *transaction costs*, if there is no longer the need to convert from one currency into another. Second, there are gains from the *reduction in uncertainty*, in the sense that there is no longer a need to forecast future movements in exchange rates — at least between participating countries. This is similar to the gains from a fixed exchange rate system, but it goes further, as there is no longer a risk of occasional devaluation or revaluation of currencies.

The extent to which these gains are significant will depend upon the degree of integration between the participating nations. If most of the trade that takes place is between the participants, the gains will clearly be much more significant than if member nations are also trading extensively with countries outside the single currency area.

## Costs

The costs come in the conduct and effectiveness of policy. Within the single currency area, individual countries can no longer have recourse to monetary policy in order to stabilise the macro economy. As with the fixed exchange rate system, one key question then is how well individual economies are able to adjust to external shocks. Thus, it is important for each economy to have flexibility. In addition, individual countries have to be aware that, once in the single currency area, it is impossible to use monetary policy to smooth out fluctuations in output and employment.

In this context, it is very important that the business cycles of participating economies are well synchronised. If one economy is out of phase with the rest, it may find itself facing an inappropriate policy situation. For example, suppose that most of the countries within the Eurozone are in the boom phase of the business cycle, and are wanting to raise the interest rate in order to control aggregate demand: if one country within the zone is in recession, then the last thing it will want is rising interest rates, as this will deepen the recession and delay recovery.

*National currencies were replaced in the Eurozone from January 1999 by the euro*

## Evaluation

Paul Krugman has suggested a helpful way of using cost–benefit analysis to evaluate these aspects of a single currency area. He argues that both the costs and the benefits from a single currency area will vary with the degree to which member countries are integrated. Thus the benefits from joining such a currency area would rise as the closeness of integration increased, whereas the costs would fall.

Figure 36.3 illustrates the balance between costs and benefits. For countries that are not very closely integrated (that is, if 'integration' is less than $t^*$), the costs from joining the union exceed the benefits, so it would not be in the country's interest to join. However, as the degree of integration increases, so the benefits increase, and the costs decrease, so for any country beyond $t^*$, the benefits exceed the costs, and it is thus worth joining.

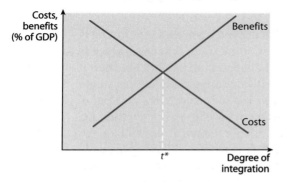

**Figure 36.3** *Costs and benefits of a single currency area*

For an individual country considering whether or not to join the euro area, a first step is to reach a judgement on whether the country is to the left or to the right of $t^*$. There may be other issues to consider in addition to the costs and benefits, but unless the country has at least reached $t^*$, it could be argued that entry into the union should not be considered.

One way of viewing the situation is that the costs are mainly macroeconomic, but the benefits are microeconomic. This complicates the evaluation process. Some research published in 2006 argued that most of the boost to trade within the euro area occurred during the initial period, and would not continue to build up over time. It was also suggested that the EU countries that decided not to join the euro (Britain, Sweden and Denmark) gained almost as much as the countries that had joined. Nonetheless, it is important to view the euro area from the perspective of possible UK entry.

### Exercise 36.2

Use an *AD/AS* diagram to analyse the problems that could arise if a country that is part of a single currency area enters a period of recession at a time when other countries in the union are in a boom.

## The UK and the euro

The UK government's policy stance on membership of the euro was set out by the chancellor of the exchequer in October 1997 after only a few months of the new Labour government. This stance was essentially that, while in principle the government was in favour of UK membership, it would be prepared to enter only at a time

when the economic conditions were right. Table 36.1 sets out the five economic tests that the chancellor specified as his conditions for deciding whether a case can be made for entry. You will see that these go beyond looking at the simple cost–benefit analysis, although clearly some of the criteria do relate to the closeness of integration, especially in terms of convergence.

| | Test | Explanation |
|---|---|---|
| 1 | Convergence | Are business cycles and economic structures compatible, so that UK citizens and others could live comfortably with euro interest rates on a permanent basis? |
| 2 | Flexibility | If problems emerge, is there sufficient flexibility to deal with them? |
| 3 | Investment | Would joining EMU create better conditions for firms making long-term decisions to invest in the UK? |
| 4 | Financial services | What impact would entry into EMU have on the competitive position of the UK's financial services industry, particularly the City's wholesale markets? |
| 5 | Employment | Will joining EMU promote higher growth, stability and a lasting increase in jobs? |

**Table 36.1** *The chancellor's five tests*                                                 Source: H. M. Treasury.

### Convergence

Sustainable convergence is seen to be crucial if the UK is to be successful within the euro area. What sort of evidence should be looked for in order to judge whether the UK's business cycle is converging on Europe? The chancellor could look at fluctuations in GDP, to see whether the phase of GDP growth in the UK is in tune with the rest of Europe. However, if the concern is with interest rates because of their importance with respect to policy, it may make sense to look at interest rates directly.

Figure 36.2 showed that, towards the end of the period 1977–2001, UK interest rates had converged to some extent, while still remaining a little higher than in member countries. Figure 36.4 shows the growth rates of GDP for France, Germany, the UK and the USA. Although there is perhaps more similarity evident towards the end of this period, there are certainly times when growth rates have diverged significantly, which would have created problems in the context of EMU. For example, look at Germany in the early 1990s.

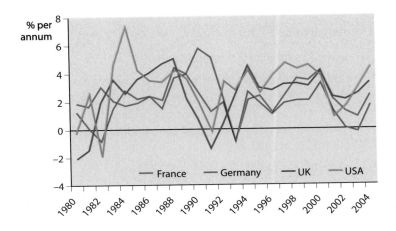

*Figure 36.4 Growth rates of GDP, selected countries, 1980–2004*

Source: OECD.

Another aspect of this issue that makes the convergence test especially important for the UK is the nature of the housing market. A larger proportion of home owners in the UK hold mortgages on a variable interest rate basis than their counterparts elsewhere in Europe, where fixed-rate mortgages are more common. This makes interest rates a particularly sensitive issue.

It is also argued that, in any approach to entry, the exchange rate is critical. The brief experience of the UK trying to tie its currency to the Exchange Rate Mechanism in the early 1990s illustrates the dangers of joining with the exchange rate at too high a level, and this is a mistake that the Treasury does not want to repeat.

### Flexibility

The convergence test is concerned with whether the UK's business cycle is sufficiently synchronised with the Eurozone. The flexibility test is about what would happen if this were not the case, or if the UK fell out of line. In other words, if the UK were to be out of phase, would the economy be sufficiently flexible to be able to get back into line in the absence of an independent monetary policy? It is about resilience.

It is quite difficult to measure flexibility in this sense, and there is no simple indicator that gives a ready judgement about whether an economy is sufficiently flexible to deal with situations that may or may not occur.

The key issues here concern the flexibility of markets, and the extent to which fiscal policy can be activated in order to help stabilise the economy, should that be deemed necessary. One danger is that inflation could become more variable if the UK joins the euro, as happened to Ireland. This is because at present the exchange rate is able to fluctuate in order to accommodate differences between national economies.

In the Treasury's assessment of the tests published in June 2003, the flexibility test was said to have been failed. Although the UK labour market was found to be relatively flexible, the Treasury identified a number of areas needing improvement. In particular, it argued that regional pay differentials were insufficient to reflect differences between the regions in the demand and supply of labour, and that there was a significant skills gap between the UK and the Eurozone members. It was also difficult to judge whether the UK tax system could be sufficiently flexible to allow rapid stabilisation. In these circumstances, it is hard to say whether or not any convergence would be sustainable.

### Investment

The issue for investment revolves around the incentives for firms to invest in the UK. There are two aspects to this. First, there is the question of UK-based firms, and whether they would find membership of the Eurozone conducive to investment. Second, there is the question of overseas firms, and the conditions under which they would be prepared to invest in the UK.

The question of whether firms would be prepared to invest more if the UK were part of the Eurozone depends in part on the success of the economy in meeting the convergence and flexibility tests. If firms have high expectations about the future,

they will be more prepared to invest, so if they see the UK as thriving within the euro area, this will be beneficial.

An additional consideration concerns the reduction in foreign exchange risk within the single currency area. This might encourage investment by reducing the risk premium required by firms considering investment.

Inward foreign direct investment (FDI) may depend on a number of factors. In particular, there may be US or Japanese firms looking to gain a foothold in Europe — will they choose the UK? Figure 36.5 shows annual FDI into the UK between 1965 and 2005, expressed as a percentage of GDP. A striking feature of the graph is the way that FDI appeared to boom towards the end of the 1990s, only to fall back quite dramatically in 2001–03. It is important to be a little careful in interpreting this pattern. It might be tempting to argue that the launching of the euro area at the beginning of 2002 may have contributed to the fall, with the UK becoming less attractive as a destination for FDI because of its decision not to join the euro. However, it is equally likely that the fall reflected the global reduction in flows of FDI following the 9/11 terrorist attacks in the USA. The graph shows that there was a recovery of inward FDI to the UK in 2004 and 2005. The fact that there are often multiple factors influencing economic decisions is a common problem in economics.

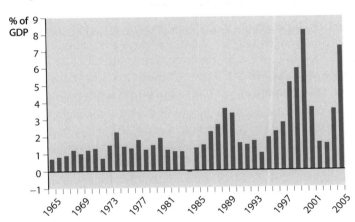

Figure 36.5
Inward foreign direct investment in the UK, 1965–2005

Source: ONS.

### Financial services

The fourth test concerns financial services. In the June 2003 Treasury analysis, this was the only test that the UK economy was judged to have passed. The financial services sector was singled out for a special mention because of its importance in the structure of the UK economy. The UK is seen to have a significant comparative advantage in wholesale financial services, and it was accepted that the City is the pre-eminent financial centre in Europe. There was thus a concern that becoming part of the single currency area would damage the competitiveness of this sector.

The evidence here seems to suggest that the UK financial sector benefits from EMU even with the UK being outside the euro area, but that it would gain even more if the UK were to join. Financial services have become a significant item in the balance of payments, with a positive balance of more than £12 billion in 2004. This is a substantial share of the overall surplus in trade in services, which was about £14.6 billion. If the UK were a full member of the single currency area, it is likely that this balance would be even more positive.

*Traders at Barclays Capital — financial services had a positive balance of more than £12 billion in 2004*

## Growth, stability and employment

The final test relates to whether becoming part of the euro zone would promote higher growth, stability and a lasting increase in jobs in the UK. This might be interpreted as an overall assessment of the potential success of the single currency in the long run. However, this test cannot be divorced from the others. In particular, sustainable convergence (i.e. convergence plus flexibility) would be expected to influence firms' expectations about the future and could affect their willingness to invest, which in turn would contribute to the rate of economic growth.

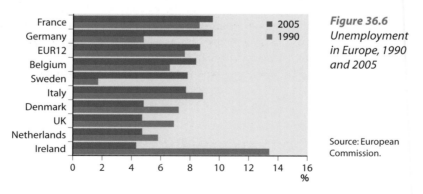

*Figure 36.6 Unemployment in Europe, 1990 and 2005*

Source: European Commission.

Figure 36.6 provides some context, showing rates of unemployment in 1990 and 2005 in a range of European countries. The countries are ranked in descending order of their unemployment rates in 2005. It is evident that the UK in 1990 experienced an unemployment rate that was below, but close to, the average of the euro area countries. However, since then the UK rate has fallen appreciably, while the euro average rate has increased. The relativities between countries seem to have altered quite a lot over this period, with Germany showing a substantial increase and Ireland a dramatic decrease.

## Summary

➤ The first step towards monetary union was the launch of the European Monetary System (EMS) in 1979.

➤ An important part of this was the Exchange Rate Mechanism (ERM), under which participating countries (which did not include the UK) agreed to keep their currencies within a narrow band (2.25%) against the average of their currencies.

➤ The Maastricht Treaty created the European Union (EU), and set out the route towards closer integration.

➤ The treaty also set out the convergence criteria, to be used to judge which countries were ready to join in monetary union. These criteria covered financial and fiscal aspects.

➤ Twelve countries adopted the euro as their common currency in January 2002.

➤ The main benefits of a common currency area are that it encourages trade by reducing transaction costs and reducing foreign exchange risk.

➤ However, the downside is that individual countries have less autonomy in controlling their macro economies. Adjusting to external shocks and smoothing short-term fluctuations in output and employment become more difficult with a common monetary policy that may not always be set in ways that are appropriate for all participating countries.

➤ From the UK's point of view, the government stated in 1997 that it intended to join the euro area, but only when the economy had passed five economic tests set by the chancellor: on convergence, flexibility, investment, financial services and employment.

## Exercise 36.3

Identify the costs and benefits that would be associated with the UK's entry into the euro single currency group of countries, and discuss whether you believe that the UK should join when the time is right.

# Chapter 37
# The transition economies of Europe

*Although economic integration was drawing countries in Western Europe closer together during the period after the Second World War, Eastern Europe was in a very different situation. Since the revolution of 1917, Russia had followed a very different path towards industrialisation, and after the Second World War, the Soviet Union brought together a group of countries in the east of Europe and in the Baltic region that adopted a centrally planned approach to economic management. During the 1980s in particular, this approach was seen to be failing, and from 1989 the Soviet bloc began to fall apart. These countries then began to introduce economic reforms that began to allow markets to play a more active role in the allocation of resources. For many, the transition towards a market system was a painful one. By analysing the path to reform, there is much to be learnt about what it is that makes the market system effective as a way of allocating resources, and what conditions are critical in the process.*

## Learning outcomes

After studying this chapter, you should:
➤ understand the characteristics of centrally planned economies
➤ be aware of the main failings of central planning in resource allocation
➤ be familiar with the nature of economic reforms in the transition economies
➤ be able to evaluate the costs and benefits of market reforms for the transition economies
➤ be able to analyse the economic performance of the transition economies
➤ be familiar with the differences between the transition economies that have chosen to join the EU and the established member economies
➤ be able to discuss the reasons behind the desire of some transition economies to become part of the SEM

## Centrally planned economies

The economic analysis so far presented has shown how the operation of markets can act to allocate resources. Consumers use markets to express their preferences for various goods and services, while firms react to price signals in deciding which goods and services to produce, and how to produce them. Governments help to provide the environment for markets to fulfil these roles, and to intervene in cases where markets do not work effectively. In particular, the World Bank's 'market-friendly' view suggests that the state should withdraw from parts of the economy in which markets can be relied upon to work effectively, and only intervene in situations of market failure. However, this is not the only way that societies have tried to cope with the basic economic condition of scarcity. Under central planning, the state takes responsibility for directing the economy, becoming actively involved in influencing the allocation of resources.

Russia became the role model for central planning, at least in the European context. In the early part of the twentieth century, Russia had lagged behind countries in Western Europe, remaining primarily an agrarian society. Karl Marx had written about communism, and predicted that there would be revolution to overturn capitalism, but he would not have expected this to occur in Russia, which had not yet reached the capitalist stage of development. However, it was the Russian revolution of 1917 that launched central planning, under a centralised socialist system.

*Karl Marx (1818–1883)*

Under the Stalinist model, the state planning agency (Gosplan) took responsibility for determining the output mix. The focus was primarily on developing heavy industry and military capability. The stress on heavy industry came from the fact that Russia had not been through an industrial revolution at the time of its political revolution, and perceived that it needed to catch up with the other industrial powers of the period. In diverting resources towards heavy industry and the military, Gosplan had little regard for consumers, whose needs were neglected during this period. This extended beyond Russia to other countries that joined Russia to form the Union of Soviet Socialist Republics (USSR, or Soviet Union) in 1924.

Gosplan operated by first deciding the desired overall mix of output. It then set targets for the key sectors — heavy industry and the military — with a much lower priority being given to consumer goods. The service sector was also perceived as being of low importance; indeed, it was seen as being unproductive. Gosplan then set specific targets for the industry managers and for individual firms. It was then up to the industry managers and firms to assess their input requirements for meeting those targets. The incentive for these managers was thus to overstate their input requirements, so that more workers and other factors would be allocated to them, making it easier to meet their targets. In other words, there was a strong incentive to build a certain amount of X-inefficiency into the system.

Further distortions were built in because firms were set targets in terms of output, and would thus set out with the objective of meeting those targets, regardless of profit. This had some unintended effects on production. An example often quoted is that of a nail factory. A typical output target for a nail factory might be expressed in terms of either the quantity of nails to be produced or the volume of nails by weight. In the case of the former, firms would meet the target by producing large numbers of small nails. However, if the target was in terms of the weight of nails to be produced, firms would concentrate on producing large nails that would weigh more. This meant that production was distorted towards over-production of some products and under-production of others. This sort of pattern was repeated across the whole economy. In addition, the planning process itself consumes resources. An advantage of a market system is that to a great extent it runs itself.

Prices under central planning were set independently of supply and demand, and were often set below market-clearing levels for basic necessities such as food, clothing or housing. This caused widespread shortages, and was to be important when the transition did begin. In any situation in which there is persistent disequilibrium, some way has to be found to enable markets to function. When there is excess demand, there needs to be some mechanism for rationing the goods. Under central planning, this rationing was accomplished simply — through queuing.

The distortion of prices from market values applied also to the prices of factors of production, and led to inefficiencies in their use. This applied not only to labour and capital, but also to the prices of materials and of energy. This resulted in the adoption of techniques of production that were highly inappropriate and wasteful. These inefficiencies were later to prove to be one of the seeds of the breakdown.

*The blast furnaces of the metals factory of Magnitogorsk, in the southern Urals, 1930s*

The achievements of central planning in the Soviet Union should not be under-estimated. In terms of the effects on industry and military development, the system delivered, and the Soviet Union became a superpower in the postwar period, with its satellite countries in the Baltic and Eastern Europe. In this period, central planning spread throughout the Soviet Union, with some countries being devoted to particular activities within the overall plan. This again had implications later.

## Exercise 37.1

Imagine that you are in charge of a firm operating under central planning. You run a factory that produces rubber tyres for bicycles, cars, HGVs and JCBs. Your target is to produce a given number of tyres during the next year. How would you go about making sure you meet the target? Think about your incentives in relation to the output mix (between different sorts of tyres), the use of factors of production, and investment in research and development and new technology.

## Summary

➤ In centrally planned economies, the state rather than the price mechanism decides how resources are allocated.

➤ In the Soviet Union, the state planning agency (Gosplan) operated the central plan, giving precedence to heavy industry and military developments at the expense of consumer goods.

➤ Gosplan set output targets for industries and individual firms.

➤ This set up weak incentives for managers to be efficient in production methods.

➤ Prices were set independently of supply and demand, often being set below market-clearing levels for basic necessities.

➤ The resulting shortages led to rationing through queuing.

## The breakdown of central planning

In the 1970s and early 1980s, the Soviet Union entered a period of stagnation, which set the scene for its collapse. By 1985, GDP per capita in the Soviet Union was estimated to be about 29% of that in the USA, and it became apparent that the system was not working. The inefficiencies in production and resource allocation became even more severe. Enterprise managers were still attempting to maximise output without regard for quality. There were still incentives for the managers to conceal their true productive capacity, and operate in ways that ensured a quiet life. Why increase output beyond the target if the result was more demanding targets for the following year?

It has been estimated that during the 1980s, the Soviet Union was using 15 times as much steel per unit of GDP as the USA. In some enterprises, the prices of inputs

and outputs were so distorted that firms were producing output that was worth less than the materials used in the production process — in other words, they were producing 'value subtracted'. In addition, managers had no incentive to keep pace with technological change, in a period when this was bringing substantial productivity improvements elsewhere in the world. In short, the central planning system simply could not cope with increasing inefficiency, poor incentives and distorted prices in what was an increasingly complex global environment.

So, in 1989 the Berlin Wall was demolished — a symbol of the separation of Western and Eastern Europe, and of West and East Germany. By 1991, the Soviet Union had disbanded.

*Dismantling the Berlin Wall, 1989*

## The need for reform

The dismantling of centralised planning created a substantial challenge. Markets could not be expected to start operating effectively overnight, and the transition period was to prove a difficult time for the countries trying to go through it. From the point of view of economic analysis, the process of reform forced a focus on the key requirements for the operation of a market system. With political changes proceeding at the same time, it was perhaps inevitable that the transition would be a painful process. The consensus view is that the reforms needed to focus on four key areas: liberalisation of markets, macroeconomic stabilisation, privatisation and the development of market institutions.

### Liberalisation of markets

A key requirement for any market-based system is that prices should reflect relative scarcity. 'Prices' here refer to both the prices of goods and services, and the prices of factors of production. If prices are to act as signals that will guide resource allocation, it is vitally important that those signals should be as reliable as possible.

As has been explained, prices under central planning had been administered by the state planning agency, so in many cases they bore no relation at all to demand and supply of goods or factors. Moving to a system in which prices would be reliable signals was bound to be a difficult process. Furthermore, managers of firms needed to learn how to respond to price signals, rather than operating to externally set targets for output. Given the length of time that had passed since the

Russian Revolution, the manager of a Soviet enterprise would have had to be over 85 years old to have experienced market prices!

## Macroeconomic stabilisation

It is widely believed that a market system can work effectively only in the context of a stable macro economy. In particular, firms need to have a stable environment within which they can take good decisions about investment.

This was an especially challenging requirement to meet in the early years of the transition, when prices had to adjust to their market values, and so would be liable to substantial short-run volatility. In addition, many of the institutions needed for implementing monetary and fiscal policy had to be put in place.

## Privatisation

The need for the state to divest itself of the ownership of firms across a wide range of sectors was a further key element of the reforms. Indeed, people in the economy needed to be accustomed to the whole notion of private ownership of assets and of capital.

## Market institutions

The development of new institutions to enable markets to operate was the final key element of the reforms. The need for institutions is something that it is easy to take for granted when a market system has been in operation over a long period of time, and the experience of the transition economies is a useful reminder of how important it is to have such institutions in place.

A prime requirement is for there to be a secure system of property rights. This is important in many ways. For example, in the absence of property rights, individuals may not be prepared to undertake saving. The notion that firms will act to maximise profits makes sense only if firms know that they can control the profits that they make. The whole framework of economic incentives rests on the existence of secure property rights, and without it, markets cannot operate effectively.

In order to achieve macroeconomic stability, effective financial markets are required. There is a need for a central bank to oversee the financial system, and to implement monetary policy. Other financial institutions are needed to ensure that savings can be channelled into productive investment. For example, a functioning stock market is important in enabling firms to raise funds for investment. There needs to be regulation of the financial system, which in turn requires there to be a system that imposes accounting standards on individual firms and enterprises. There need to be bankruptcy procedures in place, and regulation that ensures that commercial banks adhere to a responsible lending policy.

Given the past pattern of productive activity, there also needs to be a coherent competition policy which ensures that an appropriate degree of competition in markets is fostered. There need to be measures in place to ensure that monopoly firms do not exploit their new-found position in developing markets.

## Exercise 37.2

The above discussion has indicated some key aspects of the reform period. Prices needed to find their way to market-clearing levels. Firms needed to stop producing goods that nobody wanted, and start to produce new products for which there was a consumer demand. Inefficient production techniques needed to be abandoned. Incentives for investment were relatively low because of uncertainty. Privatisation led to the establishment of new monopoly firms.

Sketch an *AD/AS* diagram to try to analyse the effect of these changes on the overall price level and real income in the short run and in the long run.

## Summary

➤ Central planning broke down between 1989 and 1991 following a period of stagnation and growing inefficiencies.

➤ Without central planning, market reforms were needed to introduce the key elements of a market economy.

➤ The reforms covered four key areas.

➤ Markets needed to be liberalised in order that prices could begin to reflect scarcity of goods, services and factors of production.

➤ Macroeconomic stabilisation was needed to create an environment within which price signals could be effective in guiding resource allocation.

➤ Privatisation enabled previously state-owned enterprises to pass into the private sector.

➤ Market institutions needed to be developed to facilitate the establishment of a market system.

## Which are the transition economies?

Broadly speaking, the transition economies can be divided into three groupings. These are set out in Figure 37.1. One group of countries (the CIS group) remain allied to Russia. A second group (the EU8) have allied themselves with the EU, becoming members of the Single European Market (SEM). The third group (SEE) is made up of countries in southeastern Europe that lie somewhere in between the Russia-centric and the Euro-centric blocs, but which seem to be inclining more towards the latter. Indeed, the European Central Bank reported as early as 2003 that there was an estimated 38 billion worth of euro banknotes circulating outside of the euro area, most of it in Central and Eastern Europe, where the euro was gaining popularity in parallel to local currencies. This included some countries in the SEE group.

The performance of the groups has shown some significant differences. This is partly a result of differences in the pace at which reforms were introduced,

| The CIS | The EU8 | SEE |
|---------|---------|-----|
| Armenia | Czech Republic | Albania |
| Azerbaijan | Estonia | Bosnia and Herzegovina |
| Belarus | Hungary | Bulgaria* |
| Georgia | Latvia | Croatia** |
| Kazakhstan | Lithuania | FYR Macedonia |
| Kyrgyz Republic | Poland | Romania* |
| Moldova | Slovak Republic | Serbia and Montenegro |
| Russia | Slovenia | Kosovo |
| Tajikistan | | |
| Turkmenistan | | |
| Ukraine | | |
| Uzbekistan | | |

**Figure 37.1**
*The transition economies*

\* Countries in the process of acceding to the EU.

\*\* Candidate for EU accession.

but there have also been differences in long-term objectives and aspirations. In general, those economies (the EU8 in particular) that decided early in the process that membership of the EU was their long-term aim adopted reform at a more rapid pace than others whose long-term aims were less clear.

At the time of the transition, there was a debate as to whether countries would be better off going for 'shock treatment' — implementing reforms as quickly as possible and accepting the short-run pain — or whether a more gradualist approach would be less painful and equally effective in the long run. In the event it seems that those countries that opted for shock treatment fared better in the longer term, whereas those that were slow to begin the process of reform found the process more difficult.

## Economic performance during the transition

In terms of economic performance, two areas caused initial problems for the transition economies, in line with the adjustments that had to be undertaken. In the first place, prices had to be allowed to adjust to reflect true market values. In the second place, the transition economies needed to go through a process of structural change in order to create more balanced economies.

The price adjustment process caused substantial instability of prices for a period. This partly reflects the way that prices of many goods and services had been held below market levels, so that these needed to adjust upwards. In addition, demand had been artificially held low. The lack of goods for sale had been resolved through queuing rather than formal rationing. There was major pent-up demand to be tackled. Given inelastic supply of many products, this meant a wild acceleration of prices, with inflation reaching four digits in some countries.

Figures 37.2 and 37.3 show the situation in a selection of countries. In the cases of Russia and Belarus, data did not become available until 1993, at which time you can see that inflation was running at dramatically high rates. By this time, some of the countries that had initiated reforms at an earlier date, such as Hungary and Poland, were already beginning to get things under control.

These inflationary conditions made it imperative to put the financial institutions in place that could create a more stable macroeconomic environment. During the

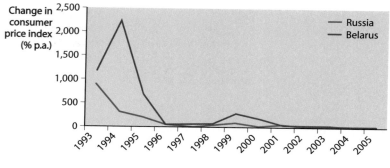

Figure 37.2
Inflation in the
transition: Russia
and Belarus,
1993–2005

Source: IMF.

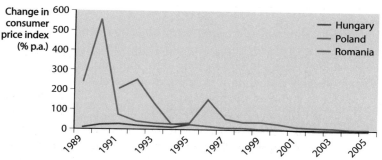

Figure 37.3
Inflation in the
transition:
Hungary, Poland
and Romania,
1989–2005

Source: IMF.

inflationary phase, real interest rates became negative, discouraging saving. With prices increasing so rapidly, people had no incentive to hold money, and it made sense to spend as quickly as possible. Nonetheless, the graphs suggest that this was a transitory stage, and that most of the economies concerned were able to bring inflation under control, albeit after a painful period of hyperinflation in some cases.

In most cases, this was achieved by a process of pegging the exchange rate. This process of committing the government to maintaining the exchange rate against a 'hard' currency such as the US dollar or the Deutschmark was effectively a promise that the government would adopt tight macroeconomic policies, and was designed to inspire confidence in the policies adopted. In a number of cases, this policy was further reinforced by granting independence to the central bank, thus removing the possibility that the government would renege on its undertaking to bring inflation under control.

As far as output was concerned, a process of adjustment and structural change was again imperative. Enterprises had to start making goods that people actually wanted to buy, and in the short run, this required firms to stop making goods that were not wanted by consumers. Coupled with a fall in investment expenditure, the short-run result was a fall in real output, which in some cases was substantial. The change in the balance of the economy away from the military sector also contributed to the fall in output, as some capital could not be readily transformed into new uses.

Figure 37.4 shows the overall annual growth rate in the region since 1990. This clearly shows the prolonged recession that accompanied the initial transition.

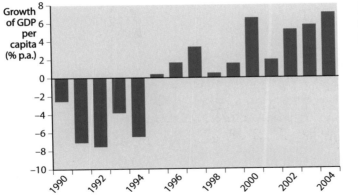

*Figure 37.4*
*Growth rate in*
*Eastern Europe,*
*1990–2004*

Source: World Bank.

As an example of how much real output fell, it was reported that real GDP in Russia in 1995 had fallen to just 48% of the level that had been reached before 1989.

In some of the transition economies, the process of privatisation added extra costs in terms of economic performance. Managers, bureaucrats, party members or government officials gained control of many enterprises that were being privatised, and engaged in asset stripping, selling off the assets for their own gain, and leaving the enterprises unable to produce. This added to the fall in output, although in some cases it may have added to the size of the informal economy, which grew very large relative to the official sector. This may have contributed to the negative growth of GDP shown in the statistics.

In many sectors, the privatised industries immediately became monopolies, and without competition authorities in place to regulate their performance and protect consumers, some firms were able to use their market power to crank up prices, further fuelling the inflation that was taking place.

It was also the case that the central planning era had left the countries concerned with unbalanced economies in terms of the structure of production. The neglect of the service sector had left economies with no expertise in certain skills that were now seen as an important part of the modern economy, such as management, design, packaging, distribution, logistics and after-sales service. Time was needed to nurture and encourage these to develop. Subsequent research has shown that foreign direct investment into the transition economies has tended to be located in those economies that made most progress in developing their service sector.

## Costs and benefits of transition

Was it all worth it? Is it possible to evaluate the costs and benefits of the transition?

A first point to note is that the growing inefficiencies of the centrally planned system were getting to such a state that things were not sustainable. So in evaluating the costs and benefits of the transition, it must be borne in mind that the alternative to reform was not a continuation of the former state of affairs, as this was not viable. In addition, as people in the East became more aware of

*International trade to the EU8: Klaipeda harbour, Lithuania*

conditions in the more prosperous countries of the West, there was mounting internal pressure for reform, especially from the countries that were geographically closest to the EU.

The more time that passes, the easier it is to put the transition years into perspective. An evaluation conducted in the late 1990s would have weighted the costs more heavily than an evaluation carried out today, when coherence is emerging from the chaos of the early years.

Economic analysis suggests that there are long-term gains to be made from introducing market reforms, and allowing market forces to dictate the allocation of resources. By allowing prices of goods, services and factors of production to reflect economic scarcity, it is expected that there will be gains in both productive and allocative efficiency. By encouraging structural change, the transition economies may be better suited to exploit their areas of comparative advantage, and to be more active in international trade.

### Could the transition have been handled differently?

There are countries elsewhere in the world that have also gone through (or are going through) the process of market reform and transition to a market economy. Most notable among these are China, Cambodia, Laos and Vietnam.

It is especially tempting to compare the performance of the transition economies with that of China, which has become such a high-profile success story. China adopted a gradualist approach. Inflation was kept very tightly under control, and the reforms were introduced in a carefully planned manner. A major difference was the size of China's agricultural sector. This contrasted strongly with the large (and inefficient) industrial sectors in the European transition economies. China thus needed to introduce reforms in the agricultural sector as well as in the manufacturing and service sectors — and did so with some success.

The market reforms were introduced gradually in China, often in small enclaves, rather than trying to reform the whole economy at once. One example of this was the development of Special Economic Zones (SEZs). These were export-oriented, and foreign firms were encouraged to become established there with minimal interference. Another part of China's success was in the way it was able to attract foreign direct investment. This has enabled technology transfer to take place — a process that has been accelerated by the Chinese authorities' relaxed view of intellectual property rights. The lure of the enormous Chinese market has doubtless helped in the attraction of foreign capital.

It seems unlikely that the Chinese approach could have been adopted in the European transition economies, as they faced a very different configuration of problems and characteristics. This is a reminder of the diversity of economies around the world. Economic policy needs to be designed in response to the particular features of the various situations that can arise in different countries.

Nevertheless, there are some general principles at work. The theme that has run through this whole book is that markets can work to bring about an allocation of resources within a society that can be efficient in terms of both productive efficiency (the use of resources) and allocative efficiency (an appropriate balance of goods and services). The centrally planned economies failed on both counts, but in lauding the move towards a more market-based approach to resource allocation, it must also be remembered that markets do fail, and that government intervention in order to deal with market failure is an important part of economic management.

## Summary

> The transition economies can be divided into three groups.
> One group comprises countries that allied themselves with the EU and worked towards accession.
> A second group allied themselves with Russia.
> A third group, in southeastern Europe, fall somewhere in between the other two groups, with some seeking accession to the EU and others retaining ties with Russia.
> The early years of the transition were characterised by falling real output and rampant inflation.
> Firms needed to adjust to the notions of profit and efficiency.
> Corruption in some cases led to asset stripping, adding to the decline in real output levels and to a substantial informal economy.
> The structure of economic activity also needed to be redressed, allowing a stronger service sector to emerge.

## The transition economies and the European Union

The question still remains as to why some of the transition economies set out to accede to the European Union, and to join the SEM, whereas others have preferred

to keep their distance. Political issues might have affected some countries after the collapse of central planning. For example, it is hard to imagine Russia becoming a minor state in the European Union, given its relatively recent status as a super-power — and having been on the 'other side' in the Cold War.

What of those who did decide that it was in their interests to join the EU? Why should this be an objective? And why should the EU be ready to welcome them in?

The key piece of economic analysis is the *law of comparative advantage.* Within the SEM, the intention is to facilitate trade between member countries as far as possible in order to benefit both firms and consumers, by enabling countries to specialise and thus make the most of their respective areas of comparative advantage.

## Exercise 37.3

Discuss what economic activities are likely to be sources of comparative advantage for the EU8 transition economies in the context of the SEM.

Remember that one of the features of the single market is that it allows for free movement of factors of production between member states. What does this imply for the nature of the relationship between the original 15 EU members and the acceding nations?

### The impact of EU enlargement

One way of seeking to assess the impact of EU enlargement is to look at population size. The new member countries vary considerably in size on this simple measure. The smallest acceding country is Malta, which was not a transition economy, but joined the single market at the same time as the EU8 transition economies: Malta had a population of 397,000 people in 2002. The largest was Poland (39 million). If Turkey were to join, this would add a massive 70 million more citizens to the EU.

Figure 35.2 showed how the enlarged EU would stand in the world rankings of big countries. This underlines the fact that the previous 15 member countries of the EU contained more people than the USA. At the time of the enlargement in 2004, the combined population of the EU member states was 455.4 million, compared with 293.5 million in the USA.

Size is not everything. It is the *effective* demand for goods and services that is important for a market, and this depends upon purchasing power, not just on the size of population. Average income levels in the new member nations are lower than in the incumbent members. This has implications both for the size and the pattern of effective consumer demand. However, this does not mean that there are no gains to be made.

### Comparative advantage and diversity

The gains from specialisation that arise from exploiting comparative advantage are likely to be greater when there is diversity between countries. It is the *difference* in relative opportunity costs of production that drives the process, so the fact that the new members are not just clones of the existing members may be a point in their favour, and suggests that there may be scope for gains from trade.

It is also important to be aware that it is not only *levels* of average income that are important, but also the rate of growth, which indicates how economies are changing through time. Figure 36.1 showed the growth rates of GDP per capita for the countries in 2001–02, just before the accession. This reveals something of the potential dynamism of the acceding countries relative to the existing members. Again, it might be argued that the existing member countries would gain from having closer trading links with countries that were enjoying these relatively rapid growth rates.

## Market integration

In thinking about the effects of the arrival of the EU8 from the perspective of the existing members, the fact that they are in transition from central planning is highly relevant. One of the conditions laid down by the Copenhagen European Council for membership was that the candidate country must have achieved 'the existence of a functioning market economy as well as the capacity to cope with competitive pressure and market forces within the Union'. By agreeing to the enlargement in May 2004, it was accepted that this condition had been fulfilled. However, it is important to bear in mind that the market systems now operating in these former centrally planned economies are relatively young, and only time will reveal whether they are sufficiently robust for their firms to withstand the rigours of international competition within the EU. Nonetheless, it might be argued that the strong growth shown by some of these countries shows the benefits that have been flowing from the market reforms adopted in preparation for membership.

## Human resources

It is also important to realise that there are some significant differences between the transition economies of Central and Eastern Europe and the less developed countries of sub-Saharan Africa or South Asia. Although income levels are lower in Central and Eastern Europe than in Western Europe, this partly reflects the inefficiency of the former centrally planned economies. However, in general, human capital levels are higher than in many LDCs, as education and healthcare systems have received investment in the past.

This was shown in Figure 35.4, which provided values of the Human Development Index (HDI). Although the HDI values for the acceding countries are lower than in most of the existing member countries, all of the countries that joined the EU in May 2004 have HDI values that place them in the UNDP's 'high human development' category. This augurs well for the future, as the availability of human capital is important if convergence is to take place. If workers are skilled and literate, this helps the spread of technology and the adoption of more efficient working practices.

## Migration

The potential effect of EU enlargement on intra-European migration cannot be ignored. One pronounced difference between the EU15 and the new EU countries is the relatively high unemployment rates in the latter, especially among young workers. In 2001, the long-term unemployment rate in the EU15 was estimated at 3.1% of the active population, and the unemployment rate among 15–24-year-olds was estimated to be 14.6%. Comparable estimates for the acceding countries were 7.6% and 31.3% respectively.

It is possible that the high youth unemployment rate will encourage migration within the single market, one of whose provisions is the free movement of workers within the Union. This could be seen as a positive supply effect of enlargement, with a boost to the labour force in the EU15 countries. However, the full effects of this are only likely to be attained if the labour market in the EU15 is found to be sufficiently flexible.

On the basis of past evidence, the majority of immigrants into the EU15 will choose to locate in the countries closest to their home countries: that is, mainly in Germany and Austria. However, a study undertaken into this issue at the time of the accession suggested that only about 335,000 people would move to the EU15 countries from Central and Eastern Europe even if there were free movement of workers immediately on accession. The EU has agreed a flexible transition period of up to 7 years, during which time the flow of workers will be monitored and controlled.

## Other issues

It is possible that the enlargement of the EU area will encourage flows of investment, which could also be beneficial overall, both for investors and for recipient countries, bringing a further impetus to economic growth within the expanded EU.

It is important to be aware of the potential implications of the enlargement for the EU Budget, which was certainly politically sensitive at the time of the enlargement and in the following years. There were a number of reasons for this. One issue arose because the new members had lower average income levels than the existing members, and thus qualified for support for their economic development. This implies a need for greater commitment from the richer members of the EU to allow a transfer of resources to the new members. It is also the case that the new EU members have relatively large agricultural sectors, and would thus be eligible for subsidies under the Common Agricultural Policy (CAP). This is another contentious area, as it is widely believed that the CAP is in urgent need of reform. The French have a vested interest in retaining the CAP farmers' subsidies and have resisted reform, but they have accepted that a review should be carried out in 2008, with the possibility of change taking place no sooner than 2013.

A study by the European Commission suggested that enlargement could increase the growth rate of the acceding countries by between 1.3 and 2.1 percentage

*Agriculture in the Czech Republic is now eligible for subsidies under the Common Agricultural Policy*

points annually, and increase the growth rate of existing members by 0.7% annually. If this were to be the outcome, it would be a significant development indeed, as even a small increase in the annual growth rate accumulates over time. This suggests that there are mutual gains to be made from the enlargement of the SEM.

## Exercise 37.4

Discuss whether the status of the EU8 as former centrally planned economies will be an advantage or a hindrance in integrating with the rest of the SEM.

Use *AD/AS* analysis to analyse the macroeconomic effects of EU enlargement for both original and acceding countries.

## Summary

➤ By joining the Single European Market (SEM), the EU8 countries could make use of specialisation in order to gain from their areas of comparative advantage.

➤ The diversity of characteristics in the new member countries as compared with the old members of the SEM suggests that there will be gains from the enlargement of the market for both old and new member countries.

➤ However, this may be a severe test of the newly established market system in the EU8.

➤ The EU8 have some advantages over less developed countries elsewhere in the world because of their relatively well-developed human resources.

➤ The free movement of people within the SEM may be expected to lead to some migration from the newly acceding members to the original member countries.

➤ There are expected to be mutually beneficial gains from the enlargement for both old and new members.

# Index

Page numbers in **bold** refer to **key term definitions**.